Letters from a Life: The Selected Letters
and Diaries of Benjamin Britten 1913–1976

Letter 224: Britten writes on 21 November 1939 to Antonio Brosa about his Violin Concerto, Op. 15.

EDITOR-IN-CHIEF: DONALD MITCHELL

Letters from a Life:
The Selected Letters and
Diaries of Benjamin Britten
1913–1976

VOLUME TWO
1939–1945

EDITED BY
DONALD MITCHELL
ASSISTANT EDITOR:
PHILIP REED
ASSOCIATE EDITORS: ROSAMUND STRODE,
KATHLEEN MITCHELL, JUDY YOUNG

First published in 1991
by Faber and Faber Limited
3 Queen Square London WC1N 3AU
This paperback edition first published in 1998

Phototypeset by Intype London Ltd
Printed by CPI Antony Rowe, Eastbourne

A CIP record for this book is available from the British Library

ISBN 978-0-571-19400-1

10 9 8 7 6 5 4 3 2 1

To the memory of Elizabeth Mayer
1884–1970

CONTENTS

INDEX OF CORRESPONDENTS
to Volumes One and Two

LIST OF PLATES

Note: Pictures from a Life (PFL, 1978) remains the most extensive picture documentation of Britten's life. We have tried to avoid duplication, but some overlap has proved necessary.

1 Britten's parents, an engagement photograph, 1900

2 Edith Rhoda Hockey, before her marriage to Robert Victor Britten

3 The wedding: St John's Smith Square, London SW1, 5 September 1901

4 R.V. Britten, 1909

5 Edith Britten, 1909

6a The family home, 21 Kirkley Cliff Road, Lowestoft, where Britten was born on 22 November 1913; Mr Britten's dental practice was on the ground floor

6b The first floor sitting room, known to the family – because of its upper location – as 'Heaven'

7 Beth; Edith Britten and her infant son, Benjamin; Barbara; Robert, 1914

8a Nursery theatricals; back row from left: Barbara; unidentified; Robert; Benjamin cross-legged in front row; Beth kneels on his right

8b Mrs Scarce, Nanny, with Benjamin, 1914

8c Benjamin, c.1915

9a Invitation to the theatricals, probably in Nanny's hand

9b Benjamin and battleship, c.1916

9c Beth and Benjamin, c.1916

KEY TO BIBLIOGRAPHICAL ABBREVIATIONS

BBAA   Benjamin Britten, *On Receiving the First Aspen Award*, London, Faber and Faber, 1964

BBST   Benjamin Britten, 'Britten Looking Back', *Sunday Telegraph*, 17 November 1963, p. 9

BC   Christopher Palmer (editor), *The Britten Companion*, London, Faber and Faber, 1984

DMBA   Donald Mitchell, *Britten and Auden in the Thirties: The Year 1936*, London, Faber and Faber, 1981

DMHK   Donald Mitchell and Hans Keller (editors), *Benjamin Britten: A Commentary on His Works from a Group of Specialists*, London, Rockliff, 1952

DMPB   W.H. Auden, *Paul Bunyan: The Libretto of the Opera by Benjamin Britten*, with an essay by Donald Mitchell, London, Faber and Faber, 1988

DNB   *The Dictionary of National Biography*

DVDM   Donald Mitchell (compiler and editor), *Benjamin Britten: Death in Venice*, Cambridge, Cambridge University Press, 1987

EMWHA   W.H. Auden, *The Complete Works of W.H. Auden: Plays (with Christopher Isherwood) and other Dramatic Writings, 1928–1938*, edited by Edward Mendelson, London, Faber and Faber, 1989

EWB   Beth Britten, *My Brother Benjamin*, Bourne End, The Kensal Press, 1986

EWW   Eric Walter White, *Benjamin Britten: His Life and Operas*, 2nd edition, edited by John Evans, London, Faber and Faber, 1983

GE   Graham Elliott, *Benjamin Britten: The Things Spiritual*, Ph.D. dissertation, University of Wales, 1985

HCWHA   Humphrey Carpenter, *W.H. Auden: A Biography*, London, Allen & Unwin, 1981

IHB   Imogen Holst, *Britten* (The Great Composers), 3rd edition, London, Faber and Faber, 1980

LFBML .   Lewis Foreman, *From Parry to Britten: British Music in Letters*, London, Batsford, 1987

MKWW   Michael Kennedy, *Portrait of Walton*, Oxford, Oxford University Press, 1989

PFL   Donald Mitchell and John Evans, *Pictures from a Life: Benjamin Britten 1913–1976*, London, Faber and Faber, 1978

PGPB   Philip Brett (compiler), *Benjamin Britten: Peter Grimes*, Cambridge, Cambridge University Press, 1983

PHFB   Paul Hindmarsh, *Frank Bridge: A Thematic Catalogue*, London, Faber Music, 1983

PPT   Marion Thorpe (editor), *Peter Pears: A Tribute on His 75th Birthday*, London, Faber Music/The Britten Estate, 1985

PPTMS   *A Tenor Man's Story*, Central Television/Barrie Gavin, 1985

PR   Philip Reed, *The Incidental Music of Benjamin Britten: A Study and Catalogue of His Music for Film, Theatre and Radio*, Ph.D. dissertation, University of East Anglia, 1988

RDBB   Ronald Duncan, *Working with Britten: A Personal Memoir*, Welcombe, The Rebel Press, 1981

TBB   Anthony Gishford (editor), *Tribute to Benjamin Britten on His Fiftieth Birthday*, London, Faber and Faber, 1963

TP   *A time there was . . . : A Profile of Benjamin Britten*, London Weekend Television/Tony Palmer, 1980

The American Years
1939–1942

Chronology: 1939–1942

Year	Events	Compositions
1939	*9 May*: Britten and Pears arrive Quebec, Canada, leaving for Montreal following day. Spend rest of month and early June at Gray Rocks Inn, St Jovite Station, Quebec Province, where work continues on *Les Illuminations* (Rimbaud) and the Violin Concerto *27 June*: Travels to New York with Pears *July*: Stays at Woodstock, New York, near Aaron Copland *21 August*: Britten and Pears return to New York and take up residence with Dr and Mrs William Mayer and their family, at Amityville, Long Island *27 August*: First performance in Toronto (CBC broadcast) of *Young Apollo*, with the composer as soloist *3 September*: Second World War begins *September*: Receives commission from Japanese government to write work for 2,600th anniversary of the Japanese Imperial House	*May*: BBC: *The Sword in the Stone* (T.H. White, adapted by Marianne Helweg) *July*: *Young Apollo*, for piano and strings *August*: *A.M.D.G.* (Hopkins) for mixed voices *September*: Violin Concerto, Op. 15 *October*: *Les Illuminations*, Op. 18 *December*: *Canadian Carnival (Kermesse Canadienne)*, Op. 19
1940	*15 January*: Soloist in American première of Piano Concerto at Chicago, with the Illinois Symphony Orchestra conducted by Albert Goldberg *30 January*: Sophie Wyss gives first complete performance of *Les Illuminations* in London *February-March*: Seriously ill in New York with streptococcal infection	*April–June*: *Sinfonia da Requiem*, Op. 20 Radio: *The Dark Valley* (with Auden) *July*: *Sonata Romantica* *August*: *Diversions*, Op. 21 *October*: *Seven Sonnets of Michelangelo*, Op. 22 *November*: *Introduction and Rondo alla Burlesca*, Op. 23, No. 1 Radio: *The Dynasts* (after Thomas Hardy)

Year	Events	Compositions
	28 March: First performance of Violin Concerto by Brosa, with New York Philharmonic Orchestra conducted by John Barbirolli, Carnegie Hall, New York *August*: Visit to Owl's Head Inn, Maine *November*: Britten and Pears move to 7 Middagh Street, Brooklyn Heights, where they live until the summer of 1941	
1941	*10 January*: Frank Bridge dies at Friston *29 March*: First performance of *Sinfonia da Requiem*, New York Philharmonic Orchestra conducted by John Barbirolli, Carnegie Hall *5 May*: First performance of *Paul Bunyan* at Colombia University, New York *22 June*: Germany invades Russia *July–August*: Visit to Escondido, California, where Britten and Pears stay with the piano duo, Ethel Bartlett and Rae Robertson. Encounters poetry of George Crabbe *21 September*: First performance of String Quartet No. 1 in Los Angeles. Britten and Pears return to Amityville *7 December*: Japanese attack on Pearl Harbor. USA enters the war	*April*: Radio: *The Rocking Horse Winner* (after D.H. Lawrence) *May*: *Paul Bunyan*, Op. 17 (with Auden) *June*: *Matinées Musicales*, Op. 24 *July–August*: *Mazurka Elegiaca*, Op. 23, No. 2 String Quartet No. 1 in D, Op. 25 *October*: *An American Overture* *Scottish Ballad*, Op. 26
1942	*2–3 January*: Attends performances of *Sinfonia da Requiem* in Boston, conducted by Koussevitzky. Receives a $1,000 commission from the Koussevitzky Foundation to compose *Peter Grimes* *16 January*: First performance of *Diversions* with Paul Wittgenstein as soloist	

Year	Events	Compositions
	16 March: Britten and Pears sail home on board MS *Axel Johnson*. On the trans-Atlantic voyage Britten completes *Hymn to St Cecilia* and composes *A Ceremony of Carols*. Among the unfinished works was a Clarinet Concerto for Benny Goodman	

172   To Wulff Scherchen

Cunard White Star "Ausonia"[1]
May 1st, 1939
[Postmarked Quebec, 9 May]

[. . .]

As there is no chance of posting letters until Sunday this will
have to take the form of a diary.

Well – we caught the train & the boat successfully – except that
I somehow lost a £5 note in the transaction – very sickening, but
I'm not going to spoil the trip over it – £5 won't make or mar us.
We had a party the night before to say goodbye – I say 'party'
but it was rather a sort of 'drop-in' with a bottle of sherry on the
floor – friends of yours came – Enid Slater, Trevor,[2] John Pounder,
Hedli (of course), both the Brosas, & others – & Beth, Kit, & the
new babe,[3] & last but not least Barbara.

Then to the train next day – Barbara & Ralph Hawkes & Trevor
– while the Bridges motored all the way to the boat – darned nice
of them.

The boat's not too bad – except that there's nothing to do. It's so
bloody boring. Eat, sleep, ping-pong, eat, walk decks, eat, eat,
deck-tennis, eat, read, sleep – etc. ad infinitum. Food's not too bad
– only there's too much of it. Weather so far good or moderate – an
aggravating swell to-day which makes ping-pong difficult. I've tried
to read, but no inclination. I suppose this mood is only reaction
after the hurly-burly of the last few weeks – & the emotional
excitement of saying 'goodbye' to people. [. . .] Peter is very
nice & a good companion. We keep to ourselves mostly – merely
because there's nothing here at all attractive to eye, ear, or
intellect. A fearfully boring crowd of English bourgeoisie on
holiday. The lower decks are crowded with refugees, poor devils
– & some of the children are sweet – but very cowed. Well – now
Peter & I've got to go & have cocktails with the Captain & I [will]
write some more later – [. . .]

This is Wednesday now [3 May] – & the last two days have been
unadultered misery. There has been a terrific gale & the ship
bumps, pitches & rolls which makes moving about & keeping still
equally unpleasant – & oh – does she creak? Sleeping at night is
almost impossible. So far Peter & I haven't been ill – but lots of
people are & have been – the feeling one has all the time is
weariness of this continual buffeting – one yearns for still & quiet.

What a fool one is to come away – the more I think of Snape
[. . .] – the more I feel a fool to have left it all. [. . .]

Monday now – we've had an exciting time since I wrote the
above. Icebergs. They were quite large, & got more & more
frequent until eventually the ship was stopped & we heard the ice
bumping against the ship all night. It was the most staggering
night ever. Then the next day was thick fog, until eventually the
ship was stopped for that <u>too</u> & the siren blew boop-boop all
night. Then we had a good morning's run, & then ice again – and
ice all yesterday – so that now we are three days late.

We've got to know the people on the ship better – & some of
them are quite nice – have you ever read a book called '1066 &
all that' – it's very funny, & one of the authors is on board.⁴ We've
got lots of addresses for Canada, & it looks as if we shall stay
East for a month or so & then across – but I'll let you know when
we settle.

[. . .]

Peter & I gave a recital last night – the old ladies adored it. Since
the people discovered my photo in the Bystander⁵ I've had no
peace –!

[. . .]

1 Britten and Pears sailed from Southampton for North America on
  board the *Ausonia* on 29 April and arrived at Quebec on 9 May,
  travelling on to Montreal the next day. On Britten's departure, Bridge
  gave him his own viola, a Giussani, accompanied by the following
  note:

  So that a bit of us accompanies you on your adventure.
  We are all 'revelations' as you know. Just go on expanding.
  Ever your affectionate
  & devoted
  Ethel & Frank
  Bon voyage et bon retour.

2 Trevor Harvey (1911–1989), English conductor. He was an assistant
  chorus master at the BBC from 1935 to 1946 (a period interrupted by
  military service) and then became a freelance conductor. He was
  responsible for some important broadcast performances of Britten's
  music, including the radio features *The Company of Heaven* (1937) and
  The World of the Spirit (1938) – it was Harvey who suggested that
  Britten should compose these scores – and the first performance
  in England of *Diversions*, Op. 21, with Paul Wittgenstein and the
  Bournemouth Municipal Orchestra, on 14 October 1950. He was
  invited by Britten in the same year to conduct *Let's Make an Opera!*

in a London season at the Lyric Theatre, Hammersmith, sharing the conducting with Boyd Neel and Edward Renton, but this proved to be a less than happy experience for conductor and composer and the old association was not resumed in later years.

3 Britten's nephew, Thomas Sebastian Welford (b. 26 March), Beth's first child.

4 Robert Julian Yeatman; his co-author was Walter Carruthers Sellar. *1066 and All That*, a comic history of England, was first published in 1930. See also Mark Lawson 'Wrong but utterly Wromantic', *Independent*, 20 October 1990.

5 London periodical, founded 1903; merged with the *Tatler* in 1940.

173   To Lennox Berkeley

Cunard White Star "Ausonia"
May 3rd 1939.

My dear Lennox,

I hope you are feeling fine & that everything is going as it should. Wulff told me that you went there to lunch on the Friday & that they enjoyed having you alot. Was Dent nice? I hope that when I get to Montreal (if ever, it seems) that there'll be a letter telling me all this.

[. . .] One has no inclination at all to work or to read seriously – so I've been dipping into an enormous range of stuff – from Hans Anderson to Boris Godonof.[1]

As usual a small boy has attached himself – a nice kid of 14, but inclined to cling rather. But they're nice animals!! Otherwise we keep abit separate from the people – very dull colonials, or refugee-emigrés from Central European who naturally keep to themselves. There is a nice Purser who's terrifically hot at ping-pong[2] & whom I've not beaten yet – but determined to do it before this interminable week is out. So far plans are not settled – but expect to stay East until June or end of & then across[3] – more later, my dear.

[. . .] This will go to-night so I'd better stop. Let me know if there are any bothers – & I <u>do</u> hope that you're feeling O.K. my dear. I think about you a great deal – really!

Love

B

1 Pushkin's play, on which Mussorgsky's opera, itself powerfully to influence *Peter Grimes*, was based.

2 Britten was an enthusiastic, skilful, and determined ping-pong player. Table tennis was a favoured form of relaxation (especially with guests) until late in his life. He liked to win.

3 Britten probably meant that he was staying East until June or the end of June and then travelling 'across' to the West, i.e. Hollywood, where he thought he had an offer of a film.

174 To Aaron Copland

Cunard White Star 'Ausonia'
May 8th 1939.

My dear Aaron,

At last, & look where I am![1] On the way to Canada, & surrounded by ice. A thousand reasons – mostly 'problems' – have brought me away, & I've come to stay in your continent for the Summer. I suppose you'll be off to Mexico? But in case you arn't going, couldn't you write me a card to my permanent address: c/o Boosey & Hawkes (Canada) Ltd. 10 Shuter St., Toronto, Ont.? And if things could be fixed – well, you know what way I'd feel. My plans are as follows: probable stay of a month or so round Montreal or Ottawa – then to motor across to Vancouver till end of August. Then I rather want to come South to the States & as there seems a possibility of a job or two to stay the Autumn. But nothing's settled. I've come with the guy I share a flat with in London. Nice person, & I know you'd approve.

You know, Aaron, I've thought lots about you even tho' I haven't written. I love the 2nd Hurricane,[2] & it's keeping your memory green at Snape. I'm jolly glad that B. & H. are printing the Salon Mexico, & I hear Koussevitzky[3] is recording it – Lennox heard it in Paris.

I've had an intolerably busy winter & was nearly crazy with work. I got heavily tied up in a certain direction, which is partly why I'm crossing the ocean! Wystan Auden tells me he's met you – I hope to be seeing him the next month or so.

So Aaron, please anyhow keep in touch with me – even if (as you probably will,) you lose this letter, a letter to Snape will always find me out!

Love,
BENJAMIN

P.S. I <u>may</u> have to go to Hollywood!!!!

1 Copland wrote in response to Britten from the Hotel Empire, New York:

How perfectly extraordinary to think of you here on this side of the water! I can't get used to the idea – but I will. It seems rather sad that since you are only a night-train ride away from N.Y. that you can't come down here for a visit – particularly with Auden & Isherwood here.

My own plans for the summer are still vague. I shall certainly be here till June 1st. I have my Billy the Kid ballet which is being premiered on the 24th by Kirstein's Ballet Caravan. I'm tempted by Mexico in June. Why shouldn't you come down there by boat from Vancouver? and get off at Acapulco. Somehow something must be arranged.

Write me where you are always.

Affectionately
AARON

See also note 2 to Letter 178.

2 *The Second Hurricane* includes a 'chorus of parents' and was purposefully didactic. A likely model for the work was Kurt Weill's highly influential school opera, *Der Jasager*, with a text by Bertolt Brecht, composed and first performed in 1930. Britten's own interest in music for children had already found expression in *Friday Afternoons* (1933–5). It is clear that the significance of *The Second Hurricane* was not lost on him (see also note 5 to Letter 138). It was with an operetta (*Paul Bunyan*) for the American high school that Britten and Auden were to try their hand in 1940–41, and later works, for example *The Little Sweep* (1949), *Noye's Fludde* (1957) and *The Golden Vanity* (1966), extend the tradition. *The Little Sweep*, in particular, combines musical instruction (how an opera is made) with a socio-historical theme (the plight of children chimney-sweepers in the nineteenth century). Typically, the instruction and information are introduced in music of great ingenuity and charm (a didactic approach would not have made much appeal to the composer).

When Britten and Pears arrived in the United States in 1939, the Works Progress Administration, a federally funded organization set up by the Roosevelt government to counter and alleviate the Depression, was still active in the field of the arts and Britten was to encounter it in his association with Albert Goldberg and the Illinois Symphony Orchestra (see Letters 210 *et seq.*). The WPA Federal Art Project, which was launched in August 1935 – on 3 April it was announced that 18,000 musicians were to get jobs in a federal 'arts relief' programme – ushered in a sponsorship of the arts by the federal government that has not been seen since in the States, sponsorship not only of literature 'but architecture, the fine arts, music, dance and drama [. . .]. Sponsored or not, much of the art of the time included a strong and self-conscious strain of social criticism. With a critical but constructive urgency artists rejected the mood of the 1920s [. . .] and often devoted themselves to political causes' (*The National Experience*, Part Two, 6th edition (San Diego, Harcourt Brace Jovanovich, 1985), p. 700 ('The New Deal', by Arthur M. Schlesinger, Jr, revised by John M. Blum). The Depression and its attendant problems, as Russell Lynes has pointed out in *The Lively Audience: A Social History of the Visual and Performing Arts in America, 1890–1950* (New York, Harper & Row, 1985), p. 405, created a mood 'in the community of the arts [. . .] very different from what had been its traditional aloofness from society's problems [. . .]. The Depression had shifted their focus to the political left. They saw a social revolution in the making, and many of them wanted to man the intellectual and political barricades with their skill as satirists and champions of people's rights.' See also Barbara L. Tischler, *An American Music: The Search for an American Musical Identity* (New York, Oxford University Press, 1986), Chapter 5, 'The National Government and National Music', pp. 127–56.

There is nothing to suggest a personal involvement in all of this on Britten's part; in any event America's joining the Second World War in 1941 put an end to the WPA, its activities and its aspirations. None the less he must have been aware of those aspirations and in some ways found them wholly familiar, since they represented the same sort of social preoccupations, and were motivated by the same political thinking, that had coloured significant aspects of Britten's work in the thirties (e.g. for the GPO Film Unit). In fact, his first introduction to the WPA, to the ethos and aesthetics of the New Deal, was in 1938, before his visit to the States, when he heard the play-through of Copland's school opera, itself a product of that era, behind which were European models from the earlier thirties. The rise of fascism in Europe meant that many of the radical creators from Europe fled to hospitable America and took their political engagement with them, and their presence must have helped fuel such initiatives as the WPA.

The political profile of some of Britten's work in the thirties was never to recur with the same sharp definition but, as has been argued in DMBA, many of the 'social' features of his work and his beliefs about it – the children's pieces noted above, for instance, and indeed his whole concept of being 'useful' (not only a duty but also an artist's right) – were in fact rooted in his formative experience in the thirties and the convictions he held.

3 Serge Koussevitzky (1874–1951), Russian-born American conductor of the Boston Symphony Orchestra from 1924 to 1949, whom Copland was to introduce to Britten at Tanglewood in the summer of 1939 (see Letter 202), was to become one of the most influential advocates of Britten's music during his years in the States and after. (See note 3 to Letter 186.) His recording of *El salón México*, with the

Boston Symphony Orchestra, was released on RCA Victor DM-546 in 1939.

Britten had first heard Koussevitzky conducting in London on 15 May 1933, when he wrote in his diary:

Dinner at Bridges at 7.15. T. Brosa & an American composer there. Go on to London Musical Festival concert (B.B.C. orch) after with Grace [Williams]. (Good seats from B.B.C.) Conductor Serge Koussevitzky. Not so startling as I imagined. He seemed too finicky & not at ease. He wasn't very enlightning in Sibelius 7th Symph, abt. which I can't make up my mind. It contains some fine things & some utter tosh. A hectic perf. of Tsch. 5th finished. An uneven work. Concert began with Prokofiev's Classical Symph. Brilliant & witty scoring. Rather dull second movement.

Koussevitzky, who had an emphatic belief in Britten's gifts, was responsible for commissioning Peter Grimes (and the Spring Symphony of 1949). (See The Koussevitzky Music Foundation: Catalog of Works (New York, Boosey & Hawkes, [1958])), which curiously fails to include the Spring Symphony.) But he was also a notable interpreter of Britten's earlier music and the performances he gave with his orchestra of Sinfonia da Requiem and the Bridge Variations were among the best that the composer heard while living in the States. In later years he also included the Four Sea Interludes from Peter Grimes in his repertory. A colourful personal portrait of the conductor, 'Koussevitzki-ana', is to be found in Nicolas Slonimsky's autobiography, Perfect Pitch (Oxford, Oxford University Press, 1988), pp. 91–107.

It was probably Koussevitzky who suggested that Britten should attend a performance of Gershwin's Porgy and Bess in New York in 1942. When Britten heard Porgy and Bess in the theatre – for the first and only time – ideas for his own opera, Peter Grimes, were already taking shape in his mind. Perhaps it is not altogether surprising that Gershwin's remarkable work would have proved to be in some respects a potent influence (one, however, that has gone largely unacknowledged because unrecognized), especially in view of some close dramatic parallels and correspondences which, whether consciously or unconsciously, played a role, we now perceive, in the making of Grimes. The general parallels are obvious, for example in Porgy, as in Grimes, the fishermen go about their business and mend their nets, while the community (=chorus) is as fundamental to Gershwin's dramatic conception as it is to Britten's. We also note that the protagonist of each opera is crippled, Grimes by his psyche, Porgy in his body. More particularly, the advent of the storm in Porgy – which one may think is symbolic of the storm of violence in Crown's mind in precisely the way that it is symbolic of the storm in Grimes's – leads to its use as a musico-dramatic device which provides a clear precedent for a similar procedure in Grimes: cf. Porgy, Act II scene 4, where the storm (already established at the end of the preceding scene; cf. *Grimes*, Act I scene 1) blows Crown into Serena's room. The bursting open of the door and interruption of the proceedings within the room by the music of the storm quite remarkably anticipates the similar sequence of events in the famous 'Pub' scene in *Grimes*. It is impossible not to believe that it was not Gershwin who provided Britten with his brilliant dramatic model and musical scheme. The parallel is strengthened by the succession of elaborate choral ensembles which, in *Porgy*, the orchestral storm music punctuates: one is reminded of the vernacular character of the choral music in Britten's 'Pub' scene, of 'Old Joe has gone fishing', above all. The communal round, sung by the inhabitants of the Borough, performs something of the same function – release of tension, among other things – as Gershwin's quasi-spirituals sung by the inhabitants of Catfish Row; and indeed more than once in *Porgy* one is struck by choral textures in a fast tempo which bring Britten's choral writing to mind (cf. in particular Act I scene 2). Another extraordinary precedent is surely supplied by the Prayer which opens (and closes) Act I scene 1, in which a vocal polyphonic hubbub is secured by solo voices each pursuing and repeating, and freely combining, their independent melodic parts, a technique that may not have serviced any part of *Grimes* but was to become part of Britten's armoury of resources from *Albert Herring* onwards. Finally, the on- or offstage drumming which in *Porgy* opens Act II scene 1, and summons the revellers to the picnic on Kittiwake Island: the sound of that seems to have echoed on in Britten's imagination and re-emerges as the drum-led procession of townsfolk in *Grimes*, Act II scene 1.

Britten rarely mentioned Gershwin. In the field of popular song, it was Cole Porter, rather, whom he admired. But the very fact that Gershwin perhaps made no strong personal appeal to him as a composer makes it all the more fascinating that *Porgy* proved to be so influential. This assimilation of Gershwin's masterpiece shows that Britten did not necessarily have to 'like' a composer in order to find him useful.

175   To Ralph Hawkes

Cunard White Star 'Ausonia'
May 9th 1939.

My dear Ralph,

Well – so far so good. We are due at Quebec to-night & Montreal the following night – three days late, well – better than never. [. . .]

B.B.C. or no BBC., I've done no work at all – but I shall get their stuff done this week & send it off to them by the beginning of June as I promised.[1] Have they communicated you about this? John Cheatle[2] is the man.

So far no definite plans – but we hear of a nice Inn in Mount Tremblante about 80° N of Montreal where we may stay for 6 weeks or so & then go across. I'll let you know later what we decide.

I hope to be able to send you the Rimbaud suite completed at the end of June[3] & the Violin Concerto will follow soon after.[4] I feel I should like to stay out here in the Autumn, so could you tell Heinsheimer that if people enquire I could do i.e. the pft. Concerto? And/or anything else.

I hope you're feeling fit now, & that business is going as well as possible. I will contact all the people you've told me about – & hope to expect you in the Autumn here!!

My love to your wife,
Yours ever
BENJAMIN

Peter sends his love.

1   The incidental music he had been commissioned by the BBC to write for *The Sword in the Stone*, adapted by Marianne Helweg from the Arthurian novel by T.H. White. It was broadcast in a series of six weekly programmes between 11 June and 16 July, with Britten's score performed by the male voices of the BBC Singers and BBC Orchestra, conducted by Leslie Woodgate. When Britten posted his score to London, he enclosed unusually detailed performing notes about each movement of the incidental music to assist Woodgate and the producer, John Cheatle. They were inscribed on the first page of the manuscript full score:

A)   Introduction: in three sections: use preferably all three but starts could be made at 4th or 7th bars. Very pompous – with free trumpet part.

B)   Boys' tunes: in three sections – No. I (Wart) being first page (repeat desirable but not obligatory). No. II (Kay) starting page 2 – rather pompously (this section may be too long – so I've marked a possible cut of four bars on page 3). No. III (last bar of page 3) – both tunes together (repeat obligatory).

C)   Merlyn is a bassoon solo – with a little counterpoint in the middle (Merlyn was well educated!) – and his mission is suggested by a quotation on trumpet on page 3 – but the end is somewhat blasé.

D)   Spell – hope this is what you want – if it isn't – alter it how you will.

E)   A lullaby – very touching this. (I beseech you use it all) – the end's a bit realistic. (Quite slow but one in a bar.)

F)   Water music – Wind instruments to sound 'gurgly' must be <u>clear</u> – so
     don't let the boys take it too fast. Repeat the end as often as you like
     – or fade it. Harp – very soft, but <u>audible</u> always.

G)   I've done the two tunes as you said   1) Trombone, '40 years on'
     2) Trumpet 'Eton Boating S.'   3) Both together and added a drum,
     horsey, accompaniment. I'm not clear as to what you wanted for the
     actual joust – I roughly sketched a percussion bit (on the 2nd page –
     end) which may be quite wrong – anyhow I suggest you explain to the
     player – and he can use my rhythms as you direct.

H)   The Jousting Song – The words wouldn't fit either of the tunes – so
     I've muddled them: suggest Pelinore has a bit at the end (in the original
     copy – end is like this) and then (as directed) both together – Key as
     you please (to suit singers).

I)   Couldn't think of Bird noises – so you'll find one original bird. (Donald
     Duck?!) on trombone – & visitors from Beethoven (Pastoral Symphony),
     Wagner (Siegfried), Strauss (Bourgeois Gentilhomme), Liza Lehmann
     (Bird Songs) & Delius (1st Cuckoo) – which may be abit incongruous –
     but it's the best I can do!!!

J)   I've done two settings of the Hymn – one solemn & an obvious parody:
     the other still parodying but perhaps less embarrassing – I prefer no. I
     – all these unaccompanied things can be transposed at will.

K)   Lustily is all I ask – & <u>accurately</u>!!

L)   Witch music – has come out as a Dance of Death, <u>please</u> use it all! The
     middle is an incantation – of sorts.

M)   <u>Please</u> may the witch have a drum background – or if not a drum, let
     her (or someone else) stamp – or hit a broom or anything. I want the
     rhythm. The song should be scarcely sung at all. The two spoken bits
     (Wart & Madame Mim) I should like over the rhythmic background.

N)   Tree music. Just sentimental background – plenty of harp, please. <u>Not</u>
     fast. It's only supposed to be a background – but if it's too short, just
     repeat from beginning.

O)   Hope it's not too long, but scarcely cuttable. Should make the hell of a
     din.

     <u>Sword Chords</u>
     <u>Must</u> have the best players possible to do justice to this deep & subtle
     music.

There have been two subsequent radio productions: in 1952 and
1982.

A suite from the score was compiled by Colin Matthews in 1983
and performed at the Aldeburgh Festival that year by the Aldeburgh
Festival Chamber Ensemble, directed by Oliver Knussen. It was published by Faber Music in 1989. See PR, pp. 396–412 and 587–93.

2 John Cheatle, BBC radio producer. Britten had worked with Cheatle
in 1937 on a radio programme, *Up the Garden Path*, in which Auden
also was involved. See DMBA, pp. 105–7, and PR, pp. 361–2.

3 In fact *Les Illuminations* in its final form was not completed until

October, by which time Britten and Pears were living at Amityville on Long Island, New York.

4 The composition of the Violin Concerto was completed while Britten was still in Canada. He left for New York on 27 June and finished the full score at Amityville on 20 September. See Letters 207 and 210.

176 To Ralph Hawkes

> Gray Rocks Inn Limited
> St. Jovite Station
> Province of Quebec
> Canada
> May 16th 1939.

My dear Ralph,

Thank you for your letter – I hope by now that you've got mine from the boat.

We eventually arrived last Wednesday (9th) & spent two days in Montreal, looking around the place. I went & saw Dr. Gagnier & M. Boudet at the C.B.C.[1] and they treated us like kings & showed us all over the place. They had actually planned to have a show of the Variations on the Tuesday – a welcome of sorts! – but the band wasn't big or good enough & anyhow, the boat was late. I am now waiting around to hear definitely whether they want me to conduct them in Toronto towards the end of June[2] – it seems pretty definite & so I thought it best to stay about until then & not miss it. So Peter & I heard of this place up in the Laurentians & it's turned out first class – abit expensive (65 [Canadian dollars] together a week), but just what we wanted. We live in a wooden cabin up the hill, away from the Inn itself – very quiet, & with every luxury! There's tennis, golf, fishing (the place is situated on a glorious lake), hunting & skiing in the winter – I suggest <u>when</u> you come over this might be a good holiday place. People are friendly & very nice.

Anyhow – I got down to my BBC. job & finished it yesterday & sent it off to-day. Could you please collect the money & send it to my Solicitor – he'll probably need it for odd things in England? I suppose they won't pay any more for it (they mentioned 20 guineas) – it was a hefty job – 15 bits, & about six playing at least a minute. What do you <u>think</u>? Another mercenary thing – the BBC I hear may be repeating the Whitsun programme[3] I did for them last year. Ellis Roberts who did the script (an outsider like myself) gets I hear a fee everytime this happens. Do I – or couldn't I?

I'm now free to start on the Violin Concerto in earnest – & shall probably do so to-day. I'm bucked about it – & hope to get a sketch done while I'm here. It would be grand if Toni Brosa could do it in America next season. I should have to be out here for it, too? We expect to be here for three more weeks – then Ottawa & Toronto for a few days. Then as time is so short it looks as if we may miss Vancouver – it's so far away, & if we motored it would only leave a fortnight or so before we had to come back. So we rather hanker after the States – New York for a little to contact Heinsheimer & others (probably Willy W.⁴ as you suggest – & Aaron Copland & Auden etc.) – & then south for the rest of the time. That's to say if we can get visas.⁵ We tried in Montreal, but they didn't like the idea of giving them to us, & asked why we didn't get them in England. I think it would help if you could write an official note saying that we wouldn't be a burden on the State if we went & that you think we're good boys & won't go blowing up things. And then if I can get Heinsheimer to write saying it's necessary for me to come – & one or two other people – with the help of the Tweedsmuirs⁶ – we may get it. But they're horribly sticky.

Sorry this is so long – but there's lots to say. I hope you're well & flourishing – & family too.

We're enjoying this trip no end – & I'm feeling terrifically fit & out to beat the world with the Fiddle conc!

Yours ever,
BENJAMIN

1 The Canadian Broadcasting Corporation, with which Britten was to establish firm links during the few weeks he spent in Canada. It would have been the French section of the CBC in Montreal, then housed in the King's Hall Building on St Catherine's Street, that Britten first visited soon after his arrival. Dr Jean-Josaphat Gagnier was a French–Canadian conductor, composer and administrator. He came from a family of Montreal-based musicians and was Regional Director of Music at CBC, Montreal, from 1934 until his death in 1949. Jean Beaudet was the Station's Program Director.

2 The performance, broadcast from Toronto, was given on 18 June, though it was not conducted by Britten. See note 1 to Letter 177.

3 *The World of the Spirit.*

4 Walton visited the States in the spring of 1939 to consult Jascha Heifetz, for whom he was writing his Violin Concerto. He completed the score in New York in early June and intended to return for the

première of the work, which was given by Heifetz with the Cleveland Orchestra conducted by Artur Rodzinski on 7 December. However, a letter Walton wrote to the conductor, Leslie Heward, in March (see LFBML, pp. 213–14), explicates the original proposed circumstances of the concerto's first performance and the reasons for its delayed première:

As you may have seen I've withdrawn my Concerto from the World's Fair not as is stated because it's unfinished but because Heifetz can't play on the date fixed (the B.C. [British Council] only let him know about ten days ago!) Heifetz wants the concerto for two years and I would rather stick to him. But actually I'm afraid there is little to be said for either the British Council or myself, so keep this 'under your hat'.

So I'm out of the World's Fair altogether. I understand that all the music programmes barring those of the B.C. have been cancelled and that nothing is happening at all.

Unfortunately I know very little about American conditions, but I am going over sometime soon to look with Heifetz on the concerto probably the same time as you [. . .]

But by then the Second World War had begun and Walton was unable to be present at the Cleveland première. The first New York performance was to take place at Carnegie Hall on 5 February 1941 (we do not know if Britten was present), just ten months after the first performance there of Britten's Violin Concerto. (Heifetz was never to perform Britten's concerto, though it seems that he expressed an interest in it, probably after Britten's return to England.) Interestingly, Walton had enjoyed the advice of another violinist while writing his concerto, Antonio Brosa, who seems to have played much the same role in relation to Walton's work as he was to play later in relation to Britten's. Walton and Brosa had collaborated in the film *Dreaming Lips* (1937), in which Raymond Massey played the role of a violinist and Walton's score was performed by the London Symphony Orchestra under Boyd Neel. The complex network of crossovers and interrelationships between musicians in the 1930s is itself of no little fascination. Britten's hopes, however, of meeting Walton were not to be realized: he had left New York for home before Britten arrived there (see Letter 186). See Neil Tierney, *William Walton, His Life and Music* (London, Robert Hale, 1984), pp. 83–8, and Susana Walton, *William Walton: Behind the Façade* (Oxford, Oxford University Press, 1988), pp. 87–92, and MKWW, pp. 96–107.

5 For entry into the United States.

6 The first Baron Tweedsmuir (1875–1940), Governor General of Canada from 1935 until his death. He was John Buchan, the celebrated author of *The Thirty-Nine Steps* (1915) and other spy thrillers of the First World War.

177   To Wulff Scherchen

Gray Rocks Inn Limited
St. Jovite Station
Province of Quebec
Canada
May 16th 1939

[. . .]

This is only a note to tell you that we are staying here for about a month. It is a heavenly spot – & we have a log cabin at the side of a hill overlooking a grand lake & lots of forests. It is very uncivilised country – quite wild – but very rugged – beautiful. We are both working very hard – & enjoying it all lots.

[. . .]

I expect we'll stay here till the middle of June – & then south to Toronto, where I've got to conduct the Variations¹ & probably play the Concerto on the Radio.² And then I want to go up to the States to see people, & Wystan & Christopher too in New York. We may spend the rest of the time³ in the States. Anyhow I'll let you know later.

[. . .]

1 The *Frank Bridge Variations* were in fact performed by a CBC ensemble under the direction of Alexander Chuhaldin. Britten, however, introduced the performance and spoke a few words after it. While in Toronto he stayed with the conductor and his wife. See also Letter 186.

2 Harry Edward Jarman, the Managing Director of Boosey & Hawkes (Canada) Ltd from 1938 to 1947, had tried to secure a performance of the Piano Concerto, with Britten as soloist, at about the same time as the broadcast of the *Bridge Variations*. This, however, never took place. Jarman made up for the disappointment by arranging for Britten and Pears to give a short recital of Britten's songs (*On this Island*?), which was broadcast in June from Toronto by the national network of CBC; it was also possibly transmitted by the Mutual Broadcasting System (MBS) in the United States.

3 This would suggest that, when writing this letter at least, Britten had in mind a limit to the duration of his and Pears's stay. Indeed, when booking their passage on the *Ausonia* Britten and Pears had in fact made 'round trip', i.e. return, reservations.

Logo for the World's Fair, New York, 1939

178   To Aaron Copland

> Gray Rocks Inn Limited
> St. Jovite Station
> Province of Quebec
> Canada
> May 18th 1939.

My dear Aaron,

It was grand to get your letter – & to know that you're still about the place. It seems very odd to be this side of the Atlantic – & at the moment I'm feeling very strange & out of my depth! But we've found a good place up in the Laurentians – & have got a log-cabin at the side of the mountain overlooking the lake, & I'm doing lots of work – & we're sticking around till I hear definitely from the C.B.C. when they want me to go & conduct my old Variations for them. Probably at the end of June. Then I want to come south to New York & after that – well, that's the problem. You say you'll be around (see how American I'm getting – my accent's getting quite the genuine article!) till beginning of June – then probably Mexico. We <u>might</u> get a boat down to Mexico from New York & spend the rest of the time there (Peter, who's with me, has to go back to England at the end of August, & I stay on <u>if</u> money lasts) – but this depends on whether the fare is expensive or not – & whether you'd know of somewhere cheap where we could stay. The alternatives are (a) Florida (b) New England. I suppose you couldn't think of coming up to either of those for abit in the summer? But tell me – is Mexico terribly <u>hot</u> in July or August?[1]

Sorry this is so vague – but I'm like that at the moment.

I do hope that Billy the Kid'll be a grand success. I've heard lots of the Kirstein people & they sound fine.[2] Will they be doing it at the World Fair[3] & is there any chance of us seeing it when we go, perhaps, in July?

Don't you dare go away without letting me know where you are
going & all that –

Love,

BENJAMIN

1 The Mexican trip did not materialize. It was not in fact until 1967
that Britten and Pears first visited Mexico, as part of their tour of
Latin America for the British Council.

2 *Billy the Kid*, a ballet in one act, choreographed by Eugene Loring (b.
1914), with music by Copland (played on two pianos), first performed
in Chicago in October 1938 by the Ballet Caravan (whose music
director at the time was Elliot Carter). The New York première (with
orchestra) was given on 24 May 1939, again by the Ballet Caravan.
The score was the result of a commission by Lincoln Kirstein (b.
1907), with whom Britten was later to work in New York, no doubt
through Copland's introduction. At one stage in the history of *Paul
Bunyan* it seemed as if Kirstein were to produce the operetta (see
Cecil Smith's column on Britten in the *Chicago Tribune*, 14 January
1940, where he refers to *John Bunyan* [*sic*] with a libretto by 'William
Auden'). It was for Kirstein and his American Ballet Company that
Britten in 1941 composed – and to whom he dedicated – a further
Rossini suite, *Matinées Musicales*, Op. 24. This score, together with
the earlier *Soirées Musicales*, Op. 9 (1936), provided the music for
the ballet *Divertimento*, with choreography by George Balanchine
(1904–1983). At about the same time he made an arrangement for a
small orchestra of *Les Sylphides*, for use by Ballet Presentations Inc.
(Ballet Theater), New York, the score of which has been lost. In 1942,
the *Bridge Variations* (in a two-piano arrangement by Colin McPhee)
were used as the basis for a ballet, *Jinx*, first performed by Loring
and his Dance Players at the National Theater, New York, with
choreography by Lew Christensen. McPhee wrote to William and
Elizabeth Mayer on 15 April 1942 from 7 Middagh Street:

Just a line to say hello, and let you know that the two-piano arrangement
of Ben's Variations seems to be a success, although I have not heard it yet.
They are doing it next week here, but alas, I shall be away lecturing, and
not back till the end of the week.

McPhee also wrote to Britten in July:

Wish you had heard the Variations; they sounded well, all except the fugue,
which was nothing. As for publishing, I'm afraid there is nothing doing here
yet.

McPhee's arrangement remains unpublished. *Jinx* was in the repertory of the New York City Ballet when the company (of which
Kirstein was the moving spirit) visited London in 1950. For the story
of the ballet, see Donald Mitchell, 'Jinx', in the *Decca Book of Ballet*,
edited by David Drew (London, Muller, 1958), pp. 414–16. See also
EWW, pp. 40 and 75, and Aaron Copland and Vivian Perlis, *Copland:
1900 through 1942* (London, Faber and Faber, 1984), pp. 279–84.

3 The World's Fair, held in New York in 1939, where English music was represented by Bliss's Piano Concerto, and works by Bax (the world première of his Seventh Symphony), Goossens (the American première of his oboe concerto with Leon Goossens as soloist), and Vaughan Williams (the world première of *Five Variants on Dives and Lazarus*). These works made up two programmes, given on 9 and 10 June, under the auspices of the British Council, when the New York Philharmonic Orchestra was conducted by Sir Adrian Boult. It was on the latter date that Solomon appeared as soloist in Bliss's concerto.

Bliss, like Britten, was caught in the USA by the outbreak of war, about which he wrote to Britten from Stockbridge, Massachusetts, on 10 September, offering shelter. This generous offer was repeated in a further letter 22 September, in which Bliss also mentions E.J. Dent, who had been in New York for a meeting of the American Musicological Society, but had left in haste in the light of the international situation.

In April 1940, a few months after the American première of Britten's Piano Concerto at Chicago, Bliss's Concerto for two pianos and orchestra was also performed by the Illinois Symphony Orchestra, another example of the orchestra's adventurous policy towards new music. Bliss was not able to return to England (by way of Canada) until June 1941. A full account of this period is given in Bliss's autobiography, Chapters XII and XIII, pp. 120–39.

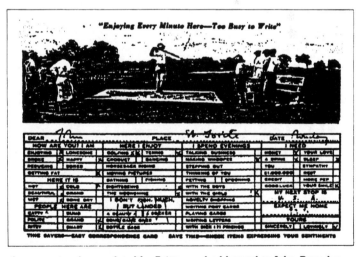

A pro forma postcard, completed by Britten and addressed to John Pounder, postmarked Montreal 23 May 1939

179   To Henry Boys

[*Picture postcard: Gray Rocks Inn,
Lake Ouiment and Mount Tremblant in background,
St. Jovite, Province of Quebec*]

[Canada]
[May/June 1939]

My dear Henry,

   This is a great spot & very quiet – with tennis golf – canoing –
& I'm doing lots of work – well on with your violin concerto.[1] We
expect to go south to the States at the end of June – & may link up
with Aaron. Hope you are well & that your father's much better –
my love to your mother & yourself.

BENJAMIN

1 The Concerto was to be dedicated to Boys.

180   To Ralph Hawkes

Gray Rocks Inn Limited
St. Jovite Station
Province of Quebec
Canada
June 1st 1939.

My dear Ralph,

I hope by now that you will have had our letters – we discover that
letters take ages to reach this out of the way spot – at least 10
days.
   Well – things are going fine. This is a good place – & I'm glad
we picked on it (although it's frightfully expensive – 65 dollars
aweek for the two – but living seems to be generally that way round
here). We've played tennis & golf lots – walked & canoed lots –
& as for work – well – I've already finished the second movement
of the Fiddle concerto – & the third should be done at the end of
the week. The scoring shouldn't take long – but I may leave that
till Toni Brosa's seen the violin part – which I'll copy & send to
him within a few weeks. I'm pretty pleased with it so far. It's very
serious – & should please the critics anyhow in <u>that</u> respect.
   We go south to Grand Rapids to stay with some friends of Peter's
next week.[1] We shall call in at Toronto on the way – but our

longer stay there will be left till after G. Raps. when I may conduct
the Variations over the Radio, & see those friends of yours. Jarman
has been very good indeed in every way, & is making lots of
arrangements too. So is Heinsheimer. I hope to go to N. York at
the end of June – & then South from there – probably with Aaron
Copland.

I've had the enclosed letter from Sir(!) Mayer & don't know what
to say. If you think it's worth it – I shall probably be doing a
Canadian pot-pourri[2] – called Grey Rocks – or St. Jovite & he might
like the first show of that (in England) – but what you will –

Post now – so I must go.

Hope you're well & everything good.

Wish you'd come out here – you'd like this spot – what about
the Autumn!!

Yours,

BEN

Peter sends his respects.

1 Harold and Mary Einecke. Einecke, an organist, and conductor of
the Park Congregational Church Chancel Choir, was closely involved
in the annual Bach Festival of Grand Rapids, in which Pears took
part in January 1941. See Letter 186.

2 A work that he was still to compose, *Kermesse Canadienne* ('Canadian
Carnival'), Op. 19, for orchestra, completed on 10 December 1939,
by which time he was resident on Long Island, New York. In the
event, the first performance was not given under Robert Mayer's
auspices. The first performance was a broadcast, on 6 June 1940,
from the Bristol studios of the BBC, conducted by Clarence Raybould.
(It was to Bristol that the BBC Symphony Orchestra had moved as
a result of the outbreak of war in September 1939.) In a letter to
Ernest Chapman, on the day of the broadcast, Erwin Stein wrote:

I was not able to get to Bristol as there are further restrictions now for aliens
and I should have had to get a Permit from the Police. Honestly I was not
very keen to do this. I wonder whether you will be able to hear it this
evening. I quite agree with your idea of sending out a press communiqué
about Britten. Thank you for your offer. I will send you a draft shortly. The
only trouble is that the boy writes so many new things at the same time.

The concert première was given by the London Philharmonic
Orchestra conducted by the composer, on 13 June 1945, as part of
the first Cheltenham Festival.

181   To Ralph Hawkes

> Gray Rocks Inn Limited
> St. Jovite Station
> Province of Quebec
> Canada
> June 3rd 1939.

My dear Ralph,

Many thanks for your letter – which I was relieved to get – I'd thought I was completely forgotten. I was very much taken by surprise, I confess, by the fact that you want the Rimbaud songs so quickly. Since your last letter, I'd thrown everything aside except the Violin Concerto – & concentrated hard on that. I have nearly finished that now – & so I shall be able to continue with the Rimbaud pretty soon – but not in time I'm afraid for letting you have it by the end of the month. What I suggest is – if Sacher[1] insists on seeing something by then – let him have a look at the two you've already got – & the following is an approximate scheme you could tell him:

1)   Introduction (Fanfare)
2)   Mouvement
3)   Being Beauteous
4)   Marine
5)   Antique
6)   Phrases
7)   Parade

The whole playing about 20 mins.[2] I warn you that the 'management reserve the right to alter the programme' but I think it'll be like that alright.

As for Herbage[3] and the proms. I don't see how I can cut the work, as I particularly don't want anymore bits & pieces done separately before the complete work. I should much prefer Sacher to do the 1st show – or Boyd Neel[4] in London – or what you will.

I sent the BBC stuff off ages ago – I hope they've got it – if they won't pay more than 20 guineas I'd better stick to that! It was a beastly job!

Peter & I set off for the South on Wednesday – Paying a visit to the C.B.C. in Montreal on the way & Jarman in Toronto too. We are going to Grand Rapids for a week. After that I've got to come back to Toronto to witness a show of the Variations & speak on the Radio first – horrible thought! Then probably south to the States but I'll let you know.

Apart from the fearful amount & viciousness of the mosquitoes we are still enjoying this place. We have made friends with several members of the fair sex & goodness knows in what state I'll come back! My love to Erika[5] – hope she liked Paris. Excuse haste but I want to catch the fast boat –

Yours ever,

BEN

P.S.   Please tell old Herbage that if he doesn't want Sophie Wyss (to do the Rimbaud) at the proms – he can't have the songs anyhow – I won't be palmed off with his old crocks![6]

1   Paul Sacher (b. 1906), Swiss conductor and generous patron and benefactor of the arts and artists, and of contemporary composers in particular. Sacher founded the Basel Chamber Orchestra in 1926 and remained its principal conductor until his retirement in 1986. Among the many eminent twentieth-century composers whom Sacher invited to write works for his orchestra were Bartók, Hindemith, Honegger, Frank Martin, Martinů, Stravinsky and Tippett. It is evidence of Sacher's exceptional awareness of the contemporary scene that he had (presumably) responded to the overtures made to him by Ralph Hawkes about the youthful Britten; or perhaps the initiative was his own? If the latter, then it is also evidence of Britten's growing European reputation. Sacher might well have been particularly intrigued by Britten's special, proven skills in the area of the string orchestra. These were the forces which Bartók, for example, used in the work commissioned by Sacher in 1939 (his *Divertimento*); likewise, Stravinsky's Concerto in D of 1946. But it was not until the post-war years that Britten's relationship with Sacher flowered both personally and professionally. It was a commission from Sacher that led to the composition of the *Cantata Academica* ('Carmen Basiliense'), Op. 62, in 1959, celebrating the 500th Anniversary of Basel University, the first performance of which on 1 July 1960 was conducted by Sacher, with the Basel Chamber Orchestra. The composition sketch and full score are now in the Paul Sacher Stiftung in Basel, as too is Britten's manuscript of the theme, for solo cello, the *Tema . . . SACHER*. Britten's homage on the occasion of Sacher's seventieth birthday in 1976 served as the basis of a set of celebratory variations contributed by other composers. See *Komponisten des 20. Jahrhunderts in der Paul Sacher Stiftung* (Basel, Paul Sacher Stiftung, 1986).

2   This of course was not the shape that *Les Illuminations* was finally to assume and it interestingly shows how, gradually and stage by stage,

the song-cycle came to be assembled, from the composition of the first songs (as isolated numbers) to the emerging of the *cycle* as we know it today. To make comparison easy, and to document the chronology of the work, we place side by side the scheme as outlined in the letter and the scheme of the cycle as published, indicating in the latter all the known dates of the composition of the individual songs. The figures in square brackets in the left-hand column indicate the placing of the songs in the final (right-hand) scheme:

	June 1939		*October 1939*
(1)[1]	Introduction (Fanfare)	(1)	Fanfare [undated]
(2)	Mouvement	(2)	Villes 4 October 1939
(3)[7]	Being Beauteous	(3)	a) Phrase [undated]
			b) Antique [undated]
(4)[5]	Marine	(4)	Royauté 6 July 1939
			[Woodstock]
(5)[3b]	Antique	(5)	Marine 18 March 1939
			[Snape]
(6)[3a]	Phrases [*sic*]	(6)	Interlude [undated]
(7)[8]	Parade	(7)	Being Beauteous 16 March 1939
		(8)	Parade 9 October 1939
		(9)	Départ 4 October 1939

Three further settings of Rimbaud were completed in composition sketch but did not form part of the final version of the work: 'Aube', 'Phrase' ('La Cascade sonne': undated; see note 2 to Letter 215), and 'A une raison' ('Un coup de ton doigt': undated). A setting of 'Un prince était vexé' was started but not finished (and is not dated). In the manuscript full score, only two songs are dated: 'Being Beauteous' (11 April 1939) and 'Royauté' (Woodstock, July 1939). There is an overall completion date at the end of the manuscript: 'Amityville, NY, 25 October 1939'.

3 Julian Herbage (1904–1976), English conductor, scholar and musical administrator. From 1927 to 1946 he was on the music staff of the BBC with special responsibility for planning the Proms. He was a noted specialist in English music of the seventeenth and eighteenth centuries. His surviving papers, including his Arne research notes, were placed in the Britten–Pears Library after his death. He was a popular broadcaster and, with his wife, Anna Instone, edited for many years the BBC Sunday morning programme, *Music Magazine*. In his musical views and enthusiasms he was very much a spokesman for the musical orthodoxy of the 1930s and 1940s in England. See PFL, plate 82.

In his role as Assistant Director of Music at the BBC, a post to which he was appointed in 1940, Herbage often found himself required to pronounce on new music. It was in this capacity that he reported in an internal memorandum dated 23 April 1942, having attended 'an audition at Boosey and Hawkes yesterday afternoon of new works by Benjamin Britten who has just returned to England from the United States'. He continues: 'With him was Peter Pears, who not only sang song groups, but also assisted at the second piano in the orchestral and two piano music.' This is a comment which illuminates a little-known aspect of Pears's remarkable musicianship. In many ways the occasion must have reflected the very many times the two men had played through new works by Britten at Stanton Cottage, Amityville, when staying with the Mayers.

Herbage's report is of no little interest, and notable for the generosity of its response to what he heard. Britten and Pears had only landed at Liverpool a few days before, on 17 April, and this preview must have been the first chance an English musician would have had to encounter the works in performance (albeit that the orchestral works appeared in two-piano guise):

Sinfonia da Requiem (20 mins)
I already had the score and a high opinion of this. Although the two pianos did little to convey the orchestral colour, I am convinced it should make a great impression, and is undoubtedly Britten's most significant contribution to the orchestral field. It has had great success in America, and Koussevitsky has played it several times.

Michelangelo Song Cycle (16 mins)
An extremely fine cycle – Italianate virility of vocal line and simplicity and extreme effectiveness of piano accompaniment have produced an unusual and notable work. The whole was sung twice, at the beginning and at the end of the audition, and confirmed more deeply first impressions on second hearing.

Scottish Ballad for two pianos and orchestra (15 mins)
A show piece for Ethel Bartlett and Rae Robinson [*sic*]: the opening chorale, funeral march, leads unexpectedly to a reel based on a well-known Scottish tune (whose name I've forgotten). Well written, effective, an ideal Prom piece and a valuable addition to the repertoire.

Irish Folk Songs for tenor and piano
The least satisfying of the four works, though quite charming and well executed, they have an ingenuousness which to my mind descends to the childish or silly clever. They make quite pleasant listening if not too critically approached.

My whole impression is that during the last couple of years Britten has grown greatly in stature as a composer and has now found a simple individual and clear cut style. With his extraordinary mastery of technique one looks for most important if not great things from him in the future.

On 8 June 1945, a day after the opera's première, Herbage was to write an assessment of *Peter Grimes* for internal circulation at the BBC, though this time one as negative in its views as his 1942 memorandum had been positive: it was addressed to the Director of Music, Victor Hely-Hutchinson. The predictions embodied in the last paragraph read a shade oddly in the light of the performance history of the opera:

Much publicity has been made of the fact that 'Peter Grimes' is the first new opera to be performed in any important capital since the beginning of the war. Certainly it was a brave and praiseworthy effort of the Sadler's Wells Company to return to their old home with a new opera.

'Peter Grimes' is certainly a work on a full scale – it lasted, with intervals, from 6.45 until just on 9.30 p.m. I see that in the press it has been compared to Moussorgsky's 'Boris', though apart from the fact that the plot is handled 'realistically' and that the Chorus (i.e. the people) replaces the traditional operatic hero, there seems to me to be little futher resemblances.

The libretto of 'Peter Grimes' makes an obvious attempt to get away from conventional opera. The subject is sordid – the life of a squalid fishing village painted in all its unpleasant colours – and there are no heroics and little love interest. In making Grimes the central figure the librettist had to steer a very balanced course in order to portray both the vicious side of his character and at the same time hold the audience's sympathetic interest. Without having read the libretto (and I could hear practically no word of what was being sung), it is difficult to judge how successfully he has carried out his task. From what I could judge, however, in spite of many effective scenes the libretto is hardly one which would carry the opera to public popularity.

One naturally expects from Britten a score of extreme technical competence and facility. Britten's greatest fault indeed is that he thinks and writes in terms of music with such fluency that he very often seizes on his first musical thought, however trivial it may be, and gives it a technical twist which produces a superficial illusion of originality. One felt throughout the opera that the score contained far too much intellect and far too little heart or, going even further, really original expression and characterisation. Certain technical devices, particularly (in the composition) the use of pedal points and (in the orchestration) decoration by means of flute figuration, were very much overdone. Britten too seemed to have little sympathy with or insight into most of his characters – they came out on the whole as rather flat and trite caricatures. Only Grimes himself and the schoolmistress Ellen were painted with any intensity of creative feeling, and many characters, such as 'Auntie' and the 'nieces' were completely thrown away.

The music, through its technical ingenuity and original and incisive orchestration, keeps one interested throughout, though in my opinion the first act is not nearly so good as the other two. The actual musical material, however, apart from its treatment, is often trivial and commonplace in the extreme. Again only in rare moments does it become dramatic as opposed to theatrical. Some moments, however, are of extreme beauty in themselves, particularly the first scene of Peter Grimes and Ellen, Ellen's conversation with the workhouse apprentice to the background of a service in the village church, the whole of the scene in Peter Grimes's hut (to my mind the high spot of the opera), the women's quartet, and the choruses in the third act. Incidentally, I cannot understand why it was necessary to break into the spoken word at the end of the third act and stop all orchestral background for a period which sounded like (to one in the audience) at least 3 or 4 minutes.

Finally I must mention that the style throughout was extremely eclectic –

one of Ellen's arias had come almost straight out of 'Madam Butterfly', while one interlude was complete Sibelius and another (the passacaglia) owed much to Berg's 'Wozzeck'.

The décor was on the whole most effective, particularly the village square, though I felt the lighting (or rather lack of it) was rather overdone. The Sadler's Wells stage, however, was not large enough for certain scenes, and the inside of the 'Boar' gave one the impression of a Piccadilly pub on VE day.

Obviously much care had gone into the production, and though the chorus as usual over-acted to the point of burlesque their team work was excellent. It is a great pity that so few words could be heard – as far as the chorus was concerned this was mainly due to Britten's treatment of the chorus as part of the orchestra, but the soloists could certainly have improved their diction if they had shouted less and articulated more. The opera was excellently cast, and apart from the usual vocal limitations of the Sadler's Wells Company, it seems invidious to pick any of them out for special praise. I should imagine, however, that never will Peter Pears (Peter Grimes) or Joan Cross (Ellen Orford) be more suitably cast. Incidentally, if Pears continues to sing his mad scene in his present throat straining manner he would be liable to lose his voice.

Much praise has been lavished on Reginald Goodall, the conductor. Certainly he had heavy odds to contend with in an indifferent orchestra, and certainly he kept things together and moving. I did not feel, however, that he showed signs of being any more than the normal competent operatic conductor, and I would certainly like to hear some of the music again in better surroundings with a better orchestra and a more experienced man on the rostrum.

To sum up, the opera was a very ambitious and praiseworthy effort for a first attempt. It undoubtedly exploited all Britten's undoubted talent as well as showing up certain weaknesses. I cannot think it will make an addition to the repertoire though if Britten ever chooses to write a further opera he will undoubtedly have gained great experience. I feel, however, that he is at present standing too intellectually aloof from his subject, and until he enters more intensely into his drama and characterisation and until he purges his style of many of his trivial and eclectic elements, he will not make a real success in the operatic field.

Yet another BBC internal memorandum (dated 11 June), this time from Basil Douglas, expressed quite another point of view:

I am convinced that the production of this opera is of the first musical importance, not only because it is a very fine work, but also because its influence on the future of opera in this country may well be decisive. Britten may write better and more successful operas – there are several factors, most of them nothing to do with music, that may prejudice a prolonged life for 'Peter Grimes', and I for one hope that the psychology of the next one will be clearer – but it is none the less an astonishing technical achievement. With the exception of one scene in the third act, the opera is 'durchkomponiert' in a succession of varied forms, each of them a genuine musical growth it itself, and the result is, in my opinion, a remarkably unified and well-balanced structure – with the one exception of the last scene, which I feel is slightly misjudged. The music is intensely dramatic and vital, exceptionally vocal and brilliantly orchestrated (the characterisation and tone-painting in the orchestra is extraordinarily vivid and subtle, and there are passages of strong emotional power and beauty). The range of his technical resources is extremely wide and varied – there are frequent hints of Verdi (the way he plunges straight into the Prologue, for example, reminds one of 'Falstaff', and the dramatic use of the chorus recalls 'Macbeth'), and for the eloquent freedom of the recitations he readily acknowledges the example of Purcell – and one could point to several other influences. But Britten has absorbed these composers into his own style, which is now quite individual.

The Performance

The two performances I have heard went extremely well. The chorus sang splendidly, though not always with complete clarity; the complicated rhythms are still giving them trouble and the producer has obviously insisted that they look at the conductor as little as possible, which doesn't help; but familiarity should breed clearer diction. The principals all came up to expectations and there was some fine singing and acting from Peter Pears and Joan Cross. In fact the standard of singing was a good deal higher than has been noticeable recently in their performances of other operas. The orchestral playing was adequate, but this music wants first-class players in every department, and more strings.

Broadcasting

I hope we shall be able to broadcast it soon, and I would strongly urge that it be broadcast in its entirety. The gesture to the enterprise of Sadler's Wells would be more complete, and besides, the organic structure of the work makes it very important that it should be heard as a whole; otherwise the listener will miss one of its most remarkable features.

Faced with so diametrically opposed opinions, Kenneth Wright (the Deputy Director of Music), in the final memorandum of this series (13 June), gave a breathtaking demonstration of how to sit on both sides of the fence simultaneously:

I do feel, having seen it myself and agreeing almost completely with the existing reports from Mr Herbage and Mr Douglas, that we ought to put ourselves out to reflect this work in our programmes, far more than merely to include some interludes in a Promenade Concert, which may, in fact, not be broadcast. This is the kind of musical event of importance which in Paris or Brussels would never be allowed to pass unrepresented in the local broadcasting; and Director Collaer [Paul Collaer, Director of Music of the Belgian radio] was most anxious to know if and when the opera, in whole or in part, would be produced by us. I would suggest that to wait until Programme C [which was to be the Third Programme] comes along will look either like lack of confidence in the most important of our young composers, or the kind of timidity in our programme building of which we are not as yet suspected by our continental colleagues.

See also note 2 to Letter 502.

4 Neel was to conduct his orchestra in the first performance of *Les Illuminations* at the Wigmore Hall on 30 January 1940, with Sophie Wyss.

5 The first wife of Ralph Hawkes. The marriage was dissolved in 1941, in which year Hawkes married Clare Zollner (1906–1989).

6 Sophie Wyss gave the first concert performance of two songs from the Rimbaud cycle – 'Being Beauteous' and 'Marine' – on 17 August 1939 at a Promenade concert at the Queen's Hall, London, with the BBC Symphony Orchestra conducted by Henry Wood.

182 To W.H. Auden[1]

Gray Rocks Inn Limited
St. Jovite Station
Provence of Quebec
Canada
June 5th 1939

My dear Wystan,

Thank you very much for your letter. The chances of meeting certainly look bad. We leave here this Wednesday – then to Toronto – & on the 12th to Grand Rapids for a few days. I'm afraid, looking at the map, that that's too far away to consider meeting you for a day or even a night – & I've got to return to Toronto on 18th to speak over the Radio (!). We expect to come to New York at the end of the following week – about 23rd[2] – & so it looks bad. I can't, seeing the circumstances of your departure, urge you to put it off a couple of days, can I?*

Anyhow – please keep in touch with me – via B & H. (Toronto) for the next few weeks & I hope something will materialise. But, how long will you be in the South? Peter & I are looking for somewhere near New York – or even Florida or Mexico (proper) – if we link up with Aaron[3] – till the end of August. The next time you write – please give me an outline of your plans for the Autumn. I may stay here (this side of the Atlantic) if money doesn't run out – or if I can get work.

Thanks alot for the songs – Calypso is grand for Hedli – & as soon as I've finished my present stuff I'm going to get down to all those cabaret ones – the other fits the tune I gave you marvellously – you are a clever fellow! – but dare I ask for a second verse with a slightly sardonic second couplet? – such as

"Most shout the names they think are fine

But I daren't mutter the name of mine – "

> Much love, old thing,
> BENJY
> Where is Christopher?[4]
> Dead?

*It now looks as if we <u>may</u> have to return to Ottawa after 20th to pay a call on the Tweedsmuirs – useful re Visas etc. – so possibility grows less & less ____

1 This is the only surviving letter from Britten to Auden, whose practice it was to destroy personal correspondence. It surfaced in New York in 1985, having somehow escaped his wastepaper basket.

2 In fact Britten and Pears travelled on the 27th (see Letter 192), by which time Auden and Kallman had left for New Mexico. On 8 June, however, Auden replied:

> St. Marks School
> Southboro
> Mass

Dear Bengy,

Dear O dear. Leave New York on June 20. Why not come and share the ruined 14 room Hacienda I have been lent in Taos New Mexico. I am so anxious for you to meet Chester, though a little frightened as he is extremely musical, and you do play so fast.

Anyway, when you come to N.Y. stay at the Hotel George Washington corner of 23rd Street and Lexington Avenue. It's much the nicest hotel in town and the manager Mr. Donald Neville-Willing (and don't forget the hyphen) is expecting you. There is a good piano.

Write to me c/o the George Washington and as soon as I know the Taos address I'll send it. Will try and think about another verse, but believe you're wrong in wanting one, at least for my song which ought to be just an encore 30 second song.

Christopher is in Hollywood   Address 1406 Franklin Avenue.

> Much love
> WYSTAN

Auden's letter clearly responded to Britten's request for 'a second verse'. We have not been able to trace the music, but Auden's text – the brevity of which clearly disconcerted Britten – has survived. It was written on an accompanying sheet of headed ('St. Mark's School') paper:

> <u>Song</u> (after Sappho)
> O What's the loveliest thing the eye (the eye)
> Can see in the black earth before we die?

____

To some it's horses, to some the Rhine, (The Rhine)
To others it's battleships steaming in line

———

Men say this, and Men say that
Say that and this,
But I say it is
The one I love
The one I love.

(for <u>one</u> read boy, man,
girl or goat
to taste)

It provides interesting further evidence of how closely Britten and Auden worked and thought together, the poet being able to supply on demand words for a text-less tune. It was a practice that showed up in their collaboration on *Paul Bunyan* (see DMPB). The Cabaret Songs, indeed, were seminal in relation to the compositional character of the operetta, which Britten himself recognized when writing to Ralph Hawkes on 7 December (see Letter 226):

Paul Bunyan is progressing well [. . .] I have sketched one or two tunes already, a little bit more serious than the Hedli tunes but very direct and simple, which is the kind of style I propose to use throughout the work.

3 See Letter 196.

4 Christopher Isherwood, who had travelled to the USA with Auden in January. In May he left New York for California (see Auden's letter quoted in note 2 above) and remained there, on the West Coast, for the rest of his life, writing, teaching, meditating, and professing the pacifism he had unequivocally declared in April. He applied to reside permanently in the USA at the beginning of May and became a United States citizen in 1946.

183 To Beth Welford

[*Full text*, EWB, *pp. 111–13*]

Gray Rocks Inn Limited
St. Jovite Station
Province of Quebec
Canada
June 5th 1939

My dear old Beth,

Thanks alot for your nice long letter. I was frightfully pleased to get it. I couldn't imagine why I hadn't heard from you – since I thought you would have had my letters long since. Any how I had a letter from Wulff this morning by Air Mail – so there's no excuse

for letters taking a long time now, although it's much more
expensive. Don't write by it unless it is very important!

So far the trip's being a great success. We are getting on well
together & no fights. This place is just heavenly & it is sickening
we've got to leave it on Wednesday. The people are very nice – we
have become bosom friends of an American secretary & the
daughter of the pioneers up in these parts – very nice people[1] who
take us about in cars & play tennis & golf with us lots. In fact
with all those occupations & walking alot, to say nothing of work
which goes pouring out – I've nearly finished a Violin Concerto
since I got here – besides a job for the B.B.C! – time has gone very
fast indeed!

[. . .]

We go to Toronto on Wednesday evening – I've got to go & see
the Boosey & Hawkes people there & then Peter and I go to Grand
Rapids (U.SA.) for about a week – & then I've got to return to
Toronto to have a personal interview on the radio! Before the
Variations are played! 7.30 on 18th in the evening – but don't try
& get it as I believe it's about 12.30 by your time! It seems odd
that you are five hours in front of us all the time!

After that is not settled yet – Ottawa probably & New York &
South after that. The Vancouver car trip fell through because of
the broadcast & King & Queen[2] not being out of the way before
end of June (we want to see the Tweedsmuirs who are occupied
with their Gracious Majesties!) – & it takes so long to go by car –
at least a fortnight.

[. . .]

Now for your news. This is exciting about Sebastian & the musical
box. But don't let him be a musician – it's too much like hard
work – but I daresay you won't have entered him for King's College
choir before I get back.

I was <u>very</u> angry to hear that Mrs. Hearn was snooty with you
– she knew perfectly well that you were coming, I told her ages
ago & repeatedly. You give her socks if she's like that again! and
please go alot. July will be freer I should think.

[. . .] Please give my love to Barbara will you, & tell her all the
news. I will write in a few days when I get to Toronto – or anyhow
Grand Rapids. I hope she's feeling better now. Where did you go
for Whitsun? None of you to Snape? – or was Lennox there?

We are going for a picnic to-day – along Devil's River – that
sounds romantic doesn't it? Especially as both our companions

are of the fair sex & pretty fair at that! Don't be surprised if I've changed my state when I get back.

Much love, my dear old thing. I miss you lots & I wish to goodness you were here. But I'll have a look round & see whether I can find a nice practice for Kit! You'd love the country & the people arn't too bad.

My love to the family & I hope Sebastian's given up waking up in the night!

See you soon, I expect!
Love,
B

Peter sends his love

P.S.   Could you possibly ring up the flat & find out what's happened to Jackie[3] – we haven't heard a word from him or even had any letters forwarded. If he can't remember what to do with our letters – he'd better send the whole lot to Snape – including Peter's.

Please!

1 See also Letter 185.

2 King George VI and Queen Elizabeth were touring Canada at this time. They left England on 6 May for Canada and crossed the border into the USA on 7 June. The American part of their journey included a visit to the World's Fair in New York on 12 June. See Keith V. Gordon, *North America Sees Our King and Queen* (London, Hutchinson, [1939]).

3 Jackie Hewit had taken over the flat at 67 Hallam Street, after Britten and Pears had left for the USA. See also Letter 227.

184 To Aaron Copland

Gray Rocks Inn Limited
St. Jovite Station
Province of Quebec
Canada
June 5th 1939.

Dear Aaron,

Where are you? Don't you dare say you've already left for the South without telling me! Our plans now are as follows: Leave here for Toronto 7th – Grand Rapids 12th, Toronto 18th (those

Variations on Radio), Ottawa (possibly) 20th, New York 25th – or
a few days later for a week – perhaps – While we find somewhere
to go for the two summer months[1] – i.e. unless you've got any bright
suggestions. We've put off decisions until hearing from you – <u>so</u>
<u>please write</u> – to 10, Shuter St., Toronto.

How was Billy the Kid? I hear the Caravan's[2] been a great success
– was that because of you?

Affectionately,

BENJAMIN

1 At this stage it is evident that Britten and Pears were not contemplat-
ing a long stay in New York. What changed their minds was their
meeting with the Mayers, who offered them a home shortly after
their arrival in the city. See Letter 194.

2 The Ballet Caravan. A publicity pamphlet about the company was
published (1938?) by the Frances Hawkins Concert Management with
an introduction by Lincoln Kirstein which unfolded the company's
philosophy:

Starting as an untested company in the summer of 1936, the Ballet Caravan
has presented some fifty performances, enjoying particular success at col-
leges and summer theatres before a successful New York début which terminated its first season. The idea of such a highly selective group of twenty
American dancers immediately pleased many discriminating audiences who
had hitherto been unfamiliar with dancing in general or the ballet in particular.

In commissioning a number of younger generation American musicians
and painters to collaborate with its dancers, the Ballet Caravan has stimulated
much provocative work. These completely new works complement other
ballets based on accepted masterpieces of classic musical literature, both
traditional and contemporary.

The repertory of the Ballet Caravan is prepared for presentation with local
orchestras. Its appearance with the Philadelphia Symphony was the first in
a series of similar engagements, which constitutes a practical solution to the
problem of presenting fine dancing, and great music without the heavy cost
of a traveling orchestra.

The Ballet Caravan itself is a permanent organization constituting the top
rank of young Americans trained in the strict classic tradition. Their style
of virtuoso dancing, while stemming from an ancient discipline is, in its
presentation, both of our country and our day.

185   To Enid Slater

Gray Rocks Inn Limited
St. Jovite Station
Province of Quebec
Canada
June 6th 1939.

My dear Enid,

Thank you for your nice letter – I was glad to get all the news. Certainly your detail about Snape was cunning propaganda! For about half-an-hour I decided that I'd have to come home at once – but then I looked at the view here – mountains & lakes & – well, changed my mind, & rather postponed my decision! This is certainly a terrific spot. Wild as oats. Mount Tremblante that overshadows us is the Northest point of civilisation before Hudson Bay (about 400 miles away). Most of it is not even detailed on the map. This Inn is a fashionable resort, started by a remarkable American family called Wheeler – Mr & Mrs. W. senior were pioneers up here in the last century & none of the descendants can bear to leave the place. It is run very haphazardly, & in the 'off' season – such as this – is very good. But in the season they have about 300 people all over the place – including sometimes about 50 aeroplanes on the lake – so that's not our cup of tea. We have got a log cabin on the side of the hill – very quiet & indusive to work – in fact I've practically completed a violin concerto (besides an odd B.B.C. job) in the three weeks we've been here. Tomorrow – unfortunately we've got to go south. The weather's been patchy. Alternately very hot & very cold. But enjoyable at all times – except for the legions of mosquitoes – which have nearly driven us crazy. As soon as you stop moving for a split second they're on you – & with terrible results. I've got 31 bites on one foot alone! All the houses have screens on, so we can sleep at nights – but the beastly animals beat the screens by one night (they appeared one day before schedule) & we couldn't sleep a wink all night – & they all sang on E & F – so much so that I almost have to avoid those two notes in my music now – so evil are the associations!

Very glad to hear about Montagu's new pageant[1] – I wish I could see it. Give him my heartiest condolences on the rain fiasco in Wales – I cannot think why people do things out of doors in England.

Go to Snape as often as you can – I'm sure it's a good thing in

every way. <u>And</u> Cambridge[2] if you can – I've just had a very
sweet letter – & nearly broken all my resolutions! Thank you for
the details about the garden – you can't imagine how welcome they
were.

Love to all the kids – I must send them cards –

& to Montagu.

Affectionately,

BENJAMIN

1 Slater's *Pageant of South Wales* had been organized by the South
Wales Miners' Federation in association with the Labour Research
Department. It was produced by André van Gyseghem, with music
arranged by Bamford Griffiths, and performed, on 1 May, in three
different Welsh towns simultaneously. For further information on
the pageant as a theatrical form see André van Gyseghem, 'British
Theatre in the Thirties: An Autobiographical Record', in *Culture and
Crisis in the Thirties*, edited by Jon Clark, Margot Heinemann, David
Margolies and Carol Snee (London, Lawrence and Wishart, 1979),
pp. 216–18.

2 Where Wulff Scherchen lived.

186   To Ralph Hawkes

The Chancel Choir,
Park (First) Congregational Church,
Grand Rapids, Michigan.
June 16th 1939.

My dear Ralph,

Yours of 5th to hand – & I'm hastening to catch the 'Yankee
Clipper'[1] airmail for the reply.

I'm being temperamental about 'Les Illuminations' at the
moment. My entire attention is being occupied by the Violin
Concerto. I've been on that this last month or so & it is nearly done
now – but I've given the other project not a thought. (You remember
when I left that you told me to take things easily – well this is the
result!) I hope certainly to be able to let you have a score of the
completed Rimbaud before long – anyhow by perhaps the end of
July – but I'm very anxious (a) not to be rushed over this (b) for
the first performances to be <u>complete</u>. So please tell BBC – with my
love & devotion – that if they want this for the proms – they must
have the lot – (& Sophie Wyss) & not tie my hands as to length –

I can guarantee not more than 20 mins. probably less. But –
actually, I don't think the proms. suitable for a first performance
of this work. Why can't they do something else? I <u>don't</u> want to be
known as 'First performance Ben'. I hope occasionally that my
things are worth playing twice!

Re the Violin Concerto. So far it is without question my best
piece. It is rather serious, I'm afraid – but it's got some tunes in
it! Probably the best scheme re Goossens[2] would be to send a sketch
score to you & Tony – & let him have a look-see at it – & if you
think wise play it over to Goossens. I'm keen to have a first show
over here. What about Boston? I may have a contact with
Koussevitsky[3] soon thro' Alexander Chuhaldin[4] who's doing the
Variations over here (Toronto) on Sunday – & who thinks I'm the
cats whiskers. In fact we're being rather a success over here! Jarman
has done us proud in Toronto – we've been meeting everyone &
accordingly fêted. Peter's giving a complete recital of my songs in
Toronto next week. Jamieson[5] was charming there too – & we
shall see him again when we go back there tomorrow. We've been
staying in Grand Rapids with the Einecke's – friends of Peter's –
& they again have done us proud – interviews with press (I'll try
& send you cuttings) – & meeting conductors etc. In fact the more
I get about here – the more I feel that – should I stay out the
autumn – lots of shows might be fixed, with the Concerto, Orch.
pieces etc., & odd playing dates. People are so friendly. However
I'll talk the matter over with Heinsheimer in New York – whence
we go next week. (Willy Walton has had to return to England by-
the-way). Perhaps you'd drop Heinsheimer a note too – or do you
think I'd better be a good boy & come home?!!

Thank you very much for your note to the Consul – we got our
visas for a year very easily.

The Concerto is fine in print – & so's the Advance Democ.[6] I'll
scatter copies of that around.

We had lunch to-day with the conductor of the Symphony Orch.
here to-day – Carl Wecker[7] – & he was eloquent about what he
called the short-sightedness of Music Publishers! He said that what
organisations of his kind wanted was modern music, of which
the material was buyable, & held for use in the libraries. He said
that he (& the 100 other similar orchestras) could afford to buy
the parts etc. – but couldn't afford the continual hiring fees &
performing fees. The same was the tale in Toronto. Chuhaldin,
the man who's doing the Variations, is distraught because he can't
buy the parts of that work. He's crackers on it, & wants to add it

to his library – so he can keep it in the regular repertoire of his orchestra. As his orch. only plays on the Radio – & I suppose the programmes are declared to the P.R.S. – what is the harm? Forgive me, but I promised I'd put in a word with you!

Post just off – so I must go.

I hope you're well, & family fine. We're both in fine spirits & enjoying ourselves no end. Thanks more than I can say for making it possible.

One matter further – I was a bit sick that Effie Hart[8] is going to do first (!?) show of Illuminations. I don't like her society for music like that – I want a more general audience – even a contemporary B.B.C. show would be better – but best of all a public show such as a Boyd Neel recital – or a Monday 'Pop'. These songs aint written for long-haired high-brows! I'm hoping for Sacher – tho' – or/and Ansermet?

Please thank Stein for his note & the press-cuttings. Would you give him all the dope re Violin Concerto & songs?

Excuse scribble – but time's short.

Yours ever,

BEN

1 A new transatlantic airmail service, which had begun to operate on 1 June.

2 Eugene Goossens, the conductor.

3 Hawkes was to write to Britten on 21 July:

[. . .] I went over to Paris on Tuesday, especially to see Koussevitzky and your ears should have burned. He promised me to do 'VARIATIONS' and I gave him a Piano copy of the 'CONCERTO', which he will study with his Pianist, for he has a very able one in the Orchestra. He asked for new works from you and whilst I mentioned the 'VIOLIN CONCERTO', I feel that I do not want to prejudice the situation with Barbirolli in view of Brosa's engagement with him. When I mentioned 'LES ILLUMINATIONS', he said that this was a work which was barely suitable for the big Symphony Orchestra but that this Harpist, Mr Bernard Zigera, had a Chamber Orchestra which gave concerts in Boston under Koussevitzky's direction and this was just the sort of work that he would be delighted to include. Soprano voice, he thought, was perfect, for they have a good singer and I, therefore, confidently look forward to a performance of this work in Boston during next season.

I suggest that you write to Koussevitzky at Boston, or get in touch with him through Aaron Copland, to cement this and if you can arrange to meet him, so much the better. He sails back in the 'Champlain' on Wednesday and will be in Boston by the time this letter reaches you. I gather he is having a festival of some sort at Berkshire, wherever that may be.

4 Russian-born Canadian violinist and conductor (1892–1951). He emi-

grated to Canada in 1927, when he joined the staff of the Toronto College of Music. He worked as a radio conductor of several orchestras, including 'Symphonic Strings', 'Melodic Strings' and 'CBC Strings'. He was to conduct the first performance of Britten's *Young Apollo* (see note 2 to Letter 192).

5 See also Letter 193.

6 Britten refers here to the arrangement of his Piano Concerto for two pianos – four hands, by Brian Easdale, which had just been published by Boosey & Hawkes, along with his motet, *Advance Democracy*.

7 Karl Wecker (b. 1894, d. ?), American violinist and conductor. He was Music Director of the Grand Rapids Symphony, 1923–40. In 1940 he held a post with the Federal Music Project in California and later became Director of the Hollywood Bowl.

8 The secretary of the London Contemporary Music Centre. (See also note 1 to Letter 248). Hawkes replied on 3 July:

I had anticipated the question of 'Les Illuminations', and, therefore, you have no need to worry. The two numbers already done from Birmingham are, however, included in the Proms with Sophie Wyss but there is no question of any others. The complete first performance of this work is scheduled for December 5th at an L.C.M.C. public concert with Boyd Neel at the Aeolian Hall. I believe this will be a very satisfactory introduction, for your long-haired high-brows, although they may be there in small quantity, will not affect the situation very much. Sacher will also do them although the date is not yet fixed.

In the event the first performance did not take place until January 1940. Paul Sacher conducted the Continental première of the cycle, with Violette Andreossi (soprano) and the Basler Kammerorchester, in Basel on 9 February 1940, in a concert that also included the world première of Martinů's Double Concerto for string orchestra, piano and timpani (1938). A notice of the concert appeared in *Weltwoche*, 327, 16 February 1940 (here translated by Paul Wilson):

Britten is a virtuoso when it comes to the treatment of the string orchestra; this is already evident in his works in variation form and our awareness of his ability to conjure rich colourful sounds from the strings is excitingly renewed in this cycle. Colours are *de rigueur* when setting Rimbaud's poetry to music. One might even ask oneself whether his 'Illuminations' requires musical expression at all; in any case these songs demonstrate intimate knowledge of the text: the musical phrase always remains completely bound to the cadences of the poetry. Striking orchestral part-writing, almost cheeky in its simplicity, develops ingeniously from the harmonies.

187   To Wulff Scherchen

Alexandra Palace,
University Avenue, at Queens Park,
Toronto, Canada.
[?19 June 1939, Postmarked 20 June 1939; per SS *Queen Mary*]

[. . .]

[. . .] I'm thinking hard about the future. This <u>may</u> be the
Country. There's so much that is unknown about it – & it is
tremendously large & beautiful. <u>And</u> it is enterprising & vital.

[. . .]

188   To Lennox Berkeley

Alexandra Palace,
University Avenue, at Queens Park,
Toronto, Canada.
June [1]9th 1939.

My dearest Lennox,

Just a scribbled line to catch the Queen Mary mail – to tell you
that things are going fine out here – to thank you for the letters
etc. – & to hope you're enjoying the combination of Snape & June!
It is honestly very nice to think of you both[1] there & enjoying
yourselves lots. Atta boy! We had a terrific time in Grand Rapids.
We were fêted like Toscaninis. Interviews to papers – house
parties – lunches etc. They think I'm pretty hot out here & I'm not
trying to disillusion them!

They did the Variations over the Radio last Sunday (quite well)
& I was interviewed in person before – horrible ordeal! Peter is
giving a complete recital of B.B. songs this week over the same
medium! I've finished the sketch of Vln. Concerto – & so far v.
pleased. We go South to New York at end of this week – but no
definite plans yet. That's approx. all the news. Let me have yours
some time.

Much love to you both & to the family when you see them. Give
D[2] a ring please & thank her for her <u>grand</u> letter & tell her I'll write
as soon as I get a moment.

Love,

BEN

P.S. Please Lennox – I'd forgotten I owed Wulff 10/-   Could you
please send it him from me & I'll pay you when I get back? Sorry
to bother you, but it's so difficult from here. He'd love a letter from
you – Just [Torn page makes this letter incomplete.]

1 Beth and her family were visiting the Old Mill.

2 Dodo, Beth's mother-in-law.

189 To Ralph Hawkes

> Alexandra Palace,
> University Avenue, at Queens Park,
> Toronto, Canada.
> June 19th 1939

My dear Ralph,

The enclosed letter has just been forwarded from my London
address, where it arrived after a round-about passage, much
overdue. Could you please deal with it? It seems alright to me – if
I'm back(!) – but if circumstances keep me here, we'll break it to
them later – don't you think.

Thank you also for the cable & letter. So glad that there's no
hurry about the Rimbaud now – that makes me feel much easier.
No 'prom' for me this year then? But it can't be helped.

The Toronto broadcast of Variations went quite well – & so far
reactions seem favourable. I've finished the sketch of Violin
Concerto & when it's sufficiently digested (& copied out) I'll send
you a copy.

> In great haste,
> & With best wishes,
> Your sincerely,
> BEN

190 To Barbara Britten

[Full text, EWB, pp. 114–15]

> Bala[1]
> June 25th 1939

Dear old Barbara,

[. . .] Now we are spending two heavenly days up in the
Moskoka lakes a singing teacher[2] Peter wanted to see lives up

here by the side of the Lake – a grand spot. We go back to Toronto tonight & then on to <u>New York</u> on Tuesday. I'm looking forward lots to that – it ought to be very exciting. No plans yet after that – all depends on Aaron (you remember him!!) who we'll see there. But I expect we'll have a good time – we have so far always managed it!

I hope you're all right, my dear. I think about you lots – more than you'd imagine! Write to me as much as possible – you can't imagine how welcome letters are! By-the-way – it is better <u>always</u> to send letters to Toronto – we move about so suddenly – I got your last one lots late. Quite a good thing is to find out when the "Queen Mary" sails & to send by that.

Have you been to Snape yet? I expect your hay-fever's on the mend now – was it a bad bout this year? Peter's had it abit.

Please tell the family all the news – I'll write <u>when</u> I get the time – but as I said it's <u>very</u> difficult.

Love to Helen [Hurst]. Take her to Snape.

<u>So sorry</u> about the Budges.[3] It is rotten for you. Requiem aeternam dona eis.

Much love,
BEN

Peter sends his love.

1 On the shore of Lake Muskoka (which Britten mis-spells), Ontario.

2 Campbell McInnes, with whom Pears had a few lessons at this time. See also Letter 221.

3 Perhaps the enforced (i.e. in anticipation of wartime) demise of his sister's pet budgerigars.

191 To Beth Welford

[EWB, pp. 113–14]

c/o Boosey & Hawkes, Toronto
June 25th 1939

My darling old thing,

I'm writing this in the train from Bala – up the Moskoka lakes to Toronto at 11.0 p.m. on Sunday. I've written a newsy letter to Barbara & I was going to send you a postcard as I wrote to you last; but I thought I would scribble a note (<u>if</u> you can read it!!) – saying that I thought lots about you on the 17th – & how did

Sebastian behave?[1] Did he cry? I wish I'd been there to do my duty officially.

Things are going quite well, though personally I'm pretty tired. They keep us so hard at it and I am being fêted rather too much – I'm not used to that sort of thing! It even got into the papers that I went on the Scenic Railway!

We are going to New York on Tuesday and it looks as if it may be the same way. But we are looking for a quiet cheap place for two months, so that will be nice. I don't know yet about the Autumn. It looks as if I shall stay over here – unless there's a war. I might as well confess it now, that I am seriously considering staying over here permanently. I haven't decided yet of course and I'm terribly torn, but I admit that if a definite offer turned up (and there are several in the air) I might take it. Use your judgement as to whether you tell anyone. As it is so much in the air I suggest you don't.[2]

Canada is an extraordinary place. I am <u>certain</u> that N. America is the place of the future. I wish to goodness you would come across. Would Kit necessarily want to buy a practice or would he work one up? But seriously, do think about it, and if I see anything at all possible I'll let you know. We've met some charming people over here – &, though certainly one is worried by a lack of culture, there is terrific energy & vitality in the place.

We're just arriving in Toronto so I must stop. It strikes me that you wont after all be able to read a word of this – but perhaps it doesn't matter!

All my love to all of you

BEN

Peter <u>sends love</u> to you all,
Please write <u>often</u> & <u>lots</u> – I live on letters!

1 The christening of Beth's son, Sebastian, whose godfather Britten had agreed to be.

2 This paragraph reveals the volatility of Britten's responses to North America. It undoubtedly reflects his enjoyment of Canada, a feeling he sustained throughout his life. 'I am <u>certain</u> that N. America is the place of the future': this sentiment of course preceded his first experience of the USA. As subsequent letters show, this particular certainty was to undergo major qualification; and indeed his Hamlet-like debate – 'To stay or not to stay' – becomes a conspicuous feature of his American years.

192 To Enid Slater

In the train to N. York
June 27th 1939.

My dear Enid,

Thank you very, very much for sending the photos. If they were
sent to make me homesick they certainly succeeded! The trees
were heavenly – & the small car did the oddest things to my heart!
I liked one of the Sophie Wyss ones alot. Thank you again – very
much – please send some more if/when you have the time.

So you are now in France? I hope you're having a grand time &
a good rest from household worries. I am enjoying that side of
this holiday alot – although living out here is fearfully expensive.

As you see we are on the way to New York – reason for the
pencil & the wobbley writing – I darn't risk a pen.[1] I'm writing
now as I don't know when I shall have a moment again – they
keep us on the run so. We had a terrific time in Toronto & really
met some charming people. They seemed to like having a real live
composer round about, & made, what seemed to me, a ridiculous
fuss! Interviews were priceless – I'll let you see some sometime!
Had two Radio shows – & I've been asked to write a special work
for the C.B.C. at Toronto & to play it myself in August.[2]

I'm looking forward to New York.[3] But also feeling abit nervous
about it – with all its sophistication & 'New Yorker'[4] brightness.
I can't do that sort of thing very well! However I hope we'll find a
nice place to settle down in for abit – near Cape Cod or Boston –
I want to do some more work.

No plans for the Autumn yet – even as far as one can possibly
plan these days. Things of course look very black to us out here
– but I'm hoping that as usual, actually on the spot, that you find
them less frightening. Here, I'm afraid, one is inclined to speak of
Europe in the past tense. I think it may be this side of the Atlantic
for me – but it is impossible to say as yet – because lots of things
will have to be got over before that decision is made. However –
no word of this as yet, please!

Go to Snape again when you're back in England & take some
more photos. { It'll be an effort to give up that!
                { It would

Love to you both, & write all the news please
BENJAMIN

1 Britten also wrote a 'wobbley' letter in the train to Wulff Scherchen in which he remarked, 'I'll write to you describing New York. It ought to be pretty exciting. I'm looking forward to seeing the skyscrapers & the Fair [The World's Fair].'

2 *Young Apollo*, a 'Fanfare' for piano, string quartet and string orchestra, commissioned by the Canadian Broadcasting Corporation. This was first performed (a CBC broadcast) on 27 August, conducted by Alexander Chuhaldin (the dedicatee), with Britten as soloist. The commission clearly arose from the successful performance of the *Bridge Variations* Chuhaldin had conducted on 18 June. After one performance in New York, a broadcast on 20 December (see Letter 227), *Young Apollo* was withdrawn by the composer and was not heard again until after his death, when it was allotted its original opus number, 16. It was revived at the 1979 Aldeburgh Festival (21 June) and published in 1982 by Faber Music. Work lists inscribed, probably in 1941, by the composer and Pears in two published scores – *A Boy was Born* and the Violin Suite – demonstrate Britten's later ambivalent feelings towards *Young Apollo*. One list (Opp. 1–26) has 'Op. 16 Young Apollo' crossed through, while the other list (Opp. 1–25) includes Op. 16 as part of the acknowledged *oeuvre*. Britten clearly had in mind adding a work to his repertory in which, as in his Piano Concerto, he could appear in the joint role of composer and pianist. He had mentioned the commission in a letter to his sister, Barbara, on 25 June: 'They've [the CBC] also commissioned me to write a special piece and play it with Orchestra on August 27th – nice of them?!!'

3 They stayed at the George Washington Hotel, as recommended by Auden. On 8 March 1981, the *New York Times Book Review* (p. 11, introduced by Edward Mendelson), published an 'Ode to the George Washington Hotel', written by Auden in 1939. It is amusing to note that this witty and characteristic salutation adopts the style and identical metre of Inkslinger's song in *Paul Bunyan*, e.g.

> The walls look unlikely to crumble
> And although to be perfectly fair,
> A few entomologists grumble
> That bugs are exceedingly rare,
> The Normal Man life is so rich in
> Will not be disgusted, perhaps,
> To learn that there's food in the kitchen,
> And that water comes out of the taps,
> That the sheets are not covered with toffee,
> And I think he may safely assume
> That he won't find a fish in his coffee
> Or a very large snake in his room.

The inscription at the end of the poem reads:

> To the Manager of the George Washington Hotel
> Mr. Donald Neville-Willing
> and to all the staff with gratitude
> and good wishes from
> W.H. Auden

It may have been that the preoccupation with food, eating and cooking in *Paul Bunyan* suggested to Auden, consciously or unconsciously, the adoption of a metre prominently used in the operetta's libretto for his eulogy of the George Washington Hotel.

4 *New Yorker*: the fortnightly periodical, famous for its urbane wit and sophistication, qualities of which Britten was preternaturally suspicious. Hans W. Heinsheimer, in an interview with Donald Mitchell (April 1977, New York; Archive) vividly related the tale of Britten's first encounter with Broadway:

> Some things you remember after so many years like they were yesterday. So maybe the first night after they had arrived from Canada, I took them out, and I was also a newcomer – I had been here maybe half a year only. So for me New York and Broadway, that was absolutely something unbelievable [. . .] of course Peter had been here before but Ben had never been here before. First night – I take them out to Broadway.
>
> I had never made a bigger mistake in my life. It was an absolute fiasco. The noise, the dirt, this man smoking a cigar and puffing the smoke out on Broadway [a 'live' advertisement hoarding], the rotating lights – and I'd said, 'Isn't it marvellous?'
>
> It was absolutely awful. I still remember this unbelievably polite smile Ben had – really Ben always smiled nicely – but really it was a flop.

For a description of the Times Square District at this time, see *The WPA Guide to America* (New York, Pantheon Books, 1985), pp. 115–16. (Ironically, one of Britten's operas was to be produced on Broadway, *The Rape of Lucretia*, in December 1948, at the Ziegfeld Theater. The show closed after a week's run. In a letter to Chester Kallman, 30 December 1948, Auden wrote: 'Tonight to <u>Rape of Lucrece</u> [*sic*], the performance of which I hear is awful.' (See Dorothy J. Farnan, *Auden in Love* (London, Faber and Faber, 1985), p. 181.) No more successful was a misconceived production of *Let's Make an Opera!*, staged on Broadway in December 1950, conducted by Norman Del Mar and directed by Marc Blitzstein. It closed after five performances.

193   To Ralph Hawkes

George Washington Hotel,
Twenty-Third Street and Lexington Avenue,
New York City, N.Y.
June 29th 1939.

Dear Ralph,

I hope by the time that this reaches you that yet another major crisis won't have arisen. Over here of course papers are having the time of their lives – every movement of soldiers in Europe is flashed across the headlines & our hearts flutter yet again.[1]

Anyhow – here I am in New York for a few days. We came last Tuesday & to-morrow go to Woodstock near here for an indefinite period to stay near Aaron Copland.

Toronto first of all. Harry Jarman turned up trumps. He was really splendid. He took us about, introduced us to everyone of note, arranged the broadcasts – & was always to hand with documents or data if the position arose. I think you've got a fine person there – he is terrificly energetic & enthusiastic, & wants to develop the place enormously. My whole impression across this side is that here is a continent just leaping ahead in the arts. Music means something here. Imagine English newspapers interviewing composers! Yet here I got a large amount of space in each of the three Toronto papers – & in 2 cases in the centre page! I will enclose cuttings if I can find them.

Here too the position is the same as Toronto (& Canada in general). I've seen Heinsheimer & had long talks with him. He has told me that the opportunities are immense – for an orchestral piece (I told him the French–Canadian idea & he was delighted),[2] for an operetta for children (for which I also have ideas & will write to Wystan Auden).[3] The Variations have apparently gone across big here – in fact I shall come back here for a big show on July 12th at the Stadium here.[4]

(I can't get this off by the Mauretania as I'd hoped, as I've got so much to say – so I'll leave it till the next boat).

Woodstock – we are just up here & it is all that we expected & more.[5] We're getting very sunburned!

– So as opportunities seem so good here & if I can manage it financially I want to stay across here for the Autumn. Heinsheimer is making arrangements for me to meet people when I'm in New York on July 12th & later on too – & I've had an offer from the

C.B.C. at Toronto to write & play a short piece for piano & strings
on August 27th – they would give the first performance, but have
no rights on it of course – Jarman would look after that sort of thing
& has been very business-like in the preliminary negotiations.
Personally I like the idea of doing it – won't take long (they want
about 5–8 mins.) – & it might be useful later on.

Rimbaud: If Sophie Wyss is definitely doing the two I've already
done at the Proms, I can send another one to go with them &
probably a fourth within a fortnight or so.[6] Anyhow I'll send the
scores for you. When is the proposed date?

Now I'm settled here for abit the piano score of the Violin
Concerto should follow soon. I shall probably have a photograph
made of it here first as it might be useful in hawking it around! I
shall get down to the full-score too, soon.

Thank you too for the efforts re 'Johnson over Jordan' & 'Sword
in the Stone'. I feel doubly delighted that you have done down
Basil Dean! Will that £40 or £50 go into the guarantee – or
(hopefully!) not? By-the-way could you please make arrangements
with Jarman about letting me have the half-year's money, as you
said you would? He doesn't think that the firm in Toronto could
stand it without help from you! There is no violent hurry, but I can
see it being needed in a month or so.

Mr. Jamieson has been charming to us. He gave us a nice time
at his Yacht Club in Toronto – & a grand dinner in the Ritz-
Carlton in New York. He seems a fine chap in every way.

No more immediate problems. I'm counting on you coming over
in the early Autumn. I shall need a lot of paternal advice at that
period, I fear, so please come! That is more of a demand than a
request!

> With best wishes to your wife & to yourself of course,
> Yours ever,
> BEN

P.S.   Could you please send two or three more copies of both the
'Ballad of Heroes' & 'Advance Democracy' – if you could send them
direct to Heinsheimer it would be best. Thank you!

P.P.S.   Aaron has just played me bits of his Outdoor Overture.[7] It
sounds fine & apparently is going very well over here.

1 In April, on the 7th, Italy had invaded Albania. In the same month
   conscription for men aged twenty and twenty-one was introduced
   in Britain and Hitler denounced the Anglo-German naval agreement

of 1935. In May, Hitler and Mussolini agreed a ten-year political and military alliance, the so-called 'Pact of Steel'.

2 See note 2 to Letter 180.

3 *Paul Bunyan*, the 'choral operetta' that Britten was to write with Auden and which was first performed in New York by the Columbia Theater Associates of Columbia University at Brander Matthews Hall on 5 May 1941. (A private recording of one of the two final perform- ances was made on 10 May, copies of which are in the possession of Columbia University and the Archive.) The work was withdrawn until Britten finally agreed to its revival towards the end of his life. It had its British première in a BBC broadcast production 1 February 1976. This was followed by a first English stage production at the 1976 Aldeburgh Festival, the last Festival Britten was to attend. When the work was published in 1978, it carried the opus number 17 (chosen by Britten himself in 1974), a number that had formerly been allocated to another withdrawn work from 1939, the settings of Gerard Manley Hopkins for unaccompanied voices, *A.M.D.G.* (Ad Majorem Dei Gloriam). See note 4 to Letter 202. For a comprehensive history of *Paul Bunyan*, see DMPB. Already in 1948, Pears was trying to arouse the composer's interest in a revision of *Paul Bunyan*. He was to write to Britten from New York on 26 October:

> Yesterday morning I spent a little time listening to the old recordings of Paul Bunyan. They had suddenly been sent from Columbia University & he (Ralph) had heard some & thought the ballads were so wonderful, and wants to take them out and use them separately. It made me cry & shudder to hear P.B. again. The performance was appalling! and some of it is faintly embarassing, though I believe by drastic cutting one could make a pleasant thing of it still. The ballads are quite sweeties! They really are. So I've copied down the tunes & Elizabeth has the words & I'll bring them back to you to fix slightly!

In his last question to Britten in his 1960 BBC interview (*People Today*; Archive), Lord Harewood asked: 'Have you ever thought of writing what one calls a musical nowadays – a musical show?'

BRITTEN: Yes, quite honestly I have recently considered that very seriously. I was asked to write the music for a musical and have very reluctantly turned it down. I don't say that I never will be able to do that, but I don't see at the moment a way of – if I can put it like this – jettisoning all one's actual technique. I don't want by any means to talk disparagingly of musicals, but their aim seems to me very different from what I'm aiming at. They aim at a kind of directness, a kind of melodic simplicity, a kind of formal simplicity that I don't feel at the moment I can manage. The best musicals of many years have been those written by essentially simple people who can turn out a short melody which fits very neatly into the conventions of harmony at that moment and which is entirely dependent on that. Now one day I would love to be able to agree to write such a thing because I feel that it's an important part of the artistic life of our time; but I don't feel my public [. . .] is quite of that kind. I think, to put it simply, that I'm aiming at [. . .] the serious popular or the popular serious, rather than the entirely commercial popular world.

4 See note 1 to Letter 196.

5 Britten and Pears must have arrived in Woodstock on Saturday, 1 July (see Letter 194). Copland's memories of this summer appear in Aaron Copland and Vivian Perlis, *Copland: 1900 through 1942* (London, Faber and Faber, 1984), pp. 293–4:

> During that summer in Woodstock we played many things through for each other; Ben was a fine pianist and a great accompanist. Always able to compose what fit his temperament, he wrote music in a modern style, yet without danger of upsetting an audience. I thought of him as the voice of England in the contemporary musical scene, and he, in turn, considered me the American spokesman. We had many of the same sympathies, musical and other kinds, and we knew we faced similar problems. Toward the end of August, Ben and Peter left Woodstock. They worried constantly about whether to return to England. I wrote to Ben: 'You owe it to England to stay here. After all, anyone can shoot a gun – but how many can write music like you?'

6 In fact it was only 'Marine' and 'Being Beauteous' that were performed by Sophie Wyss at the Proms on 17 August, when Sir Henry Wood conducted the BBC Symphony Orchestra. These were the same songs that had already been heard earlier at Birmingham on 29 April. Letters 198 and 200 make clear that the two new songs Britten had thought of adding to the 'old ones' were 'Royauté' and 'Antique'.

7 *Outdoor Overture*, a work for school orchestra, the commission for which had been stimulated by the precedent of Copland's school opera, *The Second Hurricane*. The overture had been first performed on 16 December 1938 as part of a campaign whose slogan was 'American Music for American Youth'. See also Copland and Perlis, op. cit., pp. 285–6.

194 To Elizabeth Mayer[1]
From Peter Pears

[PFL, *plate 114*]

George Washington Hotel,
Twenty-Third Street and Lexington Avenue,
New York City, N.Y.
[29 June 1939]

My dear Mrs. Mayer –

Please look at the signature first and then let me tell you that I
ought to have written to you many times since I last saw you 18
months ago. But because I haven't written it doesn't mean that I
haven't thought often of you, particularly in the hurricane of
September and then through all these recurrent crises that we in
Europe have been enduring.

But anyway the important thing is that after nearly two months
in Canada in Quebec Province and then in Toronto, I and my
friend, Benjamin Britten, composer, have just arrived in New York,
and I am so looking forward to seeing you again.

Please will you & Michael[2] have lunch or tea with us tomorrow
(Friday)? I will ring you up in the morning to see if you can. On
Saturday we go into the country near Poughkeepsie[3] until the end
of July (except for two nights in New York about the 12th) and
for August we go to the sea. I sail for England again on August
26th or so,[4] and shall have a few days in New York then so I hope
to see you a lot.

My love to you all.
Yours ever
PETER PEARS

1 Elizabeth Mayer (1884–1970), youngest daughter of the Chaplain to
the court of the Grand Duke of Mecklenburg. The remarkable Mrs
Mayer and her remarkable husband and family – two sons (Michael
and Christopher) and two daughters (Beata and Ulrica) – are among
the most important figures thronging the pages of Britten's letters
after 1939. No annotation could better the description of Mrs Mayer
found in Letters 219 (BB) and 372 (PP). The two men's eloquent words
say everything that need be said about the relationship and about
Mrs Mayer's exceptional gifts. One aspect of that relationship has
been clearly spelled out in EWB, p. 144:

It is obvious that Elizabeth loved Ben from the start and during those ghastly
war years, when he was so miserable, homesick and ill, she looked after

him like a mother and did her best to take the place of the mother he had lost only three years before.

(See also Introduction, pp. 38–9.) But that was only part of the story.

It was through Basil Douglas (see note 5 to Letter 372) that the encounter with the Mayers had come about. Douglas, himself an aspiring singer, on the recommendation of an Oxford friend had gone to Munich to improve his German. His tutor was Elizabeth Mayer:

[. . .] I had a wonderful month there. She played the piano a lot – very good pianist – and I sang a lot, and she flatly refused to speak English to me although her English was very fluent indeed [. . .] and at the end of the month I was able to put the verbs in the right place, very often.

It was through her translating and language lessons that Mrs Mayer helped support herself and her family during the pre-war Nazi period. Her husband, Dr William Mayer, was half-Jewish, and thus unable to practise as a doctor and psychiatrist. Although Mrs Mayer had long abandoned her professional musical ambitions, music none the less played its part in Douglas's studies:

[. . .] we just went through one song after another and she told me what she thought and I thought it was wonderful; and so she was not really teaching those things – just making me aware.

'Awareness' was one of Mrs Mayer's chief characteristics. In the last letter received by friends in Germany from Mrs Mayer before the outbreak of war she was telling them already to make a note of Britten's name. (The 'Interlude' in *Les Illuminations*, composed at Amityville, was to be dedicated to her, and later, the *Hymn to St Cecilia*.)

The Mayers finally succeeded in emigrating, not *en famille*, but individually. Beata had left for Italy in 1933, where she was trained as a nurse, and Michael in the same year was sent to England to continue his education. Mrs Mayer, with her remaining children, Ulrica and Christopher, sailed to join her husband, who was already working in the USA, leaving Hamburg on 5 November 1936. The ship docked briefly at Southampton, where Michael took the opportunity to go on board and spend some hours with his mother. Among the joining passengers was Peter Pears, embarking on a tour of the USA with the New English Singers.

Pears was a flatmate (with Trevor Harvey) of Douglas's, who already in October had written to Mrs Mayer to acquaint her with the extraordinary coincidence that Pears was going to be on board the same ship (the *Washington*) at the same time and entreating her to seek him out. We know from the diary Pears kept on the voyage that Mrs Mayer did just that. On 7 November he reported 'A note from Frau Mayer asking me to meet her if well enough, but won't risk it yet'. Sea sickness was afflicting the passengers, but on the 9th and 13th Mrs Mayer and Pears succeeded in meeting and on both occasions recorded 'interesting' conversations, much of them, according to his notes, devoted to conditions in Germany, e.g.

Two stories about Knappertsbusch leaving Munich. (1) he refused to allow Swastikas on the stage in the last act of Meistersinger. (2) The portrait of Hermann Levi, a great Munich conductor, was being removed from the opera for obvious reasons, and Knappertsbusch insisted on it being taken to his own private room.

(Pears's 1936 diary of his first visit to the USA is in the Archive.)

It was thus that the first meetings took place which were to have such fruitful consequences for both Pears and Britten in 1939.

The Mayers did not first reside at Amityville. They moved there in May 1937, when Dr Mayer took up his appointment at the Long Island Home, of which he was Medical Director. In December of that year, Mrs Mayer was visited by Pears when he was again on tour with the New English Singers. It was doubtless to this meeting that he refers in his letter above: 'I ought to have written to you many times since I last saw you 18 months ago.'

Britten's and Pears's letters document their absorption within the family and their relationships with the parents and children. It was Beata (b. 1912) who was closest to the two men, both personally and professionally. Moreover, she was able to put her nursing experience to valuable use during Britten's serious illness in 1940. She remained an intimate friend of each of them, until the end of their lives.

There were, naturally, tensions arising from the visitors' invasion of the family circle. The Revd Michael Mayer remarked that 'The intrusion was not something entirely new [. . .] my mother always had all kinds of people around, so it wasn't anything extraordinary.' Mrs Mayer – a *very* powerful' personality, he observed, while his father 'was all his life completely dominated by women in general' – 'I won't say she ignored us, but she really wasn't intensely interested in what her children were doing or where they were [. . .] my mother had four children because she wanted a quartet and we failed her. I never played an instrument of any kind.' Much laughter accompanied Michael's recollections, which were doubtless exaggerated in order to make a significant point, and the broad thrust of which Beata confirmed:

[. . .] as far as my parents were concerned, my mother in particular, but also father, they [Britten and Pears] could have stayed for ever [. . .]. My brothers are in agreement, so I am not saying anything to hurt them. They were the children she always wanted.

But whatever the tensions may have been, there are, too, abiding memories of youthful high spirits, for example Michael's reminiscence of Sigmund Spaeth, an egregiously popular writer on music, one of whose books (1936) was entitled *Great Symphonies: How to Recognise and Remember Them*.

[. . .] [Britten and Pears] introduced us to the words he wrote to famous pieces of music [. . .] the [scherzo of the] Pastoral Symphony [. . .] 'Peasants are dancing and prancing together, the weather is nothing to them, ha ha ha' [. . .] 'Loo-ook – what a pretty brook!' [the slow movement], and from the *Eroica*: 'I am your fate, come let me in.' Ben and Peter loved those. They loved *Kitsch* in general, you know. They went to see every Deanna Durbin movie that ever came out in Amityville [. . .] my mother was [. . .] a little startled at that because she was much too intellectual [. . .] too elevated [. . .] and it seemed strange to her that geniuses like Peter and Ben would stoop to such ordinary things.

'We were all young then', he reminded us, 'and we had a marvellous time.' (Within the family circle, no doubt with affectionate irony, Britten and Pears were referred to as 'the geniuses'.)

As for sexual decorum within the household, where Auden too was a frequent visitor, Michael had this to say:

I've read all the biographies of Wystan Auden, you see, and you get the impression from those that he did nothing all day except chase boys [. . .]. But I was never really aware of that as part of daily life.

Nor was it part of Britten's or Pears's daily life at Stanton Cottage:

I was an extremely handsome young man in those days and nobody ever made a pass at me [. . .] My mother was never aware of such things. My mother thought that Beata ought to marry Ben, you see; but she lived in another world.

Elizabeth Mayer's extraordinary gift for recognizing exceptional creativity meant that she surrounded herself and her family with creators of all kinds who were exceptionally endowed, not only Britten and Pears, but many others who were outstanding writers and painters and poets, not least among them W.H. Auden, a collaborative friendship (she co-translated with Auden Goethe's *Italienische Reise*), which was sustained until she died in 1970. In 1967 Britten and Pears were in New York; Michael recalled, 'They came up in the limousine to visit her in the nursing home where she was [. . .]. It was a great joy to her; her boys came to see her.' The poem that Auden had addressed to her on her eightieth birthday in 1964 (6 April) was read by him at her funeral:

> Here, now, as bodies
> We have no option,
> Dates, locations divide us.
>
> As You, as I, though, each
> Is born with the right
> Of liberal passage

To Dame Philology's Realm
Where, in singular,
Name may call to Name.

And Name to Name respond,
Untaunted by
Numerical haphazard.

So, today, I think that sound
To which you have answered
For eighty years

With this intent:
That you shall think it happily,
As *Elizabeth*

Through twenty-five has been
For a happiness of mine
Its Proper name

(W.H. Auden, *Collected Poems*, pp. 567–8)

Sources: Basil Douglas, Interview with Donald Mitchell, 16 November 1987, London, Archive; Revd Michael Mayer, Interview with Donald Mitchell and Philip Reed, 22 June 1988, Aldeburgh, Archive; Beata Sauerlander, Interview with Christopher Headington, June 1988, Aldeburgh, Archive. See also Aldeburgh Festival Programme Book 1988, pp. 85–7.

2 The Mayers' elder son.

3 See Letter 196.

4 The imminent outbreak of war in Europe was to change Pears's plans.

195 To Ralph Hawkes
[*Western Union Cablegram*]

WOODSTOCK NY
[10th July 1939]

JUST FINISHED TWO NEW RIMBAUD SONGS SUITABLE WITH OTHERS FOR
PROMENADE PERFORMANCE STOP SENDING SCORES THIS WEEK
CONCERTO FOLLOWING[1]

GREETINGS
BEN

1 See Letter 202.

196   To Wulff Scherchen

George Washington Hotel,
Twenty-Third Street and Lexington Avenue,
New York City, N.Y.
July 13th 1939
[Per RMS *Aquitania*]

[. . .]
[. . .] Peter & I have rented a studio up in Woodstock near the
Hudson for a month, near a composer & very dear friend of mine,
Aaron Copland. We had to come back to New York for a day or
two because the [New York] Philharmonic Orchestra gave my
Variations on 12th.[1] They were a great success & I had to come on
the stage & bow twice – !! [. . .] The papers have all given me
marvellous notices & it seems certain that other performances will
follow soon. So in that way I'm happy. [. . .] I haven't yet any
plans about returning. I want to be in New York abit in the Winter
Season. I have odd playing dates here & there – Toronto August
27th. Unless anything drastic occurs I may stay till Xmas or even
longer. Mais je sais pas encore – !
[. . .]
New York is a staggering place – <u>very</u> beautiful in some ways –
intensely alive & doing – bewildering in some ways, but always
interesting. [. . .]
[. . .]
I enjoyed the poem – please send all the new ones – I always
carry 'madrigal' in my pocket!

N.B.   If you address letters now c/o Boosey & Hawkes, Belwin
Inc. 43–45–47, West 23rd St., New York City it'll save time.

1 At an open-air concert at the Lewisohn Stadium, conducted by Frie-
der Weissmann. This was the work's first New York performance and
attracted much press attention. See Letter 197. The earliest American
performance of the *Bridge Variations* we have been able to trace was
given by the Cincinnati Symphony Orchestra conducted by Eugene
Goossens, at Cincinnati's Music Hall, on 3 March, although a letter
of introduction from Ralph Hawkes to the American Consul, written
on Britten's behalf, suggests that Goossens and his orchestra may
have performed the *Bridge Variations* in October 1938.

197   To Beth Welford

[EWB, *pp. 116–17*]

George Washington Hotel,
Twenty-Third Street, and Lexington Avenue,
New York City, N.Y.
July 14th 1939

My darling Beth,

This is only a scribbled note

(a)   to thank you for your letters, which I love having, please keep up the weekly bulletin: one adores letters when one is so far away & (secrets!) one occasionally feels very homesick for one's sisters.

(b)   to tell you to send these letters
c/o Boosey & Hawkes Belwin Inc.
43–45–47 West 23rd Street,
New York City.

(c)   to tell you that Peter & I are now settled for a month up in a place called Woodstock in the Kingston District of the Hudson River (look it up in the map) near the Catskill Mts. It's very beautiful & we've rented a studio there. Aaron C. is near & we have a great time altogether.

I'm in New York again for a few days as the N.Y. Philharmonic Orch. have just played my Variations at one of their big out-of-door Stadium concerts – & it was a great success, my dear! I had to go twice onto the platform to bow – the orchestra was very pleased & so was the audience (about 5000!). The write-ups have been marvellous[1] – so I feel rather 'started' in New York now!

You would adore this city – but be abit bewildered by it, as I am now. It is very sophisticated, but charming. It is very beautiful & the sky-scrapers are <u>incredible</u>! Everso big!

Glad to hear Sebastian is well. I'm sick to be missing so much of him as it'll be a lovely period of his development. But <u>all</u> periods'll be the best – you proud old mother, you!

I think of you lots & lots my dear – & wish you were here. No more developments about the little matter I wrote about last time – but I feel much the same.[2] I hope Kit's back with you now. Did you enjoy Snape?

Much love to you all,
& to Barbara when you write.
BEN

<u>How's the new maid?</u>

1 Among the reviews appearing on the morning of 13 July was one by 'G.G.' in the *New York Times*:

Mr Britten has frankly attempted no more than a parcel of variations that have no mutual relation beyond their common harmonic kinship with the theme, and he would probably not resent calling the entire work a pastiche. Judge for yourself: the variations bear such titles as March, Romance, Aria Italiana, Wiener Walz, Moto Perpetuo, Funeral March. This is not to say that Mr Britten has chosen the easy way. For one thing, he has limited himself to the restricted palette of the string orchestra, which he has exploited to the hilt. He has made his variations not so much from the inner dramatic values of his theme as from its harmonic material; but his work, though it has no interest in form, is far from being the exercise in surface decoration that so often passes for variations.

It is witty, most of it shrewdly built, and effective in performance. One of England's white hopes, Mr Britten romps happily in conservative harmonic fields and is unafraid to pluck a melody where he finds one. Sometimes he seems over impressed with the look of his notes on paper, as in the fugue, but on the whole he steers clear of needless complexity. As the sample of a 24-year-old writer, it augurs well from the things he has written in the last two years. He was recalled to the stage by a good-sized cordial audience.

Jerome D. Bohm, in the *New York Herald Tribune*, wrote:

The Britten Variations are an interesting mixture of serious and satirical music. The opening variation, Adagio, is perhaps the most original and profound of the eight, for the concluding section, which aims at a similar depth of expression, is strongly Mahlerian in style. Most amusing are several of the variations in which composers of the past, Rossini and Tchaikovsky among them, are amiably and wittily mocked. The work is not an easy one to perform, but barring the fugue, in which there was some muddled playing, it was capably set forth, often with flowing tonal texture.

2 Britten refers to his thoughts about 'staying over here permanently': see Letter 191.

198 To Ralph Hawkes

~~The George Washington Hotel~~
~~23, Lexington Ave, at 23rd Street,~~
~~New York~~
<u>Woodstock</u> N.Y.
July 18th [1939]

My dear Ralph,

Many thanks for your two letters of July 3rd & 7th respectively – & also the quarter's cheque – which will be very welcome in a week or so!

I expect you're now in the middle of the Mediterranean enjoying & sunning yourselves – but I daresay that there is someone left to deal with this.

I hope by now you will have received (a) my wire re the new Rimbaud songs (b) the scores themselves. If the BBC want the two old ones I suggest that you use all the pressure possible to make them do the four – military sanctions if necessary – they are very short & make a far more intelligible group than the two by themselves. I suggest too that the English translations be put in the programme – the translations, i.e., in the Faber & Faber Edition of 'Les Illuminations' trans: by Helen Rootham (Titles in English: Royalty, Antique, Being Beauteous & Marine).[1]

The Violin Concerto: I am progressing apace with the fair copy of the piano & violin version which you should have easily by the end of the month. Could you please phone Toni Brosa & tell him this? I am writing to answer his letter but I don't know if I shall be able to catch this boat. I suggest that Henry Boys be asked to play it with him in the 'try-outs'.

I have just got back here after a hectic four days in New York. The Variations were a great success at the Stadium concert & I have met lots of people. Heinsheimer is very nice & has been wonderfully efficient. He introduced me to many influential people & with luck something may materialise.

I am waiting to hear a definite date of arrival from you in this part of the world! I am sure that you're needed here. Heinsheimer is full of enterprise & wants backing as does Jarman in Toronto. I am delighted with this part of the world, I must say. Music really seems to matter!

Owing to Miss Jackson's arrival I have had to leave New York of course, lest she should find out the truth about my behaviour there.[2] But I shall write to her explaining. Seriously though – it doesn't look as if I shall be in New York while she's there; but I am going to make a great effort to make it possible.

By-the-way, I always forget to tell you that just before I left England I met Donald Tovey & he expressed an idea to get to know my stuff.[3] I said I'd try & make this possible. If you would think it worth while, what about sending him a copy or two of things? As you think.

I hope the trip is a success & that you are not 'non-intervened' with in those treacherous waters!

Love to you & your wife,
Yours ever,
BEN

---

1 *Prose Poems from Les Illuminations*, put into English by Helen Rootham

with an introductory essay by Edith Sitwell, London, Faber and Faber, 1932.

2 Hawkes had written on 7 July:

Now that the first excitement of New York has worn off and you have had a chance of looking round that extraordinary City, I have to tell you that I am sending Miss Jackson over especially to see that you are behaving yourself.

She arrives in the 'Queen Mary' – on the 17th I think – and she would certainly like to see something of you whilst there.

3 Donald Francis Tovey (1875–1940), teacher, writer and composer. He was Reid Professor of Music at Edinburgh University from 1914 to 1940 and famous for programme notes that set entirely new standards in that field. Tovey had a house at Hedenham, Norfolk, where he kept his Bösendorfer concert grand. It was here that Britten must have visited him. Part of the time, Pears recalled being told, was spent by Britten and Tovey playing piano duets (probably Schubert).

199 To Beth Welford
[EWB, *pp. 115–16*]

Woodstock, N.Y.
July 28th 1939

My darling old Beth,

I always seem to be writing to you just as the Mail for England is departing & am consequently very rushed for time. The truth is that one is kept very occupied these days. Peter & I do all our own housework (!) & gosh, what a time it takes – nearly as bad as W. Cottage Road!

Our days are generally something like this:

Get up – 8.30 (with luck)

Finished getting breakfast & washing up & clearing up – 10.30.

Then work (got lots to do too – especially with this commission for Toronto on top of everything) with an interval for cold scrappy lunch until – say – 4.30.

Then we walk along to Aaron's cottage, where we bathe in stream & sun. till 6.0.

Then tennis perhaps till 7.30 or 8.0. Then the big meal of the day at a snack-bar called Trolley Car; and after that either here or at Aaron's we gossip or play piano, or go to cinema at Kingston 9 miles away. So we're occupied – you see!

Of course this drought has been awful – everyone is running out of water – & gosh, the heat! I can't imagine the Tropics much hotter! Actually the weather has broken now – & tho' it is still very hot, it has been raining for 2 days solidly.

No plans yet for future – immediate ones are – we're here till 20th Aug – then New York to see Peter off on 23rd by Queen Mary[1] – then I go up to Toronto to play new piece on the Radio; I shall probably go up to Bala again for a few days: what I shall do in September isn't settled yet, but I may go to New Mexico to see Wystan.[2] Anyhow I shan't be in New York till October I don't think. Then we'll see how things turn out.

Let me know all the news. I suppose Kit's at Beckenham[3] now? Are you with Elinor[4] – it is so difficult to keep track of dates – being so far away.

I hope you're happy with Sebastian – obviously he's the best baby yet – everyone says so to me, anyhow!

Much love – please give Barbara my love & all the news – I'll write by next Boat.

Greetings to all 3,

BENJAMIN

Look out for bombs, please![5]

1 See, however, Letter 205.
2 Britten did not make the trip. On 14 August, Auden was to send a postcard to Britten from Santa Monica, California:

Shall get back to N.Y. (George Washington) at the beginning of Sept. Must see you there as I have several propositions to discuss with you beside longing to see you.

Much love
WYSTAN

3 Beth's husband was a locum at Beckenham in Kent.
4 Elinor Bond, Beth's old schoolfriend.
5 The war scare.

200 To Sophie Wyss
[*Incomplete*]

Woodstock, N.Y.
as from: c/o Boosey & Hawkes Ltd.
43–45–47 West 23rd St.,
New York City.
July 28th 1939.

My dear Sophie,

Thank you very much for your letter, which I was very glad to get. I had been meaning to write to you for ages – but what with

one thing & another I have been kept very busy since I got here –
more especially now as Peter & I have taken a studio in the
Catskill Mountains & have to do all our own housework!

I am glad to know that you are doing the Rimbaud songs
definitely. I am hoping (almost insisting!) that you do the two
new ones that were sent off to Ralph Hawkes the other day, as
well. It makes a much better group – Royauty, Antique, Being
Beauteous, & Marine – as the other two are so short. I am waiting
to hear whether this can be arranged. If Ralph Hawkes hasn't
communicated with you about it – please ring him. I sent piano
versions, for you to learn from, made by Peter!,[1] with the
orchestral scores.

[. . .]

1 While Britten and Pears were in North America, it was often Pears
who helped Britten with copying and the making of vocal scores, as
here. He was later responsible for the vocal score of *Paul Bunyan* and
for the fair copies of the Hopkins settings, *A.M.D.G.* In Central
Television's documentary film about Pears, PPTMS (1985), he replied
to a question about the trip to the States in 1939:

[. . .] I was really going as [Ben's] esquire, I think, in a way. [. . .] I
thought it was part of my duty, and certainly part of my pleasure as well,
to go with him [. . .] I was working really for him in America, when he
got there and we got down to the Mayers [. . .] I was copying out [. . .]
the parts and score of various things.

201   To Enid Slater

Woodstock, N.Y.
July 29th 1939.
[Per North Atlantic Air Mail]

Your letter from the sick-bed[1] has just arrived & I think if I'm
quick I can catch the air-mail back at once. I am so sorry to hear
about your illness – it sounds frantic, & I pity you more than I
can say. Your letter has enough in for me to imagine all the details
– including the agonising return to consciousness. You poor thing.
I hope you're having a good convalescence. Why don't you go to
Snape for a longer period? I'm sure it could be arranged – write
to L.B. & suggest it, tell him I told you to! It pleases me to hear
you talk about Snape & Suffolk like that. Tell it not in Gath – but
I've been horribly home-sick for it recently! I'm not making any
plans for the future at the moment – except that I shall be spending

Oct–Nov. in New York, & I've got to go back to Toronto on Aug 27th to give first performance of a new bit I've just done – piano & strings – title not yet decided but it is founded on the end of Hyperion 'from all his limbs celestial . . .' It is very bright & brilliant music – rather inspired by such sunshine as I've never seen before. But I'm pleased with it – may call it 'The Young Apollo', if that doesn't sound too lush! But it is lush!

I am glad you had some nice times in France – & took some good 'photos – if you could send me some small copies of them I'd be glad. By-the-way if in future you post letters to:

c/o Boosey Hawkes, Belwin Inc.,
43–45–47, West 23rd St.,
New York

it saves a day or so.

I had a terrific success (I admit) in New York when the Philharmonic Orch. did the Variations – & all the reviews were good! How's that!! I feel that I may be fated to have successes here & not in England – & that will be an extra incentive to live here. But o – Snape! Peter & I have taken a Studio in the Catskill Mountains – where we work, bathe, play tennis, & sun ourselves. It is all very quiet. A bit too many artists about, but one never need contact them.

I am so glad about Montagu & the Co-op² – that is indeed a leg up for him. I hope it means good money too for you all. We're feeling the pinch here – because acclamations have nothing to do with money! I'm going to try & get work to do from England I think.

I may spend September with Wystan in New Mexico.

Do see Wulff if you can manage it. But I do hope you're feeling fitter now – I think it was a rotten affair for you.

Love to all the Family & to yourself. Excuse hurry – but I want to catch this mail.

Yours ever
BENJAMIN

1 She had undergone a serious dental operation on 12 July.
2 She had written on 10 July:

Montagu's play Doomsday is being produced at the Kingsway on Sept 2nd & there may be a chance for another one later as the Co-ops have started an Entertainments plan – plays, repertory etc & are putting thousands into

it. They hope to buy a big West End Theatre & M. is on the Committee. So
if he cannot push a play through them – he's hopeless!

202   To Ralph Hawkes

Woodstock, N.Y.
Aug. 15th 1939.

My dear Ralph,

I have just posted off to Heinsheimer a nice ink piano reduction
of the Violin Concerto, which I hope will reach you by the time
you get this. I am sorry to have taken so long, but I didn't wish to
hurry it, & I have been very occupied with things over here.
Would you please have the violin part copied – fully cued – for
Toni Brosa to try over for you? I hope that something will be able
to be fixed for this season. Will you try for London this season too?
I am so fed up with small studio concerts that I think it might be
worth waiting until I can get a nice Queen's Hall show. After all I
think I <u>should</u> have a Symphony Concert show by now, don't
you think – if I can have a public show in Brussels, Geneva, N.
York, – I think I deserve one in London![1]
Woodstock has been very successful – it has been nice & hot (not
broiling like New York) & we've got nicely browned. I've done
lots of work – finished this small piece for Toronto I mentioned to
you – 'Young Apollo' (after Keats), Fanfare for Piano, Solo String
quartet, & string orchestra. It is a 'brilliant' kind of piece, playing
about 8 mins. The 1st perf. is in Toronto on Aug. 27th – 7.0 – &
Heinsheimer thinks he'll be able to arrange for me to play it over
the Radio in N. York with Wallenstein.[2] Would you care to try &
place it somewhere for performance in London?
I'm also doing a series of four-part songs for Peter & his Round-
table singers to 'first-perform' at the Aeolian Hall on November
24th.[3] I've done four so far – fairly extended, all to religious words
by Gerald [sic] Manley Hopkins – & there'll probably be two
more.[4] Peter'll show them to you when he arrives back at the end
of the month.
I may go to California for about a month at the end of the Toronto
jaunt (28th). To see Auden. (I don't want to go to New York till
October when people will be returned there).[5] Not settled yet – but
I'll let you know!
I had a charming letter from Lewis[6] saying that there is a slight

possibility of that film materialising again.[7] I'll wire you, of course, should anything happen, which I rather doubt.

So sorry you've had bother about the passage money[8] – I thought that bother was cleared up ages ago. Would you please get in touch with my solicitors again?

Now I come to think of it you must be still on holiday – I hope it is a good one – & that you won't be disturbed by bad weather or crises!

I don't know what happened to Miss Jackson. I wrote her asking her to come here, if not too far away, & I didn't hear anything. I was very disappointed.

Best wishes, & hoping you're fit,

Yours ever,

BEN

P.S.   This letter will never end – !

I saw Koussevitzky in the Berkshires twice – Aaron introduced me – & he was charming & seemed favourably inclined towards me – you'd done your stuff well in Paris! He said he'd be doing the Variations in Boston & possibly in New York too![9]

Did anything materialise about that 'Ballet' film?[10] I must say that I should like the money – & I might even do it out here?

Have been playing some hot-stuff tennis.

I suggest that Henry Boys would be the ideal person to get to play the Fiddle concerto with Toni.

1 In the event, the Violin Concerto was given its first performance in New York at Carnegie Hall on 28 March 1940 with Brosa as soloist and the New York Philharmonic Orchestra conducted by John Barbirolli. The first English performance was given on 6 April 1941 in London at the Queen's Hall with Thomas Matthews (the orchestra's leader) as soloist, when the London Philharmonic Orchestra was conducted by Basil Cameron. The composer was still in the United States. See also PFL, plate 137, where the wartime programme is reproduced.

2 Alfred Wallenstein (1898–1983), American cellist and conductor. He was principal cellist of the New York Philharmonic under Toscanini and after the latter's resignation in 1936 abandoned his desk as an orchestral player and took to radio performances and guest conducting. In 1933 he had formed the Wallenstein Sinfonietta for station WOR of the Mutual Broadcasting System and was the station's Music Director from 1935 to 1945. He also conducted the NBC Symphony Orchestra and the station's 'Voice of Firestone' programmes. Wallen-

stein conducted a broadcast performance of *Young Apollo*, with the composer as soloist, in New York on 20 December. See also Letter 274.

3 The concert did not take place. The Second World War had begun on 3 September and Pears remained in the USA. The 'Round-table singers' referred to by Britten had been formed by Pears, probably before his departure for America. The name clearly indicates an intention to perform in the Elizabethan manner, i.e. sitting around a table, which was the practice of the New English Singers of which Pears was also a member.

4 The composition sketch of *A.M.D.G.* is inscribed: 'For Peter & the Round Table Singers', and comprises the following settings for four mixed voices (with composition dates):

    1. Prayer I ('Jesu that dost in Mary dwell') – 11 August
    2. Rosa Mystica – 11 August
    3. God's Grandeur – 18 August
    4. Prayer II ('Thee God, I come from, to thee go') – 5–7 August
    5. O Deus, ego amo te – 30 August
    6. The Soldier – 15 August
    7. Heaven-Haven – 15 August

All the settings were composed at Woodstock with the exception of 'O Deus, ego amo te', which was the first composition Britten completed at Amityville. Nos. 1 and 6 are crossed through. The fair copies, in Pears's hand, of Nos. 1, 2, 5 and 7 were made for use by a small group of solo singers, formed by Pears in America along the lines of the Round Table Singers. His activities complemented Britten's conducting on Long Island of an amateur orchestra. *A.M.D.G.* was published by Faber Music in 1989.

5 In fact, Britten and Pears were back in New York in August: their names make their first appearance in the Mayers' visitors' book on 21 August (see PFL, plate 115). As Letter 203 shows, by the beginning of September they had taken up residence at Amityville. Auden in any case had left California and returned to New York by the end of August. His signature appears on the same page of the Mayers' visitors' book, dated 4 September, the day after the declaration of war by England.

6 Lewis Milestone (1895–1980), American film director of Russian birth, who was head of productions for United Artists from 1932. His best-known films were *All Quiet on the Western Front* (1930) and *Of Mice and Men* (1940), the latter with music by Copland.

7 Christopher Headington, in his biography of the composer, *Britten* (London, Eyre Methuen, 1981), p. 43, cites Peter Pears:

He [Britten] had, I think, a definite offer, which later fell through, of a film in Hollywood about King Arthur. When we arrived in America we still thought that he was going to have a film. But it must have been quite clear soon that it wasn't so.

The film was to have been entitled 'The Knights of the Round Table' (see Letter 268). See also PR, p. 172. Britten may have been approached by Milestone because of the reputation the composer had made with his incidental music for D.G. Bridson's radio drama, *King Arthur* (1937).

Ralph Hawkes had written from London to Britten on 9 June about another, unidentified film project:

John Davenport has just 'phoned me to the effect that their film idea has been shelved indefinitely; this is too bad! He also urges me to tell you that you should under no circumstances go anywhere near Hollywood!

In a later letter (29 August) Hawkes returned to the subject.

I note that you are likely to go there. I beg of you not to 'flirt' with the film people too much, until they really want you, for I think it would be a grave mistake. You must, of course, use your discretion whether you notify them or not that you are there but I feel that if they know it, they are not likely to be as generous as if they wanted you from here. That is my impression but however, I may be wrong.

8   Hawkes had evidently loaned Britten the fare for the voyage out but had not been reimbursed.

9   Koussevitzky first performed the *Variations* with the Boston Symphony Orchestra on 25 April 1941, the first occasion that Britten's music featured in the orchestra's programme. The performance in New York, however, did not take place.

0   Hawkes had written on 3 July:

There is a slight possibility that a Ballet will be required for a picture which is being made by the Ealing Film Studios. [. . .] They have been trying to get Petrouchka but what with price and Stravinsky being very bloody-minded, it seems that this will be impossible. The picture is, I think, called 'Bullet in the Ballet' and a Ballet is necessary where there is a certain character; in other words, not just general dancing. I have already told [Michael] Balcon that I think you could do a swell job of work for him but as you were in America and not likely to be back for some months, if he was in a hurry, it would not be possible. On the other hand, if this was wanted later on when you were back, this might well be arranged. The price has not yet been discussed but I feel sure there is between £300 and £500 in it. If it develops, you may expect to hear more from me. In the meantime, I should not worry about it but proceed as if I had not told you.

A Bullet in the Ballet was a humorous novel by Caryl Brahms and S.J. Simon (London, Michael Joseph, 1937).

Hawkes was to write again on 29 August:

The idea for this Ballet has now taken shape and they are using some other music by [Alexander] Tcherepnin. I am sure if you had to do it, it would involve being present almost immediately and I am afraid, therefore, that it cannot be considered, for it would barely be worth your while.

203 To Barbara Britten

[Amityville] U.S.A.
[3 September 1939[1]]

My darling,

You can't tell how glad I was to get your wire, & to know that you are well. Peter took the message which was 'phoned from New York, & didn't ask when or where it was sent from, so I don't know yet whether you are still in London or not. I hope & pray you aren't – if physically possible do get away – because the strain of waiting & expecting must be so frightful.[2] So far I am taking your advice[3] because (a) I hear that we are not wanted back (b) if I come I should only be put in prison – which seems silly, just to do nothing & eat up food. I am staying with friends of Peter's near New York & as far as possible am having a good time. Thinking of you simply all the time, too; the papers & radio are hysterical of course and one feels chronically sick about the whole thing. I've seen & am seeing Auden a lot, & our immediate future is locked with his, it seems. I'm writing lots – in desparation, for fear everything may be terminated at any moment! Barbara dear – do read, listen to music, look at pictures (try El Greco – that lovely book of reproductions), as much as possible – even if it means spending money. Remember every moment of sanity is a help in these times. If you have a moment to write, please do so. You can't imagine how homesick & bad one feels so far away, & yet brought so close by all these horribly rapid means of communication. God, what a mess man has made of things. And force has never done any good.

Would you be an angel & forward these letters for me? Get postage from Nicholson, who should have money for me!

Much much love, my darling,
& to Helen too.
BENJAMIN

1 Obviously written on or just after 3 September, the day war was declared, and the first letter home dispatched from Stanton Cottage, the Mayers' home at Amityville. Britten wrote a similar letter to Beth which was enclosed with this letter to Barbara. See EWB, pp. 118–19.

2 Britten refers to the expectation of air raids.

3 Barbara, in her cable (which has not survived), had clearly advised her brother not to return.

204   To Ralph Hawkes

U.S.A.

[3 September 1939]

My dear Ralph,

So it has happened at last. I <u>am</u> sorry for you, & hope that things arn't so entirely disrupted as you feared they might.

It looks as if I shall be out here for a bit still – I have lots of things to do, & am at the moment staying with friends on Long Island, and inspite of everything working very hard. I've nearly completed the Violin Concerto score – if you can bear to think of such things! – & have written and am planning lots of other things. If you have the time, the ability, & the inclination, could you please send the score of the four Rimbaud songs (I'm glad to hear they were a success at the Proms), the piano concerto & Hunting Fathers? I'm seeing a bit of Winkler[1] & learning some eminently practical things about American musical life – & I think that things will materialise therefrom!

I am so glad you got your holiday before everything broke, & more than I can say do I hope that things will clear & that you can go on again with the great work.[2]

When are you coming over. America needs you, you know!!

Regards to everyone – including your wife,

Yours ever,

BENJAMIN B.

I await your instructions on matters musical, of course!

1 Max Winkler founded the American music-publishing house of Belwin Inc., in 1918. The company was later to be associated with the New York office of Boosey & Hawkes.

2 Britten refers, we think, to Ralph Hawkes's success in building up the catalogue of his company, which he did with such extraordinary flair in the thirties and forties.

205 To Aaron Copland

c/o Dr. Mayer,
Long Island Home,[1]
Amityville, N.Y.
Sept. 10th 1939.

My dear Aaron,

   Thank you so much for your letter – it was honestly a great
comfort.[2] This is not a real answer to it as I hope very much to
see you soon – <u>actually</u>, Dr. Mayer (see above) is driving over to
Woodstock on Wednesday next (13th) & we're coming with him – &
may call on you in the afternoon if you're in. So please be in!
   Don't think from the address that we have been certified insane
– although I admit we've both come very near it these last few
weeks! Peter is still here – I persuaded him to stay, so that <u>if</u> we
had to go back we could at least go together. We are staying with
friends of his (a Psychiatrist – German refugee – who has a job
here) – & they couldn't be nicer or more opportune! England, at
the moment, is not too keen for us to go back – but decisions have
eventually to be made, & we can't go on for ever living on
hospitality. However we can talk about that kind of thing when we
meet – it will be grand to see my cheery 'Father' again![3]
                                  Love to you both from us both.
<u>What </u>a world. I do hope the Sonata[4] is going well – that is the
<u>only</u> kind of thing that matters – <u>I'm sure.</u>

BENJIE

1 The official description of the Long Island Home was a 'Private
   Sanatorium for Nervous and Mental Diseases'.

2 Copland must have commiserated with Britten on the outbreak of
   war in Europe.

3 Britten was not alone in this attitude to Copland. Leonard Bernstein
   (1918–1990), the American composer and conductor, with whom
   Britten was to become acquainted during his years in the USA, also
   thought of Copland as a 'substitute father' in the 1930s and 1940s.
   See the entry on Copland by W.W. Austin in the *New Grove Dictionary
   of American Music*, Vol. 1 (London and New York, Macmillan, 1986),
   p. 499.

4 Copland's Piano Sonata was composed 1939–41 and first performed
   by him in Buenos Aires on 21 October 1941.

206   To Elizabeth Sprague Coolidge[1]

c/o Dr. Mayer,
Long Island Home,
Amityville, N.Y.
September 18th 1939.

Dear Mrs. Coolidge,

I enclose a letter of introduction to you given to me by my master & very old friend Frank Bridge.[2] I wonder whether you could spare me some time, because I should so much like to meet you and talk with you of him & Mrs. Bridge. I am staying at the moment with friends on Long Island, & if you happened to be in New York I could arrange any day & any time – but if, as I gather you most probably are, you are in Washington, I could easily arrange to come there.

With best wishes,
yours sincerely,
BENJAMIN BRITTEN

P.S.   Peter Pears, who sang for you with the English Singers two Christmasses ago,[3] is travelling with me. May he come to see you with me? He would like to be remembered to you.

1   American patron of music (1864–1953). In 1925 Elizabeth Sprague Coolidge created a charitable foundation at the Library of Congress, Washington, which promoted concerts (under the Library's auspices) and administered various prizes for composition. The Coolidge Foundation also furthered musicological research through the Library's music division. In 1932 she created the Elizabeth Sprague Coolidge Medal 'for eminent services to chamber music', which Britten was to be awarded in 1941 for his First String Quartet; the quartet was commissioned by and dedicated to Mrs Coolidge. For a full account, see Stephen Banfield, ' "Too much of Albion?" Mrs Coolidge and her British Connections', *American Music*, Spring 1986, pp. 59–88.

2   Bridge – with whom Mrs Coolidge had had a long friendship – wrote a letter of introduction for Britten, dated July 1939:

Our beloved Benjamin Britten, that young friend, pupil, and quasi-adopted son, of whom you have heard us talk very often, and who is probably the outstanding composer of the present young men here, has been in Canada and we now hear he is going to New York.
I am sure you would like him [. . .] and I do so hope a meeting materializes. I am so anxious that you should meet him through me, because he is a part of me!! How I wish I could have been present to personally introduce him.

P.S.   You will remember Peter Pears who sang with the English Singers. He and Ben are together.

3 Mrs Coolidge had engaged the New English Singers to give the inaugural concert in the Coolidge Auditorium in 1937 – the first of two trips to the USA Pears had made with this ensemble.

207   To Ralph Hawkes
[*Typed*]

Boosey Hawkes Belwin Incorporated,
43–45–47 West 23rd Street,
New York, N.Y.
September 19th, 1939

Dear Ralph,

Well the war has started at last as we feared and as far as I can see, it is possible for me to stay on here. Peter is going to find it difficult, but I think will be able to pick up some jobs here and there.

Financially I am worried a bit, I admit. I suppose that all business has momentarily stopped. I am hoping against hope, that that doesn't mean my guarantee will stop too.

I have been speaking a lot with Mr. Winkler about this, and other matters. We agreed on many points, principally that I must get down to writing simple marketable works for him, which idea I like very much. In fact, Mr. Auden and I have been talking this afternoon with him about writing a High School Operetta, also I have planned writing works for Military Band and simple works for Strings.[1]

With this idea in view, he has made me an offer subject to your okay: he could pay me a royalty guarantee for this quarter, at a fixed Pound rate agreed between you and him (suggested $4.50 to the £) and subtract this amount from money owed you. I must say that I do hope this can be made possible, because I have much work, apart from these "practical works", that I wish to complete.

I have practically finished the Score of the Violin Concerto. I have completed a set of Part-Songs[2] and I have many other works of similar caliber in view.

It is possible that I could get some kind of work out here such as secretarial work at the Congress Library[3] or hack it at any of the broadcasting stations, but you will understand that I do not wish very much to do this.

Please write to me as soon as possible, saying all that is happening with you, what you would like me to do and any plans you may have for the future. I hear from Mr. Winkler that you will not come to the States at the moment, but I feel sure that somehow or other, you will be able to manage this. Meanwhile, you are very much in my thoughts and I must say that I wish I were with all my friends in England, but I feel at the moment that I am of more use doing the one thing I can do over here.

With kindest regards to you and your wife, I am
Sincerely,
Benjamin Britten

[Signed on his behalf by 'Y.G.', to whom this letter was dictated.]

P.S.   May I apologize for the length and confusion of the letter, as it is the first one I have dictated.[4]

1 Of these projects, it was only the operetta, *Paul Bunyan*, that came to fruition.
2 *A.M.D.G.*
3 The Library of Congress at Washington.
4 Britten was presumably availing himself of the secretarial facilities of the Boosey & Hawkes office in New York.

208   To Ralph Hawkes
[*Western Union Cablegram*]

AMITYVILLE N.Y.
22 September 1939

VERY INTERESTED IN BRITISH COUNCIL PROPOSAL[1]   ABLE AND WILLING PROVIDED NO JINGO EXCLAMATION MARK[2]   AWAITING DETAILS[3]

BRITTEN

1 The first intimation of the commissioning of the *Sinfonia da Requiem*, Op 20. Hawkes had cabled Britten on 21 September:

BRITISH COUNCIL ASK IF YOU ARE INTERESTED IN COMMISSION FOR FULL SCALE ORCHESTRAL WORK SYMPHONIC POEM SYMPHONY SUITE OVERTURE UNDERSTAND FEE SUBSTANTIAL EVEN HUNDREDS. I SAID YES   PLEASE CONFIRM

2 i.e. no jingoism.
3 See Letter 211.

209 To Ralph Hawkes

[*Western Union Cablegram*]

AMITYVILLE
27 September 1939

SOUNDS CRAZY BUT WILL DO BRITISH COUNCIL COMMISSION AWAITING
YOUR LETTER AND INSTRUCTIONS[1] BEST WISHES

BRITTEN

1 This cable was a response to Hawkes's letter of 23 September. See
note 1 to Letter 211.

210 To Wulff Scherchen

Long Island Home, Amityville.
[Postmarked 29 September 1939]

[. . .]
[. . .] How I wish I could get you out here, but as I am not at all
sure how long I shall be allowed to stay here myself nor is the
money position at all secure at the moment (I don't know if my
money will continue to come from England – & all depends on
getting jobs here – which isn't at all easy) – we had better wait till
things are a little more definite.[1] But my heart's set on it – both
you & Gustel, & if possible Barbara & the family too. I have a
feeling that things are going to be bad in Europe for a very long
time – & that the place will be quite uninhabitable, as it seems to
be at the moment! [. . .]

I hope you're going on working as I am – just completed the
score of my Violin Concerto & pleased with it – because it is at
times like these that work is so important – that humans can think
of other things than blowing each other up! I am reading lots
(Benvenuto Cellini's autobiography) – playing <u>lots</u> of music – & it
makes life much easier. I try not to listen to the Radio more than
I can help & the newspapers here are hysterical of course.
[. . .]
Peter sends his love, & says he's looking after me – and he certainly
is – like a mother hen!
He's a darling ——

1 Wulff and his mother were part of that larger community of friends
and family whose bodily transfer to the USA was one of Britten's
preoccupations at this time. Wulff was to find himself transferred to
North America in August 1940 in a manner somewhat less congenial

than Britten had envisaged (see Letter 281). None the less, he was to write to Wulff on 10 September 1940:

I can't say how relieved I am that you are over in Canada – I couldn't bear to have anyone else to worry about in England at this moment. You are certainly the right side of the Atlantic Ocean.

211   To Ralph Hawkes

N.B.   I should like to be paid in advance – or at any rate most of it. Could this be worked?

> Long Island Home, Amityville, N.Y.
> [October 1939]

Dear Ralph,

Thank you for your letter & all the surprising details.[1] I am just dashing to catch the return Air-mail to tell you I've received it. I certainly agree to the proposals & I'm now just sitting tight hoping to hear from Washington.

I have a scheme for a short Symphony – or Symphonic poem. Called Sinfonia da Requiem (rather topical, but not of course mentioning dates or places!) which sounds rather what they would like. Anyhow that we can settle when things become more definite. I must say I shall like the money – as that side of my present picture is none too rosy. However I'm hoping that some of the Schemes with Winkler will materialise as I expect & hope they will. I feel more & more keen to stay out here. Do let me have a line from time to time saying what & how you do. I was very interested (what a word?) in your last. Do take care of yourself. How English music (& BB in particular!) needs you! Peter sends best wishes.

Excuse violent hurry – but I want to catch this mail.

> Wishes to everyone.
> Yours ever,
> BEN

1 The history of the commission of the *Sinfonia da Requiem* – and the subsequent rejection of the work by its commissioners – is a complex and fascinating one and has never been fully told. The negotiations reveal the strangest mixture of farce and – given the context of the international events of the time – tragedy. It is for these reasons that we document the progress of the commission in considerable detail, using among other sources Hawkes's letters to Britten. His letter of

23 September, to which this letter (No. 211) was a response, set out the opening moves:

I saw Miss Henn-Collins [of the British Council staff in London] yesterday and she then disclosed to me that the Japs – of all people – had approached the British Council through their Ambassador in London to suggest and hope respectfully that an English composer could be recommended by them to write a full scale orchestral work for the 2,600th Anniversary Celebration of the Japanese Empire. The conditions are as follows:

1. Only one contribution from each country may be submitted, the choice of the composition being left to the country.

2. The composition must be a new work to commemorate the event.

3. The work, which may, if desired, be accompanied by chorus, must fall within one of the following categories:
    a) Symphony
    b) Symphonic poem
    c) Symphonic Suite
    d) Overture
    e) March

The time allotted to the performance of a), b), and c), should be approximately 15 to 20 minutes for each part, and for d) and e) 30 to 40 minutes for the whole performance.

4. If considered desirable, the Committee will grant an honorarium not exceeding Y10,000 (£580) [Y=Yen] for a symphonic piece, Y5,000 (£290) for an Overture, and Y2,000 (£115) for a March.

5. The work selected must be timed to reach Tokyo not later than May, 1940.

6. Copyright in Japan will be held by the Committee, but will be at the free disposal of the Composer elsewhere.

    and I make the following observations thereon:–

1. If you agree you will be sole English representative.

2. Is obvious.

3. Are the categories [sic]. My own suggestion is that you go for the Symphonic Poem, for I think it would be a most useful work. Actually, we have no full scale orchestral work from you of this nature and for performances elsewhere it would doubtless be most useful. On the other hand, perhaps an Overture might suit you better and I must leave this to you. I certainly do not favor a Symphony. I cannot think that the durations are at all accurate and I think perhaps you should adhere to the recognised durations of works in these categories when considering them.

4. Of course, the honorarium will be desirable and necessary and I am awaiting news from Miss Henn-Collins as to whether the sum in Yen can be exported. I understand that this is the case with permission and doubtless permission would be granted under these circumstances; otherwise the whole thing is not worth while.

5. Gives you sufficient time, I think, for the material can be made in the States and despatched from there.

6. I would be quite agreeable to the copyright in Japan being held by the Committee, for elsewhere it would be fully protected, as usual.

Two other points arise:—

(a)   In the event of Great Britain and Japan falling out before May 1940, the British Council could not accept any responsibility and with this I quite agree.

(b)   You are of military age and it is on the cards that you may have to return here in consequence. Even so, I think I could pull sufficient strings to get you made a Bandmaster or put you in a Band. This will doubtless be a point that has had your consideration already but I do not think it will arise for some months.

At the moment I have no details as to how and when the payment would be made but the invitation for the commission will be issued direct by the Japanese Ambassador in Washington to you whilst you are in America and I see no reason for you to come back here (unless, of course, you want to or have to) until you have completed the work.

Miss Henn-Collins was very nice indeed and I am very happy that she should have suggested you for this. Apparently the orchestra is about 80 or 90 players and they have a very good chorus. Walton and Delius are liked there and I saw the programmes of the Concerts for the last few years, which showed a general range of all the classics. You could, of course, find out locally in New York other details regarding the Tokyo Symphony Orchestra: I think some Americans have been over there to conduct.

Britten's instant reaction to the proposal in his first cable was that he would provide 'no jingo'. It is difficult, however, to understand how he (or his publishers) ever thought that the proposal for a *Sinfonia da Requiem* 'sounds rather what [the commissioners] would like' to mark the 2,600th Anniversary Celebration of the Japanese Empire. This was a point that seems to have occurred to Lennox Berkeley, who was to write to Britten on 21 April 1940, 'I'm glad to hear that the Jap. Government commission is really happening, though that they should commission an anti-war work seems a piece of disconcerting irony.' In an interview Britten was to give for the *New York Sun* on 27 April, he is reported as saying:

'I'm making it just as anti-war as possible,' he declared. 'I don't believe you can express social or political or economic theories in music, but by coupling new music with well known musical phrases, I think it's possible to get over certain ideas. I'm dedicating this symphony to the memory of my parents, and, since it is a kind of requiem, I'm quoting from the Dies Irae of the Requiem Mass. One's apt to get muddled discussing such things – all I'm sure of is my own anti-war conviction as I write it.'

Although he's frankly 'of pacifist leanings' Mr Britten tried to go home as soon as Great Britain entered the present war. The British authorities informed him he'd be called when he was needed, and that meanwhile, he could serve his country best by carrying on as usual.

As for Hawkes's point 6(b) on an altogether different topic, he was to pursue the same thought over two years later in a letter dated 9 December 1941, when Britten and Pears had in fact irrevocably decided to return to the UK. It seems, however, that Hawkes was still not aware of their intention to object to military service, even of a non-combatant character:

I do not know whether you have advanced your plans for return to this country but a note I saw in the paper this morning to the effect that younger men in the USA may have to return, prompts me to write and tell you what I have done here regarding your future.

If you were here, I could immediately make application for you to go into the RAF Band; I spoke to [B. Walton] O'Donnell on the telephone last week about it and he seemed quite agreeable but, of course, it would be better if you played another instrument, as well as Piano.

I have also spoken to Willie Walton and although he has not been called yet, he does not expect to have his deferment extended any longer than March. There is a Committee which applies for these deferments but I do not think they will be very successful under the new Call-up Regulations. As far as I see it, there are two courses open to you (1) Return to this country and as soon as I know you have arrived, I would make immediate application for you to be enlisted in one of the Bands (2) Go to Canada and join a Band there. My own personal view is that you will be better off here; the entire situation has, of course, been changed by the 'Japanese incident' [Pearl Harbor] and this letter will just serve to keep you up to date with the position as it may affect you here.

212 To Beth Welford

[EWB, pp. 119–21; incomplete]

Long Island Home, Amityville, N.Y.
October 19th 1939

My darlingest Beth,

I was sick when I read in your letter that you hadn't had any communications for so long from me. I hope that by now that you will have got my letters. Please don't think that I've forgotten you! Why I don't write everyday is because Air-mail is so beastly expensive – & it is the only mail that gets to places in reasonable time. Your letter took just three weeks! You seem horribly far off with communications so bad. I try to write to you & Barbara every week alternately – & please tell the other one all the news – that sort of thing.

Actually one is terribly busy here. You see it is not like England

where ones name is known musically – here people are willing
to be impressed, but one has to work hard to keep it up. And at
the moment one is in the between stage of – 'well, if you produce
the work we'll do it' – & one has to sit down & do it! However
things might be much worse. The only part that is so awful, is
that I find working so difficult. Thinking of you all day & wondering
what is happening now. The papers are hysterical here – you
complain that you're not told enough – well, we're told too much.
And half of it is false rumours. I nearly died when I heard that the
length of the East Coast had been raided, but then it turned out
that it was only a scare.

I feel terribly homesick, my dear. Yearning for things to get all
right & so that we could meet again, & go on living as before. I
can't get used to the idea that I should become an American. I
won't do it until I'm forced. But I suppose it's stupid, since these
days Nationality is only a convenience (or inconvenience!) & has
nothing to do with what one feels about countries! However, we'll
see. I shall do nothing rash – you can count on me!

The Mayers continue to be as sweet as possible. The fact that
they are Europeans is so comforting at this time. Americans are
awfully inclined to treat the whole thing as an awfully interesting
stage play, & applaud or hiss as they feel inclined. There is no
doubt on whose side their sympathy lies. Something like ½%
sympathise with the Nazis I believe.

I suppose Lennox is right about letting the Mill, but much as I
should like to I can't send money to keep it on for you. I feel
furious that he didn't take Ralph's offer at the beginning of the
war.[1] Sometimes I feel pretty black about him (his letters to me
are the only preachy ones I get) all about conscience & that kind
of thing – about really being a pacifist, but this being a just war
– and that sort of nonsense. However it is easy to sit outside &
criticise – it must be hell for him & his likes right in the middle
of this horrible thing.

I see lots of Wystan; it is nice to have him around.[2] Also Aaron
Copland – although he's gone off to Hollywood to do a film[3] at
the moment. Wystan & my opera is settled for Broadway[4] when
we have done it. We'll have our work cut out doing it, I feel! I've
also completed the rest of the 'Illuminations' for Sophie to do in
November – somewhere in London I believe, but I thought
concerts were stopped? Ask Ralph when because I should love you
to hear them – they're my best so far. You heard the grand news
about the first performance of the Violin Concerto in New York

Philharmonic? So I shouldn't be too bad tempered – but if <u>only</u>
you were over here. I think we'll <u>have</u> to arrange this, Beth, you
come over & keep house for Peter & me! Goodness me, I wish you
could persuade Kit to try that. I know it sounds hopeless, but at
these moments anything is worth trying! My great idea is for all
my friends (& nice relations!) to come & live over here, & if the
situation's possible we could go back to England for holidays.
Think it over! Barbara seems tied to Helen & her job – but it looks
abit as if her job won't last very long — — ??

Thank you for seeing about the Mill & furniture. Why couldn't
you & Barbara live there & keep it up. I might send you money
from time to time. It's <u>very</u> cheap, living in Snape.

Please forgive this rambling incoherent letter – but I've been
dictating (!) letters all the morning & I'm very wuzzy! Beata eldest
Mayer daughter, who is a trained sec., is living here at the moment,
& has been helping me with my overdue correspondence!!⁵
There's, as usual, lots to do.

My love to everyone. I shall be writing to D [Dodo Welford] in
a day or so. How's everyone? I <u>loved</u> the photos of Sebastian &
you. You both look grand. I was terribly sentimental when I got
them. I think he looks lovely, especially the close up of him – &
the one on your shoulder. You look grand too – o, how I'd love to
see you again. But sometime we MUST. Give my love to Barbara
& say how much I appreciate her long letters. She really is writing
marvellous ones – & they are well known in the State of New
York. I'll be writing to her next mail.

XXXXOOOOXXXX   BEN.

1 Hawkes had offered to rent the Mill from Lennox Berkeley.

2 For an account of 'Auden in Amityville', see Robert P. Rushmore,
   Long Island Forum, July 1985, pp. 131–5.

3 In October, Copland flew out to the West Coast to write the score for
   Lewis Milestone's film, *Of Mice and Men* (based on John Steinbeck's
   dramatized version of his novel). See Aaron Copland and Vivian
   Perlis, *Copland: 1900 through 1942* (London, Faber and Faber, 1984),
   pp. 297–300.

4 In fact the operetta, *Paul Bunyan*, was staged at Columbia University,
   New York, but the reference to Broadway is interesting. Although
   this goal was not achieved, something of the ambition certainly
   remained to influence the character of the music. See DMPB. In an
   interview with the *New York Sun*, 27 April 1940, Broadway remains

an objective. The account of *Bunyan* Britten gave his interviewer (William G. King) is illuminating in its own right:

'Sometimes strangers see such things more clearly,' he said. 'It's a matter of perspective. Bunyan in a way symbolizes the pioneers of the whole world, the men who opened up new country, who conquered without killing, who were the noblest kind of adventurers.'

The operetta was begun (possibly under the Copland influence) as a work suitable for performance by high school students. If certain plans which can't be discussed at present go through, however, it will have its first performances in a Broadway theater.

'We still intend to keep it as simple as possible,' Britten said, 'but we hope it will have an appeal for adult audiences, too. Auden has finished his script, and the music is all sketched. No, I haven't used any American folk-tunes, although I've learned a lot from them, and I've tried to capture some of their spirit.'

Britten's old teacher, Frank Bridge, was receiving news of the composer's plans via Ralph Hawkes. He was to write on 11 December to Britten: 'There are rumours of a piano Quartet with Orch. for Toronto [*Young Apollo*] and a Revue for New York. I wish I felt happier about this last.'

Britten's incidental music *was*, however, to reach Broadway in 1940: Max Catto's melodrama, *They Walk Alone*, first heard in London in 1938 (see note 2 to Letter 160), was revived in New York (see PR, pp. 532–3).

5 Beata Mayer had had a secretarial job at the Long Island Home for about a year, until August, when she left for a short vacation in Bermuda with her brother, Christopher. When they returned to Amityville they found that Britten and Pears had taken up residence in their absence. It seems that Beata then took on occasional nursing engagements for two or three weeks at a time and in between was at Stanton College, when she helped Britten with his correspondence.

213 To Antonio Brosa
[*Typed*]

c/o Mrs. W. Mayer,
Long Island Home,
Amityville, N.Y.
October 19th, 1939.

My dear Toni,

I am urgently expecting a letter from you saying how you and Peggy are, how you are existing, and also when you are going to be able to come to America.[1] I hope you were as pleased as I was

to hear that Barbirolli[2] is going to do my Violin Concerto. He
really was very enthusiastic about it and, furthermore, thinks it is
an excellent start for you in this country. Whether it will be too
late to get other performances of the work with you in this season
remains to be seen. Dr. Heinsheimer, the Boosey & Hawkes agent
over here, is indefatigable, and if it is physically possible to arrange
further performances, he will do it. Have you an agent over here?
If so, I suggest that you send his name and that he gets in touch
with the aforesaid Heinsheimer. I am afraid that Barbirolli insists
on this being a world's first performance and under the present
horrible circumstances I think he is right. Ralph[3] tells me that you
approve of the work, which pleases me more than I can say. If
there is anything which you or Paganini find impossible to play,
don't worry. We will alter that when we meet. But at the moment,
knowing your capabilities, I don't think that this can be possible.
Do please find time to write me a note as to your future plans. I
can arrange anything for you, should you wish to come to America
soon.

I myself with Peter are staying on Long Island, which is very
convenient for New York being only an hour away and it being
a very beautiful place. Peter and I were staying here with friends
of Peter's when the War started and owing to their indescribable
hospitality, here we are still. We are looking for a small house to
take for the winter, but owing to the amount of work I am doing,
and also to our present extreme of comfortableness, this house-
hunting is somewhat half hearted.[4] I cannot say more about the
qualities of the family I am staying with, since the eldest daughter
is taking down, believe it or not, this letter in shorthand.
However, I do suggest that as soon as you come to America, you
make their acquaintance.

My love to you both. I do hope that life is not as unbearable as
everyone says it is, although I'm afraid it must be. Where are you?

Much love
Yours ever,
BENJY

1 Brosa was resident in the USA 1940–46, after which he returned to
Europe.

2 John Barbirolli (1899–1970), English conductor, started his musical
career as a cellist. He conducted opera for the British National Opera
Company and Covent Garden before his appointment to the Scottish
Orchestra, Glasgow, 1933–6. From 1936 to 1942 he was conductor of

the New York Philharmonic Orchestra, returning to England in 1943
when he became conductor of the Hallé Orchestra, a post he retained
until his death. He was knighted in 1949. In 1939 he had married
the oboist, Evelyn Rothwell, who was a contemporary of Britten's at
the College, and with whom he found himself playing chamber
music in New York:

> [Britten] suggested to her that they should tackle some Mozart string quintets
> and said 'You can have a bash on the oboe.' This led to a glorious time for
> five musicians including Evelyn, attempting the first violin parts on her
> oboe, and Britten playing the viola.
> (Harold Atkins and Peter Cotes, *The Barbirollis: a Musical Marriage*
> (London, Robson Books, 1983), p. 71)

3 No letter from Hawkes exists which relates this information. Perhaps
Britten learned it from Heinsheimer? However, in a letter to the
composer of 3 November Hawkes was to write:

> VIOLIN CONCERTO: I have not written you since I heard Brosa and Boys play
> it; they came up the other afternoon and gave us a reading here. We were all
> much impressed with it; its seriousness and in particular the last movement
> seemed to show quite a different trend in your writing.

4 Nothing came of this, but in November 1940 Britten and Pears moved
into the famous house in Brooklyn of which Auden was custodian.
See note 2 to Letter 291.

14 To Ralph Hawkes

[*Typed*]

c/o Mrs. W. Mayer,
Long Island Home,
Amityville, N.Y.
October 19th, 1939.

My dear Ralph,

Thank you for your long letter. I notice that you have nothing to
do but write long letters to me which I appreciate very much,
however, and please do not think of stopping them because letters
from England are much treasured in these times.

I am continuing to live on Long Island, as I told you, and all
things considered I am enjoying myself very much. I am working
very hard and two days ago completed LES ILLUMINATIONS,[1] which
I am now hard at work scoring, and I hope to have the score
posted to you within a week. When it will arrive with you is in the
hands of God and Hitler. I must say that I am very pleased with
it and that it is definitely my Opus 1.[2] I will include with the score

piano arrangements for Sophie Wyss to study from and will write
direct to her instructions as how to sing it.[3] I shall do my best to
arrange a performance in New York of this work with Peter
singing.[4]

You will have heard, of course, the good news about the VIOLIN
CONCERTO. It was a remarkable feat for Dr. Heinsheimer to have
pulled this off. Barbirolli was very pleased with the work and
should give it an excellent performance, and I think it should be
a good start for Toni Brosa on this side of the Atlantic. I will write
direct to him about that too.

YOUNG APOLLO should have arrived with you by now. I hope that
we can arrange a performance of it here, but until concerts get
going with you again I don't think England will have the privilege
of hearing that masterpiece. I am waiting now to hear from the
Japanese Embassy, but owing to the volcanic state of affairs in the
world this moment, it is conceivable that Anglo-Japanese relations
may be broken off [Handwritten: at any time!]. So I hope it will be
possible for me to have some Yen paid in advance. The work I
am planning to do is a short program symphony which is certainly
not military in character. More than that I can't say at the moment.
It will probably be called Symphonia da Requiem, but I shall have
to discuss this kind of detail with His Excellency The Jap in
Washington.

Auden and I are set now to write a School operetta for Max
Winkler. This has the extra stimulus of a probable professional
Broadway performance by the wellknown Ballet Caravan in
January. This seems an excellent thing, since it is a first rate start
for a work of this kind, and also before the work is printed we can
have practical experience of how the work sounds and looks on
the stage. The probable subject is that of Paul Bunyan, the American
frontier hero, who has, believe me, the most extraordinary
adventures. It is certainly up Wystan's tree and also up mine.

Enough of business. Judging by your and my family's letters,
London seems Hell at the moment. The B.B.C. is obviously
worthy of all the names you call it. I don't know whether boredom
is worse than bombardment, but even then I hope you won't be
given the chance to decide that question. I admire you very much
for continuing the way you do. I think it is frightfully important
that at times like these the non-military businesses carry on as well
as the Government will permit. For that reason my presence not
being urgently required in England, as I am informed, I feel it is
wiser that I shall stay out here and go on working, and as I found

these really excellent friends, I consider myself more than lucky. Thank you more than I can say for arranging the continuance of the guarantee. As you can understand, money is not overplentiful for Peter and me over here, and so we both appreciate that very much. Peter is negotiating possible jobs and we are living in hopes that something may come of it. My love to Erika and all the best to yourself. Why don't you come to America, where I can assure you, your presence is urgently needed. By the way, I think Heinsheimer is a most excellent person and for B.H.B.[5] a gift from the Gods.

> All the best. I am thinking of you very much.
>
> Yours sincerely,
>
> BEN

[*Handwritten:*]
P.S.   Could you please forward the enclosed letter to Toni Brosa? You may have his immediate address (I've only got the St. John's Wood one) – besides Air-mail stamps are expensive!

> Many thanks –
>
> B.

1 i.e. 17 October. The completion date inscribed at the end of the full score is 25 October, eight days later. Some of the songs already existed in full score. See note 2 to Letter 181.

2 Britten had already referred in 1937 to *Our Hunting Fathers* (Op. 8) as 'my Op. 1 alright' (Diary, 30 April). See also DMBA, p. 19.

3 See Letter 215.

4 This was to take place at the Town Hall, New York, on 18 May 1941 as part of the eighteenth ISCM Festival: see note 4 to Letter 313.

5 Boosey Hawkes Belwin Incorporated.

215   To Sophie Wyss
[*Typed*]

> c/o Mrs. W. Mayer,
> Long Island Home,
> Amityville, N.Y.
> October 19th, 1939.

My Dear Sophie,

Thank you very much for your letters, it is so good of you to write so often and I appreciate them more than I can say.

I was thrilled to hear how well you sang LES ILLUMINATIONS at

the Queens Hall at the Proms, and how well they were received.[1]
I have now completed this work, which I am very pleased with,
and in a few days I hope to send you the rest of the songs. I am
afraid that you may find them rather awkward to sing, but at any
rate I hope the prosody is O.K. As the opportunity for writing
letters is somewhat rare and, of course, the posts are chaotic, I
will give you a rough idea of the songs now, in case future letters
do not arrive in time for the performance.

The work as it now stands is very much of a whole – the pieces
are to follow each other without interruption. In order that you
should not be a nervous wreck at the end of the work, I have put
in the middle an orchestral interlude. The character of the whole
work is difficult to describe since anything dealing with Rimbaud
must necessarily be enigmatic. But roughly the idea is this: Les
Illuminations, as I see it, are the visions of heaven that were allowed
the poet, and I hope the composer. That is not to say, of course, that
the visions are actually of heaven, but rather of the heavenly aspect
of the subjects. Rather like the Apostles who were given the sixth
sense at, I believe, Pentecost. The clue to the whole work is, I
think, to be found in the last line of Parade: "J'ai seul la clef de
cette parade sauvage", which I have used in all three times – one,
at the end of the initial fanfare; two, at the end of the interlude;
three, at the end of Parade. Each time it is sung to the same musical
phrase and must be made as important as possible by you.
Incidentally, the second time it happens it is marked pianissimo,
but it must not lose its heraldic character. Now roughly this is the
scheme of the movements:

FANFARE.   This is to call attention, prepare the mood, and
                give thematic suggestions for the work. Its
                character is obvious from the music.

VILLES.   This poem, I believe, was written in London
                and certainly is a very good impression of the
                chaotic modern city life (although it cannot
                apply, I gather, to London at the moment). I
                want it sung in a metallic and relentless fashion
                with the exclamation: "Ce sont des villes!"
                somewhat sarcastically sung. The end is simply
                a prayer for a little peace.

PHRASE.   This short section, very dreamy, is merely an
                introduction to

ANTIQUE,   which is a slow dance.

ROYAUTÉ.   Pompous and satirical. The idea merely is that,
                  given the right circumstances, it is in the
                  power of anyone, however humble, to imagine
                  himself King or God, whichever you prefer[2]
MARINE, about which you know everything.[3]
The ORCHESTRAL INTERLUDE is a reproof for the exaggeratedly
ecstatic mood of Marine.
BEING BEAUTEOUS. No one in the world could tell you how to sing
                  this one.
PARADE.   you will enjoy, because it is a picture of the
                  underworld. It should be made to sound
                  creepy, evil, dirty (apologies!), and really
                  desperate. I think it is the most terrific poem
                  and at the moment I feel the music has got
                  something of the poem!! After this,
DÉPART.   Should be sung quietly, very slowly, and as
                  sweetly as only you know how. "O Rumeurs
                  et Visions!" should bring tears to the eyes of
                  even the program sellers at the back of the
                  hall.

Enough of business. I do hope young Arnold is enjoying his
school. Give him my love when you next write. I will try and
send him a post card from here. I gather that Heinemanns[4] is
having the time of his life owing to the blackouts and the
consequent boom in reading. I have seen Wystan a lot. He is now
living in New York and I am living with Peter on Long Island
about an hour's ride away. We have been rescued out of an
avalanche of woe by some excellent friends of Peter's who have
made us believe that life is still worth living, which I can assure
you is these days no mean feat. I still have not given up the hope
of seeing you again although at the moment it seems a faint hope.
But I think of you and the family, including my inestimable
godson, very very often. Please write as often as you can.
    With best love and many wishes for your safety and health.
                                                    Affectionately,
                                                    [Unsigned]

1 The anonymous reviewer in The Times, 18 August, wrote:
   Miss Sophie Wyss sang finely two songs from a set, as yet incomplete, of
   poems by Arthur Rimbaud with accompaniment for string orchestra composed by Benjamin Britten. These songs show a sensitive feeling for the
   French language that is in itself rather unusual in an English composer, and
   a greater command of vocal line than has formerly been evident in Britten's

songs. There still remain occasional intractabilities like the phrase in the first song to which are set the words, 's'élargir et trembler comme un spectre', where the voice has to jump about the stave in a way that can hardly avoid sounding awkward. But the rest of this song has a genuine lyric beauty, and the elaborate virtuosity of the second, 'Marine', makes a good foil to it.

J.A. Westrup in the *Daily Telegraph*, 18 August, wrote more warmly of Britten's music on this occasion than had been his habit during the early thirties:

Mr Britten's songs mark a spiritual change which may prove to be decisive in his creative work. In the past he has been praised for his sleight-of-hand, and he has also shown an aptitude for caricaturing other people's music. But these qualities, however admirable, are not the stuff of which a composer is made.

Here in these songs is the evidence of a mind directly influenced by an idea and striving to achieve not mere cleverness, but a sincere expression of that idea. The idiom recalls that of French composers – not Debussy or Ravel, rather Fauré – but there is no suggestion of parody.

The melodic line is perfectly adapted both to the words and to the mood, the architecture of the first song in particular is beautifully contrived, the whole atmosphere is restrained and thoughtful and the writing for strings is masterly.

2 The Archive possesses a typed draft of this letter which differs from the copy sent to Sophie Wyss in one highly interesting particular. In the interpretative inventory of the cycle prepared by Britten, between the entries for 'Royauté' and 'Marine', there appeared a recapitulation of 'Phrase', described as follows: 'Again PHRASE, this time brilliant and exciting, is merely an introduction to [MARINE] [. . .].' This tells us that in October Britten was still not quite certain about the contents and sequence of the cycle and was thinking of including the additional setting of 'Phrase' ('La Cascade sonne') documented in note 2 to Letter 181. But before the letter to Wyss was finally typed, this entry was deleted and the setting itself discarded.

3 This song and 'Being Beauteous' had been performed independently before the completion of the cycle as a whole, hence Britten's comment.

4 William Heinemann Ltd, the London publishers, for whom Arnold Gyde worked.

216 To Beth Welford

> Long Island Home, Amityville, N.Y.
> Oct. 23rd 1939

My darling Beth,

Your letter of 9th got here this morning. I was very glad to hear that you & all are well, & also honoured that you have named

me advisory guardian to Sebastian! Such a responsibility appalls
me – but lets hope & pray it won't be necessary for a <u>very</u> long time!

Now – re alarums & excursions: I was certainly piqued by the
things you said. The sooner Mr. Nicholson[1] realises that these are
exceptional times, the better. His letter to me (I have only received
one) took <u>one month</u> to arrive. There are only about two mail boats
per month now & letters are held up in England & here – especially
if they come via Canada. This one letter from him I answered by
<u>cable</u> the same evening & by a long letter the next air-mail. So you
can hardly call me dilatory! I'm very angry with him. Why didn't
he let us know before that Hallam Street was being a bother?[2]
Besides he knows that I'm (& Peter is) responsible for the rent –
surely he knows us well enough to be able to advance the £7 or
whatever it was to Mrs. Walker (landlady). I told him I had money
coming to me – what about Sewell's[3] rent forinstance? At least he
might have written by air – or has the old fogey never heard of
air-mails? Any how that should all be cleared up by now – I've told
him to write to B & H where there is enough money to pay the
rent till the end of the lease (November 27th). Mrs. Pears[4] & Barbara
will I hope be able to look after the furniture – & we've written
to them re that already.

Of course I realise that Lennox has got all worked up about the
war – both physically & financially – But your letter was the first
intimation I've had that he was keeping the place up grudgingly.
After all he knew that I was going to be away indefinitely (I never
even suggested to him that I might be back for Christmas) – & he
<u>put in writing</u> that he would be responsible financially for the Mill
(ask Nicholson for the letter – he's got it). I understand that the
new Income tax has hit him badly – but after all the house cost
him nothing to be built & I'm perfectly prepared to waive the rent
he's paying me (until the end of this year I've received it). It's
nothing to me if he prefers to go & live with the Davenports.[5] He
should know his own mind earlier – I know this war situation is
difficult, but God knows everyone is feeling it. Another thing that
makes me angry is that Ralph Hawkes tells me he 'phoned him at
the beginning of the war & offered to rent the Mill – & Lennox
couldn't make up his mind whether to do it or not – so Ralph
(evidently piqued) couldn't wait. I'm sorry to feel like this about
Lennox – but his letters to me have been dreadful – moany &
whiny, pompous & preachy, however well they may have been
meant – but I suppose that's how he's made, so I can't blame

him. Barbara said some choice things about him in a letter a week or so back.

To get down to plans – what I'm doing is this – I shall write (air-mail of course) to Nicholson. Tell him to sell out my Life Insurance (I mean it), pay off the overdraft at the bank, & whatever charges are due to him. Then if Lennox won't stay at the Mill – Nicholson must hunt for a tenant – & if that can't be managed, he must shut the place up. After all he's my attorney. I shall have to send money from here (if I can find any – God knows it's hard enough at the moment) if the Insurance won't cover all this. I won't bother you, old thing, because I know that you've got lots to think about – but I should think that would be an advantage at these times. Sometimes I feel a bomb on Snape might not be a terrible thing – but I don't want to sell it. I still hope & pray that I'll be able to come back & enjoy it. Let the garden go – that's unimportant – & I don't think that the place shut up will come to much harm. I'm sorry Mrs. Hearn will have to go – sorry for her to[o] – but that'll be on Lennox's conscience.

I'm sorry that I still haven't time to write letters to the Welford family – but you must realise that I am working terrifically hard – you see the quicker that I can get things written, the sooner we can make money by having them performed. Life's not easy even if one's out of the reach of bombs. By-the-way, for the benefit of Lennox, Nicholson & all true patriots, the time has not yet come to talk of 'duty' & 'conscience' because we've been officially informed that our best duty is at the moment to stay put. Our beautiful English accents are such good propaganda – I don't think.

I loved the photos of Sebastian. Please send more at the earliest opportunity.

Much love, my dear; gosh – how I want to see you all again.

Hope you're well.

BEN.

P.S. John Nicholson's 'letter about a job' – if it is the only one I got from him – was merely a forwarded one from Rudolph Holzman, requesting some works from B & H. This was done by Ralph Hawkes who I presume told Nicholson. When I next had to write to Nicholson I acknowledged it – but it was hardly necessary to write specially. After all it had already cost me 6/8d.[6] Please use air-mail in the future.

1 Britten's solicitor.

2 See also Letter 218.

3 Laurence Sewell, Mr Britten's former assistant, had continued the dental practice in the same premises. The Britten family still owned the house and Sewell paid a rent of £25 per quarter.

4 Pears's mother, Jessica (Jessie) Elizabeth de Visnes Pears, née Luard (1869–1947). His father was Arthur Grant Pears (1863–1948).

5 Friends of Berkeley and also of Henry Boys. Berkeley wrote to Britten from Snape on 24 September,

> [. . .] the Davenports have asked me to go and live with them – it certainly is a bit depressing to be here all alone in these times. So I'm probably going to do that with occasional visits back here to see that everything is all right. Mrs Hearn is quite happy to carry on.

On 21 November, he wrote from the Davenports' home in Wiltshire:

> I love being here and don't know what I should do without them. Henry Boys is here too, and we often talk of you. Tony Brosa was here a short while ago and played your Vn Concerto with Henry – unfortunately it was while I was away, so I haven't heard it.

6 One-third of £1 in 1939 and a standard lawyer's fee.

217 To Hedli Anderson

c/o Mrs. W. Mayer,
Long Island Home,
Amityville, N.Y.
[? October 1939]

My darling Hedli,

I know – I know – I know. I deserve it all – but darling Hedli – arn't we all human? I'm sure you've done dreadful things like this before. I tell you what it is – or rather was. Peter & I talk & talk about you – you are in my mind so often – because you know how warmly I feel about you – but every time I sat down to write letters (not very often, I admit) – 'I can't write because I've not written those songs'[1] – & since you gave me that cheque (which was so very useful – you can't imagine) I felt worse. To be honest, I couldn't get myself into the mood. It's difficult to think in that medium over here, because everyone writes & thinks of 'swing' & does it so well that I say – 'o well it's their forte, I'll stick to my highbrow' – specially as since I arrived over here I've written & written & written – finished the Rimbaud series of songs (best thing I've done so far) – written a big heavy-weight Violin Concerto (first performance with New York Philharmonic in March) – a new piece for Piano & Orchestra called 'Young Apollo' (after Keats very Romantic) which I played in Toronto in August – 8 religious part songs from G.M. Hopkins – so I've been busy, my dear, you see! But, Hedli, I promise you – you will get your songs one or two or possibly three (God help me!) by air-mail either at the end of this or most probably next week. See I swear it – swear it – swear it – wish that I may die – cross my fingers – & if I'd cut myself shaving this morning I would have put my blood on it.

I bet you're having a lousy time. Hope you get Ashley Duke's job – because I suppose the Trocadero one is off.[2] London sounds so awful now – I have long letters from sister Barbara & Ralph Hawkes describing it. You can't imagine how bad one feels over here too – our news is nothing if not full (much fuller than reality!) – & one suffers heart attacks at every newspaper & radio bulletin. I loathe America's attitude to the whole business – rather like people in the stalls watching an interesting play, & being oh – so critical about the actors. They certainly don't sympathize with the Nazis – but they don't like Chamberlain, they don't. We arn't wanted back, & there doesn't seem any reason to come – except to see people like you Hedli. My affairs are in the most awful muddle, because (i) letters take such ages to get to here & everything cris-crosses all the time (air-mail is the only possible means of communication) (ii) the two tenants – at the Mill and Hallam St – have proved such weak-kneed, incompetant fools. Jackie has just gone off & paid nothing apparently – & Lennox frets & doesn't make decisions, writes letters about conscience & duty (King & Country etc.) & complains about neglect – oh, Hedli, what a bloody fool I was about all that – one sees so much more clearly when one's away. He's just NO GOOD.

We're staying with adorable friends in this Lunatic Asylum in Long Island (not as inmates) – he is a refugee Psychiatrist from Munich who has a good job here – & his wonderful wife who was the great maecenas of artists, poets, & musicians in Bavaria & is gradually achieving that position in New York State. She has a grand family of four – & Peter & I have been admitted to that select circle & now there are 6!! Wystan's in New York & he comes down here nearly every week-end. He's working well & we often talk about you – & plan, & plan! One never knows, Hedli – but I won't raise your spirits too much! So life might be worse – if only one could look ahead & could forget about the world's horrible troubles. But it's no good, one can't.

I must post this now because the mail's just off. Do you forgive me, Hedli – I shall understand you if you don't – but you <u>must</u>!!

Everso much love. I'll write more with the songs.

BENJAMIN

P.S.   Did you get the piano from 67 Hallam Street?[3] If not now that everything has to be cleared (at the end of the lease November 28th – or sooner) – could you have it now? Please, Hedli, do take it if you possibly can – Barbara is arranging all this stuff – 11 Tryon House, Mallord Street, SW3 (Flaxman 6202) – please 'phone her – there's a darling.

I hear-by authorise Miss Hedli Anderson to have my piano for as long as she cares to keep it –

BENJAMIN BRITTEN

So there!!!!

1 Britten refers to the so-called 'Cabaret Songs'. See note 2 to Letter 126. Hedli Anderson had clearly commissioned further songs, for which she was urgently waiting.

2 In 1989 Hedli Anderson was unable to recall what the Ashley Dukes job might have been, unless it was some involvement in the revival of *The Ascent of F6* at the Old Vic in June. But she did recall still that Britten, in the music he wrote for her, 'stretched me to my vocal limits'.

3 Hedli collected the piano and cared for it until Britten took possession of it again on his return from the States.

218   To Ralph Hawkes
[*Typed*]

c/o Mrs. W. Mayer,
The Long Island Home,
Amityville, N.Y.
October 27, 1939

My dear Ralph,

Dr. Heinsheimer has received the full score (complete) of LES ILLUMINATIONS, is having it photographed, and with luck will catch the Manhattan[1] tomorrow. I have also made piano scores of the new numbers for Sophie to learn from, and I hope they are legible enough for her. Peter wrote two of them,[2] so at least those two ought to be allright. You don't say when the first performance is, but please let me have a note saying how it goes. If you could let my sister Barbara know, I shall be pleased. Name, Miss Barbara Britten, address, 11, Tryon House, Mallord Street, S.W. 3. I shall try and arrange with the invaluable assistance of Heinsheimer a performance on the radio over here, probably with Peter. I have contacts with NBC, CBS, and also Mutual.[3] I did not have time to put the Metronome markings on the score and I enclose them here, so perhaps you could be good enough to put them on for me. By the way, there are one or two alterations in the old ones. Could you please have them carefully checked, score and parts. Notably in Royauté there are considerable alterations in the vocal part. Please tell Sophie this. There is also an extra bar in the beginning of Antique. Enough of Illuminations.

Re the Japanese commission, I have not heard any more since your last letter, when you say that you have had official notice from the Jap Embassy in London. I am feeling slightly worried about the Japanese silence over here since, if I am to get this work completed by May, I want to start thinking about it very soon, as it is to be a heavy work as you say. Shall I myself write to the Embassy in Washington, or shall I just wait till he coughs up something? You might let me have a note by the next airmail re this.

There have not been any more developments in my other activities. Auden is at work, I hope, on the script of the opera to be produced here in January, but Winkler will have told you all about this. It sounds to me a grand idea, but it is going to take a hell of a lot of work to get it done by then. However, doubtlessly we shall succeed. The Violin Concerto dates are settled, as you obviously will know. I am still waiting to hear from Toni Brosa as to when he expects to come and as to what he thinks about the work, etc. If you can get in touch with him, you might poke him in the ribs for me.

I hope that life is a little more bearable for you now – that the BBC has emerged slightly from its gloom and is giving you something worth listening to. Life is continuing here as pleasantly as possible. I am doing a terrific amount of work. The muse does not seem to be affected by the international situation, I am glad to say, although at times working is an effort.

I have been somewhat disturbed by letters from England re my various estates etc! My poor stuffy old solicitor does not seem to

realize that letters take a day or two to reach me, especially if he
sends them to Canada by the slowest possible boat, so if they
should bother you at all, please divide their emotions by two and
don't worry and tell them to go to Hell as politely as you think
suitable. It seems that Lennox has at last decided to leave the Mill.
I feel very sick that he did not take your original offer, but I hope
that now he will succeed in letting it to someone. The Hallam Street
flat has been a pest too, since the person we let it to has
disappeared and paid no rent since the end of July. However, I
think that the moneys from the BBC "Sword in the Stone" show
should cover this till the end of the lease in November. I am sorry
you should be troubled by this. If you see Lennox, please explain
to him the difficulty of answering letters one has never received. I
am sorry to appear slightly bitter about this but when one receives
day after day complaints and similar sour comments on one's
behavior, I think it is excusable, because I am trying really to be
a good boy.

   My love to Erika. I hope she is enjoying the seclusion of the
country side and not finding it too boring. I hope Miss Jackson has
not lost all the good effects of her American holiday.

Yours sincerely,
BEN

1 Presumably the ship that was carrying mail to England.
2 'Villes' and 'Départ'.
3 These three were all major national radio networks in the USA. NBC
   was established in 1926, CBS in 1927 and MBS (the Mutual) in 1934.
   See also obituaries of William Paley (Chairman of Columbia Broadcasting System), *Independent on Sunday*, 28 October 1990, and *Independent*, 30 October 1990.

219 To Enid Slater

You know, even <u>before</u> the embargo, letters were taking 3 weeks
to get here? Now they'll never arrive, almost – so <u>please</u> be
extravagant & send them air-mail (even that takes 14 days now!)

c/o Mrs. W. Mayer, Long Island Home, Amityville, Long Island,
N.Y.
November 7th 1939.

My dear Enid,

   At long last I have time to answer your two letters – <u>and</u> your
cable to Toronto. The crisis, which I believe has caused you in
England such acute boredom, has taken us very differently here –

by 'us', I mean English people stranded over here – with little
possibility of return (either inclination, or actual possibility). I
have been terribly busy – working, seeing people & making more
plans to work. Peter & I have found some wonderful friends –
who are (luckily) devoted to us – & on no account will let us depart.
They are German émigrés (from Munich). He – is a Psychiatrist &
an assistant at this mental Home. She – is one of those grand people
who have been essential through the ages for the production of
art; really sympathetic & enthusiastic, with instinctive good taste
(in all the arts) & a great friend of thousands of those poor fish –
artists. She is never happy unless she has them all round her –
living here or round about at the moment are lots of them – many
refugees. Wystan comes here from New York nearly every week-
end – an excellent German painter lives here, too, – Scharl[1] –
friends include the Manns,[2] Borgesi,[3] Einstein.[4] That's the kind of
person she is. She did wonderful work under Hitler; incredibly
brave things. I think she's one of the few really good people in the
world – & I find her essential in these times when one has rather
lost faith in human nature. There are four children – 2 Girls, 2 Boys
– 3 of them splendid specimens – one not so hot, & at the moment
a great worry to all. Living in a mental home is worrying in many
ways – but one gets used to it – the occasional shrieks used to
get me down, & still do abit; but the patients are treated so well,
& the doctors are so civilised that it isn't so bad. The grounds are
certainly lovely – Long Island too is in spots very beautiful – so like
Suffolk you'd never believe.

I can't possibly tell you all I want to – it would take so very long
& would cost dollars & dollars. I'll just wander on until it's time to
stop. I hope you'll find some coherence in it. Besides I'm a bit
afeared of it being opened, & I have no desire to have my intimate
feelings examined by Whitehall officials. They wouldn't appreciate
them at all I fear.

Thank you more than I can say for going to Cambridge, it was
the first news I'd got since the beginning of the war. I can't
understand why he hadn't got any letters from me, as I've written
one or twice, at least, every week by air-mail. So I'm going to
enclose a note to him in this – just in case it can get through – so
do you think you could forward it to 136 Blinco Grove for me?
I'm afraid alot of resolutions have gone up in thin air – especially,
funnily enough since the war. But re other little problems my mind
is firmly made up. You cannot think what distance does! Things
can be examined in the cold light of 3000 miles, & don't look so

nice! Besides letters from the Mill have been so dreadful. The only person who wrote to me about 'duty', 'conscience' – 'being a pacifist at heart, but this was a war, etc. . . . – (sic, sic SIC!!!); was he of that noble ancestry. Besides too – the man (sic) has no sense. He now writes whiningly of his obligations to the Mill (as if anyone wouldn't adore to live at the Mill!) – & wants to let it; & what am I going to do? – Ralph Hawkes offered to rent it at the beginning of the war & L.B. couldn't make up his mind. Oh – this all sounds silly – but when letters take months to come, if they ever actually do come, complaints, & grumbles sound so ridiculous. There's been a wonderful correspondence between me & family complaining of no letters, when I know all the time we've all been writing hard & the letters haven't arrived! I got so ill at one time with these snarky, barky letters that now Peter opens my letters – I don't want to!

My poor Enid – things seem bloody with you. I do wish that I could be with you. You can't imagine how homesick one is for England & Europe. That's why living with the Mayers is such bliss. Of course it is easy to be snarly about Americans – & one mustn't do it, because they have been terribly kind to us, & they are a vital, go-ahead race. But in so many things they have the faults of Europe without the attractiveness. The present chauvanism in their arts is horrifying – & most of their art is pretty lousy. But as soon as the war is over I'm coming hopping back – may-be before if they call us back, & we have to go to prison & all that – Opinion, as far as we see it, is hate for Germany, horrified surprise at Russia, patronisation(?) for England & France. Chamberlain has no following, & I suppose had the war not happened, the Allies' name would have been very muddy. Still, one's English accent is still much sought after.

One short note re work. Since I left I've done this Violin Concerto (First performance New York Philharmonic March with Brosa & Barbirolli – that's a let up!), Young Apollo (thank you very much for your cable. I got it when I arrived by air, very dejected late at night, & lonely – as only one can feel in Canadian cities! – & the cable cheered me lots. The performance went well, & I like the little thing), & I've now finished the Illuminations – which have turned out better than I dared hope. It's a big work, & so far I think my 'opus one'. I thought a very lot about the work & it's my favourite . . . I think Peter will sing it on the Radio soon here. Sophie's doing it in England sometime soon – please consult Ralph Hawkes re this as I'm particular about you hearing it. Much love,

Enid, my dear – & to Montagu too. I'm so glad that he's so well – how's the Novel?[5]

Be good, & well (how are you?), & keep up spirits. I'll be back soon or you'll be over here.

xxxooo

BEN

1 Josef Scharl (1896–1954), Munich-born artist, who emigrated to the United States. Britten and Pears possessed several examples of his work, including one of his many portraits of Einstein, of whom he was to become a friend. He was a member of the Mayers' circle in America, having known them in their Munich days. Mrs Mayer was an admirer and active on his behalf. A pen-and-ink portrait of Britten by Scharl was reproduced to accompany Britten's article, 'An English Composer Sees America', *Tempo*, 1/2, American Series, April 1940, pp. 1–3. See also Aloys Greither and Armin Zweite, *Josef Scharl 1896–1954* (Munich, Prestel-Verlag, 1982), in which a pen-and-ink portrait of Wolfgang Sauerländer sitting at the piano appears. (In 1971 he was to marry Beata Wachstein (née Mayer).)

It was with Sauerländer that Scharl emigrated to the USA on 26 December 1938. The Sauerländer and Mayer families had been friends in Munich, and both Scharl and his fellow immigrant soon found themselves re-established as members of the Mayer circle centred on Amityville. Indeed, the indefatigable Mrs Mayer found living and working accommodation there for Scharl on his arrival in the States, and he lived in Amityville until taking up residence in Manhattan in 1940. This was a period when he would have got to know Britten and Pears well, along with many other mutual friends and acquaintances – the Steiners, for example, and Lotte Jacobi, the photographer, who took many of the photographs of Britten and Pears during their American years. Scharl then moved to a studio at 160 Claremont Avenue, which he shared with Sauerländer. See Greither and Zweite, op. cit., pp. 52–9, and note 1 to Letter 258.

2 Thomas Mann (1875–1955), the German novelist, had settled in the USA in 1936 and was followed by his daughter, Erika (whom Auden married in 1935, to provide her with a British passport), his son, Golo, the historian, and his eldest son, Klaus, the novelist. See also note 2 to Letter 291.

3 Giuseppe Antonio Borgese (1882–1952), Italian essayist, historian and academic. He emigrated to the United States in 1931, and in 1939 married Thomas Mann's youngest daughter, Elisabeth (b. 1918). Borgese was a political commentator and strongly anti-fascist in his views. He was to write the libretto for Roger Sessions's opera, *Montezuma* (1941–63).

4 Albert Einstein (1879–1955), the German-born mathematical physicist, author of the general theory of relativity. Einstein was a keen amateur musician (violinist) and was introduced to Britten and Pears by David Rothman, whose wife was a patient of Dr Mayer's. (See also note 1 to Letter 301.) Rothman's hardware store served local yachtsmen and fishermen. Einstein had a cottage on Long Island and a boat, which made him a customer at Rothman's store. The great scientist and Rothman discovered a common interest in music, which led to Einstein participating in chamber music at Rothman's home. Rothman recalled the meeting with Einstein, in TP, in these words:

My wife's a pianist, my daughter was studying music, and we had a lot of musical people in the home at all times. And the understanding was that maybe I could do something for these boys, help them get along in this country.

So we had a string quartet here one evening and I suggested that the Mayers come and bring Ben and Peter. And on that particular Quartet Evening, we had Albert Einstein here. I asked Einstein, 'Tell me, what do you think of these two young fellows?' And he said to me, 'You know, they are very talented, and they will go very far.'

On another occasion Rothman recalled a different evening of music-making, with Mrs Mayer and Britten at the piano, Einstein playing the violin and Pears singing. What Britten and Pears remembered of their encounter with Einstein was the physicist's somewhat unreliable intonation.

Rothman's association with Einstein was recalled in Alden Whitman, 'A North Fork Remembrance', *New York Times*, 28 January 1973.

Another visitor to Stanton Cottage, and friend of the family, was Alfred Einstein (1880–1952), the musicologist and Mozart scholar, who took up residence in the USA in 1939 and was a cousin of the physicist. But it was surely Albert that Britten had in mind when writing to Mrs Slater.

5 Probably *Once a Jolly Swagman* (London, John Lane, 1944).

220 To Beth Welford
[EWB, *pp. 121–2*]

Long Island Home, Amityville, N.Y.
[7–11 November 1939]

My darling Beth,

There really isn't any news – I told Barbara everything in my last letter – which I hope you heard about, & I do nothing here except

Benjamin Britten: Sketch by Josef Scharl, reproduced in *Tempo*, American Series, 1/2, April 1940, p. 2

work, while Peter goes around looking for possible jobs; – But I couldn't bare the thought of an air-mail going to England without something in it for you from me!

Life here is as good as possible under the circumstances. It is very quiet (except when the patients start kicking up a fuss & screaming & shouting the place down!) & I'm doing lots of work. Mrs. Mayer is the most marvellous person – motherly & comforting. The fact that she's European is so important at these times. She is terribly keen on music, & we spend all our time at that, it seems. The children & Dr. Mayer are nice too – & so are the Titleys,[1] in whose house we are actually staying (tho' we eat chez Mayer). We expect to stay here until we know definitely about things (money etc.) & we <u>may</u> take a small house in Amityville – which is a lovely place & the sea looks more like the North Sea & the coast like the East Coast than can be believed. I may be having a good commission to write a big work through the British Council, but until that is signed & settled I am not rejoicing! I've had too many false alarms in my day! But I'll let you know of course as soon as anything materialises. <u>If</u> I can afford a house – I want so much to get you all over here – I'm building <u>such</u> castles in the air! Do write a note as soon as you can saying how you are. Try air-mail direct to here it's so much quicker. Other letters are held up terribly.

Air-mail just going so I must stop.

Love to everyone (including Robert if & when you write – tell him I'll write soon) & to D [Dodo Welford] of course I hope she's well.

My love, my darling, keep well – I'm sure we shall all survive!

BENJAMIN

1 See also Letter 284. Dr William Titley was Superintendent of the Long Island Home and an enthusiastic amateur pianist. His wife, Dr Mildred Squire (see Letter 225), was also a psychiatrist at the Home; at one time Zelda Fitzgerald (the wife of the novelist, Scott Fitzgerald) was one of her patients. It was for Dr Titley that Britten composed, in 1940, a four-movement *Sonatina Romantica*, which was completed but abandoned while he was revising the finale. Peter Pears recalled the circumstances of the work's composition in a note he wrote for the first public performance of the work given at the Aldeburgh Festival of 1983, on 16 June, by George Benjamin:

[. . .] Titley had been struggling with the *Invitation to the Waltz* and Ben presented the *Sonatina Romantica* as a tactful suggestion that he change his tune. But the doctor, I seem to remember, remained determined to master Weber!

In the light of Pears's recollections, perhaps Britten's dedication of the fair manuscript copy of the *Sonatina* has a certain edge to it: 'For Dr. William B. Titley to play.' The manuscript is inscribed 'July 1940 Amityville, N.Y.' The first and second movements of the *Sonatina* were published by Faber Music, London, in 1986.

221 To Ursula Nettleship
From Peter Pears

c/o Dr. Mayer.
L.I. Home. Amityville.
N.Y., U.S.A.
November 11th [1939]

My dear Ursula –

Here is the letter which should have been the first of several written these last months. You must please forgive me. I cannot imagine (or perhaps I can) what you have been thinking and

(knowing you and your downright ways!) probably saying about
me – . I deserve it all. It only remains for you to write it to me! We
have been thinking of you so much and what you may be doing
and your feelings. You aren't I suppose still at Cheyne Walk or are
you? Because I seem to remember that it was a particularly nasty
spot for air raids. Perhaps you are 'excavating'[1] children? I'm afraid
London must be a quite ghastly place – completely dead – and
the war atmosphere under Chamberlain – oh dear. We do so long
for England and to be with our friends, yet it's obviously better
for Ben to be out of it, and as of course all my plans for the season
are ruined, I decided to stay here too, anyhow until April when
Ben's new and very beautiful fiddle Concerto has it first show
under Barbirolli with Brosa. After that we might come back, I
don't know. I feel in a way that I want to come back and object
actively. One is too detached here in a way, liable to become too
smug, surrounded by American luxuries, and the odious American
press. Some wonderful friends of mine from Munich have put us
up now for 2 months and we are staying indefinitely. We couldn't
be happier in the circumstances. Ben is writing hard, an opera for
Broadway in January, a Canadian suite,[2] a symphony perhaps.[3] He
has just finished his cycle of Les Illuminations of Rimbaud. They
are his best so far. Most lovely. I'm hoping very much to do them
here sometime perhaps broadcast. I am working hard now.
During the Summer our travels got in the way of sustained work,
though we started off with 6 very profitable weeks in Canada,
and in August there was another clear month for work, but
inbetween times, we have been running backwards & forwards
which is bad for exercises. However, there is no doubt whatever
that my voice is much better than it was six months ago, bigger,
easier, brighter, more telling. I've been working with Shakespeare
(a very good book)[4] with an occasional dip into Aiken,[5] and my
B flats and Bs really do sound like them now, although I still get
stiff with nerves sometimes. My breathing's a lot better, though
no doubt it could be better still but my efforts on my back in the
early morning are quite Herculean, and although I now weigh
200 lbs., I'm sure a lot of it is diaphragm! How I wish I could sing
to you now, Ursula. O this bloody war. Things have gone wrong
in England with our respective abodes too. The Hallam St flat we
let (without an agreement) to a friend who has walked out without
paying the rent, leaving everything in a ghastly mess. My mother
has had to go & clear up – and Lennox decided he couldn't keep
the mill on and is trying to let it (I expect you have heard) – Ben
was terribly sick about it. He is so homesick for it, and wanted

Ralph Hawkes to have it earlier, but he didn't get it from Lennox. Have you seen people lately? How is everyone? Letters take a quite incredible time getting here, and now since the Repeal[6] here I imagine it will be worse. I am keeping your Shakespeare and Aiken very carefully here with me, as I thought it would be too risky and difficult sending them. However if you cant do without them I will send them. We get an immense amount of news in the papers out here, but how much of it is correct I don't know, and of course now is the ideal time for the armchair politician to sit back and advise just how the war should be run and why it is all wrong now and so on. It needs all one's control to stop one being very angry, but that does no good. No one considers that war is wrong, and that the only step to be considered is the way to stop it. We are so lucky in our hosts, who are the nicest people who ever lived – very musical and great patrons of the arts in the old days, he is a psychiatrist in a mental home here (I should have warned you earlier that we haven't been forcibly detained here by the Government because of our mental condition, and so far as one can judge we are still sane). She has four very sweet children, and we are completely two of the family.

I heard from my friend Esther Neville Smith[7] that she had seen you at Glyndebourne, which probably seems a long time ago now. I wonder how it went; well I expect? It was exciting to see that they proposed Carmen for next year; I can well imagine Carmen at Glyndebourne would be marvellous. But I suppose John Christie will have to give up next summer in spite of his hope that Glyndebourne had become so rooted in people's hearts (and pockets) that they wouldn't give it up even in a war – but I should doubt it – unless he lowers his prices and has an English cast. Perhaps he might do that.[8]

While we were in Toronto, I went and called on Campbell McInnes and had a couple of lessons from him. Interesting and he is a very charming old man and wanted to be remembered to you and all his other English friends. I'm not sure that the lessons were enough to be of much use – but I think he helped to loosen me up a bit. You will be pleased to hear that I am not frowning so much as I used to! Just as well, you will say! Yes, Ursula – I only frown now in the direst agony. It would be so nice to have you out here, Ursula; come. There is something tremendously alive about it out here, although sometimes crude & sometimes very depressing – but we have met many very lovable people. Come and add yourself to them, Ursula. Much love to you, my dear.

Do look after yourself, and remember me to all the people I want
to see again so much. Write if you have a moment.

Yours ever,

PETER

Hullo – Ursula – how are you? I'm burying myself in writing
musič – perhaps the only reality these days!

BEN

1 i.e. 'evacuating': children were moved out of the capital because of
   the danger of air raids. Lennox Berkeley had written to Britten on
   24 September:

   Snape hasn't changed much, except for the influx of what Mrs Hearn calls
   'excavated' children and it's funny to hear cockney in these parts. I wonder
   whether the Snape children will talk cockney, or the Londoners Suffolk as
   a result.

2 Pears refers to *Canadian Carnival*, completed a month later than this
   letter. Britten himself at this time seems to have thought of it as a
   Suite: see the postscript to Letter 223.

3 *Sinfonia da Requiem*.

4 Probably William Shakespeare's *The Art of Singing*, 3 volumes (New
   York, Ditson, 1898–9).

5 Pears probably refers to W.A. Aiken, in *The Voice: An Introduction to
   Practical Phonology*, which was re-issued by Longmans, Green & Co.,
   London, in 1951.

6 Repeal of the Neutrality Act of 1935 which had remained the greatest
   obstacle faced by Roosevelt in making American aid available to
   the Western democracies fighting Hitler. The neutrality-revision bill
   which Congress passed and the President signed on 4 November
   placed the arms trade on a cash-and-carry basis. The new law enabled
   Britain and France to buy war materials in the United States so long
   as they were willing to pay cash and to carry their purchases away
   in their own ships. Throughout 1940 Britain was able to use this
   system but by December 1940 both aspects of the arrangement were
   in peril – 'cash' because Britain's supply of American dollars was
   nearing exhaustion, and 'carry' because of the effectiveness of the
   German submarine campaign against British shipping. In January
   1941, the Administration introduced the so-called lend-lease bill,
   authorizing the President to sell, transfer, exchange, lend, lease or
   otherwise dispose of war equipment and other commodities to the
   government of any country whose defence the President deemed
   vital to the defence of the United States. Despite bitter isolationist
   opposition, Congress passed the bill, which became law on 11 March
   1941. 'Through this legislation,' Roosevelt said, 'our country has

determined to do its full part in creating an adequate arsenal of democracy.'

7 The wife of H.A.N. Neville-Smith, a master at Lancing College, Sussex, and a friend of Pears from his schooldays. It was she who, in 1947, suggested that Britten should write a work to celebrate the centenary of Lancing. The composer obliged with the cantata, *Saint Nicolas*.

8 The Glyndebourne Opera House closed after the 1939 season and was not to re-open until 1946 (with *The Rape of Lucretia*).

222   To Antonio and Peggy Brosa

Long Island Home,
Amityville, N.Y.
November 12th 1939

My dear Toni & Peggy,

This is just a note enclosed in the Brits[1] saying how much I think of you both, & how much I am longing to hear from you. I had tea with Mrs. Norton[2] the other day & she sent very much love to you, & she, like us all, is longing for the time when you both will be living out here. Now <u>when</u> are you coming? I hope so very much you can make it soon. I am sure, if you think it will be difficult for you, that we could find some way of managing it. Out on Long Island living is very cheap, & Peter & I are going to take a small house, that will be <u>quite</u> large enough to house you, <u>whenever</u> you come – & <u>please</u>, the sooner the better.

I had a talk with Heinsheimer, the advisor of Boosey & Hawkes here, & he seemed insistent that you didn't take any engagements before the Philharmonic one. But after that I am sure that there are possibilities – in the summer there are all these out-door concerts – Stadiums & things. But he has written to Ralph H. about all this, who has doubtless communicated with you. But <u>please</u> come out soon – if you can find a boat! Anyhow do write & say how you are both – & also, Toni, how you find the Concerto.

Very much love from Peter & me,
Yours ever,
BENJAMIN

1 Britten would have enclosed this letter in a letter to the Bridges and asked them to forward it on to the Brosas.

2 A friend of the Brosas.

223 To Ralph Hawkes
[*Typed*]

c/o Mrs. W. Mayer,
The Long Island Home,
Amityville, N.Y.
November 21, 1939.

My dear Ralph,

ｌｄｌｄｌｏｌ Thank you very much for your long awaited and much appreciated letter which arrived on Sunday. I was glad to hear that you are well and sane. Let us hope that nothing happens to alter this state of affairs.

♩♩♩ I am still going on working hard on Long Island. In fact, since I last wrote you, among other things I have completed the Canadian work, which I suggested to you a long time ago and about which Heinsheimer has always seemed so keen. It is quite short, plays about 13 or 14 minutes, and very lively. Heinsheimer and his wife are coming down here tonight to hear it and help me decide on a title for it. I dare say you will hear from him direct whether he thinks it will suit the American market or not. You see how commercially minded I am growing.

I seem to have been to New York a lot recently. The Robert Mayers[1] are over here now and, entre nous, are kicking up much the same kind of dust that they kick up in London, and it is of course getting into some people's eyes, a very unpleasant state. Peter and I went to a meeting of the American I.S.C.M. and it seems likely that the Festival will be held here next fall.[2] We also went to the Philharmonic Concert on Thursday where Bliss conducted. I am on very good terms with Barbirolli now, especially since I knew his wife in England. Of course, every time one goes to New York one comes back with scores of addresses and having given one's own address scores of times – America is so hospitable! We have met some most charming people over here.

Now for business:–

♩♩♩ LES ILLUMINATIONS. I hope by now that you have received the score and piano score of the complete work. You do not say when the English performance is, but I presume that it won't take place as originally scheduled.[3] Ditto the Basle performance, since we hear direct from there that things are completely topsyturvy. I have been seeing the musical director of Columbia with favorable

results and on Friday next Peter and I probably shall go and perform
the work for him. I presume that it would not worry you re first
performance etc., should anything materialize fairly soon. About
the publication of the work, as it has turned out to be such an
instrumental work (the orchestra part is so important), I feel
strongly that the score should be issued instead of the piano part,
or even better to combine the two. This has been done, I remember,
in the miniature score of L'Impresario [Mozart's opera, *Der
Schauspieldirektor*, K. 486] in the Philharmonia edition with, I think,
excellent results. I feel that the work simply makes no sense on
the piano, and as I fear that it is never likely to be performed very
often, I don't think there will be a demand for the piano score
separately (the work is more likely to be bought by students than
by performers!). If by any happy chance one or two of the
numbers became popular, they could of course be issued separately
with piano accompaniment (such as Antique or Royauté).
Probably when you get this letter you will have started on the
publication of it; anyhow I trust your unerring good sense over
the matter.[4] However, I hope it can be arranged for me to see a set
of proofs.

VIOLIN CONCERTO. I am very glad that this work impressed
you at the trial run. I feel quite pleased with it, I must say, and
much look forward to hear Toni and Phil play it. I will, of course,
do all I can to get Toni dates here, but I gather that it will be
tactless for him to take engagements before the date of that concert,
and of course after it is very near the end of the season. But I am
convinced that if he is over here and has a good agent, he will be
able to get plenty of work. There is broadcasting and all the legion
of outdoor concerts in the summer. It would be crazy for him to
turn down the date, as everyone thinks it is a heaven-sent
opportunity for him here in America, and marvellous publicity. Re
the printing of this, it seems a little risky without me having heard
Toni play it to engrave it, but I have written to him, asking him to
be honest and tell me what passages are ineffective and what
alterations he suggests. Also I am hoping that he will finger and
bow the part for the edition ("edited by Antonio Brosa").[5] There are
one or two slight alterations, which I enclose. Could you please
forward these to Toni who, I presume, has the Violin part and
Piano score.[6]

YOUNG APOLLO. No hurry over this. Over here I may frolic
with it on Columbia, but nothing definite yet.

SCHOOL OPERETTA. Wystan has completed one act of "Paul

Bunyan". He is coming down tomorrow with it to discuss it and I will find out how he has cast Paul Bunyan's feet. However, I gather that Paul Bunyan never appears on stage, so that avoids the problem of his size of boot. It is excellent that Auden is associated with us over it, since he has a very big name over here.

♩♩♩ JAPANESE EMBASSY. I await as usual your instructions over this. I hope with all my heart that the Japanese Government does not break relations with the British before May, but things don't look so hot at the moment, I must say. I wish they'd buck up, because there isn't all that amount of time.

♪♪♪: PIANO CONCERTO. I expect Heinsheimer will have told you of the projected W.P.A. performance[7] of this with me in Chicago. Since the W.P.A. don't pay soloists, the British Council don't function in USA, our respected Ambassador[8] loathes music and propaganda equally, <u>and</u> Chicago is a good step away, it does not seem likely that this will take place with me. However, we will see what happens.

♭♭♭ I do hope that you will find a reason for coming over here, since it would be marvellous to see you. If you want an excuse to come, I can think up plenty. I will write again in a week or so to tell you what happens. Meanwhile, all the best to you and the family.

Yours sincerely,
BEN.

P.S.   The Mill and the flat have been a something nuisance for the last few months, but things show signs of clearing up now. I hope they have not bothered you too much over the business.
[*Handwritten*:]

   Heinsheimer's just been & gone, & approves heartily of the Canadian Suite, which he'll try & place over here pretty soon. Name: 'Kermesse Canadienne' – that do?

1 Was Britten referring here to adverse views on the Robert Mayers' part of 'absentees' from the war effort?

2 The eighteenth ISCM festival did not in fact take place in New York until 1941.

3 The performance was to take place two months later than originally planned.

4 Ralph Hawkes seems to have taken Britten's advice. The score was issued with the piano reduction added below the orchestral lay-out. At a later stage, however, an orthodox vocal score was published.

5 Brosa did indeed edit the original solo violin part, but perhaps rather more extensively and ambitiously than the composer had originally intended. In his revision of the work in 1958 Britten took out Brosa's virtuoso accretions, which were no longer to his liking.

6 See Letter 224.

7 See Letter 229.

8 The eleventh Marquess of Lothian, Philip Henry Kerr (1882–1940), English diplomat, Ambassador to the United States from October 1939. He succeeded Sir Ronald Lindsay (1877–1945), who had been Ambassador since 1930.

224 To Antonio Brosa

[21 November 1939]

A facsimile of this letter appears as frontispiece to this volume.

Brosa: a drawing by Marjorie Fass

225 To Beth Welford

[EWB, *pp. 122–3*]

c/o Mrs. W. Mayer,
Long Island Home,
Amityville, N.Y.
November 28th 1939

My darling Beth,

I am writing this in a New York Psychiatrist's office – Dr. Squire's (alias Mrs. Titley) in whose house Peter & I are sleeping. Peter & I are in N.Y. for the day – a typical business day – seeing odd

people, having lunch with an eminent organist, tea with an arty
'socialite', & going to the flat of a Columbia broadcasting official
after dinner to-night.[1] I discovered yesterday that there is a Clipper
going to-morrow so I brought my pen & paper up here – actually
I discover that I only brought one sheet of air mail paper & so the
letter'll have to be shorter than I intended. Well – thank you very
much for the cable. I loved having it & it was nice of you to
remember your poor little bro. – especially as no one has any
good words to say for him at the moment (although for anything,
he can't think what he has, or hasn't done!). I had a nice birthday
– the Mayers were sweet & gave me lots of presents, & cake, &
candles, & party. Wystan came & with Peter, Titleys & family we
had a grand time. But one did miss the old family ties – gosh, it's
awful how home-sick one feels – & especially Suffolk-sick – but
I'm glad, overjoyed that you & Kit are at the Mill – you got my
wire? There's no need to pay L.B.[2] money if you don't use his
room or his studio. But incase he kicks up rough I've sent Barbara
£50 – all I can spare at the moment – & £25 of that can be used
for him (blast his eyes). The rest I want her to spend on herself &
you – she seems so awful in her last letters, so sad, & poor, now
she's lost her job that my heart bled.[3] I wish she & Helen could
come to the Mill too. If you are having bother in keeping up the
place do let me know & I'll struggle to send some more money.
By-the-way, re this £50 – don't fight over it – just divide it as you
both honestly think most fair – at this distance you can't tell who
needs it most – & I had to send it to Barbara since it'll be more
convenient for her to change the draught. So don't write abusing
letters saying I favour one or the other – because honestly, my
darling, I can't stand any more of these letters (at 3000 [miles]
distance & a war on, letters cool off & lose their points, if they're
only destructive criticism). Anyhow, I do want, if physically
possible, you to go on living at the Mill – to regard it as yours, not
to think of letting it (unless of course you can't possibly keep it
up), & from time to time I'll send you what monies I can spare.
I was terribly pleased with your last letter – it was so nice & chatty,
telling me all the things I wanted to hear – I adore hearing about
Sebastian, he sounds a grand kid. If I saw him now, I bet I wouldn't
recognise him!

    Time's getting on & I've got this lunch date, so I must buck up.
Don't worry about me old thing – I'll get along all right. People
are terrifically kind & I'll never be destitute or starve! It is horrible,
of course, & we get an overdose of radio, & paper news – & one

feels hopeless & distraught – poor old Kit, I bet he feels like hell.
But tell him to read (Jane Austen!) lots & play the gramophone
(Mahler!).

I'm working hard – just starting a new opera with Wystan – but
I find working terribly difficult.

Much love to you all three. <u>Remember</u>, stay at the Mill, consider
yourselves joint owners of it, & I'll help out with ex. if poss.

XXXXOOO   BEN   XXXOOO
Love from Peter

1 These 'odd people' remain unidentified.

2 Britten had cabled his sister on 16 November:

OVERJOYED HEARING YOU ARE AT MILL   DONT CONSIDER LEAVING   DONT
PAY BERKELEY ANYTHING   USE MY FIXTURES   WRITING

3 In EWB, p. 124, Beth Welford writes:

Barbara's job came to an end because the clinic where she worked was a
voluntary one and a lot of children left London to go to the country or were
sent to the U.S.A. It was not long, however, before she was appointed
Assistant Superintendent of the Child Welfare Department of the Middlesex
Hospital in London. She was happy there [. . .].

226   To Ralph Hawkes
[*Typed*]

c/o Dr. W. Mayer,
The Long Island Home,
Amityville, N.Y.
December 7, 1939.

My dear Ralph,

I saw Max Winkler yesterday and he gave me the great news of
your proposed trip over here. I was highly delighted and hope
you will make the stay a very long one. Your influence is needed
in every way, you can be sure. I gather that I am going to be
privileged to meet you and to accompany you to the Middle West
immediately on your arrival. That sounds excellent and I am much
looking forward to it. (Heinsheimer may be able to arrange a
performance of the Piano Concerto during our sojourn in
Chicago.) You can't imagine how good it will be to see you over
here. I have lots of people I want you to meet and thousands of
schemes to discuss (as usual!). I am waiting for an answer to my
long letter of November 22nd[1] – really, the posts get worse and

worse every day. Airmail now takes nearly three weeks and so I
am going to send this by boat – I hope for the best.

Nothing much has happened since that letter. I shall enclose, if
I remember, the timing of "Les Illuminations" and the "Violin
Concerto" as Chapman requests. I note that the engraving of these
two works is going ahead. When is the first performance of "Les
Illuminations", by the way?

I am still waiting for news of the VIOLIN CONCERTO from Toni
Brosa and also probable date of his arrival which is worrying us a
little over here.

YOUNG APOLLO is tentatively booked for December 20th on
Columbia with the composer as pianist. I think rehearsal time is
the only query with this.

PAUL BUNYAN is progressing well and quickly on Auden's side,[2]
but rather spasmodically on mine, since I am busy completing the
score of Kermesse Canadienne. However, I think you will be
delighted with the idea and materialization of the libretto. It is
very witty but nevertheless serious in the fundamental idea. I have
sketched one or two tunes already, a little bit more serious than
the Hedli tunes[3] but very direct and simple, which is the kind of
style I propose to use throughout the work.

By the way, I hear from Hedli that you suggest she makes records
of some of her songs[4] with an Arthur Young, a friend of yours.
That sounds good. She also asks me whether you could print one
or two of these songs. The position with regard to them is this:
They were all suggested by Hedli and I think it would be unfair to
print them before she has used them for her own personal success,
and anyhow I don't think these songs would be any use printed
until they were first launched (successfully we hope) in a show
or over the radio. Hedli always seems to have a big possibility
around the corner. I was under the impression that she was going
to have a show at the Mercury Theatre at which they could be
sung, which would be a good start for them. I am so much out
of touch that I don't know whether this has happened or not.
Anyhow, please decide this with her. You obviously know best
about this kind of thing. If you want any more to go with them,
let me know and I will do them.

JAPANESE EMBASSY. I have given up hope that anything shall
materialize from this. Time seems impossibly short to do a big work
now. I admit however I have still a sneaking hope that something
should come out of it, as the money would be only too welcome.
I am having to send a certain amount of money to England to help

the family who are in a very sticky position because of this beastly war, and also debts seem to run up as much in my absence as in my presence, which is saying a good deal.

I hope Erika is well and that she will not miss you too much when you are away, but I fear she will. Have as good a Christmas as possible under the black-outed circumstances. It will be grand to have you over here and to discuss my "problems" with you in the flesh instead of on paper.

Yours ever,
BEN

1 See Letter 223, dated in fact 21 November, though he probably signed it on the 22nd – a day he would remember.
2 We know, for example, from a brief note of Auden's to Britten that the texts of the 'Dog and Cats songs' (Nos. 8, 21 and 22 in the libretto) were delivered to the composer before 16 December.
3 The Cabaret Songs.
4 The proposed recording was not made.

227 To Wulff Scherchen

c/o Mrs. W. Mayer,
Long Island Home,
Amityville, N.Y.
December 8th 1939

[. . .]
[. . .] The mails are completely impossible now. There is so much I want to know about you – how you are, what you're doing, what troubles you & Gustel have had to go through (if any!).[1] We have heard lots of stories of German emigrés in England & France, but by all accounts the British ones weren't bothered like the French, who were all without exception cast into Concentration Camps. [. . .] I hoped that you wouldn't be molested by any stupid warmongering English patriots. I was abit scared that you might feel terribly sad about everything & go & do something crazy. It is an absolutely bloody position for you both, I realise only too well.

Well, life here is going on just the same. I am terribly busy with one or two projects – & people are extremely friendly, & I'm having a pretty good success, as far as is possible in a strange country in these particular times – when America is very much anti-Europe, & pro-American ——— It's a great pity that they won't

learn from the mistakes of Europeans, but they seem only too
keen on their Nationalism. I see Wystan an awful lot; he is a great
friend of the Mayers, & comes to stay here often. In fact he was
here this morning when your cable arrived – & was terribly glad
for my sake. He sends his love. You know I'm writing an operetta
with him to be put on at the end of January? It's very good so far
(at least, his part is – customary modesty (!)). I am playing my
'Young Apollo' which I wrote for the Canadian Broadcasting Corp.
– on Columbia on Dec. 20th,[2] sometime in the middle of your
night – you know whom that's written about – founded on last
lines of Keat's Hyperion [. . .] O – if all this bloody business
would clear up – or if you could come over here. That's what I
want most of all. You know, in some ways, I'm glad that the
Mayers are German – & refugees – because there is so much about
them which reminds me of you. You'd adore them – especially
Mrs. – an absolute saint, & extremely intelligent. How is Gustel? I
must write to her for Xmas. Next week is the last air-mail leaving
in time for Xmas so I'll try & get letters off by that.

I have had a terribly bad time over matters in England. You know
that Jackie Hewitt took our flat – well, he behaved abominably –
ran away with a month's rent due – left the place filthy – they had
to put new locks on the doors – had the C.I.D. men after him – he
robbed the Gas meters – left large bills (including telephone bill
with a trans-atlantic call of £3 odd!) – & it has cost Peter & me
untold bother & expense. Also the Mill's been a trouble – Lennox
hasn't been too sensible over that – decided it was too lonely for
him – refused a good let (from Ralph Hawkes) & complained that
because he hadn't heard from me that I wasn't taking an interest
in it – forgetting, dear boy, that mails are disrupted & letters get
lost. It's all silly, but people's tempers are so frayed nowadays.
Poor old Barbara's lost her job, Robert's poor, ditto Beth & Kit. I
had to send them all the money I could spare the other day.
Luckily my publishers are being generous here so I'm not too badly
off. How's your financial problem? Do you have communications
from your father? I must stop this now because I'm crazy with
sleep, having worked all day, & the post leaves early tomorrow
morning, & I want this to go to you at once – to say how pleased
I was to hear you were all right. [. . .]

[. . .] Also, I met Sigurd Rascher[3] in New York the other day – &
we had a grand pow-wow – you remember him? The Saxophonist
with the Red Hair? He's coming down here to see us soon I think.
O – what memories – what heaven it all was when things were

(more or less) peaceful! But I suppose this'll all end sometime, &
people will be able to get on with their lives again. Although one
is away from it, one seems to be even more concerned – our Radio
& Newspaper reporting is so bloody efficient. Working is
damnably difficult, but it is the only thing that keeps one sane. So
don't forget, [. . .] work hard, read hard (try E.M. Forster, or
Somerset Maugham). Have you seen Ian?[4] Play the <u>piano</u> <u>alot</u>.
[. . .]

1 Wulff and his mother were German nationals and thus came to be
classified as 'enemy' aliens. See note 1 to Letter 281.

2 The programme also included the *Bridge Variations*, conducted by
Britten.

3 Sigurd Rascher (b. 1907), German–American saxophone virtuoso.
Several distinguished composers wrote works specifically for him,
including Ibert, Hindemith, Eric Coates and Frank Martin, and it is
likely that this would have been the motive for his visit to Britten.
In an interview Britten gave to William G. King, 'Music and
Musicians: About Benjamin Britten and a Symphonic Première', *New
York Sun*, late March 1941, a saxophone concerto for Rascher is among
a list of works in progress, along with a cello concerto for Emmanuel
Feuermann. Although King writes that Britten 'expects to have
[. . .] them ready for next season', neither concerto materialized
and no sketches survive at the Archive. See also Letter 258.

4 Ian Scott-Kilvert.

228 To Julianne Painter

Long Island Home,
Amityville, N.Y.
Dec. 14th 1939

My darling Aunt Julianne,

I don't know whether this will reach you in time for a Christmas
wish, but the post-office here says it will – I rather doubt it,
knowing the state of the Mails these days. Anyhow – for whatever
Festive season this is topical for – the best wishes I have are for
you. I know it won't be a very pleasant one, with all these beastly
events going on all round, but do try & forget them for abit. It
doesn't help to remember always, does it?

Well – as you see I'm still over here. Stuck, rather. I was staying
with these very charming friends on Long Island when the war

started – & – here I am still! My friend, who'se been with me, is
here too. They are German emigrés. He is a Psychiatrist, & Dr.
at this mental home (don't worry, I'm not a patient yet!) & she, is
a great artist, musician & a very cultured woman, who is friends
of very famous people both in Europe & America. She has become
like a mother to me, & you can imagine how, at these times
especially, I needed that! There are four children (26, 23, 21, 16) &
we have a splendid time together. They gave me a lovely birthday
& we shall have a grand Xmas I'm sure. It was indeed a God-send
to find them, as I simply don't know what we should have done.
You see, both Peter's & my season in England was wrecked so we
couldn't return (besides England doesn't want us – so she says)
– & it is very difficult to get started in a new country. However I
have been terribly lucky & had some good success. I have had lots
of work to do, & people seem to like your little God-child alot!
There is a complete broadcast concert of my works on Dec. 20th
from New York – I go to Chicago to play on Jan. 15th & am writing
an operetta for Broadway – so they keep me busy. I like New
York & Americans very much – although they are quite different
from Europeans. They are more sophisticated & (perhaps) more
excitable, but terribly hospitable. The only things I don't like are
their newspapers & Radio. The way they scream about the war –
& most of the news is untrue – too. So you see – my life could be
alot worse – I am lucky to be spared the immediate horrors of the
war-conditions – but, believe me Aunt J., it is horrible to be away
from one's nearest & dearest at these times, & I feel terribly
homesick for England – Snape especially. I'm longing & living for
the day when I can return & see you & all of it again.

I hope that you are as well as possible, & keeping up that grand
improvement that you were making when I left. Are any of the
family with you? And the Link?[1] My love to any & all of them. And
do write a note from time to time as one lives for letters.

Very much love, my dear, as good a Christmas as possible,

Your loving,

BENJAMIN.

1 Possibly Malvern Link, near Great Malvern, Worcestershire, where
Julianne Painter lived after her husband's death.

229   To Albert Goldberg[1]

[*Typed*]

c/o Dr. W. Mayer,
The Long Island Home,
Amityville, N.Y.
December 14, 1939

Dear Mr. Goldberg,

   Thank you for your letter of December 12th. I can assure you
that I am delighted that it has been possible to arrange for the
performance of my Concerto with you. I am looking forward to it
exceedingly as I have heard such good things of your orchestra
and the concerts that you give.[2] I feel also very honored[3] by the
trouble you are taking in order to give me good publicity. It is an
excellent start for me in Chicago.

   The program you suggest seems excellent and I quite understand
that the Mont Juic Suite would not be suitable for it. I hope that
you will be able to play it some other time, but I am naturally a
little bit disappointed that I cannot hear this performance of it.[4]
Thank you for the offer of your services. I shall not hesitate to take
advantage of this.

   In the meantime I am much looking forward to January 15th.

With best wishes,
Yours very truly
BENJAMIN BRITTEN

BB:bem

1 Albert Goldberg (b. 1898), American critic, pianist, conductor and
   musical administrator. He wrote about himself (Goldberg/Britten
   papers in the Archive):

   For virtually the entire existence of the US government-sponsored Works
   Progress Administration (WPA), I was the state director of the Federal Music
   Project in Illinois. I started as a lowly district supervisor on 1 December,
   1935, was promoted – to my horror, and under protest – to the top post of
   State Director in June, 1936, and served in that capacity until the project's
   demise with the advent of World War II, in February, 1943.

      In addition to arduous administrative duties, my job consisted of setting
   local policies throughout the state, selecting soloists and conductors for all
   instrumental and vocal units, and making or approving all programs for
   public performance. In addition, I shared the conducting of our major Unit,
   the Illinois Symphony Orchestra, with Izler Solomon.

      It was the Illinois Symphony that gave the American première of
   Britten's Piano Concerto, with the composer as soloist and Goldberg

conducting, at Chicago on 15 January 1940; already in February 1939 the orchestra had performed *Soirées Musicales*. A photograph of Goldberg and Britten on the former occasion appears in PFL, plate 129. The liveliness of Britten's letters to Goldberg – the correspondence in its entirety, both sides of it, forms part of the Archive – speaks for itself. It was clearly a most cordial relationship and Goldberg deserves his special place in the history of Britten's music and its performance in the United States, where he was one of the composer's earliest champions. Goldberg's extraordinary enthusiasm and encouragement led to a series of performances in Illinois under the WPA umbrella which stand out as one of the most positive features of the American years. (See also *The WPA Guide to Illinois* (New York, Pantheon Books, 1983), pp. 137–45.) To Britten's letter of 20 January 1942 (No. 363) Goldberg was to respond with clearly genuine feeling:

Your farewell note touched and saddened me. I hate to think of you on the briny deep at this time and of your returning to what must be anything but pleasant conditions at home. [. . .] I can only wish you and Peter bon voyage and hope that you will be back with us again at the earliest possible moment. Your appearances were among the highlights of the turbulent history of this project, and I am happy that it's all in the record.

In the autumn of 1949 Britten and Pears returned to the States on a recital tour which took them out to the West Coast where they renewed their old acquaintance with Goldberg. It was a reunion remembered with pleasure by Britten in the last letter that he seems to have written to Goldberg in October, 1950: 'We often talk of you and our time in Los Angeles – Quite the nicest time we had on our tour.'

This was not, however, the last time they met. Goldberg came to the 1955 Aldeburgh Festival. He also met Britten and Pears in Montreal at Expo '67 and saw Pears once more in Los Angeles after Britten's operation in 1973.

Goldberg worked on the music staff of the *Los Angeles Times* from 1947 until his late eighties. See also Albert Goldberg, Interview with Donald Mitchell, 23 May 1989, Pasadena, California; Archive.

2 In Goldberg's own words (his 'Vignette' of Britten, which is among the Britten/Goldberg papers), his policy was to present

as many new composers and new compositions as possible, mainly American, but also including many currently active European and South American composers. For example, we gave the first Chicago performances of the Shostakovich symphonies, as soon as the scores became available. The Chicago Symphony was nearing the end of its thirty-nine years under the direction of Frederick Stock, and mainly it played standard repertory for its ultra-conservative clientèle. We made an attempt to supply the adventurousness and up-to-dateness that Chicago Symphony Orchestra programs lacked.

The name of Benjamin Britten was just beginning to be known. I had heard some of his music and had been impressed by it. A letter from Hans Heinsheimer late in 1939, representing Britten's publishers, Boosey & Hawkes, informed me that Britten was in the United States and had not yet been heard in public performance. Heinsheimer offered to send Britten to Chicago to play the U.S. première of his First Piano Concerto with our Illinois Symphony Orchestra. It would also be Britten's American début as a pianist.

Britten arrived and everyone was enchanted by his youthful charm – he was then twenty-seven – his spontaneous wit, his British accent, and his complete naturalness and friendliness. He also quickly proved himself to be a remarkable pianist. Had he cared, he could easily have followed a virtuoso's career. Everyone loved him. He was outgoing and congenial and perfectly agreeable to participating in all the little functions we planned in his honor. During the week that Britten was in Chicago, his and my friend, Aaron Copland, turned up, and we enjoyed an innocent but jolly night on the town.

3 The spelling, as on occasion elsewhere, reflects American usage and the fact that Britten's 'business' letters were now being dictated to Beata Mayer, who was lending him a secretarial hand and naturally followed American practice.

4 See note 1 to Letter 264.

230 To Antonio Brosa
[*Typed*]

c/o Dr. W. Mayer,
The Long Island Home,
Amityville, N.Y.
December 31, 1939.

Dear Toni,

Thank you very much for your letter which I was delighted to get. I am immensely relieved that you find the Concerto good to play. Certainly make the alterations you suggested in your letter. Play on the G string for 7 bars at No. (4) (if you prefer you can play the whole work on G string – I am sure you would make it sound fine that way!) Play Octaves in the 2nd movement and in the 3rd movement before (36) also G string. I have seen Barbirolli recently and he is still excited about doing the work with you. I think the recital in the Town Hall is a splendid idea and I must do lots of propaganda about it. By the way, would you like me to play for you at that concert to save you the expense of an accompanist? If you think it political to have one of the stock accompanists from Manhattan I shall certainly understand, but I just make the offer to see what you think.[1]

I am glad you have been seeing the Bridges and sorry to hear about Marjorie[2] being so ill. I have written quite a lot to the Bridges but in the beginning of the war a large number of letters from this country were lost (we hear complaints from all sides about this). It is usually only the air-mail ones that get through although they are often delayed. We have seen your friend, Mrs. Norton, a lot and like her immensely. She has asked us to go to her country house, but at the moment I am terribly busy working on a new opera with Auden for possible production soon and have not had time for much recreation. I go off to Chicago on the 2nd with Ralph Hawkes and will play my Concerto there on the 15th.

Give my love to Peggy and yourself and let us know as soon as possible when you are coming, because I want to make grand preparations for it. I hope it will be soon because I gather that life is not at all pleasant in England. I heard from Michel Cherniavsky[3] that you are playing with him in Ipswich and that most thunderous of pianists, Mark Hamburg.[4] I hope it was a success and that you received your expenses at least. I cannot think how people are existing now. We are still very happily living on Long Island and working very hard although it is terribly difficult to get started in a new country. I feel certain you will have a great success out here and I will do all the work I can to get you jobs over here. I am on good terms with Columbia at the moment; that may be useful.

Best wishes for 1940 and let it not resemble 1939 at all.

Yours ever,

BENJAMIN

1 For Brosa's recital, held on 8 April 1940, he was accompanied by George Reeves. However, on 17 May, in the recreation hall of the Long Island Home at Amityville, Britten and Brosa gave a recital which included music by Granados and movements from Lalo's *Symphonie espagnole*.

2 Marjorie Fass.

3 Michel Cherniavsky (1893–1982), Russian-born cellist.

4 Mark Hambourg (1879–1960), Russian-born pianist who came to Britain as a child in 1886.

231 To Beth Welford
[EWB, *pp. 125–7*]

c/o Dr. W. Mayer,
Long Island Home,
Amityville, N.Y.
New Year's Eve 1939

My darling Beth,

This is only a note to wish you a happy New Year – faint hope,
but if possible a better one than 1940 [*sic*], which shouldn't be
difficult. Heaven knows when you'll get this letter, the posts seem
to get worse & worse, now that the air mail's so disorganised, but
you may get it in time for next New Year's day!

First of all – what sort of Christmas did you have? All at
Peasenhall[1] I expect? Hope it was not too gloomy and that all the
Festivities weren't entirely 'blacked-out'. God – it must be hellish
for you! You can't imagine how much I feel for you, & think of
you. When I read all these things in the papers (half of which aren't
– luckily – true) it is odd to think that they're happening to you –
the nice person I shared 559 Finchley Road with – that your food's
being rationed, that your M.G.'s[2] headlights are dimmed etc. etc.
I'm feeling abit blue tonight – God how I hate anniversaries – &
what with my birthday, Mum's birthday,[3] Xmas & now New
Year's eve – we seem to have had a good supply of them recently.
Anyhow – thank you everso much for your letter. It was worth
£50 to get cheerful letters from you & Barbara! But mind you, don't
start writing grumpy ones again, because it won't always work!

We had a nice Xmas – the Mayers gave us all a fine one. In the
German custom it was Xmas Eve which was the great hour – at about
6 o'clock a bell was rung & in we all trouped into the living-room
& there was an enormous Xmas tree hung all over with candles,
candies & cookies & all round the room in little piles were our
presents – & lots too – everyone was very generous to us – which
made up for lack of correspondence from England! Did you, by the
way, get some little presents from me – I shan't be surprised if
that little scheme went wrong – but anyhow the thought was there!

I played 'Young Apollo' on Columbia a week or so ago – it went
well & everyone was pleased. Ralph Hawkes arrives to-morrow
& I go with him to Chicago (about 1500 miles!) the day after – &
play the Concerto on 15th – it is going to be nice to see him, but
I don't want to leave here. I am becoming a very retiring boy at

the moment – I loathe going up to New York, & all I want to do is to sit still & play Chinese checkers – that's a game that is rampant over this Continent at the moment!

Wystan's been here for a week & we've done lots of work on the opera – I know you'd like it – it's full of nice tunes & blues & things. No date for production yet.

Must stop now as all the mid-night celebrations are about to begin. Ugh! Wish you were here my dear.

Much love to my God-child – send a photo sometime. He sounds sweet. Also to Kit – tell him to write to me again soon & lots to you, yourself, darling,

Be careful,

BEN.

Could you be a saint & forward these letters for me – air-mail is so expensive.

Laulie: Miss Austin, Flat No. 4, Gambier Terrace, Liverpool
Mr. Nicholson

1 At the Welford family's home.

2 The famous sports car.

3 On 9 December.

232   To Barbara Britten

c/o Dr. W. Mayer,
Long Island Home,
Amityville, N.Y.
Jan. 1st 1940.

My darling Barbara,

Well it was quite worth the cheque to get that letter from you! But I told Beth that it won't always work – I mean if you write nasty meany meany letters I won't always send you a large cheque to improve your temper! But seriously I hope from time to time to send you cheques – principally to keep up the Mill as a cottage where you & Helen & Beth & family etc. can always go as a refuge, in case things get worse & you can't go on living in London. You see I don't want to let it. At the moment I don't need money from it – & what's the sense of having a place like the Mill if one's nearest and dearest can't use it. But look here old thing – there's no sense in putting it in savings or whatnot for me because even if I

needed it you can't send it to me! No money <u>at all</u> is allowed to
go out of England – Wystan has over £300 in England & can't touch
it – he's going to give it away – rather than let the government
get it! I sent the money for you & yours. Let me know if Lennox
takes the money! I may have been hard on Lennox – but from
this distance (with the irregularities of the posts complicating
matters) his behaviour has seemed inexplicable. I can understand
people losing their heads & going all hysterical – but he seems to
have kept his – financially at anyrate!

Well – a happy new year, my dear old thing. It seems a faint
hope – but let's pray that it is an improvement in every way over
1939. That shouldn't be difficult, should it? Thank you very much
for your nice little present – it arrived surprisingly quickly considering
that it was sent by boat. I loved having it & getting your wishes. I
missed all the family celebrations terribly – but the Mayers gave
us a lovely time & it was as nice a second [?home] as you could
imagine. I am working very hard now – & this week sometime I
go off to the middle-west for a fortnight or so – with Ralph Hawkes,
who is due to arrive to-day in the Clipper, but I don't think he'll
be here yet, as the clippers are all terribly delayed. Wystan's been
here this week & I've done lots of work with him on the new
opera – very light – full of tunes!

What sort of Christmas did you have? Abit gloomy was it? I had
a nice letter from Robert the other day, & he is naturally abit
down about things. But he seems to be able to continue in a small
way next term, doesn't he? My god – what worries you family
give me – lucky that there's one member who is able to keep head
above water! – for the moment that is! When does your new job
start – don't be too down about it. I know it must be beastly for
you – but it is only temporary, & anything is better than doing
nothing – although <u>I</u> can't think why you don't go down & organise
Snape Welfare & use the Mill rent free? Still I suppose you won't. I
am afraid this isn't a proper letter, but I wanted to write you a note
before I go off on my excursions into the mid-west, & I don't
know when I shall have time again to write. If you only knew the
number of letters I have to write – after all you have only <u>one</u>
relation abroad, & I have God knows how many & friends as well
to write to!

Much love my dear – keep up – the night-mare will be over sometime – & we'll all be together again.

Could you please send the enclosed letter[1] to Hedli Anderson,

6, Maiden Lane, <u>W.C.2.</u> & David Layton, 6, Abbott's Place, <u>N.W.</u>
<u>6</u>. & give the other to Helen –

Be careful, Go to Snape often,
Love,
BENJAMIN.

1 This has not, it seems, survived.

233 To Lennox Berkeley

[1 January 1940]

My dear Lennox,

   I am enclosing this in Barbara's letter – & hope you'll get it
sometime. I'm sorry I've not written for such a long time (but
neither have you!) – but letters at this time seem so futile. Here of
course we know so much that we know what is going to happen, &
often what hasn't happened. Everyone talks Europe, & the only
subject on the Radio is Europe. And neutrality of course. I'm
working terribly hard – all in desparation, thinking that one may
be stopped any moment. I hope you're getting something done
too. Art is <u>all-important</u> at this time – & faith, if you have it! – I'm
soaking myself in El Greco, Benvenuto Cellini, & Buxtehude.[1] Do
you know the latter? He is absolutely outstanding. Since my
discovery of Mahler I haven't been so excited over anything. I
think he's so much better than Bach!!! He has a wonderful harmonic
sense & a most extraordinary tonal feeling – he writes often in
one key with no modulations for a whole piece, & the result is
eminently successful. And his figuration is wonderfully inspired.
I don't know, my dear, if you've got the patience to read this – you
will have skipped it if you haven't – but it's difficult to know what
to write about at these moments. But more & more I am being
pushed off my old materialistic beliefs – excellent for me, no
doubt, you will say! – I feel I'm <u>at last</u> growing up! Don't laugh.
I've seen Wystan – a very changed Wystan – alot & it looks as if
we shall be doing the same things for a period of time now. If you
have time & the inclination do write, if you don't – I shall
understand. Do what you like with Snape or anything – I hereby
give you 'carte blanche'!

Much love,
BEN

1 The discovery of Buxtehude is memorably recorded in Auden's 'New Year Letter', dated 1 January (the very date of this letter), and dedicated to Elizabeth Mayer (which suggests that perhaps the enthusiasm for Buxtehude owed something to her):

> And the same sun whose neutral eye
> All florid August from the sky
> Had watched the earth behave and seen
> Strange traffic on her brown and green
> [. . .]
> The very morning that the war
> Took action on the Polish floor,
> Lit up America and on
> A cottage in Long Island shone
> Where Buxtehude as we played
> One of his *passacaglias* made
> Our minds a *civitas* of sound
> Where nothing but assent was found,
> For art had set in order sense
> And feeling and intelligence
> And from its ideal order grew
> Our local understanding too.
>   (W.H. Auden, *Collected Poems* (1940))

Colin McPhee, the composer (see note 12 to Letter 312), and another member of the Mayer circle, showed a similar enthusiasm for Buxtehude at about the same time (see Carol J. Oja, *Colin McPhee (1900–1964): A Composer in Two Worlds*, Ph.D. dissertation, City University of New York, 1985, work list, pp. 473–4). Two of his two-piano transcriptions of Buxtehude, the chorale prelude 'In dulci jubilo' and 'Ciacona', were performed by Ethel Bartlett and Rae Robertson in New York on 9 December 1941, on which occasion the first performance of Britten's *Mazurka Elegiaca* was also given. In 1944, at Friends House, London, a concert in which Britten and Pears participated included two cantatas by Buxtehude. He remained an admired composer and his music was occasionally included in an Aldeburgh Festival.

Pears had written to his Cousin Barbie in August 1940 from the Owl's head Inn, Owl's Head, Maine:

How is your piano going? I do hope you are playing a lot. At Amityville, they have a large stock of piano duets, and Ben and I have been making ourselves familiar with all sorts of stuff. Some marvellous Mozart sonatas and fantasias – lots of Schubert – and Buxtehude too. He's a very good man in these times. After any particularly harrowing news from France, we would play a really wonderful Prelude & Fugue in F♯ minor. We have seen a bit of Wittgenstein, and he talked much of Margaret Denneke & Ernest Walker, and that brought back such memories of your party and our recital in Balliol.

There are many other illuminating glimpses of musical and literary life at Stanton Cottage, Long Island, in 'New Year Letter', as well as a discourse on the theme of

> That order which must be the end
> That all self-loving things intend
> Who struggle for their liberty,
> Who use, that is, their will to be.

This section of the poem opens:

> To set in order – that's the task
> Both Eros and Apollo ask

– a theme that surfaced in letters of Auden's and Britten's from this period and was to remain a preoccupation of the composer's until its final embodiment in *Death in Venice*. See Letters 364 and 367.

234   To Benjamin Britten
From Elizabeth Mayer

[Amityville]
Jan. 3, 1940

My darling,

It is late afternoon, very quiet, everybody is in town, Mildred [Titley] was twice here to see me. It is a lovely winter day, and I thought the whole time of you flying high above all the snowy beauty, you blessed bird. How I miss you, dear boy, how I miss you! and yet I am glad that the first day is nearly gone, one day less, one day nearer to your return![1] I do hope everything went alright on the air-field, and that you got a breakfast and a little sleep in the plane, and that you arrived safely, my dear. I prayed hard for you, and the gods filled my heart with peaceful thoughts.

Everything here awaits you patiently. Your table at the window, the little piece of red blotting paper, which made me cry silently, the ruler . . . the trees and squirrels and the sky. Here is your home now – waiting for you – I went around the house all morning, tidying up things, mending, reading a little, and now and then playing the piano. How perfectly lovely is: A boy was born. Why didn't you tell me before, and played some to me. How I love: Lullay, Jesu – and: In the Bleak Mid-Winter, and now I should like to hear the whole done. Is it possible that you knew at 19, that "exacte Phantasie" is the secret and force of the genuine artist, that method has to be absolutely reasonable, sure, able, accomplished, but the aim, the whole, the conception an eternal poem . . . I don't worry about you,

Ben, less than ever. I detected everything I love in your music – the immortal something – in this youthful work. Good night, darling, I hope you'll have more rest in Ch. [Chicago] than here. Please, tell me what you need, what you are missing . . . did you leave your camera here on purpose?

I long to see you again.

ELIZABETH

1 Britten had left on a trip to the Midwest, which was to culminate in the first American performance of his Piano Concerto, with himself as soloist, at Chicago a few days later (see Letter 241).

235 To Elizabeth Mayer

Inman Hotel, Champaign, Illinois.[1]
Jan. 5th 1939 [recte 1940]

My dearest Elizabeth,

Your sweet note has just arrived, & before I embark on another day of this madness, I want to write you a little note in return. It'll be short but scarcely sweet – that's to say with regard to the writing – because who could write properly with the temperature 6° below zero?

I hope you got my night-letter saying I got here O.K. – You dear, I knew those Gods of yours would bring me safely here! Now, please, let your Gods bring me an answer from Kay Leslie[2] because I don't relish a week alone in Chicago! So far things have been entertaining if tiring here. I can't attempt to describe the 'goings-on' but believe me, my dear it's like another world. I'm like a visitor from Mars to them – they pull me, & poke me, take photos, talk about me, & admire my accent no end – but it is all rather sickening. When I see the young men & boys, who make up the bands here, straining to get something good to play, trying to enjoy the stuff they do play with such spirit & skill – & get served with this muck, & so badly directed – I feel more than ever that this European culture is not just snobbishness – but merely superior knowledge in how to train & entertain. Poor kids – they are just as wonderful as the conductors & managers are dull & pompous.

No-more now, my dear – I'll write later. I don't have much time as I'm hauled about so – but I did take off this morning to try & get some work done on P.B. [Paul Bunyan]. Goodness – what a breath of fresh air that stuff of Wystan's seems.

Now – down to lunch – with poor old Max Winkler to whom everything published by him is so good and everything else just bunk. But at least he's honest – & doesn't talk about 'modernist' music. So glad you find the old 'Boy' [*A Boy was Born*] to your taste. Gosh, what years ago that was.

Much love to you all – Beatta & Herr Doktor esp.

Your very loving

BENJAMIN

Only 11 more days?[3]

1 For details of the motivation of the trip to Champaign and of the trip itself, see Letter 243. The 'wind band' was then – and remains still – a peculiarly American phenomenon and lucrative market for composers and their publishers. In the *Chicago Daily News* on 15 January, under the heading 'School Band Din Called Vital by British Pianist', it was reported:

> Most of us prefer to forget the din from a school band in rehearsal. But to Benjamin Britten, London composer and pianist, those same sour cornet notes are the voice of America's musical vitality, and composers should give attention to these high-school virtuosos.

In the same interview Britten expressed the hope that the operetta he was writing with Auden (*Paul Bunyan*) might 'one day win a place with the Gilbert and Sullivan operettas as a high-school vehicle'.

2 Before the war Kay Leslie had taken German lessons from Mrs Mayer in Munich. She lived in Winnetka on Lake Michigan, north of Chicago.

3 Until his return to Long Island.

236 To Benjamin Britten
From Elizabeth Mayer

Jan. 5, 1940.

My dear Ben,

Thanks a lot for your night-letter! I was not worried, thanks to my means of aerial communication, but, dear me, how good it was to read your lines, characteristic even in the mechanical lettering, your "stops" etc. It was read to every member of the family, Jip included, and thereupon solemnly deposited in the archives of B.B. Yesterday was a dull day (with the exception of your Telegram and a lovely cake baked by Peter) I had to drive around with the German doctor's wife, who is with us for 2–3 days, and who is simple but acceptable, in the evening Brigitte[1] and her mother were invited (Peter was fortunately with Bill and Mildred) and, oh, how dull it was, narrow and shallow. I mended your socks and tried to be a polite hostess, but how boring is that role. Still lovely pure snow, sunshine, cold . . . Beata finishes typing two new songs that may have reached you by now. Fine Kahler[2] wants to have her in Princeton on Monday for at least two weeks; she hesitates to go, but I think it would be the best, although I hate to see her go. Perhaps she can find an "amoenus" [pleasant] job in Princeton; I know she hates to look for a job in N.Y., – this would be a kind of transition and adjournment. All this will be quite far from you now and should be; I am sorry, but I am so accustomed to talk over everything with you . . . My darling, I hope that you have a good time and that everybody spoils you, that you got in touch with Kay and have good rooms for the week before the concert.

Colin[3] called up last night, and asked for you – nothing particular – he wants to come out soon, talked yesterday on the radio on Balinese music, I was in the car, turned on and was pleased to hear his voice. I invited him – he'll come when you are back – everything will be nice and alive when you are back, dear presence, dear Ben!

E.

1 Brigitte Steiner; see note 2 to Letter 315.
2 The Kahlers were friends of the Mayers, rich immigrants from Vienna. Erich von Kahler was a philosophical writer, a friend of Stefan George, the poet, and other members of the George circle. In the family, and to Britten and Pears, Josephine von Kahler, his wife, was known as 'Phine' ['Fine'].

   Beata had been invited to Princeton to type the manuscript of a book. The 'two songs' to which Mrs Mayer refers were probably additional texts for *Paul Bunyan*, on the typing of the first draft of the libretto of which Beata had already been engaged. Her typescript is to be found in the Berg Collection of the New York Public Library.
3 Colin McPhee, the composer; see note 12 to Letter 312.

237   To Benjamin Britten
From Peter Pears

> Boosey Hawkes Belwin Incorporated
> 43–45–47, West 23rd Street
> New York, N.Y.
> <u>Tuesday</u> [9 January 1940]

My darling Ben –   It was marvellous to get your letter. The first
from Champaign and then from Chicago – I don't suppose you'll
get my last letter for abit, as I sent it care of Goldberg at Chicago.
I only hope he doesn't open it, as my letter was compromising to
say the least of it! You poor little Cat, frozen to death in 12° below
zero weather – I do hope it's not quite so cold now. It's 5° above
here and that's summery compared to you. I got your night letter
by post yesterday morning, and it was quite a bit different from
the way I got it over the phone on Sunday. I was so sad that you
were so depressed and cold – I wanted to hop into a plane and
come and comfort you at once. I would have kissed you all over &
then blown you all over there & then ‿‿‿ & ‿‿‿ & then you'd
have been as warm as toast!

I'm writing this, sitting in a large chair in Mildred's office,
balancing it on my knee – (not the chair). I came up with her &
Bill this morning & gave old McNamee her lesson – and I rang
Heinsheimer to see if he knew anything of Ralph. The Rex
[steamship] isn't due according to the papers till Saturday, that
may mean she won't come till Sunday, but H. imagines he'll fly
straight to you (grr!) you little much too attractive so-and-so – in
order to hear the Concerto (so he says – Personally I don't think
he gives a damn for the concerto). Mildred has been terribly low
lately – not on edge but just sort of worn out, so while Bill goes
to his bloody lectures tonight, I thought I'd give her dinner & take
her to a movie somewhere. I'm finding it pretty difficult to face
sitting with them in the evenings now, it's easier when you're
there. Dr. Mayer misses you very much. Everyone does – except
me, and of course I don't care a brass farthing how long you stay
away, because if you stay away a day longer than Wednesday I'm
going to come & fetch you, wherever you may be, & as long as I'm
with you, you can stay away till the moon turns blue.[1]
 [. . .]
I'm reading Of Human Bondage of Somerset Maugham[2] & it's
terribly good – some wonderful school stuff, & of course the

whole thing, in his subtle way, is quite <u>itching</u> with queerness. Perhaps I'll send you a copy to Chicago to read in bed.

Please give Harold & Mary a whole lot of my love – I feel foul at not having written to them before, but I have every intention of writing to them in the next day or two. I shall never forget a certain night in Grand Rapids. Ich liebe dich, io t'amo, jeg elske dyg (?), je t'aime, in fact, my little white-thighed beauty, I'm terribly in love with you.

P.

1 One thinks of the Prologue of *Paul Bunyan*:

> Once in a while
> The odd thing happens,
> Once in a while
> The moon turns blue.

When listening to the BBC recording of that chorus from *Bunyan* which initiated the work's revival in 1976, Britten remarked (to Donald Mitchell), 'That was Peter'.

2 Maugham's autobiographical novel (an account of a lonely boyhood) was published in 1915.

238 To Benjamin Britten
From Elizabeth Mayer
[*Typed*]

Amityville, N.Y.
January 9, 1940, Tuesday.

My dear, my last letter, scribbled at midnight, must have been pretty illegible therefore I shall write this one on the typewriter, and I do hope that you will feel all the warmth I try to inspire the mechanical letters with. In this moment I receive a message from Kay by wire, she just tried to reach you in Champaign and failed. I wired back, and hope she can reach you very soon and make arrangements for you. My poor Ben, I am so sorry not to be with you and take a little care of you. It seems to be very cold in Chicago, and I know what murderish winters happen in those parts. I do hope you have your scarf and take care of yourself in any way! We have a rather severe winter here too, more snow every day, but sunshine . . . and the landscape is lovely. I even ventured to Nassau Shores and celebrated a little with you. Everywhere a flawless beauty! Every morning, driving with Michael to the station, I enjoy the freshness and purity.

The house is very quiet. Yesterday Beata left for Princeton. I miss her very much, but I arranged this visit because I think it will do her good, it is a little break, probably a kind of transition to the work people want her to do, and a relief from the strain in the relationship to U. [Ulli] whose problem is not yet solved. But we see a little clearer, and I think I shall have time this week to start something for her. Everything is very peaceful in our house, and you know perfectly well who it was who brought peace, and blessings on him for ever and ever! Peter and I are often together, and we have good talks and read and even play duos. Last night we tried the Wolf-Mörike, Peter did very well, but I felt very ashamed of my stammering on the piano, particularly knowing so well how it should be. I am going to practise again regularly.

Every day we start talking of you and calculating where you are and what you may do at the moment. I wonder if you are to-day in Grand Rapids, and if it is even colder there than in Chicago. I hope and I think you will every-where meet people who love you and do everything for you, my darling! Yes, we too count the days, will you be back on the 17th? and what about Ralph? has he not arrived yet? [*Handwritten:*]

Peter just went into town with Bill and Mildred. William told me that there had been a letter from you. As he is coming home early, I'll hear soon from him! Good-bye! my dear.

I just sent an Air-Mail to the Borgeses. They live Hotel Windermere. I hope Kay reaches you to-day!

E.

239　To Elizabeth Mayer

Stevens Hotel,
Michigan Boulevard at Balbo Drive,
Chicago.
[9 January 1940]

My darling Elizabeth,

There never seems time for more than a scribbled note to you – I'm sorry but I'm kept awfully busy. I have enjoyed your letters so much – they've simply kept me alive. I don't remember ever feeling so black – it was being away from Amityville & having no one to talk to about things – I've got so firmly fixed in the Mayer family now that I can't stand being uprooted! In some ways, tho', I am very glad to have made this trip. This is much more what I

had imagined America & Americans to be. I'll tell you all about
it when we meet next week (<u>next week</u>!) as there isn't time now –
and I haven't really decided what I really think about things here
– being slow of intellect it takes me ages to make up my mind! One
thing – I met the Borgeses last night at the WPA concert when
Sessions new piece was played (<u>not</u> very good I'm afraid).[1] I
couldn't make much of <u>him</u> – besides teeth – but I talked alot to
<u>her</u> – she seemed a poor little thing I felt – & seemed terribly glad
to talk to someone her own age! (or more or less!!).   And she
giggled quite nicely when the orchestra and/or Sessions made a
particularly funny noise! Signor B. didn't seem to approve. If &
when Wystan comes here[2] we're going together to eat with them.
I've met some nice people here so far – a little more polished
perhaps than the bluff bandsmen of Champaign! but still typically
mid-western, I gather. The Orchestra isn't bad. I have my first
rehearsal this afternoon – & so I shall know how they take to
Concerto no. 1 in D major in a few hours, now! Then I go off to
Grand Rapids[3] by the 5.0 train & back early Friday morning for
rehearsals again.
    It is now 11.0 a.m. & I'm still in bed – but I've had breakfast &
so it's not as slack as it seems – especially as I was up terribly late
last night, & I <u>can't</u> sleep in this town – it's too noisy. I usually
take a seditive about 1.30 in desparation – & much against my
conscience! (If you happen to have an odd seditive around could
you put it in an envelope for me sometime?) I shall be coming
back here on Friday unless I can't get a room – that I shall know
when I check out after lunch & will let you know. Do you know
when I'm by myself I'm pretty efficient at arranging matters –
booking rooms, tickets etc. & getting about. It's only when Peter's
around that I become so shy & retiring – what – what! Don't tell
him tho' —
    Very, very much love, my dear. Write often – & see you Tuesday
– as far as I know I shall fly back then – as soon as possible!

Love to all, esp. Pitt(!)[4]

BEN

1 Roger Sessions (1896–1985), American composer. The 'new piece'
  was Sessions's Violin Concerto, composed 1930–35, and first performed at Chicago in the Blackstone Theater on 8 January, in which
  Robert Gross was the soloist and the Illinois Symphony Orchestra
  was conducted by Izler Solomon. On the back of the programme the
  orchestra announced 'with pleasure the American début of Benjamin

Britten, who will give the first American performance of his Concerto No. 1 in D major for piano and orchestra', a week later. The American conductor, Izler Solomon (b. 1910), had worked for the WPA during the 1930s as Music Director for the State of Michigan. He was conductor of the Illinois Symphony Orchestra from 1936 to 1941, and was, as this Sessions première shows, an enthusiast for contemporary American music.

2 The intention, presumably, was to work on *Paul Bunyan*, but it seems unlikely that Auden made the trip.

3 See Letter 243.

4 Dr Mayer: a pet name used by his wife.

240 To Albert Goldberg

c/o Dr. Mayer,
Long Island Home,
Amityville, N.Y.
Jan. 18th 1940

My dear Albert,

Just a note – in my inimitable long-hand – to thank you and your delightful, tho' occasionally insubordinate, assistant,[1] for the grand time that you gave me in my stay in Chicago. I enjoyed every moment (except the one when the piano went wrong!)[2] of it – & I hope you aren't too much out of pocket because of all those meals you paid for me! I should call some of those feasts 'business – to be stood by the W.P.A.' – if I were you.

Well – the journey back was fine – we were 40 minutes early the wind was so strong! Not too bumpy for me to have a big meal on the plane – served free of charge of course! Since I got back I seem to have spent most of the time in bed (that's what the Mid-west does for you) – but I've got to get started on work now, especially as life has become complicated by the arrival of two enormous sets of proofs – the Violin Concerto & this 'Les Illuminations' for Tenor & strings I told you about – & do I hate proofs ——!

Well: the best of luck to you – with plenty of goodspeed & British Consuls.[3] Best wishes to you & Harold – thank him very much for the terrible journey he had to make on my behalf to the air-

port, & tell him my nerves have by now settled down beautifully
(but he <u>does</u> drive well, Albert – have courage!)

With good wishes to all the boys (orchestra)
Yours
BENJAMIN BRITTEN

P.S.   Could you please 'phone the Stevens[4] & ask them to send
on any mail to the above address – if you can read it?

1 Harold S. Bailey (1909–1985). His official function in the Illinois Music
   Project was Chicago Supervisor. Goldberg (Interview with Donald
   Mitchell, 23 May 1989, Pasadena, California; Archive) remembers
   him conducting 'school choirs and that sort of thing', which was
   doubtless the reason why Bailey was later to make a particular inquiry
   of Britten about his choral music (see Letter 314). He was not, at
   least in these times, 'a trained musician'. Post-war, however, he was
   a voice teacher for some years at the Chicago Musical College (later
   incorporated into Roosevelt University), and he maintained a 'studio'
   for private pupils until the time of his death.

2 See Letter 241.

3 See Letter 243 which mentions the party for Britten given by the
   British Consul in Chicago. 'Plenty of goodspeed' is clearly a joking
   reference to the Mrs Goodspeed (a Midwest patroness of the arts?)
   who turns up again in a later letter of Goldberg's to Britten of 21
   June. He was to write regretting that the composer was unable to be
   present at the performance of *Mont Juic* (see note 1 to Letter 264) on
   17 June adding:

   I had anticipated the subsidiary festivities which would have attended your
   visit. (This does not include the luncheon which the British Vice-Consul had
   planned in your honor with Mrs Goodspeed as the main exhibit.)

4 The hotel at which Britten had stayed while in Chicago.

241   To Beata Mayer

c/o Dr. Mayer
Amityville.
18th Dec. 1940. [18 January 1940][1]

<u>Ralph Hawkes comes down to-morrow</u>
Love from
everyone.

My dearest Beata,

   O this long-hand – how I hate writing letters – this is the third
to-night, & you'll be lucky if you can read it! But I did want to

thank you for your note which arrived just before my concert – & was I jittery?! – & it did it's cheering up job magnificently, & I was terribly pleased to get it.

Well – it was a great success & the audience & critics both seem to find the work (& the pianist!) much to their taste.[2] What actually won their favours, though, was something apart from the music – because the piano in the first movement broke down on me – (part of the key-board was insecurely fixed) & I had to stop the orchestra, apologise to the audience (who found the old British accent 'charrrrrming'!) & restart the work.[3] After that I had no difficulty – such are manners – ugh!!

I picked up a vile cold in Chicago somewhere & felt abit lousy abit of the time (I can hear my secretary tick me off for saying 'abit . . . abit' – but I'm not going to alter it – ha! ha!) – especially as I had so much to do & so little time to do it in – they kept me horribly busy. But I've spent two mornings in bed – & of course the house, is very quiet nowadays! – & I'm feeling better. Seriously, the house is much too quiet. Everyone misses you terribly – especially der liebe Papa; there is no one to tease him, & Peter & I can only beat him once out of every ten times in Chinese Chequers. Mildred's been abit low apparently but is feeling better now. But I expect you've been told all the news, so I won't bore you with that. How are you? I hope things are getting abit cheerfully. Why not suggest you move furniture around the place if things get too bad – Fine likes that I think? Give my suitable regards to Erich – I liked him alot. Tell him that the red trousers are hibernating – but a red sweater of mine caused much feeling (pro & con) in the middle west!

Much love, my dear – I'll write again soon.

Be good (or careful)

BEN

1 Britten erroneously dates this letter December. It clearly belongs to January.

2 The performance was reviewed by Edward Barry in the *Chicago Tribune*, 16 January, under the headline 'Pianist Britten Well Liked in Own Concerto':

Yesterday was British day in Chicago music. Benjamin Britten, English composer and pianist, made his American concert debut in the Blackstone theater last night, playing his own concerto with the Illinois Symphony orchestra under Albert Goldberg's direction.

    [. . .]

Mr Britten – tall, slim, and 26 – is as English as rain. His music, however, indicates that he has been influenced not only by such of his own compatriots as John Ireland but also by schools and composers outside his own country.

The concerto has a patness, lightness, verve and humor more suggestive of France or even of Russia than of England. This is not meant to imply that Mr Britten has slavishly imitated any one or anything but merely to indicate that in the expression of his own vigorous ideas he was influenced by the modes current in various parts of the world.

The audience liked the concerto's quaint, out-of-focus melodies, its pungent but never extravagant harmonic touches, its odd, percussive rhythms, and the free, almost improvisatory character of the whole. The audience also liked Mr Britten's competent, off-hand manner of playing, and gave him quite an ovation at the end.

In the *Chicago Daily News*, 16 January, Eugene Stinson wrote:

The brash young piano concerto which its pianist–composer brought with him from England had its first American performance on Monday night – and so did the composer – when Benjamin Britten all but astonished us with it at the Illinois Symphony's concert at Blackstone, Albert Goldberg conducting.

It is in four movements and is full of the bad boy spirit which only recently commenced to subside in 20th-century music. Mr Britten has been strongly influenced by other composers, which is quite as it should be as he has completely assimilated the influence and has used them in his own way.

I suspect that his work is not as strong as it is bold and not as deep as it is entertaining. Yet certainly it is good music to hear, it is full of mood and it has the gusto of a gifted extemporaneous speaker. Mr Britten admits that its various passages are energetic, angry, mocking, grim, growling, menacing, tense, fierce, tender, rather ominous, impertinent, wrathful, warm, jingoistic, doubting, solemn, reflective, furious, agitated, muttering, excited, swaggering, headlong and confident. There was not much to add unless one were old-fashioned enough to find it in general dire, which I did not. I found it rather loosely constructed, but its invention like its orchestration, was excellent. Its popularity will be somewhat limited by the fact that it asks more from a performer than it gives him.

Mr Britten, however, did not mind playing it at all, and play it he did, with a splendid facility of that magnificently ready sort which does not mind adventitious imperfections. He was vigorously applauded, and I believe that this will be the case wherever he plays in America.

The term 'bad boy' came to be particularly associated with the music and personality of George Antheil, whose 1945 autobiography was to be entitled *Bad Boy of Music* (New York, Doubleday).

Further reviews appeared on 16 January, by Herman Davies in the *Herald American*, and by Claudia Cassidy in the *Journal of Commerce*. We quote from the latter:

Mr Britten is a good pianist with a sense of humor – he smilingly stopped the whole orchestra early in the first movement when his piano threatened to disintegrate – and his concerto was received with roars of approval.

It is an attractive, amusing and often stimulating work which manages to be young without undue gaucherie and to stir reminiscence without blatant imitation. The waltz movement is engagingly subtle and admirably balanced and the third movement, marked recitative and aria, begins with a beguiling dialogue between piano and woodwind and builds to a broad, vividly accented theme which has power and dynamic excitement. Mr Britten has touches of Stravinsky's instrumentation and of Gershwin's use of rhythm and he uses them well. But he has, too, an expansive talent for couching contemporary music in terms an audience understands and likes. His American debut is plainly marked 'come again'.

3 In his 1989 Interview with Donald Mitchell (Pasadena, California; Archives) Goldberg recalled the incident:

And we'd just started, you know, a few introductory measures, and I felt a tug at my sleeve – 'stop the orchestra, Albert! Something's wrong with the piano!' So we investigated and it was easily fixed and just [as] I had my arms up, like this, ready to start again, Britten stood up looked at the audience and said, 'I hope you don't think it was I who was to blame.' And that won the audience you know.

Goldberg added:

In the week he'd been there, we'd loved him. When he arrived in kind of ragged clothes, we wondered if he had anything decent to wear for the concert, but [on the night] he was immaculate [. . .]

Another memory: 'One day we were in a basement' when Britten needed a lavatory, 'and there was a sign up, ten cents. He said, "Ten cents, Albert? Ten cents for shitting?" [Laughter.] That shocked him.'

'In Chicago,' Goldberg told us,

we were extremely fortunate because at that time the Chicago Opera folded, and we inherited intact the Chicago Opera Orchestra, about sixty men [. . .] and that became the nucleus of the Illinois Symphony [. . .]. So we had a head start on that – we had a good trained group of professional musicians [. . .]. We held Sunday afternoon concerts for fifty cents in the Great Northern Theater in downtown Chicago, and they were a great popular success.

The works that accompanied the American première of the Piano Concerto were Brahms's Second Symphony and a suite of pieces from the Fitzwilliam Virginal Book transcribed for orchestra by Gordon Jacob (his *William Byrd Suite*, 1922, revised 1939).

ILLINOIS SYMPHONY ORCHESTRA

Unit of
Illinois Music Project, Work Projects Administration

BLACKSTONE THEATRE
MONDAY, JANUARY 15, 1940
AT 8:15 P. M.

ALBERT GOLDBERG
CONDUCTOR

BENJAMIN BRITTEN
COMPOSER-PIANIST
(American Debut)

This Concert is Presented by
WORK PROJECTS ADMINISTRATION

ILLINOIS MUSIC PROJECT
DR. EARL VINCENT MOORE, National Director
ALBERT GOLDBERG, State Supervisor
HAROLD S. BAILEY, Chicago Supervisor

Chicago, the American first performance of the Piano Concerto, 15 January 1940: the cover of the programme.

242 To Beata Mayer
From Peter Pears

> L.I.H. A. N.Y. U.S.A.
> [Long Island Home, Amityville, New York]
> [19 January 1940]

Béatté darling – Now don't blame me at once and say "Why haven't you written before? You said you'd let me have something every day" – because you have had something every day haven't you? Your mother says she's written to you each day – but of course really I should have too. Verzeihe mich, meine schöne Schwester [Forgive me, my beautiful sister].

Well, I missed you so very much when you went, and Ben was away too. The only thing I could do was to work, so I practised v. hard every day at new sounds, straight through the nose and very loud. Ben of course says he thinks it sounds lousy so I shall have to start all over again on another line – perhaps not through the nose this time!

Ben came back on Tuesday [16 January] looking like a corpse – he had much too strenuous a time & a cold – so now of course your mother is spoiling him quite unbearably and stuffing him with food and he is swelling visibly. Are you putting on weight too? How many pounds? I hope it isn't too depressing for you. I didn't go away to Philadelphia because I thought I was doing such good work and didn't want to interrupt it. Don't be too long away dear

Beata – we all miss you very much – even Gippy[1] has only found
Mrs. Keins'[2] clothes to eat and they are not nearly so appetising as
yours. Were you here when your Mother tried to cut some of his
fur off? He looks now just like a poodle, and it has had a strange
effect on his psyche. He minds very much being laughed at – but
one can't help laughing at him he is so absurd, and of course smells
to high heaven. Your mother has just finished "Where Angels
fear to tread".[3] The fight at the end of it nearly killed her – You
could see her still panting for breath for about an hour after!

　　Ralph Hawkes is coming down for the day today & dining tonight
chez Titley. I wonder how they'll mix. I'm a bit scared.

Much love to you Beata – Come back soon –

PETER

1　The Mayer family's dog, whose name was variously transcribed, e.g.
　　Jippy, and which may have been the model for Fido in *Paul Bunyan*
　　(see PFL, plate 120).

2　Mrs Keins was one of the many refugees from Europe offered tempo-
　　rary shelter by the Mayers.

3　The novel (1905) by E.M. Forster.

243　To Beth Welford

[*Full text*, EWB, *pp. 128–9*]

c/o Dr. W. Mayer, Long Island Home,

Amityville, N.Y.

Jan. 21st 1940

My darling old thing,

　　I was highly delighted with your letter (Jan 4th[1] – another
anniversary, how they get me down!) which came after what
seemed a long silence. But anyhow one is letter-greedy nowadays
& it probably wasn't as long as it seemed. It was a beauty – &
told me lots of news about things I wanted to know. You do write
nicely, you know – just anything that comes into your head, about
everyday things, which is what one really is interested in. Robert's
letters (entre nous) get me down alot – he is always talking about
'duty' 'uniform' 'Hitlerism', & reads like a leading article of the
Times. However – it's him, poor thing – & he seems very unhappy
under all the veneer of patriotism. I was overjoyed with the
calendar – & it makes my heart beat faster everytime I see it – it
was a grand idea. I love the picture of the Aberdeen trawler – &

the pictures are excellent & remind me – o, how they remind me!
However –

_____

Well – there is so much news that I don't know where to begin
– all letters must necessarily (??) be so sketchy in detail; <u>when</u> we
meet you'll hear all the details – shall we ever stop talking? I had
a <u>terrific</u> success in Chicago – like one dreams of! 14 calls – &
cheers & shouts of speech! [. . .] Anyhow I'm re-booked for
Chicago in May.[2] So <u>that's</u> good. I had two weeks' trip. Started
in Champaign, Illinois (flew there), where I heard lots of wind-
bands & met conductors – got to do an article on it for a paper[3] –
then I went to Chicago where I rehearsed the Concerto. Then to
Grand Rapids, Michigan (where I was in the summer), saw lots
of people I had to (some friends some business), flew back to
Chicago – with vile cold & flu' (temperature was 14° below 0°ˣ one
day – you've never dreamed of such cold!) which has only just
cleared up. I was back in Chicago on 11th – where I had a terrific
time – with interviews & parties (British Consulate threw one for
me!) – & after the show on Monday flew home. Marvellous
journey – we had tail wind, & did it (to New York) in 3 hours 20
minutes (it's about 780 miles!) I felt completely dead on arrival –
but I'm fine now – Mrs. Mayer is such an angel & looks after me
like a mother. Besides Ralph Hawkes has been down here which is
fine. It was lovely to see him – could tell us so much about general
conditions. He's going to be over here for a long time I think – &
is full of schemes.

Now, my dear, I am so glad you're back at Snape. I am perfectly
all right as regards cash – & if you're in need of any, let me know
at once. You see we're living very cheaply & altho' we're not rich,
we're managing quite nicely. We've got to make new plans for
the future, as things won't always be as easy as they are now – but
we'll let you know as soon as anything is settled. I'm writing to
Barbara to tell her to use the money – to send you some for the
upkeep of the Mill. I want you to consider yourselves (you & Kit)
as temporary owners of the Mill – to do anything you like with it.
I <u>don't</u> want you to let it – unless you want money yourself – or
Nicholson wants money for me – because anyhow you <u>can't</u> send
money out of the country for me, you know? <u>Do</u> try & live there
indefinitely – it's the next best thing to living there myself to know
that you three are there.

I'm all right – I felt abit bad over Xmas – & abit hopeless about
the future – but since Ralph turned up & I had the success in

Chicago, I feel better. And now to get <u>you</u> over here. What plans! ——

Love to Kit & Sebastian. Tell Kit to write again I love his letters.

Please excuse writing – but I'm snowed under with important proofs to be corrected at the moment – & I wanted to catch this mail.

×The weather – not <u>my</u> temperature!!

xxxoooxxxx Love

BEN

Love from Peter.

1 Britten's father's birthday.

2 See Letter 257 *et seq.*

3 'A Visiting Composer Looks at Us', the *New York Times*, 24 March (reprinted as 'An English Composer Sees America', *Tempo* 1/2, American Series, April 1940), in which Britten wrote:

> Besides having the largest concert organizations in the world and the obvious advantages of Hollywood, this country has an educational system unparalleled in size and scope, and the demand for good, simple music in this direction is enormous. There are school operas to be written, pieces for the numberless school children learning to play instruments, and, above all, there are the bands which are such a feature of this country and have been so neglected by the serious composers.

244 To Barbara Britten

In the papers to-day the British Censors have let through the news of the ghastly weather you have been having.[1] My poor dear – that on top of everything – it isn't fair – is it. Let's hope it'll get better soon.

c/o Dr. Mayer,

Long Island Home,

Amityville, N.Y.

Jan. 28th 1940.

My darling Barbara,

[. . .] there's been little time for letter-writing, especially as Beata Mayer, who helped me with my correspondence – dictating and typing – is away & I have to manage it all myself!

[. . .]

[. . .] I am fairly O.K. as regards money. R.H. will continue as long as possible with the guarantee, & I can pick up odd things.

I had such a good success in Chicago, that I'm sure I can get dates
playing in the future. Anyhow – as soon as poss. Peter & I are
going to get on the British Quota – which allows us to work
normally instead of being just 'visitors'.[2] We shall go probably to
Mexico or Cuba (a formality) & return as under this Quota. A curse
& an expense but it must be done. I didn't want to do it as it
seemed somehow to cut another English tie – but it isn't binding
at all and I can return to England whenever I can (pray God –
soon!), & Ralph & all are insistent.

Much love my dear. Hope a good job turns up – it seems a pity
that you should have to take a Council job but it's better than
nothing – & I'm sure something better will turn up later.

Love to Helen. I hope she's well & bearing up.
Be careful. Go to Snape.
XXX OOO
BEN

1 The winter of 1940 in England was an exceptionally severe one.

2 The quota system was introduced as a result of the Red Scare in 1919
and 1920:

> Nativism set the stage for a major reversal of immigration policy which had
> for so many decades kept the gates of America open to newcomers. In
> February 1920, over Wilson's veto, Congress passed a law limiting the
> number of immigrants in any year to 3% of the foreign-born of each national
> group who had been living in the United States.

Further controls on immigration were introduced in 1924 (National
Origins Act) and while in 1938 Roosevelt, to aid the alleviation of
persecuted Jews, arranged 'for some 15,000 refugees or visitors permits to remain in the United States, [. . .] he did not combat con-
gressional and public opinion that opposed any relaxation of the
immigration quotas'. (See John M. Blum *et al*, *The National Experience*,
6th edition (San Diego, Harcourt Brace Jovanovich, 1985), pp. 619–20,
637, and 714–15.) This was the background to the preoccupation of
Britten and Pears with the renewal of their visas which runs like a
continuous theme throughout the correspondence from the American years (and which in 1939 was also a concern of Auden's). However, they did not make the trip to Mexico or Cuba as envisaged in
this letter. See also Letters 248 and 256.

245   To Sophie Wyss
[*Fragment; typed*]

[?early January 1940]

[. . .]

Perhaps one day you will be able to come and sing Rimbaud with them.[1]

That is about all the news. Give my very best love to my godchild and young Arnold. I will try and find some nice thing to send them as a belated Christmas present, if it does not get lost crossing the ocean. In the meantime you have all my prayers for your continued safety and good health.

Yours ever,

BENJIE

P.S.   You asked for some contemporary American songs. Unfortunately song writing is not a forte of American composers today and I cannot find any that are really worth your while. Aaron Copland, who is by far the best American composer, has not written any.[2] The only composer whose songs are performed is a man called Charles Ives,[3] who is almost without exception the worst composer I know of. He is pretentious, has nothing to say and can't even say that. However, I may send you, if I can find one, a volume of his songs for your amusement.

1 It is possible that Britten refers to his recent appearance with the Illinois Symphony Orchestra.

2 This was not quite correct. Copland had written some songs pre-1939 but a significant number of them were unpublished. It was not until the composition of the *12 Poems of Emily Dickinson* in 1944–50 that Copland emerged as a songwriter. His *Old American Songs* (Set 1) were written at the invitation of Pears and Britten and first performed by them at the Aldeburgh Festival on 17 June 1950.

3 Charles Ives (1874–1954), American composer. Volumes of Ives's songs were in circulation pre-1939, including *114 Songs*, the collection privately printed in 1922. Britten's assessment of Ives is a typical composer's judgement, i.e. one influenced by temperament and above all (in Britten's case) by convictions about the overriding importance of a preternaturally acute ear. It would be hard to think of two composers whose ears were seemingly more mutually opposed and exclusive. For all that, Ives was occasionally heard at Aldeburgh, though principally after Britten's death.

246 To Beth Welford

[*Pencil;* EWB, *p. 133*]

Saturday 24th Feb. [1940]

My darling Beth,

Please forgive the long silence, but I gather that Peter has explained things[1] – & I hope I won't seem so unbrotherly when you've read his letter. Anyhow its ages since I had a letter from you! I can't remember actually whether I answered that last one with photos of Sebastian in. Anyhow I adored them – he looks a grand kid – give him his godfather's love won't you. I liked his signature in Kit's letter too – shows his uncle's influence! Thank Kit too for his excellent letter. I will answer it as soon as [I] get sufficiently "up" to hold a pen & think distinctly! I hope things are going on well with you still. Has Kit any form of job[2] – or will he just wait until this bloody war is over? It's awfully funny – being in bed one has just got miles away from it – just like being up in the stars. It has really been a marvellous rest – & I feel fine now – only longing for the rash-irritation to go – which must be soon now. I have had really marvellous nursing! Beata is a trained nurse & managed all the bed-pans etc. marvellous[ly] – although I can't pretend I like them (B.P. I mean!) – do you remember when you had to bother with all that?[3] Peter has been sweet & nothing too much trouble for him & everyone is marvellous. I couldn't have better attention even at Snape – so don't worry will you – there's nothing to worry about at all – I am fine & will be better than ever before.

I will write next week when I'm convalèscing. I shall have lots of time then. Write soon & tell me all the news. Love to all. Hope Kit occasionally gets a New Yorker[4] –

Much love,
BEN.

1 Pears had written to Beth on 20 February:

[. . .] the reason I am writing just now is to tell you that Ben has been ill in bed but is now very nearly allright though still in bed. I'll start at the beginning. You know he went to Chicago last month to play his concerto and all, and was away 2 weeks in the bitterest weather (12° below zero etc.) and he came back with a horrible cold and feeling lousy. Well he stayed in bed for a day or so but I think he never quite got rid of his cold, and on Thursday night (the 8th Feb.) he had a long and horrible nosebleed which left him pretty weakish – and it seems that a streptococcus

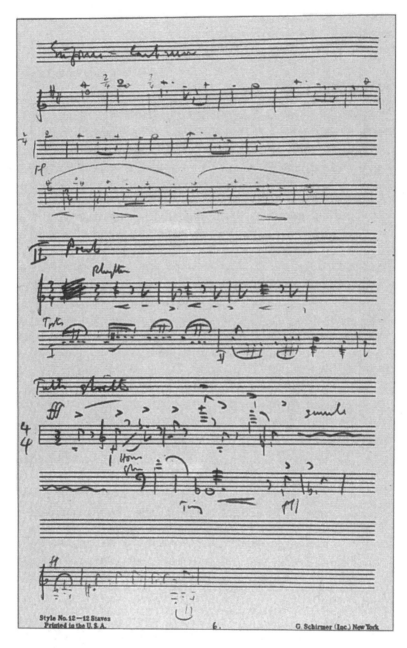

Two pages from the sketchbook to which Pears refers in note 1 to Letter 246: the left hand page includes sketches from the *Sinfonia da Requiem*, in this order: the opening of the last movement) then ideas for the central Scherzo; the right hand page: the opening of the first movement, at the bottom of the page, sketches for the First String Quartet (slow movement)

of some sort seized upon that moment to attack him and of course found him pretty easy material. He got up Friday and Saturday but his face was sore, his nose blocked and a rash on his chin. He stayed in bed Sunday and has been there since. His temperature ran high – up to 104° and a bit on the Wednesday. You can guess it was a bit alarming. Luckily he was in the hands of many doctors (almost too many!) and Dr. Mayer who was in charge was confident about it, but when his temperature suddenly went up to 107° for a bit last Sunday night, he got a specialist to come down on Sunday and look him over. Well apparently he's allright and taking it very well (heart, chest, lungs, etc in perfect condition) but his tonsils are quite rotten apparently and must come out at the first suitable moment (perhaps June). Also he has to take it very easy indeed for 3 or 4 weeks, as I gather after these sort of things there are always possibilities of complications (the kidneys are always the danger). So he's having an easy time in bed for another week or so.

Friday Feb. 23rd

[. . .] Ben continues getting better and should be out of bed in a day or two. The specialist was emphatic that he mustn't get out of bed until his temperature was completely normal for four days, and as it generally goes up a few points in the evening, he's still there. Beate Mayer (the eldest daughter) who is a trained nurse, did night duty with him for a week and now she stays with him for most of the day. She was quite marvellous. But now I am back in the room with him, and he really is pretty well, except that he is rather weak still, and his face still irritates rather at night. They are being exceedingly thorough (as well as being marvellously kind) and his urine is analysed twice a week, and from time to time they test his blood and his throat swabs. But everyone agrees that as long as he's careful and looks after himself, there's not the least likelihood of anything untoward happening – and believe me, he will be looked after very well here, you may be sure. He's very cheerful, considering the boring business of being two weeks and more in bed. Everyone adores him here, and can't do enough for him. He never need be alone unless he wants to be, and there are always people to talk or read to him, there's a portable radio by his bedside, in fact he's in clover – and really getting better every day. He's full of musical ideas, and has a little sketch book by his bedside (à la Beethoven!) which he fills with notes. Mrs. Mayer has written a note to Barbara, I think, and don't be alarmed for a moment, Beth, because he will get all the attention he can here. We'll see to it.

(EWB, pp. 131–2, complete)

Britten often said that Beata had 'saved his life'. There is no doubt of the severity of this bacterial attack. It was an example of one of the many illnesses to which Britten – seemingly so healthy, spare and athletic – succumbed throughout his life, a contributing factor to which may have been the original infant illness of 1914 (pneumonia), which could have left his heart and constitution permanently impaired. See EWB, p. 30. Characteristically, Auden thought the illness psychosomatic in its origins, the result of Britten's 'indecision about emigrating permanently' (source: Caroline Seebohm, 'Con-

scripts to an Age: British Expatriates 1939–1945', Archive; and see
note 2 to Letter 291).

2 Kit had taken a locum at Orford, Suffolk, in January. See EWB, p. 127.

3 Beth's (and her mother's) illness in 1937.

4 Presumably Britten had taken out a subscription to the magazine for
his brother-in-law.

247 **To Arthur Nicholson**[1]
[Typed; carbon copy]

c/o Dr. W. Mayer
The Long Island Home
Amityville, N.Y.
February 26th, 1940

Dear Mr. Nicholson,

Your letter of December 12th, which took nearly a month to
come, reached me when I was paying a visit in Chicago. I
apologise for not having answered it before this, but since then I
have been stricken with a serious form of tonsillitis and general
streptococcic infection which is taking its time about leaving me,
and I still have not reached the convalescent stage, I am afraid.

I am glad that the flat trouble seems finished and I hope that the
telephone company were amenable, although I shan't be
surprised to hear the contrary. In that case, as Hewitt is so elusive,
I think we had better pay it without much further ado.

I don't know what you are doing about money. I hope you
received the £20 from Boosey & Hawkes. If you needed other
small amounts, Barbara can let you have them as she has a little
money on deposit for me. Any other amounts you had better let
me know direct and I will see what can be arranged.

That brings me to a matter which is seriously bothering me. As
the position with regard to my return to England has not
apparently changed, and this ghastly war shows no signs of
stopping, I have got to be prepared to support myself here for
some considerable time. That means I must leave the country
(possibly going to Mexico) and re-enter on quota, so that I am
free to earn money in this country (at the moment I am here on a
temporary visitor's visa). For that reason I have cabled today to
you for a copy of my birth certificate. I don't think you will have
any bother in getting that for me. The other documents needed for
this I can get here, I think, but if not, perhaps you would be good

enough to help me if I give you the details. I do, of course, keep
my British passport in spite of all this, but I should like to know
my position in regard to British Income Tax. The royalties I
received from Boosey & Hawkes are being paid to me through their
New York branch and, as they are royalties which are collected
all over the world, it is immaterial in which country they are paid
me. Does that mean I have to pay English income tax as well as
American? You will understand that the sum, not very great, will
dwindle to an embarrassingly small amount if subject to both
these taxes. American income tax, of course is compulsory if I am
here on quota.

I have been told that owning property in England makes one
liable for taxation there. Of course one is taxed on that property,
but does that mean on one's income not received in that country?
If this is the case would it perhaps be wise to make the Mill over
to perhaps Beth or Barbara (the former seems most suitable to me)?
I am in your hands about this and want you to do whatever you
think wisest straight away without consulting me for it, but I should
very much like a detailed reply as soon as you conveniently can give
it to me. About my income tax for the last year, after I left England
I received no moneys other than the guaranteed royalties from
Boosey & Hawkes mentioned above, which for 1939 came to £350.[2]
I have earned only the small amount of £23 : 12 : 6d from the BBC
which Boosey & Hawkes sent you in October, I think, and the
reading fee for Boosey & Hawkes which comes to 10s. a week.

I think my financial position over here ought to be secure after
a short time, but it is very difficult starting in a new country,
especially at this particular time when America is very "American".
However, I have been lucky in making good friends and good
contacts and so am not too despondent.

I hope this letter has been clear. Please forgive me if it is not,
since my brain has been of necessity idle the last few weeks. I
have had marvellous attention here and the Mayer family has given
me every kindness, and so I must consider myself very lucky.
Please give my love to Mrs. Nicholson. I hope she does not find
rationing too much of a worry. Is John still in England? Give my love
to him when you see him which I hope is frequent. I hope you
yourself are not too upset by the terrible events that happen so
frequently these days.

With best wishes,
Yours sincerely,
[unsigned]

1 The Britten family's solicitor.

2 The earnings equivalent in 1989 would be approximately £23,600 per
   annum. Based on changes of average earnings over the period, £1
   of income in 1938 = £67.50 in 1989.

248 To Sophie (Wyss) and Arnold Gyde
[*Typed*]

c/o Dr. W. Mayer,
The Long Island Home,
Amityville, N.Y.
March 15, 1940.

Dear Sophie and Arnold,

Thank you both very much for your letters about the performance
of Les Illuminations.[1] I am very sorry not to have answered them
before this, but I have been rather ill for the past five weeks and
have been unable to do any correspondence. However, I am much
better now and my amiable nurse–secretary is taking this down
from my broken and rather hoarse dictation.

I was delighted to hear that the performance was so good,
Sophie. I hear you have never sung better and I know what that
means. It must have been a terrific show. I was delighted with
several of the notices which I have seen,[2] but I only saw the
section of them which referred to the work itself and so I don't
know whether you got your due from those snarky old critics –
but anyhow, I hope you did. Thank you too, Arnold, very much
for your very detailed account of the whole show. I think it is
wonderful that so many people turned up in spite of the appalling
weather. It was sickening that the Bridges could not make it. I
hear from them that they were completely snowed up for several
days. I feel rather surprised that our indomitable and efficient
secretary[3] could not control the weather, but seriously, I think she
did a marvellous job in getting the place so full.

How is my godchild? I hope he is flourishing. He sounds as if
he is getting very grown up now, and young Arnold too. I
suppose he is away at Kelly College[4] still, or rather by the time you
get this I expect he will be at home for his Easter holidays. Give
them both my love and say I think lots about them.

Since I last wrote to you I have not done very much because of
this wretched germ (streptococcus). I played my Piano Concerto
in Chicago in January, which I am glad to say was a success. The

old Variations have been done from time to time about the place, and now the great event is the arrival of the Brosi [Antonio and Peggy Brosa] on Monday on the Manhattan.[5] It is very sickening that I shan't be able to go and meet them at the boat, but Peter will go. It will be marvellous to hear first-hand news of you all, because letters, through terribly welcome, seem a little dry and cold after they have been three or four weeks on the sea and in the censor's office! The performance of the Violin Concerto is on March 28th and 29th. I don't know how long the Brosi are going to stay, but I hope a long time. Future plans are vague, but Peter and I expect to go to Mexico within the next month or so, so that we can get on the quota which allows us to work freely here for money. Wystan has done this already. Thank you both very much again for your nice letters about the concert. It was a very extraordinary feeling to realise that the first performance of this work was going on in one's absence – not a very pleasant feeling either, because it is a work I am rather especially fond of and I think the best so far. Can't you persuade Decca to record it with Boyd? He makes lots of records for them and as it had such good notices it ought to sell quite well.[6] Is there any chance of doing it for the BBC? One very interesting thing has happened. Peter is now having lessons with Therese Schnabel[7] in New York where she is now living. It turns out that she knew you, Sophie and Colette[8] quite well. In fact, Colette seems to have had lessons from her. Peter is terribly pleased with her, finds her charming and [?an] extremely good (if severe!) teacher. The improvement in his voice after only a month is quite staggering. It is much clearer, more resonant, and much more controlled. I think you would be delighted with it. He is singing your Illuminations in Chicago in May and he certainly sings them very well. How is Heinemanns, Arnold? I hope the paper rationing has not affected you very severely. Have you anything new and exciting on the stocks? Much love to you all. I am looking forward terribly to seeing you again, but it looks as if it will be a long time ahead since the position with regard to our returning is the same as it was – but while the rationing[9] is on, our absence is more valuable than our presence. Anyhow, if you have any nice snapshots of any or preferably all of you, please send them and I shall be very, very pleased.

With much love
Yours ever,
BENJAMIN

[*Handwritten:*]
Please forgive the typed letter – but I'm not supposed to write much at the moment – much love to all.

1 The first performance of *Les Illuminations*, with Wyss as soloist and the Boyd Neel Orchestra conducted by Boyd Neel, had taken place on 30 January at the Aeolian Hall, London, in a concert promoted by the London Contemporary Music Centre (LCMC). The programme also included Herbert Howells's Concerto for string orchestra, the first performance of Berkeley's *Serenade* for strings (1939), and the first performance of Lord Berners's *Adagio and Variations* and *Hornpipe*.

Sophie Wyss had written to Britten on 1 February:

I wish you had been there as I think we gave a very good performance of it. In another way I was glad you were in America as I might have felt more nervous if I had thought you were in the audience.

It was of course the best work of the evening. Lennox has improved, it was very attractive but still a little thin. Now it is to be given in Switzerland by Sacher and I am writing to Emilie [Wyss's younger sister] to see if she can do the work either for Beromünster or Radio Geneva. I will let you know if something comes out of it!

We had a good audience. Unfortunately the Bridges could not come because of the terrible weather. The Slaters came, Brosa of course and Mrs Behrend! [. . .]

I still feel tired after the nervous strain of presenting a new work but it was worth it. I think I sang at my very best. Boyd was very pleased.

Lennox Berkeley wrote a few days later, on 4 February:

The 'Illuminations' are marvellous – even better than I had expected. It's grand music from beginning to end, and I don't know how to wait to get hold of a score. I must see if I can get B & H to lend me a proof. I think it's an absolute knock-out, and the best thing you've done (of what I've heard). Sophie sang very well – better, I think, than I have ever heard her; and considering that there was very little time for rehearsal, it was a pretty good performance. You've had a wonderful press – but no doubt the cuttings will be sent to you.

Among others who attended the concert were Kathleen Long and Dr Alfred A. Kalmus.

It is of some interest to read what Pears wrote to Britten in 1943 about a proposed recording of *Les Illuminations* by Wyss:

I just felt that perhaps I was rather cross the other night over the phone about the recordings of Les Illuminations. But I do mind so terribly about them. It's grand that Sophie should do them so often [. . .] but not permanently on wax! I couldn't bear to think that people will imagine that's the right way to sing them. Besides a performance like that surely can't wear so well – I mean when you've heard it twice, you've heard it all. Which is wrong.

2 *The Times'* review appeared on 31 January:

The close season in new music imposed on us by the war was triumphantly broken last evening at Aeolian Hall with a concert of works for string orchestra gallantly provided by the Contemporary Music Centre. Four works of substance by English composers were presented, three of them in the nature of suites and the fourth a song cycle, with string accompaniment. This last by Benjamin Britten and called 'Les Illuminations', consisted of some 10 settings of French prose-poems by Rimbaud, whose moods and pictures were touched on with the utmost economy and effect. Britten's natural talent is enormous, and his facility, which sometimes seems to make things too easy, has enabled him to seize upon these short scenes with the required swiftness and concision.

The critic of the *Daily Telegraph*, 31 January, thought that 'greater range and variety marked the Cycle for voice and orchestra' than in Britten's previous work, and that the composer was 'one of the modern musicians fully aware of the importance of true lyrical expression'; he further remarked that 'Sophie Wyss's soprano voice did perfect justice to Benjamin Britten's delightful song cycle'.

Ferruccio Bonavia contributed a review to the *New York Times*, 31 January:

Not one of the four works performed by the Boyd Neel orchestra failed to interest: two of them, Benjamin Britten's 'Les Illuminations' and Lennox Berkeley's 'Serenade', had outstanding merit. 'Les Illuminations' is a setting of ten prose-poems by Arthur Rimbaud describing moods aroused in the poet by the interplay of thought upon thought. They have been treated by Britten with a sure grasp of the psychological problem set by the words. This work alone would suffice to place Britten in the front rank among the composers of the younger generation. The Serenade of Lennox Berkeley is not of equal merit throughout its four movements. But the first has the jollity and ease associated with times different from ours, and wholly foreign to the restless, seeking, tormented artist of today. The other movements, if less original and striking, constituted nevertheless a very praiseworthy effort.

3 Effie Hart.

4 The Church of England boarding and day school at Tavistock, Devon, founded in 1877 by Admiral Kelly, which maintained strong links with the Royal Navy.

5 Date of arrival: 20 March. However, newspaper cuttings record that Brosa

was taken to Ellis Island from the United States liner Manhattan for a hearing by a special board of inquiry [. . .]. Officials at Ellis Island stated he was listed as 'a doubtful visitor', but that more specific reasons for his detention could not be disclosed until after the hearing.

He was released, however, in time to undertake the première of Britten's concerto on 28 March and a Town Hall recital on 8 April which included the American first performance of Van Dieren's Sonata for solo violin. A report of Brosa's arrival in the USA – 'Brosa

Finds American Stay Rewarding Despite Brief Joust with Ellis Island'
– appeared in the *Musical Courier*, 15 May:

The Spanish violinist, who has maintained his nationality despite a twenty-
six years' residence in England, laughed as he recalled how he had been
detained at Ellis Island on his arrival. 'They feared I might become a public
charge, you know,' he said.

Mrs Brosa, charming and talented British wife of the violinist, joined in
the conversation and both pointed out that this visit had been planned long
before the outbreak of the war. Mr Brosa added: 'I had the engagement with
the Philharmonic and John Barbirolli, under whose baton I have played
several times in England, and also my recital in Town Hall on April 8 already
scheduled. So we decided, owing to the war in Europe, to remain here for
our vacation. A pupil of mine [Winifred Roberts] is coming from England to
continue her study with me. I should like to hold some master classes and
do some quartet coaching and teaching. But my principal reason in coming
was to fulfil the engagements I had entered into with the Philharmonic and
to give Mr Britten the finest show I could in the work he wrote for me.'

Brosa and his quartet had already visited the USA in 1930 and 1931
under the auspices of Mrs Coolidge (the link here no doubt had been
Frank Bridge).

6 In fact *Les Illuminations* was not first commercially recorded until
1954, with Peter Pears as soloist, and the New Symphony Orchestra
conducted by Eugene Goossens (Decca LXT 2941). However, Edward
Sackville-West once owned acetate 78 rpm discs of 'Being Beauteous'
and 'Marine', sung by Wyss at the 1939 Proms, and recorded off-
the-air. The discs have not survived.

A Boosey & Hawkes internal memorandum from Ralph Hawkes
to Leslie Boosey, dated 6 May 1943, notes that HMV's Walter Legge
proposed a recording of *Les Illuminations* to be sung by Maggie Teyte.
It was a suggestion that Britten firmly opposed, in spite of Teyte's
considerable reputation in French song. Hawkes wrote:

I think you will find that Britten will raise some difficulties about Maggie
Teyte and I have the strongest feeling that it is Walter Legge, who is very
friendly with her, who is trying to engineer this, as he does not like Britten
or Pears.

7 Therese Behr (1876–1959), German alto, who married the pianist
Artur Schnabel in 1905.

8 Wyss's elder sister. Britten composed his *Two Ballads* – 'Mother Comfort' (Slater) and 'Underneath the abject willow' (Auden) – for Sophie
and Colette Wyss in 1936. However, as his diary for 15 December
1936 reveals, Betty Bannerman took Colette's part at the first performance:

[. . .] meet at 7.15 Wystan Auden & Louis MacNeice for a meal – very
rowdy and pleasant. W. being slightly drunk & arguing hard with the
waitress about 2nd helpings (having always a collossal appetite). Then we

go on to Hallis concert at Wigmore Hall. This is run by him on a Subscription basis (all partakers buying up a certain number of seats). Sophie Wyss & Colette Wyss (her first appearance here) Shadwyck Str. Quartet Natalie Caine & Adolphe take part – as well as Betty Bannerman who takes Colette W's place in my duets as she is scared of the English.

'Music in the Making', *Tempo*, 1, January 1939, reported that Britten had plans for 'a work for three voices and string orchestra to be performed by Sophie Wyss and her sisters'. A handwritten note in the 'Britten file' at Boosey & Hawkes's London office indicates that the proposed work was intended for two sopranos, alto, string orchestra and percussion. The idea, however, came to nothing.

The *Temporal Variations* for oboe and piano were also first performed at the same concert as the *Two Ballads*, by Natalie Caine and Adolph Hallis:

My Oboe Suite which they play well if not brilliantly & which goes down very well – surprisingly – as also do the duets – Montagu Slater's & Wystan's words. After the concert Wystan, Louis M., Peter Burra & Lennox Berkeley, Beth & I all go to Café Royal & have nice supper – back by 12.45.

A notice of the concert appeared in *The Times*, 18 December:

Benjamin Britten's 'Temporal Suite' (does the adjective mean 'ephemeral' in this context?) for oboe and pianoforte is a triviality. It is the kind of music that is commonly called 'clever'. The suite was given an excellent performance by Miss Natalie Caine and Mr Hallis. Two duets, by the same composer, sung by Miss Betty Bannerman and Miss Sophie Wyss, seemed to have a parodistic intention, but, without the words, it was difficult to see their point.

Richard Capell's notice appeared in the *Daily Telegraph*, 16 December:

In his Suite for oboe and piano, faultlessly played by Natalie Caine and Adolph Hallis, Mr Britten is again a sly and nimble Harlequin of music. The neatness of his leg-pulling amounts to grace.

But the fun of his new duets – if fun is not too gross a word for so dry a humorist – which were sung by Sophie Wyss and Margaret Bannerman, was rather missed in the absence of the text (Slater and Auden) from the programme. How much singers rely upon our reading the words as they sing!

Britten and Hallis (1896–1987), the South African pianist and composer, had become acquainted in 1935, and the following year Britten composed two two-piano works – *Lullaby* and *Lullaby for a Retired Colonel* – for the piano duo they had formed. However, an unsuccessful BBC audition on 19 March 1936, at which *Lullaby for a Retired Colonel* was probably heard, seems to have put paid to the possibilities of a partnership: '[. . .] at 1.0 we go to B.B.C. for audition. In concert hall, with vile pianos, & gloomy atmosphere. We play 3 pieces & depart in silence.' Efforts to set up the duo and engage the

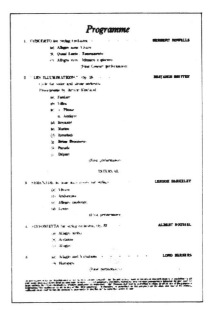

The first complete performance of *Les Iluminations*, 30 January 1940

BBC's interest dragged on but finally petered out. From 1936 to 1939, however, Britten served in an advisory capacity to the series of contemporary chamber music concerts Hallis promoted in London.

Lullaby and *Lullaby for a Retired Colonel* received their first public concert performances on 22 June 1988, as part of the Forty-first Aldeburgh Festival, performed by Peter Frankl and Tamás Vásáry. Both pieces were published by Faber Music in 1990.

9 Food rationing had been introduced in Britain on 8 January.

249 To Ralph Hawkes[1]
From Edwina Jackson
[*Telegram*]

[21 March 1940]

JAPANESE EMBASSY ENQUIRE DATE COMPLETION BRITTENS COMPOSITION ALSO DETAILS REGARDING LENGTH AND NATURE OF WORK

EDWINA JACKSON

1 c/o Boosey & Hawkes, New York.

250 To Albert Goldberg

[*Typed*]

c/o Dr. W. Mayer,
The Long Island Home,
Amityville, N.Y.
March 26, 1940

Dear Albert,

You must have been cursing B. Britten these last six months for
his dilatoriness and general slackness, but for once in my life I
got a good excuse. I have been at death's door these last six weeks,
and only now am I my usual spritely self. I have been in bed and
generally incapacitated with a foul bug of a streptococcic nature
since the beginning of February (I knew no good could come out
of that Chicago visit and those arctic temperatures!) However, I am
now staggering about the place and talking in hoarse whispers
and beginning to pick up the threads of my busy existence once
again. Your letter of February 17th stares up at me from a pile of
unanswered correspondence. So – here goes!

I have still got May 27th pencilled in for Les Illuminations and
Peter Pears. By the way, these have just had their first European
performances, and the London notices are something you dream
about. If you would like those for publicity's sake, I expect
Dr. Heinsheimer would be only too pleased to send you a copy.
Anyway about the date, could you let me know within a week or
so whether I ink it over or rub it out? I inquire because of the other
dates in the district that are being negotiated now. Thank you for
the other press clippings. I must say I enjoyed the Sibelius
symphony with you that night – anyhow you got the key right.[1]

Yes, much as I would like to deny it, I cannot deny the presence
of a Simple Symphony by E.B. Britten. This, I must confess, is as
near as you can get to a best seller with music in England, the
reason being, I suppose, that I wrote it when I was about 12,
which is about the mental age of most conductors (Present company
excluded, of course!). There is nothing exciting about the E. in
the composer's name; I'm sorry to disappoint you. It is merely my
first initial which I dropped for the simple reason that it took so
much longer to sign checks. By the way, if you ever think of
performing this auspicious work, for God's sake don't tell
Heinsheimer, because, as you see, it is not B.H.B. but O.U.P.

I am sorry that the Violin Concerto is not being broadcast,

because Brosa, the violinist, gives the most superb performance
of it, it being terrifically difficult, and compared with it the Sessions
was a five-finger exercise. However, perhaps some other time you
may have an opportunity of hearing those dazzling scales, luscious
harmonies, and heartfelt melodies that always characterize my
music, as you of course know.

I am glad that your concerts at the Studebaker[2] are successful.
Personally, whenever I hear that name I connect it with a very
old and rickety car we had way back about 1919, which hardly ever
went and always best with the brake on.

Enough of this bauble [sic]. Greetings Herr State Supervisor! Let
me have a note soon. How is your underling Harold?

Yours ever,
BENJAMIN BRITTEN

1 This must have been Sibelius's Second Symphony, in the same key
(D) as Britten's Piano Concerto.

2 The motor-car manufacturers and sponsors of musical events. The
Studebaker Theater, Chicago, was one of the venues for the Illinois
Symphony Orchestra's concerts.

251 To Antonio Brosa

c/o Dr. W. Mayer,
Long Island Home,
Amityville, N.Y.
March 31st 1940.

My dearest Toni,

Thank you – thank you – & thank you for a most marvellous
show.[1] I was most terribly pleased – more than I can say. The
work will never be better played or more completely understood
than it was by you on Thursday & Friday, & I am more than
grateful to you for having spent so much time & energy in learning
it. I hope it wasn't altogether a thankless task, but certainly
judging by the rapturous notices you had from all the critics,[2]
people realised what a task you had & how marvellously you
overcame all the difficulties. Let us pray that lots of jobs for you
come as a result of it – & do, if you can manage it sometimes!,
occasionally play the little work that was so proud to introduce you
to Carnegie Hall!! Ralph Hawkes is going to try to press Toronto
for it.[3]

When shall we see you & Peggy? Everyone is keen for it to be soon. We (Peter & I) shall be in New York on Thursday & Friday – but I hope you can make it before that! Perhaps Tuesday?

My love to you both – & many thanks to the most accomplished, intelligent, natural & sweet-sounding (sounds like a M.G.M. [Metro-Goldwyn-Mayer] advertisement, but it's true!) violinist in the world!

Yours ever,

BENJY

1 The first performance of the Violin Concerto on 28 March. As Britten writes in the preceding letter, this première was not broadcast, unlike that of the *Sinfonia da Requiem* when it came to first performance in 1941. Sunday afternoon performances from Carnegie Hall were regularly broadcast. The repeat performance of the *Sinfonia* fell on a Sunday, hence it was broadcast. The performance of the Violin Concerto, however, took place on a Thursday, and the repeat performance the next day.

A curious narrative is attached to the first performance of the Violin Concerto by the New York Philharmonic. Brosa had originally been engaged by Barbirolli to perform the Berg Violin Concerto, on the mistaken assumption, it would seem, that this would have been the first New York performance (Brosa had already appeared as soloist in the work in Geneva). But in fact, Louis Krasner had played the work with the Boston Symphony under Koussevitzky at Carnegie Hall on 11 March 1937 (he had given the American première with the same forces at Boston on 5 March). As alternative, the orchestra then proposed the first American performance of a new concerto by the Russian composer, Nikolai Miaskovsky (1881–1950). His Violin Concerto had been first heard at Leningrad in November 1938. But this proposal too ran into difficulties because of the outbreak of hostilities between Russia and Finland from November 1939 to March 1940. This created tension between the USA and the USSR which made a performance of the Miaskovsky impolitic. Despite these two setbacks Barbirolli did not give up the struggle to get Brosa to the States, and it was the violinist (who of course was well acquainted with Britten's concerto) who suggested that it should be given its world première in New York. Indeed, a letter from Ralph Hawkes to Britten (29 August 1939) suggests that an audition of the Violin Concerto was held in London for Barbirolli's benefit, some time during mid-September prior to Barbirolli's return to the States on the 27th. It was performed by Brosa, with Henry Boys at the piano. (An earlier play-through of the concerto had been arranged by Hawkes for Eugene Goossens.) Barbirolli responded positively and the rest is history. Brosa, according to his wife, memorized the concerto on the transatlantic passage. (Source: Peggy Brosa, Interview with Donald Mitchell, 9 September 1977, London; Archive.)

A recording of the concerto made by Brosa, with the BBC Scottish Symphony Orchestra conducted by Ian Whyte, is in the Archive.

2 Olin Downes, in the *New York Times*, 'Britten Concerto in Première Here', 29 March:

Mr Britten has given us something that has a flavor of genuine novelty in the violin concerto form. Whether a part of this novelty would prove to be a product of misleading glibness and of only exterior value is not to be discussed here. There were many and positive virtues in the music.

There are distinctive melodic ideas. The violin part is more than an obbligato to the orchestral fabric, on the one hand, or the vehicle for an old-fashioned display piece on the other. This is genuinely a concerto for violin and orchestra, with both agencies assuming special responsibilities in the matter. Of certain places it could be said that the violin takes almost the position of accompanist of the orchestra. The moods of the music traverse those of the poetical, the satirical and elegiac. There is modern employment of percussion instruments – perhaps too persistent employment of these devices, which involve not only effects of percussion, but rhythms that become organic parts of the musical development.

The instrumentation, sometimes very simple, often very brilliant, is nevertheless so expert that the violin is never covered when it is intended to show forth, while at no time does the writing appear impractical or ineffective. The concerto is not overlong, but it is of substantial proportions. The effect of length and substance is increased by the close connection of each of the three parts of the concerto. The ending is uncommon, very earnest and far from the conventional 'hoopla' finale. It is probable that greater familiarity with the music would disperse, at least in a measure, the impression of segments rather than of a continuous tonal fabric. How organic, balanced in its proportions, closely interrelated in its material and development will this concerto finally prove to be? The question is only to be answered after repeated hearings.

Mr Brosa, who played with taste and evident authority, presented the work not only with virtuosity, finish and insight, but in a way which suggested strongly the sanction and the deserved approval of the composer. Mr Barbirolli gave of his best to the orchestral part. At the end of the performance the composer appeared, with the conductor and the violinist, to acknowledge long and cordial applause.

Jerome D. Bohm, 'Philharmonic Plays Britten Work for Violin', *New York Herald Tribune*, 29 March:

The first movement, the shortest of the three, is moderato and rather rhapsodic in form. There is no long orchestral introduction, as in the concertos of the classic and romantic periods, but the violin enters after a few introductory measures with a lyrically sustained melody which is opposed to a stubbornly reiterated five-note figure in the orchestra. Unfortunately, Mr Britten has abandoned this promising material too soon and it gives way for a brief period to an 'Eulenspiegel'-like subject which in turn makes way for a Hungarian Gypsy-like episode which brings the movement to an unexpected close.

The second movement, a scherzo, is more conventional in its architectonics and it, as well as the final Passacaglia, owes much to Hindemith of 'Mathis der Maler'. There is a cadenza of considerable length which serves to bind the second and third movements. Two of the variations in the Passacaglia, including the final one, which is suggestive of a wailing lament, reveal promising touches of originality. The violin part makes enormous demands on the capacities of the player, and these were triumphantly met by Mr Brosa, who not only gave a technically brilliant and tonally persuasive account of the music, but obviously believed in it. The instrumentation is effective and Mr Barbirolli provided a carefully adjusted accompaniment. Mr Britten appeared on the platform and modestly acknowledged the liberal applause. Mr Brosa, too, was warmly received.

In Louis Biancolli's notice in the *New York World-Telegram*, 29 March, the composer's onstage appearance was described:

Mr Britten, a tall, gangling lad of 26, came out after the performance and bowed rather shyly and awkwardly. Frankly, he didn't look like the composer of his D minor concerto.* But, then you never can tell in music.

The first performance of
the Violin Concerto (*recte* Op. 15),
28 March 1940: the programme

---

*In the programme, the title of the work was given as 'Concerto for Violin and Orchestra in D minor, Op. 16'. There is no attribution of key in the manuscript of the concerto and none in any of the published versions of the work. Likewise, the title on the occasion of its British première, which confined itself to 'Concerto for Violin and Orchestra, Op. 15'. See Letter 287 and its list of opus numbers.

Mrs Brosa (Interview, op. cit.) recalled that

at the second performance – on the Friday – where usually we were told the ladies of the Philharmonic Society arrived in kid gloves and were afraid to clap too much for fear of busting their gloves [. . .] they must have bust their gloves, because there was a terrific applause after it [. . .]. Ben and Barbirolli and Toni, they had a terrific success.

A photograph of Brosa and Barbirolli backstage at Carnegie Hall after the première was published in *Musical Courier*, 15 April, together with a brief notice of the concert, which opened with Rossini's *Semiramide* overture and ended with Beethoven's Fifth.

3 i.e. to press the Toronto office of Boosey & Hawkes to secure the first Canadian performance of the concerto. But this was not to materialize. See Letter 275.

252 To Leslie Boosey
Boosey & Hawkes, London
[*Cablegram*]

AMITYVILLE
[2 April 1940]

TITLE SINFONIA DA REQUIEM OR FIRST SYMPHONY   SUBTITLE TO MEMORY OF MY PARENTS THREE INTERLINKED MOVEMENTS ABOUT TWENTY MINUTES[1]

GREETINGS
BENJAMIN BRITTEN

1 This was Britten's response to Edwina Jackson's cable of 21 March (No. 249). At this early stage Britten evidently was thinking of the work as his 'First Symphony'. (He had likewise designated his Piano Concerto 'No. 1', and indeed it was originally published as such.) The dedication was finally formulated: 'In memory of my parents'.

253 To Kit Welford
[EWB, *pp. 135–9*]

Long Island Home, Amityville, N.Y.
April 4th 1940

My dear Kit,

I got your last long & extremely interesting letter when I was in New York last week, & as I was feeling extremely low, being convalescent after this beastly strep. bug, it cheered me up enormously. It is so grand to hear all you're doing & with your

extremely intelligent comments – besides you write about the plans
& people [I] want to hear about. When one is as far as this I find
one doesn't think of England in terms of Chamberlain, or London
but in terms of Suffolk, East Anglianites, & ones friends.

Although I was sick that you've had to leave the Mill, I was glad
for your sake that you got a job, & delighted that it was a country
one such as you like, I know.[1] I don't remember Swaffham well –
but I have a vague idea I've had a lunch at the George. I'm hoping
to hear soon that you've got a nice cottage to live in for the period
you'll be there – which I hope will be long, at anyrate for the duration
of this wretched squabble. Thanks for looking after the Mill so well
– I'm sorry that you had the bother with the burned-out pump
engine – hope it didn't cost much. If there's any outstanding
account to be settled, you'd better send the bill to Nicholson (not
that he's got much money to pay it with, I'm afraid, but it'll look
nicer on his desk than yours!) Barbara says she'll help you to pay
for Hart.[2]

Well – we seem to have had a few excitements here. I managed,
the first time for 2 months, to get into New York to hear Toni
Brosa & Barbirolli's boys play my Violin Concerto last week. The
bug hasn't completely left me yet – I still get periodic sore throats
& a form of Uticaria[3] on my face – but I dare say till I have the old
tonsils removed I shan't get completely fit. I've had one of the
best New York internists, Dr. Benjamin Ashe, looking after me –
in addition to Dr. Mayer, & 3 or 4 other M.D's round here! – &
he isn't likely to let any harm come to me – so you might reassure
Beth & Barbara on that point! I don't think I'll have to face
Tonsilectomy until the Fall. Anyhow I was able to make the
platform in Carnegie Hall – & bow to the cheers. I had an excellent
show (Toni played marvellously) & a wonderful reception. The
criticisms were pretty violent – either pro. or con. The N.Y. Times
old critic (who is the snarkyest & most coveted here) was won over,
so that was fine. But two gave me hell in such personal terms
that opinion is that they were political. One of them compared me
to the Bermuda crisis (seizing of American mail –)[4] & said it was
risky, at this moment of shakiness in the British foreign policy, to
produce such a work!!! and said I was an international incident.
I will try & get copies of some of these & send them to you, because
they're very funny – especially one which called me a 'kick-in-
the-pants of a young Englishman' – I was also called 'gangling' –
'loose-jointed'. . . . . . . these Americans! However it's all
publicity.

I want to give you a rough idea of how this country strikes one,
because I hope one day that you'll consider making it at least your
temporary home, but it is an almost impossible job – because it
simply isn't a country. What one state thinks will be laughed at
by 45 of the others – what is possible for the West is impossible for
the East – the New Yorker is as much like the Southerner as a
Norwegian is like a Turk – and says so too. There is only one thing
in common with them at the moment & that is disagreeable – that
is that they are all American – & chauvanistically so, I'm afraid.
They're fed up with Europe – they didn't like it's peace – and
they're suspicious of it's war. They're full of advice as how to run
the rest of the world – & refuse to take any of the consequences.
(I will paint the blackest side of America, first!). Their politics are
the dirtiest so far (except perhaps Canada, which has the
corruption but none of the vitality of the U.S.A.) – & anything from
a Kidnapping case to a War will be used to their own political
ends – at the moment the anti-Rooseveltians, who are anyone from
the bankers to the small capitalist class, are using the German
discoveries in the Polish archives (about Kennedy[5] & Bullitt[6] getting
the States involved in war) to try & prevent Roosevelt from
running a third term.[7] In some ways this country seems to have
the corruption of the Old World & little of its tradition or charm.
There is, too, something very frightening about this conglomeration
of people (& this is true of everywhere – from East to West, &
South to Middle-West) – & that is how terribly easy it is to rouse
the masses (& that is nearly everyone) into a hysteria. The things
that were done to pacifists or pro-Germans in the last war were
unbelievable – & since then there have been plenty of examples of
crowd-hysteria – the Klu-Klux-Klan – negro-lynchings & burnings
– the Martian visit (the broadcast a year or so back)[8] the present
Dies committee with its – "pro-American" searchings – in which
anyone vaguely liberal is labelled as Communist & treated as
such.[9] And another dreadful shock has been the present Bertrand
Russell case – in which the Irish Catholics have prevented him
taking a job at the N.Y. University which was O.Ked by the board
of Directors of the University & one of the student's mothers
objected to a book he'd read![10] The Irish Catholics are the great
curse of this State – that's why the police in New York are so
unscrupulous, hard & rude. The British Bobby is an angel in
comparison! You see, Kit, in so many ways this country is such
a terrible disappointment. Sometimes it seems to have, forinstance,
all the infuriating qualities of youth without any of its redeeming

qualities. Of course I judge mostly from this State – & the little of New England that I've seen – the Middle-West when I went there was quite different, & had nothing of the ultra-sophistication of, say, New York. I <u>hate</u> New York – Wystan compares it to a great Hotel & it's a damn good comparison. It is like the Strand Palace[11] – all glitter, & little gold – nothing stable – everyone on the move – & terribly fashionable (in the worst sense of the word). Everything here is crazes – crazes – crazes. You see – I'm gradually realising that I'm English – & as a composer I suppose I feel I want more definite roots than other people. But against all this one must put the facts that U.S.A. is <u>not</u> engaged solely with killing people (altho' she may be thinking of it more every day) – enterprise <u>still</u> is rewarded in this country, & I'm sure there is a future for this country altho' the next decade or so may be very black. What I want so much is for you to come out here for a visit before you decide anything. I'm going to try & find out for you the <u>medical</u> possibilities here. You know that every emigré has to pass an exam.? Luckily speaking English, you won't have to take the language exam. which is one of the worse bogies. I have an idea that there are some states which have no exam. – I'll find that out for you. We could easily find affidavits for you – & by that time I <u>may</u> have taken out my 1st Citizen papers – which, incidentally, arn't binding in the least. Don't take this tirade too seriously, Kit, because I'm still feeling abit (convalescentally) down after my bug – & I happen to have met lots of Americans recently (R. Hawkes gave a party for me & Toni last week) & I always feel blue after hearing Americans talk about Europe – as they <u>all</u> do, because they are jealous of it – tho' God knows why at this particular moment of history!

My plans for the Summer are this: In May, I go to Chicago for a concert or two: then Peter & I settle down in a small cottage near here & work hard for the rest of the season – he to go back & forwards to N.Y. where he has lessons with Teresa (wife of Arthur) Schnabel – & me to write score after score – because altho' one might have one success, one's got to keep oneself before the public all the time. You I suppose will stay around Swaffham unless any bloody emergency calls you elsewhere (pray God it won't).

Please tell Beth that Mrs. Mayer was delighted with her letter – & that I'm in completely angelic hands here – the Mayers, Titleys, & Peter all treat me as if I were soluble material about to take a bathe! I'll write to her by the next mail. Give my love to Sebastian – & – o, Lord, I've forgotten his birthday – please give him the season's greetings from his devoted God-father & when I have

some spare cash I'll send him some to buy a prayer-book or what
he will———

Much love, & best wishes to you all,

BENJAMIN

Could you please forward the enclosed to Barbara, please? By-the-
way, would you like the Mill as a present? Ask Nicholson, if you
would!!

1 See EWB, p. 135:

After Kit's job at Orford was finished and the snow departed, he hung
around for a while wondering what to do next. So far there was no sign of
his being called up and he thought he might as well look for another locum.
One of the doctors in a partnership at Swaffham in Norfolk had joined the
Army and they were looking for someone to take his place. Kit applied and
was taken on as a locum for as long as he could stay.

2 A gardener/handyman at the Old Mill, Snape.

3 Urticaria: a rash which takes the form of an itchy red weal on the
skin. Britten had written about his illness to Beth on 15 March:

You should have seen my beard & hair. . . . it was marvellous . . . just like
Jaggers Chraggers. And I've got all new skin over my face, hand & feet –
so for once I'm quite clean! (don't whisper it about – but it's possible that
I've had a strange kind of scarlet fever!!)

(See EWB, pp. 133-4 for full text)

'Jaggers Chraggers': Schoolboy slang for Jesus Christ.

4 On 28 March mail was removed by British authorities from a Pan
American westbound Atlantic clipper when it made an unscheduled
stop at Bermuda.

5 Joseph Kennedy (1888–1969) was appointed American Ambassador
in London in 1937, but resigned in 1940, believing that a Nazi victory
was inevitable. He advocated a policy of isolationism for the United
States. His son, John F. Kennedy, was to become thirty-fifth President of the United States, 1961–3.

6 William C. Bullitt, American Ambassador to France (1936–41), and
co-author with Sigmund Freud of *Thomas Woodrow Wilson*.

7 Franklin Delano Roosevelt (1882–1945), thirty-second President of the
USA, was first elected in 1933. He was re-elected on 5 November for
a third term, and on 7 November 1944 for a fourth, an event unique
in American constitutional history.

8 This was the famous Orson Welles broadcast on CBS, *The War of the
Worlds*, based on H.G. Wells's novel of the same title but updated
to give an account of Martians invading New Jersey. Although the
programme (which began at 8 pm on Hallowe'en, 31 October 1938)

was introduced as 'Orson Welles and the Mercury Theater of the Air in *The War of the Worlds* by H.G. Wells', some listeners who tuned in late were panic stricken to hear seemingly realistic communiqués of an assault on Earth by Mars, interrupting a programme of live dance music. 'Fiction' was taken for fact and led to much public disturbance (and disturbances). Next day the banner headlines on the front page of the New York *Daily News* read: 'Fake Radio "War" Stirs Terror Through U.S.'. See also a syndicated feature article by Michael Oricchio on the occasion of the fiftieth anniversary of the programme, *Austin-American-Statesman*, 30 October 1988. For a full description of this celebrated event in the history of radio, see Barbara Leaming, *Orson Welles* (London, Weidenfeld and Nicolson, 1985), pp. 158–62. The most graphic account of the public impact made by *The War of the Worlds* is John Houseman's 'The Men from Mars', reprinted in *The Thirties: A Time to Remember*, edited and with commentary by Don Corigdon (New York, Simon and Schuster, 1962), pp. 583–97, a useful guide to the decade through American eyes.

9 This was a committee of the House of Representatives, chaired by Martin Dies of Texas. The so-called 'Dies Committee', on Un-American Activities, was dedicated to the harrying of radicals in and out of government and became an instrument of conservative retaliation against the New Deal. See Arthur Schlesinger and John M. Blum, 'The New Deal', in John M. Blum *et al.*, *The National Experience*, 6th edition (San Diego, Harcourt Brace Jovanovich, 1965), p. 694.

10 Bertrand Russell (1872–1970), had been invited to teach at New York City College, but the invitation was withdrawn at the last moment:

> An Anglican Bishop was incited to protest against me, and priests lectured the police, who were practically all Irish Catholics, on my responsibility for the local criminals. A lady, whose daughter attended some section of the City College with which I should never be brought in contact, was induced to bring a suit, saying that my presence in that institution would be dangerous to her daughter's virtue.

See *The Autobiography of Bertrand Russell* (London, Allen & Unwin, 1968), Vol. II, pp. 218–19, where a full account of this incident appears. See also Ellen W. Schrecker, *No Ivory Tower: McCarthyism and the Universities* (New York, Oxford University Press, 1986), p. 76 *et seq.*

11 A well-known hotel located in the Strand, London, near Charing Cross and the river Thames, and built in a thirties 'Babylonian' style.

254 To John Pounder

c/o Dr. Mayer,
Long Island Home,
Amityville, N.Y.
April 7th 1940.

My dearest John,

This is an odd place to be answering your very nice & welcome
letter – in the grounds of a lunatic asylum – but, although there's
plenty of reason for it, I am not an inmate of the place! The real
reason is simple enough – on September 1st last year (oh –
memorable day!) Peter (you remember Peter?) & I were staying
with some friends of his; they were Germans, refugees from the
Sturmer[1] & such-like, & well — — — here we still are! You see we
were placed in a rather awkward situation when England decided
to fight the Nazis – Peter's winter season in England was cancelled
(a complete financial crisis for him), & tho' I was desperate to see
my friends & family in England in this new form of Hell, you know
what I feel about fighting and all that. So when we were told by
the Brit. Ambassador that it was our Patriotic duty to stay away
from the home-country (more mouths to feed etc!) we decided
we'd better stay put. Not being financially too happy, this most
delightful family saw our need & pressed us to stay with them –
he is a brilliant Psychiatrist & head M.D. at this home for Mental
diseases – & so, as I said before, here we are – & very happy too.
Peter has been having extensive singing lessons in New York – &
I have worked liked blazes – & had quite alot of performances &
made lots of friends. Of course – when I say we are happy, please
understand that it means under the circumstances. Personally I'm
crazily homesick, & if it were not that Peter looks after me like a
lover,[2] & the family Mayer were surely made in heaven, & that
Wystan Auden's about the place & always coming down here, I
should be home, war or no war, like a shot. Well – let's be honest
about it, John, – America is a great disappointment. I don't know
whether it's just one's acutely sharpened sensitiveness of the
moment, or just that it's a bad patch in American history, but I
find it almost unbearable. [. . .] When I saw the way things were
going in Europe I used to think that the only hope was America –
now I'm sadly disillusioned. This country has all the faults of
Europe & none of its attractions. Where that hope is to be found
now I can't think – except of course in art, & in one's friends. I

personally have never worked so well as at the moment – perhaps as an escape, but I don't think so – but that is a long story & must wait till we meet.

I'm sorry this is so late in coming – but I've been sick for 2 months & unable to write. I was nursed night & day & had 5 doctors in attendance – so I was well looked after. However I was able to struggle up for the premiere of my Violin Concerto at the N.Y. Philharmonic last week, which Toni Brosa played marvellously, & which was a great success – thank God – tho' one or two critics loathed it – in fact one called it an 'International incident' & compared it to the American mails being seized in Bermuda!! Grand to be so important. I am longing to hear from you if you've had your tribunal & what was the result.[3] Good luck, my dear, – what ever you decide to do, in what ever way, will always be understood by me, because I know your integrity & admire it – so be brave! I suppose America will be in this war within a year & then I'll be back ——

Give my love to your parents. Peter sends lots to you & so do I.

Courage mon ami, le diable est mort,[4]
Love,
BENJAMIN

1 A reference to *Der Stürmer*, the violently anti-Semitic newspaper, established by the Nazis and edited by Julius Streicher.

2 Already, in 1937, Britten knew he could address Pounder as a wholly understanding friend. On 17 April he wrote in his diary for that year – after visiting with Beth their parents' graves and attending a wedding – '[. . .] I meet John Pounder for a long walk & much "queer" talk – he's a sympathetic dear [. . .].' This conversation took place two weeks or so after he had had similar confiding conversations with his brother Robert (see note 1 to Diary for 23 August). These 1937 conversations are in themselves suggestive of the freedom to talk that Britten found after his mother's death at the end of January.

3 Pounder had intended to register as a conscientious objector in the UK.

4 'Courage my friend, the devil is dead.' Quotation from Charles Reade's *The Cloister and the Hearth*, often exchanged between friends at times of misfortune.

255   To Enid Slater

c/o Mrs. Mayer,
Long Island Home,
Amityville, N.Y.
April 7th 1940.

My dear Enid,

All right – please forgive me – I know I've been very dilatory but
this time it really is not my fault. Since Christmas life has been
just one thing after another. I had to go & play my piano concerto
in Chicago & stay in the district for abit, meeting people & seeing
conditions – that took quite a time – & also I was incapacitated by
a blasted 'flu cold which wouldn't go, & which developed at the
beginning of February into a severe attack of a Streptococcii germ
which laid me low for nearly two months – until about a week
ago when I struggled up to New York for the first performance of
my Violin Concerto. So I've got some pretty good excuses! I was
delighted with your letters – & the children's contributions – I feel
very guilty about them – I must find up some nice postcards for
them. I was terribly bucked that you find 'Les Illuminations' to
your taste – I must say I'm pleased with them myself, & yearn to
hear them on an orchestra. So Sophie sang them well – but I bet
you'd get a shock if you heard Peter do them – he's been having
lessons from Terese (wife of Artur) Schnabel & singing 100% better;
he sings them wonderfully & we're going to do the first U.S.A.
performance in May in Chicago I think.[1] I'm looking forward to
your hearing the Vln. Concerto, which Toni plays so marvellously.
It was really a great success here – the audience really was moved
I feel (especially for the Phil. Audience, & for a work which is
very quiet and subtle) – & the critics were quite excited (60% pro.
40% con). One was so angry as to compare it to the seizing by
the British of American mail in the Bermudas, saying it was unwise
to produce such a work by an Englishman in such a shaky period
in English foreign policy! However, that may be quite a good thing,
controversy (tho' unpleasant for the controversee) being good
publicity – & everything in this country is valued by publicity. God,
how I hate it all. I always make a resolution never to attend any
more first performances – it is terrifying, & I make everyone all
round me uncomfortable, by feeling sick, having diarrhoea, &
sweating like a pig! I have now got lots of things on the stocks.
I've got a sudden craze for the Michael Angelo Sonnetts & have

set about half a dozen of them[2] (in Italian – pretty brave, but there
are people here who speak good Italian, & after Rimbaud in
French I feel I can attack anything! I've got my eye on Rilke, now
& Hölderlin!)[3] And a crazy commission from the Japanese
government has come up again & I'm planning a work with plenty
of 'peace-propaganda' in it – if they will accept it – And a String
Quartet[4] – & arranging some Tschaikovsky,[5] etc. etc. All this must
sound pretty callous to you, living as you are in a pretty awful form
of hell – with life going to pieces all round you, with sensible people
doing stupid things for apparently sensible reasons, & not knowing
what to expect from day to day. My dear, I do sympathise – as I
know what you particularly are going through – & as far as I
understand you, you haven't got any blind creed to carry you
through it.[6] But if you're living in an active form of hell, we're
living in a passive form of it over here. I hate to have to admit it,
but America seems to be letting us down in every way. I don't mean
us personally, so much as all the things one believes in. She is so
narrow, so self-satisfied, so chauvanistic, so superficial, so
reactionary, & above all so ugly. People & Scenery. I know that
there are striking scenes, grand canyons, & water-falls, but the older
I get (& perhaps the longer I stay away from England & Europe!)
the more I realise, that beauty (in people as well as things) doesn't
consist in striking features, but in character, expression & general
atmosphere. This country is dead, because it hasn't been lived in,
because it hasn't been worked on. It may come in several hundred
years but I doubt it, if the Americans go on as they are going on
at the moment. Everything comes too easily – success, wealth,
luxury. They have no standards; no culture – or rather the culture
they have is acquired in three terms' work (each term – (1) Art –
(2) Appreciation – (3) Renaissance – perhaps!) at a University. I
get mad at them for the way they talk about this war, too – as if it
were a rather boring play or film that didn't start moving as it
should. I wonder if they realise that every day – so [some] poor
wretch gets killed on the Western Front – how taxes are soaring
in England – what hell it is to be living in Germany at the moment
– or how much the Russians must have loathed freezing in the
Finnish snow. Of course it does all seem silly at this distance – &
peoples mistakes seem more obvious – but these bastards have
no imagination. I'm sorry – it's probably Spring that makes one so
bad tempered – England is so heavenly at this time – & I've got
to let Snape – o dear, o dear . . .

Don't bother anymore about Wulff. Thank you for being so sweet about it. Your photo of me has been used in several papers . . . !

Much love – write again soon – I adore hearing about you & all your doings.

Love to the kids & Montagu.

BENJAMIN

I have no definite plans for the future – but have of necessity to stay here quite abit longer ——

1 In fact the American première was to take place in New York, on 12 May 1941.

2 These were finally to become *Seven Sonnets of Michelangelo*, Op. 22, for tenor and piano, completed at Amityville, on 30 October. Mrs Mayer collaborated with Pears in providing the English translations of the sonnets for the programme of the first performance, at the Wigmore Hall, on 23 September 1942. These same translations also appeared in the first published edition of the songs. See also note 2 to Letter 391.

There is some evidence to suggest that Britten may have thought of setting Michelangelo in the late 1930s. Was he introduced to Michelangelo as poet by Auden, who was likewise to introduce him to the poetry of Rimbaud? Across the top of a letter from Auden to the composer dating from November 1937, Britten has noted, 'Holyroyd – Michael Angelo a life of / Duckworth'. Perhaps Auden had recommended this biography (by Sir Charles Holroyd, first published in 1903) to the composer. But see also note 2 to Letter 313.

In 1989, Wulff Scherchen recalled 'Ben complaining of a "mental block" over a Michael Angelo Sonnet & "putting it away". I'm sure I saw the Italian text.' Scherchen's memory must date from the prewar period (1938/9), for when he and Britten met again in England in 1942, the *Michelangelo Sonnets* had been in their final shape for nearly two years. If Britten had attempted some Michelangelo settings before his departure to America, then his return to the texts in 1940 would be entirely characteristic of his creativity (see, for example, note 3 below).

3 Britten was not to set Rilke. Hölderlin, however, he tackled at a much later stage, in 1958 – the *Sechs Hölderlin-Fragmente*, Op. 61, where once again the English translation was prepared by Mrs Mayer and Pears and published in the Boosey & Hawkes edition. This was another and wholly characteristic instance of a long period of creative gestation.

4 The first mention of Britten's String Quartet No. 1 in D, Op. 25, composed during the summer of 1941 at Escondido, California.

5 The Tchaikovsky arrangement remains unidentified. Was it perhaps something for Lincoln Kirstein and his ballet company, who were to perform Britten's instrumentation of Chopin's *Les Sylphides* in 1940? See note 2 to Letter 310.

6 Probably a reference to the inflexible political convictions of Enid Slater's husband, Montagu.

256 To Beth Welford

[EWB, *pp. 139–42*]

c/o Dr. Mayer, Long Island Home,
Amityville, N.Y.
April 28th 1940

My darling old Beth,

I feel dreadful about not having written to you for so long – in fact I haven't written to anyone these last three weeks. It is partly that I simply have had no time, & partly that at these beastly 'eventful' times one just doesn't want to sit down & write about current events, & the trouble is one cannot think of much else to write about. Besides when posts are so slow & irregular one knows one's letters are hopelessly out of date & untopical when they reach their destination. Anyhow I am going to send this 'surface' mail since the air-mail is hopeless – the Clippers have been delayed at Horta[1] these last three weeks.

Thank you very much indeed for the socks & tie that Peggy brought with her – I am afraid I forgot to thank you in Kit's letter, but anyhow I do it now, & I did really appreciate them <u>very</u> much. The socks are fine – you can't get nice woollen socks in this country, people don't seem to wear them, & the weather has been bitterly cold – until to-day, which is marvellously hot & sunny in fact I am writing this in the garden of the Mayers & nearly frizzling in the heat. The tie is just the right colour – what impeccable taste you have, old thing! Thank you also for the sweet thought. It was lovely to have Peggy arriving with a parcel from you – a real contact. She tells me she's written to you & told you all the news – probably more than I could or would think of telling you – & Mrs. Mayer's going to write again. She would have written before but has been away & busy since she got back. I'm feeling fine now. I am having a long 'doing' at the dentist at the moment, & I find that the American dental art, so boosted, is not so hot after all – nothing compared with Pop or Mrs. Harwood[2] even, – but

perhaps this is just the local man's failing. Certainly they have all
the gadgets imaginable – including portable X-ray – but the
handling is so uncouth. Then within the next month or so Peter
& I are going to have our tonsils removed – & then we'll be as good
as new, I hope. Poor Peter, by the way, has had the most horrible
carbunkle these last weeks; they are horribly painful (or rather,
irritating) things. Take ages to drain. I think it's probably just
one's mental condition that gets one down these days. One just
feels so hopeless & helpless – & impossible to settle-down. In the
normal way it wouldn't be so difficult to decide whether to stay
British or change to American – but at the moment I am just
marking time until I can get back to England! I suppose there
wouldn't be much sense in coming at the moment – because my
work is the most important thing, & I suppose it is best to stay
where [I] can work most easily, & that is it over here. But the
idea of spending one's life here appalls me at the moment. Probably
in normal times it would be O.K. – but at the present time one is
inclined to see all America's bad points & England's good ones.
When Americans start telling one what to do about Nazis & there
are Englishmen dying by the 100 in Norway[3] one's inclined to be
unreasonable, I find.

However for the moment I am stuck here. The proposed Japanese
Government commission has materialised & I now find myself
faced with the proposition of writing a Symphony in about 3 weeks!
Something went wrong with negotiations – which started last
October & I only heard officially on Friday![4] However financially
it relieves one of worry for abit, & I should have written the work
anyhow – it is a Sinfonia da Requiem, combining my ideas on war
& a memorial for Mum & Pop.[5] So I shall be pretty occupied for
abit. Then I go to Chicago to do the first American show of Les
Illuminations with Peter, & that'll take a week or so. Then Tonsils.
Then probably Mexico for quota. Then I've lots of work to do for
Ralph Hawkes for the Summer – & Paul Bunyan which was held
up through my being sick. God grant that something will have
materialised in the world situation by then – & that I can come
home & see you!

I am longing to hear your news – I pray that you haven't had
your lives affected by this new turn of events, & that you are still
at Swaffham. I had a long letter from Robert all about his new
school-job. I must say I'm relieved that he is out of the way safely
– surely he can't be called upon for service – with this job & his
bad sight. I must write to Barbara – but anyhow give her all the

news & lots of love. I hope to be able to send some more money
soon to her – & you all. You must let me do this as it pleases me
so much! Any news of the Mill? I'm waiting for a note from
Nicholson saying whether you've let it – but personally I should
like to have it kept open in case Barbara/&/or you want to go there
ever – & I'll send money for Hart. What about Lennox sending
money occasionally, because after all we're storing his furniture for
him?!

Blast! – I've started a new page & I meant to stop now because
it's getting so late, & I've got to go to the dentist at 9.0 in the
morning. Well, I'll keep this & write some more to-morrow – I
don't think it'll matter as there are probably only very few boats
going at the moment, & they never advertise sailing times anyhow.
So sleep well, my dear, although by now you must be well asleep
– 11 p.m. here – 4 a.m. with you – you, Kit & Sebastian – how nice
it seems!!

––––––

[continued 30 April]

I am sorry not to have finished this yesterday but I had a hectic
day with much writing & an awful visit to the dentist – no more
of that man for me – he's an old butcher, the most callous thing
you could imagine. So I'll find another one in New York. I enclose
a copy of the N.Y. edition of 'Tempo' which reprints an article that
I wrote (with Peter's considerable aid!) for the [New York] Times,[6]
& also some criticisms of the Violin Concerto – only the good ones
of course! If I can find any other amusing things I'll put them in.
This is only to bring your 'lost' brother a little closer to mind! I
hope it doesn't need it, because you are terribly much in my
mind. Strictly entre nous, this spring gets me down a lot – and
homesickness is not a pleasant disease – personally I think
Streptococcic infection is preferable!

Much love to you all three,
& good luck to you,
Love,
BENJAMIN.

1 The Portuguese Azores in the North Atlantic, about 900 miles west
  of Lisbon and a staging post for the clippers *en route* for the USA.

2 Britten's London dentist in Sloane Street who treated him after his
  father's death.

3 On 9 April Germany had invaded Denmark and Norway, and on

the 14th British naval forces landed in an unsuccessful attempt to take Trondheim.

4 Although it seems that there was inordinate delay in Britten's receiving official confirmation of the Japanese commission – in Letter 226 (December 1939) he had given up hope that the commission would come off – already in February, on the Japanese side, there was advance notice of the invitation to Britten and no suggestion that it had not been offered and accepted. The *Japan Times*, 25 February, under the heading, 'Leading European Composers Writing Symphonic Work for 26th Centenary':

Promoting international friendship through the medium of music, Europe's leading composers are writing symphonic works which they will dedicate to Japan and in which the 26th centenary of the Japanese Empire will be glorified, it was revealed Saturday night.

Through their diplomatic envoys stationed in Japan, the governments of several nations have expressed the desire to contribute toward the celebrations, being held in the course of this year throughout the Japanese Empire, and proposed to have their leading composers write symphonic works for the occasion.

Thus far, it has been decided that Richard Strauss, of Germany; Jacques Ibert, of France; Ildebrando Pizzetti, of Italy; Sandor Fellesz [Veress], of Hungary, and Benjamin Brittain [*sic*], of England, dedicate their compositions to Japan.

A further report appeared in the same newspaper on 12 May, but this time, interestingly, a cloak of anonymity had descended on the British contribution. Presumably this reflects the delay in the confirmation of the commission to which Britten himself refers, very possibly the result of the difficulties of wartime communication between Tokyo, London and New York. The first work to be delivered was by Sandor Veress, and the report continues:

[. . .] it is expected that compositions from Richard Strauss, the venerated German composer, and from an English composer whose name was not available this morning at the British Embassy here, will be received in Tokyo by the end of this month. Early in June the scores of works by Jacques Ibert, leading French composer, and by Ildebrando Pizzetti, prominent representative of the modernistic Italian school, are to reach Japan.

The final report that we have been able to trace was published in the *Japan Times* on 21 July. It records the arrival of Strauss's *Festmusik* – an autographed photocopy 'bound in parchment, engraved in silver letters on the cover page, and . . . to be presented to His Majesty the Emperor' – and Ibert's *Festive Overture* (the original manuscript!), and continues:

The number of compositions expected here from Europe for celebration of Japan's anniversary will be completed early in autumn, as a work by Benjamin Britten, English composer, is expected to arrive on the Tatuta Maru, about August 10, and the score by the Italian composer Ildebrando Pizzetti is to reach here before the end of September.

No work of Britten's has a more complex history and chronology. At this point when Britten himself documents confirmation of the commission, it is perhaps important to remind ourselves that when the proposal was originally made in the autumn of the preceding year, it was the scheme for the *Sinfonia* with which Britten had responded. It was therefore somewhat ingenuous of him to suggest after his return to the UK (see note 2 to Letter 297) that 'When [confirmation] finally arrived I was working on the "Sinfonia da Requiem" [. . .] and I replied that the only work I could provide in the time would be the said "Sinfonia da Requiem".' In fact, this had been the project from the outset of the protracted negotiations.

5 A particularly important comment this, which throws fresh light on the *Sinfonia*. The work has generally been regarded hitherto as a tribute to the composer's parents. But Britten's own words show that the *Sinfonia* was also a specifically wartime piece, with its *Dies irae* scherzo clearly written in the vein and spirit of earlier 'Dances of Death' (in *Our Hunting Fathers* (1936) and *Ballad of Heroes* (1939)).

6 See note 3 to Letter 243.

257   To Albert Goldberg

c/o Dr. Mayer,
123, Louden Avenue,
Amityville, N.Y.
April 29th 1940

Dear Albert,

Enclosed are programme notes for 'Les Illuminations' & a note on Peter Pears's career which I thought might be useful to you.[1] Photos (decent ones this time!!) will be following in a day or so. By-the-way are you going to let me conduct the old work? – no aspersions being cast of course, but I do like to wield the old baton! How would the band like it? Or would my English accent worry them – but I promise to learn the American names for the notes![2] When do you want us – I presume the week before the show? Let me have a note about that.

No more now – fearfully busy writing a symphony (& how).

Love to all,
Yours,
BENJAMIN B

1 Britten's [and Pears's?] programme notes have survived among the Goldberg papers at the Archive and include these two paragraphs:

[Rimbaud's] short life as a poet was an erratic and turbulent one, generally near starvation and often homeless, sometimes with his friend Verlaine sometimes alone, and much of it was set in the most sordid surroundings, in Paris London and Brussels; but throughout it, the boy's inspiration remained radiant and intense. The word "Illuminations" suggests both the vision of a mystic and a brightly coloured picture, and Rimbaud's biographer, Enid Starkie, says that at this time Rimbaud did in some way identify himself with God, and imagined these poems to be directly inspired. Intensely original and in many places obscure, they are in fact visions of the world he lived in, violent and sordid, which was for Rimbaud at the same time so horrifying and so fascinating.

The composer has taken seven of these poems, six in prose and one in verse, and has made them into a cycle. As a recurrent motto he has chosen the arrogant cry from "Parade" – J'ai seul la clef de cette parade sauvage – I alone hold the key to this savage parade. It appears in the opening Fanfare and in the Interlude, thus serving to bind the work together, as well as to remind the listener of the visionary quality in Rimbaud's utterances.

2 American nomenclature follows the German system, e.g. ♪ = semiquaver (UK) = sixteenth note (USA).

258 To Beata Mayer

c/o Mayer,
123 Louden Av.,
Amityville, N.Y.
May 1st [1940]

My dear Beatty,

So you see I couldn't come up to New York after all.[1] I may come up on Friday, but I can't be certain, as my new baby is giving me the hell of a trouble being born, & as that is at the moment rather an important matter I must let other things bow before it – much as I should like to do them! I'll let you know so that when I do come up you won't be all booked up & so forth.

How are you? I hope that you're still being treated like Porcelain – & that no one has cracked you yet. How's Ralph? I haven't written a letter in weeks, & am quite resigned to watching the pile on my table grow & grow. I can't even be bothered to put them in the right folders anymore!

Life goes on a pace here. Ulli [Ulrica] has now honoured me with black looks & we have wonderful duels at meals; I've got the head-shaking act taped now I think – quite the genuine article!

Mr Squires[2] is v. bad – & Mildred's all upset, poor dear. The
Carbunkle is much better & so Peter's spirits improve – unless he
sees a newspaper. Rascher here to-day – the Brosas over the week
end – unless anything happens to Mr Squires, I suppose. And I
should be writing music & here I am writing a letter to you – well –
well. But I must stop. So good-bye, old thing. Be a good girl –
won't you? Not too much tippling!

Love,

BENJAMIN

1 Beata was staying with Joseph Scharl and Wolfgang Sauerländer in
New York. 'Every two or three days,' she replied to Britten, 'Ralph
[Hawkes] employs me as a secretary for an hour or so and I like it
very much.' Later in the year he was to employ her on a more
substantial basis (see note 3 to Letter 267). In her undated letter she
wrote further:

I'm sorry to hear that your newest baby [*Sinfonia da Requiem*] gives you so
much trouble. I just wrote a very businesslike letter to the Jap Consul in
confirmation of your interview there. Ralph even trusted me so far as to let
me sign it, because he had to go out.

The letter in question was addressed to Tomio Mori, the Japanese
Vice-Consul in New York, and confirmed the terms for the commissioning of the *Sinfonia da Requiem*. The most important clauses
were (1) and (3):

(1) You will pay him the sum of 7000 Yen, approximately $1650. 2000 Yen
of this will be paid now in New York, and the remaining balance upon
delivery of the orchestral score.
[. . .]
(3) He will deliver the orchestral score of a work of symphonic character,
to play for about 20 minutes for full orchestra, and your people in Tokio
will arrange to have the parts copied out there.

Beata's letter ended:

Why not take an afternoon and come up to Claremont Avenue and dictate
all the letters you like? You can even do it on the roof, unless it rains, and
the view might inspire you. So long, dear. I miss you rather, because I have
no Symphony to write which keeps me busy.

2 Mrs Titley's father.

259 To Albert Goldberg
From Elizabeth Mayer
[*Typed*]

Amityville, N.Y.
The Long Island Home.
May 7, 1940

Dear Mr. Goldberg,

Benjamin has asked me to write an answer to your letter of May 4 to you, as he is at present very busy with a new work. He has given me a short sketch of his answer on the different questions, and I do hope to deliver them to your satisfaction.

1. Time of LES ILLUMINATIONS 22–23'.
2. It will be the first <u>American</u> performance.
3. B.B. is communicating with Boosey and Hawkes re English text.
4. He will try to be in Chicago for the Wednesday rehearsal.
5. He is giving the following suggestions for the programme: The Overture <u>must</u> be classical and lightly scored. Why not
GLUCK, Iphigenie in Aulis, – or BEETHOVEN, Prometheus, – or ROSSINI, La Scala di Seta, – MOZART, Così fan tutte, – or a Concerto Grosso by HANDEL? Then:
LES ILLUMINATIONS –
– Intermission –
Symphony: MOZART, Jupiter Symphony
    or SCHUMANN, II, III, or I.
        ,, BEETHOVEN, VI.
        ,, MAHLER, IV.
        ,, SCHUBERT V. or VII.

Benjamin and Peter's American "family" is very glad of your friendship toward B. and your interest in his work, in which we have such great faith. We do hope to see you here some day on this island, when you are coming east! All the best for the concert!

Warmly,
ELIZABETH MAYER

260 To Albert Goldberg
From Peter Pears

c/o Dr. Mayer, Amityville, L.I.

[May 1940]

Dear Mr. Goldberg,

Benjamin asked me to send the enclosed texts (both French and English) of "Les Illuminations". I hope you will be able to print one or the other in the programme. If you print the English text, the quotations from it in the Programme-note we sent you before will hardly be necessary.

I am looking forward so much to singing with your orchestra. I know I shall enjoy it enormously. It's a lovely work and I'm determined to give it a good show.

With regards from us both

Yours sincerely

PETER PEARS

261 To Elizabeth Sprague Coolidge

c/o Dr. Mayer,

Long Island Home,

Amityville, N.Y.

May 16th 1940.

Dear Mrs. Coolidge,

Thank you so much for your letter – which I was delighted to get. I am so sorry that we have been unable to meet this winter, but for me it has been a terrible time with great pressure of work, considerable illness, & of course terrible anxiety & disruption of one's normal life by this dreadful war in Europe. I was disappointed not to be able to come to your Washington Festival, of which I hear such excellent accounts from my friends the Robertsons[1] & Antonio Brosa.

About the quartet I am writing for the Grillers,[2] the arrangement at the moment is that they should play it in their scheduled tour over this country next season, which should mean a considerable number of performances – & so far I haven't heard that their tour will be cancelled through the present circumstances.[3] So it would seem that it will have been played a good deal before your Pittsfield Festival[4] in September, perhaps too often for you to

consider it advisable for inclusion. But as I have always wished
to have a work included in one of your Festivals, would you
perhaps let me write a work specially for you? Perhaps a Piano
quintet (I should love to play the piano part myself!) – or what
combination of instruments would you consider suitable?[5] I am
afraid that I have no other chamber work which would meet your
requirements.

I have sad news from the Bridges[6] – it is tragic that they should
have to go through this terrible time in England – & I fear worse
is to come.

With kindest regards,
yours very sincerely,
BENJAMIN BRITTEN

1 Rae Robertson (1893–1956), Scottish pianist, and his wife, Ethel Bart-
    lett (1896–1978), English pianist. From 1928 the Robertsons toured
    extensively as a duo in Europe and North and South America. Britten
    was to compose his *Introduction and Rondo alla Burlesca*, Op. 23, No.
    1 (1940), and *Mazurka Elegiaca*, Op. 23, No. 2 (1941), and the *Scottish
    Ballad*, Op. 26 (1941), for them. The composer and Pears visited the
    Robertsons in California in the summer of 1941.

2 The Griller String Quartet, whose members remained unchanged
    throughout the quartet's lifetime (1928–61): Sidney Griller, Jack
    O'Brien, Philip Burton (who had been a member of Boyd Neel's
    orchestra), and Colin Hampton. Apart from the standard quartet
    repertory, the Grillers played many twentieth-century works, several
    of which were dedicated to them.

3 The Griller Quartet had started its successful tours of the USA in
    1938–9. The projected 1940–41 tour was in fact cancelled and the
    members of the Quartet joined the RAF Orchestra. Britten's First
    String Quartet, Op. 25, originally was to be written for the Grillers,
    but in the light of the changed circumstances of wartime, with the
    composer resident in the USA, the commission was undertaken by
    Mrs Coolidge and the first performance of the work was given under
    her auspices and performed on 21 September 1941 by the Los Angeles
    Coolidge String Quartet. It was the Grillers, however, who gave the
    first English performance of the quartet at the Wigmore Hall,
    London, on 28 April 1943, after Britten's return from the USA, when
    the music critic of *The Times*, 29 April, wrote:

    Two new works of chamber music made an eventful programme at Wigmore
    Hall last night. Gordon Jacob's clarinet quintet and Benjamin Britten's string
    quartet were played for the first time here.
    [. . .]
    Britten's quartet is more unconventional and more experimental. These

are qualities not normally found in this composer, who has a way of unobtrusively going straight to his point. Certainly his last three vocal works did not prepare one for the striking juxtaposition of sharply, almost harshly, contrasted elements in three of the four movements of this work. Only in the finale is there his old decisive handling of a clear and forceful theme, which brings exhilaration to the ear after some slight sense of uneasiness. Not that there is any cause for alarm: on the contrary, it rather looks as though he has begun to advance from his easy accomplishment into some new phase of development in his thought which will be watched with interest.

4 The Berkshire Festivals of Chamber Music were held at Pittsfield, Massachusetts, under the patronage of Mrs Coolidge. They had begun in 1918 as the South Mountain Chamber Music Festival.

5 Alas, this proposal never materialized.

6 The Bridges had evidently been troubled by air-raids, in addition to which Marjorie Fass had been ill during April with sciatica and had convalesced at their Friston home.

262   To Albert Goldberg

c/o Dr. Mayer,
123, Louden Avenue,
Amityville, N.Y.
May 16th 1940

My dear Albert,

I am distressed that this has happened. Peter & I were both looking forward so much to coming to perform with you, in fact our lives at the moment seemed to pivot round that date – "yes, we can do that after Chicago" – kind of thing ——— but the circumstances are just too much for us. For one thing we have this appalling financial news from England, which just makes our whole future extremely precarious;[1] then, the other job we were coming for in Grand Rapids[2] fell through (conductor was ill); again my publisher was going to pay for me to go to Battle Creek (to hear more brass bands!) & they have now suffered great losses and couldn't do it – so it meant we would have to come to Chicago on our own steam – & well, Albert, it just couldn't be done! I am personally very sick about it, as I wanted to see you again so much (& that assistant of yours!) & also because I wanted to hear 'Les Illuminations' which has been done so often in Europe & which I shall now have to wait ages to hear. However let's hope that things will be straightened out by Autumn (sorry, I mean Fall!) &

that we can come to you then. In the meantime – I suppose you couldn't do Mont Juic instead on that programme – I don't want to be dropped altogether, you see! – that would be a first American performance.

By-the-way, what would you say if I wrote a special orchestral piece for you, as a peace offering, for you to do next season?[3]

In the meantime – all my apologies, & I do hope this hasn't made havoc of all your arrangements – but if Europe insists on blowing itself up, I suppose it is not surprising to have repercussions as far away as North Dearborn Street![4]

> Yours most apologetically & lacrimosely![5]
>
> BENJAMIN B

1 Britten had cabled to Goldberg on 15 May:

FRIGHTFULLY SORRY   TERRIBLE FINANCIAL NEWS FROM EUROPE   DON'T
SEE HOW WE CAN AFFORD TO COME AND PERFORM.

This message probably also indicates the notional fees that Britten and Pears were likely to receive from the Works Progress Administration engagement. Some of the difficulties of Britten's personal financial position at this time – and in particular an overdraft at his bank in the UK – are made clear in Letter 275. But all these troubles were precipitated by the wartime decision made early in 1940 in England that there were to be no further transfers of monies overseas, a constraint that cut Britten off from his principal source of finance, his publishers in London. It is clearly this 'crisis' which prompted Britten's telegram.

2 Britten had been in Grand Rapids in January. In a letter to Goldberg of 3 February outlining his plans for a visit to the Midwest, he had written: 'It looks as if the Grand Rapids affair will be about the 10th [May].'

3 Nothing came of this suggestion.

4 The address of the Illinois Music Project of which Goldberg was State Director.

5 An oblique reference to the first movement of the *Sinfonia* on which Britten was engaged, i.e. the *Lacrymosa*.

263 To John G. Coffrey
[*Typed*]

c/o Dr. W. Mayer
123 Louden Avenue
Amityville, N.Y.
May 23rd, 1940

Dear Mr. Coffrey,

Your letter of March 31st had an exciting journey before it
eventually reached me on Long Island where I have been staying
for the past year. It spent some time in the Channel Islands, where
Dr. Ireland is now staying, before visiting my publishers in
London who sent it to their branch in New York. Naturally I was
pleased to get such a travelled missile.[1]

I was delighted to hear that my piece had been so well received
in Berkeley.[2] It is always encouraging to hear of successful
performances. You ask whether I am a struggling young composer
and I should say that just about describes my present condition.
True, I have had a certain amount of success in Europe and recently
a little in this country and I have a very generous and helpful
publisher, but when does writing music ever cease to be a struggle?

I hope you won't despair of getting your beautiful dream
compositions down on paper. Don't be disappointed if the result
falls short of the initial glorious idea. It is only a matter of practice
and experience, and believe me, when you get near to your goal it
is a pretty exhilarating sensation and well worth the years of weary
labour.

If I can remember it I will write the theme on the programme as
you asked me.[3] Forgive me for not writing more at the moment but
I am horribly busy.

Yours sincerely,
BENJAMIN BRITTEN

P.S.   Yes, in one spot the strings are divided into eleven parts, not
including four soloists, but this is nothing to be imitated.

Enc.

1 In the first instance the letter must have been sent to England, c/o
   John Ireland, Britten's former teacher. The news of Britten's residence
   on Long Island seems not to have reached California.

2 The *Frank Bridge Variations* had been performed at Berkeley on 31
   March by the University of California Symphony Orchestra con-

ducted by Albert I. Elkus, a concert in commemoration of the Seventy-second Charter Anniversary of the University. In the same programme Arthur Bliss conducted four dances from his ballet, *Checkmate*.

3 Britten returned the programme duly inscribed with his signature and the theme of the *Variations*.

264 To Albert Goldberg

c/o Dr. Mayer,
Long Island Home,
Amityville, N.Y.
May 26th 1940

My dear Albert,

Just in case you have time and/or the inclination this is the explanation of all the hullaballoo: The enclosed letter [i.e. Letter 262] was written immediately after my first wire to you & is, I think, self-explanatory. Just as I was about to send that, the good doctor with whom I've been staying these last nine months offered me the cash to come with Peter Pears & so I immediately re-wired you.[1] You couldn't re-alter it – which I understood perfectly & anticipated. Then Peter P. made an arrangement to have his tonsils out, & now the Doctor forbids him to sing as soon as June 17th, & that coupled with the complete disorganisation of our plans makes the new date impossible. So – there we are. Let's hope & pray for better times in the Fall – with no money shortage, no tonsilectomy, & no doubtful plans. Panic-stricken as I admit we were, & still are, by the horrible European war (I don't like to think how many near & dear, or how many contemporaries at school, are lying dead at this moment) – that <u>wasn't</u> the reason of not coming. I'm sticking to music as hard as I can – & working 16 hours a day. Honest!

Probably after all you won't be able to read this – but it is late – & – well – what the hell . . . !

All the best,
BENJAMIN

1 The cable of 16 May reads:

JUST HAVE UNEXPECTED FINANCIAL OFFER TO ENABLE US TO COME WEDNESDAY AFTER ALL   PLEASE WIRE IF WE ARE FORGIVEN AND PERFORMANCE CAN STILL TAKE PLACE

The 'good doctor' to whom Britten refers in his letter was the ever generous Dr Mayer. On 17 May Goldberg cabled:

SORRY PLANS FOR REVISED PROGRAMME ON MAY 27TH CANNOT BE ALTERED   COULD PUT YOU ON JUNE 17TH   PLEASE ADVISE

To which Britten responded on 24 May:

SORRY JUNE 17TH TOO RISKY   BETTER POSTPONE TILL FALL   WRITING

Out of all this confusion of cables and letters emerged the first American performance of *Mont Juic*, though the composer was not present. Goldberg wrote to Britten on 21 June that *Mont Juic*

made a great success with the audience and was, in fact, the popular hit of the evening. [. . .] Solomon liked the pieces and wants to play them on his NBC programs in September. [. . .] I also recommended them to Robert Whitney, conductor of the Louisville Symphony Orchestra for his programs next season.

A notice of the concert appeared in *Music News*, 'Music in Chicago':

One of the most interesting works heard all season was the first American performance by the Illinois Symphony Orchestra June 17, of the Lennox Berkeley–Benjamin Britten Mont Juic Suite of Catalan Dances. Based on folk tunes, these two composers have constructed a work that is at once vital, full of bright, vivid contrasts, somewhat dissonant at moments, but always moving with a tremendous drive and certainty. The charming Allegro grazioso, a gavotte form, was exquisitely played. Izler Solomon, the conductor, gave the entire suite a flexible and stirring reading.

In the programme *Mont Juic* was attributed to Lennox Berkeley, 'in collaboration with Benjamin Britten'.

265   To Aaron Copland

c/o W. Mayer,
123 Louden Av.,
Amityville, N.Y.
[?Received 27 May 1940]

My dearest Aaron,

Forgive not writing, forgive no lunch & well – forgive everything. Things are just up-side-down at the moment. Peter's had his tonsils out – I've gotta have mine done too (blarst!) – & well – news is bad from Europe & apart from pure sentiment & all that it is practically bad for me – no cash & innumerable worries. However. Thanks a hundred times for the Hollywood bizniss – having consulted big boss (R.H.) – see no reason why I shouldn't (in fact plenty why I should) sign it – I am now signing it & off it goes.[1] Good luck to it.

I 'phoned you when in town last week, but just dead silence –
am probably in next week, & Do want to see you so much. Can't
you & Vic.[2] drive out here? Suggest a date – almost any is good
for me.

Missed your broadcast this afternoon (blarst again). Hear that
you're good at that.

Peter wants to see his pictures so can you ask Victor to send
them please?

That Chavez[3] of yours is damned elusive.

Much love & all that,
please ring or write about coming – do.
Regards to Vic,
BENJY

One positive thing about the last year or so is that I have now a
N.Y. driving licence – so there's no excuse now for not letting me
drive Posh[4] – or is there?

1 Copland recounts in his autobiography, Aaron Copland and Vivian
   Perlis, *Copland: 1900 through 1942* (London, Faber and Faber, 1984),
   p. 293:

   Ben had financial problems, so when I went to Hollywood in 1940 and got
   an agent (Abe Meyer of MCA), I arranged for a film contract for Britten. 'If
   this gets you no work in 4 months,' I wrote, 'the contract is null and void.
   I think it's safe to sign it. Anyhow, I signed one just like it.'

   It was to the signing of this contract that Britten refers in this letter.
   See also Letter 268, in which Britten returns the contract to Meyer.

2 Victor Kraft (b. ?, d. 1976), Copland's 'pupil, companion, secretary
   and friend' (see Copland and Perlis, op. cit., p. 213), whose photograph of Britten and Koussevitzky appears in PFL, plate 156.

3 Carlos Chávez (1889–1978), the Mexican composer. Chávez and Copland were close musical friends – they shared in some significant
   respects a common musical aesthetic – and Chávez championed
   Copland's music in his own country. Copland was clearly attempting
   to introduce Britten to Chávez, who had an outstanding reputation
   for the performances of contemporary music in Mexico, where he
   was principal conductor of the Mexico Symphony Orchestra for many
   years.

4 Was this a pet name bestowed on Copland's car as a result of his
   visit to Snape in 1938? 'Posh' was the nickname of a friend of Edward
   Fitzgerald, the translator of *Omar Khayyám* and Suffolk eccentric; but
   the naming of Copland's automobile may have had quite other origins. (Vivian Perlis tells us that Copland once had a dog called Nadia,
   presumably named after his teacher, Nadia Boulanger.)

266 To Beth Welford

[EWB, *pp. 145–6*]

> Long Island Home, Amityville
> N.Y.
> June 11th 1940

My darling old Beth,

Your letter came a day or so ago – with all the usual complaints! I'm so sorry, but I hope by now that you have had my long letter with press cuttings etc. which I sent by boat (as air-mail is so variable (& expensive!) these days), & anyhow I have been so terribly busy these last months. My Japanese Symphony has had to be finished & despatched, all in a terrible hurry – & besides I have had lots of sessions with the dentist & you know how that takes up time & energy. I had my awful old front tooth out – & that did the dirty on me – it had an abcess on it, & had what they called a 'dry socket' which gave me violent toothache for a fortnight! Nothing serious but you know how I bare pain! However it's all getting better now & soon I shall have a beautiful gleaming smile – like advertisements for Pepsodent! I was glad to hear all your news. It must have been, & still be, absolute hell for you. I'm afraid in this country it has been obvious that things would get to this point, & the complacency of the French & British was rather worrying. However this country was as much to blame not to have helped before – still let's hope that it's not too late now – lots of people think it isn't, thank God. I'm sure one feels out here nearly as bad as you do – because all the news services are so damnably efficient & one feels so terribly helpless – one can't even drive a car and help. However one can talk to people, sign petitions for immediate help to the Allies, & go about & exercise the old charm on people & every little helps to swing public opinion round towards the Allies – & my God, how it has swung since old Chamberlain went![1] Enough of that. I hope that you are able to do & think of other things. If there's anything you're short of & I can possibly send, write or cable for it. – Even money! I'm terribly grateful for what you're doing re the Mill & Nicholson. I feel so much easier since I knew that you were taking an interest in it. Nicholson is an old fool – never writes – I never know what's happening. I suppose he's disgusted with me – but after all personal opinions shouldn't get in the way of business. However I enclose a cheque (through Peggy Brosa) for any little expenses that may crop up. (Nicholson doesn't send me accounts so I won't send it to him – you might ask to see accounts of Sewell's money or the Craske div.).[2]   Also for any thing you or Barbara may be needing – just use your judgement, my darling. It's all I can spare at the moment. My love to you all – hope & pray Kit's still with · you – let's all be together soon, somehow! Always thinking of you.

BEN.

1 Neville Chamberlain, the British Prime Minister, had resigned on 10 May and was succeeded by Winston Churchill as head of a National Government.

2 Laurence Sewell, who had taken over the dental practice. The Craske dividend was an investment in Craske Ltd, coal merchants, Bridge Chambers, South Quay and Admiralty Wharf, Lowestoft.

267 To Beata Mayer

Long Island Home,
Amityville, N.Y.
12th June 1940.

My dear Beatty,

How are you? It seems ages since anyone heard anything of you. Have you left for San Francisco? Or are you still in the riotous neighbourhood of the Brass Rail Woodstock.[1] Things here have been going on more or less as usual. Peter's been singing (& well) this last week or so, & so he's made a rapid recovery. Dr. MacA[2] is pleased with him. Everyone else is well. Mike has had a cold & that's gone now. Ulrica has had one too & as she coughed abit her boss sent her down here – but she goeth back to-morrow. William & Elizabeth are fine. But only poor me has been seriously in the wars – teeth – blasted teeth. I had an extraction which did the dirty on me & I had 14 days of lousiest pain (& between you & me I'm not keen on pain). That's more or less gone now – but I have a lovely gap right in front which makes me look even more adolescent than ever! And to-day I've a lousy cold & throat so I've stayed in bed. So everything is fine you see.

That's over – thank goodness – now I can get on with my real message. I saw R. Hawkes yesterday & he told me to tell you that he is definitely opening an Artist's Agency in connection with BHB – & if you want a full time job, he wants you to come & work for him.[3] See? I don't know what salary you'd get – but just write to him, will you please? saying whether you're interested or no. He goes to-morrow to Canada for 2 or 3 weeks so you wouldn't have to start right away – & I should think might put it off even longer if you're tactful. Letters will be forwarded to him.

May I say that I miss you alot? I almost forget what you look like. Hope you're not too depressed by all the news. Personally I hover from hopeless optimism to blackest gloom – the latter when I get letters from England – which are pretty terrible as you might guess. Any how whatabout a letter?

How's Fine? My respects to her & Erich if he's about.

And much love to you, my dear,

BEN

1 Beata was staying at Woodstock, where the Kahlers had rented a house for the summer in the artists' colony. The 'Brass Rail' was a bar.

2 This was probably the doctor who had removed Pears's tonsils. There was a natural anxiety about the effect of the operation on his voice.

3 In the autumn of 1940, Beata worked as a secretary (one of two girls) in the offices of Boosey & Hawkes Artists' Bureau, Inc, on West 57th Street, New York. At this time she moved to Manhattan with her brother Michael and returned home to Amityville for the weekends. As this letter suggests, she undertook the job at the invitation of Britten and Hawkes.

268 To Abe Meyer

c/o Dr. W. Mayer,
123, Louden Avenue,
Amityville, N.Y.
June 17th 1940

Dear Mr. Meyer,

I am sorry not to have returned the enclosed contracts to you before, but as you will understand, my plans & arrangements have been somewhat upset recently. However I have now signed them & initialed the riders: I would be grateful if you could do the same & return me one copy for my files.

As I believe Mr. Copland told you I was very nearly signed to do a picture with Albert Lewin when he was with Paramount (the picture was The Knights of the Round Table) – but when he left Paramount it fell through. I have been in contact with him since

& I gather he wants me to work for him sometime in the near future. So will you approach him for me?

I am sure you will appreciate my point when I say that at the moment I am very busy with 'straight work' (commissions & otherwise) & I am not keen to come out West unless it be for a really good picture & a good fee.[1]

With many thanks,
Yours sincerely,
BENJAMIN BRITTEN

1 Hawkes was to write to Britten on 13 August requesting the particulars of the contract Britten had signed. He explained:

[. . .] that now the Boosey & Hawkes Artists Bureau is functioning and if I may add in no uncertain manner, I think we ought to take up the cudgels on your behalf, and for this purpose and others, of course, Andrew Schulhof, who is Bartók's manager here and associated with us as you know, is going to California in two weeks' time, and he will be there about five or six weeks. He has a great many friends in the picture game of Hungarian origin and will, I feel sure, make a lot of excellent contacts. I want him, therefore, to handle your work out there, and for this purpose I must have the information regarding MCA. My intention is that we should talk about you for a feature picture only and not just as a writer of sequence music. He will, of course, see Lewin and renew that contact that we had some time ago.

269 To Beth, Kit and Sebastian Welford

[EWB, *pp. 146–8*]

Long Island Home, Amityville, N.Y.
June 30th 1940

My darling Beth, Kit & Sebastian,

I'm writing to you all together because I hope rather superstitiously that it'll mean you are still all 3 together. I don't know how much this evacuation of danger zones has affected you, but to be on the safe side I'll send this to Aunt Julianne to forward. Thank you both for your grand letters. I was delighted to get them. And you, Beth for your cable, saying that you were all right & had got the money – before I forget, talking of money, will you please get in touch with Leslie Boosey, B & H, 295 Regent Street, & get him to send you direct my money – which he can't send to me here. I'm not sure how much it is, but for a start ask for £50, & if it's more I'll let you know. I don't need money at the moment (in fact I'm so rich that I'm going to buy an old Jaloppy for about £20!!) – & I thought that you might be able to use the amount that

I'm owed by the firm. I'm writing the same to Barbara, incase this
letter miscarries, so don't be disappointed if L. Boosey tells you it's
already been sent to her. If you don't need it yourselves, perhaps
you know of someone who needs it: or Gustel Scherchen may need
it to pay transportation fares if they want to send her or Wulff to
Canada. Anyhow I want it sent to you rather than to Nicholson as
I don't know what he's up to. By-the-way, while we're on this
dull subject of business – I don't think there's any sense in selling
the Mill at the moment – since it's in such a dangerous position &
I'm clinging to the hope that one day I'll be able to come back &
live there! But I do think we ought to sell the Life Insurance (as
I suggested last year!) so will you tell Nicholson I authorise him to
do so. I'll sign.[1]

Of course life here is just hell. I find it impossible to work or
think of anything but what you're going through. Everytime we
have a thunderstorm (& they're pretty bad & frequent here) –
I imagine what it must be like in your bombardments. Everyone
here takes a gloomy view of things, & rather enjoys being gloomy
– that's what makes one so sick. I do hope & pray that you, Beth
& Sebastian will soon be able to evacuate yourselves. As I said on
my cable[1]

<u>Long Island Home, Amityville N.Y.</u>

(I) can guarantee your maintenance in this country – & that of
any young relations or friends you know of who can get away.
Then I'll sign that too –

BENJAMIN BRITTEN

Kit as you are so marvellous with children, have you never thought
of applying for a job on one of those Transport ships[2] & looking
after kids on this side? It's an idea that's struck us. Excuse me if I
seem a little over-anxious, but I feel convinced that the more
people that manage to get away from Europe at the moment, the
better. Food shortage everywhere may become a serious problem
– & here I am a rich parasite, so why shouldn't I do something to
help!

I expect you have all read about America's great swing – over
towards the Allies – it's been astonishing, but rather depressing
that it needed the fall of Paris[3] to cause it. At the moment it is being
rather eclipsed by the fact that the time is come to find a new
President – you see the world may be going up in flames (as it
seems to be), but nothing must stand in the way of the American's
political games. It makes one sick. Roosevelt strikes me as being a

great man – & strangely enough for a man who has ideals, good
at the political side too.

At the moment we haven't got many personal plans. Everything
is in a state of flux. I don't feel inclined to plan for weeks ahead
as no one knows what'll be happening then. So I'm going on
writing as much as I can; people are just discovering that Peter
can sing & he's getting an agent & some jobs. Toni Brosa & Peggy
are living down here now & it's grand having one's friends
around. They're having a difficult struggle I'm afraid since America
is a beastly hard country to get going in – & this is just the worst
possible moment. But they'll manage to survive, I've no doubt. The
Mayers are well – Elizabeth has written to Stella Churchill (an old
friend of hers)[4] as she may have some say about Doctors for
evaquation of children. I've had beastly trouble with my teeth,
but it shows signs of clearing up now. I've also had a boil & a rash
– but I'm afraid it's mostly Psychological. I find, as you do too,
that if one's mind's upset, that one's body usual[ly] gets that way
too. Did I say how much I enjoyed your letters? Please write again
if you have time. It's so terrible – the papers only give general news
– & never say how people react. The worst side of wars never
gets into the news. Sebastian sounds a grand kid – I'd give anything
to see him again – & you too. Let's pray it'll happen soon. Glad
you saw Barbara – must stop this now.

Love to all the families – & more than I can say to you three.

BENJAMIN

1 A strip *c.* 4.5cm deep has been cut out of the letter at this point. It no
   doubt contained Britten's signed instructions to his solicitor. Britten
   expected his sister to show this letter to his solicitor as evidence of
   the authorization to which he refers. This also explains the signature
   that appears in the body of the letter, together with the address
   added at the start of a new page, guaranteeing his support of his
   family in the event of their moving to the USA.

2 Britten was thinking of the transatlantic shipping of children in wartime to safe locations in North America. This is borne out by a later
   reference in the final paragraph of this letter.

3 The Germans had entered Paris on 14 June.

4 Also, it seems, a friend of the Bridges and living with them in Friston
   during 1941. See PHFB, p. 192.

270 To Abe Meyer
[*Typed; BB's copy*]

123 Louden Avenue,
Amityville, N.Y.
July 2, 1940

Dear Mr. Meyer,

Thank you for your letter and for returning a copy of the contract.

I enclose a list of my published works as up to date as I can make it, but there are new pieces being added all the time. As a matter of publicity for you, I have just completed a Symphony[1] which the Japanese Government commissioned through the British Government – strange as it may seem in these days!

The Film work I did in England was chiefly connected with Documentary (non-commercial) films; but two of these (Night-Mail and Coal Face) became quite famous because of their sound tracks and were shown in this country. The one big commercial picture for which I wrote the score was "Love from a Stranger" – produced by Max Schach, directed by Rowland V. Lee with Ann Harding and Basil Rathbone. It was a big success in Europe, but I don't know how it went in this country.

I have done a great deal of Radio work with the B.B.C. in London, the biggest production being "King Arthur" and a serial "The Sword in the Stone", and I just recently did a score for the C.B.S. production, New York, (a play "The dark valley" by W.H. Auden).[2] I have done no stage work in this country, but in England I did a great deal – the last show being "Johnson over Jordan" by J.B. Priestley, which had a lot of music in it, ballets and interludes etc.

I have not much on phonographic records yet, but Decca Ltd. (London) have recorded the Variations, Soirées Musicales, and the Simple Symphony.[3] The first and last named are obtainable in this country, but I am not sure about the others.

I enclose a copy of "Tempo"[4] giving further details which may help you. Anything else you wish to know please write and ask.

With kind regards,
Yours sincerely,
Benjamin Britten

P.S. Aaron Copland was out here this weekend talking about his "Our Town"[5] experiences. Please give my best regards to Albert Lewin when you next see him.

1 Britten refers to completing the full score, not the composition, of the work. The composition sketch was laid out by Britten in the form of a piano duet. Pears recollects (in PPTMS) that the 'first sketches' at this time

> were often for a sort of four hands at a piano, so that we could bang things through more convincingly perhaps than with two hands. And I played (in private, of course) to various people the *Sinfonia da Requiem* [. . .]

See also Letter 290.

2 Auden's monologue, *The Dark Valley*, was first broadcast by CBS as part of their experimental 'Columbia Workshop' series on 2 June 1940 in a production by Brewster Morgan. The English actress, Dame May Whitty (1865–1948), played the role of the Old Woman and Britten's slender score was conducted by Bernard Herrmann. See PR, pp. 379–86, and 594–5.

3 The *Frank Bridge Variations* had been recorded by the Boyd Neel String Orchestra, conducted by Boyd Neel, on Decca x226–8; *Soirées Musicales* by the Charles Brill Orchestra, conducted by Charles Brill on Decca AK 873–4; and *Simple Symphony* by Boyd Neel on Decca AX 245–7.

4 The first American edition of *Tempo*, March 1940, p. 9, included information about Britten's recent activities:

> BENJAMIN BRITTEN played his Piano Concerto with the Illinois Symphony Orchestra, Albert L. Goldberg conducting, with unusual success. He will be present at the first performance of his new Violin Concerto on March 27 in New York, which will be played by Antonio Brosa, noted Spanish violinist at his American debut at a concert of the New York Philharmonic Orchestra under John Barbirolli. Britten just finished a new piece for orchestra, 'Kermesse Canadienne', based on Canadian folktunes and is now working on an operetta 'Paul Bunyan' with W.H. Auden, the eminent poet. Paul Bunyan, says Auden, 'is an American myth'. He is the incarnation of the spirit of conquest, of the men who went in the wilderness to fell trees, to settle in a new land and eventually to 'provoke a general impulse towards settlement and cultivation'.

5 In 1939 Copland had written the music for the film version of John Steinbeck's prize-winning play, *Of Mice and Men* (based on his novel of the same title). As a result of the success of this he was invited to write the score for the film version of Thornton Wilder's play, *Our Town*. A full account of Copland's work on this project, at a time when he was in close touch with Britten, appears in the composer's autobiography, Aaron Copland and Vivian Perlis, *Copland: 1900 through 1942* (London, Faber and Faber, 1984), pp. 302–4.

271 **To Beata Mayer**
From Peter Pears

Amityville
[4 July 1940]

BeAtty my dear –

Please forgive me not having written eight and a half days ago
or more to thank you for your lovely birthday present[1]. The thin
mints went of course in twenty four hours, and I curled up on a
sofa with Somerset Maugham until I had finished him. It was a
new one to me and marvellously disagreeable and exciting! So acid
it nearly burnt! The manuscript paper book I am keeping for my
old age when I start composing to show these young men how to
do it!

Being thirty is no joke I can tell you! It seems to have had an
immediate reaction on my figure, for I weighed myself in a
subway the other day, and the gross total has now reached 215 lbs
you will [be] sorry to hear – I really must start reducing –
Tomorrow perhaps –

Woodstock doesn't sound so bad after all – I'm very glad – It
must have been nice having Wolfgang[2] up there – and Fine is
hoffentlich [hopefully] not too depressed (though a voluminous
letter to your mother a few days ago sounded a bit confused,
though full of your praises –)

Ben's thinking hard of buying an old car when Bill[3] comes back
next week – George Welsh[4] is even now looking for one. And
then we thought all your four great Amityville brothers[5] might drive
up & see you at Woodstock for a weekend – perhaps weekend
after next if we have a car by then. I took my test, by the way,
triumphantly – Very easy –

I have been going on with my lessons with my hexe [witch][6].
She is very sweet and has done me a lot of good – but she goes
off tomorrow to Colorado, and no doubt I shall relapse. Our
immigration arrangements are still very hazy. The Japs have paid
Ben which is a good thing – He may be commissioned to write a
concerto for a one handed pianist called Wittgenstein.[7] We went
& had a long talk with him the other day. He was rather stupid,
couldn't understand Ben's music (!), & Ben nearly got terribly
cross, but just managed to contain himself –

Ben had a boil on his chin recently but otherwise has been
allright. I have been rather stricken with hayfever –

33a   The trip to North America, April/May 1939: Britten on the deck of the SS *Ausonia*

33b   Pears and a young passenger (see Letter 173)

34a Pears in Canada, May/June 1939

34b The World's Fair, New York, 1939: Pears with Donald Neville-Willing, the manager of the George Washington Hotel, where Britten and Pears stayed on their arrival in the city

35a Stanton Cottage, Amityville, Long Island, the Mayer family home

35b The Mayer family, Amityville, c.1942; left to right: Elizabeth Mayer, Sgt Michael
G. Mayer, Dr William Mayer, Christopher Mayer, Dr Max Wachstein, Beata Mayer
(Ulrica Mayer, Beata's sister, was absent when this photograph was taken)

36a Upstate New York, July/August 1939: Pears with Copland and Victor Kraft (photo, B.B.)

36b July/August 1939: Pears, Copland, Kraft (photo, B.B.)

36c Peggy Brosa, Toni Brosa, Kraft, Britten, Copland, ?1940 (photo, P.P.)

37a Woodstock, July/August 1939: Copland, Kraft, Pears (Britten clearly left his seat at the table to take this snap)

37b Chicago, 15 January 1940: Britten rehearses with Albert Goldberg and the Illinois Symphony Orchestra for the American première of his Piano Concerto

38a Jones Beach, Long Island, c.1940: Britten and Pears

38b Jones Beach, c.1940: Mrs Mayer, Beata Mayer and Pears (photo, B.B.)

39a Paul Wittgenstein and Britten, discussing the *Diversions* for piano (left hand) and orchestra, 1940

39b Britten in the Toronto studios of the CBC in August 1939 when appearing as soloist in his *Young Apollo*; he talks to the producer, John Adaskin

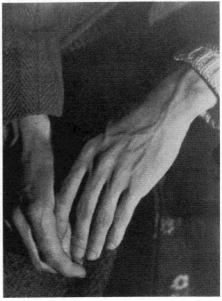

39c Britten, December 1941 (photo, Lotte Jacobi)

39d Britten's hands, 29 December 1941 (photo, Lotte Jacobi)

40 Auden and Britten, New York, 1941, at the time of the rehearsals of *Paul Bunyan*

41a The Prologue in the original production of *Paul Bunyan*, New York, 5 May 1941

41b Slim, the cowboy, rides into the loggers' camp

42a Britten and David Rothman, c.1940

42b David Rothman and his son, Bobby, to whom Britten dedicated his folksong arrangement 'The trees they grow so high'

43 Stanton Cottage, 29 December 1941: Pears and Britten (photo, Lotte Jacobi)

44a   Antonio Brosa, c.1940, who was to give the first performance of Britten's Violin
Concerto at Carnegie Hall, 28 March

44b   Amityville, 29 December 1941
(photo, Lotte Jacobi)

44c   Amityville, 29 December 1941
(photo, Lotte Jacobi)

45 Britten and Pears rehearsing *Les Illuminations* in the CBS studios, New York: this performance formed part of the ISCM Festival in May 1941 and was both the American première of the work and the occasion of Pears's first performance of it

46a   Portland, Maine, 16 September 1940

46b   Group photograph, ISCM Festival, New York, May 1941: Britten in the back row, with Martinů on his left; Bartók, front row, seated second from the left

47a Amityville: Ethel Bartlett and Rae Robertson with Elizabeth Mayer and Pears
(photo, B.B.)

47b Escondido, California, summer 1941, when Britten and Pears were staying with
the Robertsons

48 New York, 14 March 1942: Britten and Pears with Elizabeth Mayer, the day before they left New York at the start of their return journey to England

Just now they're letting off crackers outside (to the terror of Gip) in celebration of pushing our great-grandfathers into the sea![8] Let's hope they won't do the same to us!

Much love to you, Beatty, from Ben and me, and let us know if you don't want us, or if another time would be better. Remember us to the Kahlers.

PETER

1 Pears's thirtieth birthday, on 22 June.
2 Wolfgang Sauerländer: see note 1 to Letter 219. He too was a friend of the Kahlers.
3 Dr Titley.
4 Probably the man who looked after the cars at the Long Island Home, or a local garage proprietor.
5 i.e. Michael, Christopher, Britten and Pears.
6 His singing teacher, Therese Schnabel.
7 See note 1 to Letter 272.
8 Independence Day: 4 July.

272 To Paul Wittgenstein[1]
[Draft]

[9 July 1940]

Dear Mr. Wittgenstein

Thank you for your kind letter. I should be delighted to come & have supper with you 'à l'autrichienne'. May I suggest towards the end of next week, because then I shall have some sketches of the proposed concerto to show you? Could you perhaps let me have a postcard saying what evening would suit you?

With kind regards,

BB

1 Paul Wittgenstein (1887–1961), the Austrian pianist (and brother of the philosopher, Ludwig). He lost his right arm in the First World War. Britten was to compose his *Diversions*, Op. 21, for piano (left hand) and orchestra, for him, the première of which was given on 16 January 1942 by Wittgenstein with the Philadelphia Orchestra under Eugene Ormandy. Wittgenstein commissioned similar works from Ravel, Richard Strauss, Prokofiev and Franz Schmidt. See PFL, plate 157, and E. Fred Flindell, 'Paul Wittgenstein (1887–1961): Patron and Pianist', *Music Review*, 32, 1971, pp. 107–27. Britten had first

heard Wittgenstein in 1929, when he was still at school. He wrote in his diary on 14 February,

In the afternoon after a lie down [he was convalescing] I listen to the wireless, a concert, orchestra & Paul Wittenstein (I think that's his name, the left-handed pianist). Quite good, tho' I didn't like the programme very much.

The first meeting with Wittgenstein had taken place in Manhattan on 1 July, at the pianist's apartment, 310 Riverside Drive. On 2 July, Heinsheimer wrote to Britten:

I called Mr Wittgenstein once more this morning and asked him if he could please make up his mind quite clearly and sincerely. He said that this is exactly what he did yesterday and that if it sometimes looked a little bit strange, the reason was that he wanted to be as sincere as possible. He didn't consider this meeting as the proper occasion or the proper opportunity to pay nice compliments, but as a sort of meeting of a doctor and a patient, where only the utmost sincerity should be applied. He apologizes if he made the impression of being a little bit too persistent and he really thinks that your music would be the right thing for him. He highly appreciates your offer to show him parts of the work before the deal is completed. After thinking the whole matter over a little bit more, and after this conversation this morning with Wittgenstein, I think I should encourage you to try it.

In the light of that first encounter it is not surprising that the ensuing relationship with the pianist was fraught with difficulties.

273 To Gustel Scherchen
[*Night letter telegram*]

[Postmarked 18 July 1940]
NEW YORK

ELIZABETH MAYER IS MAKING EXTENSIVE INQUIRIES ABOUT WULFF THROUGH REDCROSS PLEASE CABLE IF YOU HAVE NEWS DONT WORRY

LOVE
BENJAMIN BRITTEN

274   To Benjamin Britten
From Elizabeth Mayer

Hotel Pemaquid,
Pemaquid Point,
Maine,
July 21 1940[1]

Dearest Ben,

This is a place where you would like to be – and where you should be for a while – I feel quite guilty enjoying all this – and knowing you are in the heat and humidity and too great nearness to worrying news. I want you to go to a place like this, Ben, where one is put up well and peacefully and informally, and where just behind the house a delightful trail leads in 15 minutes to perfectly lovely and utterly lonesome coves, where we are lying for hours on the big rocks, listening to the cry of the sea-gulls and the immense sound of the ocean. William is very happy and relaxed, and enjoys every minute. He was another person since we sat in the car and drove away. We had a very pleasant time with Wystan, who lives on a nice old farm, some miles away from Mina Curtiss, Lincoln's sister.[2]   M.C. was not there at the moment but I promised Wystan to come back in August and spend some days up there. To see Wystan's face did me a lot of good, I instantly forgot all my worries and depressive thoughts, and got new courage through that great human being. You should go and see him and then come here. I miss you, Ben, although I think that it is good for you not to see the Mayers for a while, at least not to see me. I have been so un-balanced the last months, being very unhappy to the roots of my being, and I am afraid you have noticed it even if I tried to control myself. I would give any prize not to have to go back to Amityville. Everything there seems to me a big failure of mine – (in regard to the L.I.H. and particularly the Titleys). But you, dear Ben, you have been a blessing, I think with ever so many good feelings of you, my darling, of you and Peter! I miss you both, and I miss news about everything concerning you. What about the Austrian supper at Wittgensteins and the piano-concerto [Diversions], Peter's audition,[3] letters from England, plans to drive to Mass. etc., Toni's journey . . . Beata's visit . . .

Next Tuesday Wallenstein plays again the Variations – we'll try to listen. The piano here is quite good, I play sometimes, the old Professor on Arabian dialects is still alive and here, with delightful

French books, we talk every morning half an hour, – some of her people of last year, <u>verry</u> New England, indeed Victorian – we were received very cordially, William plays all kind of games, is a great favourite with the ladies, I am reading and resting. The short drives around are lovely, and the car – the car – [4]

I hope everybody cares for you sufficiently – how do you feel. How was the ominous Monday?   I'll think of you to-morrow with special sympathy.

Good bye, my dear,
very, very affectionately,
E.

<u>Dear Peter!!</u>

1 The Mayers were on holiday.

2 See note 5 to Letter 276.

3 Perhaps an audition with Thea Dispeker, whom Pears later described as 'my first "agent" in New York in 1940' (Peter Pears, 'The New York *Death in Venice*', Aldeburgh Festival Programme Book, 1975, p. 12).

4 A reference to Britten's setting of Auden's 'As it is, plenty' in *On this Island*.

275   To Beth Welford

[*Full text*, EWB, *pp. 148–51*]

c/o Dr. Mayer,
123, Louden Avenue,
Amityville (alias L.I. Home!)   N.Y.
July 26th 1940

My darling Beth,

It is ages since I heard from you, & I am afraid, ages since I wrote to you – the reasons for the latter are manifold, but the principal reason is always that I don't know what to write about. I don't know how it affects you to hear of one's normal (un-warlike) doings overhere – if it just makes you vomit, well, just tear the letter up, I'll understand. As a matter of fact, although one is not actually drilling or rolling bandages etc., it would be untrue to say one's life is unwarlike, because everything is clouded by the blasted situation. Although we <u>can</u> go bathing everyday – we just can't get up the energy to do it, or enjoy it properly when we do – it's dumb, but there it is! As amatter-of-fact,[1] when we actually did go down to the ocean for the first time the other day, we got such

fiendish sun burns (forgetting that the American sun is not so
innocent as the English!) that life for a week was hell – & of course
we said this was a punishment for enjoying ourselves while you
were in agony over the seas. Sadly, but that's another result of war
– losing all reasoning powers. Another reason for not writing
more often is that I had never before experienced a Long Island
summer – & that is saying something. When the temperature is
permanently in the 90°'s & humidity in the 90%s life is unbearable.
One has no energy to do anything, but sit still & even then almost
drown in one's perspiration!

I was scared to get your cable until I remembered I'd sent your
last letter to Aunt Julianne & the cable was I suppose pointing
out that you're still in Swaffham. I'm damn glad, because bad as
Norfolk is, to judge by the papers Western cities are not healthy
places to be in at this moment. I hope you aren't too bothered by
the cable I had to send you – but it had to be arranged as I don't
want the bank to turn nasty & sell the Mill (at a hopeless loss) to
redeem my overdraft. In England at the moment my money
situation ought to be O.K. – if you can sell my life insurance. The
position with regard to Boosey & Hawkes is this: I'm owed, by
contract, £100 per quarter, I've had $300 (i.e. £80) paid over here
from B.H. New York. So I have £220 due to me in England (I'm
paid quarterly in advance, Jan., April, July.) Could you collect this
& use it in whatever way is best? I don't want anymoney to sit in
the Bank doing nothing. Just leave a little to keep the account going
& pinch the rest – see? Have a good time yourselves – buy some
rum & forget for abit – the same for Barbara!

I hereby authorise you to tell Nicholson to do anything you like
with my money –

BENJAMIN BRITTEN –

he is my attorney so can write cheques – but he himself is hopeless
to make decisions. I haven't had a note from him since February.

I've had plenty to occupy myself with recently. The Japanese
government paid up on the dot – & I'm now in contact with the
British Embassy in Tokio who wants me to go there in the Autumn
to witness the festivities. So I may be leaving for the rising Sun
in September – right into the arms of the Mikado – hope he's nice.
In the meantime I've been commissioned by a man called
Wittgenstein – a one-armed pianist – to write him a concerto.
He pays gold so I'll do it. I bought a cheap car (Ford 1931) – for
95 dollars (about £25) – & we now rattle along merrily over the
park-ways. It is a 2 seater open (almost the only open car on Long

Island!) & though the body is dilapidated the engine's fine. We can touch 55 going down hill, if we hold on tight. We've got alot of going about to do in the near future & it's cheaper than train fares.

The Mayer parents have been on holiday these three weeks & Peter & I have been alone here with Michael & Christopher. We see lots of Toni & Peggy (they are very depressed as Toni's big date in Canada to play my Concerto with the Toronto Symphony was cancelled, since he couldn't get an entry visa). Toni & I are working on an orchestral book together[2] for Ralph Hawkes, & it means lots of copying – in which Peggy, Peter & Christopher all join. We haven't been to New York much lately as it's too damned hot – but we were there for a dinner party in our honour last Sunday – an all British party, which sounded gloomy but was quite pleasant after all. We have an invitation to go up into New England next week-end as a result, from the head of the British Board of Commerce in New York – so we're quite official now! A friend of Peter's who is in the Admiralty[3] has arrived here on the purchasing committee so it's nice to get some first-hand news of England.

I have been having some anxiety over Wulff since I had a letter from Gustel saying he was being shipped to Canada with some other German internees – working it out he should have left England on the day that the Andora Castle[4] went down with hundreds of his kind – so I've been hopping round Red Cross Societies & making inquiries in official circles trying to trace him & to bring some comfort to his poor mother. I had a cable from her this morning saying he missed disaster & arrived here O.K. So I shall now be doing up parcels for him.

Now for a serious word. I do want you all to realise – if by hook or by crook you can get visas to come across, I will guarantee everything this end – if the authorities won't take <u>my</u> guarantee I can <u>easily</u> get the necessary ones from friends. This goes for any other relatives or friends you know. I've already cabled Sophie to send her kids, but she's '<u>waiting</u>', as if every moment weren't precious – because even if the invasion doesn't come off, life is going to be, if it isn't already, a particularly nasty form of hell; & the more people who can get away the better for everyone. All that has to be done is to arrange for passage & permission <u>your</u> end & I'll do everything here – the Government's made it very simple too. I wish to God you three would come – you can't imagine how much I yearn for a sight of the old faces again!

Much love to you all, & be careful (!)

BENJAMIN.

P.S.   Please write on only one side of the paper in future –

P.P.S   I have just completed my dental tortures – thank God. I've now got a brand new front tooth which looks as good as – if not much better than (!) – new. <u>Beootiful</u> gold covered with porcelain. I have a wonderful grin. I'm very glad to have that done, but it was bloody expensive!

1   A phrase that had a special resonance for the family because of a much-quoted childhood poem of Britten's in which 'a matter of fact' was used as a kind of refrain. See EWB, p. 41, where the poem is quoted in full. See also Letter 402.

2   This was the first volume of *Violin Passages*, 'Extracted by Benjamin Britten and Antonio Brosa', and published by Boosey & Hawkes, Inc, New York, at $1.00, in 1941. The title page is reproduced in PFL, plate 134. A further volume of excerpts (from the nineteenth century) was planned but seems not to have materialized. The idea of the volumes was to produce practice materials for aspiring violinists, Britten choosing the excerpts while Brosa edited them from the performer's point of view. This was a time of close collaboration between Britten and Brosa, shortly after the première of the Violin Concerto, the editing of the violin part of which Britten had entrusted to Brosa. Beata Mayer wrote in a letter in July to Wolfgang Sauerländer:

> [. . .] music in the evenings with Toni Brosa, bathing on Jones beach during the day, drives in Ben and Peter's old Ford. Everybody helps copying music for a book Ben and Toni are publishing, about the difficult violin passages in music literature. [. . .] Then as usual, when I am around, Peter got sick with temperature and aches all over, diagnosed by me as influenza, and I have to play nurse [. . .]

3   Richard Powell (b. 1909), a friend of Pears from the 1930s. He was a member of the British Merchant Shipping Mission in the USA, 1940–44, and was knighted in 1954.

4   The *Arandora Star* was torpedoed and sunk by a German submarine on 2 July, seventy-five miles off the coast of Ireland. The loss of life was heavy and included some six hundred German and Italian internees and prisoners of war.

276   To Elizabeth and William Mayer

Amityville, N.Y.
July 29th 1940.

My dear Elizabeth & William,

Two apologies – one: that I haven't written to date & two: that the present letter won't be as long or lucid as I should like to make it. Reason – the same reason as for all the woes of the past week or so – the weather. It has been appalling – I've never known anything like it. We have all just sat & dripped – moved about abit & still dripped. Going to the beach has been the only relief, but that needs energy to get one there & there is no surplus energy these crazy days. How I envy you your lovely spot – & the seagulls. I liked them alot. I feel that a sight of some real big seagulls & the sound of them no less would rouse my drooping feelings no end.

Well – things have been fine here – no snags nor hitches. Edith[1] is marvellous & works like a bee – she has a great washing craze at the moment, to such an extent that she almost seizes the clothes off one's back to dip them in the tub. Jippy is well – but as you would expect not exactly lively. We've been stern but nice to him & he's been quite good – except for his early morning barking & one or two skirmishes after legs. He's well fed & sleeps well.

We spent a pleasant week-end mostly at Jones Beach with Michael, Chris & Peter. The Brosas & Bill & family were there on Sunday afternoon – & several other people had the same bright idea we discovered – whew!   I've never seen such a crowd. The little car got us there & back most efficiently at all times. Chris has been slaving on it – the top was very ragged & we went round to the Ford Co. & "Top-menders" & the former said it would cost $50 to renew & latter $25 to renew so we weren't having any. So Chris upped & took the thing to bits & hopes to get it finished by the time he leaves for Maine to-morrow – lucky blighter, but he deserves it as he's been working so hard. He's helped Toni & me lots with our book which is progressing fast – we have regular "copying-bees"[2] with Peggy & Peter also helping.

I pulled off the deal with Wittgenstein. I had a dinner with him – which was much more pleasant than I'd feared – he's much easier to manage alone!   I've even started the piece which I think may be quite nice.

So Peter & I start on our holiday on Friday – D.V. & W.P.[3]   We

leave early on Friday morning & hope to make Pittsfield by the
afternoon – if the little car will stand the weight of Toni & Peggy
as well! We then go to Lennox for a festival concert[4] & Peter & I
will drop Toni & Peggy to get to Cape Cod on Sunday & proceed
to Wystan[5] – so if you call on him we may be there on Monday
or Tuesday! All the plans are very vague – & all depend on the
amenability of the 1931 model!

Thank you, Elizabeth, for sending on Mrs. Bridge's letter – poor
dear she is unhappy. I had a cable from Wulff's mother saying
that he's in Canada & gave me an address to write to – so that's a
relief.

Much love to you both. I hope you'll have a grand run back.
How's the automatic car?[6]   I hope you don't go to sleep driving it!
                    I'll let you know our plans as they develop.
                                                                      BEN

P.S.   You won't know me when you see me next – with my
wonderful row of gleaming teeth —— !!

Beata was here for nearly a week & we had a good time altogether
– but she went up last Friday to help look after a neighbour of the
Kahlers. We couldn't drive her as Peter wasn't too well – ran a
temperature of about 100° one evening – no symptoms & he was
O.K. next morning – probably just heat.

1 The Mayers' maid.
2 Copying sessions.
3 God Willing (Deo Volente) and Weather Permitting.
4 Britten refers here to Tanglewood, an estate near Lenox, Massachusetts, the site of an international festival of music and Music Center.
   The Festival began in nearby Stockbridge in 1937 and was moved to
   Tanglewood in 1938.
5 Auden in 1940 was teaching one day a week at the New School
   for Social Research in New York. Part of the summer he spent at
   Williamsburg, Massachusetts, on a farm in the company of Chester
   Kallman. After a break in California, visiting the Mann family and
   Isherwood, he returned to the Williamsburg farm, which was close
   to the house of Mina Curtiss, the sister of Lincoln Kirstein, where
   Britten and Pears also stayed for a few days after visiting Auden.
   Curtiss was later to write a biography of Bizet and edit and translate
   Proust's letters. See HCWHA, pp. 296-7. In a letter to Beth on 25
   August, but completed after their return to Amityville, Pears writes:
   We're staying on a farm, where Wystan Auden has been spending the
   summer, it's all very like an English farm – the Cotswolds, except that

they make most of their money from corn (Indian) and maple sugar. [. . .]
We had a very nice time with Wystan and then stayed some days with
a friend near there. She [Mina Curtiss] had a lovely house with lots of
records and many so-called "Primitive" American paintings i.e. colonial
eighteenth century stuff. She had a wonderful cook too and fed us very
well. But it was rather high up in the hills and cold and Ben caught an
awful cold which he has still got, although back here it's very warm.

On 24 August, Pears had written to Mrs Mayer: 'Could you send
Ben c/o Wystan, his Music MS of Paul Bunyan? It is in the top of the
cupboard in drawing room.' See EWB, pp. 157–9, for a complete text.
Clearly the opportunity was taken while staying with Auden for
further work on the operetta, and also on the *Hymn to St Cecilia*.
Auden in fact had sent a reminder to Britten on 15 July: 'Please bring
Paul Bunyan with you as I want you to try it out on MacLeish.'
MacLeish was Archibald MacLeish (1892–1982), the poet, who in the
thirties addressed himself to social issues and wrote two verse
dramas for radio. He was Librarian of the Congress, 1939–44. See
also Letter 290 and Dorothy J. Farnan, *Auden in Love* (London, Faber
and Faber, 1985), pp. 24–5, who writes:

Peter Pears had an old Ford Model T flivver for twenty-four dollars in which
he, Dr Kallman, and Malcolm [Chester's father and younger brother] roared
all day through the New England countryside while Wystan and Benjamin
worked on *Paul Bunyan* and Chester wrote poetry.

6 Presumably a car with an automatic gear change.

277 To Barbara Britten

c/o Dr. Mayer, Amityville, N.Y.

Aug. 1st [1940]

My darling Barbara,

I feel terribly guilty about not having written for so long, but
things have been hectic here – & worse than that there has been
heat that I never thought could have existed. It is probably difficult
for you to realise what it's like, – to sit perfectly still indoors &
for sweat to pour down one. You see, here the humidity is the
great problem – when the thermometer goes up it's bad enough
but when the air is so damp (it hit 100% the other day) it is
impossible to think or work or do anything. So much for grumbles!
I have been sending messages to you through Beth, who has been
managing my things thro' Nicholson (who is not exactly helpful
at the moment), so I hope you realise I haven't forgotten you! Far
from it – you two are in my thoughts the whole time – it is

impossible to think of anything else besides England at the
moment. In some ways I should love to be called back: one feels
helpless here: but still the official order (from Washington) is that
unless one is a trained pilot or technician, then one must stay put.
So I'm carrying on here – but only on the condition: that if you let
me know whenever there is anything to be done – permission (or
affidavits) to be got for friends or relatives to come here – or money
to be sent – I can easily raise it. I have lots of grand friends who
will do anything in their power to help – in fact everyone is crying
out for something to do – 5,000,000 homes have offered to take
children! We have had a scare over Wulff whom we thought had
gone down on the Andora Star – but it appears he got another
boat & probably by now is in Canada. Poor Gustel was in a bad
way. I'm trying to trace him now & send food & stuff to him.
Lots of anti-nazi friends of the Mayers were in France, and are now
missing. It is a hell of a time.

Beth writes that she's seen you – & that you are working too
hard as usual. I'm so sorry – & wish I could do something to
help. I suppose it's naughty to suggest this to a member of our
family[1] – but, do try a bit of drink from time to time – it does
help!!!   Beth ought to have plenty of money if she sells my life
insurance – which she must – & I don't want any money saved
– see? You never know what may happen & I'm sure I can easily
earn more. I've got a new commission for a one-handed concerto
[Diversions], so I'm well off now!!   So spend away my dear – even
if it's only on sherry & new hats!

Peter & the Brosas & I are off to-morrow on a sort of business-
pleasure trip up to New England (wish it were Old E.) in an awful
old 1931 car I've just bought. I hope it'll get us there. Driving in
this country is quite easy – the traffic is well controlled only there's
too much of it. The trouble with this country is that everything is
too controlled and organised. Bathing is only from special places –
picnicing is all organised – most places have tables to eat off – there
are few side-roads to go along – the ones there are are too bad –
everyone travels on big park-ways – marvellous roads with ordered
scenary – but they are deadly dull.

You've heard that I may have to go to Japan? The British Embassy
in Tokio has cabled saying that I ought to go to the First
performance of my Symphony there – but I don't think it'll come
off now, with all this arrest business going on.[2]   Anyhow I don't
want to go – they have too much rice, earthquakes and hari-kari
(or mata-hari, or whatever that is).

Have you seen Robert recently? I hope he's well. It seems a good
thing that he got out of that school in Norfolk when he did.
People aren't keen on the East Coast at the moment, I shouldn't
think. By-the-way (secretly) it's abit sickening that of all the
relatives & friends I've been trying to persuade to come here – the
only ones who may come are Marjorie & kids – !!!!!³   But shush
– shush – – –

My love to Helen. I hope she's bearing up, poor dear. Where's
Mrs Hurst⁴ now? I wish I could think of you two anywhere but
in London. I know London <u>may</u> be safe at the moment – but finally
I'm sure things will happen. Oh – Blast, Blast, Blast, Blast, etc.
ad libitum.

I must stop now my dear. Much love to you. Wish to God that
I could see you. But you will swear that if there's anything I can
do for you, however crazy it may seem, you'll let me know & I'll
do it. Never Unprepared⁵ & how.

> Be careful & not too good.
>
> BEN

1 One of Britten's uncles, William Hockey, was an alcoholic, as was
William's mother, Rhoda. Beth writes in EWB, p. 17: 'Because of this
and because one of her brothers [William] also took to the bottle
later, my Mother always dreaded that one of us would turn out to
be alcoholic.' This was a bit of family history of which Britten was
aware, and while he certainly enjoyed a drink, he was as cautious
and economical in his drinking as he was in most areas of his life.

2 The arrest of US citizens of Japanese origin whose loyalty became
the object of arbitrary and ill-founded suspicion, which led to their
internment. It was only in 1989 that final reparations were made by
the US government. See also John Armor and Peter Wright, *Manzanar*, with commentary by John Hersey and photographs by Ansel
Adams, (London, Secker & Warburg, 1989), and Russell Lee,
'Japanese Relocation', in Carl Fleischhaus and Beverly W. Braman
(eds.), *Documenting America, 1935–1943* (Berkeley, University of California Press, 1988), pp. 240–51.

3 Robert's wife and children. But this did not happen.

4 The mother of Helen, Barbara's lifelong friend.

5 See note 1 to Letter 5.

278 To William Mayer
[*Picture postcard: Bald Head Cliff, Ogunquit, Maine;*
in PP's hand]

[8 August 1940]

We arrived here last night on our way to Pemaquid, and go on to-
day. The car started off to the Berkshires in perfect style; then there
were three days of temperament, when it seemed to have an attack
of Beziehungswahnheit (?).[1]   Several mechanics turned it inside out
& couldn't find anything wrong, and now it's behaving very well.
We have been through lovely country and are enjoying ourselves.

Much love –

PETER

BEN

1 Beziehungswahn = Paranoia. The word to describe the car's malfunc-
tioning was obviously chosen to amuse Dr Mayer, the psychiatrist.
The postcard also reminds us that a whole chapter in any life of
Britten could be devoted to the trials he experienced with old cars,
from the days of his youth until he was able to afford a car that
was trouble free. However, none of the tribulations diminished his
enthusiasm for motoring. This epic journey in the temperamental
Model-T Ford is also vividly described by Pears in a letter to Beth
(see EWB, pp. 157–9).
    The car was bought
with some of the proceeds of [Ben's] Japanese commission and we trundled
off in it last week up to the Berkshires, to hear Koussevitzky & his Boston
boys play. They make the sweetest and most sublime sounds I ever heard.
They played Ravel's Daphnis and Chloe and it was so beautiful one wishes
it was a sin! We also saw a lot of Aaron Copland, who is a very good
friend of ours, and a long way the best American composer now-a-days.
When we get back to New York, I'll send you his
Piano Variations. They are pretty grim and awkward, but they are
considered the sort of classical modern American piece.

(Pears to his Cousin Barbie, August 1940)

279 To Elizabeth Mayer

Owl's Head Inn,
Owl's Head, Maine.
[12] August, 1940.
[recte 26 August 1940]

Dearest Elizabeth,

    Just a note in haste to put in Peters.[1] Il y a une crise over M.S.
paper – in other words I've run out! Could you please have a

good look round to see what there is about the place. In the first place I <u>don't</u> want:

a) Orchestral stuff i.e. with Flutes, & clarinets & clefs & what-nots printed down the side
b) the enormous great Schirmer stuff with 36 odd staves.

But any other is very acceptable – there should be quite alot of 24 lines (parchment brand No. 19 – 24 lines) – could you send me about 2 quires of that. There <u>may</u> be some 20 lines & I should like as much of that as there is. But there may not be – don't worry if there isn't. Sorry to bother!   Peter mentioned the musical sketches of Paul Bunyan I think. Please!

Just finished the Wittgenstein piece & am pretty bucked.

Much love to you,
BEN

Thank you for sending on the Red Cross letter. I don't know whether there is any sense in writing again to Canada until I have an answer saying he [Wulff] is actually there. What do you think? If you think it advisable to write again (I wrote about 2 weeks ago) the address is on the bed-room table – in a pencil written copy of a cable from Gustel Scherchen.

1 Pears had written a letter to Mrs Mayer on the same day.

Owl's Head Inn

OWL'S HEAD, KNOX COUNTY, MAINE

LLOYD G. KEMPTON, PROPRIETOR

280 To Antonio and Peggy Brosa

Owl's Head Inn,
Owl's Head, Maine.
August 13th 1940.

Dear Toni & Peggy,

Just a note to tell you that we have at last settled down for a few days & please write & tell us how things are going with you in that lovely house which made me feel quite sick with envy![1]

We eventually made Pemaquid Point, but found the place most disappointing – not on the sea, & full of the most terrible Bostonian old ladies, that we left after one gloomy night. Then we came on here which is a grand spot – very unpretentious – but quiet & right on the sea. We can work & there are tennis courts nearby. It is too cold to bathe unfortunately – but there is plenty else to do.

The car did well after we left you & apart from one or two ominous hiccoughs brought us here without mishap. But the roads are <u>terrible</u> – you'd both have been sea-sick in the dickie-seat!

We've made no definite plans yet, but if we like it we shall stay on quite abit. We definitely shan't go back to the Berkshires – too far & expensive. But we might make some arrangement to pick you up <u>if</u> you're still around. Let us know how you're enjoying yourselves & how long you can stand it or them you!

How's the painting? Felix Salmond is also in these parts – we saw him playing Golf yesterday – <u>what</u> a sight![2]

Love to you both from us,
BENJIE

1 The Brosas had been dropped off *en route* at Cape Cod: see Letter 282.

2 Felix Salmond (1888–1952), the English cellist and teacher, resident in the USA. He was the soloist in the first performance of Elgar's Cello Concerto. Salmond was exceptionally tall.

281   To Wulff Scherchen[1]

> As from: 123, Louden Avenue,
> [completed] Amityville, N. Y.
> (3.9.40)
> Owl's Head Inn, Owl's Head, Maine.
> [letter begun] August 15th 1940

My dear Wulff,

At last we have traced you! Your mother and I have been writing & cabling each other across the Atlantic the last few weeks, & I thought you would never be traced. However I shall write her air-mail at once saying that I'm in contact with you & now I can start sending you things – if I can think of anything besides the lists of things I am <u>not</u> allowed to send you! I have friends in Canada who will be able to send you things more easily than I can myself from here.

Well – I am sorry about the long silence, but for me as well as for you the last six months have been hectic. I was seriously ill for a month or so & only just recently has it all cleared up. Inspite of this and the general misery & worry one has felt I have had to do lots of work. My comissioned Symphony from the Japanese Government via the British Government had to be finished – & they may want me to go to Tokio to hear the first performance. I have a left-handed piano concerto to write for Wittgenstein (the Viennese pianist) now – so I've been busy.[2]

Peter has been well & is up here with me. We drove in a second-hand car I bought & had lots of trouble with it on the way – blast it! However it is marvellous now we are here. It is the first time I've been cool for ages it seems. Long Island was unbearably hot. We shall go and see Wystan in Massachusetts on the way back – & I'll give him your love. He is well & working hard.

I have news from the family in England regularly – they are all well.

I will send things as soon as I can get to a town or make

arrangements. I hope that things aren't too bad, my dear.
Although I haven't written I have thought about you constantly.
[. . .]

1 Scherchen was in Internment Camp 'Q' and the letter was addressed
to Army Base Post Office, Ottawa. In 1940, in wartime England, even
those who had fled from the Nazis were temporarily interned in
camps, some of which were far away from England. The fear was
that in the event of an invasion, the enemy forces would find a
ready-made fifth column awaiting them. This ill-judged, ill-founded
and ill-considered assumption led to much hardship among those
who had already, one would have thought, suffered enough. It was
in these circumstances that Wulff was shipped out to internment in
Canada. There is a good account of this unhappy wartime episode
in Ursula Vaughan Williams's biography of her husband, *R.V.W.*
(Oxford, Oxford University Press, 1964), pp. 236–7. Vaughan Williams, to his honour, was much dismayed by the government's action
and was eloquent and active on behalf of those who were so shabbily
treated. Matters improved when he was appointed Chairman of the
Home Office Committee for the Release of Interned Alien Musicians.
For a complete history of Britain's internment and overseas expulsion
of its wartime refugees, and the sinking of the *Arandora Star* in July
1940, see Peter and Leni Gillman, *'Collar the Lot!'* (London, Quartet
Books, 1980), and Letter 285. See also François Lafitte, *The Internment
of Aliens* (1940; new edition, London, Libris, 1990), and for accounts
of internees' experiences ' "Enemy aliens" remember war', *The Times*,
15 May 1990.

2 Wittgenstein was busy too with ideas and suggestions, among them
the dispatch to Britten (on 3 August) of a work by Franz Schmidt.
This must have been one of the two works for piano (left hand)
and orchestra that Wittgenstein had commissioned from Schmidt
(1874–1939), the two concertos of 1924 and 1934, the first of which
was a set of variations on a theme by Beethoven. That Wittgenstein
should have thought that Schmidt's score (whatever its merits) was
likely to be useful to Britten as a model, suggests that he had little
perception of the character of the composer from whom he had just
commissioned a work – or the character of his music. Mrs Mayer
wrote to Britten from Maine on 9 August: 'The music which Wittgenstein sent, is here, I don't send it.'

282   To Aaron Copland

Owl's Head Inn,
Owl's Head, Maine.
August 15th 1940.

My dear Aaron,

We've found the most glorious spot up here & are firmly settled here for abit working like the dickens & happy as kings. We had considerable adventures after we left you – the car started O.K. but we hadn't gone 5 miles when all the trouble started <u>again</u>. So we pulled in at a Ford Agent & he worked all Monday morning & most of afternoon on it – & apparently cured it – all went well as far as Worcester, & believe me, if it didn't start <u>again</u>. That of course upset all the Brosas' plans – they missed their connection in Boston – & so after tinkering about abit at the third garage that day we limped slowly to Milford – & then took Toni & Peggy by degrees actually to Cape Cod the next day. After that the car decided to reform (all by itself) & now apart from back-fires it goes well enough. So the trouble was probably neurotic – being associated with loupy musicians – what! So being here after all that – we feel inclined to stick around abit so will have to forgo the last Berkshire week-end. Very sorry! We'll contact you when we get back so please leave word if you've gone to the Guatamalas or wherever it was.

Hope your bad boys are still bad. In absent-minded moments we're still inclined to hum Shapiro's[1] trumpet-tune – curse him from us!

Be good & get on with the Sonata![2]

Love from us both,
Yours,
BENJY

1 Harold Shapiro (b. 1920), American composer. In his early years Shapiro was much interested in jazz and popular music and was well known as a pianist and dance-band arranger. Britten must be referring here to Shapiro's Trumpet Sonata in C, composed in 1940. His preceding remark about 'bad boys' might possibly be an allusion to composers, some of them close to Copland, who were involved in or influenced by jazz and popular music. The term 'bad boy' some years later came to be identified with George Antheil's well-known autobiography.

2 Copland was working on his Piano Sonata.

283   To Elizabeth Mayer

Owl's Head Inn,
Owl's Head, Maine.
August 22nd 1940

My dearest Elizabeth,

Thank you so much for forwarding all our letters that have arrived quite quickly & have so far been quite cheering – better than recent correspondence has had a habit of being I'm afraid. I was delighted to get Barbara's cable, because we had got rather a bad wind-up about the bombings that seemed to get nearer & nearer. Beth's & her other letters have been splendid – full of life & hope & interested in things far away from the scheme [i.e. scene] of war. I think they're being very brave & keeping their integrity remarkably. Barbirolli is going to do the Sinfonia some time this winter.[1] That may (or not) be a good thing. I hope all this correspondence hasn't cost you too much in postage – I hope (but it's a faint hope) that you have kept an account of it!

As you see, we are still here – & as a matter of fact we have had some acquaintances up here. We came in to dinner the other evening & heard some pretty sophisticated talk going on & recognised Kurt Weil![2]   He was spending a few days here with Mr. & Mrs. Maxwell Anderson (Key Largo fame – or infame!).[3] We saw quite alot of him & he really was awfully nice & sympathetic, and it was remarkable how many friends we had in common, both in Europe & here. He tells me that Werfel[4] was not shot & may be coming here, & that Goland [sic] Mann[5] apparently has been contacted with – other news not so good. I am terribly relieved to be in contact with Wulff – don't worry I'll send a first tentative parcel from here, to see how much gets thro' (he wrote me lists of things forbidden) & then we can make up good parcels from Amityville – please!

Our other acquaintance up here was Beata Mayer whom we prevailed upon to visit us for a few days! We can then take her back with us when we go South at the beginning of next week – perhaps stay a night at the Whites[6] & then drop her off when we get to Williamsburg. It is lovely having her up here, & the weather after a skirmish over the week-end, a most exciting storm (not thunder!), is perfect; & she seems to be enjoying it a lot.

I don't know how long we shall stay with Wystan – but I'll let you know from there. It depends on how my work is going;[7] so far it's going quite well & I haven't much more to sketch – but there's many a slip . . . as I found in the Sinfonia!

I had abit of trouble with my throat & tonsils, but that has cleared up now. Luckily Beata knew all the right things to do so it isn't any more trouble at the moment. But I must have those old offenders out pretty quick when I'm back.

Peter is well & cheerful & sends his love, & so does Beata, to you both. We are so glad you rubbed in[8] the Maine idea!

Much love,
BEN

P.S. We expect to leave here on Monday 26th – letters after c/o W.H.A. please.

1 The first performance of the *Sinfonia da Requiem*, Op. 20, was to be given at Carnegie Hall, New York, on 30 March 1941, when the New York Philharmonic Orchestra was conducted by John Barbirolli.

2 Kurt Weill (1900–1950), German composer (he became an American citizen in 1943), of *Die Dreigroschenoper* and *Mahagonny* and, in his American years, *Knickerbocker Holiday*, *Lady in the Dark*, *Street Scene*, *Lost in the Stars* and many other shows and scores. He also wrote *Down in the Valley*, a college opera (1945–8), a late 'American' contribution to the genre which he had so powerfully initiated in Germany in 1930 with *Der Jasager* (see also DMPB, pp. 108–13).

   When Britten and Weill met in August, Weill was still working on *Lady in the Dark*, which was to open in Boston on 30 December and in New York (Alvin Theater) on 23 January, where – with Gertrude Lawrence, Bert Lytell, Victor Mature and Danny Kaye – it was still running when *Paul Bunyan* was launched on 5 May 1941. It seems certain that the virtuoso patter song, 'Tchaikovsky', from the show, made famous by Danny Kaye, provided the model for the verbal acrobatics of 'The Love Song' in *Paul Bunyan*. See DMPB, Appendix B, pp. 78–82 and 145–6, and Philip Reed, 'A Rejected Love Song from *Paul Bunyan*', *Musical Times*, June 1988, pp. 283–8, which includes a facsimile of the song from Pears's vocal score of the work. It was a number, however, that Britten discarded when revising the operetta in 1974. The 'Love Song' appeared in 1990 on Virgin Classics, VC 7 91107-2, together with the discarded finale to the original Act I and the unperformed Overture, in an orchestration by Colin Matthews.

3 Maxwell Anderson (1888–1959), American playwright, who collaborated with Kurt Weill in many musico-theatrical projects, e.g. *Knickerbocker Holiday* (1938) and *Lost in the Stars* (1949). *Key Largo* (1939) was a verse play by Anderson, in which an idealistic American serves in

the Spanish 'Loyalist' forces, i.e. the army of General Franco. Hence, no doubt Britten's 'infame', i.e. 'infamous'.

4 Franz Werfel (1890–1945), Austrian poet, playwright and novelist, author of *The Song of Bernadette*. When in the USA (from 1940) Werfel was to marry Alma Mahler, the widow of the composer. He had collaborated with Weill in 1934–5 on the panorama of Jewish history the first title of which was *Der Weg der Verheissung*, which was finally staged in New York in 1937 in a revised format as *The Eternal Road*. See also Peter Stephan Jungk, *A Life torn by History: Franz Werfel 1890–1945* (London, Weidenfeld and Nicolson, 1990).

5 Golo Mann, Thomas Mann's elder son.

6 Mr and Mrs Homer White, friends of the Mayers. Anne White had known the Mayers in Munich. Her husband was a writer and an amateur musician. Mrs Mayer wrote to Britten on 9 August:

He [. . .] is a good musician [. . .] and has a very simpatico and cultured voice, baritone, thank heaven not tenor. He plays the piano very well, and having hurt his right hand with a combination of typing and tree-felling, you, Ben, might use him as a guinea-pig for the lefthanded piano-concerto [. . .]

7 On *Diversions*. On 12 August Pears had written to Mrs Mayer:

We're wondering about your friends the Whites. Is it really an invitation, and could they really face putting us up for a few nights? If it honestly would not be an imposition, please send us a card by return and we will write and invite ourselves, perhaps for late next week. Ben would like them to have a piano to work his left hand on!

8 'Rubbed in', i.e. persuaded Britten and Pears to make the trip to Maine.

284 To Beth Welford
[*Full text*, EWB, *pp. 152–6*]

Owl's Head Inn, Maine.
As from: Amityville, N.Y.
August 25th 1940

My darling Beth,

I got your grand long letter about aweek ago up here where Peter & I have been staying a week or so having a much needed rest from Amityville – heat & so on. I am delighted that you don't find my letters too unsympathetic & casual in these beastly times & if you want everyday news you shall certainly have it. Personally it is a relief for me not to write of war, because it is almost the only topic of conversation now & certainly one thinks about it most of the time. I nearly went dotty during the very bad raids[1] the last

week (& as you can guess they are reported pretty 'hot' here!), &
was overjoyed to get Barbara's cable. So she's away on vacation
– that's fine – wish she could stay out of London altogether. Your
& Kit's letters I may point out have been grand – it has been very
illuminating the way the war has been reflected in people's letters
– & I'm damn proud the way my family has come out of it. Of course
you can't help showing you're depressed now & then, Barbara too,
poor dear – but you three (B.B. & K.)² have kept your integrity
marvellously. Robert's letters have changed since Wellingboro'³ –
full of scandals & school affairs (most amusing – I enjoyed it no
end) & only a slight patriotic peroration at the end. Lennox – poor
dear – all brave. Sophie – sweet, all bound up in Music & children.
Enid Slater – just desparate, she doesn't seem to have anyone to
talk to much. The most depressing is Ethel Bridge who has gone
wildly flag waving & bloodthirsty – I just dread her letters.⁴ Still
she is probably in the happiest state, living where she is. Frank
is more balanced. And so on – very interesting, if one weren't so
emotionally hit by it all. This is all to point out how very much
your letters are appreciated! Please continue.

Thank you most awfully for looking after the money side of my
things – I feel relieved to know you are doing it. I at last had a
letter from Nicholson saying nothing in particular rather
distractedly. Poor dear, having to run that business without much
help. Anyhow I signed a form authorising him to sell life insurance
& telling him to send you the residue (if any) after paying off the
overdraft. And don't bother to put my money on deposit unless
you really want to – because I want you consider it the money as
yours & nothing to do with me – none of this keeping some incase
of future. If I come back I'll come back with enough (D.V.W.P.!)
to live on. So – don't go asking my permission to buy a new coat
– buy 20 if there's enough money. I'm glad you could pay
Barbara's bill for telephone. Does she need any more? Oh dear –
oh dear I do feel so bad that I can't send any more – but I daren't
because now B & H can't pay me any more here I have to rely on
commissions & they aren't very frequent – & poor Peter's jobs
aren't coming in very fast as yet. But if there is any urgent need –
cable & I can get money easily; you've no idea of my resources!!!

Well – Peter is telling you all about our trip up here & the
adventures with the little green Ford (blast it). I shall be sorry to
leave to-morrow altho' our holiday isn't over yet as we are going
to stay with Wystan in the Berkshire mountains (Massachusetts).
Get out your map & see where we are – 200 miles from Canadian

border – right on the ocean. A grand spot – but sea is too cold
for comfortable bathing. Rockland is nearest town – & Portland
nearest big place (150 miles S.W. of us). I don't know how long
we shall be in Massachusetts – all depends on weather & money.
I have been busy up here & finished all the sketches for my latest
commission (the one-handed piano-concerto for Wittgenstein); but
I still have lots of things to get done. Good thing to be busy – &
so far the ideas come rolling in. Then I suppose we shall go back
to Amityville for abit – at anyrate until I've had my old tonsils
out – which will be as soon as my throat is fit. Incidentally ask Kit
if he knows about the great Sulfa's – Sulfamilamide & Sulfapyridinc[5]
– which are all the rage here now & judging by accounts amazingly
successful. One is for pneumonia & one for Streptococcic
infections – I can't remember which is which. I know that I had
one of them last week & certainly it brought down my temp.
which was round about 103° on Sat. evening to 98.7° on Sunday
morning! And the Dr. Brown who attended me has had some
staggering results with the pneumonia one. Wish we had had it in
1937![6]   They've only been out here for about a year, but
apparently were invented in Europe & not much used for a long
time. Anyhow – nice to think of people inventing things to save
lives nowadays! I expect to have tonsilectomy at the beginning of
September – & I expect I shall go on living in Amityville, for when
Christopher goes back to school & Michael takes an apartment
(American for flat!) in New York instead of 'commuting' (going
up & down in a train to N.Y. everyday!) & as Ulli has a job & Beata
will be living in New York the parents will be lonely & press us
to stay with them – & certainly it is very cheap to do so. Actually
one gets abit tired of it – you see the Home is really a small village
where everyone knows everyone & everyone's business, & the
intrigues & scandals are unbelievable. Dr. Mayer gets very tired
of the work too – he had his own practise in Munich, & it is difficult
for him not being the boss. Dr. Titley, the boss, is a younger man,
not such a fine psychiatrist, but a good organiser & there is a certain
amount of friction – & of course it is the old story about the wives
of all the doctors, & asking the staff to meals – this person sulks
because that person has been asked twice a week & she has only
been asked once. Not that lots of the people aren't nice, but it
seems impossible for people to be shut up together without
squabbling. And Mrs. Mayer, darling as she is, is inclined to put
people's backs up by not being tactful; Of course she is very
intelligent & has met lots of poets & writers & can speak six

languages, but that doesn't excuse her in the eyes of the assistant-
secretary who has been snubbed for talking of the new doctor's
lady-friend – etc. etc. etc. So it's all abit trying. Luckily Mrs. Titley
(who is also a doctor & practises in the home) is one of the most
charming people I've ever met, & she makes life well bearable
there, altho' she herself has a packet of trouble. This has been a
tough year with innumerable crises – the Long Island home crises
(most acutely emotional!) are famous – & she has come out tops
every time. I'm longing for you to meet these people. God how
I hope you come over here – or I bring them over to England – the
Mayers & the Titleys are well worth knowing! Peter & I are (when
we are there) living with the Mayers now – we slept at the Titley's
home for about 8 months & eat at the Mayers – shucks! I'd better
draw you a map of the place:

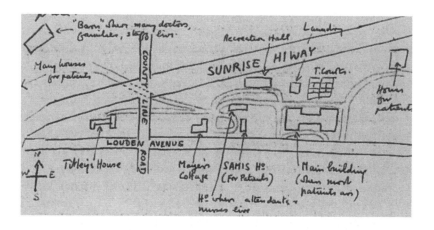

The pencil is the road system actually on the grounds – the ≡ ≡ ≡
is a tunnel under the Sunrise Hiway (American for Highway!).
The County Line Road divides Nassau from Suffolk county –
actually the county line goes through the Titley's house & the
East being Suffolk – we have been sleeping in Suffolk all the time.
    Everything is done very well in the place of course. The
arrangement about food is that cooking is done in the actually
[sic] houses & cottages individually, but the food is bought by the
central Main building & distributed from there, & paid for by the
Home! Servants – Titleys have three & a nurse for Rachel (aged 4).
Mayers – one, a black (actually coffee-coloured) – Edith – abit
clumsy & slap-dash (slap-<u>dish</u> would be more appropriate!) but
with a heart of gold & never gets upset although ten visitors may

arrive unexpectedly for dinner – which often happens! So you see,
apart from the little extras (such as Coca-Cola – the American
national drink – made from a Cola bean, which is not immediately
attractive, but is a slight stimulant, & grows on one lots!) we don't
<u>cost</u> the Mayers anything. So our consciences are easy on that – &
both Doctor & Mrs. M <u>do</u> seem to like having us; at least when we
go away they write & say they miss us & want us back quickly!
Actually Peter ought to be more in New York next season, so
we'll have to see whether we can afford a room for him somewhere
& I'll go on living at Amityville.[7]   But it seems hopeless to try &
make plans – one can only speculate these days. It has been fun
having Peggy & Toni living in Amityville too, & as Wystan often
comes down, & Ralph Hawkes too, we have been quite a colony.
People still seem to like the English here – at least one's accent
makes people prick their ears up, even if they don't understand a
word! You've no idea how difficult it is to make people understand
often – especially in shops – & quite often people think you're being
snooty – which I don't like being considered – even if it's true! But
on the whole people envy us being English – altho' we have made
such a goddam mess of our politics – though the American system
is pretty lousy too.

Thank you so much for the photos which I carry about with me
in my pocket book. Sebastian looks a grand kid, I'd love to see
him. Give him a pat where he likes it best from Uncle Ben!   I'm
sorry you didn't like my picture. I thought it rather impressive,
although the wind was doing it's damnedest that day, I remember.
Certainly the garb was yankee – but rather comfortable, & people
wear most highly coloured stuff over here, you know. And, by
general consent, brushing my hair <u>slightly</u> back (<u>not</u> right back)
instead of only sideways, helps matters by giving me a forehead,
which I didn't have much of before. Of course now with my new
tooth I've got a real Kolynos grin. Anyhow I've got to have some
nice press photos taken soon & then I'll send you some to judge.

I must stop this screed. The trouble is (don't laugh) that I take
up so much time writing to you & Barbara that I don't write to
anyone else – so I get numerous bitter complaints from other
sources. Incidentally – Lennox has <u>no</u> right to the jumper – at
least I paid for half of it, & anyway he just pinched the AC which
was a present to me, & besides I am storing his beastly furniture
for him. No – don't you dare give it up – see?!

Much love to you all three. Even if the invasion <u>doesn't</u> come,
do still try & come over – the winter isn't going to be much of a

picnic – to be avoided if possible. Anyway remember that if there is the slightest chance & you want something done this end, just cable & it'll be done. Why I said just write on one side of the page was because censors have a habit of cutting bits out of your letters & when you write on both sides I lose <u>two</u> sections of interesting news not only one. See? So please get <u>thin</u> paper. I'm in touch with Wulff who is safely in Canada & seems in not too bad a way. Thank goodness he <u>is</u> over here now. Best place for him.

Much love my darling, write again & often,

BEN

Beata, who's here with us, sends her love. Peter hasn't completed his saga of our trip & will send it in a day or so.

Love B.

1 Air-raids on London – the 'Blitz' – had started in earnest on the night of 23 August. This was the period of the 'Battle of Britain', from 10 July to 31 October.

2 Beth, Barbara and Kit.

3 Wellingborough, the public school where Robert was now teaching.

4 On 2 June Ethel Bridge had written:

Goodness knows how long we shall be able to remain here as now that the Huns are so very near, we are not in a safe area. [. . .] We had the army cutting places all along our land & hiding with guns & rifles, as they expected a raid, so for once I felt 'Well now the soldiers are in our garden they'll look after things for us & so we could go to sleep without the fidgets' [. . .] we are all so <u>proud</u> of all the little boats which have proved so wonderful during this miraculous evacuation, it's more than one can speak of.

5 Sulphanamide = the class of drug. Sulphanilamide was the earliest type of antibiotic drug and was to save many lives in the war.

6 Britten refers to the death of his mother.

7 However, when the move was made from Amityville, Britten and Pears moved together. See note 2 to Letter 291.

285 To Gustel Scherchen

as from: c/o Dr. Mayer,
Long Island Home,
Amityville, N.Y.
August 26th 1940

My dearest Gustel,

Thank you for your letters & cable – it is a great relief to be in touch with Wulff again, & I know how you must feel: it was a terrible time of anxiety. However it is much better that Wulff should be over here on this side of the Atlantic, things being as they are, for altho' anything else than an allied victory is hard to imagine there is another possibility, and again war-fever is definitely at a lower pitch in Canada than in England, & I could imagine that must mean alot to a person like Wulff. You speak about obtaining his release – but I should think that Dent's letters to Macmillan[1] would do as much as anything to obtain that. I can't think of anyone who could help as much as he would – but, I admit, I am very skeptical about this being obtained – actually whether it would be wise, unless of course the Canadian Government decided to release alot of the prisoners. Suspicions are running very high at this moment. Entry into this country would be impossible – however powerful the influences that could be used – the quota is filled for four years, & besides it is highly probable that he might become an 'enemy alien' in this country pretty soon, I'm afraid, & the position would be even worse here. At the moment all societies are working overtime for the German refugees caught in France, Holland etc., & are inclined to think Wulff in a rather fortunate position – ! My dear Gustel, I know how you feel. It is tragic for the dear boy, but we must, & he must, just regard it as a period of 'marking-time' (as it is for everybody else). I will get all books that he wants for the continuation of his studies & I will send him everything I possibly can to make the physical discomforts less, & I have such faith in him that I feel sure that he will pull through all right. It is the period after the war that will be most trying – but pray God there will be someone around who can help him – & I am sure there will!

I hope you are as well as possible. I am glad you are going to live with your sister – she will be a great comfort to you – although I wish it wasn't going to be in London.

It is a terribly worrying time – & of course we get all the news

(with considerable additions!) over here 'all hot', & one's feeling
of helplessness just grows & grows. However I have had lots of
work to do & that has kept me sane. I have written a new
Symphony (commissioned by the Japanese Government thro' the
British Government – & I may have to go to Tokio for the first
performance!) – & a one-handed piano concerto for Wittgenstein –
you know him? Peter is also working hard & is singing with
Klemperer next season.[2] He & I have been staying up in Maine
(working at the new concerto) & enjoyed it very much, & who
should arrive at the same little Inn, miles away from anywhere, but
Kurt Weil. Naturally we had long talks about you & the old days.
He is such a nice man.

   Well – I must write some other long overdue letters now. I will
let you know at once if anything develops about Wulff & believe
me, I shall do my utmost.

   Don't be too unhappy, my dear.

   We shall meet one of these days.

Much love,
BENJAMIN

1 Presumably Harold Macmillan (1894–1986), politician (later Prime
   Minister, 1957–63), who was Parliamentary Secretary to the Ministry
   of Supply (1940–42) in Churchill's wartime government.

2 This engagement with Otto Klemperer (1885–1973), the German conductor, materialized in October. Klemperer had been conductor of
   the Los Angeles Philharmonic Orchestra from 1933 but was struck
   down by partial paralysis in 1939 and for a number of years conducted only very rarely.

286 To Ralph Hawkes

c/o W.H. Auden,
Clary Farm,
Williamsburg, Mass.
September 2nd 1940.

My dear Ralph,

   I presume you are still here in this country, since I haven't heard
to the contrary – anyhow I sincerely hope so, since the other side
is not a healthy place to be in at the moment. Have you much news
from there?

   Please tell Doc [Heinsheimer] that I am now writing out a

beautiful copy of the Wittgenstein piece & will send it off at once
when it's done. I've written to him direct & told him all about the
piece – which I'm very pleased with – hope he'll like it! It's quite
substantial, but attractive, I think. It plays about 22 minutes (with
possible cuts) – title 'Concert Variations'[1] – any comments?

Our New England tour staggers on – we had an alarming run
down from Maine – with Battery trouble & flats. We're just
wondering what else can go wrong. We met some charming people
in Ipswich (E. Mass.) & are going back there for next week-end
(address: c/o Mr. Homer White, Ipswich, Mass.) & will then come
back here for next week – to stay with Lincoln Kirstein's sister
(Mrs. Curtis, Chapelbrook, Ashfield, Mass.), until the 16th. I find
it very easy to work up here – & as we are having grand hospitality
the going is cheap! Incidentally we have been discussing plans &
have decided that (i) we must get our papers in order, which
means quota & Cuba[2] (ii) we must therefore be in the centre of
things & must live in New York – so we shall be hogging it round
Manhattan soon. I think it's wise, don't you, in these days, when
one must be on the spot.

Auden has been in Hollywood & has made some excellent
contacts for him & me (& Christopher Isherwood who is on
contract there now) to do a musical film.[3]   His agent is Mrs. Edna
SCHLEY (10480 Troon Avenue, Los Angeles, (Ardmore: 862010))
and the man he is in contact with is Mr. McKenna, M.G.M. Story
department. Could you tell this to Schulhoff[4] & get him to follow
it up with Abe Meyer of MCA? I feel there's something there.

Do let me have a line here. We don't go east till Thursday.

All the best,
Yours,
BEN

Greetings from Auden & Peter.

1 An early title for *Diversions*, Op. 21, inscribed on the composition
   sketch. The location of the fair copy of the manuscript full score,
   which Britten would have given the pianist as part of the commissioning arrangements, is unknown. The Trustee of Wittgenstein's Estate
   and his widow, Hilde Wittgenstein, tell us they have no knowledge
   of its whereabouts.

2 Cuba may have been in Britten's mind because it was there that Paul
   Wittgenstein had sought a visa.

3 While in California in the summer of 1941 'Auden also saw Isher-

wood, who was living near Hollywood and was working on film scripts for M.G.M.' (HCWHA, p. 296.)

4 Andrew [André] Schulhof, the Hungarian-born head of Boosey & Hawkes Artists' Bureau and Beata's employer. In *Fanfare for 2 Pigeons* (New York, Garrett Publications, 1949), p. 106, Heinsheimer wrote:

Boosey & Hawkes, in order to assist Bartók and his wife, the pianist Ditta Pásztory, in their attempts to get engagements on the concert stage, had started a little concert bureau of their own. Thus I worked for him in a double capacity as publisher and as manager, to the last days of his life.

Schulhof's Hungarian origins would have placed him in a unique position to assist his exiled compatriot in the search for concert engagements.

287 To Peter Pears and Benjamin Britten
From Elizabeth Mayer
[*Typed*]

> William Mayer, M.D.
> The Long Island Home,
> Amityville, N.Y.
> Phone: Amityville 2
> September 4, 1940

Dear Peter,

your very important and upsetting letter arrived just this minute when we left for New York. I take the chance to send you all the affidavit-forms quickly to Ipswich where you may be by now. I was afraid the letter would not reach you any more in Williamsburg. I shall refrain from any comment on your plans – only – you have to send the right form personally to Bill and ask him yourself – I really cannot do it in any form, because I even do not see him at all. We are at this moment only on greeting terms – since we are back from Maine they have never asked us over to the house, and I really do not know, what it is all about, neither does William. We have just decided to wait and not to bother. But you know how sensitive he is about my "mothering" you two, and I would never dare to say a word about you, or ask for something. Don't take it too serious – we know after all his moods etc. By the way, he has rather angrily mentioned to William that he once came into the empty house to look for his tennis-racket and did not find it, if you took it with you? You better mention it and apologise . . . you know the irritability of the young man.

I had already mailed – air-mailed the Letter of Ben to Kay [Leslie], and realised only afterwards that you meant me to send her also a form. But I am not quite sure which one. I enclose some Air-Mail-envelopes, so that you can send the right things quickly. Kay's address is 609 Sheridan Road, Winnetka, Illinois. My dear boys, everything I can do for you, I love to do. Give me all kind of orders and requests . . . for ever and ever. Ben gets his list to-night. I cannot do it this moment, perhaps I can still enclose it . . .

In a big hurry, William already in the car, Love from all of us, also to the Whites. I am so glad that you got on well together. I'll go up there too very soon,

Be careful!
E.

[*Handwritten:*]
Dear Ben: here is your list.

op.	1.	Sinfonietta
op.	2.	Oboe Phantasy
op.	3.	A Boy was Born
op.	4.	Part Songs – Simple Symphony?
op.	5.	Holiday Tales
op.	6.	Violin Suite
op.	7.	Friday Afternoons
op.	8.	Our Hunting Fathers
op.	9.	Soirées Musicales
op.	10.	Variations on a Theme of Frank Br.
op.	11.1.	On this Island (Songs) [i.e. the first of a probable two volumes of Auden settings]
op.	12.	Mont Juic (Catalan Suite) with L.B.
op.	13.	Piano Concerto No. 1 in D
op.	14.	Ballad of Heroes.
op.	15.	Violin Concerto.
op.	16.	Young Apollo.
op.	17.	A.M.D.G.
op.	18.	Les Illuminations
op.	19.	Kermesse Canadienne.
op.	20.	Sinfonia da Requiem

(written on Grand Central [Station] I'll send you some typed sheets. But Anne and H. [the Whites] have a typewr. probably).

Love: E.

288   To Ralph Hawkes

The Clary Farm, Williamsburg, Mass.
Sept. 8th 1940.

My dear Ralph,

Many thanks for your wire. I got in touch with Gene Goossens immediately, & as I was supposed to be staying this week-end with friends only 80 miles from where he is staying I made an arrangement to go to lunch with him on the 9th. Actually, the week-end fell through and I developed a bad cold & I didn't like to risk a 200 miles drive possibly bringing on another streptoccus attack, so I phoned Gene last night & had a long & very friendly talk – the result of which is that I may drive up & see him for a night at the end of this week (cold, car & strep. willing) or anyhow see him in New York. So I think that ought to cover everything. How are you? How's business?

The article of mine in Tempo[1] seems to have caused a rumpus in London, I am sorry to say. Truth is always impalatable, especially when one is in the middle of an air-raid. I feel sick it was issued there just at this moment.

B.H. are cutting up rough with me in London. I had a letter from my solicitor saying that they didn't like giving him information about my monies (they said that they had 'no remuneration' for work of that kind) – but he can't have asked much, only details for income-tax & so I think that's inreasonable, don't you? Could you perhaps mention . . . . . . ?? Another thing, I had a pathetic note from Sophie Wyss saying that L.B. [Leslie Boosey] had written asking for her M.S. copy of Les Illuminations & she wants to go on singing from it – "sentiment . . . it was written for her . . . first performance . . ." – as the firm has the M.S. of the score, I think she might be allowed to keep that copy, don't you?[2]   Could you also perhaps mention that . . . . . . ???

Meanwhile I have practically finished the neat copy of 'Concert Variations' for Wittgenstein & hope to post it to you to-morow.

I'm making lots of contacts here. Nearly fixed a show of Illuminations & a new short ballet with Lincoln Kirstein.[3] I'm going to work like hell this autumn – it's the only way to keep sane. I want to do some incidental music for Columbia [CBS].[4]

We stay with: Mrs. Mina Curtis,
   Chapelbrook,
   Ashfield, Mass.

for a week from to-morrow.

> All the best; many thanks etc.
> Sorry to be a blithering nuisance.
> Yours ever,
> BENJY

1 This was the article which had already appeared in the USA in April
(see note 3 to Letter 243). It was probably comments like the following
that caused the 'rumpus':

> Let me say straightaway that, in my opinion, the American composer has
> little to grumble at; compared with English composers, nothing. Whatever
> struggle American music may have had in the past for its fair share of public
> recognition, today the composer here, compared with his English brother
> even in normal times, has a very rosy prospect.
>
> In the first place, as far as I can see, there does not exist in the minds of
> most audiences here the deadening distinction so common in England,
> between 'music' and 'contemporary music'. This in part may have been
> caused by the British Broadcasting Corporation's mistaken policy of giving
> a full-sized concert once a month by music of contemporary composers
> (generally of the most formidable and unattractive kind); and with this
> gesture, having done its duty to 'contemporary music', it returns with a sigh
> of relief to the normal programs of 'music'.
>
> [. . .]
>
> Contemporary music should take its place in concert programs side by
> side with the well-tried masterpieces; it should be judged solely on its merits
> as music.
>
> American audiences appear to be less prejudiced in this respect than
> English ones. Most of the symphonic programs include a twentieth-century
> work, and the halls do not seem to be any the less full. American composers
> should be very definitely helped by this attitude, in their efforts to be heard,
> and, to judge from the concert and radio columns of the Sunday papers, it
> is undoubtedly the case. Since the beginning of the season, modern music
> generally has been continually broadcast, and American music in particular
> has received outstanding encouragement from such festivals as the ones
> organized by ASCAP [American Society of Composers, Authors and Pub-
> lishers] and, more recently, by WNYC [radio station], as well as the fine
> concerts of American music given by Dr Koussevitzky. The programs of the
> Boston and New York Symphony Orchestras contain American works, as
> do the programs of the symphonic bodies all over the country.
>
> In England, too, there is no such organization as the WPA, which accord-
> ing to the press, has performed 7,332 American compositions by 2,258 native
> or resident composers! I wish that the American musician could see the
> programs of the BBC Symphony, the London Philharmonic Orchestra and
> the London Symphony Orchestras. He would not think himself so hardly
> used.

2 The original manuscript vocal score was written out by Britten, Pears
and Berkeley. Berkeley copied only two songs, 'Marine' and 'Being

Beauteous'. Sophie Wyss retained the score, which is now in the Archive.

3 Probably *Divertimento*, the ballet based on *Soirées* and *Matinées Musicales*: see note 4 to Letter 315.

4 See note 1 to Letter 298.

289 To Elizabeth Sprague Coolidge

The Clary Farm, Williamsburg, Mass.
as from: Long Island Home, Amityville, NY.
Sept. 8th 1940.

Dear Mrs. Coolidge,

We (Peter Pears & the Brosas) enjoyed the festival concert in Pittsfield at the beginning of August very much; but I was much disappointed that I had not an opportunity of meeting you. When do you return to the East? I should be very pleased if you could let me know as I much look forward to making your acquaintance, and talking about our many mutual friends, and also the project for your next Festival, which you mentioned to me.

I expect to spend the winter in New York as it seems that still the British Government does not wish any one to return – one's absence and possible means of sending currency being more precious than one's presence. I feel very lucky in being in a country where one is able to work and to think about other things than destruction, but it is a terribly anxious time. My family is scattered over the East of England and in London, & I have friends in every part of the country.

In order to be able to work freely in this country I must change my status from that of a visitor to that of an emigré, in other words I must leave the country & re-enter on the quota. This procedure is made much easier if one has letters of recommendation from prominent people, and I know of no one whose word would carry more weight than yours. Would you be so kind as to let me have something of this sort, which I can show the Consul in Havana where I propose to go? I should really be most grateful.

I hope you are well and not too worried by the terrible happenings of these dreadful days. One really needs music to restore one's faith in humanity.

With best wishes and many thanks,
yours very sincerely,
BENJAMIN BRITTEN

290 To Elizabeth Mayer

c/o Mina Curtiss,
Chapelbrook,
Williamsburg, Mass.
Sept. 12th 1940? Anyhow Thursday
[which was the 12th]

My dearest E.,

Thank you as usual for everything, including your very sweet letters, which we both love having.

Well – our tour is very nearly at an end. We go up to Maine to-day to see Eugene Goossens about matters musical.[1] Then back here for the week-end. Then on Monday we set our noses South. We expect to stop in on Dr. Williams[2] in Connecticut for lunch – & be back home fairly late on Monday evening. I don't know my dates, but I believe we shall just see you before you go off with Chris. the next day, which will be nice – but <u>don't</u> be away too long – there is too much to talk about! Of course all these plans are weather-permitting as the car is <u>impossible</u> in the rain – the top is completely non-weather proof! But we'll wire you if there's any cancellation. Thank you for being so bright about the Japanese Consulate. I'll see him when I get back. I have a sinking feeling that they want me to go to Tokio.

We are enjoying our stay here. It is a lovely house & Mina Curtiss is a sweet person & very intelligent. Lincoln comes for this week-end. We have lots of music. Yesterday Peter & I went in to Northampton & tried over the new Concerto on 2 pianos & it sounded quite nice. I'm going to play it to you. It's not deep – but quite pretty!

Much love to you all. By-the-way – Bill T. [Titley] wrote Peter a sweet note & said he'd certainly do the affidavit and for me too if I had need of it. (I haven't heard from Kay[3] yet). I do hope things are easier with you – I think it was very wise to have them over for music. I'm so glad you're playing for Toni – now no more need for bashfulness when I'm around![4]

Very much love & thanks, & looking forward
everso much to Monday.

BENJAMIN

Ralph Hawkes is off to England, had a long & depressing conversation with him in Toronto[5] last night.

1 Britten had written to Wulff Scherchen on 10 September:

Today Peter & I drive up to Maine to Eugene Goossens. He may be doing some things of mine next season & I've got to go & be nice to him. Luckily he's a very pleasant person [. . .]

2 Unidentified.

3 Kay Leslie: Britten was inviting his friends to support his current visa application.

4 Mrs Mayer had studied piano at the Stuttgart Royal Conservatory of Music, where she was taught by Max Pauer. The birth of Beata put paid to her professional career. She was a capable pianist but clearly could be shy about playing in Britten's presence.

5 By telephone.

291 To Beth, Kit and Sebastian Welford

[EWB, pp. 160–61]

Amityville, N.Y.
[18 September 1940]

My darling Beth, & Kit & Sebastian,

This is only a scribbled note to put in with Peters[1] as it is late & I want to go to bed, but I didn't like to send his off without a word. Your letter Kit has just arrived; thank you more than I can say. It was a grand description, & gave me a very vivid picture of what you are going through. My God, if I could only get you out of it all. I'm praying that something will materialise out of our scheme, but I've had no news from Dr. Churchill as yet. If anything whatever occurs don't hesitate to come as I can always get friends to guarantee your existance – see? That of course goes for Barbara too. Where is she? Surely not in London still? Can't you persuade her to leave. Sorry if this is all hysterical (& out of date when it arrives probably) but all one can think of at the moment is the News, & that is pretty ghastly. I'm afraid I've got very bad wind-up, probably much worse than you all have, but it's only not hearing from you, & not having an idea of what's happening to you.

We got back here the day-before-yesterday, & it is grand to be back with the family again. They are such dears & such a comfort in these bloody times. Peter & I are going to take a flat with Wystan Auden for the winter in Brooklyn[2] – one of the districts of New York City. We feel we have to be nearer the big city where things go on & jobs are born. But I loathe the idea of living in a town again –

I expect I shall always be hopping down to Amityville again. The flat ('apartment' here) is quite nice – but small – with a grand view of the river, which is something. It is very cheap by New York standards – but hideously expensive by English (& the current exchange) – nearly £5 a week! It's a terribly dear place to live in. Luckily all parts of America are not the same.

There are lots of problems to be settled at this moment, & it is very worrying. There are so many alternatives as to what to do, & what one <u>wants</u> to do too – that I, who never was good at decisions, don't know where I am. I wish to God I could be back with you, but that's no use, because obviously if I were back I couldn't be <u>with</u> you – so that's not much sense. One feels bad about not suffering as well – & of course many militant people here are very cross with us for being alive at all (esp. old ladies) – but one must try & be realistic, & that's what I'm trying to work out now – where one is most use & least bother. If you have any ideas let me know! (Officially one must stay put).[3]

By-the-way I was horrified to find that the selling of the Life Insurance didn't cover the overdraft, Beth. If the Boosey And Hawkes money doesn't cover it from next quarter (i.e. if they can pay at all, which I doubt) – you'd better let me know. But at the moment I'm abit broke and can't send any – what with the new tooth in front, my tonsils, the blasted car that would go wrong & now the flat! I wish I could sell that Mill.

I must stop now, my dears. All luck to you.

Keep your heads – & don't get caught by any emotional hullaballoos ('duty' & what not) – but I know you will.

Much, much love to you all,
BEN.

1 On 25 August Pears had started a long letter to Beth ('the saga' to which Britten refers in his postscript to Letter 284). Pears's letter was not completed until after 16 September, when he and Britten were back in Amityville.

2 Britten and Pears were about to move into a house, 7 Middagh Street, Brooklyn Heights, owned by George Davis, at the time the literary editor of *Harper's Bazaar* and himself a writer. (He was in later years to marry Kurt Weill's widow, Lotte Lenya.) Pears was to send his mother, on 19 October, a description of the new abode and the reasons that motivated the move:

We are down here only for the weekend this time, as Ben and I have taken 2 rooms in New York. We feel that we really <u>cannot</u> stay here any longer

altogether. The Mayers have been so kind that I cannot hope to describe
it, and they have received us as their children, and we have felt to them as
to our mother and father, and although they really begged us to stay and
we are of course no expense to them, we felt that we didn't ever want
to become a burden to them. We are quite easy about having lived with
them so long – They have loved us, and loved having us. But you understand
how it is, we don't want to feel they have to take us into consideration in
all their plans. So, as a friend of ours has just bought a house in Brooklyn
(the south part of N.Y. City, across the river) & he offered us rooms on
the top floor very cheap, we decided to take them. We are buying a very
little furniture and I hope it will be comfortable. We went up last week to
try and get into it, but the plasterers & painters and carpenters hadn't nearly
finished. They're incredibly slow! Don't you believe that this country is so
marvellously efficient! because it isn't – the workmen seem to work when
they like and only then. So it was cold there – no heating, and dust &
plaster everywhere! so we came down here!

In this Brooklyn brownstone Auden was proxy landlord to a household that surely must be among the most remarkable ever to have
been gathered together under one roof. At various times, and for
various periods, the residents included the writer and composer Paul
Bowles (and his wife, Jane); Britten (who moved a Steinway into the
communal living room); Davis; Gypsy Rose Lee; Louis MacNeice (a
brief visit); Carson McCullers, the novelist; Golo Mann (who was
often visited by his sister, Erika, whom Auden had married in 1935)
and his eldest brother Klaus; Pears; and Oliver Smith, the theatrical
designer (who was later to design several notable musicals, including
On the Town (1944) and *Billion Dollar Baby* (1945), and the Tanglewood
production of *Peter Grimes* in 1946; see PFL, plate 205). He was a
cousin of Paul Bowles. If one adds to these 'founder' residents the
friends and acquaintances – most of them associated with the arts –
who visited the house from time to time, then what Denis de Rouge-
mont wrote about 7 Middagh Street as it struck him in 1941 seems
free of exaggeration: '[. . .] all that was new in America in music,
painting, or choreography emanated from that house, the only center
of thought and art that I found in any large city of the country'.
(Quoted in Virginia Spencer Carr, *The Lonely Hunter: a biography of
Carson McCullers* (New York, Anchor Books, 1976), pp. 124–5: the
whole of the seventh chapter of this study is devoted to an account
of 7 Middagh Street from 1940 to 1941.) Much information about the
owner of the house, George Davis, is to be found in Donald Spoto,
Lenya: A Life (London, Viking Penguin, 1989).
See also HCWHA, pp. 303–7; Christopher Sawyer-Lançanno, *An
Invisible Spectator: A Biography of Paul Bowles* (London, Bloomsbury,
1989); and Paul Bowles, *Without Stopping: An Autobiography* (New
York, G.P. Putnam's Sons (1st edition), 1972), pp. 233–5. Mr Bowles
remembers the 'big black Steinway' Britten had installed in the 'first

floor parlour'. (He had an upright piano of his own in a small room 'in the cellar behind the furnace' where he worked on his ballet *Pastorela* for the American Ballet Caravan.) He recalls that Auden, Britten and Pears occupied the third floor of the house. George Davis was on the first floor, Oliver Smith and Paul and Jane Bowles on the second and Golo Mann in the attic. 'It was an experiment', he writes 'and I think a successful one, in communal living. It worked largely because Auden ran it; he was exceptionally adept at getting the necessary money out of us when it was due.' Mr Bowles supplemented his published recollections with a private communication dated 8 December 1982 which contains a few further illuminating details of the Middagh Street household:

I'm afraid I have very little to tell you regarding Benjamin Britten. My sojourn at the Middagh Street house lasted only about four months. And although we all ate together each day at the same table, he and I had nothing memorable to say to one another. One might say that the household was segregated rather than integrated: there were British and there were Americans, and the members of each group appeared to find its own nationals more sympathetic, thus easier to converse with, than the others.

I first met Britten at Aaron Copland's studio somewhat earlier. At that time he was not talkative; he struck me as obsessed by his work. In the house at Middagh Street he had a concert grand in what was called the front parlor; and when he was not using it, Wystan Auden sometimes played Chopin. My own workroom was in the sub-basement, as far as I could get from the sound of the piano! (I had my own upright which I was using to compose a ballet.) As far as I can recall, Britten and I never had a disagreement about anything, but doubtless that was because Auden would not allow what he considered 'controversial' subjects to be discussed at meal times. (I approved whole-heartedly of his injunction: nothing interfered with our digestions save perhaps a bit of overindulgence at times, for the food was good.)

We are indebted to Caroline Seebohm (Mrs Walter Lippincott) for allowing us access to her unpublished account of 7 Middagh Street ('Conscripts to an Age'), which contains much material of interest, including this description of the colourful household:

A more different atmosphere from Amityville could hardly be imagined. Instead of a small, well-organized household where serious work could be and was done [Britten and Pears] now belonged to a huge, rambling society of creative eccentrics, living in varieties of squalor. Auden ruled the roost after a fashion; he collected rents, paid bills, organized food, calling meal times. The rest of their days were less structured. Many of the rooms were unfurnished, although George Davis's quarters were elaborately decorated with Victoriana, a mixture of camp and kitsch. He had written a novel in the early thirties which became a *succès d'estime* (it was the childhood story of a writer in horrifyingly claustrophobic family surroundings), and he had lived some time in Paris, where he was part of Cocteau's circle. [. . .] 'He looked like a frog. But he was charming,' said James Stern's wife, Tania.

(They had known him in Paris.) 'The first time I ever went to Middagh Street,' Stern recalled, 'Carson was sitting crouched up in a corner with a gallon of sherry under her left arm. George was sitting at the piano. There was no floor, just rubble. George was sitting at the piano with nothing on at all, smoking a cigarette. A black mamma they all loved hovered in the background, coming in and out.' Middagh Street was odd, but it was lively.

In New York in 1941 James Stern collaborated with Auden on the dramatic adaptation for radio (CBS) of D.H. Lawrence's short story, *The Rocking-Horse Winner*, for which Britten wrote the incidental music. For further information on the Sterns, see HCWHA, pp. 200–21, *passim*.

The twentieth birthday of Auden's friend and collaborator Kallman was celebrated in the house on 7 January 1941. Auden wrote a special poem for the occasion; Lincoln Kirstein and Marc Blitzstein were among the guests, and Pears sang 'Make Believe' from *Show Boat*. See Dorothy Farnan, *Auden in Love* (London, Faber and Faber, 1985), pp. 25–7. (There were to be further encounters with Blitzstein, who in August 1942 came to London as an enlisted member of the United States Eighth Air Force.)

For a graphic description from Britten of life at Middagh Street see Letter 303. The first extant letter from the new address is No. 297. A description of the house appears in *Time*, 16 February 1948, p. 65: 'It was a ramshackle, remodeled four-storey brownstone whose architecture had fascinated Auden and his friends: from the street it looked something like a Swiss chalet.' See also *The WPA Guide to New York* (New York, Pantheon Books, 1982), pp. 441–4, and Susan Edminston and Linda D. Cirino, *Literary New York: a History and Guide* (Boston, Houghton Mifflin, 1976), pp. 348–53.

See also Richard Channing, 'An Audenary House', *Harpers and Queen*, March 1988, pp. 208–10, in which a photograph of Britten accompanying Pears in the drawing room of Crag House, Aldeburgh, is wrongly attributed to New York. In 1945 the house was torn down to make way for the Brooklyn–Queens Expressway.

3 On the same day that Britten wrote this letter, Pears was writing to his mother:

I am wondering whether I shall come back to England soon or wait till we are called – I suppose they have enough men or they would have called us back before – but on the other hand I might be some use in the fire-brigade or carrying a stretcher. What do you think?

An account in Auden's hand rendered to Britten and Pears for two weeks' accommodation at 7 Middagh Street

292 To Ralph Hawkes

c/o Dr. Mayer,
L.I. Home,
Amityville, N.Y.
October 7th 1940.

My dear Ralph,

I was overjoyed to get your letter; to know that you'd arrived safely and found that you could stand up to the strain of the "orchestra"[1] and the other inconveniences! How you can sleep through it beats me, as the softest thunderclap or fire syren shoots me out of bed – but I suppose one would get used to it. I see in to-day's [New York] 'Times' that you had a night of respite yesterday – let's hope you have lots more. I think it is grand the way the firm is able to carry on. I was very much afraid that the destruction of so many buildings close to you might have affected you, & relieved to find it hadn't. I hope by the time you get this that nothing will have happened to alter that.

I am afraid what you say about performances of my things in England & what some people are saying doesn't surprise me, much as it hurts me.[2] But it is absolutely understandable, and I want you please not to press my works at all. If people want to play them over there, they will,[3] but I don't want you to embarrass yourself in any way. A propos of this I have a financial scheme

to propose to you. Why not, for the 'duration', wash out all
payments to me in England. If you like you could continue a
minute 'token payment' so as to prevent the contract being broken.
I don't want to break it – & hearby give you my word I won't
offer any work to another publisher in England or elsewhere,
without first offering it to you. But I simply don't see why you
should continue paying me when conditions have so completely
changed. If I could receive the normal share of what B H earns
from my things in this country I should be grateful. Write me please
what you think about this.

To return to the matter of my absence from England at this
moment – I have been desparately worried, not really about what
people are saying (I feel that one's real friends in England will be
unselfishly pleased that one is being spared the horrors – that is
in fact what every letter says so far), but about the fact that one is
doing nothing to alleviate any of the suffering, that both of us
again asked official advice on what we had better do. The answer
is always the same – stay where you are until called back; you
can't do anything if you do go back; get on with your work as
artistic ambassadors etc. etc. Incidentally – if the latest
developments hadn't developed I should be on the high seas to
Japan at this moment. There has been an awful lot of commotion
about my attending this Tokio festival. I have to see the Consul in
N.Y.C. [New York City] early this week to get final instructions,
but the head of the Brit. Board of Commerce has been helping me
over the matter & now advises me not to go. Anyway I'll let you
know what happens.

Otherwise nothing much. I've refinished the Sinfonia to my
satisfaction at last.[4] I'm scoring the piano concerto with which
Wittgenstein seems pleased. Seen alot of Gene Goossens who is
very favourable at the moment. Peter most probably will do Les
Illustrations (sic.) at Cincinnati[5] as well as Chicago.   Hollywood
seems to be waking up. Have been discussing Mahler projects
with Heinsheimer (he was out here yesterday).[6] Am writing 2 piano
suite for les Robertsons.[7] Very friendly letter from Mrs. Coolidge;
no definite plans yet about next Festival – but hopes . . . . .
Koussey & his Boston boys are definitely doing Variations next
season. We're not coming in on quota yet awhile – feel this is the
wrong moment to change our status & anyway we may be called
back . . . . Moving to our apartment end of this week or beginning
of next. That's all, I think.

Please give my very kind regards – & wishes of good luck to all

my friends you see – especially Miss Jackson. I hope she's well &
bearing up.

And all the best to you, Ralph, old boy – hope to see you by
Christmas over here if I don't meet you over there before!

Yours ever,
BENJY

P.S.   Toni and I have just finished Vol. I of the Violin book, & will
be consulting Max [Winkler] about it this week. Shall we proceed
on Vols. II, III, IV, V, VI . . . . . yet?

1 A reference to the London Blitz.

2 Much heat in wartime England was engendered by the departure of
   Auden and Isherwood for the United States in January 1939, followed
   by Britten and Pears in May, though in fact the motivation and
   consequences of the two sets of exits were in many respects very
   different. Isherwood referred to the climate in England in a letter to
   Britten in New York, written from California on 18 March 1940:

   I wonder so much what your plans are. Are you on the quota, etc? Or will
   you eventually go back? Wystan and I, as you know, are branded as traitors
   by the English press – and even our so-called friends are joining in the
   chorus. It's all so unutterably silly and sad and messy. The whole war is
   such a lousy mistake that one can't even work up a good hate against it.
   And suppose it will just spread and spread, in a kind of nasty festering way.

   Isherwood probably refers to an ambiguous editorial by Cyril Connolly in the February issue of *Horizon* (see Charles Osborne, *W.H.
   Auden: The Life of a Poet* (London, Eyre Methuen, 1980), p. 199); and
   on 13 June a Question was asked in the House of Commons about
   Auden's and Isherwood's absence in the USA, an exchange that
   ended with the MP, Major Sir Jocelyn Lucas, who had asked the
   original Question, asking another:

   Is my Hon. Friend aware of the indignation caused by young men leaving
   the country and saying they will not fight? If they are not registered as
   conscientious objectors will he see that they lose their citizenship?

   (Osborne, op. cit.)

   There was a moment of high comedy in this parliamentary
   exchange when it appeared that the Minister in replying confused
   Auden with the tennis star H.W. ('Bunny') Austin (see HCWHA,
   pp. 291–2). But in fact the raising of the matter in the Commons
   was evidence of the hostile attention now being paid in England to
   absentee 'intellectuals'. There was denunciation in the popular press
   and yet further debate in literary journals and circles, in which E.M.
   Forster and Louis MacNeice joined.

   On his return to London in September, Ralph Hawkes wrote to

Britten on the 26th, the final paragraph of his letter sounding a cautionary note:

As I have only been back a few days, I have not yet seen anybody that you know but I have seen evidence of a situation which I think I must bring to your notice immediately. There is no doubt at all that we are going to have difficulty in getting performances of your works and caustic comment has been passed on your being away. I remember what you told me and again I would say that I do not wish to influence you in any way, for after all you must be your own master but I feel it my duty to tell you of this situation.

Britten's friends, as early as April, seem to have been aware of the circulation of hostile opinions. Marjorie Fass, in a letter to Daphne Oliver, wrote:

Bill [Ethel Bridge] tells me that there have been lots of writings in various papers about Benji & Auden & Co. so much so that possibly they'll never be able to come back to England again.

In the summer of 1941 the controversy, that had hitherto largely centred on literary figures, suddenly opened up in the columns of the *Musical Times*. This long correspondence was initiated in June by a letter from Pilot-Officer E.R. Lewis, and continued in August, September and October. His letter appeared under the heading 'English Composer Goes West', and with some ingenuity not once mentions Britten by name, though that Britten was the target can not have been missed by a single reader:

The favour recently shown to a young English composer now in America, has, to my knowledge, caused discontent which calls for notice. The taking of American citizenship by the group to which he belongs invites mockery of the sociological ideals which it formerly proffered at considerable length, and I must protest at the continued description of this musician as a 'British composer' when, by his own action, he disclaims the title. Moreover, though his work should have the same chance of performance within these shores as has other imported work, is the particular favour shown by concert-givers, particularly the B.B.C., in the best of taste?
  The one justification of such prominence is overwhelming merit, and this composer's reputation hardly fulfils that condition. A large body of critical opinion was unenthusiastic towards his first essay in concerto form, yet the work received many concert and broadcast performances. His next venture is published, puffed, and arranged for piano and violin even before the several performances waiting for it have allowed consideration of its worth. To the gifts of any artist who uses them consciously, I wish to do nothing but honour, and I am well aware that the boundaries of art are international (in this case they need to be!), but I call for justice and a sense of proportion. Why should special favour be given to works which are not of first rank when they come from men who have avoided national service, and when so many British artists have suffered inroads upon their work so as to preserve that freedom which, musically, they have not yet enjoyed to the full? It is not encouraging to see others thriving on a culture which they have not the courage to defend.

As the letter makes clear, the writer's indignation had been aroused by the first British performance of the Violin Concerto on 6 April 1941 (see Letter 312). (On the matter of Britten's citizenship, Mr Lewis, of course, had got it wrong.)

Gerald Cockshott, from Norwich, wrote in Britten's defence, without knowing, of course, that the official advice given to the composer in the USA after the outbreak of war had been to stay put:

I have seen no statement of Mr Britten's private reasons for leaving this country at the beginning of the war, but it seems to have been generally assumed that he wishes to continue his work undisturbed. If that assumption is correct, all praise to him. The artist's place in society is not something that has been defined once and for all by divine law or precedent, and the fact that Mr Britten's personal solution of the problem is not necessarily that of the majority of the general public is no excuse for bad taste. The general public doesn't write works like the 'Variations on a Theme of Frank Bridge' or 'A Boy was Born'.

I can sympathize with those persons who feel that the attention that has been given to some of Mr Britten's more recent work is not justified by the quality of the work itself; but that is an entirely different matter. If this composer fulfils his early promise, posterity will not care a brass farthing how he behaved or did not behave as a member of society. They will rather thank their stars that Mr Britten had the sense to act as any government with a genuine regard for art would have *made* him act. And we have no real reason for assuming that Mr Britten's talent has 'dried up'.

Let the would-be wits ask themselves this question: which would they honestly prefer – Gurney, Butterworth and Denis Browne alive and composing in America, or the tragedy that we all know so well?

It was at this stage that the editor of the journal, Harvey Grace (1918–1944) intervened, and his final paragraph conspicuously raised the temperature:

Mr Cockshott's final hypothetical question is a mere quibble that takes no account of the millions of other tragedies incident to war. After all, there are even worse fates than being unable to go on living and 'composing in America', and one of them may be the consciousness of having saved one's art and skin at the cost of failure to do one's duty.

Mr Cockshott was not to be put down, and restated his arguments with what strikes one still as admirable eloquence:

I personally believe that by continuing to serve his art Mr Britten is rendering the best service to the country. He may not be making any immediate contribution to the national cause; but ultimately it is by its cultural achievements that a nation will be judged. If Mr Britten has something original and important to say, we shall be the poorer if he is not allowed to say it. I am fully aware that 'there already exists more music than can get itself performed'; but time will sift out the ephemeral from the enduring, and Mr Britten has already given us clear indication that he is capable of producing the kind of music that will endure.

I do not agree that my hypothetical question was no more than a quibble.

One composer may well affect the whole history of a nation's art. Where would English music be today if those men who happened to survive the last war had shared the fate of their less fortunate colleagues? Can we honestly say that a government has a genuine regard for art when it is content to leave such tremendous issues to mere chance? It seems to me fantastic that our rulers should take care to safeguard the artistic achievements of the past from damage and at the same time display such complete indifference towards the men who bid fair to produce the achievements of the future. For Heaven's sake let us at least try to preserve our sense of spiritual values even amid the distractions of these detestable times.

In the meantime, the lists were entered by Mr Eric Halfpenny, whose letter the editor does not print, but from which he quotes a comment on conscientious objectors and entertainers and musicians who 'have managed to excavate for themselves convenient vocational funkholes within the armed forces, from which they not infrequently emerge to give recitals and concerts and broadcasts'. The editor, to do him justice, refutes Mr Halfpenny's assertion, but in doing so makes clear where *his* contempt is directed:

[. . .] this discussion began with, and must be confined to, the position of artists of military age who are living in safety abroad. Those attacked by Mr Halfpenny have at least not 'ratted'; and if they can combine their military service with musical work, mostly for the benefit of their brothers in the Forces, so much the better.

'Ratted' is revealing of how high feelings could run in the early years of the war.

The correspondence continued in the October issue, with Mr Cockshott making a sharp comment – 'I had thought that tolerance of unpopular viewpoints and the freedom of the individual conscience were the very things that all of us wish to maintain. If so there can be no harm in pointing out that Freedom, like Charity, begins at home' – with Mr Halfpenny complaining that his views were misrepresented, and with E.J. Moeran, an old family friend, writing to remind readers that

It seems to be assumed that Mr Britten went to America at the beginning of the war. [. . .] In fairness [. . .] I would point out that he left this country many weeks earlier, and that at the time of the outbreak he was already fulfilling engagements in the U.S.A. Provided that he keeps valid his artistic integrity, I consider that he is doing his duty in remaining where he is.

The editor provided a long coda:

[. . .] nothing brought forward in this controversy has convinced us that gifted young composers are more important than gifted young creators in any other art, or even than the possessors of outstanding ability in any kind of work that is of vital importance to the country; and we believe that this is the view of the public and of the bulk of musicians themselves.

It can not have been by accident that his final column of comment was juxtaposed with a report of Shostakovich discharging his obligations as a fire-fighter in Leningrad, with parts of his broadcast message editorially italicized, e.g. *'The cultural workers of Leningrad are doing their duty like all other Leningrad citizens.'*

How much of all this was known to Britten and Pears is not clear. Although they may not have known of the detail of the *Musical Times* correspondence (there is no evidence of their having seen it), like Isherwood they must have been well aware of the climate of hostility aroused by their absence. One might think that the controversy was confined to the period of the American years from 1939 to 1942, but in fact the hostility spilled over into the years after their return to England and manifested itself in attitudes with regard to Britten's employment by the BBC and the undertaking of the première of *Peter Grimes* by Sadler's Wells. Indeed, it was only on 20 March 1941 that the ban on the employment of conscientous objectors by the BBC had been lifted. British intolerance of pacifists and homosexuals, we sometimes wonder, may have contributed rather more than has been recognized hitherto to that retiring 'privacy' for which Britten was renowned. Perhaps it was also, in part, forced upon him by circumstances and adopted as a means of self-defence. The controversy and hostilities of the 1940s may have cast a longer and more influential shadow than we had imagined.

(Gerald Cockshott (1915–1979) was a schoolmaster, writer and composer, who had studied privately with Vaughan Williams. His works included two one-act operas, a Symphony in B minor, and songs, carols and choruses, among them many arrangements of folksongs.)

3 Of the works Britten composed after leaving England in 1939, only the following were performed in England during his absence: *Les Illuminations* (first complete performance), 30 January 1940; *Canadian Carnival* (first broadcast), 6 June 1940; and the Violin Concerto (first performance in England), 6 April 1941. In respect of the last, Hawkes was at pains to explain to Britten, in a letter dated 20 December 1940, that the suggestion for the performance of the Violin Concerto came from the London Philharmonic Orchestra and not through undue pressure from himself. He was evidently complying with the composer's wishes as expressed in this letter.

4 Since delivering his manuscript full score of the *Sinfonia* to Tokyo, Britten had made some revisions to the last movement. Thus the fair-copied autograph full score does not represent the composer's final version of the *Requiem aeternam*. The revisions were mostly significant but minor contractions, with the exception of the movement's final bars which Britten rethought. The first two movements were untouched.

5 This suggestion was probably the result of Britten's discussions with Eugene Goossens who was permanent conductor of the Cincinnati

Symphony from 1931 to 1946. As Letter 303 makes clear, the proposal evaporated. Goossens had already heard an impromptu performance of *Diversions*, from the composition sketch, which was laid out for two pianos. Heinsheimer had written to Britten on 3 September:

Will you be in town on the 21st? Eugene Goossens will be having dinner at the home of a friend of mine, that young American composer John Haussermann, who is very anxious to meet you and asked me several times to bring you out to him. Would you accept an invitation for the 21st? This would, by the way, be a very good opportunity to play the Wittgenstein Concerto for Goossens. Haussermann has two pianos, and if Peter would join you, we could have a perfect show on two pianos, with your right arm bound behind your back or at the ceiling as you please.

Goossens wrote to Heinsheimer on the 27th:

It was good to see you the other night at Haussermann's. What a delightful evening we all spent – an evening made really conspicuous by the first hearing of the Britten left-hand concerto. This is a truly amazing work and confirms again one's knowledge of the fact that Britten is the outstanding young man in the world of creative music today.

6 The upshot of this discussion was Britten's arrangement for 'reduced orchestra' of the second movement from Mahler's Third Symphony, the Minuet 'Was mir die Blumen auf der Wiese erzählt'. The arrangement was commissioned by Boosey & Hawkes, New York, and published (in 1950) under the title 'What the Wild Flowers tell me'.

Britten outlined the principles guiding his arrangement in an article, 'On Behalf of Gustav Mahler', which appeared in *Tempo*, 2/2, American Series, February 1942, p. 5:

The reduction of the scoring will not make as much difference as might at first be thought, as the movements chosen for this edition are mostly the middle ones, in which the extra instruments (such as 4th Flute, E flat Clarinet, and Double Bassoon) are only very occasionally introduced, and so may be omitted with small loss of effect. The complete orchestra is usually reserved for the big first and last movements. Mahler himself set the precedent of performing the movements out of their contexts, giving in fact titles to some of them. And though one has to admit that these movements must lose something of their special significance when performed thus, I am convinced that it is an excellent way of introducing Mahler's music to more orchestras and a wider public, and of helping to remove his 'hard-dying' bad reputation.

It is of some interest to note that other Mahler arrangements by Britten of a like kind were contemplated. The movements proposed were the second movement from Symphony No. 2; the second and third movements from Symphony No. 1, and the third movement from Symphony No. 3. In the event, Britten arranged only the Minuet from the Third Symphony. Erwin Stein's reduced orchestration of the Andante from the Second Symphony was published by Boosey

& Hawkes. Britten's article on Mahler was reprinted in *Tempo*, 120, March 1977, pp. 14–15.

7 *Introduction and Rondo alla Burlesca*, Op. 23 No. 1, for two pianos, completed in November. It was first performed on 5 January 1941 as part of a two-piano recital given by Ethel Bartlett and Rae Robertson. Jerome D. Bohm wrote in the *New York Herald Tribune*, 6 January:

Penned in the autumn of last year, the music reflects, at least in its slow introduction, something of the tragic fate which is overtaking the composer's native England, although neither the subject matter nor its treatment exhibit much originality. Mr Britten has discovered that the juxtaposition of the major and minor modes produces an effect of tension and relief; but Schubert and Wagner have exploited that device more tellingly and the leading theme of this slow introduction, a descending figure consisting of a series of long notes connected by a short-valued two-note figure, is similarly wanting in individuality. The Rondo itself, 'ironical and bitter' in intention, is labored and ineffectual.

Ross Parmenter in the *New York Times*, 6 January, wrote:

The Britten work, which was played here for the first time, had in it some of the same disturbed quality to be found in Hindemith's work of the early twenties. It was interesting and its ideas were well worked out. The performance was expressive and skilful.

The *Mazurka Elegiaca*, Op. 23 No. 2, 'In memoriam I.J. Paderewski', was not composed until the summer of 1941, when Britten was visiting Bartlett and Robertson in California.

293 To Wulff Scherchen (51628)

c/o Dr. Mayer,
Long Island Home,
Amityville, N.Y.
October 8th 1940

[. . .]

I have been glad to get your occasional letters and post-cards, but we must both get used to the idea that correspondence is very disorganised & one doesn't get answers for a very long time. For that reason, since I haven't heard yet that you have received the books I sent, nor the gum-boots, I am not sending very much money with this letter. As soon as I hear that you are getting my letters & parcels all right I'll send more.[1]

I hope that conditions are not too bad for you now; that you have the clothes you want. If there is any specific clothing you need – write & tell me it, because I have no idea of what you've got or want. See?

I have not had much mail from England recently, which is rather worrying. Barbara is still in London, which cannot be pleasant; I suppose Gustel is in Hampstead?

Life goes on much the same – I find it more and more difficult to concentrate on music these days – but one must pull oneself together & go on working. Luckily there is quite alot I <u>must</u> do, so I have no alternative but to do it. Peter is singing a certain amount in concerts, & singing very well. He also finds it difficult to work. There has been alot of talk about my proposed trip to Tokio for the Symphony I wrote – but the British Consulate advises me not to go, for which I am very grateful!! I may have to go to Hollywood,[2] which I should hate; but if I had the chance I must take it, since it is a grand way of making alot of money quickly, and I'm afraid the family in England will be needing it soon. Things are so disorganised for them.

Barbirolli is doing my new Sinfonia da Requiem at the Philharmonic this Season – how I wish you could be there to hear it! I wonder how long it will be before we can take up our normal lives again. I am terribly sorry for you, my poor old thing, but I know you are strong enough not to get demoralised by it all. I think about you and wonder what you are doing all the time.

Have you any news of your father? Do you know where he is? I wish he could get a job over here, but the profession is so hopelessly overcrowded that it would be stupid for him to come unless he had some actual engagements.

Well, my dear; I must get on with my work. Much love to you, & all good luck to you.

[. . .]

Peter sends love too,

Yours ever,
BENJAMIN

1 Britten had written to Wulff on 10 September:

> I feel so sorry that I haven't yet made up a parcel for you – but since I got your address I have again been ill, & as soon as I got better I have been travelling round the country & had no time to do it. Anyhow when I get back to Long Island on Monday I'll send one, & don't be cross if it hasn't got things you want in – because I don't know what you want. Anyhow next time you write, tell me <u>exactly</u> what you want, having found out what you're allowed to receive, and I'll send it all along quickly.

2 For Britten (unlike Johnny Inkslinger in *Paul Bunyan* – 'A telegram, a telegram, / A telegram from Hollywood'), the summons never materialized.

294   To Elizabeth Sprague Coolidge

c/o Dr. Mayer,
Amityville, N.Y.
October 14th, 1940.

My dear Mrs. Coolidge,

I ought to have written to you before this to thank you for your very kind & helpful letter. When I re-enter the country I will show it, as you say, to the Consul & I am sure it will make things much easier. Owing to the tragic news coming daily from England, I have decided not to change my status at the moment, since if there is anything that I can do to help eleviate some of the terrible suffering there I must be free to be able to go there. Still, at the moment, we are told to stay where we are & to go on working, which is very, very difficult, however.

We hear regularly from the Bridges – they are having a terrible time, but so far they seem to have escaped any actual harm to themselves or their property, for which I am very relieved. I do wish that some reason could be arranged for them to come to this country; it is so tragic for them to have this worry & disorganisation at their time of life. But I feel that neither of them would leave unless there was some specific reason.

If it is at all possible I wish so much to come to Washington at the end of this month to be present at your celebrations.[1] There are one or two 'buts' – uncertainty of immediate plans as usual, & a small operation I have to have[2] – but I am living in hopes that these may be overcome!

Once again, thank you so very much for your most helpful letter. I hope that you are in the best of health.

With best wishes,
yours most cordially,
BENJAMIN BRITTEN

1 Probably a birthday celebration. Mrs Coolidge was born in October 1864.

2 See also Letter 298, in which Britten announces that his troublesome tonsils have at last been removed. Britten was in the New York Hospital, Room 1214, on East 68th Street, from 21 to 24 October. On leaving he paid a total fee of $54.60, at 12.47pm. (The receipted account is in the Archive.)

295   To Hans Heinsheimer

c/o William Mayer, M.D.,
The Long Island Home,
Amityville, N.Y.
November 4th 1940.

My dear Hans,

Here after three & a half solid days of heart-breaking work, leaving my temper for ever bruised & battered, are the Sinfonia proofs! They are quite well written & actually few copying slips – the trouble is that the copyist is obviously completely inexperienced. I have made all the <u>additions</u> necessary, but the alterations & eradications she must do, & I have indicated them all. So will you send them back to her with the following mild comments.

1.   <u>Cues</u>. Choose the obvious instruments playing <u>striking</u> passages – it is no use choosing the 2nd Flute if the whole orchestra is playing ff. It is no good giving the middle of an 'ostinato', as no one knows where on earth the 'ostinator' is. <u>Above all</u> in the transposing instruments (Clarinets, Cor Anglais, Horns, Sax. etc.) the cues <u>must</u> be transposed into their pitch. This will entail alot of work but it <u>must</u> be done. I have indicated this through out.

2.   Expression marks. It is allimportant where these start and stop, i.e.

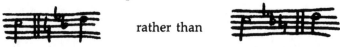

is <u>not</u> the same as

Again common sense must be used in deciding to which instruments expression marks refer. Forinstance, in several places crescendos have been put under rests – not easy to play, that!

3.   It is usual when changing key to put the <u>correcting</u> accidental first & then the remaining accidentals; and again the double bar not after the accidentals e.g.

rather than

4.   Turns of pages must be arranged where possible for players convenience & <u>not</u> in the middle of important solos. Sometimes this is difficult but in this particular work there is no difficulty whatsoever. In most cases here it is just annoying but I am afraid

the three Trombone parts will need re-copying – I have marked
why – unless the copyist has exceptional ingenuity with sticking
plaster etc.!

5.   There is no title of the work on any part – this is unfortunately
necessary owing to the existence of many other orchestral works (see
Beethoven, Mahler etc.) And why should the movement headings
be so secret in pencil?

6.   The Percussion parts are a great muddle. How four players are
expected to play off two parts, I don't know, especially when they
are scattered over the ends of the earth as percussion players
usually are. I don't know how this is going to be arranged. A
separate Timp. part must be copied. Probably if a separate
Xylophone part too were copied that might solve matters. But
who knows definitely about this? The Philharmonic Librarian? Also
for 2 harps – 2 parts?

I am afraid all this will be a shock – but break it gently. When
she has digested it all I'll be pleased to recommend her – as she
writes clearly & accurately.

How was Washington? Just had a nice letter from Ralph H. – but
no mention of the Mahler scheme.

I'm much better in the throat now & will be in town some day
this week.

How's Bartók?[1]

yours, in haste,
BEN

Have written a note to Wittgenstein.

1 Bartók and his wife, after an arduous journey from Europe, had
   arrived by ship at New York on 29 October and disembarked the
   next day. Ralph Hawkes, after Germany's seizure of Austria in March
   1938, had already been in touch with Bartók and entered into a
   publishing contract with him. His music had previously been published by Universal-Edition of Vienna.

296   To Beata Mayer

[?November 1940]
[recte 1941]

Dear Beatty,

Here is the agreement – duly signed sealed & settled. Thank you!
Thank you also for sending the other things by William [Mayer].

I'm not terribly impressed by the printing of the Wittgenstein piece – it's so small. I hope Dr. H. [Heinsheimer] will sell magnifying glasses with it. Besides the paper is so dark & the ink so grey – gives me a liver attack to look at it!

Hope your cold is progressing well – or rather I hope it is leaving you? By-the-way has Michael got a morning coat I could borrow for Sunday's Riverhead concert? (American for Morning coat is 'Cutaway' I think – anyhow it is cutaway & got tails)

Excuse scribble & haste.

Love,

BENJY

1 Since *Diversions* was published in 1941, this letter must have been written that year.

Identification Card.

Name BENJAMIN BRITTEN
Street 7 MIDDAGH ST
City BROOKLYN HEIGHTS
State N.Y. Tel. No. MA.4.3009
In case of accident or serious illness, please notify
Name Mrs. ELIZABETH MAYER
Address LONG ISLAND HOME, AMITYVILLE, N.Y.
Tel. AMITYVILLE 2.

297 To Hans Heinsheimer

7, Middagh Street,
Brooklyn Heights, N.Y.C.
[?November 1940]

Dear Hans,

Here are (a) agreement duly signed[1] (b) another letter to the Japs.[2] The latter is not final by any means; the historical part of it can be extended a great deal, if we decide to use this kind of method for them, when I come in next week & go thro' your documents on the case – this is compiled solely from my own. I think it is more dignified than the one we wrote the other day – & considering the present American & British attitude towards Japan, I think we ought to be quite direct. Could you tell me the man from the British Library when he phones you?

I'll think about the Szell matter.[3]

Best regards,
Yours ever,
BEN

P.S.   Sorry to bother you, but it is essential that we have the
<u>complete</u> letter from Konoye (in translation of course!) – in order that
we get his attitude & tone exactly. Could you please ask Mr. Mori?[4]
In such a matter as this we must really insist.

1 A letter of agreement that allowed Britten to be paid royalties on
   performances of his works in the USA by the New York office of
   Boosey & Hawkes, thus mitigating the serious financial position in
   which he found himself when wartime regulations no longer permitted the transfer of funds from London.

2 Earlier in the month the crisis over the commissioning of the *Sinfonia
   da Requiem* had been precipitated by a letter of rejection from the
   President, Prince Konoye, of the Committee for the 2600th Anniversary, addressed in the first instance to the Director of the Cultural
   Bureau of the Japanese Foreign Office in Tokyo, a copy of which was
   then forwarded to Hans Heinsheimer in New York by the Japanese
   Consul General. Heinsheimer had then informed Hawkes of this
   serious hitch.

   Prince Konoye's letter, which is of historic interest, follows complete, in the translation Britten requests in his postscript:

                                      Re: Mr. Britten's composition
   Dear Sir:
   Mr Benjamin Britten's composition is so very different from the anticipation of the Committee which had hoped to receive from a friendly nation
   felicitations expressed in musical form on the 2,600th anniversary of the
   founding of the Japanese Empire.
   We are afraid that the composer must have greatly misunderstood our
   desire or that we did not understand each other fully enough.
   It seems to us that this is a composition in the nature of a 'Requiem
   Symphony' composed in memory of the composer's own parents and does
   not express felicitations for the 2,600th anniversary of our country.
   Besides being purely a religious music of Christian nature, it has melancholy tone both in its melodic pattern and rhythm making it unsuitable for
   performance on such an occasion as our national ceremony.
   We are puzzled and should like to ask that you make further inquiry in
   this matter. Meanwhile the Committee will hold Mr Britten's composition.
                                                    Yours very truly,
                                         PRINCE FUMINARO KONOYE
                                                          President.
                           Committee for the 2600th Anniversary.

   Britten and his publishers embarked on drafting an appropriate
   reply, one version of which was included in this letter to Heinsheimer. The reference to it – 'more dignified than the one we wrote
   the other day' – suggests that it was a copy (or draft) of the letter
   that was sent to Mori on 27 November (No. 299), on which day
   Britten also wrote to Hawkes (No. 298), enclosing a copy of No. 299

and describing it as 'dignified & firm'. It is clear that the formulation of a reply to the Cultural Bureau of Tokyo cost Britten (and his friends and colleagues) no little labour and ran through a number of versions before the final text was established.

After Britten's return to England in 1942 and after a BBC broadcast of the *Sinfonia da Requiem* on 5 December 1945, there was some discussion in the correspondence section of the *Radio Times* about the history of the work's commission. Several listeners drew attention to a book by John Morris (who was to become the first Controller of the BBC Third Programme), *Traveller from Tokyo* (London, The Book Club, 1945), in which a description appeared of the concert in Tokyo for which the *Sinfonia* had been destined but at which of course it was never performed:

The year 1940 was celebrated throughout Japan as the 2,600th anniversary of the accession to the throne of the first Emperor, Jimmu Tenno, who is alleged to have commenced his reign in 660 B.C. However this may be, the government commissioned several well-known foreign musicians to write special compositions in honour of the occasion. Some declined the honour, but scores were received from England, Germany, France and Italy. As an official of the Foreign Office I received an invitation to the concert at which these compositions were performed for the first time in public. It was held in the huge *Kabuki* theatre, and in order to do justice to the occasion the New Symphony Orchestra was augmented by the inclusion of practically every living Japanese musician; it must have been well over two hundred strong, but as this was a diplomatic occasion Mr Rosenstock was debarred from conducting. The concert opened with the playing of the Japanese National Anthem in full, throughout which the Axis representatives remained in the 'Heil Hitler' position, much to the discomfort of those seated immediately in front of them. The French had submitted a suite by Jacques Ibert, but the chief item of the concert was the 'Festival Music' of Richard Strauss. This is scored for a gigantic orchestra and contains parts for special drums, temple bells, gongs and various other exotic instruments. I was looking forward to hearing this, but it turned out to be a sterile composition. Although technically clever, it gave me the impression of being a piece of patchwork containing rejected passages from most of Strauss's earlier works.

To my disappointment the concert was a purely Axis occasion. This was not intended. It was due to an unfortunate occurrence which it was not possible to make public. Mr Benjamin Britten had agreed to submit a composition, but the letter inviting him to do so was apparently badly worded in that he was asked to write something *in memory* of the defunct Emperor, and no hint was given that the occasion was a joyful one. Not unnaturally, Mr Britten submitted a dirge. Unknown, I imagine, to him, experiments were made in altering the tempo, but no matter what liberties were taken with the score, there was still very obviously nothing festive about it. It was decided that his composition could not be performed; but in order to save the face of all those concerned it was made known that the English offering had not been received in time to permit of adequate rehearsal.

Morris's ear-witness account is undeniably of interest, though not always quite accurate, but it seems as if Britten himself was anxious in 1946 to set the record straight, which led him to write a letter to the *Radio Times* (18 January) himself:

In the early autumn of 1939 I was approached by the Japanese Government through the British Council to compose a work to commemorate the two thousandth [sic] anniversary of the Japanese dynasty. I replied that I would be willing to do so on condition that I was left free in the choice of subject and medium, and specified that I was unable and unwilling to provide any jingoism.

The reply to this was definitely in agreement to my conditions, but for six months I waited for the actual contract. When this finally arrived I was working on the 'Sinfonia da Requiem', which was a tribute to the memory of my parents. Owing to this delay I was left with something like six weeks in which to complete the required symphony, and I replied that the only work I could provide in the time would be the said 'Sinfonia da Requiem'. I discussed the suitability of the work with the local Japanese consul, indicating its nature, and telling him that each movement had a Latin title – Lachrymosa, Dies Irae, and Requiem Aeternam. He communicated, I presume, with his ambassador and I was notified that the work was considered entirely suitable. I accordingly completed the score, delivered it to the consul, and for at least six months heard no more.

In the autumn of 1940 I was summoned to the consul. He then read, with gradually mounting passion, a long letter from Prince Konnoi, brother of the then Prime Minster of Japan, who was organising the festival. This letter accused me of insulting a friendly power, of providing a Christian work where Christianity was apparently unacceptable, that the work was gloomy, and so on. I replied to this letter in as dignified a manner as possible, saying that since I was a Christian and came from a Christian country, the work was (not surprisingly) Christian, denying that it was gloomy, denying the insult, and so on. This letter was sent for approval to the local British consul and other British officials, and sent off to Tokyo. I awaited the next move.

Owing to the steadily worsening relations between England and Japan, and finally the incident at Pearl Harbor, it is perhaps not surprising that I never heard any more about it, but I am told that in several books there are descriptions of the arrival of the score in Tokyo and its subsequent rehearsal.

However, this 1946 account does not quite match up with the account he gave to William G. King of the *New York Sun* in April 1940:

[. . .] Japanese Government representatives in London had suggested that he compose a symphony to be played during the celebration of the 2,600th anniversary of the Imperial Dynasty, which takes place this summer and fall. He was informed, very flatteringly, that the only other occidental composer who had been asked to contribute was the veteran Richard Strauss. After the preliminary negotiations, however, Britten heard nothing further from the Japanese and forgot the whole business until, a few weeks ago, he was notified that they expected the score of the symphony to be delivered in Japan by the middle of May. (The work is scheduled for performance under the direction of Viscount Konoye, leading exponent of occidental music in Japan.) Britten says he will have it ready on time.

If Morris was not always correct in his facts – for example, he was mistaken in thinking that Britten's score was the first to be received: as was reported in the *Japan Times* of 21 July, works by Strauss, Ibert and Sándor Veress had already been delivered, while Britten's was still expected – the composer's own account raises certain queries. For instance, while it is more than likely that he had the *Sinfonia* in mind and wanted to compose it, there is no evidence that he had started work on the *Sinfonia* in advance of the Japanese commission or that he had ever thought of any other response but this to the invitation. We also find it difficult to read Prince Konoye's surely rather mild and courteous letter in the terms of Britten's reaction to it, as expressed in the *Radio Times*.

The manuscript full score of the *Sinfonia da Requiem* is in the possession of the National University of Fine Arts and Music, Tokyo. The autograph corresponds to the published edition, but for the third movement, in which – before the first performance of the work in New York – Britten made cuts in three places (32 bars in all), revised the movement's climax (Figs. 42–3), and reconsidered and abbreviated the coda. The most significant excision was made three bars before Fig. 40, where a rhapsodic string passage of 28 bars, of Mahlerian character and intensity, was contracted to the existing 4 bars in the published score. This original form of the slow movement was heard for the first time on 2 February 1989 at Birmingham, when the *Sinfonia* was performed by Simon Rattle and the City of Birmingham Symphony Orchestra. See also Atsushi Miura, 'British Conductor Finds Missing Work by Britten', *Asahi Evening News*, 5 June 1987, p. 3.

Tailpiece: On 14 September 1943 the BBC Eastern Services Organizer wrote to John Morris about the performance of the *Sinfonia da Requiem* scheduled for 30 September, 'I would like to have your confirmation', he asked, 'that we still want to take full rights in a recording of this work and to process the particular section which we selected some weeks ago as a signature tune for the Japanese Service.'

Given the history of the work's commission, this would indeed have been an ironic outcome. Morris replied on the 20th that he would prefer to stick to the signature tune with which the Japanese Service had been started: the chimes of 'Big Ben'.

3 George Szell (1897–1970), Hungarian-born American conductor. The only association of Britten's name with Szell's appears in an advertisement in *Tempo*, 1/4, American Series, January 1941, which lists a forthcoming performance in March of *The Bewitched Violin*, with the NBC orchestra under George Szell. Szell was indeed guest

conductor of the NBC at this time and it may well have been this proposal to which Britten refers. The work never materialized but for a
handful of sketches, one of which we reproduce overleaf. In Elizabeth Mayer's diary for 12 February we find the following entry: 'William
in town. Spring air. Ben stuck with "Zaubergeige" [*The Bewitched
Violin*]. Wonderful performance of early works and *Hunting Fathers*.'

These last would have been performances of his own works by
Britten at the piano. Mrs Mayer's diaries record many such occasions,
and also the progress of a particular work. For example, 18 January,
'Schubert with Ben'; 21 January, 'Ben does the "wild geese" ' (part
of the Prologue to *Paul Bunyan*, vocal score, Fig. 5); 24 January,
'Scoring Paul Bunyan. "Lied von der Erde" '; and 11 February,
'Southold with the Rothmans. Scanty orchestra' (a reference to the
Suffolk Friends of Music Orchestra that Britten later was to conduct).

In a 1941 calendar Mrs Mayer records on 26 April, 'Ben and Peter
leave for the West'; and the day after, this generous woman was
out at Middagh Street, 'to collect the boys' "Nachlass" ', i.e. the
belongings they had left behind. She lunched that day with Auden,
George Davis, Oliver Smith and Golo Mann, all of them at one
time residents of the Brooklyn establishment. On the way home she
collects Gordon Green and Colin McPhee. On 2 June, 'Colin for
lunch; reads to me his article on Ben, on Nassau Shores' (see note 4
to Letter 308). On 5 September, she makes an entry, 'Records of "Les
Illuminations" ' (see note 2 to Letter 315) and on the 21st celebrates
quietly 'Ben's Quartet (first perform. in Los Angeles. Sell Ben's old
car for 40 Dollars to George Haff'; 2 October, 'La Vita Nuova: Peter
and Ben back at noon. wonderful workshop.' On the 6th 'Ben plays
Weber Sonatas marvelously' and on the 7th is working at 'an
Occasional Ouverture' (see note 2 to Letter 343). The overture was
finished on the 16th, 'Unforgettable evening We three working in
music room till 2.30 a.m. Peter reading aloud from Forster: A Room
with a View. – myself preparing score with ruler on piano.' 17 October: Pears gets the extension of his visa. 'P. and B. playing Mahler
VII.' 22 October, 'Ben flies to Boston with Ralph: first rehearsal of
his Sinfonia Boston Philh. Koussewitski' (see note 1 to Letter 361).
He was back on the 23rd, and on the 25th was working on the
score of *Scottish Ballad*. On the 30th, 'Early to Washington. Hotel
Continental. Ben and Peter. We lunch at French Restaurant. Concert
3.30. Mrs. Coolidge giving Ben the medal before the Kroll Quartett
plays Bens Quartet, Tea with the Wallings, meet there Dick Powell.
We five delightful dinner at Pierre's. Walk back to Hotel, wonderful
talks on way and later' (see Letter 326). 1 November, 'rainy. a bit
low. Ben plays Mahler like an answer'. 3 November, 'We three [i.e.
EM, BB and PP] have quiet evening, reading Lear: Nonsensebook.
Chateaubriand on America. Ben plays heavenly Pachelbel and

The first page of the sketch for the unfinished *Bewitched Violin*

Obrecht.' On the 6th, 'after lunch Ben to Southold, stays till Nov. 8. had a good time with the Rothmans, played at salesman in store, brought presents for us all, for me glass-waterkettle.' Late in November Mrs Mayer accompanied Britten and Pears to Chicago for their performance of *Les Illuminations* (see Letter 347). On 22 November, 'Peter a bit coldish but better. Ben alone to rehearse. (photo!) We drive at 3 p.m. to Madison, Wisconsin. Lovely landscape. Swedish farmers. Roadside stands with cheeses. Have a short blizzard. Evening with Toni Brosa and Peggy.' 24 November, 'Very cold but sunny. Drive with Ben and Peter to rehearsal in the Civic Theatre. even. Concert.'

We have been selective in our annotations, but they convey with remarkable vividness the texture of life at Stanton Cottage in 1940 and 1941. On 16 March 1942, the entry in Mrs Mayer's diary reads: 'I bring B. and P. to the boat at 3 p.m.'; and she added in the margin, 'The Ides of March'.

4 Japanese Vice-Consul in New York.

298 To Ralph Hawkes
[*Typed*]

> Boosey & Hawkes, Inc.,
> 43–47, West 23rd Street,
> New York, U.S.A.
> November 27th, 1940.

Dear Ralph:

Thank you very much for your very welcome letter. I think the new contract clears up the whole matter. I hope, by now, you have received the signed copy sent by Dr. Heinsheimer. I personally am very glad that we have been able to arrange matters like this because neither of us now can feel an uncomfortable amount of obligation to the other!!

Things are going on more or less the same here, and I am very busy. I did a show for Columbia on Sunday which seemed to satisfy everyone.[1] I am seeing Szell this afternoon about another possibility, in fact, I am writing as hard as I possibly can in case there may not be much opportunity to work in the future. I hope that your luck still holds good – we are all crossing our fingers for you. Make up your mind to come back here as soon as you possibly can because everyone needs you.

A little bother has arisen about our friends from the Japanese Festivities. I enclose a copy of a letter from them (it was translated in case your Japanese isn't as good as it has been). After much consultation with the British Consulate and a member of the British Library of Information, I decided to write a short reply which was dignified but firm (copy of which is also herewith enclosed for your inspection).[2] I wonder if you could ask any member of the British Council in London – who is within reach at the moment – what his or her opinion of the matter is. I am in a quandary myself: if I am a private citizen in the matter, there is not the slightest doubt in my mind as to what I should do. I feel that the matter is not artistic but political, i.e. that at the moment they cannot possibly perform a British work in Tokyo. There has been no secret from the beginning of the nature of the work. In fact, if you remember, I cabled Leslie Boosey on March 30th, 1940 the title and dedication of the composition which, I presume, was communicated to the British Consul and subsequently to the Japanese Embassy. Incidentally, if you have a copy of this cable to Leslie Boosey, I wish you could put it out of the way of bombs for the moment since, if any legal action by the Japanese is contemplated, this will be an important part of my evidence.

On the other hand, if in this matter I am temporarily an official of the British Government, I do not feel so free about the matter. The British Consulate and Library of Information agree with the steps I have already taken, but feel that if the British Council is still interested in the matter, they should let me know their opinion. I am more than sorry to bother you with this since, I know, you have so much to worry and think about. Personally, I do not think the matter is very serious: after all, I have had the money and spent it, so they can't do much in the way of getting it back. No one seems to think here that they would go to any legal action about it. If they do, I have so much evidence that, I think, the case is water tight. Anyhow, the publicity of having a work rejected by the Japanese Consulate for being Christian is a wow.

I haven't yet heard when Barbirolli is playing it, but I gather it will be quite soon after Christmas.

I have now had my tonsils out and am enjoying food again. Let me know – if you can – how your personal matters are.

With all good wishes, I am
Yours,
BEN

1 Britten had written some incidental music for a CBS (Columbia Workshop) adaptation of Thomas Hardy's Napoleonic epic, *The Dynasts*, first broadcast on 24 November. Virtually nothing is known about this score – the manuscript is lost – but for a solitary review by Charles Mills which appeared in *Modern Music*, 18/2, January–February 1941, p. 132:

The score of [. . .] Thomas Hardy's *Dynasts*, was by Benjamin Britten. Largely a military affair of brass and percussion, it was appropriate enough, only there was too much of it. As background, the music seemed over-prominent and to lack subtlety of timing, though there was an exception in the string mood accompanying the verbal soliloquy of Napoleon.

See also PR, pp. 390–91, and 596.

2 Letter 299. What has also come to light is a response to the Japanese
   complaint, drafted by Auden. This is a much longer document than
   Letter 299. It was probably prudent of Britten to make a briefer reply.
   However, as a comparison with Letter 299 shows, he takes over the
   concluding sections of Auden's draft to form the central part of the
   letter to Mori. Quite apart from the draft's intrinsic interest – it is yet
   further evidence of the close friendship between the poet and the
   composer in these American years – it also sets out in detail and
   with admirable clarity the tragi-comic story of the commissioning
   of the *Sinfonia da Requiem*, and it is for that reason we quote from
   the draft, prefaced by an editorial note from Professor Edward
   Mendelson, the Auden scholar and the poet's literary executor, who
   has transcribed the draft and generously made it available to us:

[Transcribed from a partly illegible pencil draft in a notebook Auden used
in 1940; now in the Berg Collection at the New York Public Library. Para-
graphing and layout have been regularized, and minor spelling errors silently
corrected. Words in [square brackets] are reasonably confident guesses at
partly legible words in the manuscript; words in <angle brackets> are
supplied by the transcriber, generally from deleted versions of the same
sentence. A question mark that does *not* appear within brackets is Auden's
own.]

I am in receipt of your version of Mr Konoye's letter dated ? re the symphony
commissioned from me by the Committee for the 2600th Anniversary Celebration of the Japanese Empire.

   I must confess that I am at a complete loss to understand its tenor.

   I would like to give you a brief account of the circumstances surrounding
the commission of this work.

[Paragraphs 1–3, which consist almost exclusively of the exchange of known
telegrams setting up the commission, have been omitted. The draft begins
here with an account of the first meeting between the interested parties in
New York.]

4. At the beginning <of April> Miss Rothe and myself visited yourself.
    You showed me a letter from Tokio naming terms. No mention was
    made in these of a symphony being [?ever] of any specific character
    [?istic]. The terms being satisfactory I began the work.
5. Around the end of May I had a further discussion with <you> during
    this I asked you whether in your opinion the [*illegible*] titles to the
    movements [could] cause any offence.
    Your answer was no. On May 27th I received [*illegible*] cheque for [*illegible*].
6. On ? I delivered the completed score to you.
7. On ? I received your final cheque.
    Except for a claim of copyright and a number of discussions as to whether
it [might] be possible for me to go to Tokyo to be present at the first
performance, I received no comments on the manuscript until my interview
with you on Nov 12th, i.e., not until the Committee had been in possession
of the ms for 3 months.

As you will see from this.

1. At no time did the Committee specify the kind of music they required, and by the [*illegible*] they had already been informed of the title and character of the symphony I proposed to write;
2. Mr Konoye objects to the Christian character of the work. If the Committee were unwilling to have a Christian work, I do not understand why they commissioned one from a composer belonging to a Christian nation;
3. Mr Konoye calls the work gloomy. This is, of course, a matter of opinion, but I cannot help feeling that he has not examined the Symphony very carefully.

The structure is such that the conflicts of the first two movements must move to a solution in the final Andante, which is a movement of peace and quiet rejoicing.

I can only hope that the discourtesy of Mr. Konoye's letter was no more deliberate than that of which he so gratuitously and without any foundation accuses me.

I much regret that you should have to trouble with all this, and I would like to take this opportunity of thanking you for your unfailing helpfulness and patience.

Friede F. Rothe (paragraph 4) worked for Boosey & Hawkes in their Artists' Bureau.

299 To Tomio Mori
Japanese Vice-Consul, New York
[*Typed; BB's copy*]

7, Middagh Street, Brooklyn, New York.
November 27, 1940.

Dear Mr. Mori,

I must apologize for not having answered your letter and the enclosure from the Director of the Cultural Bureau of Tokyo before this, but the matter which is raised therein must necessarily be given great thought.

I must say at once that I am grievously shocked and hurt by the contents of the letter. My position in regard to the matter is quite clear.

At no time did the committee give any indication of wishing for some special kind of work, and they were informed of the nature of the work and its titles at the end of March through the British Council in London.

Mr. Konoye[1] objects to the Christian nature of the work. If this is his real objection, it is difficult to understand why the committee ever commissioned a work from a composer who is a member of a Christian nation.

Mr. Konoye calls the work melancholy. This is, of course, a matter of opinion, though I cannot but feel that he has not examined the score very carefully and has possibly been misled by his perhaps false idea of what the title means. An examination of the structure of the music would dispel any doubts as to its real nature. The conflict of the first two movements, one a slow march, the other a desperate dance, moves to a solution in the final movement which is one of peace and quiet rejoicing.

If the committee wishes me to go further into the matter, I shall be only too pleased to do so. Permit me to say that I deeply regret that you should have been bothered with all this and allow me to take this opportunity of thanking you for your unfailing helpfulness and patience.

Yours very truly,
BENJAMIN BRITTEN

1 Britten's reference to 'Mr.' Konoye raised the ire of Ralph Hawkes: see the opening paragraph of the letter we quote below, dated 20 December, in which is exposed the embarrassment and confusion generated by the commissioning of the *Sinfonia da Requiem*, not just on the Japanese side:

[. . .] the Japanese question. I promptly communicated with the British Council, for I had perforce to do this and I gather that they are somewhat worried by the development. It appears that some mistake was made at this end in advising that the work bore a dedication to your Parents and had this not been mentioned, I think the position generally would have been easier. The circumstances altogether are unfortunate and the delivery of the Score must have come at the time when everything possible was being done politically to boost Axis prestige in Japan and I am now informed that the works submitted by Richard Strauss and Pizzetti – the great Axis Composers – bore elaborate dedications of celebration and dynastical import, thus bringing into the limelight the fact that your work had no such dedication; I suppose, therefore, that this was contributory to their attitude. Your letter to Mr Mori, however, does not appear to have helped the situation in the opinion of the British Council here and I must say that I think you might have addressed Prince Konoye with his correct title instead of plain 'Mr' and – as Miss Henn-Collins remarked – was there any need to be quite so flippant?

I endorse your statement, however, regarding the objection being raised on account of the music being of a religious and Christian nature and I feel that this is the excuse they have provided to protect themselves and in order to make it a political matter. My conception of a work being written for any Festival, whether it be my birthday or the 2,600th Anniversary of anybody else's birth or death, is that it is the Festival which is the point and not the actual character of the work written for it. If they had wanted 20 minutes of trumpeting, they should have said so but seeing that they asked for a Symphony or Symphonic Poem, clearly their request was for 'a work' and I have made this position quite clear to Miss Henn-Collins.

Another point, which seems to have been overlooked by them, either purposely or due to their complete inability to understand your music, which I suspect as being the real reason, is that the work, as I recall it, might well describe the 2,600 years of Japanese life, which the Festival celebrates. After all, the first two movements represent struggle, whilst the third movement represents peace and I should have thought that this was an apt interpretation to put on such a period of life; doubtless, however, the Japs think differently. More than this I cannot say at the moment; it is quite clear that there could be no question of refunding the money and I well recall that we made it clear to Mr Mori in New York at our interview that the work consisted of these three movements and the matter of parental dedication was mentioned.

I may add that I think you should now make it clear that there has been a misunderstanding as far as you are concerned and had they made it obvious to you that they wanted a work not as a pure composition but of a specialized nature to deal with this particular 2,600 years of incident, then you might have done something different; this might have the effect of smoothing out the position and easing a political controversy. I simply loathe introducing this form of comment into anything to do with the composition of music and before you act on my suggestion, I advise you to await further developments, if there are going to be any.

300 To Beata Mayer

as from Middagh Street
Sunday [?15 December 1940]

My dear Beatty,

Could you be an angel & take on a temporary salaried job for one day this week! I can't get on with my letter writing, & I am sure the impetus of your personality & the convenience of your capability would do the trick. So I suggest that if you are able and willing – could you come to Brooklyn (or I can come to West 4th St.[1] if it suits you better for a few hours (at union rates of course!) – & help me get the stuff done? I am back in town on Wednesday & will 'phone you to get your reaction.

How are you both? I am just staggering out of an acute depression – probably into another one. A great friend of my sister Beth's has just arrived from England with lots of news & messages.[2]

Much love,
BEN

1 An apartment in the Village, on the corner of 4th and 11th Streets, which Beata was sharing with her brother, Michael, at the time she was working for the Boosey & Hawkes Artists' Bureau.

2 Lilian Wolff.

301   To Albert Goldberg
[*Typed*]

> 7, Middagh Street, Brooklyn, New York.
> [*Handwritten:* also: Long Island Home, Amityville, N.Y.]
> Dec. 20, 1940

My dear Albert:

Thank you for your letter which I received about three years ago. I am sorry not to have answered before but one way or another my time has been exceedingly occupied and apart from little things like writing music, I have had attacks of various low diseases, including a visit to the New York Hospital, and also various worries connected with the other side of the Atlantic Ocean, and last not least I have entered your field as a rival and become, believe it or not, director of the Suffolk Friends of Music Symphony Orchestra,[1] a post which requires a great deal of energy, a certain amount of skill and an infinite amount of tact. Another reason why I have not written before this to you is that there always seems to be just around the corner the possibility of having an engagement somewhere in the Middle West which would enable me to come and pay you a visit. So far none of these have materialized and frankly the outlook is not good. And I have to admit that my financial state is not so rosy that I could pay you a visit just for the fun that I know it would be.

You ask several questions in your letter which I suppose I had better answer. I do not know Thaddeus Kozuch,[2] though he sounds from his name an exciting gentleman. If he is still interested in the old [piano] concerto, I should be delighted to meet him and would turn on all the charm taps that might persuade him to play the work. If he is ever within a thousand miles of this place, tell him to look me up.

Question 2: The violin concerto is printed,[3] but I think there are only two copies in this country. The rest have either been lost in the Atlantic Ocean or destroyed by a bomb at the source (it is of course printed in England). But the score and parts in manuscript are in this country. You mention Brosa. He is now at Madison,

Wis., leading the Pro Arte String Quartet, but is able to fulfill his solo jobs.[4]

Question 3: I am still in this country and very thankful of that fact, although my status is extremely insecure and a word from either the USA or the British governments could make me cross that very unsafe piece of water, the Atlantic Ocean. However, I am "making hay etc." and writing a terrific amount while I have the chance. My family in England are all safe so far, but have lost a certain amount of property.[5]

How are things with you? I hope you have been able to continue inspite of your apprehensions expressed last summer. Let me have a note from time to time because I am always intensely interested in what you are doing. This goes for that assistant of yours as well. I hear you are doing a piece of Copland's[6] in which, since I brought you two together, I feel a certain fatherly interest. What other new works are you doing? I am still living in hopes that Peter and I will be able to pay you a visit and that a performance of "Les Illuminations" might be the result. I will let you know if anything materializes and hope something can be arranged.

We have now actually got an old car which admittedly does not go so well but which might carry us the 800 odd miles to Chicago next summer, but that is so far ahead that one could not dream of planning anything definitely.

Very best Christmas greetings to you and that assistant of yours.

Yours very sincerely,
BENJAMIN BRITTEN

1 A semi-professional orchestra named after Suffolk County, Long Island, the membership of which was drawn from 'professional musicians, adult amateurs, and advanced students of high school age'; Douglas Moore and Sigmund Spaeth were on its advisory board. In *Time*, 16 February 1948, p. 66, it was reported of the orchestra under Britten that 'the amateurs got so they could play a Mozart Symphony creditably, then began thinking about a professional concert. Britten thought that amateurs should be content to stay amateurs'; and Howard L. Koch, in 'Benjamin Britten: A Reminiscence', *New York State School Music News*, February 1977, p. 15, recalled: 'At one rehearsal, on hearing strange sounds, [Britten] addressed the group: "Gentlemen, what I hear sounds vaguely familiar, but I find nothing like it in my score!" ' Britten was brought into touch with the orchestra by the Regional Chairman, David Rothman (1896–1981), who owned a hardware store at Southold, and to whose

family Britten and Pears had been introduced by the Mayers. (Mrs Rothman was a patient of Dr Mayer's.) The announcement of Britten's engagement for the 1941 series of the orchestra read as follows:

The Suffolk
Friends of Music Orchestra
Season 1941
Benjamin Britten, Conductor

The Suffolk Friends of Music announce with pride the engagement of the noted English composer, pianist and conductor, Benjamin Britten as their conductor. A graduate of the Royal College of Music, the London Daily Telegraph speaks of him as 'unquestionably the most brilliant of the younger British composers'. Though he is now but 27 years old, his compositions have been featured by the major festivals of England and the Continent in the United States. Britten compositions have been performed by Albert Stoessel's Chatauqua Orchestra, Wallenstein's WOR Sinfonietta, and the New York Philharmonic Orchestra, under Barbirolli. Mr Britten's new 'Sinfonia da Requiem' will be played by the New York Philharmonic on March 29 and 30, 1941.

As conductor, Mr Britten has appeared with the British Broadcasting Company Orchestra, the London Philharmonic and the London Symphony, and also has spent a period as conductor of the English government film project.

This was a time of financial difficulty for Britten and certainly one of the reasons for his taking on the job would have been the possibility of earning additional income (he received $10 per rehearsal). For the same reason, and about the same time, Rothman arranged for Pears to conduct the Southold Town Choral Society during the 1940–41 season. Rothman's wife, Ruth, was a member of the Society, which Pears trained and directed and from which he supplemented his earnings (he received $15 per rehearsal). In the programme we reproduce on pp. 926 and 927, McPhee and Britten appear as a two-piano duo in Handel and Arensky and Britten participates in McPhee's arrangements of sea shanties for male chorus, from his *Sea Shanty Suite* (1929).

For information on Bruce Boyce, see note 4 to Letter 473.

For the reproduction of the orchestra's 1941 prospectus, see PFL, plate 140; and also plate 139.

2 Goldberg had written to Britten on 12 August:

Just the other day, I was trying to interest a very good pianist in your concerto and may persuade him to learn it yet. He is Thaddeus Kozuch, who was awarded an Orchestra Hall recital appearance last year on the Adult Education Concert Series. He is very gifted and is beginning to get quite a few dates, so might have a chance to play a piece of this type.

3 A reduction for violin and piano was first published by Boosey & Hawkes, London, in 1940.

4 Mrs Brosa (Interview, with Donald Mitchell, 7 September 1977, London; Archive) related:

[. . .] the first four years we were at Madison, Wisconsin, with the Pro Arte String Quartet. The leader of the Pro Arte got leukaemia, and they asked Toni to join the Quartet as its leader for a year. But he [the former leader] died, so they asked [Toni] to take it on permanently and during those four years they were engaged [. . .] as permanent Quartet.

5 Barbara's flat had been bombed in the Blitz.

6 Goldberg replied to Britten on 6 February 1941 but made no response to Britten's query about Copland and we have not been able to trace any reference to the performance of a specific work.

302 Questionnaire from Jay Leyda

This document is to be found in the New York Public Library (Mus Res * MIT (Leyda)) alongside replies to the same questionnaire by Marc Blitzstein, Paul Bowles, Aaron Copland, Henry Cowell, Ernst Křenek and Karol Rathaus. Leyda (b. 1910), the American film-maker and film-historian (who was also to write books on Mussorgsky and Rakhmaninov, and on Emily Dickinson and Herman Melville) appears never to have published the results of his inquiries. See also PR, pp. 18–23. Our transcription combines the questions with Britten's answers. These were supplied on a separate sheet, headed with the Middagh Street address and telephone number (Main 4–9079) and inscribed: 'Sorry this is so late. Hope it's what you want. BB.'

CORRESPONDENCE RECEIVED FROM COMPOSERS IN ANSWER TO A
QUESTIONNAIRE CONCERNING THE COMPOSITION OF FILM MUSIC

(by Jay Leyda)

In answering the following questions, illustrate, wherever this is advantageous and possible, by a reference to a film for which you have written the music, and quote from the score.

1. *Do you assist in the choice of sequences for which music is to be written?*
A: If possible – in my experience, in documentaries yes, in commercials, no.

2. *To consider first the single film sequence – do you work on the music from the script or from the finished film sequence?*
A: All depends on the kind of film – in some documentaries I have done, the picture was cut to the music after the latter was recorded – a luxurious procedure.

3. a) *Does your musical imagination have to fit itself to particular details*

dramatic or visual of the film sequence; or is it free to produce its own musical terms for the essence or quality of the sequence as you see it?

A: a) It depends on the character of the film. Usually if the picture is lighter, or a cartoon, a lot of synchronisation with details on the screen can be used.

3. b) *What – in one case or the other – is the effect of your procedure on 1) the music, 2) the film?*

A: b) (1) If the music is free of the fetters of synchronisation it can be more interesting qua music – but that is not so important, as I don't take film music seriously qua music anyhow – (2) See 3(a) above.

4. *Do you take anything into account outside the dramatic and visual elements of the film sequence – for example, the level of musical understanding of the film audience?*

A It is usually impossible to underestimate the musical intelligence of the film audiences – certainly commercial ones. Documentary audiences incline to be more high-brow, but not necessarily more intelligent.

5. *What difference are you aware of that is produced in the music by the fact that you are composing it for a film sequence and not for a sequence in any other dramatic medium?*

A: The technical side of recording. The possibility of gradual fades in and out. And most obvious of all, that only $\frac{1}{10}$th of the audience's attention is on the music.

6. *Is the possibility of the length of a particular film sequence being reduced or increased after the entire film is completed a difficulty for you in composing the music for the sequence?*

A: One usually allows for that kind of thing when writing the score – marking possible 'cuts' or 'repeat bars'.

7. *Do you find that the special facilities of sound-recording for films – for example, the number and placing of microphones, the combining of sound track in re-recording – provide additional resources for your music?*

A: Certainly. The possibilities of re-recording are endless. Interesting sound perspectives can be achieved by the use of several microphones.

8. *Do you orchestrate the music, and if not do you feel this is a limitation?*
A: Always.

9. *Bearing in mind the degree to which you as a composer of an opera would*

control the dramatic shaping of the libretto, are you as the composer for a film, consulted about the dramatic or visual elements?

A: In documentaries nearly always – in commercials never.

10.   *Is there anything in composing music for the film sequence that necessitates a change in your usual method of composition?*

A: Usually greater speed, so that one is not so free to reject as when composing in one's own time. In moments of greatest emergency, one has to write straight into the orchestral parts, which is not my usual method! Personally, even in times of ease, I always write film music straight into score – which is not such a feat as it sounds since I use as small an orchestra as possible.

11.   *To proceed now from the problem of the single film sequence to the problem of the entire film:*
       a)   *Do you feel the need of unifying the passages of music within a film as you would unify them in any other musical work?*
       b)   *Have you found that the film permits this, or that it makes it more difficult or even impossible?*
       c)   *Have you been able to satisfy this need?*

A: a)   Certainly. I believe that the audience (usually unconsciously) gets a feeling of satisfaction from that.
       b)   It is usually possible.
       c)   By using the same kind of scoring throughout; same kind of musical material.

12.   *Are the conditions under which you compose music for film satisfactory or would you like them to be changed, and if so, how changed?*

A: No. I should always like to be consulted during the writing of the script; have what time & materials (kind of orchestra) I want; have as much money & publicity as the star actors get. Faint hope!

BENJAMIN BRITTEN

303   To Antonio and Peggy Brosa
[*Typed*]

7, Middagh Street, Brooklyn, New York,
Dec. 20, 1940.

My dear Toni and Peggy,

   I am so sorry not to have written to you before this and it seems years since you deserted us all for Madison, but life has been

hectic here. I seem to have had an immense amount to do and no
time to do it in and it is only because Beata has grumbled about
the size of my unanswered-letters file that I am doing anything
today with her not inconsiderable help (you didn't guess that this
beautiful typing is not my own, did you?). Seriously though, letter-
writing is such a luxury that it is only in this way that I can get
any done.

I was very interested to get your letter, Peggy, and to hear all
the details about the quartet. Things seemed very gloomy to start
off with, but I am sure Toni's amazing tact and powers of
persuasion will have made some tangible improvements by now.
How do you get on with your conducting, Toni? We must have a
competition some day; you with your orchestra and I with mine.
I am sure mine makes more noise than yours, although it probably
is not nearly as accurate and we would not think of playing
anything as high-brow as the Brandenburg Concertos. We only
play Slav music which seems to suit the enthusiasm of the Long
Islanders; so much so that last Tuesday I strained my back and I
am now groaning whenever I move. The house in Brooklyn is
still in a great deal of a mess, although things by imperceptible
degrees are getting cleared up. We gave a housewarming party
two or three weeks ago, at which Gypsie Rose Lee was a feature
and we played murder all over the house and you could not
imagine a better setting for it. The evening or rather morning ended
with Peter and George Davis, owner of the house, doing a ballet
to Petrushka, up the curtains and the hot water pipes – an
impressive if destructive sight.[1]   Living is quite pleasant here
when it is not too exciting, but I find it almost impossible to work,
and retire to Amityville at least once a week. Everyone is well and
quite cheerful, but Amityville has not quite recovered from the
blow of losing the Brosas. Peter and I substituted for your concert
at the Long Island Home the other day and it went well, apart from
the fact that Peter had laryngitis and I had not practised.

I was terribly sorry that the scheme that Peter and I should go
out to Cincinnati for Christmas fell through, but you know what
these conductors are. Personally I always get taken in by their
promises and then get disappointed. Of course, it may still
happen later in the season, but I have my doubts and am afraid it
is too far for us to come on our own steam, so to speak, much as
we should love to see you. Something may yet come of the Art
Society in Chicago suggestion, about which Heinsheimer wrote

you, I think. But now I never get excited about things until contracts
are signed.

How is the Sibelius concerto going, Toni? Have you had your
try-out with the orchestra yet? Here we have been inundated with
Sibelius. He had his 105th birthday,[2] or something, recently and all
conductors have been trying to outdo each other in performing
his music and singing his praises, a gloomy state of affairs. Poor
Barbirolli has been getting it in the neck too from the critics. We
saw him and Evelyn[3] the other night after his tour. Incidentally we
heard Benny Goodman[4] play the Mozart Clarinet concerto, very
beautifully only he was pathetically nervous all the time and even
played with the music. We went with Ethel and Rae [Robertson],
who incidentally are coming to Amityville for Christmas; but they
won't make up for your bright presences. I hope you will have a
good seasonable holiday and try and forget the horrors for a bit.
What news have you from England? I expect to have some first-
hand news from Beth within a day or so, because her partner from
her Hampstead business has just arrived on her way to Trinidad
and saw Beth in town before she left. Beth was well, but Barbara
not so good. I must say I cannot think how people stand it night
after night. I told you that Barbara lost her flat, didn't I?

The strain is beginning to show on Beata's face (which is not true
at all – b.)[5] and so I [had] better stop this long ramble. Very much
love to you both. I still curse the day when the offer came from
Madison, but I suppose it was a good thing, anyway financially –

Yours ever,

BEN

P.S. Have you registered?[6] December 26th is the last day and the
fine for neglecting to do it is $1000!

Much love from me too

BEATA

1 It seems likely that the house-warming party and a celebration of
Britten's twenty-seventh birthday were combined. Michael Mayer
clearly remembers the occasion (Interview with Donald Mitchell and
Philip Reed, 22 June 1988, Aldeburgh; Archive):

It was Ben's birthday in 1940 and [Beata and I] were invited to Middagh
Street [. . .]. It was a marvellous house. It was a broken-down house. We
played 'ghosts' later on [. . .]. It was a great place for that and present at
the time [were] [. . .] Gypsy Rose Lee [. . .] quite definitely she was there
[. . .]. Carson McCullers was there [. . .]. Her husband dropped in some
time later in the evening [. . .]. Aaron Copland was there, Wystan was

there and [. . .] I've forgotten now who else. [. . .] We played children's games most of the evening: charades, and 'ghosts' and games like that. Of course a certain amount of drinking [was] going on. I always tell people, 'Gypsy Rose Lee once sat on my lap with a gin bottle in her hand!' [. . .] I had to act out 'You can't take it with you' and I did it by trying to carry Carson McCullers across the threshold, but it was very easy to carry her because she weighed nothing at that time [. . .]. That was 22 November 1940, the only day on which that could have happened [. . .].

2 Actually, of course, Sibelius's seventy-fifth birthday: he was born in 1865.

3 Barbirolli's second wife, Evelyn Rothwell (b. 1911), English oboist (now Lady Barbirolli). She studied at the College, with Leon Goossens, and married Barbirolli in 1939.

4 Benny Goodman (1909–1986), the celebrated jazz clarinettist. In the 1930s Goodman proved that it was possible for a jazz musician to succeed also in the classical repertory; and towards the end of the decade he commissioned *Contrasts* from Bartók. Later commissions included clarinet concertos from Copland and Hindemith (both in 1947). Goodman was also in touch with Britten about a concerto, a work that was partly sketched before he returned to England in March 1942. In a letter dated 9 December 1941, Ralph Hawkes wrote: 'I am delighted to hear that you have finished the Mahler [arrangement of the Minuet from the Third Symphony] and that you have concluded arrangements with Benny Goodman.' A complete composition sketch of the first movement, *Molto Allegro* (26 pages, including deletions) is in the Archive. The movement was realized by Colin Matthews and given its first performance at the Barbican Centre, London, on 7 March 1990, with Michael Collins as soloist and the Britten–Pears Orchestra conducted by Tamás Vásáry.

It seems clear that Britten had every intention of completing the work on his return to England. There were many references to a Clarinet Concerto among the works that he had brought back with him; and Britten himself at one stage had allocated an opus number – 28 – to the work.

5 An interpolation from Beata Mayer, who was typing this letter from Britten's dictation.

6 Presumably an obligatory form of registration for aliens?

304 To Gustel Scherchen
[*Typed*]

7, Middagh Street,
Brooklyn,
New York.
December 22, 1940

Dearest Gustel,

I am afraid this is the first letter you will have received from me
in a long time, but I know you will be tolerant with me because
I have had so much work to do and other business to deal with. I
am afraid also that at the beginning when Wulff was sent to
Canada, our letters crossed and for a long time you did not realize
that he had been located. Letters seem to have been very delayed
at that time. I expect you have heard from him now and know that
he has volunteered in the Auxiliary Military Pioneer Corps[1] and
that he is probably now on his way back to England. Though I
realize what difficulties there may be for him in that position, I
was very glad when I heard the news, since if he had been released
in Canada, I don't quite know what arrangements could have
been made for him to continue his studying, and anyhow the
situation would have been filled with all sorts of difficulties. For
one thing, I never had any hopes of his getting permission to come
to the States, since the quota business is extremely complicated
and the red tape at the moment very exaggerated. It will be grand
for you to be able to see him again and I am sure that if it is the
kind of service I imagine it to be, his duties will not be very heavy
and he will have plenty of leave to come and see you.

Thank you very much for your Christmas wishes and for your
very sympathetic and sweet advice. I have had plenty of
opportunities to work and since the only time that one can partially
forget the present situation is when working, I can consider myself
very fortunate. The opera which I was working on with Auden
will, I think, be produced in late spring, and the new symphony
will be done at the Philharmonic concert in March, and there are
several other probabilities which give one something to look
forward and to live for. I have also been playing a great deal of
piano, both chamber music and solo and occasional recitals with
Peter who has been singing very well recently, and I have added
to my various musical activities that of conducting. I was
appointed director of an amateur organisation on Long Island and

every Tuesday I hold a very energetic rehearsal of three hours. I find it is very stimulating work, both in studying the music so thoroughly and in dealing with the members of the orchestra which is mostly composed of music professors and their best students. We give concerts in the spring and possibly in the summer season too. I don't know whether it will have a depressing effect on you to hear of a place in which the normal things of life are still functioning, but I think I know you well enough to suppose it will have the opposite effect instead. Of course, though things have the semblance of normality here, there is a great feeling of desperation in the air, rather as if people were doing things for the last time. But I think people are realizing that although the arts do not seem immediately very important, it is very difficult to exist entirely without them. I hope for that reason that in England the BBC is still able to function and is giving you better music than it did at the beginning of the war.

What news have you of Hermann? Is he still in Greece? It must be difficult for him to get in and out of Switzerland these days. Perhaps he will go to Palestine again. If I see any opportunity here for a job for him, I will certainly do my best to arrange it, but you have no idea how many applicants there are for every job in this country now, and it would certainly not be worth his while to come unless he had a first-rate job.

I was delighted with your suggestion about Mexico and I will certainly see if anything can be arranged for next summer. I know very good friends of Chavez and also I could get in touch with Jesus Bal.[2] Perhaps Peter and I could arrange a tour there and in South America.

Very much love to you and best wishes for a brighter New Year. Please give my regards to your sister when you see her next.

Yours ever,
BENJAMIN

1 As a result of which Wulff was released from internment. He was to meet Britten again shortly after the composer's own return to England in 1942.

2 Rosita Bal's husband. See note 5 to Letter 155.

305   To Antonio Brosa

7, Middagh Street, Brooklyn, N.Y.
Dec. 31st 1940.

Dear Toni,

A very very prosperous New Year to you both. Let's pray that it won't be such a catastrophic one for our friends & relatives in Europe as this blasted 1940 has been! How thankful I am to say good-bye to it!

I hope you'll be having pleasant celebrations this evening – how I wish you were back in Amityville with us all. As a matter of fact Peter & I can't leave New York to-night, & so we are spending the evening with Ethel & Rae, which will be pleasant.

Thank you so very much, both of you for the lovely parcel of surprises which arrived for us all. We were all thrilled & excited by it – especially Jyppy, who barked & nosed & bit our shoes in his fervour. I love my jig-saw & one of these days when I can get a moment to relax I am going to indulge in a good session & no-one is going to be allowed to help me!

Would you be an angel & look through the proofs[1] which should arrive with you anytime now? Both Chris and I have looked thro' them thoroughly & so there shouldn't be any mistakes, but I thought you might like to change your mind over abit or two & anyhow there are the new bits of Bach to bow & finger (which I selected after you left). If there are any queries you might note them on a bit of paper & then I can check them up in the Library. Be an angel & do it quick because as usual there is a hustle on!

Excuse rush, but I'm in a bit of a jam,

Much love & many thanks to you both,
& longing to see you again,
Yours ever,
BEN

Peter sends love & thanks, & hopes to write in a day or so – but he's horribly busy – really!

1 Of the first volume of *Violin Passages*.

306 To Elizabeth Sprague Coolidge
[*Typed*]

123, Louden Ave.,
Amityville,
L.I., N.Y.
January 20, 1941

My dear Mrs. Coolidge,

I know that this is a terribly busy time for you, and I feel guilty in adding to your great correspondence but I do wish you to know that if you have any concert or ceremony in mind in memory of our dear friend Frank[1] that you can always call on me to help you in any way necessary.

There are so many friends of his here who would be keen to help, that there should be no difficulty in finding artists – I mention especially Antonio Brosa, Rebecca Clark[2] (viola), Peter Pears (tenor) and several others of whom you doubtless know.

I am trying to be in Washington at the beginning of February; perhaps you could spare me a few moments to talk over possible plans?

With best wishes and hoping you are in the best of health,

[*Handwritten:* Yours very sincerely]

BENJAMIN BRITTEN

1 Bridge had died at his home at Friston, Sussex, on 10 January 1941.
2 Rebecca Clarke (1886–1979), English viola-player, violinist and composer, a composition student of Stanford's at the College. She settled in the USA in 1939. See also Calum MacDonald, 'Rebecca Clarke's Chamber Music – I', *Tempo*, 160, March 1987, pp. 15–26, and Diane Peacock Jezic, *Women Composers: The Lost Tradition Found* (New York, The Feminist Press (City University of N.Y.), 1988), pp. 157–62.

307 To Peggy Brosa

7 Middagh Street, Brooklyn, N.Y.
Monday Feb. 24th 1941.

My dear Peggy,

You <u>poor</u> thing! I am so sorry about your ankle – I hope you are having good treatment, & obeying the doctor implicitly – no independance, please! Don't go walking around too soon. Let me know how it goes on.

I got your letter this morning & after the remarks about the photo I couldn't help answering it at once, altho' I have <u>no</u> business to be writing letters! Life is just one hectic rush at the moment – I have a final play through of the opera on Wednesday evening to the cast & there are still <u>four</u> complete numbers to be written[1] – & what else I've got to do before that evening just doesn't bear innumerating (rehearsals, 2 recordings,[2] visit to Southold & orchestra conducting, business lunches (ugh!!)) etc. So you see I am nicely occupied – thank God.

What you say about Heinsheimer doesn't surprise me, but it does shock me no end. I think it's appallingly bad business not to mention Toni in M. Courier[3] – but I'm sure it's just inefficiency – not anything personal – because whenever I go there things seem to be going concerning Toni – his name always comes up. Still – it is unbelievable & if I get a chance I'll make my feelings felt there. By-the-way the 'photo being in was nothing to do with B & H – I happened (tactfully) to give lunch to a member of staff a few weeks ago & the inclusion is just the result of the charm tap having been full on all the time!!!

I hope Toni's travels are going on well, & that the atmosphere of 4tet is less electric. Any chance of Maaaaass[4] (forget how many a's there are) coming over?

Peter sends his love, & is very busy. He's getting together another group of singers like English Singers[5] & is up in the air with arrangements & interviews. He's changed his teacher[6] much for the better I think, & is already showing signs of improvement. We were up in Providence last week for a Relief concert[7] & it was such a wow that we shall probably be going back there for <u>our</u> Relief soon. Elizabeth is here for lunch & sends love & will reply to your letter soon.

Hope ankle gets better quick. Be careful. Much love to you both,

BEN

1 Still to be completed were the Ballad Interludes for Narrator, Slim's Song (No. 12a) and Tiny's Song (No. 15a). See DMPB.

2 Britten possibly had in mind the forthcoming broadcast of *The Rocking-Horse Winner* (see note 1 to Letter 310) or the forthcoming gramophone recording of *Balinese Ceremonial Music* with Colin McPhee (see note 12 to Letter 312).

3 The *Musical Courier*, a long-established periodical (first published under this title in 1884). A photograph of Britten (by Ernest Nash) had appeared in the issue of 1 February, to publicize the forthcoming

première of the *Sinfonia da Requiem*. Presumably Heinsheimer, on behalf of the Boosey & Hawkes Artists' Agency, had promised to ensure that Brosa would receive similar publicity for his concerts with the Pro Arte Quartet.

4 Robert Maas, for many years cellist of the Pro Arte Quartet. He was to receive the Coolidge Medal in 1946 for his services to chamber music.

5 This group was to be named the Elizabethan Singers, the members of which were Meg Mundy (daughter of Clytie Mundy), Helen Marshall (Tiny in *Paul Bunyan*), Jane Rogers, Peter Pears, and Bruce Boyce. Sample programmes designed for universities, music clubs, schools, and so forth, included English madrigals, American folksongs arranged by McPhee, vocal music by Purcell, Debussy's *Trois Chansons de Charles d'Orléans*, and 'Three Songs for St Cecilia's Day' by Britten, destined for first performance at the ensemble's projected New York recital. This last was clearly an early concept of the *Hymn to St Cecilia* (see note 4 to Letter 374). A Christmas programme included Holst's 'In the bleak mid-winter' and Vaughan Williams's arrangement of 'We've been a-while a-wandering'.

6 Clytie Hine Mundy (1887–1983), Australian-born singer and teacher. She studied at the College and was a leading member of Beecham's Opera Company, 1911–19. She emigrated to New York in 1920. Peter Pears wrote in his obituary notice of Mrs Mundy, *The Times*, 12 August 1983: 'I had the pleasure of studying with her for some time and was much helped by her straightforward direct teaching.' Her husband, John Mundy, was principal cellist in the Metropolitan Opera Orchestra.

7 Given at the Elks Auditorium, Providence, Rhode Island as the first of the Friendship Concerts in aid of British War Relief Society.

308   To David Ewen[1]
[*Pencil draft*]

[?March 1941][2]

Dear Mr. Ewen,

Please forgive me for not having answered your letter of Feb. 16th before this – but I have been most terribly busy, & also have been held up over some information that I wished to obtain before answering your kind letter. Of course I shall be delighted to cooperate with you in your new book.[3] Unfortunately I have so far been unable to obtain copies of the best articles written about me. They were published in periodicals in England some time ago

& I am afraid I have not got them with me. But Mr. Colin MacPhee
is engaged in writing a comprehensive survey of my work at the
moment, which Modern Music is considering using sometime –
but at anyrate not before the fall – & anyhow there would be no
objection to you using it I know.[4] This I am convinced would be
the best possible for your book, since, even were I able to obtain
the others from England they would be somewhat out of date.
Could you please let me know about how many words you
would like the article to be? I will send the 'credo' as soon as I have
time to do it.[5] When is the dead line?

Yours sincerely,
BB

1 David Ewen (1907–1985), American editor and writer of Polish birth.
   He produced a number of popular reference works on American
   composers and the American musical theatre.

2 This date is an editorial guess, based on the supposition that it would
   have been only after Britten had had time to acquire some sort of
   reputation in America that Ewen would have approached him.

3 The book to which Britten refers was *The Book of Modern Composers*,
   first published in New York by Knopf in 1943. It contains, however,
   no entry on Britten.

4 If indeed McPhee completed this survey, it seems not to have survived among his papers. (See also note 3 to Letter 297.) The proposal
   provides further evidence however of the close association of McPhee
   and Britten at this time. See note 12 to Letter 312.

5 Ewen's method was to include in each entry a section entitled 'The
   Composer Speaks'. This, clearly, was the 'credo' to which Britten
   refers. A second edition of the book published in 1950 includes a
   Britten entry contributed by Erwin Stein.

309 To Peggy Brosa

Amityville, N.Y.
[April 1941]

My dearest Peggy,

   Thank you so much for your wire & sweet letter – I was very
touched by them both. I am sorry not to have answered them
before this but I have seriously miscalculated the time it would take
to score Paul Bunyan & every moment of the day (& most nights!)
is taken up with that – so that is why this will only be a short note

(more excuses!!). I have also been sick with one of the plagues of
Egypt (guess which –) which has held me up a day or two.

The concert went quite well.[1] John B. was very serious & took
great pains over it[2] – & the orchestra liked playing it a lot – so the
show was a good one. The audience was friendly & some of the
critics (not the Times tho'!)[3] – so I am feeling quite pleased.
Personally, I think it is the best so far, & since it's the last opus,
it's as it should be – although to me it is so personal & intimate
a piece, that it is rather like those awful dreams where one parades
about the place naked – slightly embarrassing! I don't think the
family heard it – although I wish they could have done; but in some
way it isn't the kind of piece to play in a country at war. Poor
dears.

How I wish Toni & you could have been there. Ethel & Rae gave
a party for the Mayers & the Barbirollis & it was all quite gay –
but would have been much nicer if you'd been there too. How
were Toni's concerts? Is he back with you yet? By-the-way – this
is only a suggestion – but would he consider (if dates fit in) giving
a recital (with me!!) at Riverhead next winter for only $250? They are
trying to start a new concert series – including some orchestral
concerts (by my orch.) – & if we could have his name on the list
it would be much easier to sell the series to the public. What do
you think? I shall easily understand if he says no.[4]

Apart from work, illnesses (Peter's had infected feet & a slight
operation on them),[5] conducting my orchestra in rehearsals &
3 concerts, nothing much to say – & anyhow I must get back to my
bloody (please excuse!) scoring.

Much love to you both, & thanks awfully for the lovely messages.

Yours ever,

BEN

Not much news from England – but so far what there is, is good,
except that I can't persuade old Barbara to leave London.

1 The first performance of *Sinfonia da Requiem* on 29 and 30 March, for
which Britten supplied the following programme note:

I.   Lacrymosa (Andante ben misurato). A slow marching lament in a persistent ⁶⁄₈ rhythm with a strong tonal centre on D. There are three main motives:
(1) a syncopated, sequential theme announced by the 'cellos and answered
by a solo bassoon; (2) a broad theme, based on the interval of a major
seventh; (3) alternating chords on flute and trombones, outlined by the piano
and harps. The first section of the movement is quietly pulsating; the second

a long crescendo leading to a climax based on the first 'cello theme. There is no pause before:–

II. Dies Irae (Allegro con fuoco). A form of Dance of Death, with occasional moments of quiet marching rhythm. The dominating motif of this movement is announced at the start by the flutes and includes an important tremolando figure. Other motives are: a triplet repeated (note figure in the trumpets), a slow smooth tune on the saxophone and a livelier syncopated one on the brass. The scheme of the movement is a series of climaxes of which the last is the most powerful, causing the music to disintegrate and to lead directly to:–

III. Requiem Aeternam (Andante piacevole). Very quietly over a background of solo strings and harps; the flutes announce the quiet D major tune, which is the principal motif of the movement. There is a middle section in which the strings play a flowing melody. This grows to a short climax, but the opening tune is soon resumed and the work ends quietly in a long sustained clarinet note.

Prior to the performance, Boosey & Hawkes issued a press statement which briefly spelt out the work's strange history:

The 'SINFONIA DA REQUIEM' was commissioned by the Japanese Government through the British Council for Cultural Relations with Other Countries, for the celebration of the 2600th anniversary of the Japanese Imperial Dynasty in December 1940. Mr Britten was then in America and cabled acceptance of the offer on the condition that he was to have a free hand as to the character of the work, and mentioned the plan he had for this Sinfonia together with the titles of the movements. This condition, he understood, was acceptable; accordingly he went to work over the score, and delivered the Sinfonia as agreed in June 1940. The work was to be performed in December 1940. In November, however, Mr Britten received notice that the Japanese Government did not consider the work as suitable for this particular festival, partly because of its Christian nature. It has not been performed, therefore, in Japan, and the present performances will be the first.

2 A private recording of the performance made by 'Melotone', taken from the broadcast of the concert by CBS on Sunday 30 March, is in the possession of the Archive. For Britten's comments on the recording see Letter 352. An estimated audience of 9 million in the USA and Canada listened to these Sunday afternoon broadcasts from Carnegie Hall.

3 Because the performances of *Sinfonia da Requiem* were given at the weekend, the work's première did not receive the press attention usually accorded such an occasion. A brief notice by 'R.L.', however, appeared in the *New York Herald Tribune*, 31 March:

The promising and frequently eloquent 'Sinfonia da Requiem' of Benjamin Britten, twenty-seven-year-old English composer, was repeated yesterday afternoon in the Philharmonic Symphony Orchestra's concert at Carnegie Hall. As on Saturday night, when the work was first presented here, Mr

Britten appeared on the platform to acknowledge applause, sharing honors with John Barbirolli, who had conducted with authority and imagination.

This performance was preceded by a dank reading of Rossini's overture to 'L'Italiana in Algieri' and followed by the Beethoven violin concerto, in which the artistry of Ericka Morini, appearing as soloist, was chiefly responsible for the maintenance of the musical flow. Except for his fine work in the 'Sinfonia da Requiem', this was not Mr Barbirolli's afternoon.

The critic of the *New York Times* (Ross Parmenter), 31 March, chose merely to mention the new work as an afterthought to his review of the remainder of the programme – 'Benjamin Britten's *Sinfonia da Requiem* [. . .] had its first performance on Saturday night.'

4 Nothing seems to have come of this proposal.

5 According to Pears, he was bitten by bedbugs, unwelcome tenants at Middagh Street and part of the 'Bohemian' living conditions there which he and Britten found temperamentally unsympathetic. Pears recalled this aspect of the Middagh Street days in an interview in the *Advocate*, Los Angeles, 12 July 1979, pp. 37 *et seq*.:

Well, it was just Bohemia – which, in fact, didn't really appeal to Ben or myself, though I'm better at Bohemia than he was, I think. He was much too methodical a worker. Auden, for instance, had some very routine parts of his life. He was obviously a highly disciplined writer, but outside his writing hours his life was much freer and wilder than what ours was naturally. We were more conventional, I suppose. For a short time Middagh Street was kind of fun, but after the tremendous warmth and happiness of Amityville, it wasn't quite home. It was filthy, untidy. Just Bohemia.

310 To Albert Goldberg

7, Middagh Street,
Brooklyn, N.Y.
Main 4–9079
April 28th 1941

My dear Albert,

I know – I know – I know – but if you had had to score an operetta, a Sinfonia, write a 2 piano piece, a Radio score,[1] score 'Les Sylphides'[2] & God knows what else in such a short time – you'd have been dilatory too – and I haven't got no secretary to dictate too, neither. Any-how, please forgive me & thanks for all your nice letters and all.

I am sorry the press was so bitter about the Variations[3] – I thought that old piece was accepted by them now; certainly in most places it is – but perhaps Chicago is behind (or in front of) the times!

Anyhow the audience liked it, & that's what matters.
Koussevitsky did it last week[4] – By-the-way.

I'm sorry that you didn't like the Sinfonia,[5] because I think it's
the best so far – & people here (intelligent people – ha! ha!) think
so too. Maybe something happens in the air between Carnegie Hall
& Chicago. But you'll hear it again – don't worry!

I hope you aren't too wildly busy, & that things aren't too hectic
– but it's a faint hope, I know. I wish that there was some excuse
for me to come out to see you – but things are quite drastic with
me, as you can imagine, what with things being as they are on
both sides of the Atlantic. Still, I suppose one day things will get
straight – & then – what fun we'll have! How's that assistant of
yours? Give him my regards.

I'm just in the middle of rehearsals of my 'Paul Bunyan' operetta
– &, believe me, compared with conditions there the Work
Projects Administrations of Illinois is a mixture of the Boston
Symphony, the Ritz-Carlton,[6], & the Gestapo (for efficiency only!)

So long – be good.

Greetings & thanks,

BENJAMIN B

1 An adaptation by Auden and James Stern of D.H. Lawrence's short
   story, *The Rocking-Horse Winner*, with incidental music by Britten,
   was broadcast by CBS on 6 April, a Columbia Workshop production.
   See PR, pp. 396–91, and 597.

2 A version of Chopin's music for small orchestra made for Lincoln
   Kirstein's ballet company, for which Britten received payment of $300
   for 'all and every right in the instrumentation'. It was presented for
   the first time on 11 February at the Majestic Theater, New York, with
   choreography by Michel Fokine. When the company visited Covent
   Garden in 1946, Britten's version of *Les Sylphides* was performed. The
   score has since been lost. Britten in post-war years remembered
   its existence and showed some interest in locating it. But so far it
   has proved impossible to trace. A gramophone recording (Capitol,
   CCL 7518) purporting to use his arrangement was disclaimed by the
   composer when he heard it.

3 Cecil Smith (1906–1956) was the music critic of the *Chicago Tribune*
   (and later of the London *Daily Express*). He wrote on 25 March:

   In last night's Illionois Symphony orchestra concert Benjamin Britten's 'Variations on a Theme of Frank Bridge', played for the first time in Chicago,
   and Ottorino Respighi's 'Autumnal Poem', for violin and orchestra, presented here for the second time, were set down in the midst of more familiar
   items. Herman Clebanoff, one time concert master of the Illinois Symphony

orchestra, was soloist in the Respighi work and in Bach's Concerto in E major.

Mr Britten, who at 27 is regarded as one of the brighter lights of the younger generation of English musicians, has based a series of 10 brief and rather light variations for string orchestra upon a none too weighty theme by the late Frank Bridge. The best feature of the variations is their almost unfailing warmth and color of instrumentation. Mr Britten does not allow his orchestra of strings alone to become monotonous or dull.

In actual musical content the variations are thin almost to the point of emaciation. Mr Britten, a graduate of the famous Royal College of Music, has neither the contrapuntal skill nor the constructional ability to make anything sustained or fully developed out of his thematic material.

The *Bridge Variations* had been performed for the first time in Chicago at the Great Northern Theater on 24 March, conducted by Izler Solomon. Goldberg had written to Britten on 1 April:

Cecil Smith's review is absolutely misleading. The Variations were received by the audience with far more than the usual enthusiasm. There were even shouts, and Solomon was recalled far more than the average number of times than is customary preceding an intermission. I think it is a very fine piece, particularly the funeral march and chant.

In reply to Britten's comments in the present letter, Goldberg was to write again on 2 May '[Solomon] really did a right smart job with your Variations', and in response to the mention of Koussevitzky's performance of the work (see note 4 below) adds, 'I was surprised to see that Koussevitzky omitted three of the best variations.' The performance file of the Boston Symphony Orchestra suggests that the omitted variations were the *Wiener Walzer*, *Moto perpetuo* and *Funeral March*.

4 Performances of the *Bridge Variations* given by the Boston Symphony Orchestra, on 25 and 26 April.

5 Goldberg had written to Britten on 1 April:

Glad to have had the opportunity to hear your Sinfonia da Requiem on Sunday's broadcast. Certainly, it achieved the mood you desired although, on first hearing, I am inclined to prefer the Variations.

6 A leading hotel in Boston.

311 To Benjamin Britten
From Elizabeth Mayer
[*Typed*]

Amityville, May 6, 1941

My dear Ben,

Just a last thought before we leave for Virginia, our heads still filled with your sweet melodies![1] We were both very happy last night, even with all the imperfections in the performance, and our only 'fight' was about the greater genius and inventiveness of either the writer or the musician, William obstinately taking your side. This morning came a letter from Michael, quite contented, and very pleased to see us soon. We may drive straightways into the Fort – he is off every afternoon after 5 p.m. and will get probably a pass to go out with us.[2] That is a wonderful prospect!

[. . .]

I have read this morning several notices[3] – the majority of them lacks everything a critic should have – knowledge, flair, enthusiasm (even if refusing) decent language etc. Let them stew in their own juice, and go on working. I did not think that the photo in P.M.[4] was so bad – my scrapbook is waxing. Do you think I might get one or two of the photos you showed me in Brooklyn?

Give Wystan my love, and dear Peter who did not look too well – tell him to be careful, and sleep and rest more – my children, I love you all – God bless you! Ben, courage, I am always around you. Tell Slim[5] that he is a terribly nice creature, I think the best personification of that part – I always hear the lovely tune!

Goodbye, Sunday!!

ELIZABETH

Please don't forget to bring out the DOUBLE MAN with Wystan's dedication to Norman![6]

1 The first performance of *Paul Bunyan* had taken place on 5 May. A preview had been given on the 4th, which some critics had attended.

2 Michael Mayer had been drafted for peacetime military service. US Registration for military service had become obligatory for all men between the ages of twenty-one and thirty-five on 16 September 1940. In 1941 Michael was a private at Fort Foster, Kittery Point, Maine.

3 Olin Downes wrote in the *New York Times*, 6 May:

The first official public performance of the choral operetta, 'Paul Bunyan', by W.H. Auden and Benjamin Britten, respectively librettist and composer, was given last night in Brander Matthews Hall of Columbia University, following the 'preview' performance of the same work, for the benefit of the members of the League of Composers, one of the sponsors of the production, given the preceding evening in the same theatre.

This work, and its production, were witnessed by the present reviewer with mixed feelings. They arose from the possibilities of a form of intimate and modern opera unfolded by this score and spectacle, and by the superficial and inconsistent way in which these possibilities have been exploited.

Mr Britten had prepared us for the eclectism and adroitness of his composing by symphonic works which have met with a considerable measure of success in concert halls on both sides of the Atlantic. He is a very clever young man, who can provide something in any style or taste desired by the patron. He scores with astonishing expertness and fluency. He has a melodic vein which is perfectly plausible, though one without marked physiognomy. He shows what could be done by a composer whose purpose was deeper set and more consistent than Mr Britten's appears to be. For this very reason the respects in which he was lacking were disappointing, at times irritating.

As for Mr Auden, we had expected better of him. It need not have been anticipated that a modern English poet of his nature and antecedents, would impart a very characteristic flavor to an essentially American legend. Nor need it have been expected that a literary man's early venture into the theatre would have the salient strokes and developments of stage-craft that would thrust home his interpretation. But we had a right to hope for something from him that would have consistently developed purpose. Whereas his libretto, like the music, seems to wander from one to another idea, without conviction or cohesion. In the plot, as in the score, is a little of everything, a little of symbolism and uplift, a bit of socialism and of modern satire, and gags and jokes of a Hollywood sort, or of rather cheap musical comedy.

Of course the treatment of a subject which presents fantastical contrasts, the broad and salty kind of humor, and the braggadoccio which carries within itself something more than mere laughter and a spirit not less gigantic and heroic than the terrain of the fable, would justify ostensible incongruities in treatment – would be, in fact, inappropriate without them. But the operetta does not have a convincing flavor of inevitable conglomeration. It seems a rather poor sort of a bid for success, and possibly the beguilement of Americans.

What is done by Mr Britten shows more clearly than ever that opera written for a small stage, with relatively modest forces for the presentation, in the English language, and in ways pleasantly free from the stiff tradition of either grand or light opera of the past, is not only a possibility but a development nearly upon us.

The flexibility and modernity of the technical treatment were refreshing. That they are derivative does not alter this salient and striking fact. We do not know whether the authors of this piece are conversant, for example, with the terse social satire of 'The Cradle Will Rock' [Blitzstein], of recent and highly honorable achievement. But it seems likely.

As for the sources of Mr Britten's style, they are numerous and extremely varied. They range everywhere from Prokofieff to Mascagni, from Rimsky-Korsakoff to Gilbert and Sullivan. Few operas are neglected a bow of recognition as he proceeds. One would say that he was thoroughly conversant with the entire repertory of the lyric theatre and that as a modern craftsman he could write in any style known to man regardless of period.

He knows how to set a text, how to orchestrate in an economical and telling fashion; how to underscore dialogue with orchestral commentary, terse or more elaborately descriptive, and how to treat all this with an ingenuity that only palls when he has exhausted devices and is faced with the necessity of saying something that is genuine. Then the music begins to fail, the set numbers to become wearisome and the listeners to tire of ingenuities which are seen before the evening is over as platitudes and notion-counter devices of salesmanship.

The performance of the opera was meritorious in view of the fact that many of the singers were amateurs, that rehearsals had been fewer than were necessary and that every one entered into his task with enthusiasm and intelligence. A soloist who showed out with particular credit was Mordecai Bauman, the Narrator. But there were many soloists and no stars in the libretto or in pretenses of performance. The English text went over often, though not always, and Mr Auden is an accomplished craftsman with it. The scenery was simple and reasonably effective. Mr Ross conducted with authority and animation, showing a talent for stage music as well as choral and orchestral manifestation.

Virgil Thomson, *New York Herald Tribune*, 6 May:

Benjamin Britten's music here as elsewhere, has considerable animation. His style is eclectic though not without savour. Its particular blend of melodic 'appeal' with irresponsible counterpoint and semi-acidulous instrumentation is easily recognizable as that considered by the British Broadcasting Corporation to be at once modernistic and safe. Its real model is, I think, the music of Shostakovitch, also eclectic, but higher in physical energy content than that of Mr Britten.

Mr Britten's work in 'Paul Bunyan' is sort of witty at its best. Otherwise it is undistinguished. It is not well written for voices. Neither is it very apt as musical declamation. And the accompaniments tend to obscure rather than to sustain the soloists. Melodically and harmonically it lacks the tension that we recognize as style. There is every reason to suppose Mr Britten can do better. He usually does.

What any composer thinks he can do with a text like 'Paul Bunyan' is beyond me. It offers no characters and no plot. It is presumably, therefore, an allegory or a morality; and as either it is, I assure you, utterly obscure and tenuous. In addition, its language is not the direct speech of dramatic poetry. It is a deliberate parody, for the most part, of the attempts at intensity on the part of our least dramatic poets. Its subject, consequently, is not Paul Bunyan at all, nor even the loggers and farmers of the Northwest that it purports to depict. Its subject is literature itself, as is that of most of Mr Auden's work. Every sentence is indirect and therefore unsuited to musical declamation. Every dramatic moment has the afflatus taken out of it before the composer can get it over to the audience.

The rendition of the piece was amateurish but not dull. Mr Mordecai Bauman sang nice ditties to a guitar between the scenes. The scenery itself was adequate, if not very interesting. It did its worst at the beginning, where for a full scene and a half the music was choral, the chorus both invisible as to bodies and incomprehensible as to diction. During all this time we watched a dim stage with nobody on it but a couple of ducks and wondered if the show would ever stop talking about itself and get going. Finally some people came out on the stage, and the whole thing lasted till half past eleven; but it never did get going, and I never did figure out the theme.
[. . .]

Robert Bagar, *New York World-Telegram*, 5 May:

The allegories brushed each other aside in their mad rush for the spotlight. Paul Bunyan, lumberjack super-myth of epic proportions and derring-doodles, received a few more powers from the bountiful authors. He was, to start with, 'a projection of the collective state of mind of a people whose tasks were primarily the physical mastery of nature'. Then he became Courage, Hope, the Good Companion, the Present, the Future, the Infinite. He was all of these, but he couldn't imitate four Hawaiians.

In conveying the idea to a rather befuddled public Messrs Britten and Auden depended heavily on a conglomerate throng of characters – 'many small parts rather than a few star roles'. Thus, there were singing trees, singing geese, singing cats, a singing dog, and many, very many, singing people. Most of these talked too.

Anachronism was part of the scheme, by way of a Western Union Boy, two Film Stars and two Models, all in the typifying garb of today. There is no need to go further into the plot – who wants a plot, anyway? – suffice it to say that much was sung, much was said and time went as slow as the dickens.

Mr Britten, who is an up and coming composer, has written some worthwhile tunes in this score. It ranges, in passing, from part writing to single jingle. Its rhythms are often interesting and the harmonies fit rather well. There are arias, recitatives, small ensembles and big choral sequences. Most of the last named are good. The music makes occasional reference to Cavalleria Rusticana and one time, a stuttering bit, goes right back to The Bartered Bride.

Paul Bunyan, being such a magnificent physical specimen, obviously, could not have been interpreted, save by a giant. So, instead of appearing as one of the stage characters, he makes his influence felt by voice. Milton Warchoff was the Voice, and a rattling good job he did of it, too. Mordecai Bauman, the singing narrator, acquitted himself well, indeed.

Part of the text was clever, part of it literature, but most of it was plain jumble – and 'significant' jumble, at that. Of the numbers a Blues, sung by a quartet, The Defeated, proved effective as to both words and music. Helen Marshall, William Hess and Charles Cammock offered likeable voices.

The sets were O.K., and the costumes, ditto. The orchestra played decently more often than not. It is only necessary to add that the piece will run nightly all during this week with a matinée scheduled for Saturday. Last evening's showing was a preview for the members of the League of Composers.

See also DMPB pp. 130–35. An article by Auden about the operetta, 'Opera on an American Legend: Problem of Putting the Story of Paul Bunyan on the Stage', had appeared in the Sunday edition of the New York Times on 4 May.

4 The New York magazine in which a review of the operetta by Henry Simon appeared, along with a photograph of Auden and Britten. Simon wrote, 'The music is an ingenious mélange of Marc Blitzstein (No for an Answer) technique, motets, canons, Rossini, Gilbert and Sullivan, American ballads and others too humorous to mention.' Another famous theatre piece by Blitzstein, The Cradle Will Rock, was also quoted as a source by the anonymous reviewer in Time (19 May).

However, we have no evidence to suggest that Britten and Auden were familiar with either work. See David Ewen, *The Story of America's Musical Theater* (Philadelphia, Chiltern, 1961), pp.151–3, and Cecil Smith, *Musical Comedy in America* (New York, Theatre Arts Books, 1950), pp. 294–5; and Carol J. Oja, 'Marc Blitzstein's *The Cradle Will Rock* and Mass-Song Style of the 1930s', *Musical Quarterly*, 73/4, 1989, pp. 445–75.

5 Slim, the cowboy in *Paul Bunyan*, was played by Charles Cammock.

6 *The Double Man*, a volume of Auden's poems, was published in 1941 by Random House (the English edition was retitled *New Year Letter* (London, Faber and Faber, 1941)). 'Norman' was Norman Holmes Pearson (see note 2 to Letter 315). The poem 'New Year Letter' had been published originally as 'Letter to Elizabeth Mayer' in *Atlantic*, January and February 1941.

312   To Beth Welford

[EWB, *pp. 162–5*]

<u>Still</u> – Amityville, N.Y.
May 12th 1941

My darling, darling old Beth,

Your very sweet letter arrived just now – as, believe it or not, I was just about to take up a pen to break the long silence. I was terribly glad to get it, & to know that you are still all right – that means I shall have a few moments relief from anxiety about you until something else happens to start me worrying again! I am delighted that you have got Barbara away from London, at anyrate for the nights – I have been on tenter hooks about her being in that bloody inferno all this time. I hope it isn't too tiring for her to 'commute' (American word, meaning – 'to go backwards & forwards by train or bus to a large town to work'[1] – convenient, isn't it?!) everyday. And I am also delighted that Kit can see you so often. It would have been hell for you to go through all this & never see him. I hope he's not too unhappy about his work – he is still <u>medical</u>, isn't he? I mean, he doesn't have to fly – just tend broken legs, etc . . . ??[2] Some day – some day – I shall be able to get you over here & he'll do work he really likes, in a small place, near the sea & miles away from noise, fashion & sophistication & all the things he hates. I am feeling like that too now. A winter in New York is just about the limit for me – especially in these times when everyone is so het up & panicky – you can't imagine how hysterical Americans can be – especially in places like New York. If the British Navy sink a ship – the war is won; – if a British General is captured – then there's no sense in going on with the war, better give up. When one is feeling racked because of family & friends in bombardments, & with the anxiety & hard labour in trying to establish a reputation in a new, & not particularly friendly country, it's just about as much as one can take. However I have very good friends & of course Amityville I can flee to, if it gets too much for me – such as this present moment.[3]

I am afraid one of the reasons that I've been so long in writing is not that I have been occupied <u>every</u> waking moment (I know you wouldn't believe me if I said I have been!), but that I haven't had the time to settle down to the kind of letter that was worth writing to you after the long gap.

Now I have got this one off my chest I am going to write short letters more frequently, and not always by air-mail because it is so expensive. I am delighted that you liked my Violin Concerto.[4] I gather that it was a pretty bad performance – by the notices & by Ralph Hawkes' account.[5] How I wish you could have heard Toni do it with the New York Philharmonic – that is really something! I was sent most of the notices & was surprised that they were so good[6] – because after all they might easily be sour about me being able to go on working regardless of everything. I am glad you'd the feeling that I have 'grown up' – well, may be I have at last! If I haven't with all this, I don't think there's much chance of me ever doing so! I think I look more or less the same – I'm <u>not</u> going bald as someone (Barbara I think) suggested – merely brushing my hair further back instead of across. Gives me a fine forehead – that's why! I must see if I can get a photo to send you – maybe I have one in New York, only there's been rather a run on them recently, with all the performances that have been occuring. Well – I have produced my first Symphony (the Requiem one, in memory of Mum & Pop, paid for by the Japanese Government – nice touch that – don't you think?) & my first opera. Neither could be called an unqualified success, but the reaction was everywhere violent which I suppose is a good thing, but personally I hate it. I'd much rather it was praised mildly everywhere – I feel embarrassed at being the subject of animated debate. Roughly speaking – the reaction of the public has been excellent – in every case much applause (three or four calls for me at each performance of the Symphony) – the reaction of the intellectual composers has been bad (I am definitely disliked (a) because I am English (no music

ever came out of England) (b) because I'm not American
(everything is nationalistic) (c) because I get quite alot of
performances (d) because I wasn't educated in Paris[7] – etc. etc.)
– the reaction of the press mixed – usually the respectable papers
(like the Times) bad or puzzled – the rag papers or picture papers
good – funny, isn't it? The opera 'Paul Bunyan' I think you'd like
alot – full of tunes that people even whistle! and it's quite good
entertainment – but the labour involved was enormous – a whole
evening's work is no joke to write & score, let alone supervise
the rehearsals. The performance wasn't too good, but there are
future productions in sight, which may be better.[8] Besides this I
have conducted three concerts with my Riverhead orchestra, which
were strenuous but not altogether unrewarding; they are so
enthusiastic, although not exactly efficient. I may go on next season
– if they can raise the money to keep it up. I hope so, because in a
way I feel it is doing something tangible in return for the hospitality
of the country. I have also written several articles for periodicals,
with great effort, & with the aid of Peter & Wystan over the
grammar & spelling![9] Peter is singing 'Les Illuminations' (first
performance in America) over the Radio on Sunday afternoon – &
if I can get permission from the Unions (the great new American
racket at the moment) I shall conduct. I have also written a large
two-piano piece for Ethel Bartlett & Rae Robertson, which they
play from time to time. So you see I've been occupied, which is a
blessing these days. I hope your reaction to all this nonsense
won't be aggrevation, which I could easily understand tho'. I know,
compared with what is happening everywhere, all this has little
importance – but I feel that it is the only thing I can do well, and
after all music does give alot of comfort to those not actually in
the firing line as you are – infact it's quite extraordinary how music
is flourishing at the moment, & agents tell me that bookings are
going wonderfully for next year, when everyone knows America
will be in the war.[10] That by the way is the general opinion. There
is still a great deal of anti-war feeling, but Roosevelt is being very
cunning in being just sufficiently far ahead of public opinion, but
not too far so as to be over thrown & some reactionary quasi-fascist
power be put in instead.

Our plans for the summer are of course abit vague – but Peter &
I have had an invitation to go to spend some time in South
California (with Ethel and Rae Robertson) & as we want to go to
Mexico so as to get on to the labour-quota (you have to go out of
the country & then come back, so as to be able to work without

hindrance) that all fits in well. I also have a great deal of work to get done, & if possible I want to land a Hollywood job[11] – & then how rich we'll all be – I shall be able to send you lots of money! That, quite seriously, is the only reason I want to make money – so that you can live a little easier & have the little creature comforts that make life abit more bearable. I'll see about the parcels of food, but the boats don't go very often so don't expect it too soon, will you?

I feel bad about my God-son – but perhaps in a few years it will be a good thing to have a rich uncle in America (who knows!)

May 13th   I meant to have finished this yesterday, but I had to leave to go & play in a concert (2 piano duets with an American composer called McPhee)[12] when Peter was conducting his choral society. It went very well & there was much animated applause . . . & promises of future dates, which may or may not materialise. However, one lives on promises these days.

I am just about to leave for Brooklyn by train (about an hour away). I have a lot of business to do in the city & I shall stay a few nights in our house there – the house that Peter, Wystan & I share with a man called George Davis (one of the editors of Harper's Bazzaar). It is quite nice and convenient, tho' a trifle too bohemian for my liking – I like the ordinary dull routine more & more, the older I get! I can't live wildly and work! I don't think your brother would shock you, my dear, if you met him. He is still quite a sober, God-fearing person – & altho' you never believe it, he does work pretty hard! But he only lives for the day, when he can meet his sisters & bro.-in law & nephew – whom he thinks of continually, altho' he fails to write as often as he should. Please forgive me, my darling old Beth, but I have been horribly busy. Please tell Barbara that I'll write in a few days, but I'm going to send this right away without waiting – Much love to Kit & Dopey.[13] Just had a nice letter from Peter Welford,[14] & Piers Dunkerly.

All my love, my dear.

Bear up – le diable est mort!

BEN.

1 Evidence that Britten had by him, as was his habit throughout his life, the dictionary to which he needed to turn to check his spelling.

2 See EWB, p. 161: 'Kit was centred in London, examining air crews.'

3 Hence the inscription above the date of this letter.

4 The Violin Concerto had been given its first English performance at Queen's Hall, London, on 6 April, when the London Philharmonic

Orchestra was conducted by Basil Cameron and the soloist was Thomas Matthews (the leader of the orchestra). The programme note (by Edwin Evans) made no reference to the composer's absence in the USA. The concert was the sixteenth in the so-called Beecham Sunday Concert series. See PFL, plate 137.

5 Hawkes had written to the composer on 8 April:

Basil Cameron conducted the Orchestra and, I think, very well but one rehearsal had been largely wasted because the parts were poorly done here, chiefly, I think, owing to difficulties in reading the photographed Score and another rehearsal would undoubtedly have improved things. Thomas Matthews played the solo part as well as he could but I could never say that he is a 'Brosa'; his tone is not so big nor has he that feeling of passion that Toni has in his playing and which your work calls for on more than one occasion. Technically, he performed pretty well and made unquestionably a big personal success at the end of it. As I was the only one who had heard the work played in New York, I was asked numerous questions regarding the tempi and general style and I found it not very easy to offer concrete advice. I did think during the performance that parts of it were inclined to drag and it could have been taken faster. Clarence Raybould is going to conduct the BBC Concert on 28th. and I think he will do better. I hope this will be on the Short Wave and, if so, I will try to get a cable off to you to indicate when you should listen.

6 However Britten could scarcely have been enthusiastic about the reception of the work in *The Times*, 7 April (almost certainly written by Frank Howes):

The Sunday afternoon concerts at Queen's Hall rarely offer debateable music. Yesterday, instead of the smooth and beaten tracks of violin music, we were invited to stumble along the stony path of a new violin concerto by Benjamin Britten produced a year ago in New York and now heard for the first time in London. The effort was creditable and no doubt salutary.

Mr Thomas Matthews, who played the exceedingly exacting solo part, did not stumble, and Mr Basil Cameron kept the orchestra on the road. If the audience found some of the way heavy going they put a brave face on it and applauded with heartiness when it was over. Our own feeling was one of disappointment that so little is achieved from so large a display of ingenious effort. Not one of the old tricks of the bravura style which used to be thrown off for effect in the old-fashioned kind of concerto was neglected. They were all there, yet they never made the effect which was formerly their justification.

The first movement, starting from a drum rhythm and what was nearly a cantabile tune, became increasingly desultory as the movement proceded. The scherzo gathers rather more momentum, but becomes heavy handed just at the moment when lightness is most needed. For the third time hopes are raised by a skilful point in which the theme of the final Passacaglia is introduced pianissimo by trombones while the violin is still dreaming over that cantabile tune with which it began: but the variations which emerge seemed not sufficiently cumulative to justify the extreme solemnity of the peroration. What is a solo concerto for but to concentrate effect? The general impression was that this dissipates effect.

Edwin Evans also contributed a notice to the *Liverpool Daily Post* on 7 April, in which he finally made reference to the absent composer:

Benjamin Britten's new violin concerto, which Antonio Brosa introduced at Carnegie Hall, New York, just over a year ago, was performed for the first time in England this afternoon at Queen's Hall. It was conducted by Basil Cameron, and the soloist was Thomas Matthews, leader of the London Philharmonic Orchestra. It is a brilliant work. The only doubt it leaves in one's mind is whether it is not really too clever – whether its most piquant orchestral effects of the difficulties with which the solo part bristles are not, when considered in cold blood, so many 'stunts'. But against these there are moments of genuine tone-poetry – especially when the music assumes a meditative mood, as it does at least once in each movement. Of these there are three, except that the more satanic portions of the Scherzo seem at cross purposes with the rest of the work, they hang well together.

The solo part will probably make it popular among go-ahead violinists, but its success with the general public is less assured. Meanwhile, Thomas Matthews's playing of it is a feather in his cap. It may be apposite to mention that the composer was the other side of the Atlantic when war broke out.

7 Britten refers obliquely to the celebrated French teacher, Nadia Boulanger (1887–1979). Copland had studied with her, along with many other American composers. (Colin McPhee had also studied in Paris, but with Paul le Fleur and Isidore Phillip.) Among Britten's close friends in England, Berkeley had been a Boulanger pupil. Britten profoundly distrusted the 'school' of composition which he felt to be the result of her influence. In his eyes, the ideal teacher was one who developed – or released – a pupil's own personality and individuality, who abstained from imposing his or her aesthetic on the young composer. It was partly the fear of unduly influencing those young composers who approached him that made Britten unwilling to consider teaching.

8 An interview Britten gave to William G. King, in the *New York Sun*, late March 1941, indicates just how pressed for time the composer was: 'When he left me the other afternoon Mr Britten announced that he was going home to finish the last bit of the overture to his new operetta, *Paul Bunyan*.' The last item from the opera to be written, it survives only as a composition sketch, laid out for piano duet, and may, in fact, never have been scored, for the overture was not used when the work was first performed. Nor, indeed, did Britten choose to revive it in 1976. The overture was orchestrated by Colin Matthews in 1977 and published by Faber Music in 1980.

There were no further stage performances of *Paul Bunyan* after the first until the work's revival in 1976, although it is clear from a letter from Heinsheimer to Britten (18 June 1941) that the Berkshire Festival at Tanglewood had intended to mount the proposed revised version of the operetta during the summer. Britten and Auden were to discuss possible revisions of the opera after its première (see Letter 321 and DMPB) – Milton Smith, who was responsible for the original production, recalled (in 1967) talking to Britten about 'the possibility of trying to make a more simplified version that might be useful in schools' – but these never reached a final stage, and Britten's return to England in March 1942 meant that the whole project was shelved. Britten put his American years behind him and it was not until the end of his life, and the years after his death, that the richness of the period and its unique features came to be recognized.

9 Britten refers to his article 'England and the Folk-art Problem', *Modern Music*, 8, January/February 1941. His mention of 'grammar and spelling' reminds us of his calling on Auden for help in the drafting of the reply to the Japanese about the *Sinfonia da Requiem* affair.

The article itself includes some interesting thoughts on what Britten perceived as 'the two major schools' of composition in England and the conflict between them:

[. . .] The outstanding figures whose personalities may be said to have given each school its particular character were Elgar and Parry.

Elgar represents the professional point of view, which emphasizes the importance of technical efficiency and welcomes any foreign influences that can be profitably assimilated. Parry and his followers, with the Royal College of Music as their center, have stressed the amateur idea and they have encouraged folk-art, its collecting and teaching. They are inclined to suspect technical brilliance of being superficial and insincere. This difference may not be unconnected with the fact that Elgar was compelled to earn his living by music, whereas Parry was not. Parry's national ideal was, in fact, the English Gentleman (who generally thinks it rather vulgar to take too much trouble). From Parry and his associates there arose a school of composers directly influenced by folksong, to which belonged virtually every composer known here until recently, except of course, Elgar and Frank Bridge. This may seem surprising to many Americans who have come to regard Elgar as synonymous with England. But he is, in fact, a most eclectic composer, his most obvious influences being Wagner, Tchaikovsky, and Franck.

But since 1930 the influence of Parry has largely disappeared. Now the Elgarian approach, with its direct admission of continental contemporary influence, has asserted itself. The great success of Walton's *Façade* and Lambert's *Rio Grande*, both with the public and the intellectuals, left no doubt in the minds of the younger composers as to which was the more profitable path to follow. Elizabeth Maconchy owes much to the strong rhythms and acidulous harmonies of Bartók; Lennox Berkeley to the later works of Stravinsky and the younger French school; Christian Darnton and Elisabeth Lutyens have adopted a modified version of the twelve-tone system, as used by Webern and Berg; Alan Rawsthorne's general intellectual approach and his avoidance of tonal centers remind one of Hindemith; Howard Ferguson and Edmund Rubbra derive largely from those heavy-handed late-romantics, Brahms and Sibelius (which, I admit, is a criticism).

He continues:

Those circumstances which prompted the whole movement of Nationalism in England have been not above suspicion. Any cultural 'movement' (especially if it ends in 'ism') is more often than not a cover for inefficiency or lack of artistic direction. If one is unsatisfied with a piece of work it is useful to have some theory to shield it, and Nationalism is as good as any other – especially when one is dealing with foreigners! But there is another more sympathetic aspect of the picture. For nearly two centuries English music had been second-rate, with no more than local importance. The composers had been too ready simply to imitate their European (and especially Viennese and Italian) colleagues. The fault lay not in the influences but in the lack of talent and inability to assimilate them. It should be obvious that the national character of a composer will appear in his music, whatever technic [sic] he has chosen or wherever his influences lie, in the same way that his personal idiosyncrasies cannot be hidden. The case of Elgar we have mentioned above. Perhaps the piece of music that brings tears most easily to the eyes of an expatriate Englishman is Delius' *On Hearing the First Cuckoo in Spring*, which is founded on a Norwegian tune and written by a man who spent most of his life out of England, who responded most to the influences of Grieg and Liszt, and whose publishers were Viennese. To push the argument further, would anyone really mistake the Italian or Spanish *Capriccios* for anything but Russian, or *Ibéria* and *Carmen* for anything but French? People often cite the Russian school in the defense of Nationalism, but it is worth noting that the composer who immediately strikes one as the most Russian of Russians is Tchaikovsky who all his life was berated for being too occidental. And it was the influence of Mozart on Tchaikovsky which helped to make the texture of his music so marvelously clear and his form so much more satisfactory than that of his Nationalistic compatriots.

10 The attack on Pearl Harbor, on 7 December, forced Roosevelt's hand. The USA declared war on Japan the following day and, on 11 December, on Germany and Italy.

11 When in California in the summer (see Letter 333) Britten was to take the same opportunity as Auden had done a year earlier, to sound out the possibilities of employment in Hollywood, which, for so many visiting writers and musicians – and whatever their misgivings – remained a goal. Hence no doubt the climactic moment in the 'Christmas Party' finale of *Paul Bunyan*, when Johnny Inkslinger (Auden's self-portrait) received

> A telegram, a telegram,
>   A telegram from Hollywood.
> Inkslinger is the name;
>   And I think that the news is good.

INKSLINGER: (*Reading*) TECHNICAL ADVISER REQUIRED FOR ALL-STAR LUMBER PICTURE STOP YOUR NAME SUGGESTED STOP   IF INTERESTED WIRE COLLECT STOP

A lucky break, am I awake?
　　Please pinch me if I'm sleeping.
It only shows that no one knows
　　The future of bookkeeping.

CHORUS:　　We always knew that one day you
　　　　　Would come to be famous, Johnny.
　　　　　When you're prosperous remember us
　　　　　And we'll all sing Hey Nonny, Nonny.

Auden and Britten were not to receive the call. Of the three friends, it was Isherwood who was to achieve success in Hollywood.

12 Colin McPhee (1901–1964), Canadian-born American composer and ethnomusicologist. McPhee was a patient of Dr Mayer's, and it was through the Mayer household that Britten first met McPhee (see PFL, plates 115 and 125). The encounter with McPhee was to have historic consequences, as it was also to represent Britten's first encounter with Balinese music. McPhee had lived on Bali between 1931 and 1938, studying and transcribing Balinese gamelan music and absorbing the island's rich dance culture. He returned to the USA and busied himself proselytizing Balinese music and himself exploring as a composer a possible synthesis of Western and Balinese techniques (his remarkable work *Tabuh-Tabuhan*, composed in 1936, attempted just such a synthesis). In 1940 McPhee published a set of transcriptions for two pianos entitled *Balinese Ceremonial Music*, and it is to a performance of these pieces that Britten undoubtedly refers in this letter. Britten's copy of the published edition of the transcriptions (G. Schir-

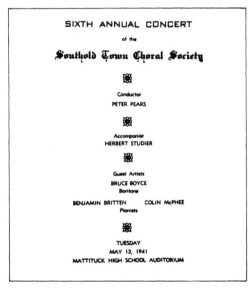

The Southold Town Choral Society, 13 May 1941

Programme	**Programme**
And The Glory of The Lord .... Handel Ave Verum .... Mozart Potapan (French Carol) .... Arr. Shaw Chorus	INTERMISSION
Arrival of The Queen of Sheba (from Solomon) .... Handel Romance .... Arensky Waltz Two-Piano Solos COLIN McPHEE and BENJAMIN BRITTEN	My Love's An Arbutus .... Irish The Nightingale's Message .... Spanish Fireflies .... Russian I'm Seventeen Come Sunday .... English Folk-Songs for Chorus
Would You Know My Celia's Charms? (Catch) .... Webbe Lullaby .... Mozart Soloist — Mrs. Dorothy Bergmann Ah! How, Sophia, Could You Leave? (Catch) .... Calcott Women's Chorus Tales From The Vienna Woods .... Strauss Waltz for Women's Voices and Piano	Billy Boy Stormalong What Shall We Do With The Drunken Sailor? Tom's Gone To Hilo Highland Laddie (Sea Shanties Arr. for Baritone Solo, Male Voices and Two Pianos by Colin McPhee) BRUCE BOYCE, COLIN McPHEE and BENJAMIN BRITTEN, Men's Chorus
Where E'er You Walk .... Handel Tally Ho! .... Franco Leoni The Roadside Fire .... Vaughan Williams Song of The Flea .... Moussorgsky BRUCE BOYCE — Baritone	Choral Dances from "Prince Igor" .... Borodin Chorus and Two-Pianos

The Southold Town Choral Society, 13 May 1941; the programme

mer Inc., New York) was inscribed by McPhee, 'To Ben – hoping he
will find something in this music, after all. Colin. April, 1940.' (See
PFL, plate 176.) (The pieces were not only published but also recorded
(in 1941) and issued as an album on 78 rpm discs.) Britten's interest
in McPhee's transcriptions as a performer continued after his return
home from the States in 1942: he played them with Clifford Curzon
at the Wigmore Hall on 29 March 1944 (see PFL, plates 174 and 176).
The immediate impact of McPhee's advocacy of an 'exotic' music
shows up first in Britten's music in the Prologue to *Paul Bunyan*, in
the heterophonic orchestral passage (Figs. 11–12) that announces the
birth of the giant logger. For documentation of the long-term musical
developments which we may ascribe to the meeting with McPhee in
1939, see Donald Mitchell, 'What do we know about Britten now?',
in BC, pp. 21–45, and two contributions to DVDM: Mervyn Cooke,
'Britten and the Gamelan: Balinese Influences in *Death in Venice*',
pp. 115–28, and Donald Mitchell, 'An Introduction in the Shape of
a Memoir', pp. 1–25, and p. 205, notes 3, 4 and 16. See also Cooke's
thesis, *Oriental Influences in the Music of Benjamin Britten*, Ph.D. dissertation, University of Cambridge, 1988, pp. 28–67. For the possible
influence of McPhee on *Peter Grimes*, see David Matthews, 'Act II
scene 1: An Examination of the Music', in PGPB, pp. 122–4. Unlike
Britten's interest in McPhee's transcriptions, his friendship with
McPhee seems not to have long survived the return to England in
1942. McPhee was to receive the Coolidge Medal in 1946 for his
services to chamber music. See also note 6 to Letter 463.

Percy Grainger and James Scott-Power must also be counted
among the pioneers. They had already transcribed 'Balinese Religious

Ceremonial Music' from a gramophone record (Parlophone MO 105) for a largely percussion ensemble.

13 Beth's baby son. Dopey was one of the dwarfs in Walt Disney's *Snow White and the Seven Dwarfs*.

14 Kit Welford's brother.

313 To Barbara Britten

7, Middagh Street,
Brooklyn Heights, N.Y.
May 14th, 1941.

My darling Barbara,

You can't imagine how thrilled I was to get Beth's letter with your enclosure yesterday saying how at last you have decided not to sleep in London any more – and only spend the days in that poor old place. I really feel as if I can breathe again! I have been most desperately worried about you, but absolutely understood your reasons and respected & loved you all the more for staying where you were. However this does seem a sensible compromise, because you can go on with your work, & after all you will now avoid the worst air-raids & be able to get a decent night's sleep. Besides it is so wonderful for Beth to have you & Helen around – the more one sticks to-gether these times the better. Gosh – what I wouldn't give to be able to be with you all now, and for times to be normal and to be able to work & think a few weeks' ahead, instead of living in the unpleasant present! I am working feverishly now – so that if a stray bomb, or conscription, or other act of God cuts my career short, I shall have something to have made life worthwhile – I am lucky to be able to go on working under these conditions, some people can't; as it is a wonderful thing to be able to retire from time to time into an abstract world of composition where only rhythms are at cross-purposes, and peace is disturbed by timpani and not by bombs! I have told Beth all the news – I hope she'll let you read it, it's not at all private!! This is only a note in hers, and I'll write you a proper letter in a day or two. I feel guilty about not having written for so long; the trouble always is that one can never find time for a decent, worth-while letter – only for little scrappy things, which seem unworthy of the occasion. However, I dare say you'd rather have that sort than nothing, so I'll promise to be better in the future. I was glad you got the money – I hope to send some more soon. As soon as

I can get my budget made out for the Summer (I have to go away and do lots of writing and shan't be able to earn much), I'll see what can be done. You can't imagine what pleasure it gives me, sending things to you – much more than you get receiving it, I know! But you needn't always send a cable – don't waste your money on it – write a letter. Another thing – if you have the strength, write more often, not necessarily long letters – & send them by <u>boat</u> – very few boats get lost coming <u>from</u> England – far more going <u>to</u> England. Just an occasional air-mail if you feel rich! I so love a hullo from time to time. I'm glad you liked the Violin Concerto[1] – but I wish you could hear the newer things, the Symphony, or Opera (this is <u>really</u> your cup of tea!) or the new songs[2] or Piano Concerto.[3]

Please tell Helen that I think of her everso often & always with great affection. One day I'm going to open a child Welfare centre somewhere in America and you two can come & run it for me! – That's when I'm a millionaire – or marry one (about an equal possibility!!)   Excuse me if I drivel a little to-night but I'm feeling very weary after a long time at the Musicians' Union this afternoon, trying to persuade them to let me become a member (altho' not an American citizen) so that I can conduct Les Illuminations on Sunday[4] over the Radio. I finally succeeded, with aid of my beautiful English accent, but it took some doing and $62!! (You will probably think I'm awfully Yankee in my ways, but, believe me, people here think I'm still very obviously a Britisher!). My darling old thing – the very best of luck to you in every way. Keep up, even with the aid of an occasional sherry! I think of you all the time – and if there's <u>anything</u> I can do just wire, & it'll be done! I had a sweet letter from Piers the other day. If you see him – tell him I'm writing.

My love to you – & lots to Helen too,

Courage mon amie!

BEN

1 Barbara would have attended the first London performance on 6 April.

2 The *Seven Sonnets of Michelangelo*, Op. 22, which Britten had completed at Amityville on 30 October 1940. His composition sketch (Beinecke Library, University of Yale, where it forms part of the Osborn Collection, MS. 510) provides some clues to the work's chronology:

1. Sonetto XVI:	'Sì come nella penna e nell' inchiostro': 5 April 1940
2. Sonetto XXXI:	'A che più debb' io mai l'intensa voglia': 15 March 1940
3. Sonetto XXX:	'Veggio co' bei vostri occhi un dolce lume': undated
4. Sonetto LV:	'Tu sa' ch'io so, signior mie, che tu sai?': undated, but a discarded ending is inscribed 1 April 1940
5. Sonetto XXXVIII:	'Rendete a gli occhi miei, o fonte o fiume': undated
6. Sonetto XXXII:	'S'un casto amor, s'una pieta superna': undated, but an earlier version is inscribed 12 June 1940
7. Sonetto XXIV:	'Spirto ben nato, in cui si specchia e vede': 30 October 1940.

Among the composer's discarded sketches at Aldeburgh is a single rejected page of a setting of Sonetto LIX, 'Non più che'l foco'.

Britten's textual source was *The Sonnets of Michael Angelo Buonarroti*, with parallel translations by John Addington Symonds, second edition (London, Smith, Elder & Co., 1904). The book originally belonged to Marjorie Fass and Britten's marks in it show that he used her copy while composing the songs. This means that Fass must have given him the book before he left for the USA. Was it then through her that he discovered the sonnets, or perhaps a combination of introductions by both Auden and Fass (see note 2 to Letter 255)?

Although the last song of the set was composed in October 1940 at Amityville, it was not until 1942, in England, that Pears and Britten first performed the songs in public. (See note 2 to Letter 391.) While in America, they confined themselves to private performances for their immediate friends and acquaintances. (One such performance was to be given for Alma Mahler, to whom Britten inscribed 'with love' a dyeline copy of a copyist's copy, dated February 1942.) It is clear that the main reason for the delayed première was Pears's wanting to wait until such time as he felt vocally ready to give the best possible account of the work (see Letter 473). In this connection it is perhaps interesting that a private recording of the songs was made in New York (in 1940 or 1941) by the two men, a kind of documented run-through and try-out of the new songs (the recording still exists in the Archive), which must have enabled singer and composer to discuss and assess their interpretation. Perhaps too there was also a certain reluctance to bring these passionate avowals of love – for his singer, for his singer's voice above all – into the public domain. These are considerations that make sense, we think, of the lengthy preparatory period that preceded the launching of a key work and the initiation of Britten's and Pears's historic partnership. See also Letter 320, where Britten writes to Enid Slater of his feelings of frustration with regard to performing the Michelangelo

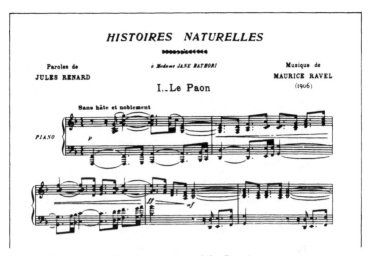

Ravel's *Histoires naturelles*: the opening of 'Le Paon'

Britten's *Michelangelo Sonnets*: the opening of the last song

settings. The right time, the right circumstances and the right location did not come together until 23 September 1942 in London, at the Wigmore Hall.

The *Michelangelo Sonnets* have rightly been recognized for their revealing of the composer's unique 'voice'. For that very reason it is of particular interest to observe that it was another and much admired composer, Ravel, who provided him with the model for the last song of the set. Compare the opening of the first song of Ravel's *Histoires naturelles* (1906) with the last of Britten's settings (see p. 931)

3 *Diversions*.

4 On 18 May, the American first performance of *Les Illuminations* was broadcast by CBS as part of the eighteenth ISCM Festival, held from 16 to 27 May in New York (the first ISCM Festival to be held in the USA), with Pears as soloist and Britten conducting. The rest of the programme comprised Henk Badings's *Prelude to a Tragedy*, the *Meistersinger* overture and music by Balakirev (see Letter 337) conducted by Howard Barlow, conductor of the CBS Symphony Orchestra. The Festival was managed by Boosey & Hawkes Artists' Bureau, Inc., by whom Beata Mayer was employed. Among the members of the Society's international jury for the 1941 Festival was the composer, Roger Sessions, who was also president of the ISCM's USA section and a member of the Festival's Program Committee. Among the performers who took part were the harpist, Carlos Salzedo (Vicepresident of the USA section), whose harp manual was to be used by Britten when writing *A Ceremony of Carols*, and the flautist, George Barrère, who had recorded McPhee's transcriptions of Balinese music with McPhee and Britten in April.

For full details of the 1941 Festival's programme and a history of the ISCM, see the *Musical Record*, New York, 2/1, June 1941, pp. 2–3 and 6–12.

314 To Albert Goldberg

7, Middagh Street,
Brooklyn N.Y.
Main 4–3009
May 24th 1941

My dear Albert,

Your note re Sinfonietta & Les Illuminations has just arrived. Thank you so very much. I am so glad that the old Sinfonietta went well & that the audience liked it (that's much more important than the stuffy old critics!!).[1] I think you might have mentioned that it is a work of my youth tho' (it is nearly ten years old!). Peter

Pears and I are delighted that you liked Les Ill.[2]   It was a splendid
performance – and the orchestra (90% Philharmonic men) did their
stuff admirably.

Well – this is only a scribble, because I am horribly rushed before
leaving for California next Tuesday in an old Ford! I have lots of
work to do & have a nice long invitation to stay in a grand house
near the sea & in an orange grove! By-the-way we are motoring
(i.e. P.P. & self) back in early September & might come via Chicago.
Will you be around? It would be grand to see you & that assistant
of yours again. By-the-way – please tell him that I have lots of
choral works – if I could only remember their names. O – yes –
A Ballad of Heroes (Chorus, Tenor & Sop. solo & orch.) B & H –
several partsongs (S.A.T.B., & S.A.T.B. & piano all B & H – &
some S.S. & piano – Oxford Press) – & a big unaccompanied piece
'A Boy was Born' – Oxford Press – that's all I can think of at the
moment. The Ballad might be his most likely bet.[3]

Greetings to all my friends. Have a good summer – let's hope
you get some rest.

My address in California is   c/o Rae Robertson,
                             Route 1, Box 345
                             Escondido, Calif.

– drop me a line sometime.

With best wishes to you & H.B. –

Yours,

BENJAMIN B

1 The first Chicago performance of the *Sinfonietta* had taken place on
   12 May, at Kimball Hall. Goldberg had written to Britten on 2 May:

   [. . .] we are doing your Sinfonietta for Chamber Orchestra on May 12th.
   The lay-offs [i.e. reductions in the strength of the orchestra] hit the Illinois
   Symphony Orchestra below the belt but we found ourselves left with a good
   body of strings . . . and with this as a basis, we are presenting a series of
   concerts devoted to string orchestra music and other pieces such as your
   Sinfonietta, with a modest number of wind and brass added. The new child
   has been christened the 'Illinois Symphonic Ensemble' and will be conducted
   by Leo Kopp of the Civic Opera, a very fine musician. [. . .] The Sinfonietta
   looks good and Kopp is quite enthusiastic about it, though there has not
   been a rehearsal yet.

   On 21 May Goldberg sent Britten 'the only two press notices
   received concerning your Sinfonietta. The performance was excellent
   and the piece enjoyed a very good success with the audience.'

2 Goldberg's letter of 21 May ends:

   Harold and I were agreeably surprised Sunday while making the long trek back from Southern Illinois to turn on the radio and hear 'Les Illuminations' [. . .]. It seemed to me to be one of the best things you have done. I also thought your friend did a remarkable job with the singing.

3 Goldberg had written on 6 February:

[. . .] Harold would be interested in getting some shorter numbers for our chorus and he is also a member of the Swedish Choral Club and would like to show some of your longer works to their conductor.

Britten had carried with him to the States a number of copies of his published works, to be used for 'promotion', among them most of the works he lists here.

315 To Elizabeth Mayer
From Peter Pears[1]

[?June 1941]

Dear Elizabeth –   So sorry if my note was confusing. They already had one copy (for Titley) and the master (i.e. first copy they made) for Chester, and Miss Paterson had fetched hers, so only one more was required (for Norman). Is that clear? I wanted them to send the bills enclosed in the records, so that we should only have to send them a cheque for the one set we have here. Can they do that? I'm so sorry if this needs a lot of work. If Brigitte wants one, will you order them to make one more from the master before it goes off to Chester? (They can make copies from any of the other copies, but they prefer to make them from the so-called master – at least so I understood them to say.)[2]

We meant to tell you to take the bottle of Château la Tour which was sitting in the clothes closet at Middagh St.   Perhaps Wystan will have found it. If not, drink it together when you are next with him.

Our journey over here was good on the whole. Very cool after we left Washington, until the last day. We didn't have a flat [tyre] at all until we got to the Mojave Desert, and then on the only hot day, and before breakfast, miles from anywhere. However we changed the wheel allright, and had breakfast – and then the other mischance occurred.   We met the Border Patrol and they didn't like me, because I hadn't had my last extension confirmed (whereas of course Ben has)[3]. So we had to empty all our suitcases and find papers etc and I had to go to the police station and answer endless questions, and then had to call on someone else in San

Bernardino, and so on. But they were all amiable and I just have to let them know when I get my confirmation.

I must stop as we have to go into San Diego to post this & Ben's first 2 numbers of the new Soirées⁴.

Much love to you all

from us both

PETER

1 Pears writes from California: see Letter 316.

2 This first paragraph of Pears's letter refers to a private recording that had been made by Guild Recordings (545 7th Avenue, New York) of the broadcast performance of *Les Illuminations* on 18 May, copies of which Pears was distributing among his friends – Dr and Mrs Titley and Chester Kallman among them. Ruth Paterson was an Amityville resident, a schoolteacher, a friend of Michael's and a fan of Britten's and Pears's. Norman Holmes Pearson had been a pupil of Mrs Mayer's in Munich and had a strong interest in music. He was later to become a professor at Yale, and edited an anthology, *Poets of the English Language*, with W.H. Auden (1950). He probably helped with the provision of the affidavit that was required to secure the entry of émigrés from Europe to the USA. Brigitte Steiner, whose husband was a local doctor, lived in the neighbouring village of Lindenhurst, a few miles east of Amityville, a friend (originally in Stuttgart) of the family. In TP appears a home-movie sequence taken on the lawn of Stanton Cottage by Mrs Steiner, who had just acquired a movie camera. Mrs Steiner's copy of the recording, on three 78 rpm discs, is now in the Archive. Mrs Mayer's copy seems not to have survived.

3 Pears refers to the extension of his visa.

4 The *Matinées Musicales*, Op. 24, second suite of five movements from Rossini, for orchestra. The note in the Complete Catalogue of Britten's published works (London, Boosey & Hawkes/Faber Music, 1973) reads (p. 18): 'This suite was written at the request of Lincoln Kirstein to form with *Soirées Musicales*, 1936, a ballet with choreography by Balanchine for the American Ballet Company, produced in 1941.' The ballet, *Divertimento*, was first performed on 27 June, at the Teatro Municipal, Rio de Janeiro, conducted by Emanuel Balaban. The scenario was as follows: 'A series of costume dances at a party. Near the end a guest costumed as a rat is chased by other guests; unmasked, he is discovered to be an acrobat. On at least one occasion, Balanchine appeared as the rat. Made for the South American tour and not performed elsewhere.' See *Choreography by George Balanchine: A Catalogue of Works* (New York, Viking, 1984), p. 151.

Kirstein writes in his *Thirty Years: The New York City Ballet* (New York, Alfred A. Knopf, 1979), p. 295:

When we called ourselves the American Ballet Caravan, on our way to a tour of Latin America, we asked Benjamin Britten, then living in Amityville, Long Island, to score a series of Rossini piano pieces from his *Soirées Musicales* (1941). This we furnished with costumes by the painter André Derain, left over from Balanchine's Ballets 1933 for *Les Songes* (Darius Milhaud).

The ballet was conceived 'as a divertissement to conclude an evening' (p. 109). Kirstein goes on to write:

I first met Britten through Wystan Auden; they were collaborating on a folk-opera commissioned through Columbia University's department of music. I admired both words and music, but Britten withdrew his score unpublished, and Auden reprinted only the lovely dialogue of Cat and Dog [No. 8 in the opera] – 'The single creature leads a partial life'. *Paul Bunyan*, revised, could have been an attractive repertory piece, but it vanished, one more work ploughed under in two dauntlessly prolific careers.

Kirstein's company was associated with two other scores of Britten's, the *Bridge Variations*, for the ballet *Jinx* (1942, revived 1949), and *Les Illuminations*, for *Illuminations* (1950, and frequently revived). See also chapter 6, 'South American Adventure: May–December 1941', in Richard Buckle (in collaboration with John Taras), *George Balanchine: Ballet Master* (London, Hamish Hamilton, 1988), pp. 128–37:

Franklin D. Roosevelt, re-elected for a third term in November 1940, had Kirstein's friend Nelson Rockefeller, Coordinator of Inter-American Affairs, charged with facilitating commercial and cultural relations between the United States and other American republics. Thus it came about that Kirstein and Balanchine were given a subsidy to take a ballet company on tour in South America.

316 To Ralph Hawkes

Route 1, Box 345,
Escondido, California.
June 12th 1941.

My dear Ralph,

Well – here we are, and in pretty good time. We had to take it pretty easy at the beginning because I had to write the extra numbers for the Rossini ballet as I went, and had to stop early in consequence. But we averaged 450 miles a day the last five days, which isn't bad for an old jalloppy (or however you spell it!). She behaved quite well except that the cooling system failed to work – we had to have 3 new water-pumps, and a new cylinder head in consequence. Actually we had only one very hot day – & of course on that day we had a blow out in the middle of the Mohave Desert!

Changing that tyre was something! This place is very lovely – just the place for work. Not too hot (nice & high up) but plenty of sun. Do try & pay us a visit if you can.[1]

One or two bits of business. Could you let me know sometime how you straightened out all my money matters? – because if I am anything to the good at the end of it, I should like to have it in the bank as soon as possible.

I had a statement from the P.R.S. that £25:0:7 had been paid to B & H for me. Under our present arrangement that will go to my sisters won't it? I ask because they need some money there at the moment, & if this has gone to them there's no need to send any more for abit.

Have you got round to hearing the records of the Sinfonia da Requiem yet? I am very keen for you to hear them before you come out here. If there is not a set immediately available, the Mayers have one in Amityville & would love to let you hear them, and incidentally want to see you yourself very much if you can manage it. The thing is, the old piece aroused quite alot of interest & I think something should be done about it before too long – at anyrate have scores available for conductors to look at. I feel particularly interested because I think it's my best (if not my only!) so far!

All good luck & good travelling to you. Drop me a line from time to time saying how you are, & how's business.

Looking forward to seeing you out here.
Regards from Ethel, Rae & Peter.
Yours ever,
BEN

1 Hawkes was in New York.

317 To Elizabeth Mayer

Route 1, Box 345,
Escondido, California.
June 14th 1941.

My dearest Elizabeth,

Please, please forgive me not writing before but I have been very occupied since I got here, & to-day is the first chance I've had. Thank you so much for your letters – and for forwarding the others so promptly – by-the-way have there been any sent on from Middagh St.? I wonder whether you could call there when you are next in town? – just to make sure that there are none left lying about the place. Not that I want letters (except from you, of course!!) but there just <u>might</u> be something important (such as Peter's visa extension).

There have been many excitements, of course, since we left you that damp evening after the Ballet.[1] (Did you ever get your Variation records,[2] by the way?) I think Peter told you about the journey – & how the car behaved. As a matter of fact, she ran splendidly except for the boiling business, & it's too bad to complain. I enjoyed <u>alot</u> of the journey over (inspite of the fact I had to work in the evenings on Lincoln's ballet, which was a bore). I didn't like the skyline drive much – too much the same & too many trees – but I loved alot of the West of Virginia & alot of Tennassee. But best of all was a bit of Oklahoma & most of Arkansas. New Mexico I'm afraid I found boring – at least the bit we came through – Arizona was more exciting, except for the lousy roads. We only had one hot day – & that was the awful last day – when we had a blow out in the middle of the Mohave desert & before breakfast! and the day we were stopped & had so much trouble about Peter's visa (which he hasn't got extended yet). This is a lovely place – & <u>not at all</u> hot – infact the first few days were definitely cold. But now the Sun has elected to shine it's lovely – & the house delightfully cool. We are really very happy – Peter goes off to the village to practise every morning. Now I have got my ballet finished & despatched I am having a few days' rest & enjoying it madly. Rae, P. & I motored yesterday to see Toni & Peggy near Los Angeles – & found them blooming. We had a lovely day with them & they are returning the compliment by coming here to stay a few days next week. Mrs. Coolidge came over to see us in the afternoon – & has definitely commissioned me to do a quartet for her – to be played next <u>September</u> over here! Short notice & a bit of a sweat to do it so quickly, but I'll do it as the cash will be useful!

Well – my dear – I am so glad you have Gordon[3] with you & see Colin & Wystan occasionally. Altho' my body is here enjoying itself – you know where my heart is – & September is not far off is it? When do you go off to Maine? Give my love to William & thank him very much for his letter – I will answer it in a day or two – only I have so many letters to write to-day – beastly over-due business ones.

Lots of love to Gordon, & thanks for the drawing! I'll write him
a card.

And to you, dearest Elizabeth. I think of you & miss you
continually.

Greetings to Mrs. Keins & everybody.

Love

BEN

O – please, Elizabeth can you find Wystan's Ode on St. Cecilia's
day (in his folder) & send it to me?[4] I want to do some work on
it. There are three numbers (3 pages I think).

1 Probably a visit to Kirstein's company, to brief himself in preparation
   for his work on the *Matinées Musicales*.

2 A private recording, like those of the *Sinfonia* and *Les Illuminations*.

3 Gordon Green, the schoolboy son of Kenneth Green, the artist and
   designer-to-be of the first production of *Peter Grimes*. Gordon and his
   mother had been evacuated to the USA and for occasional periods
   the boy stayed at Stanton Cottage, where he was visited by his
   mother, Miriam. For a while he was at school in Amityville. He later
   married and lived in Canada. It was as a result of this chance encounter with the Greens that contact with Kenneth Green was established:
   Britten got in touch with him on his return to England in 1942, to
   bring him news of his son. As it turned out, Green, who was a
   Suffolk man, had been a patient of Britten's father, but he had not
   met the composer at that time. It was Green who was to design the
   cover for the first publication of the *Michelangelo Sonnets* in 1943.

4 The first mention in the extant correspondence of the work that was
   to become the *Hymn to St Cecilia*, Op. 27, the composition of which
   was to be completed on board ship on the return voyage home in
   March–April 1942. Auden's text, under the title of 'Three songs for
   St. Cecilia's day', was first published in the December 1941 issue of
   Harper's Bazaar, thus appearing in print before Britten had finished
   his setting. (It will be remembered that the owner of the house at
   Middagh Street where Auden was still living was George Davis, the
   literary editor of *Harper's*.) The composer had already considered the
   possibility of a similar work, although not to a text by Auden, as early
   as 1935. His diary for 19 January reads: 'I'm having great difficulty in
   finding Latin words for a proposed "Hymn to St. Cecilia". Spend
   morning hunting'; and on the 25th: 'I have the scheme but no notes
   yet for my St. Cecelea Hymn.' This particular 'scheme' was abandoned until the collaboration with Auden produced an appropriate
   text. See also note 4 to Letter 374.

318   To Elizabeth Sprague Coolidge

c/o Mr. Rae Robertson,
Route 1, Box 345,
Escondido, Ca.
June 16th 1941.

My dear Mrs. Coolidge,

I am writing to say how delighted I am to be writing a string-quartet for you, and to be played in your concerts next September. It has been a great ambition of mine to write a piece for you, and I know that our dear Frank, now that he can write no more for you himself, would be tremendously pleased that you have asked me.[1]

I shall start work very shortly, and feel confident that it will be finished to my satisfaction by the middle of August.[2]

It was so nice meeting you the other day – if only for such a short time. I had such a nice impression from all I had heard about you, and from our correspondence and I know you will excuse me if I say how much this meeting enhanced that impression! I do hope to be in this part of the country when you return next August, & I do so hope we can meet again.

With very best wishes and many, many thanks for your kindness.

Yours sincerely,
BENJAMIN BRITTEN

1 Bridge had written to Mrs Coolidge on 3 November 1940:

Our Benji's publisher, Hawkes, told me that you have commissioned him to write you a work. I am awfully pleased to know this, and in my view, he is one of the few young composers that really count. I could enlarge upon this only too easily, but to find Benjamin Britten in the company of all the other composers who have written works for you gives me an especial delight.

2 The work was to be completed earlier than Britten had anticipated: the composition sketch is dated 28 July 1941, Escondido, California. See also Letter 328.

319 To Barbara Britten

Route 1, Box 345,
Escondido, California.
June 17th 1941

My darling Barbara,

I should have written days ago, but I have been pretty occupied
with one thing and another, & also I had hopes of a letter from
you – but I expect you've been pretty occupied too, & I'm sure one
will come in a day or so. Well – I've changed my address slightly,
as you will see, for a month or so. I had finished my immediate
dates in New York, and have lots of work to do (Peter, the same) so
we accepted the invitation of Ethel & Rae Robertson (2 pianists)
who have taken a house in South California, near Mexico, for the
summer, & so we can live rent free for a time & work more easily
out of the rush & bustle of the East. They had bought an old Ford
V8 and Peter & I drove it across country for them (3375 miles – no
mean job!) and arrived here little over a week ago, since when
I've had a rush job of a ballet to get done & despatched. And now
I'm having a few days relaxing before pushing the old pen through
several thousand crotchets & quavers again! The journey across
was incredibly interesting – like going through a dozen different
countries, ranging from quite cool flat countries, to mountains, &
finally about 1,000 miles of desert! The people are <u>much</u> nicer
when you get out of the Eastern cities – & our hearts broke to see
everyone looking so English, & all the names sounded Anglo-
Saxon – this was mostly in Virginia, Tennessee & Oklahoma. You
see, in New York, the percentage of fair hair is very small – &
most names are Italian or Jewish, with sprinklings of Polish and
Irish. It was such a change. And the people are so simple &
honest, compared to the sophisticated scheeming masses of New
York. I felt I liked America for the first time! The driving was
easy, most of the roads are straight for 50 miles at a time, and the
car behaved well except for a tendancy to boil (which it did one
morning on top of mountains miles away from garages – and
cracked a cylinder head!). We did it in nine days – not terribly
fast, because for the first few days I had to stop early & do some
work which had to be posted back to New York.[1] We stayed the
nights at little road-side cabins, specially built for motorists such as
us, & quite cheap. We picked up quite a lot of 'hitch-hikers'
(mostly young men or boys who make their way across the

continent asking for lifts), and heard some amazing tales of luck in getting lifts for nearly 2000 miles, of free meals – & of bad luck in waiting for days with no money or place to sleep. Some were regular tramps – one aged 18, awfully nice person, had been doing it for 5 years – picking up jobs here & there – from Mexico up to Chicago – we dropped him in Memphis where his foster-parents lived; knowing he'd been away all this time I asked him how long he was going to stay, to which he replied 'only an hour or so to pick up some clothes!' One small boy aged scarcely more than 10 had hitch-hiked over 1000 miles to stay with his grand-mother, & we picked him up on his way back. As casual as anything!

This place is very nice & quiet, tho' rather hot. But luckily being fairly high up, quite cool in the evenings. We all motored over to see Toni & Peggy Brosa who are staying near Los Angeles (about 110 miles north) – & met old Mrs. Coolidge (Frank's friend) – who gave me a good commission to write a quartet. So I feel the journey has been worth while already! So I plan to stay out here working till the beginning of September & then God knows what, with America just on the brink of war. Still, one lives in the present – if the present is bearable – otherwise in the future, I suppose!

I am going on sending letters & things to Peasenhall as Beth told me, since I've got no other address.[2] I hope you'll get everything. Do you go back to Tryon House[3] ever – or are you going to move out alltogether? You can't imagine what a relief it has been to know you are at anyrate sleeping out of London. Is there anything you want particularly, that I can send to you? I'm sending food from time to time in small quantities.

Much love to Helen & to Beth & all. How is Kit bearing up, poor dear? – I feel sorry for him. I'll write again in a few days. Much love, my darling.

Bear up & BE CAREFUL!

BEN

1 See Letter 315.
2 Beth and her family had left Peasenhall and

found a house in Northwood, Middlesex, within commuting distance of London but just far enough away to avoid the worst of the bombing. The good thing about the place was that Barbara and Helen could also commute and so get some relief. The house was large enough to house all of us, plus two maids.

(EWB, p. 161)

3 Barbara's previous address.

320   To Enid Slater

Route 1, Box 345,
Escondido, California.
June 17th 1941.

My dear Enid,

You cannot imagine what a joy your letters have been to me, &
I apologise heartily for not having answered for so long. But I
know you understand how busy I have been, how one must keep
at it & at it all the time in trying to keep afloat in a New country
– especially such a place as the States which has every form of
competition good and bad, local & emigré, trying to do one down.
I have had to work terribly hard, & actually I am quite pleased with
the result, because although there are plenty of downs as well as
ups, I think I am pretty well established – judging by the way I get
jobs & commissions & get written up, and at any rate I haven't
starved yet! Your letters have been a great comfort & I look forward
to them greatly. I think it's sweet of you to write so often & at
such length because I know you're off your head with work &
worry. I am terribly impressed with all you've done & with the
way you seem to be keeping your head up thro' all this hell. The
studio is a grand venture & I am delighted that it's been the
success it deserved. Do take some pictures of my friends & family
& send them if you have time & can get them through the censor.
You'd better not have any suspicious backgrounds or uniforms in
the pictures tho'! I have had some photos taken here, but mostly
glamorous publicity ones & not worth sending – & snapshots are
always so embarrassing, I think. By-the-way, did I tell you that
your Xmas card of the children has become a classic over here? I
have shown it to several people over here, mostly keen
photographers & they have been tremendously impressed. One
painter, Feiniger[1] (father of the well-known photographer here)
thought it most moving. So you're not without your public here!
My dear Enid – I was terribly touched that you went to London
for the Violin Concerto, and terribly pleased that you liked it so.
It certainly is the best you've heard of mine, I'm sure. But I can't
wait for you to hear the Sinfonia da Requiem, which is such
streets ahead of anything I've yet done. I believe there'll be a
performance of it in England this Autumn.[2] It was given, really
very well, by the New York Philharmonic with Barbirolli, and,
although I say it who shouldn't, made quite an impression. It is

quite short & concise, but the form is better than any of my stuff before. I wish you could hear the Michael Angelo Sonnets – but there's no chance for things like that these days, either with you or over here. One only does them for one's own pleasure, and only occasionally can they be aired in public, I'm afraid. Still – one day. . . .

Louis MacNeice[3] wasn't very accurate when he said I was ill & all that. Of course, one can't be at the height of one's scintillating form all the time these days. But I should be a liar if I pretended that one never forgets reality – at anyrate for a short time. I have some wonderful friends over here, who have been wonderful to me, & I've managed to go on working pretty hard, so things might be worse. But I admit I <u>am</u> homesick, & really only enjoy scenery that reminds me of England, and I yearn for a consistent form of society & race round me – get so fed up with mixtures. Of course New York is the worst – a struggling mass of scheming, shallow sophisticates & the lowest kind of every race under the Sun. It is only when one gets away from the Eastern border that one can like America. Peter & I have just motored across the continent – an extraordinary experience – & our hearts nearly broke when we got into Virginia & Tenassee to see all the Anglo-Saxon types & names. The people are everywhere so much simpler, more direct & honest. We have been invited to spend the Summer months with Ethel & Rae Robertson (2 pianists) who are devoted friends of ours – & as we both have gallons of work to do, & this means we can live rent free in a lovely spot, it seemed the obvious thing to do. It is in the mountains about 40 miles from Mexico. My poor, dear Enid – this must make you feel envious – but surely one day these hellish times will be through & I shall be able to show you all these lovely places. In the meantime I suppose one has to go on doing one's job as well as one can manage to – I am afraid I am horribly lucky in my job, in one way, because after all it has nothing to do with an immediate reality – when the only fighting elements are rhythms & one is not shocked by anything worse than a drum stroke!

Give my love to Montagu & the children – I'll send them some picture post-cards. I hope the bees go well & don't sting!![4]   I'll try & write again soon.

Much love,

BEN

1 Lyonel Feininger (1871–1956), American painter. An example of

Feininger's work – *An der Ilm* (ink and watercolour) belonged to Peter Pears and is in the possession of the Britten–Pears Foundation.

2 In fact, the UK première took place significantly later, at the Royal Albert Hall, London, on 22 July 1942, when the London Philharmonic Orchestra was conducted by Basil Cameron.

3 Irish poet and playwright (1907–1963), a member of the Auden circle. An accomplished classical scholar, MacNeice made a translation of Aeschylus's *Agamemnon*, first produced by the Group Theatre in November 1936 with incidental music by Britten (see note 2 to Letter 89 and PR, pp. 504–8). He also collaborated more substantially with the composer the following year, when the Group Theatre produced MacNeice's play, *Out of the Picture* (see PR, pp. 520–24). Harold Hobson wrote in the *Observer*, 12 December 1937:

When an oracular poet enters the theatre he brings strange properties with him. His characters are both larger and smaller than life, and when they speak their words are apt to soar away into the lyrical ether and harmonise with the music of the spheres. Mr MacNeice is such a poet. [. . .] His backchat, his incidental burlesque, mask a divine discontent with the blindness, the greed, the casual folly of men who, through war, would encompass their own destruction. He arraigns their insensitiveness to beauty, their lip-service to art, their prostitution of love, and their suicidal proclivities. Meanwhile, his 'commentators' who are masked and musical, express themselves in ejaculatory chorus, and serve the dramatist's turn as did the classic choruses of old. One feels at times that this poet, sceptical perhaps of his instrument, uses the theatre awkwardly. The mixture of sacred and profane is not too smooth, and some of its more playful elements jar. But the play contains enough true poetry and righteous indignation to absolve its crudities and make the performance memorable. The Group Theatre has an enthusiastic audience, whose political sympathies are apt to cloud its critical faculties. Not all the fun in this play merited the Homeric laughter that greeted it last Sunday; but the quality of Mr MacNeice's best writing is rare, and its impact was stimulating.

From May 1941 to 1961 he worked with great distinction and originality for the BBC Features Department and was able again to collaborate with Britten, in three wartime propaganda programmes for a series entitled *Britain to America* (1942), and, most significantly, *The Dark Tower* (1946) (see PFL, plates 210–11, and PR, pp. 625–34, and pp. 656–65). Britten also made a setting of MacNeice's 'Sleep, my darling, sleep', for voice and piano (?1942), which remains unpublished. See also note 13 to Letter 397.

MacNeice had travelled to the USA early in 1940 and did not return to England until December. In November he visited Auden at 7 Middagh Street, and spent Thanksgiving Day (the 28th) with him, Britten, Pears, Carson McCullers and Gypsy Rose Lee. In chapters 2 and 3 of his unfinished autobiography, *The Strings are False* (London, Faber and Faber, 1965), p. 35, MacNeice writes:

I was staying now in a household on Brooklyn Heights, still being painted and without much furniture or carpets, but a warren of the arts, Auden writing in one room, a girl novelist writing – with a china cup of sherry – in another, a composer composing and a singer hitting a high note and holding it and Gypsy Rose Lee, the striptease queen, coming round for meals like a whirlwind of laughter and sex. It was the way the populace once liked to think of artists – ever so bohemian, raiding the icebox at midnight and eating the catfood by mistake. But it was very enjoyable and at least they were producing.

MacNeice was to marry Hedli Anderson in 1942.

4 The Slaters kept bees at their cottage in Buckinghamshire. During the war the Slaters' children were moved to the cottage, where Mrs Slater's mother-in-law was living, while Montagu Slater continued to work in London. See also Donald Mitchell, 'Montagu Slater (1902–1956): Who was he?', in PGPB, pp. 22–46.

321 To Douglas Moore[1]
Director, Ditson Fund[2]

c/o Rae Robertson,
Route 1, Box 345,
Escondido, California.
June 24th, 1941.

My dear Douglas,

I feel very touched that you thought of me in connection with the Albuquerque job, and I do hope you don't feel hurt that at the moment I cannot consider such a position.[3] You see, at the present time, when one hasn't the foggiest idea of what the future will show, I feel that I want to spend my whole time writing down what musical ideas may be in my head, and unless threatened with starvation I don't want to spend my time doing what would be primarily an executive job, which incidentally I feel would be much more efficiently done by many other people. Also, at the moment, I do not want to spend much time away from the East coast, where I have so many friends and where most of my occupation lies. Later on I may find it necessary to hold such a position, but for the time being I think I'll risk just being a freelance composer, doing hack-work maybe, but in the composing line, and what little teaching just confined to composition. I do hope you understand.

I have been meaning to get in touch with you for so long, by telephone before I left, only I was so rushed there wasn't a second, to thank you from the bottom of my heart for all your sympathy and great encouragement through the viccisitudes of the past months! I really do appreciate what you did for both Auden & myself, and I want you to know that inspite of moments of depression, I look back on the Paul Bunyan episode with great pleasure, and gratitude. I feel that I have learned lots about what not to write for the theatre, and incidentally on how not to behave in certain circumstances. You may be interested to know that the old piece is now undergoing thorough revision, which I shall be delighted to show you when I return to New York in the Fall. Apparently the wreck is worth salvaging because inspite of the bangs it received there is genuine interest being shown in it in various quarters.

I am spending the summer months with friends of mine in South California – and in the intervals of high-pressure work – getting sun-burned on the beach. Where are you spending the vacation period? I do hope you will have a rest and plenty of time to do your own work.

The Russian bomb-shell has just burst[4] – what a crazy world this world of realpolitik is!

With very best wishes to Mrs. Moore and your charming daughters, and infinite thanks for all your great trouble on my behalf,

Yours sincerely,

BENJAMIN BRITTEN

1 Douglas Moore (1893–1969), American composer, teacher and administrator. Moore (who had also studied with Boulanger in Paris) was Chairman of the Music Department of Columbia University, New York, at the time of the first production of *Paul Bunyan*. The programme announced that the performance was given by 'The Columbia Theater Associates of Columbia University [. . .] with the co-operation of the Columbia University Department of Music', and it was this event which brought Moore and Britten together, as this letter itself confirms. Moore himself as a composer had a particular interest in the musical theatre and was himself author of two successful theatrical works, *The Devil and Daniel Webster* (1939) and *The Ballad of Baby Doe* (1958).

2 The Alice M. Ditson Fund, the administration of which was the responsibility of Moore. The fund was restricted to non-academic uses and its most famous beneficiary perhaps was Bartók, who was

appointed visiting Assistant in Music at Columbia from January 1941
to December 1942 on a Ditson grant, in the arrangement of which
Moore played a prominent role. See Halsey Stevens *The Life and
Music of Béla Bartók* (London, Oxford University Press, 1964), pp. 90,
94–5 and 97 for a full account of how the Fund operated in relation
to Bartók. There is only one reference to Bartók by Britten in the
extant correspondence from these years (see Letter 295, where he
inquires of Heinsheimer after the Hungarian composer, recently
arrived in New York). There is also one memory of a meeting at this
time. Rosamund Strode recalls Pears telling her that Britten once
encountered Bartók at Boosey & Hawkes's New York office, where
he was shocked to find him in a corner counting out his stipend.
Clearly the circumstances of both composers – that they had a
common publisher, were both 'exiles', and were further linked by
an association with Columbia University – might have led to further
meetings in addition to the meeting that must have taken place
during the New York ISCM Festival in May, of which photographic
evidence exists.

3 Heinsheimer had sent a telegram to Britten in California on 21 June:

WOULD YOU BE INTERESTED POSITION HEAD OF MUSIC DEPARTMENT UNIVERSITY
OF NEW MEXICO AT ALBUQUERQUE   NICE OPPORTUNITY FOR DEVELOPMENT OF
SYMPHONIC AND CHORAL MUSIC GENERAL ORGANIZATION OF MUSICAL LIFE IN
SOUTHWESTERN   TERRITORY   SALARY   AROUND   THIRTY-TWO   THOUSAND
DOLLARS   IF SO PLEASE WIRE DOUGLAS MOORE COLUMBIA UNIVERSITY WHO HAS
BEEN ASKED TO MAKE A RECOMMENDATION   ANSWER URGENT

4 Britten refers to the invasion of the USSR by Germany on 22 June.

322 To Elizabeth Mayer

[5 July 1941]

Dearest Elizabeth,

This is just a prelude to the letter Peter is about to write to you,
to thank you for sending on Wystan's Ode [and] all the other
letters so promptly.

Things go along finely here. We have just begun the hot weather
(& my pen objects – vide the blot above!), but the house is
beautifully cool, & so work is not too difficult. We don't go out
much except to the beach to bathe, just mostly go our own ways
working. Poor Ethel & Rae still have to go along to the neighbours
to practise since their 2 pianos promised a month ago from N.
York have so far failed to materialise. I have started work again,
have just about finished the Paderewski piece[1] and about to launch
into Mrs. Coolidge's quartet. Peter works hard & is singing well,

but is mostly engrossed in exercises. I hope you can forget the incredibly horrible & muddled world sometimes – are you practising at all? Try some Schubert & Buxtehude – they help abit! Yesterday we were all in San Diego & saw the lovely El Grecos, & Goyas – they have some wonderful pictures there . . . there was a Ruysdael landscape that was as peaceful as the Suffolk (Constable!) countryside – how I am looking forward to the time that I shall be able to show you that place!

The Robertsons have some very nice friends out here – one Lyell Barbour,[2] who was well known in England as a pianist but who got ill, is a real charmer, but, as I said before, we stick to ourselves mostly – and there are remarkably few frictions!

Have a good holiday, you dear two. I'll think of you on the lovely coast of Maine – lovely as the Pacific is, I prefer the Atlantic although it is colder for swimming! Let me have a card occasionally telling where & how you both are.

Much love to you, my dear,
Be careful how you drive drive –!
BEN

I have just read most amusing musical criticisms of Bernard Shaw (Corno di Bassetto)[3] – well worth reading!

1 The *Mazurka Elegiaca*, Op. 23 No. 2, for two pianos, of which the dedication reads: 'In memoriam I.J. Paderewski'. This was originally intended for a Paderewski memorial volume – *Homage to Paderewski* – published by Boosey & Hawkes Inc., New York, 1942. Composers who contributed to the volume of the solo piano music included Béla Bartók, Arthur Benjamin, Eugene Goossens, Frank Martin and Darius Milhaud. Although Ralph Hawkes originally intended to include Britten's composition in the volume, a problem was created by its two-piano format. The published volume contains the following note: 'Because two copies are required for performance, Mr Benjamin Britten's contribution to this album, "Mazurka Elegiaca for two pianos-four hands", has been issued in separate form.' Paderewski had died in New York on 29 June. The form of the mazurka was chosen to salute Paderewski's nationality.

Britten's seemingly inexplicable two-piano contribution apparently arose from his response to a cable sent him by Ralph Hawkes which should have asked for 'two piano pieces', but through an error in transmission, which converted a crucial plural into the singular, requested instead a 'two piano piece'. Britten faithfully fulfilled the faulty commission and thus excluded himself from the published solo volume.

A handwritten list of compositions inscribed on the inside front cover of a copy of Britten's Suite, Op. 6, suggests that the possibility of a further two-piano work was contemplated, i.e. there is the listing of an untitled Op. 23 No. 3.

The first performance of *Mazurka Elegiaca* was to be given by Ethel Bartlett and Rae Robertson on 9 December, at the Town Hall, New York, as part of a programme that also included McPhee's Buxtehude arrangements and Berkeley's *Polka*. Francis D. Perkins wrote in the *New York Herald-Tribune*, 10 December:

> Mr Britten's score, which sometimes suggested the influence of French impressionism, showed imagination and often set forth a duly elegiac mood, but the dance rhythms toward the middle of its course seemed more Spanish than Polish in atmosphere.

Howard Taubman, in the *New York Times*, 10 December, thought that the *Mazurka* 'was a tender and fitting tribute, for it had dignity and a touch of nobility'.

2 Lyell Barbour (1896–1967), American pianist and composer, and a friend of Lucille Wallace (see note 2 to Letter 388).

3 Shaw wrote his earliest music criticism for the *Hornet* in 1876, and between 1888 and 1894 he contributed reviews to two papers, the *Star* and the *World*. He adopted the pen-name 'Corno di Bassetto' in 1889 on his appointment as music critic of the *Star*. His collected writings on music were published in two volumes, *Music in London 1890–94* (London, 1932), and *London Music in 1888–89 as heard by Corno di Bassetto* (London, 1937).

323   To Elizabeth Mayer
From Peter Pears

Saturday July 5th [1941]

Dearest Elizabeth,

Thank you very much for your lovely letter – It is so comforting to hear from you, we miss you both so much. Many times a day, sighs of "Elizabeth" can be heard rising on the Californian air!

Since I last wrote, we have had one or two ripples on our quiet life's surface. Mildred and Bill and Margaret & Rachel[1] (not to mention Peggy and Toni) all appeared in the new Cadillac and we had lunch by the sea together. M. was looking a different person altogether – so much better. We hope to see Peggy and Toni for a week in August before they go East. It was lovely to see them. On one of our trips over to them, we stopped in at San Juan Capistrano. It was so lovely although a little trippery – Hearing

American accents in a place like that made one think one was in
Europe again – !

On Tuesday I drove Rae & Ethel into Los Angeles to see the
British consul over money.   They had to sign an affidavit to say
that they weren't using the money they use here for anti-British
activities! Really this world – –

I went in too in the hope of seeing the agent who will I hope be
interested in my singers. But he wasn't there – so I spent 3 hours
wandering round L.A. It is the most awful city, isn't it? The only
good thing in it was a marvellous Rare Book shop, wherein I
browsed contentedly.[2]

On Thursday a week ago we had tea with two old ladies in San
Diego, and all the élite of San Diego musical life was asked to
meet us. I sang and Rae played a bit for me and later Ben (that was
better!!). Apparently they were all very impressed and very
complimentary – but you know very well how boring these
functions are, however good the intentions are and however kind
the hosts. We had lunch there again this Thursday too just en
famille.

A very sweet and rather wealthy friend of Ethel & Rae is probably
going to ask Ben and me to give a little recital at her house (fee
$100!) which will be lovely.

I am working very hard, Elizabeth, I wish you could hear me. It
goes really very well.

I am enclosing a cheque – for 2 copies of "Les Ill..s",[3] one of
ours, and one for Kay (you are quite right, she must have
one).   Could you see about them? and one more thing – –

Would you be very kind and drop a line or ring up the "Brooklyn
Eagle" and see if they still have a copy of May 19th Monday
afternoon or evening edition? They noticed our broadcast very well[4]
– & I haven't seen it yet and would like to.

So goodbye 'dear Elizabeth, dear friend', and have a lovely
vacation. There is nothing we would like to do more than to take
our car and drive straight over to Maine to be with you and
William.   At least we are with you in spirit.

Much love to you both and to Gordon if he is still with you –

Your
PETER

1 Rachel was the Titleys' infant daughter and Margaret their Scottish
   nanny.
2 Pears was never quite sure whether it was in Los Angeles or San

Diego that he came across the copy of Crabbe's poems which contained the text of *The Borough*, the discovery of which triggered off plans for an opera, based on the story of Peter Grimes. In his last years Pears tended to opt for San Diego but this specific reference to a 'marvellous Rare Book shop' in Los Angeles makes us wonder if this was not the shop where the historic volume was located.

3 See Letter 315.

4 We have been unable to trace this review.

324 To Beth Welford

[EWB, *pp. 165–7*]

Route 1 Box 345,
Escondido, California.
July 6th 1941

My darling old Beth,

Your letter arrived yesterday morning & I was so glad to get it – not that I can say it was seven months since I heard, but it was fully three! Actually, although I know I have been sadly dilatory, it isn't quite as long as that since I wrote, because I know I wrote (by Air-mail, too) at least twice since Christmas – one describing the concert in N. York when Bartlett & Robertson played my piece[1] and another about the Brooklyn flat – but they went astray somewhere I suppose – like the parcels of food I sent the Bridges & Peter sent his mother. It is sickening, but these are the consequences of this present bloody period of history. How I wish I were born in another time – when things weren't universally so bloody.

Well, Peter & I continue to have a nice time out here – it is pretty hot, but the house remains cool & the ocean is fairly near. I have been working pretty hard, and shall not have much unoccupied time this summer, I can see – what with Mrs. Coolidge's new commission & the odd concertos I have to write for people.[2] However I'm not complaining – it's damned lucky to have work to do, & to be able (so far) to do it. Peter is working hard at his singing, & singing like a real opera star, very loud & high. The ocean bathing (I'm afraid this must make your mouths water, poor dears) is lovely, with surfing, but the latter isn't nearly as good as Cornwall was. The rollers are big, but not nearly so long. The Pacific doesn't look any different from the Atlantic, you know, & certainly tastes the same. The fish that come out of it aren't as good

as the North Sea – take it from me – & I'd give anything for a
good Kipper! The Pacific is full of battleships & what-not, & the air
is full of aeroplanes – San Diego, the big Naval base, is near here –
& one sees as many uniforms about almost as in England. I know
it (this apparent American indifference) must seem infuriating to
you all, but Roosevelt is being very smart. You see, this is such an
enormous country, & takes such a long time to move – Europe
seems so far off from the Middle-West or West – Roosevelt is just
moving a little ahead of public opinion all the time, & that is
gradually swinging round to realisation that something's got to be
done. After all England & France took a long time to make up
their minds about Spain, Austria etc. – but there's no doubt that
America will be 'in' it before very long. The real trouble is the
Nazi-influence in South America, which is really dangerous. No
more of that – I expect you get as sick of News-commentators as
we do. Now, we hardly ever listen to the wireless – one always
seems to hear what news there may be sooner or later, & it's no
use going all of a flap every five minutes with hysterical news
revues.

It is so grand to think of you all living together. I suppose that
Barbara & Helen will be with you permanently now they've had
to give up the flat. I'm glad that you are O.K. financially – but if
anything goes wrong & you want any little things that make life
more worth living, don't hesitate to write or Cable for it. It can
always be raised however large!   Please give the enclosed letters
to Barbara & Helen. Please tell everyone who complains that I'll
write sooner or later, but I've got so many letters to write & if I
write I want to write to you!

Much love my darling
P.T.O.

Give my love to Kit & Sebastian – he does sound a grand kid;
how I wish I could see him. I hope Kit isn't too down about the
job he's got to do, but impress on him that it's only temporary &
that all bad things come to an end. I am regarding this only as a
period of marking-time, & living for the future which will be the
same as it was always, with us all together either there or here!

Much love again, my darling.
Bear up. Love to the Welfords when you see them –
BEN

I do hope I've got your address right, but it's somewhat obscurely written – it looks like GATEHUGS[3] to me, but that's too good to be true.

I shall be at this address until at anyrate the end of August – so write here direct will you, please?

1 The first performance of *Introduction and Rondo alla Burlesca*, Op. 23 No. 1, for two pianos, had been given by Ethel Bartlett and Rae Robertson in New York on 5 January.

2 Probably the *Scottish Ballad*, Op. 26 for two pianos and orchestra, composed for Ethel Bartlett and Rae Robertson, who were to give the first performance with the Cincinnati Symphony Orchestra, conducted by Eugene Goossens, on 28 November 1941. The *Ballad* – occasionally referred to as a 'two piano concerto' – was completed at Amityville on 27 October.

3 In fact, Gatehurst, Gate End, Northwood, Middlesex.

325   To Barbara Britten

> Route 1, Box 345,
> Escondido, California.
> July 6th 1941.

My darling Barbara,

I can't let a letter go off to Beth with-out just a scrawl (literally I'm afraid – my writing doesn't seem to be improving with my grey hairs!), if only to thank you for your lovely long newsy letter which arrived yesterday. I <u>am</u> so sorry to hear of all your troubles – & I feel grieved that you will have to give up your flat, which I know you were so fond of.[1] Perhaps it's a good thing in some ways, since one never knows but that a bomb might choose it to fall on one of these unlucky days, & at anyrate all your things will be out of it. But I do know what it means to you not to have a real home of your own – but do remember, my dear old thing, that this is <u>only</u> a temporary thing & soon we shall all be back in a normal way of living. Take it from one who has spent 2½ years living in suit-cases, & who loved to be settled almost as much as you do now! But I do sympathise, old thing.

About the financial side of moving & storing etc. I had a notice the other day that the Performing Right Society had paid to Boosey & Hawkes for me a cheque of over £20. I wrote at once to Ralph H. (who is over here now) telling him to pay it to my sisters, & he wrote at once to the London branch telling them to do this. If

that hasn't arrived yet please ring them (speak to Miss <u>Jackson</u>)
and ask her for it. Please use that for any expenses you may have
– and also, <u>if</u> there's any over, to buy yourself some nice little
things that you want (what about an occasional bottle of sherry,
forinstance??) If, by any miserable hap, the money is needed for
anything else (Nicholson or something) cable me <u>at once</u> & I'll send
some money from here to cover expenses. I can always raise
money, you know – said he magnanimously – & besides it gives
me a hell of a kick to be able to help you in anyway – quite
selfishly, I'm afraid.

Well, apart from external newses and things life is quite quiet
here. We work all the morning & most of the afternoon, & then
motor down to the ocean (Pacific – isn't that funny? But it doesn't
look much different from the Atlantic or North Sea, except that it's,
maybe, a little bluer), for a bathe. We usually go to bed fairly early.
The Robertsons are really very sweet, but of course anywhere where
your bad-tempered bro. is there are usually some scraps, and this
place is no exception. However Peter usually stays serenely on
the outside and soothes things over, & so far there haven't been
any physical injuries. As a matter of fact (as you've also
discovered, I believe) there are very few people that one can live
with in complete harmony for any length of time – luckily Peter
& the Mayers are examples of those few.

The country is very beautiful – only rather dry; the rain-fall being
negligible, all the watering is done by irrigation – dams and what-
not. Until about 30 years ago this was just barren desert like lots
of the country we motored across. There are lots of mountains,
& nice trees. One gets bored with fire-flies & humming birds – but
how one longs for a cuckoo or a nightingale which apparently
don't exist in this country. It seems funny to have orange & lemon
trees growing in one's garden – but one gets used to it very
quickly – it's odd how, after the initial excitement, these things
don't mean much.

Do send a photograph of yourself, my dear, some time – try to
get one too of the whole family group, Beth, Helen, Kit & Kid, –
I'll try & send one, but you know how I love being photographed
– I have the kind of physiog which needs plenty of animation and
a strong light behind! You once remarked that you thought I was
going bald – that is only my new coiffure (I brush the hair off the
noble forehead), and generally approved of round here. As far as
I can see, in shaving it, every morning, my face hasn't changed
much. My temper is a littler sourer, and I have lost a little weight

(was down to 8 stone 10, about a month ago, but I have put on
10 pounds since then!) – apart from that, I'm still the same old
person who used to aggravate you & keep you from going to bed
& talked so much!

Au revoir, my darling – write again as soon as poss. – your letters
keep me alive.

Your devoted
BEN

1 See however Letters 336 and 338.

326   To Ralph Hawkes

Route 1, Box 345,
Escondido, Ca.
July 23rd 1941.

My dear Ralph,

It was fine seeing you this week-end; I was encouraged no end
by your enthusiasm and all your plans. You cannot imagine what
it means to have a publisher like yourself to back one, especially
in this precarious & none too cheerful times. Thank you very,
very much!

I have noted all the duties, which shouldn't be too onerous. The
quartet is still going strong & I'll send the score off to N. York
right away when it's done.[1] I'm sending the Mazurka to D. Lawton[2]
– or would you rather it went straight to Hans H.? The Mahler[3]
I'm looking forward to doing – & should have it completed well
before November.

I am sending back the folk-songs to await your arrival in Toronto.
My considered opinion is: that there are some fine tunes in the
book,[4] but that the piano accompaniments are (a) not interesting or
with personality enough for their elaborateness (b) too
complicated for school or community work. I'm sorry – but that's
what I feel.

Spivak[5] tells me that Mrs. Coolidge wants me to receive the
Elizabeth Sprague C. [Coolidge] medal for 'eminent services to
Chamber music' for this year. So that means I must go down to
Washington on Oct. 30th all in my best & accept it. I hope you'll
be there to hold my hand! I think that's the date of the 2nd
performance of the Quartet.

I'm having a slight altercation with Herr von Wittgenstein over my scoring[6] – if there is anything I know about it is scoring & so I'm fighting back. The man really is an old sour puss.

Ernest Newman's second defence of me in the Sunday Times has just been sent me (the Battle of Britten!!) and I feel really grateful to the old boy for his support.[7]

All the best in your businesses – see you in New York in September or so. In the meantime – good hunting. (I hope you got the book).[8]

Yours ever,
BEN

1 Pears had described the circumstances of the composition of the First String Quartet in an undated letter to his mother:

> Here we live a very quiet existence in beautiful but strange country. 40 years ago it was a desert, now it is full of orange & lemon trees. Our house is very pleasant and there is an orange & lemon grove attached to it. I go down to a house of an Englishwoman in the village and practise every morning from 9.30 till 12.45, and I'm doing a lot of good work. Our host & hostess practise all morning on their two pianos, and Ben sits in the toolshed and writes his new String Quartet which he has been commissioned to write by an old American patroness of music, Mrs. E.S. Coolidge. So, altogether you see the place is a hive of industry. The sea is 20 miles off and we often go over for a dip.

2 Dorothy Lawton, Librarian of the Music Library (New York Public Library) on 58th Street and also Secretary–Treasurer of the US section of the ISCM. She may have undertaken copying for Boosey & Hawkes. See also Letter 328, in which Britten refers to the dispatch of the score of the new string quartet to New York where it would be photographed and copied.

3 His arrangement of the Minuet from Symphony No. 3.

4 Unidentified.

5 Harold Spivacke (1904–1977), Chief of the Music Division of the Library of Congress from 1937 to 1972.

6 Pears was to write to Mrs Mayer on 23 August:

> Wittgenstein is being stupid and recalcitrant about the scoring of the Diversions, & has been trying to get Ormandy on his side. It means a series of tactful but firm letters from Ben.

Britten was not alone among the composers Wittgenstein commissioned (he was in the company of Strauss and Ravel) in suffering the strictures to which Pears refers. The harassed composer must have wondered if the $700 commissioning fee was adequate compensation. None of this discouraged the pianist from asking Britten to extend the period of his exclusive right to perform the work when it came up for renewal, c.1950. See also Trevor Harvey, 'A Personal

Reminiscence: Paul Wittgenstein', *Gramophone*, June 1961. See also Ray Monk, *Ludwig Wittgenstein* (London, Jonathan Cape, 1990), pp. 11–15 and 396–400.

We find some penetrating insights into Wittgenstein's singular personality in Brian McGuinness's biography of Ludwig Wittgenstein (*Wittgenstein: A Life, Young Ludwig 1885–1921* (Harmonsworth, Penguin, 1990)). 'Paul's was a quite different nature from Ludwig's', writes McGuinness (p. 30). 'He wanted all his life to carry everything with a high hand. It was more important to be respected or even feared than to be liked. He certainly had the power and determination necessary to secure this reaction.' 'He seemed in many respects', McGuinness adds,

to force nature and his own powers [. . .] He had, or came to have as a result of adversities and the strain of overcoming them, a harsh and secretive strain in his personality. Thus he lived with his family until the Second War but only some accident revealed to them anything of his private life.

For all that, McGuinness describes him in New York as 'Able, quick, well-read, with the manners of a grand seigneur', carrying with him as a professor 'all the atmosphere of a vanished age'.

7 Ernest Newman had favourably reviewed the first British performance of the Violin Concerto in the *Sunday Times*, of 4 May:

That in Mr Britten we have a young talent of unusual quality is now beyond question. His mastery of his matter is indeed astonishing from whatever angle we look at it.[. . .] If anything had been required to strengthen my former feeling that Mr Britten is a thoroughbred, this fine piece of writing [the *passacaglia* finale] would be enough. So intimate a fusion of technical device and fluid imaginative thinking is a rare thing in music nowadays.

On 8 June, Newman reported in the paper that since his original article appeared he had been fighting 'single-handed the battle of Britten':

A few weeks ago I used the word thoroughbred in connection with Benjamin Britten's new violin concerto; and ever since then I have been fighting single-handed the battle of Britten. Various correspondents have been at no pains to conceal from me that they think less highly of this young composer than I do. Whatever else they have done, they have at least thrown a little fresh light for me on the eternally interesting problem of aesthetic criteria.

Newman defended his position and it is to this defence that Britten refers. An unsavoury tailpiece to the exchange of views exists in the shape of a letter from George Baker (the singer and organist, and Hon. Treasurer of the Royal Philharmonic Society) which appeared in the paper's correspondence columns on 15 June (see also note 2 to Letter 292):

Sir – In your last issue, Mr Ernest Newman, under the heading 'Thoroughbreds', said he had 'been fighting single-handed the "battle of Britten" '.

There are a number of musicians in this country who are well content to let Mr Newman have this dubious honour. The young gentleman on whose behalf he fights, Mr Benjamin Britten, was born in 1913. He is in America. He may have had perfectly good reasons for going there, and may decide to return to his native land some time or other. In the meantime I would like to remind Mr Newman that most of our musical 'thoroughbreds' are stabled in or near London and are directing all their endeavours towards winning the City and Suburban and the Victory Stakes, two classic events that form part of a programme called the Battle of Britain; a programme in which Mr Britten has no part.

8 Britten was probably referring to the first volume of *Violin Passages* that he had compiled with Antonio Brosa, which had been published by Boosey & Hawkes, New York.

327 To Elizabeth Sprague Coolidge

Route 1, Box 345,
Escondido, California.
July 24th 1941.

My dear Mrs. Coolidge,

Mr. Spivacke has just written to tell me the exciting news that you intend to award me the 'Coolidge medal' this year, & I am writing to tell you at once how touched and flattered I feel about it. It is such a great honour to be included in the very distinguished list of recipients of the medal,[1] and a great stimulus to climb to great heights in the future!

Our quartet is progressing very well to date – I am just completing the third movement (the slow one – there are four altogether) and feel that it is my best piece so far, which is rather extraordinary for me, since at this period of work I usually am in a deep depression. Let us hope it is a good omen!

My publisher, Mr. Ralph Hawkes was here this week-end, and we completed arrangements to send Mr. Kroll[2] a photographed score as soon as that is ready – in about two weeks' time I should think. Could you perhaps send me his address, so that I could send it direct to him? The parts and the original score for yourself will follow shortly afterwards.

I hope that you are enjoying your stay in the North. This part of the world is developing a great fascination for me, – what a miraculous country it is!

Thank you again so much for the great honour you are giving me – it means to me more than I can say. I am sure nothing will prevent me being in Washington to receive the medal.

Ethel & Rae Robertson & Peter Pears all send their best wishes, and so do I, dear Mrs. Coolidge, & believe me to be

> yours most cordially,
> BENJAMIN BRITTEN

1 The medal was awarded annually from 1932 to 1949. W.W. Cobbett, the English encyclopaedist of chamber music, was among its recipients, as was Frank Bridge. In 1941 a triple award was made. Britten's companion recipients were Randall Thompson and Alexandre Tansman.

2 William Kroll (1901–1980), the leader and one of the founding members of the Coolidge Quartet, established at the Library of Congress by the Coolidge Foundation. The Quartet appears to have made its first public appearance at the Library in 1936.

328 To Elizabeth Mayer

> Route 1, Box 345,
> Escondido, California.
> July 29th 1941.

My dearest Elizabeth,

It was grand to get your lovely letter yesterday because it had seemed ages since we heard anything of you. I am so pleased you're having such a lovely holiday – the going about seeing people must have been entertaining, but I can imagine that sitting still and watching the gulls, and waves breaking on the rocks, must be more to your taste! What a lovely little picture you sent – it brought back poignant memories of the East Coast and Maine. Lovely as the Pacific can be, and it is very glamourous at times, it can never mean what the Atlantic means to me. I feel very homesick for it! However I'm sure we shall be seeing it fairly soon – sooner than we've planned (which is the beginning of September) – but, nothing is settled yet. Thank you so much for sending, and having sent, on all the letters and matters so promptly. Didn't we mention the extension forms? Actually, my extension doesn't run out till the end of September – and Peter's hasn't yet been renewed (from February!!), although he wrote again the other day asking about it, and they replied that they were very busy & were still considering it. So for the moment we are O.K. – thank you everso much tho' for having sent the forms – they'll be useful sometime I'm sure. We haven't yet made any definite decision – but I think we'll emigrate from Canada (Peter has this friend, who is son-in-law of the Minister of Emigration of Canada (very useful!)) at the beginning of the Fall.[1]

Well, my dear, I've been very busy since I wrote last. You know I wrote a 2–piano Mazurka (for the Paderewski book) and since then I've completed the quartet for Mrs. Coolidge! It is quite a big work (about 24 minutes) and I'm very bucked with it so far. It's got a few rather lame bars in it, but I hope to have them 'hotted up' in a few days. After I copy the score it is going to N.York to be photographed & copied before its first performance in Los Angeles in September. It seems doubtful whether I shall be there for that, but anyhow we'll all hear it together in Washington on Oct. 30th! By-the-way at that concert I'm to be presented with the E.S. Coolidge gold medal for services to chamber music – by her own hand! Won't you be proud to know me!

Peter is going on working hard – and really singing very well. I think Clytie'll be very pleased with him. Life goes on here much the same – one can't expect it to be always peaceful, I suppose, but, then, an awful lot of energy is wasted in unnecessary emotional scenes, I'm afraid.[2]   However Peter & I get away to the beach alone & drown our sorrows in the big waves, and I can work pretty easily in my tool shed at the back – their 2 pianos have arrived and I can't work in the house any more.

I suppose you've heard that Toni & Peggy can't come East this year? It is a great disappointment for them, and for you too, I should think – but it is our gain, because they may stay a month near here & it would be balm indeed to see them. Please don't think, my dear, that we are very miserable or nervous wrecks – but one just doesn't find an Amityville everywhere, & I am afraid we are rather spoiled for anything else!

I had the enclosed interview with a sweet old lady who is the San Diego Union musical correspondent, and thought you might be interested to see it. I also have an amusing discussion that Newman has been carrying on, on my behalf in the Sunday Times, which I'll send later.

We've just re-discovered the poetry of George Crabbe (all about Suffolk!) & are very excited – maybe an opera one day . . . !![3]

The Quartet is in 4 movements (Rondo – Scherzo – Andante – Finale) & in – would you believe it? – D major!!

All my love –

BEN

1 Like all the other proposals to solve the visa problem by re-entering the USA from another territory – Mexico, Cuba, and so forth – this one also came to nothing. By the autumn, in any event, Britten and Pears had decided to return to England.

2 The 'emotional scenes' to which Britten refers were caused, it seems, by Ethel Robertson falling hopelessly in love with him during this Californian summer, a situation further complicated by the bizarre attitude of her husband who was apparently prepared to make a 'gift' of his wife to the embarrassed and reluctant composer.

3 This is the first reference in the extant correspondence to the plans for an opera based on Crabbe. E.M. Forster's article on the poet in the *Listener*, London, of 29 May – the opening sentence of which reads: 'To talk about Crabbe is to talk about England' – reached California in the summer and was happened on by Britten; where, precisely, we do not know, but it stimulated Pears to find the volume of poems to which Britten refers. The date of this letter and Pears's mention of the 'marvellous Rare Book Shop' in Los Angeles three weeks earlier seem to us to put it almost beyond doubt that it was in Los Angeles that the volume was found, which was how Britten remembered it in his Aspen Award speech of 1964 (BBAA, p. 21):

[. . .] it was in California in the unhappy summer of 1941, that, coming across a copy of the Poetical Works of George Crabbe in a Los Angeles bookshop, I first read his poem, 'Peter Grimes'; and, at this same time, reading a most perceptive and revealing article about it by E.M. Forster, I suddenly realized where I belonged and what I lacked.

The volume itself – *The Poetical Works of the Rev. George Crabbe*, edited, with a life, by his son (London, John Murray, 1851) – is in the Archive. See also PGPB, pp. 53–60.

In a discussion about E.M. Forster with Leonard Woolf and William Plomer (BBC Radio, 11 August 1965) Britten remarked, with a slightly different emphasis, that when he came into possession of the poem in California, 'in a flash I realized two things: that I must write an opera, and where I belonged'.

329 To William Mayer

Route 1, Box 345,
Escondido, California.
July 29th 1941.

My dearest William,

Just a note to say hullo, and how-do-you-do, and how are all the ladies at Pemaquid Point? – and other pertinent (or <u>im</u>pertinent!)

questions. We miss your bright & cheery presence (not to say, puns) alot, as we also miss the Atlantic Ocean, nice as the Pacific can be on occasions. Usually we drive down (about 20 miles) for a bathe about three or four days aweek, but no walking on the rocks or watching the gulls at all hours as you can, lucky thing. However Californian weather makes up for alot.

I was glad to hear you'd met Carson.[1] I hope you can do something about her vile habits, and emotional crises. May be a course in cold-packs at the L.I. Home might be good for her! By-the-way, I should think you are quite happy to give the old place a rest for abit – have you news from them at all? We saw them for abit while they were in this direction – Titley in his old form (unfortunately) and Mildred in <u>her</u> old form (fortunately!). Give my regards to Michael if you see him – is he permanently stationed there, now? Poor thing, it looks as if he'll be stuck soldiering for quite abit now. Still if the Russians can stick it for abit, then maybe something really good will happen for a change! What a crazy world. Everyone out here, of course is terrified of the Japanese, & there is a terrific prejudice against the poor wretched Japs who have settled down and become perfectly respectable citizens. There are terrific 'goings-on' in 'defense preparations' round here – but of course San Diego is the biggest naval base on this coast.[2] I expect you see alot of that sort of thing round you, too.

I've written lots of music since I left you – a Mazurka which Ethel & Rae play with much spirit – a new Quartet for Mrs. Coolidge (for which I am to receive a gold medal) – a new Rossini Suite – and have lots of ideas, so I'm not wasting my time exactly.

I'm afraid I must stop this now as two rich old ladies are just arriving from San Diego, and must be treated with much pomp and circumstance.

Much love to you, William – you can't think how much we both miss Amityville!

BEN

Please excuse the mess, the writing, the spelling, and general lack of style – it's too hot to think straight to-day!

1 Carson McCullers (1917–1967), American novelist, one of the res-idents of 7 Middagh Street, and a patient of Dr Mayer's. For details of McCullers's crises at this time see Virginia Spencer Carr, *The Lonely Hunter: A Biography of Carson McCullers* (New York, Anchor Books, 1976), p. 180 *et seq.* Dr Mayer, whom McCullers came to consider 'her protective angel', was still treating her in 1949 (Carr, pp. 301

and 329). Something of Mayer's character and reputation – and the atmosphere of Stanton Cottage – comes across in a comment from a doctor, a friend of Mayer's, whom McCullers first consulted in 1941: '[. . .] if she had come to see Dr Mayer,' he said, 'he simply would have invited her to come home with him to play Beethoven Quartets' (Carr, pp. 180–81). It was after this that McCullers got in touch with Mayer, who thenceforth became her medical adviser and good friend.

2 In March 1942, after the outbreak of the Pacific War, 100,000 Japanese Americans were to be evacuated from a huge area of the West Coast, which had become a military zone.

330 To William Mayer
From Peter Pears

Escondido, Cal.
[29 July 1941]

Dear William[1] –

Thank you very many times for your letter from Pemaquid and also your Psych. Paper from Amityville. I should love to have been watching the gulls with you in Maine on that lovely coast. Here it is lovely too, but more exotic and, if one must confess it, a little artificial. Everything is irrigated and forced. The most sensational news has been the 4 days of rain we have had in 3 months – Unheard of! Raining in California in the summer! The climate is going to the dogs! They will probably blame the Communists for it. There is more fear of the "Reds" here than anywhere I have been in the States. It will take a lot to make them come into a war on the same side as Russia.

Your paper on migraine was very interesting and depressing. Luckily I have never had migraine and so shall not end up with permanent headaches, I hope.   There were lots of new words, which I am trying to memorize, and seeing our old friend "pyknic" in print was very refreshing.

We have all been working hard here. Ethel & Rae work here each morning, Ben goes out into the tool-shed and turns a fan on so that he shan't hear them, and I drive down into the village to the house of an Englishwoman with a piano. And we all variously work. Then lunch & often a bathe in the ocean, a little more work in the evening, supper & bed. We have made two excursions to Los Angeles – horrible place – the real 'Auspuff'[2] of America! You probably read all about San Diego in "Life" 2 or 3 weeks ago. It's all very true – nothing but sailors & marines, & the whole country is spoiled by camps. It was good to see a snap of Michael looking so well, and lovely for you to see him.

We went last night to the new Marx Brothers movie "The Big Store".[3] It's not one of their best, but still very funny. You mustn't miss it.

I am looking forward eagerly to seeing you again.   It seems such ages since May. I hope to be back about the middle of September. We would <u>like</u> to come via Chicago and see Kay Leslie, but I'm not sure –

Much love to you all,
especially Jibi –
Your
PETER

Much love from Ben, & Ethel & Rae.

1 Pears was clearly responding to the same communication from Dr Mayer to which Britten was replying in the preceding letter.

2 'Exhaust pipe' is the implication.

3 Directed by Charles Reisner.

331 To Elizabeth Sprague Coolidge
[*Picture postcard: Escondido*]

Route 1, Box 345,
Escondido, Calif.
1 August 1941

Thank you so much for your letter – I am following your instructions about the score & parts of the quartet, which is at last <u>finished</u> – and in the throes of being copied.[1] I am very pleased with it! I hope you are well; when do you come South again?

Best wishes,
BENJY (BRITTEN)

1 The manuscript fair copy of the quartet was given to the Library of Congress (Music 1589) by Mrs Coolidge in October 1941.

332 To Robert Britten

Route 1
Box 345
Escondido, California.
as from Amityville.
August 4th 1941

My dearest Robert,

It was very good to get your letter and to hear your news from you direct. I get odd snippets about you from the sisters and so I knew you were all alive and on the whole well. I was sorry to read about John's sinus trouble, and hope it's better now – although I had no idea that people had sini (sinuses??) in Europe. I thought that it was entirely an American trouble. Over here five out of ten are having trouble with their sinio (if 'with' takes the ablative), or having their sinos removed. Another craze over here, incidentally, is having an allergy, or being allergic to something or other – from cats to strawberries – which means you either sneeze or are sick at the sight of/at smell of/at taste of/etc. etc. the thing. To my mind most of it is imaginery; anyhow the amount of notice people take of their bodies is nauseating – everyone has 'food-delay' (guess what that is?)[1] and the number of vitamens they take is equivalent to a class distinction. Anyhow, I hope John's sini get better quick, and also Alan's glands. From all accounts the latter is an awfully cute kid – do you realise I've only seen him once?[2] I'm afraid I'm a lousy uncle, but one never knows; one day I may come home with my pockets bulging with silver dollars, and then they'll be proud of their uncle. By-the-way I'm to be presented with a <u>gold</u> medal at the Library of Congress in Washington in October, by Mrs. Sprague Coolidge (the rich patroness of music, friend of Frank Bridge) for services to chamber music! Gettin' quite distinguished arnt I?   But it doesn't mean any money, unless I sell the medal, which wouldn't be quite quite.[3] Still the old girl has just bought a string quartet off me for quite a sum, which will keep the wolf away for abit, so I can't complain. Thanks for your enquiries about my progress over here. Things might be much, much worse – with conditions as they are – everyone scared stiff of the future, & the place swarming with refugees (except the English, every composer whose name is familiar is over here now) – I haven't starved yet; I've had quite alot of success and a surprising lot of performances, and next season looks even better.

What is most encouraging is the number of real friends I have in many different places, who believe in me and make no bones about it – such as the Mayers in Amityville, and Ethel & Rae Robertson with whom Peter & I are spending the summer out in California. Don't imagine I'm just lazing about, sitting in the tropical sun – I've already written a Mazurka for 2 pianos, scored a new Soirées Musicales suite, and written a String Quartet since I arrived. But it is a lovely spot – the house is in an Orange Grove (we pick Oranges for our breakfast!) – about 20 miles from the Pacific Ocean where we occasionally go to swim. The Pacific doesn't look much different from the Atlantic, except maybe it is a bit bluer, but the beach is rather like Crantock. The country is very like Spain or Mexico, palms etc., with fireflies and humming birds, and Koyotes (cross between dog & wolf which come down from the mountains at night). Did you hear that we motored across the continent in an old V8 Ford? We did it in about 9 days (about 350 miles a day). It was very interesting, but an awful long way! Driving in California is crazy, by-the-way – most reckless, one takes ones life in ones hands each time one goes out. We go to Hollywood at the end of this week to see some friends – I'll give your love to Simon Simone[4] if I see her! Much love to all the family & continued good luck & prosperity etc. etc.   Forgive this being so short, but I can't get anymore sheets into Barbara's letter and can't afford another 30 cents. I'll write longer later. Much love old sport,

Yours ever,
BEN

1 cf. *Paul Bunyan*, No. 7, 'Cooks' Duet':

> Soups satisfy,
> Soups gratify.
> Ten beans a day
> Cure food delay.

The Duet continues:

> Beans for nutrition,
> Beans for ambition,
> The Best People are crazy about soups!
> Beans are all the rage among the
> Higher Income Groups!

2 Robert's younger son, Alan (b. 1938).

3 Britten was over-optimistic. The medal was not a gold one.

4 Simone Simon (b. 1911), French film star whose films include *La bête humaine* (1938) and *Cat People* (1942).

333 To Beth Welford

[EWB, *pp. 168–70, incomplete*]

Escondido
(but please send letters to
Amityville in the future)
August 19th 1941

My darling old thing,

I have been carrying this paper around for three hectic days in
Hollywood, hoping to get a chance to write to you, but, not
surprisingly considering what that place is like, it didn't materialise.
However, when I got back here there was a letter from you waiting
for me, so I can answer it, and also say thank you very much for
it. I was getting a wee bitty worried since you usually write so
regularly, so I was relieved as well as pleased to get it, & such a
nice long one too! Heavens, how I wish I could see you all again
– goodness knows when that'll be. But actually, for the first time
for years one has almost been able to look ahead – since the
incredible Russian resistance, and also America's waking up to facts
at last. In fact Washington's official opinion is that Germany is
beaten & knows it – but I'm abit scared that in going down she
may drag so many others down with her. God grant that a great
man may arise who can organise a better kind of peace than 1918.
Please excuse the digression into politics, but everyone talks them
& one can read nothing else but long prophecies, usually
completely false. Actually I am short-sighted enough only to
worry about the present, and can only be happy when those I love
arn't living a hell-on-earth existence. By the way, old thing, please
forgive me if this letter is a little more disjointed and stupid than
usual, because I'm writing it in the heat of a Californian afternoon
and that's <u>something</u> I can tell you, it was 90% in the shade a few
hours ago!) – and also Ethel & Rae are practising downstairs and
if anything is more disturbing than one piano it's two! Life is going
on much the same as usual here with occasional excursions into
Hollywood – to concerts that Barbirolli conducts at the Bowl,[1] and
to see odd people that are, have been, or may be useful to anyof
us. It is an extraordinary place – absolutely mad, and really horrible.
I can't really attempt to describe it, because it has no relation to any
other place on earth. It actually isn't a place by itself but a suburb
of Los Angeles, which is the ugliest and most sprawling city on
earth. The chief features of Hollywood are that the things that one

worries about so much don't matter a damn – money, time,
distance, behaviour, clothes (especially for men). It is completely
unreal. Peter & I stayed with friends[2] – enormously rich, altho'
they have only average jobs. One house we stayed in was built like
a boat, with a moat round it, – in the middle of all the other
houses – which anyhow are any & every stile from a native-mud-
hut to an Indian temple – via Pagodas & Spanish villas – it would
drive Mr. Welford mad![3]   The driving is mad – I saw a wonderful
little argument between 2 cars the one on the right wanting to go
left, across the other which wouldn't give way. After blowing its
horn madly for about 1 minute (they were both travelling about
45 down a main Boulevard), it started to swerve madly about – like
this

until finally it just barged straight into the side of the other, & there
was an awful crash – just because neither would give way! Typical
of all Hollywood driving – and Peter & I had enough of it, because
as no distance one ever goes is less than 5 miles, one is driving
all the time! As amatter of fact, one has to get just as hard as the
other drivers, although I didn't go so far as crashing cars I didn't
like!
     I am glad Kit seems to be liking his job more, and that you got
away for abit of leave. How are the Welfords? I feel rather bad
about not having written for so long – but I have been so really
terribly busy, & the only time one gets for letter-writing is after
dinner, & something about the Californian air & sun makes me so
tired then. Please tell Barbara I'll write to her in a few days, but
I don't want this to wait any longer. By-the-way would you please
send the enclosed to Who's-Who[4] for me – I'm about a year late
already with it!   I feel so embarrassed with this sort of thing – they
are alright for film-stars or politicians but poor old hack composers
have such dull lives, and nothing to fill books with!
     Peter and I are probably going East again in a few weeks – when
I get the present work finished[5] – lots of things one can't do by
letter have got to be done – & also, frankly, I'm abit sick of California
– there is a feeling of unreality about it which is not so pleasant as
you'd think. My dear, how I should love to speak to you on the
telephone – but anyhow even when it not so expensive, it's not
allowed for private people at the moment (Wystan raised heaven
& earth to be allowed to when his mother was ill, to no avail).

But I have a feeling that we'll be together again sooner than we think – I don't know why I'm feeling so hopeful to-day, pray something awful hasn't happened by the time you get this.

My love to Kit & the child – he sounds marvellous now, but if he grows up like his mother he'll even improve I know! Love to Barbara & Helen and lots to yourself, old thing – I'm always thinking about you!

BEN

1 The Hollywood Bowl: the open-air auditorium – a sixty-acre canyon – which has on occasion attracted audiences of over 20,000. Percy Grainger was married there in 1928, before an audience of 15,000.

Barbirolli made his début at the Bowl in July 1940 with the Los Angeles Philharmonic Orchestra and he was invited to return in the summer of 1941, when Britten was among the audience. Pears had written to Elizabeth Mayer on 23 August: 'The Barbirollis were nice but very nervous, & the Bowl is allright but nothing to do with music, as <u>we</u> know it, Elizabeth.' See Michael Kennedy, *Barbirolli* (London, Hart-Davis, MacGibbon, 1971), pp. 147–51.

2 Pears had written to Mrs Mayer on 23 August:

We went into Los Angeles last week for Thursday night [the 21st] and stayed with Catharine & Nicholas Bela. She's such a lovely person. We made great friends. I had hardly met her in Amityville and was greatly impressed by her this time. [. . .] Nicholas at first sight is not so nice as Catharine – we had enormous & rather heated arguments with him (Ben very cross!) but he's really an <u>aimable</u> old thing & I'm sure improves on acquaintance. We seemed to meet an unusual number of silly & pretentious people in Hollywood on our two trips there, but I suppose you would expect them in a place like that.

On 25 August, Mrs Mayer wrote to Britten who was now back in Escondido, 'I hope to hear by word of mouth everything about your adventures in Hollywood, did you see Christopher?' But there is no record of a Hollywood meeting with Isherwood, who may in fact have been out of town at a retreat at La Verne. See also note 4 to Letter 340.

3 Beth's architect father-in-law.

4 The first *Who's Who* entry for Britten appeared in 1943.

5 In the letter to Mrs Mayer on the 23rd Pears wrote:

Ben is now in the middle of the Scottish Rhapsody or some such name for Ethel & Rae. Before he started it he hated the idea, but the more he writes the better he likes it!

334 To Elizabeth Sprague Coolidge

Route 1, Box 345,
Escondido, California.
August 26th 1941.

My dear Mrs. Coolidge,

Your very generous cheque has just arrived, and I am writing at once to thank you, and to tell you what a great pleasure it has been writing the work for you. I am very keen for you to hear it, and I am delighted that the Quartet likes it as I think it is a good omen when the players like a piece, because they are the most severe critics!

I am so sorry that you were given anxiety last week over the non-arrival of the parts. The fact that I was away in Los Angeles for a few days did not help matters, I'm afraid. But within a few days everything was satisfactorily arranged, and I even was able to correct the parts before sending them to Mr. Kroll, which I always like to do if possible.

Please let me know when you come south again to Los Angeles, as I should love to pay you a visit, if you are not too busy. I do want to get to know you better.

With many thanks again, and the very best wishes,
very cordially yours,
BENJIE

335 To Elizabeth Mayer
[*Incomplete*]

Escondido.
Sept. 6th 1941

My dearest Elizabeth,

It is only because of the rush on the 2–piano Concerto that I have been so silent for so long. I have had terrible trouble over that piece – haven't had such 'constipation' for ages – actually because at no time could I get any interest up in it! – (swear to secrecy, my dear). It's horrible using other people's tunes and trying to make an original composition out of it – different with the Rossini because I was only <u>arranging</u> that. However it's finished now, & everyone seems pleased with it (except the composer who knows better!) It was lovely having your letters, they cheered me up enormously because entre nous, there has been a good deal of depression about – in spite of the lovely place, the lovely (not too hot) weather, good food and all that. Perhaps it is that very thing – the fact that so few people in the world can have it to-day – that is depressing. Perhaps it's those perpetual jig-saw puzzles – personal relations. Anyhow – both of us are living for the 22nd of this month when we expect to leave by car (cheapest way) for the East – probably via Kay if she's around. We can't leave before because of the première of the Quartet in Los Angeles on the 21st & I ought to go to that. How disappointing that you can't be there – that will be the first première of mine that you've missed for a long time! So with luck we'll [be] back with you before the end of this happy month.

You've heard of poor Toni? – isn't this scyatica (however you spell it) dreadful – and, poor dear, with his concerts coming on so soon. I'm afraid it's been a terrible expense, as well as worry for them; with the hospital and the treatments. It is really the damnedest luck. We go over occasionally to see them, but not nearly as often as we should like, I'm afraid – but then with only one car as transport for 4 independant people it isn't always very easy.

336 To Barbara Britten

Escondido
[On or after 7 September 1941]

My darling Barbara,

I cannot for the life of me remember whether I wrote last to you or to Beth, because I like to alternate so that no favouritism is shown! Anyhow – if I wrote last to you, please tell Beth I'm very sorry – no harm meant – & I'll write next to her. How are you, my dear? I hope you will still be free from serious raids when you get this. It is such a relief to know that you're not having to go thro' that hell – & I bet it's a relief for you, too! Have you been able to have any form of summer holiday, or has all that been cancelled on account of the 'emergency'? I suppose it's impossible for anyone to get to Snape – I suppose that it wouldn't be very pleasant even if it were possible – too many military things around I'm afraid. This place is a complete miltary hive now – crammed with soldiers, sailors & marines, with planes all over the sky, &

lots of gun practice going on & rattling the windows. I suppose it's on account of the Japan scare.

Did I thank you for your last letter? The one when you told me you'd be staying on in the Flat, which pleased me such alot. You mention financial troubles on my account – but Beth didn't say a word about it, so not being particularly flush at the moment I didn't send any. But it can always be raised if wanted – just let me know.

Well, Peter & I expect to spend another two weeks out here and then into Hollywood for the first-performance of the Quartet which I've just written for Mrs. Coolidge, and then the great trek back East. We shall go by bus as the Robertsons want the car left out here, and the train fare is too expensive. It's a nasty thought – 3000 odd miles by motor-coach, but people have been known to stand it, & so I'm living in hopes that I'll still be alive at the end. O – but I wish I were a little fatter; sitting on one's behind for a week or so at a stretch gets me down! However I have put a few pounds on, but I haven't made the 10 stone mark yet, in spite of the good food here. By-the-way, do say in your next letter, what kinds of food you need most & I'll send things off from here (or New York). We haven't been able to send chocolate from here the last few months, as it would probably melt going across the desert – which is as hot as hell. One doesn't usually think of America as being a deserty place – but actually most of the S.W. is only just reclaimed & irrigated. Still the place looks awfully sandy & is only green for a very short time.

I haven't done much since I last wrote – only work. I have finished a new Concerto for Ethel & Rae to play next season, first performance with Goossens in Cincinatti.[1] I don't think it's so hot, between you & me, but other people seem to think it's all right – so I'm praying that at least it'll make some money. It's based on Scottish tunes – & everyone says that it is full of the Scottish landscape; difficult, as I've never been there! You know, it's odd how little I travelled about England, now that I've been about this continent so much. Here one thinks nothing of going the distance of Lowestoft to London & back for lunch! But it's a crazy country, & I don't think I altogether like it. I know old England is a stuffy place, the BBC is horrible, & the plumbing is bad; but there are lots of things about this 'ere place that arn't so good, either. Their driving – their incessant radio – their fat and pampered children – their yearning for culture (to be absorbed in afternoon lectures, now that they can't 'do' Europe) – and above all their blasted stomachs, with their vitamens, their bowel movements (no one ever 'goes' naturally here – only with a good deal of stimulus!), & their bogus medicines. Still they aren't blowing each other to bits so far, & perhaps that's something.

How's the family, & Helen & Amrid[2] & all? Do write again soon, old dear. I love hearing from you, because one feels so far away these days. It's horrible to think of that explosive bit of water in between us. Still people are at last beginning to talk about the end of it all – God grant that it isn't so far off as one fears it may be. Do let me know if there are any little things you could do with – it gives me such a thrill to be able to send things.

Could you please forward the enclosed letters for me? — air-mail postage is so expensive, & the other way so risky – & I hate to think of letters <u>not</u> getting to their destinations when I make the effort to write them!

Much love my darling,
Keep well, write soon.
BEN

P.S.   Your letter has just arrived – thank you so very much for it. It was such a nice, normal cheerful one & made me very relieved about you! I am looking forward to the family portrait – buck up & send it, please! I always mean to send a photo of me, but they are so hideous, & always when I go to enclose one it makes the letter overweight, & I'm very stingy these days! Could you post the letter to Miss Sophie Wyss, Earlstone Cottage, Grey House, Burghclere, Newbury, Berks;[3] and the slip to the address on its back – please – thank you!

Much love————

1 *Scottish Ballad*: Britten probably refers here to the completion of the composition sketch. The fair full score is inscribed 'Amityville, N.Y., 27 October 1941'.

2 Amrid Johnstone, an artist and friend of the Brittens' in Lowestoft, who later shared a flat with Barbara Britten and Helen Hurst. In 1933 she designed the cover for the first edition of *A Boy was Born*.

3 See Letter 337.

337 To Sophie Wyss

Escondido, California.
as from: Amityville.
Sept. 7th, 1941.

My dear Sophie,

I have enjoyed your letters so very much – I feel I have been kept in touch with a very real bit of English life (musical & otherwise!) and it is so wonderful to know that it still exists in the lovely way you describe it. What a grand amount of work you've been doing – and what interesting programmes! And gramophone records too. I must try & get them over here as soon as they are released. It is nice to know that you have temporarily made your home in Burghclere¹ – it is a lovely spot, near good friends of yours, and a relief to know you are out of the London district – because although this lull is wonderful, one has a feeling it may not last for ever. I feel glad that Barbara has a place to go to (Beth is living at Northwood) if things start again.

Yes there <u>was</u> an 'international' festival in May – & 'Les Illuminations' was very beautifully sung by Peter & I conducted. We took records, and one day we will compare his reading with yours! But the Festival itself was a wash-out – no real community feeling – no friendliness – all the people there one knew already, they're living here anyhow – no trips, or local colouring, and the Festival was absolutely broke – in the richest country in the world! They couldn't even afford a complete orchestral concert – had to rely on [an] occasional, isolated piece in an ordinary orchestral programme – my piece was introduced by the Meistersinger prelude & some Balakirev! Shades of Paris, & Barcelona!² I had a terribly hard winter – had to write lots of things & superintend lots of performances – some good, some not so good – so when Ethel & Rae Robertson asked me out to their house in S. California I excepted [sic] with alacrity. So here Peter & I have been all the summer – working very hard, & very quietly. I've written a quartet for Mrs. Coolidge, a 2 piano concerto for the two, a Mazurka in memory of Paderewski, and done other odd jobs – so I haven't exactly wasted my time! How I look foward to the time when I can show you some of these things, and when we can do some more concerts together! (I feel quite jealous of your accompanists nowadays!) I have a feeling that it will be sooner than either of us expect. How are the two Arnolds, and my god-child? I think of them a very great deal, & wonder what they are doing & look like now. Please give them a great deal of my love – all three of them. Wystan Auden is well – I haven't seen him for abit, as he is still in the East. We plan lots of work together. He only escaped being drafted into the Army very narrowly[3] – but he is alright for a bit now I think. Give my love to all my friends when you see them – especially the Behrends – I often think about them.

And lots of love to you, my dear Sophie, write again whenever you have time. Best wishes from everyone here.

BENJAMIN

1 The village in Berkshire where the Behrends lived.
2 ISCM Festivals held respectively in 1937 and 1936.
3 In October, Auden was to begin teaching at the University of Michigan at Ann Arbor, where the university authorities were to make 'special efforts to arrange with the Military Draft Board that Auden should not be called up for war service until he had finished his year of teaching', as an Associate Professor of English. See HCWA, p. 322, and Jonathan Fryer, *Isherwood* (New York, Doubleday, 1978) p. 201, who quotes a letter from Isherwood to John Lehmann:

Later plans are still very vague. I may go East to see Wystan, but this depends on whether or not he has been conscripted: he had been ordered to report for duty on July 1, and I haven't heard from him since.

It should be remembered that conscription was introduced in the USA before Pearl Harbor and the consequent outbreak of hostilities. See also Charles H. Miller, *Auden: An American Friendship* (New York, Scribner's, 1983), pp. 56–7, who describes a visit to Auden at Ann Arbor made by Britten, Pears and Elizabeth Mayer, during the course of which Auden remarked to the author about his two compatriots, 'Now there's a happily married couple.' See note 1 to No. 354.

338   To Wulff Scherchen[1]

Escondido, California
as from: Amityville, N.Y.
Sept. 9th 1941

[. . .]

It was a great joy to get your letter not long ago – it was such a nice letter and so typical of the Wulff I remember so well, & with such affection – yet plus a little something that all the trials & tribulations of the past few years have added, and maybe, just a little of what being 21 means? Anyhow, it was fine to read of all your doings – how the army life is not so bad; how you're able to work abit, & above all see friends from time to time. That must be a real blessing. I was very touched by your description of the afternoon with Trevor [Harvey] – glad that all the time which we spent together hasn't been completely effaced by the long time that I have been away. I also, surprisingly enough, have changed a great deal. I feel much, much older &, well perhaps wiser as well. I can take a more reasoned & objective view of things, & my own work too. I am longing for you to hear the new things – especially what I have done this summer. I wonder if you will like them – & rather feel you will, actually. However – pray God it will be soon – & I rather have the feeling it'll be sooner than either of us expect.

In many ways this summer has been terrible for us – I have never felt so completely out of harmony with America. You see – over here Europe seems very remote – the only thing occasionally that reminds one of the state of things to-day is the threat of Japan, & of course the everlasting Military propaganda for American defence and all that. What I mean is, the luxury & abundance & thoughtlessness & selfishness of so many of the people, makes one feel slightly hopeless. We have been in Hollywood quite abit – & that is like another world, from the world we know. Money, time, distance – nothing has the old meaning. It explains why so many of the films that come from Hollywood, although technically so good, are artistically so rotten. All the weaknesses of the civilised world, all the lack of direction, find their epitome in California. So this summer I have taken refuge in that old convenient muse, music, and written & written. Peter & I go back East in about 10 days – I have a concert to attend in Los Angeles on 21st, the first performance of a Quartet I have just written for Mrs. Coolidge, the great American patroness of music. I shall be very glad to get back, for, although I loathe New York as a city, one at least feels one is doing something there & has some connection with reality. I will write to you from there and tell you my plans for the winter, which are at the moment extremely vague, and depend on lots of contacts that I must make when I get back. At the moment my greatest wish is to write as much as I possibly can, while I am still able & allowed to – because one never knows how long it will last, & I have such a hell of a lot to want to say —— !!

My dear boy – I don't know why I'm writing you all this stuff – it can't be of much interest to you, faced as you are with the very grim realities of a very grim world. Anyhow if you can't read it –

just tear it up – I'll understand. It is only that I like to get it off
my chest, and I have a feeling that you are still somewhat
sympathetic to me. When you write, tell me details of your
friends. Very little is ever censored in your letters – only the address
usually & any actually names of places you visit – so you can feel
quite free! If ever you go to London, do call in and see Barbara,
she is still at the same flat – you know 11, Tryon House, Mallord
St., S.W.3. – and would love to see you. She occasionally goes to
Beth & Kit's to stay & occasionally to sleep over nights, but is
usually in London, since she still has her job.

   You see – my writing gets no better. Perhaps it is having to write
so many letters these days – but I still can't use a typewriter –
have to go to Peter to get that done. Do you remember the old
rattling machine I had in Snape? Dear old Snape – I wonder if
that's still standing.
   [. . .]

1 Wulff was now back in England, serving in the Pioneer Corps at
  Avonmouth, Bristol.

339 To Elizabeth Sprague Coolidge

(Route 1, Box 345)
Escondido, Calilfornia.
September 9th 1941.

My dear Mrs. Coolidge,

   I was over in La Jolla on Saturday visiting poor Toni Brosa, and
he told me that you were not well, and not able to come South
again this Summer. I am so sorry about this, to hear that you are
not feeling fit, and also disappointed for myself because I had so
much hoped to meet you again soon. But I do hope that it is
nothing serious, & that our meeting is only put off for a short
time, and that nothing will prevent you being in Washington for
Oct. 30th – do take care of yourself, so that it doesn't!

   Poor Toni Brosa was really in dreadful pain when we saw him –
and so upset about the concerts next week. I'm afraid their visit
to La Jolla this summer won't be a very happy memory for them.

   Are you still staying at the Hotel Oakland? I am sending this
there, as I am a little afraid that my note to you, a week or so
ago, that I sent to the University at Berkeley thanking you for your
very generous cheque, may not have reached you yet. Have you

any idea when Mr. Kroll is coming South to Los Angeles? I have written to him but had no reply as yet, and I am most anxious to attend a rehearsal before the concert.[1] What a disappointment that you can't be there for it! I am more sorry than I can say.

With very best wishes for a speedy recovery

from your

BENJY

1 The first performance of the First String Quartet on 21 September.

340 To Elizabeth Mayer

Escondido

[Postmarked 13 September 1941]

My dearest E.,

Your lovely note has just come & Peter is just going down to practise so I am scribbling this to give him to post.

2 items: 1). We are driving E. & R.'s[1] car back to New York for them – nicer & cheaper than bus.[2] We'll leave on 22nd as before unless . . . 2). The acknowledgement of my application for extension of Visitor's visa hasn't arrived. I applied for it last Monday (8th) and should have it by then, – unless there's some delay. It'll probably come to Amityville, so if it does could you please send it right away air-mail, special delivery??!! You see, one daren't travel at all these days without all one's papers in order. The visa expires on 24th – & I must have a covering note.

So sorry to hear about Wystan's mother.[3] I'm writing to him. Glad you'll meet Christopher [4] – & have got Gordon with you.

In great haste, my dear,

love to all,

BENJAMIN

1 Ethel's and Rae's.

2 On 11 September Pears had written to Mrs Mayer:

We have just been comparing times & fares of buses & trains across the Continent – & will let you know the minute it's settled.   How we are longing to come East!   Oh! oh! oh!   much love to you all dearest Elizabeth –

3 Auden's mother had died. See also Letter 333.

4 Christopher Isherwood, who later this year was to work for a time at the Quakers' Co-operative College Workshop at Haverford, Pennsylvania, where Britten and Pears met him on their return

journey to New York. Isherwood later recalled the visit in Caroline Seebohm's unpublished 'Conscripts to an Age':

We discussed the whole business of going home [. . .] in particular, the idea of going back and being a Conscientious Objector. I came to the conclusion that for me personally, it was a little bit like insisting on being a vegetarian in a group of people who aren't. [. . .] Ben and Peter argued that after all I was fixing to live in America, whereas they weren't, they were planning to spend the rest of their lives in England, and therefore they felt they should go back and through with the pacifist thing. And I think they were absolutely right.

The move to Pennsylvania gave Isherwood an opportunity to visit New York and see his friends there. Thus Mrs Mayer's reference (in her letter to Britten of 25 August) was related to his move east (he returned to California in July 1942). See Jonathan Fryer, *Isherwood* (New York, Doubleday, 1978), pp. 203–4, and Brian Finney, *Christopher Isherwood* (London, Faber and Faber, 1979), pp. 181–2.

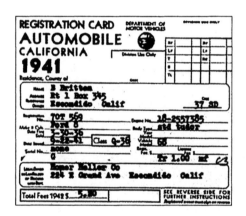

341 To Elizabeth Mayer

Escondido.
[20 September 1941]

My dearest E.,

In haste. Your letter came this morning & I have had the thing signed etc & send it back at once – what an angel you are to arrange things so easily for me! Envelope & everything –.

The acknowledgement that I've been praying for all this time hasn't arrived yet – but Peter & I are so anxious to be back that we are going to risk it & start early Monday morning. So if you get an urgent wire from us, stuck somewhere, I hope you won't get

too much of a shock!   But I have faith that the combined powers
of you, Kay & Walling[1] can get us out of most scrapes!

The Quartet rehearsal was very exciting yesterday – they (the
Coolidge Quartet) are very good.[2] The concert is 4.0 tomorrow at
the Occidental College L.A.

We saw poor old Toni yesterday – looking terrible after his
operation, but everyone says he's turned the corner now. But
what a time they've both had – it's one of our chief grumbles that
we haven't been 'able' (dare I say 'allowed'?) to see him more often,
& to help Peggy in all her worries.

Much love my dear. I can't wait till we meet . . . . . !

BEN

Love from us both to you all.

1 Metcalfe Walling, from Rhode Island. He was a lawyer, active in
politics and government and a friend of Roosevelt's. He was the first
administrator of the wage and hour laws introduced by the Roosevelt
government. He helped William Mayer secure his first post in the
USA, in 1936 at a hospital for the criminally insane at Cranston,
Rhode Island. He would undoubtedly have been consulted by Britten
and Pears about their visa problems. Walling was an amateur
musician, and art lover: his collection included at least one painting
by Josef Scharl. Britten and Pears had stayed with Walling on their
journey to California. In a postcard to Mrs Mayer from Nashville,
Tennessee, on 31 May, Britten had written: 'We got to Washington
rather late on Wednesday [28th] but the Wallings lent us their sitting
room floor to sleep on. We liked them very much.'

2 The Coolidge Quartet was composed of the following members when
Britten's Opus 25 was first performed on 21 September, at the Belle
Wilber Thorne Hall, Occidental College, Los Angeles: William Kroll
and Jack Pepper (violins), David Dawson (viola) and Naoum Ben-
ditzky (cello). The Quartet seems to have been disbanded in 1943.
Kroll later formed his own quartet, the Kroll Quartet.

342 To Elizabeth Sprague Coolidge

c/o William Mayer, M.D.,
The Long Island Home,
Amityville, N.Y.
October 5th, 1941

My dear Mrs. Coolidge,

Please forgive my long silence. You must have wondered where
I (or my manners) had disappeared to . . . !   Actually I left Los

Angeles the day after the Occidental concert, and I have been on
the road ever since, with the exception of a day or two spent visiting
friends in the Middle-West. Anyhow I expect you have heard from
Mr. Kroll how the concert went. I was delighted with the way
that they played my quartet – really first class, both in musicianship
and technique. The public was really quite enthusiastic, & the
only press-notice I have seen quite friendly![1] But it was such a pity
that you were unable to be there. It would have been twice as
nice had you been able to attend the concert. Please don't let
anything prevent you coming to the Library of Congress concert,
will you? I am planning to motor down with friends, and am
looking forward so much to meeting you again. Our acquaintance
is having, alas, a very checkered career!

I saw poor Toni Brosa just before I left, and he was just suffering
acute discomfort after his operation. But Peggy writes that he is
making good progress now, and should be on his way to Madison
– but I expect you have more detailed news than I have.

I haven't heard from Ethel Bridge for ages – I am afraid some
letters may have gone astray. Have you any news of her?

I am missing the weather of California acutely to-day – it being
a typical hot, humid Long Island day. But, on the whole, I am
glad to be back at work in the East again – somehow the West
Coast, especially Hollywood, seems a little remote these days.

With very many thanks for the great opportunity you gave me,
and the most sincere wishes for a speedy recovery,

Yours affectionately,
BENJY

1 Isabel Morse Jones wrote in the *Los Angeles Times*, 22 September:

The new Coolidge Quartet formed by William Kroll, first violinist, played
Ravel, Benjamin Britten and Beethoven quartets in Thorne Hall on the Occidental campus yesterday afternoon. The attendance was capacity and the
interest keen. This was the last, for the time being, of the programs given
the community by Elizabeth Sprague Coolidge. For such intelligent giving
of music, her name is revered wherever musicians gather.

Britten has written his Quartet in D for this benefactress. It is not a
conventional work nor is it of the 12–tone or dissonant or atonal school. It
is distinctly contemporary and the work starts in a wholly unique ethereality.
Upper partials barely heard usher in the first subject most gently. Then a
rhythm-cleverness changes the whole picture.

Britten wanted to bring the music to consciousness mysteriously, as from
another world. The idea was all right but the music was not effective. In the
'Allegretto con Slancia' – and slancia means swing-rhythm, not American

slang but garden swaying swing – there are patterns of musical figures moving in grace.

The 'Andante Calmo' is the most important movement in point of achievement. It might be titled 'In Memoriam for a Lost World.'

The last movement 'Molto Vivace', is a brilliant success. The recurrent underbeat, the revealing passages given the viola and the patterns and shapes of the phrases, molded by rhythm, are the characteristics which show themselves in a first hearing.

343   To Albert Goldberg

c/o William Mayer, M.D.
The Long Island Home
Amityville, N.Y.
Phone: Amityville 2
October 7th 1941

My dear Albert,

It was so good of you and Harold to drive over to Winnetka to see us the other day[1] – it was famous to have that glimpse of you after all these long years! We continued on our way at 6.0 the next morning, in the storm rain, and eventually with many stops (luckily all intentional!) arrived back here the following Thursday, i.e. last Thursday. Since then I have been rushing round trying to collect my scattered thoughts, and also pushing a pen as fast as I can over the manuscript paper in an effort not to be late for Mr. Rodzinski.[2] What I have discovered in my rushings is that it could be made convenient for Peter Pears and me to be round about Chicago on November 10th or so – possible dates appearing in Ann Arbor & Grand Rapids etc. etc. – and if, if, you could possibly arrange for us to perform for you that little 'Les Illuminations' for you, we will swear not to let you down this time! Do you think it is possible? I think we could arrange to be in the vicinity for 3 or 4 days before for rehearsals – and if you like I could wave the stick at the orchestra through yet another number for you – or again I could accompany Peter through another group on the piano in the second half (for instance I have arranged a few British folk-songs[3] which have been a 'wow' wherever performed so far!) These are just suggestions – to take or leave as you feel. But if, if, you could arrange this, it would be such a pleasant round-up to our American visit before our trip across that particularly nasty bit

of ocean in December.[4] It would also be vastly amusing to work
with you all again . . . . ??!!
  Greetings to you both,

Yours
BENJAMIN B.

1 Britten and Pears had broken their return journey to New York at
  Winnetka, where they stayed with Kay Leslie.

2 Artur Rodzinski (1892–1958), Polish-born American conductor. He
  was appointed conductor of the Cleveland Orchestra in 1933, a post
  he filled until 1943 when he succeeded Barbirolli at the New York
  Philharmonic.
    The work that Britten was hastily composing 'for Mr. Rodzinski'
  was *An Occasional Overture* for orchestra, which was completed, given
  an opus number 27 (which was later allotted to the *Hymn to St
  Cecilia*), but – for whatever reason – never performed (possibly never
  delivered to those who had commissioned it: see also Letter 347).
    In an undated letter (? August 1941) to Britten, Ralph Hawkes
  wrote, 'a 4/5/6 minute overture for Rodzinski would be grand & I'm
  sure he would do it in 1942 early, on tour & record it', and followed
  up the proposal in a further letter of 18 August:

  I have just been up to the Berkshire Festival [. . .] Everybody is up there
  at some time during the three weeks and this last week-end I was lucky in
  meeting quite a number of people.
    First and foremost of interest to you is Rodzinski, who told me of his
  admiration for your work, and when I informed him that you had in mind
  writing a short 5 or 6 minute overture for him, he was particularly delighted.
  The point about it however, is that he wishes to give it in New York about
  the second week in November when he conducts the Philharmonic, and
  under these circumstances I am wondering whether you will be able to do
  it in time. I know that you are busy with the Robertsons' two piano concerto
  and it looks as if you will have to put the Mahler transposition [*sic*] on one
  side in order to complete this overture. This, I don't mind, for I am anxious
  that you should make good with Rodzinski and get this New York performance, for most certainly if he likes the work it will go in a number of his
  programs subsequently.

    On 16 September Hawkes sent a cable asking the composer to
  lay aside the scoring of *Scottish Ballad* in favour of undertaking the
  'Rodzinski overture'. Two days later Heinsheimer wrote to Britten:

  I had a word today with Mr Rodzinski saying that he is delighted to learn
  that you want to write a short overture for him. If possible, he would like
  to have it in early October, in order to play it in Cleveland and during the
  second half of November in New York. [. . .] I think we will have the score
  copied for Mr Rodzinski.

  A letter of 16 December 1941 confirms that the manuscript full score had been photocopied, but we have no evidence that it was dispatched to Rodzinski. The final communication about the overture is dated 14 January 1942, when Heinsheimer writes to Britten:

I quote from a letter received this morning from Dr Artur Rodzinski:

I have just received the score of Benjamin Britten's <u>Sinfonia da Requiem</u> and will give it a thorough examination. If it is the most important piece of art written by Mr Britten, then I would rather play it than his Overture. At any rate, I am going to decide about this before the first of February.

We have been unable to discover whether in fact Rodzinski conducted a performance of the *Sinfonia* with the Cleveland orchestra.

When Britten left the USA in March 1942 he did not bring the manuscript of the overture with him. This came to light only shortly before the end of the composer's life, when Joe Bailey Cole, a cataloguer at the New York Public Library, wrote to Britten in July 1972, explaining how the library had acquired the manuscript 'from Alfred Mapelson who used to own a music rental agency in the old Met Opera building':

When I spoke with him on the phone, Mr Mapelson said that he couldn't remember exactly <u>why</u> he had the work, but that many times in the past he had held composer's scores for reproducing and, after several years, he would give them to the New York Public Library. I think that the Library acquired the work in the mid-1950s.

Britten replied to Cole on 18 August 1972:

About five years ago or so, a photograph of this work was brought to my notice. Although the writing was clearly mine and the music had obviously some of my mannerisms (not my happiest!), I had absolutely no recollection whatsoever of writing the work. [. . .] My recollection of that time was of complete incapacity to work; my only achievements being a few Folk-song arrangements and some realisations of Henry Purcell. I was in quite a psychological state then and so I suppose it is not impossible that the writing of even such a large and fully-scored work could have escaped my memory! [. . .]

I should love to have the work destroyed, but that is a little bit too much to ask of you! I should like, however, to have the assurance that, even if the work is allowed to be examined by your visitors, on no pretext whatsoever is it allowed to be reproduced in part or in toto. I hope you do not think this is too much to ask, but I am sure you will understand it is because of the unhappy conditions in which the work was (may be) written by me!

See also note 1 to Letter 351.

The overture was given its first posthumous performance on 8 November 1983 at Birmingham when Simon Rattle conducted the City of Birmingham Symphony Orchestra. It was performed under the new title which had been adopted for its publication, *An American Overture*, to distinguish it from the *Occasional Overture* that Britten was to compose later for the launch of the BBC Third Programme in

1946. This later overture was also withdrawn by the composer. It is interesting to note that the overture Britten wrote for Rodzinski shared some features with his earlier overture, *Canadian Carnival*, Op. 19, composed in 1939. It has been recorded on EMI EL 2702631 (1986), with a sleeve note by Donald Mitchell.

3 There are seven in the set, all of them composed during Britten's American 'exile', and each dedicated to an American friend:

1.	Salley Gardens	To Clytie Mundy
2.	Little Sir William	To William Mayer
3.	The Bonny Earl o'Moray	To Mildred Titley
4.	O can ye sew cushions?	To Meg Mundy
5.	The trees they grow so high	To Bobby Rothman
6.	The Ash Grove	To Beata Mayer
7.	Oliver Cromwell	To Christopher Mayer

These make up Volume I (British Isles) of Britten's Folk-song Arrangements, published in 1943 in versions for high and medium voice and piano.

4 Although Britten and Pears had decided to return to England, they had not realized how difficult it would be to secure a transatlantic passage. December proved to be a far too optimistic expectation. In the event, they were not able to start on the journey home until March 1942.

344 To Elizabeth Sprague Coolidge

c/o Dr. William Mayer,
123, Louden Avenue,
Amityville, N.Y.
October 18th 1941.

My dear Mrs. Coolidge,

I am so sorry not to have answered your sweet letter of October 2nd before this, but all my time has been taken up these last ten days with doing a rush job-of-work (which was only completed at 2 a.m. yesterday!)[1] I am so pleased to hear that you liked the quartet – because I enjoyed writing it so much; it was so wonderful to do it under such circumstances – wanting to write it so much, and knowing one was writing it for someone who would appreciate it, and who also made it so worth while for one – thank you so very much again and again.

My pleasure in hearing your opinion was, however, very much dampened by the fact that you may not be coming East for your birthday. Of course I should like to say – disregard the doctors and come – but I know that would be foolish, and might mean some unnecessary suffering for you, which might be easily avoided by just convalescing the sufficient length of time. But it does look as if we shall never be able to meet again – something always prevents it! – and here I want to tell you something on my part. I have made up my mind to return to England, at anyrate for the duration of the war. I am not telling people because it sounds a little heroic, which it is far from being – it is really that I cannot be separated any longer from all my friends and family – going through all they are, and I'm afraid will be, in the future. I think I shall be able to continue with my work over there, which is what I most want to do, of course. I don't actually know when I shall be sailing, since boats are so scarce & heavily booked up – and anyhow I have so much to get finished here, so I may not be leaving much before Christmas. But please be back before I go! I can't bear to leave our friendship like this.

By-the-way, Dr. Heinsheimer of Boosey & Hawkes says that you can have as many sets of the parts as you wish – he has the master copy and there can be as many made as you wish. Would you let me know how many, please? I have the original score here, and am making one or two alterations[2] – as soon as that is done I will send it direct to you.

With very best wishes for a most speedy and complete recovery, & many, many thanks for everything.

affectionately
BENJAMIN BRITTEN

1 The completion of the overture for Rodzinski.
2 Britten made three alterations to his ink fair copy. He adjusted the end of the introductory *Andante sostenuto* of the first movement, a section that had already caused him some trouble (there is a complete discarded sketch of the introduction); he removed two bars from the *Allegro vivo* of the first movement; and he changed one bar in the third movement. These minor changes had been suggested to him on hearing the work's first performance.

345 To Albert Goldberg

123, Louden Avenue,
Amityville, N.Y.
October 20th 1941

My dear Albert,

You'll stop swearing & cursing me for not having answered your nice prompt letters before this when you know that we're in yet

another crisis, and it is still abit doubtful whether we'll be able to
come along & sing & wave a stick for you on 24th.[1] I hope that it'll
be straightened out in a day or two & then I'll wire you & say O.K.
go ahead with the arrangements. I can't pretend that 24th is as
convenient as the 17th might have been, but I see all your reasons,
& no doubt things will be straightened out, as I hope they can be
– as I'm very keen to do this and other things around the middle
west before we set out on our rather doubtful journey across the
Atlantic.

It is extremely nice of you to suggest I conduct other things
beside the Illuminations – it would be very pleasant to share a
programme with you, (I suppose it would be possible for us to
wind up with a triumphant number conducting _together_?). Dare
I try the Sinfonia with your boys? Do you think it would upset
them? Anyhow have you got triple wood-wind, which is, I am
afraid, obligatory. (The 5th & 6th Horns, Saxophone & 2nd harp
can be managed without.) Personally I should love to do it,
because inspite of some slightly doubtful comments (where from,
I wonder??)[2] I still think it my best opus to date. Only alternatives
are – Kermesse Canadienne, which would be fun to do, – & the
old Mont Juics, Soirées Musicales, Variations, Simple Symphony
etc. etc. Yer pays yer money (or yer doesn't!!) & yer mikes yer chice
– translate that, if you can. Anyhow let me know. Would you like
Peter to do a more popular number (with orchestra & you) perhaps,
an operatic aria – just to show he can do something besides this
modern stuff. All this hangs on whether I send you a wire within
a day or two, but I think there's a 10 to 1 chance. Can you wait
that long?

> Greetings to all (meaning Harold)
> & all apologies for complications.
> Yours ever
> BENJAMIN

The crisis, as you may have guessed, is about visas[3] – life is pretty
complicated even on the less stormy side of the Atlantic!

1 Goldberg had written to Britten on 14 October:

> I have just now received a word that the Great Northern Theater will be
> available for our opening concert on November 17th. [. . .] if you could
> possibly arrange to be here for the November 24th concert, you would be
> welcomed with open arms and fêted to the extent of our ability. [. . .] I
> would be very happy to give you the lion's share of the programme – the

British lion, if you know what I mean, and the louder he roars, the better. I'll not plan anything for that concert until I hear from you . . .

2 See Letter 310.

3 Enclosed with this letter of Britten's was a letter to Goldberg from Pears in which he writes:

> For some strange Washingtonian reason, I have been denied an extension of my visitor's visa, while Ben, who is in exactly the same position as myself, has been granted one. We are going to Washington next week to plead my cause, which I hope and expect will be successful. But it would help me no end to persuade them to let me stay a little while longer if I could show them a letter from you saying how important it is from every point of view that I should be allowed to come to Chicago to sing on November 24th. Could you be so very kind and do this for me?

On 1 November Pears telegraphed to Goldberg:

> EVERYTHING OKAY THANKS MILLION YOU[R] LETTER WITH YOU NOVEMBER
> 24TH WRITING

346 To Albert Goldberg

123 Louden Avenue,
Amityville, N.Y.
Nov. 3rd 1941

My dear Albert,

As Peter's wire no doubt told you, our troubles are temporarily over, & we can come to you & sing & dance on Nov. 24th – thank Heaven, or Roosevelt or the powers that be. We now plan to motor leaving on the 19th – & so can rehearse on the Thursday morning, if the car behaves itself. Is that alright? If you'd like Danny Saidenberg to rehearse Les Illuminations for you, I know he'd be tickled pink – will you ask him, please?[1] About the Sinfonia you can do as you please. He doesn't know it as far as I know. But if, if the orchestra could know the notes before I arrive – I should consider it an honour etc. etc. . . . !! No insinuations meant – so don't get offended! About the orchestra for the Sinfonia – so glad we can have 3 woodwinds (Eb Clarinet?). What about one alto Saxophone? If we could manage to have two extra horns just for the last one or two rehearsals I should be pleased. It does just make all that difference – tho' it's not absolutely essential – the same with the Sax.

About the programme I don't know what to say since I don't know how long your programmes usually run. The Sinfonia plays just under 20 mins & the Les Ill. about 21 or 22 mins. Peter could sing an operatic aria if you wanted it (Boheme or Carmen) – but thinks 22 minutes of him may be enough for you. I <u>could</u> conduct Soirées Musicales at the end for you – but I think I've got the lion's share of the programme already. So what about something like this . .

Your Faithful Shepherd[2] – or a little Haydn symphony (say La Reine – No 15 – in Bb) if that's too short. Then the Sinfonia. Then Intermission – After that Les Illuminations & then one of the more succulent classics to end with – say one of the L'Arlésienne Suites (preferably no. 2) or the second Peer Gynt Suite (v. good)?[3] How's that?

Let me know what you think.

In great haste – best wishes to all
Yours,
BB

Thank you <u>very</u> much for the <u>excellent</u> letter you wrote for Peter.

1 Goldberg responded on 7 November:

> I would be willing to have Danny come in on Wednesday to do some work on 'Les Illuminations' except that he is one of those conductors who never knows when to stop when he gets a stick in his hand. Perhaps if I set a definite time limit it can be arranged?

> Saidenberg followed up the success of this Chicago performance of *Les Illuminations* which he had helped prepare with a further performance in New York, which he conducted himself and which was clearly an outstanding occasion; see Letter 360. Saidenberg and his Little Symphony had given the first performance of Copland's *Quiet City*, in New York, on 28 January 1941.

2 A suite from Handel, arranged by Beecham, and published by Hawkes and Son in 1941.

3 Grieg's opus 55. Goldberg was to write to Britten on 7 November:

> To be honest, Benjamin, I am a bit surprised and ashamed that the modern Elgar would recommend Bizet and Grieg. From my lonely outpost of modernity, I have settled upon Tschaikowsky – the Third Suite in G major. [. . .] perhaps the last movement – the Theme and Variations – will suffice.

347 To Peggy Brosa

Amityville, N.Y.
November 4th 1941

My dear Peggy,

I know – I know – but if you could imagine what a hectic existance we have been living here, you would understand & forgive me for not having written before – Coupled to my usual badness about writing letters of course! Anyhow, this is just to say how delighted I am to hear that Toni is so much better & playing, and travelling & standing up to the life at Madison. It is really grand – & I am relieved no end. I hope too that the atmosphere is quieter for you – with that incubus of a 'cellist gone. How is the new one? I hope he is fitting into the scheme musically, socially & spiritually! Poor dear – you must be feeling very exhausted after all you've gone through – I do hope you can have a little quiet now to get thoroughly rested. Can you do any painting? By-the-way, I've been reading some Lear[1] recently, & when I even read the Recipes (however you spell it) I can never get your inimitable Amblonguses[2] out of my mind. What a pity Lear never saw them!

Peter & I had an uneventful journey back – quite quick – paying visits to friends on way. Actually we both felt like released prisoners & so anyhow the journey would have been pleasant – even if the car had behaved badly – which it didn't. Since I got back I've been working very very hard – wrote my overture for Rodzinski (which I don't think he's going to play after all – disappointing after the hurry) – went to Boston to see Koussevitzki (who's doing my Sinfonia there & in New York) – had a fearful scare over Peter's papers (he was ordered out of the country, and all the strings that Elizabeth knew had to be pulled to keep him back!) – had my Coolidge medal at Washington (Mrs. C. caused quite a stir by calling me Benjy in front of the assembled audience!) etc. etc. etc.

Now our great plan is to motor to the middle-west, & I really do think it's going to come off. Peter is singing (& I am conducting) in Chicago on Nov. 24th – & could we come to see you for the night of the 22nd? We have a rehearsal on the morning of the 22nd & 24th & so I thought, maybe, in between that we could come to see you? Will you be there? please do be. The lovely thing is that I do believe Elizabeth will be able to come too! She is so looking forward to seeing you – so do let's have a card saying if you are there on that day – because if poss. we are all champing to see you both. It'll be so heavenly to see Toni looking his old bright self – instead of the poor dear thing in La Jolla. What a summer! Love from everyone here to you both, & lots of repentance from your very affectionate

BENJY

1 Edward Lear (1812–1888), artist, traveller and writer. Among his
extensive nonsense verse are to be found the 'Recipes' that Britten
mentions. See 'Nonsense Cookery' in *The Complete Nonsense of Edward
Lear*, edited by Holbrook Jackson (London, Faber and Faber, 1947),
pp. 123–5.

2 One of the ingredients required to make 'an Amblongus pie'. This
inspired recipe ends: 'Serve up in a clean dish and throw the whole
out of the window as fast as possible.'

348   To Beth Welford

[EWB, *pp. 171–3, incomplete*]

Long Island Home,
Amityville, N.Y.
November 4th 1941

My darlingest Beth

I am so dreadfully sorry not to have written for so long but since
I wrote last things have been really hectic. First of all there was
all the business of leaving California, which was complicated by
Rae Robertson having a smash in the car and all the repairs had
to be done before we could leave, and also I had a concert in Los
Angeles when my quartet (for Mrs. Coolidge) was first-performed,
and Peter's & my journey back had to start from there. I won't bore
you with all the millions of details about all these things, & I'll
try to stick to the main items. First of all we were incredibly glad
(between you & me!) to get away from California – it was a lovely
enough place, but the personal relationships got in such a
deplorable mess that any normal kind of life was impossible – &
all the time we were caught in a web of 'gratitude' since they were
paying for us. However I have paid them off now, by writing a
concerto for them, so I can't be accused of 'looking a gift-horse etc.'
– but I have never been so thankful to leave a place. The real trouble
is that they are 'performers' in the worst sense of the word – in
other words, selfish, self-indulgent, conceited to an incredible
degree – & the dismal fact is that they're not very good performers!
It is my fault I admit to have gone in the first-place, since I knew
roughly what kind of people they were – but the temptation of
staying rent-free, in such a lovely place for so long (especially as
I had so much work to get done) was too much. However I have
learned my lesson now, and only complain that the punishment
(3 months living on an emotional volcano) was so great! Excuse
this, my dear, but I wanted to get it off my chest. It seems silly

to make so much fuss about this little thing, when there are so
many big things wrong in the world – but you know how
important the little personal things can be – (e.g. toothache!!). The
journey back was very pleasant – we motored of course and took
about ten days, staying with friends here and there & taking a
rather devious course as a result. But at the beginning we went
pretty fast – about 2300 miles in 4 days! When I got back here I had
to sit down at once & write an overture for a conductor here – it
had to be done in a great hurry, and I'm afraid (again, between
you & me!) I didn't do an awfully good job – it is so difficult to
think clearly sometimes these days. However it'll pass muster for
the moment & I hope to rewrite it sometime. That done – I had
to go off to Boston to see Koussevitsky & hear the Boston Orchestra
rehearse my Requiem Symphony which they & he are playing
this year in Boston & New York. As you know, from records, they
are the most wonderful orchestra and played it marvellously – so
I was thrilled to pieces. This piece of news is the best thing that's
happened to me here so far – because it has the best propaganda
value – to have them play ones work in New York – so congratulate
me!!

The next thing to occupy me (and to make letter writing difficult)
was a fuss about Papers – and in these times that is no joke, because
the amount of red-tape is terrible. Actually it was Peter who was
directly concerned, but having similar papers to him I was hauled
in as an example. It caused a terrific lot of letters – & finally a
journey down to Washington to see unpleasant officials. Luckily,
owing mostly to Mrs Mayer who knows all the 'right' people and
seems always able to get one out of tight spots, it was put straight
– & anyhow the journey to Washington wasn't only on that account
since I had my 'medal' to receive. This was at the Library of
Congress and was presented by Mrs. Coolidge for 'eminent services
to chamber-music'!! It was quite an alarming ceremony, but Mrs.
Coolidge, who is really a sweet old thing, made things easier by
publicly referring to me as 'Benjy', which made everyone smile
sweetly! The Coolidge quartet played my quartet with quite good
success. We got back late on Friday last – this week-end Thomas
Matthews (whom you heard play my violin concerto)[1] & his wife
were here on a visit – they are simple & nice people, on their way
to Singapore. Yesterday I spent most of the day in New York on
business – seeing my agent about things (possibly a commission
from Benny Goodman!) – which brings me to to-day, & is, I hope
a good enough excuse for not having written before – but I'm
sorry, my dear & promise to be better in the future.

Thank you so very much for your lovely letter & the 'photos –
I am terribly proud of my nephew & show him to everyone with
pride – I was also delighted with the picture of you not exactly
prepossessing, but very typical, with cigarette & frown!!! I had
to use all my Britten fortitude to keep from spilling a tear or two.
Gosh, what I'll do when I see you I can't think – probably be
quite dumb & not be able to think of anything to say (which usually
happens on such occasions)! About the question of America &
Kit after this bloody war – I have inquired & <u>every</u> place you go to
to become a Doctor, I'm afraid you have to take a medical exam.
I don't know how hard it is, although the Americans have a
reputation of being rather advanced medically. However I know
quite a few doctors who have passed it, – so I'm sure Kit could.
But I shouldn't dream of coming unless you could bring some
money out (which will probably be easy after the war), because
there are hideous stories of doctors all qualified who can't find
work & are starving. Anyhow, wait & see what the position is –
maybe I'll be so rich that I can support you all!![2] Consider it tho',
because America I should think will be the place after the war, &
I can arrange all the necessary papers for you. Damn – I'm on the
4th page & I want to put one in for Barbara. Excuse the abrupt
finish – but you know what I feel about love and wishes & all
that, so please take lots & lots of love for granted to you all from
your devoted bro.

BEN

1 Thomas Matthews (1907–1969), English violinist. See note 4 to Letter
   312.
2 On a sheet of Long Island Home writing paper, Britten listed the
   sources of his income for the year:

			$
Receipts:	Jan 30th	Ballet Comm.	231.00
	March 1	[?] Boyar production	40.00
	March 19th	Schirmers	100.00
	April 10th	Columbia commission	75.20
	April 26th	Wittgenstein	130.00
	June 11th	B.H. Royalties	75.47
	June 23rd	Lincoln [Kirstein]	190.00
	Sept 2nd	Mrs. C. [Coolidge]	400.00
	Nov 17th	B.H. Advance	200.00
	Dec 22nd	B.H. Advance	200.00

This, if correct, would have given him a total income in the USA for
the year 1941 of $1641.67.

349   To Albert Goldberg

123 Louden Avenue,
Amityville, N.Y.
Nov. 11th 1941

My dear Albert,

Sorry not to have replied before, but I have been away & only got your somewhat hectic note on my return. You poor thing – you _are_ having a time over us – but I hope things will get straightened out about rehearsals. As I am afraid there isn't a dog's chance of us being in Chicago for the Wednesday rehearsal I am afraid we shall have to make do with the Friday, Sat. & Monday rehearsals. What I suggest is that you go ahead with your part of the programme on the Wednesday, & maybe if you feel inclined give a short time say – 40 minutes – at the _end_ of the rehearsal to Danny Saidenberg to go thro' the Illuminations. I should leave the Sinfonia[1] till I arrive & concentrate on your own part. About the instruments – don't worry about the E♭ Clarinet part. The Bass Clarinet doubles with it, & it isn't very important so if he blows a few bubbles it won't kill us. The B Cl part is much more important so it's better this way round than the other. Sorry you disapprove of my programme suggestions – personally I like Grieg no. 2 & Bizet no. 2 – but maybe I haven't heard them as often as you have! I have told B & H to send you pictures – but have they sent you programme notes? In case they haven't (& you have lost the original ones of Les Illuminations I sent you for our aborted trip last year) I enclose new ones.[2] You just use what you want of them – but I suggest that the _detailed_ bit about Les Illuminations be included. I mark a possible cut in the Rimbaud biographical bit. You have data about the distinguished composer? If not – wire me & it'll be sent right away.

I expect to arrive in Chicago latish on the Thursday & am staying in Winnetka where we met last time – 609, Sheridan Road (c/o Miss Kay Leslie) in case you want to contact us. If you don't hear from me again that's what'll be happening.

All best wishes, & looking forward lots to seeing all you again,

In haste,
BENJAMIN

P.S.   If I have to conduct out of doors I shall just perish on the spot, what with my bronchitis & my pneumonia etc. Have mercy on a couple of poor Englishmen not used to this savage climate——

1 On the day that this letter was written about the preparations for
the performance of the *Sinfonia da Requiem* under Goldberg's auspices
on 24 November, the work received its first Canadian performance
by the Toronto Symphony Orchestra under Sir Ernest MacMillan
(also broadcast by the CBC). A notice of Goldberg's concert – in
which Britten was billed as 'composer–conductor' – appeared in the
Chicago Daily News, 26 November:

Three 'firsts' for Chicago were heard in the Illinois WPA Symphony program
Monday evening at the Civic Theater, Albert Goldberg conducting. Benjamin
Britten conducted his own works, 'Sinfonia da Requiem' and 'Les Illuminations', song cycle, with Peter Pears, tenor soloist. Handel's Suite, 'The
Faithful Shepherd', Mr Goldberg permitted to speak for itself. Britten's song
cycle from poems by Arthur Rimbaud, great French poet, were illuminatingly
intelligent. 'Sinfonia' failed, in contrast, to be at all understandable.

Albert Goldberg recalls that Britten's (and presumably Pears's)
appearances with the Illinois Symphony were unpaid:

As a government relief program we could not pay his fee on either occasion
[the first was in 1940, when Britten played his Piano Concerto]. None of
the soloists or conductors was paid, even the eminent ones. The orchestra
musicians qualified for WPA employment and received wages of $94 per
month.

He continues:

This time [i.e. in November 1941] Britten offered to conduct the Chicago
première of his recently completed (1940) *Sinfonia da Requiem*, written in
memory of his parents. He also asked to bring with him Peter Pears, then
a young tenor entirely unknown to the public, to sing the first Chicago
performance of Britten's song cycle *Les Illuminations*, likewise composed in
1940.
    Frederick Stock [1872–1942], the conductor of the Chicago Symphony
Orchestra, and while theoretically a rival, always a supporter of the Federal
Music Project, attended that concert in the Civic Theater, 24 November 1941.
The next day Mr Stock phoned me and commented favorably on the condition of the orchestra. Naturally, I asked him what he thought of Britten's
compositions. 'Very talented,' he replied. 'But more manner than matter.' I
was disappointed. I had hoped that he might like the *Sinfonia da Requiem*
well enough to play it with the Chicago Symphony. As nearly as I can recall,
the only Britten work Mr Stock ever conducted was the early *Variations on a
Theme of Frank Bridge*.

The Britten connection with the Illinois Symphony was to continue
after his departure from the States in March 1942. On 22 April the
first Chicago performance of the *Simple Symphony* was given as part
of a series of 'Mid-day Victory Concerts' at the Fullerton Hall of the
Art Institute of Chicago by the Illinois WPA Symphonic Ensemble.
These concerts were sponsored by the Institute as 'an aid to citizen
morale' under the auspices of the Illinois WPA's War Services Program.

2 See note 1 to Letter 257. It is possible that the notes we reproduce there were in fact the 'new ones' mentioned here. They are the only set to have survived and are undated. The programme note for *Sinfonia da Requiem* is identical to that used on the occasion of the first performance (see note 1 to Letter 309) with the exception of two additional prefatory paragraphs:

> This work was written in Amityville, Long Island, in the spring of 1940, and is inscribed to the memory of the composer's parents. In spite of being short for a symphony, it was conceived on festival proportions and scored for a large orchestra including triple wood-wind, saxophone, six horns, piano and a considerable array of percussion.
>
> The scheme and the mood of the work are indicated by the Latin titles which are taken from the Requiem Mass; but the connection to the great Catholic ceremony is more emotional than liturgical.

It cannot pass unnoticed that Britten resolutely avoids mentioning anything about the circumstances surrounding the Japanese commissioning of the work; only 'festival proportions' hints at the *Sinfonia*'s origins.

350 To Mrs David Rothman

7, ~~Middagh Street, Brooklyn, N.Y.~~
c/o Dr. Mayer, Amityville, N.Y.
November 12th, 1941.

Dear Mrs Rothman,

Please forgive me for not having written before, but I have been terribly busy since I got back here. Anyhow, I enjoyed myself terribly in my stay with you all in Southold. It will be one of my happiest memories of America. I am glad that you 'persuaded' (don't laugh!) me not to work that day, because we had such a wonderful time out on Orient Point.[1] I don't think I have ever eaten so much in my life!

I am off to the Middle-West in a day or so, but I am sure I shall turn up again in Southold when I get back – it is a dangerous thing to make a person feel so much at home!

With best wishes to you and your delightful family,

yours sincerely,
BENJAMIN BRITTEN

1 Orient Point is on Long Island to the north-east of Southold. It could well have been home-movie shots of this memorable picnic that were included in TP.

351   To David Rothman

~~7, Middagh Street, Brooklyn N.Y.~~
Amityville N.Y.
November 12th, 1941.

My dear David,

I had such a fine time with you those two days – so thank-you
so very much for having put up with me. I feel abit guilty in
keeping you away from your work so much – but, you know, you
didn't take much urging! – neither did I, I know, but still, I'm
sure it did us a world of good that day at Orient Point. You are
such a delightful family, I have scarcely ever felt so easy and at
home with people, as I do with you all. And you, especially, David,
I feel a real source of inspiration & encouragement, such as I have
rarely met. I am very touched by your urgings on a certain
important decision[1] – please don't be injured if I seem to treat
them lightly, that is only to cover how seriously I consider them.
In spite of my jocularity, I am a great believer in 'Fate' or 'God'
or what-you-will, and I am for the moment going on with the work
in hand (which is plenty, I can assure you!) and letting the future
take care of itself.

I am off to the Middle-West soon, and will be back round the
end of the Month. May I come & see you again then? If you can
arrange that little show for Peter & me,[2] you'll be doing us a great
service. He suggests the 14th (Sunday?) as a good day, or even
after Christmas – if you think people would be still willing to spend
their dollars. But before the 14th isn't too good, and the 21st is
impossible. Let me know what you think.

In the meantime, all my greetings to your family – the charming
Emma, the very gifted little Joan,[3] and the grand kid Bobby – &
your dear wife & self,

from a grateful
BENJAMIN B

1 It was about this time, in the autumn of 1941, that Britten was
suffering from one of his periodic fits of creative paralysis. He had
experienced severe difficulty in 1940 when working on the *Sinfonia*
and the problem recurred, as is clear from the letter he wrote in 1972
to the New York Public Library (note 2 to Letter 343) about the
genesis of the *American Overture*, where he refers to his then 'psychological state' and 'complete incapacity to work'. It seems likely to
us that he unburdened himself to the understanding and admiring

Rothman, who evidently made the right kind of sympathetic and above all encouraging response. In short, he urged Britten to continue composing. That, surely, was the 'important decision' that was reached.

This was by no means the first crisis in which Rothman was consulted. In an interview Donald Mitchell conducted with Rothman for TP, an earlier event was recalled that showed some similar features:

[. . .] so they used to come here, to Southold, at weekends and stay with me; and I'd drive them down to Riverhead where he'd conduct [the Suffolk Friends of Music Orchestra]. And it came the time to give a public performance; and when we got there, there were more people in the orchestra than in the audience. And Ben was so upset that he was actually crying. He wanted to stop writing music, and wanted to work in my store. So I pleaded with him and said, 'Keep going.' I told him, 'Look, you're only about twenty-six years old; you've already done well because Koussevitzky and the Boston Symphony have performed your work. They did a violin concerto with the New York Philharmonic. What do you want? Blood?'

It may have been that Britten's attachment to Bobby – David Rothman's son who now runs the family business – was another reason for his suggesting (perhaps not too seriously) that he would work in the store.

2 Pears and Britten were to give a recital under the auspices of the American Women's Hospitals Reserve Corps, in the auditorium of the Southold High School, on 14 December. The programme included songs by Purcell and Dibdin; arias by Handel, Donizetti and Puccini; Liza Lehmann's *Three Cautionary Tales*; four British folksongs arranged by Britten, including two unpublished settings, 'The Twelve Days of Christmas' and 'The Crocodile'; and two of Britten's Cabaret Songs, 'Funeral Blues' and 'Calypso'. In addition Britten played two solos: Beethoven's F major Sonata, Op. 10 No. 2; and Chopin's B flat minor Scherzo.

A notice of the recital by 'K. De W.' appeared in the *North Fork Life*, Mattituck, Long Island, New York, 19 December:

Mr Peter Pears, baritone [sic], sang a varied group of songs last Sunday evening at the Southold High School auditorium.

Mr Pears makes the most of a somewhat limited voice, but this listener felt that his choice of material could have been more in keeping within the range of his dynamics. His middle register is mellow and warm, and when his songs were confined to that register, his singing was well worth hearing. A little more development of his upper register would make him a musician to be reckoned with.

Accompanying Mr Pears was the well-known pianist [sic], Mr Benjamin Britten, who also played a Beethoven Sonata and a Chopin Scherzo.

His performance of these works was truly electrifying and one could sense that here was a master pianist. Some technical flaws marred an otherwise magnificent reading of the Chopin opus, but we understand that Mr Britten

approaches music as a composer–conductor, rather than as a keyboard virtuoso. On the whole, however, we left feeling that we should like to attend
some further concerts by these two.

3 Emma and Joan (a talented pianist), the Rothmans' daughters.

Southold High School Auditorium, 14 December 1941, recital programme

352 To Serge Koussevitzky

7, ~~Middagh Street, Brooklyn, N.Y.~~
123, Louden Avenue, Amityville, N.Y.
November 18th 1941.

Dear Dr. Koussevitzky,

I hear from my publishers that the new score of my Sinfonia da
Requiem has already been sent to you, and also the records of
the New York performance.[1] I am afraid the latter are not very
satisfactory since they were taken 'off the air' and have bad
surfaces, and also I find some of the speeds rather unsatisfactory
– the first & last movements being too slow, and a bad slow-up
in the middle of the 2nd movement. But I do hope that soon I shall

be [able] to come to Boston soon, as you suggested, so that I can play you the work. I have to leave to-morrow for the middle-west, and shall be away until the end of next week. Would it be convenient for me to motor to see you at the beginning of next month?

I did so very much enjoy meeting you and talking with you in Boston last month; I felt it a great experience. At the present moment my plans for the future are still rather vague, but I expect to leave for England in the middle of January. I do hope that I shall carry back with me the thrilling memory of, what I consider, my best piece played by you and your glorious orchestra.

I hope you are well.

> With best wishes,
> Yours sincerely,
> BENJAMIN BRITTEN

1 The 'new score' to which Britten refers was presumably an engraved score to replace the reproduction of a hand-copied score published at the time of the work's première.

353 To Peggy Brosa

> 609, Sheridan Road,
> Winnetka, Illinois.
> Tuesday.
> [25 November 1941]

My dear Peggy,

Here is Eth's letter – a much brighter one than the others I think, although poor darling, she really is going thro' hell, isn't she? You needn't have worried about me seeing all the letter – because I have known about the situation (from Marj's side, mostly) for a time! But thank you so much anyhow for letting me read it.

It was lovely seeing you both again, to see you looking so well & cheerful, & Toni really his old self again. What a great relief! I feel now that the wounds of that horrible summer are now quite closed up. Let's forget about it altogether!

The concert went well last night – the orchestra played well, Peter sang splendidly & had a good reception, & I wasn't too bad (except for 2 up-beats in one spot!) with the stick. The notices are pretty catty,[1] but that is to be expected.

I am afraid we have to leave for Grand Rapids[2] right away – but I'll write longer when we get back East. This is just to send Eth's

letter back & to say how heavenly it was to see you, and to give
you both lots of love from Kay, Elizabeth, Peter

and

BENJY

1 Edward Barry reviewed the concert in the *Chicago Tribune*, 25 November:

The Civic Theater housed a première of unusual interest last night when the
English tenor, Peter Pears, and the Illinois WPA Symphony orchestra gave
a first Chicago performance of the song cycle, 'Les Illuminations', by the
English composer, Benjamin Britten. Mr Britten conducted.

The song cycle is based on the feverishly mystical outpourings of Jean
Arthur Rimbaud, the curious French poet whose creative life fell entirely
between his 16th and 18th year and who during this short period saw and
imagined and expressed the world with an almost epileptic intensity and
perversity. His intuitions resemble Dostoevski's rather than those of anybody
of his own western world.

The music closely follows the wild invention of the words. It is dissonant,
asymmetrical, sometimes almost hysterical.

The vocal part was ably handled by Mr Pears, who had done it on the
occasion of 'Les Illuminations', first American performance in the east last
spring.

Mr Britten introduced another work of his, the 'Sinfonia da Requiem'.
Seldom does one encounter a new piece so completely incomprehensible.
The ear is baffled by its instrumental texture and passes nothing on to the
mind. Either the composer himself has failed in the task of communicating
to others by means of his music what he himself felt or the orchestra (still
far from its mid-season form) put before us something considerably different
from what the composer intended.

Before Mr Britten's appearance Albert Goldberg, one of the orchestra's
regular conductors, presented a first downtown performance of Beecham's
transcription and arrangement of excerpts from Handel's 'The Faithful
Shepherd'. The conductor handled his tempi and his instrumental intensities
sensitively and achieved a persuasive performance. The concert closed with
the Theme and Variations from Tschaikowsky's Suite for Orchestra, No. 3.

Remi Gassmann wrote in the *Chicago Daily Times*:

Over at the Civic Theater, the Illinois Symphony was devoting most of a
program to works by the young British composer Benjamin Britten. I heard
Mr Britten conduct only his 'Sinfonia da Requiem', Opus 20. The work over-
emphasizes a musical approach that would have seemed startling back in
the good old days of chaotic musical composition immediately after the last
World War. Today, the final impression falls completely short of anything
approaching structural integration.

Mr Britten does not write for the orchestra in the sense that he provides
it with music to play. He merely uses the orchestra to produce a variety of
instrumental sound-effects. By such methods, I am afraid Mr Britten can no
more cajole the listener into hearing these as music of content and substance,

than one can convince a hungry man that pepper, paprika and mustard make up a satisfying meal.

2 The concert took place at Grand Rapids the next day, and gave rise to a review (from an unidentified newspaper) which must rank as one of the most perceptive from the American years. The programme opened with *Les Illuminations*:

The cycle originally written by Mr Britten is for high voice and string orchestra. It was given here with the composer giving at the piano an arrangement of the orchestral score. Even with the handicap imposed by the lack of an orchestra the work showed itself as one of striking vitality and originality.

Britten is modern in spirit more than in outward devices. He does not shun melody, has in fact a gift for strangely moving song. One lyric of the group, No. 7, 'Being Beauteous' even brings to mind, though not by any reminiscent phrase, some of the troubling, beautiful songs of Schumann with their exquisite accompaniments.

Modern as is his tonality, he does not use strange progressions merely for their strangeness and his tonality never falls into chaos. Even in the piano transcription the orchestral score showed for something rich and beautiful, adding much to the expressiveness of the music, which is required to suggest the spirit and possibly something of the form of the images that haunted the poet's mind as he wrote his mystical verses.

The audience, a good-sized one for a recital scheduled at such short notice as this one was, was extremely enthusiastic over the new work, and recalled Mr Britten and Mr Pears repeatedly to the platform. Mr Pears' singing indeed deserves special mention in any account of this work. He gave the music, stormy and lyrical by turns, a sympathetic interpretation such as few new works receive.

The remainder of the program, while less novel was thoroughly delightful. Mr Pears has a tenor voice of fine quality and robust strength and considerable dramatic gifts. He sang Handel and Haydn selections skillfully but the most interesting portions of the program aside from the new Britten work were the groups of old English songs and British folk songs presented by the two artists.

Mr Pears added two numbers to the announced program, 'Sally in Our Alley' and by request Bach's 'Come Sweet Repose'.

The two musicians are guests here of their friends, Dr C. Harold Einecke, minister of music at Park church, and Mrs Einecke. At the conclusion of the program Wednesday evening the recitalists were tendered a reception in the parish house arranged by the United Workers society.

'Les Illuminations' will be given in Town Hall, New York, Dec. 22, with Daniel Saidenberg's orchestra. Soon after, the two young Englishmen expect to return to their native land.

The day before the recital, Britten and Pears had rehearsed the church choir in a performance of *A Hymn to the Virgin*.

ILLINOIS W. P. A.
SYMPHONY
ORCHESTRA

CIVIC THEATRE
MONDAY, NOVEMBER 24, 1941
AT 8:15 P. M.
SECOND CONCERT — SIXTH SEASON

ALBERT GOLDBERG
CONDUCTOR

BENJAMIN BRITTEN
COMPOSER-CONDUCTOR

PETER PEARS
TENOR

This Concert is Presented by
ILLINOIS WORK PROJECTS ADMINISTRATION

CHARLES P. CASEY, Administrator
EVELYN S. BYRON, Director, Division of Community Service Programs
ROBERT L. McKEAGUE, Chief of Public Activities Programs

ILLINOIS MUSIC PROJECT
ALBERT GOLDBERG, State Supervisor
RAY H. MANN, Chicago Supervisor

The first Chicago performances of *Les Illuminations* and *Sinfonia da Requiem*,
24 November 1941

354 To Beata Mayer
From Peter Pears
[*Western Union Dayletter*]

ANN ARBOR MICH[1]
1941 NOV 28 PM 12.57

DEAR BEATTY   WOULD YOU BE AN ANGEL AND SEND TELEGRAM TO ETHEL
AND RAE CARE CINCINNATI SYMPHONY WISHING GOOD LUCK FOR TONIGHT
AND LOVE FROM BEN STOP[2]   THANK YOU MY DEAR YOU CAN UNDERSTAND
WE ARE TOO NEAR HERE EXCLAMATION MARK   HOW ARE YOU   MUCH
LOVE   BACK SUNDAY

PETER P[E]ARS

1 On 28 November, Britten, Pears and Mrs Mayer came to stay with
Auden at Ann Arbor, where Auden was teaching. He had begun to
write his 'Christmas Oratorio', intended for setting by Britten, and
the composer had gone to Ann Arbor to discuss the project with
him. See also note 2 to Letter 397, and HCWHA, pp. 318–24.

2 The first performance of the *Scottish Ballad* on 28 November, when the Robertsons were soloists and the Cincinnati Symphony Orchestra was conducted by Eugene Goossens. The last sentence of the cable reflects the 'emotional volcano' of the summer at Escondido. A notice of the concert appeared in the *Cincinnati Enquirer*, 29 November:

Mr Britten described his treatment of the Scottish tunes as personal. He was not exaggerating. But that accounts for the lean strength of his music – a kind of rugged strength which one commonly associates with Scotland. It all worked up to a high degree of intensity. The pianos served chiefly as part of the orchestra, but the composer occasionally let them take over, often most eloquently, as in the middle section of the funeral march with the touching melody 'The flowers of the forest'.

In addition to its merits as a bold and positive piece of music, the Scottish Ballad gave signs of being a good show piece for the two pianists who helped to introduce it. I believe they realize as much from the generally favourable impression it created yesterday.

355 To Serge Koussevitzky
[*Telegram*]

1941 DEC 15

PLEASE WIRE ME WHEN SYMPHONY WILL BE GIVEN   I AM LEAVING
SHORTLY FOR ENGLAND AND WOULD LIKE TO ATTEND PERFORMANCE[1]

BENJAMIN BRITTEN

1 This telegram has its reply pencilled over it: 'Could you come Boston for rehearsals Wednesday & Thursday and attend performances Friday Saturday Jan. 2–3.' See Letter 359.

356 To Albert Goldberg
[*Picture postcard*: *Pablo Picasso* – *Study for* Guernica
(*Museum of Modern Art, New York*)]

[December 1941]

With all good wishes for Christmas to the "Maecenas" of Modern art

from PETER & BENJAMIN

(is the Sinfonia as obscure as this??)

357   To Elizabeth Sprague Coolidge

c/o William Mayer, M.D.,
The Long Island Home,
Amityville, N.Y.
December 21st 1941.

My dear Mrs. Coolidge,

Please forgive me for having let such a long time elapse before
answering your kind letter. The truth is that I have been expecting
to come to Boston to hear Dr. Koussevitzki conduct my Sinfonia
da Requiem & only yesterday did I get the exact dates of the
performance – January 2nd & 3rd. Is it possible that you will still
be in Boston on those dates? I do hope so, as I expect to leave for
England soon after, & might not have an opportunity to go to
Washington – and I am so very keen to see you again, & to take
a personal message from you to Ethel Bridge & our many mutual
friends. Could you perhaps let me have a postcard letting me
know if you will be able to see me – I will make it possible to see
you whenever you say.

I am delighted that you are feeling so fit and that your physician
has given you such a good report – that is good news!

I had a long letter from dear Ethel – she seems on the whole
more cheerful, though missing Frank terribly still, of course. I am
afraid she has had to give up the lovely Bedford Gardens house –
which will be a wrench for her; but still, I am glad she will not
be in London for a time, because one can never be sure how long
the present lull will last.

By-the-way, did you ever receive the sets of parts of the Quartet
that you wished for? If you still need them I will do a little
agitating from my end. Actually I hear that they are to be printed
over here now, which will be nicer for the players, since it is
always uncomfortable playing from MS. however good.

Wishing you a very happy Christmas, and a prosperous
New Year with a continued clean bill of health, and with very
much love,

yours affectionately
BENJY

358 To Elizabeth Sprague Coolidge

c/o William Mayer, M.D.,
The Long Island Home,
Amityville, N.Y.
December 28th 1941.

My dear Mrs. Coolidge,

Thank you so much for your telegram and your kind invitation
to dine with you next Friday, which I shall be delighted to accept.
I hope to arrive in Boston at noon; then attend the Boston
Symphony Concert in the afternoon (when Koussevitzky is doing
my symphony); and it will be lovely to spend the evening with
you.

I went last night to the Washington Irving school in New York
to hear the Coolidge quartet play our quartet, which was really a
very good success with the large audience.[1] The quartet played it
wonderfully, & they say they feel really at home with the work
now, having played it so often over the country.

I hope you are feeling still as well as when you last wrote, & that
the New Year will bring you continued good health & prosperity.

With all good wishes,
yours affectionately,
BENJY

1 The first performance in New York on 27 December of the First String
Quartet. See Letter 360. We have been unable to trace any reviews
in the New York press of this event.

359 To Serge Koussevitzky
[*Telegram*]

30 DECEMBER 1941

COULD BE IN BOSTON FOR REHEARSAL THURSDAY   PLEASE
WIRE TIME   WILL STAY FOR PERFORMANCES FRIDAY AND
SATURDAY   REGARDS

BENJAMIN BRITTEN

360   To Antonio and Peggy Brosa

William Mayer, M.D.
The Long Island Home, Amityville, N.Y.
Dec. 31st 1941

My dearest Toni & Peggy,

A very, very happy New Year to you both – as happy as the circumstances permit, & may this year see the end of all this bloody mess, so that we can go forward without the encumbrances of registration, applications, quotas etc. – to say nothing of bombs & torpedoes! Above all – no more scares from you, Toni my dear, like last summer. (and ppp sotto voce, no more summers like last for us!!)

Thank you so very much for the tie; it was sweet of you to think of us, and to think so nicely, as it is a beootiful one –   One that I can often, & shall, wear.

It was sickening that we couldn't get to Boston, Toni, especially as everyone has such glowing accounts of your playing – and I expect to hear lots more tomorrow when I go to Boston to hear the old man play the Sinfonia. But things just got too complicated, & Boston, even judging by American standards, is quite a way off. However, we are all just looking forward to when you come East, and it looks almost certain now that Peter & I won't have left on our uncomfortable journey across the water, by then. We have already our priority on the boat (from the British side it's O.K., that is), but we still haven't got our exit permits, and when we get them, we've got to wait for a boat –   So it looks alright for at least a fortnight or so. By-the-way I have to be in Philadelphia on the 16th & 17th[1] – aren't you playing around there then, Toni? In that case I might be able to connect pleasure with business!!?

Things are hectic here as you'd imagine. Peter sang Les Illuminations with really <u>rounds</u> of success the other day at Town Hall[2] – and, apart from old stinker Virgil Thompson in the Tribune, had wonderful notices[3] – masterpiece, sang magnificently . . . . . and so on – quite encouraging! The Coolidge played my quartet in N.Y. the other day, & quite successfully. Koussey's probably doing the Sinf. in N.Y. next week, as well as Boston on Friday – so things are humming, aren't they?

I do hope you're feeling better, Peggy. Your letter sounded very depressed, my dear – I think after a time one gets into a routine of things, and just lives from day to day. That's what has happened to me – I've even started to work again!

I had a sweet letter from Eth, seemed much more cheerful, and confident. By-the-way, you won't mention to anyone that we're going back, will you, please – because I think Beth & Barbara would have forty fits if they knew I was sailing at this time.

Everyone sends love – Peter is writing – please excuse haste, but I have to go up to town immediately.

Much love to you both & every good wish,

Yours ever,

BENJY

1 For the first performance of *Diversions*, Op. 21, for piano (left hand) and orchestra, in which Paul Wittgenstein was the soloist and the Philadelphia Orchestra was conducted by Eugene Ormandy. The press was full of acclaim for Wittgenstein's prowess, but generally unenthusiastic about the work itself. The notice by Edwin H. Schloss in the *Philadelphia Record*, 17 January 1942, is a characteristic example:

As the name implies, Mr Britten's 'Diversions' are in the form of a theme and variations. The 11 movements are ingeniously written and include with deliberate daring (in the case of music for the left hand) two brief toccatas. Musically the 'Diversions' are of no great importance but the score served admirably to exhibit the soloist's special gift, which is remarkable.

Mr Wittgenstein gets unbelievable effects with one hand and has achieved a special artistry of expression that makes an asset of his liabilities. He was warmly received by the audience.

Linton Martin wrote in the *Philadelphia Inquirer* on 17 January:

A one-armed pianist, whose right sleeve hung empty at his side while his left hand swept the keyboard with fairly magical mastery, thrilled the Philadelphia Orchestra audience in the Academy of Music yesterday with a performance of virtuoso brilliance that would have spelled triumph for a greatly gifted artist exercising all ten digits.

An interesting chronicle and assessment of Wittgenstein as a pianist appears in Brian McGuinness's biography of his brother, Ludwig Wittgenstein, the philosopher (*Wittgenstein: A Life, Young Ludwig 1889–1921* (Harmondsworth, Penguin, 1990), pp. 30–31):

A pupil of Leschetizky and destined for a career as a pianist (an evident sign of the mitigation of his father's regime), he made his concert debut in 1913. But in the early months of the war he lost his right arm on the Eastern Front. Returned by the Russians in an exchange of prisoners, he contrived both to be sent back to serve as an aide-de-camp and to teach himself to play with the left hand only (there was the the precedent of Count Zichy for whom Liszt wrote pieces). He commissioned and performed pieces by Richard Strauss, Ravel, and others and continued his career as a concert pianist and a teacher with great success. It will already be apparent that the family provided its own severest critics and Paul's style of playing was not always to the taste of his brother and sisters, let alone of his mother. There was a violence about it which was only in part explained by the exigencies of execution with the left hand. They, who had heard Joachim and turned up their noses at Sarasate, were suspicious of any effect not strictly demanded by the music. (Ravel was to share these doubts.) On recordings and to a modern ear he sounds like a virtuoso indeed but an Austrian virtuoso of the past, richer and less brilliant than a modern performer. The recordings of course, are thicker than those of today and the unnaturalness of his mode of execution, which the Wittgensteins felt sharply, is not there to be seen.

2 The performance was conducted by Daniel Saidenberg, with the Saidenberg Little Symphony, on 22 December. The work – and Pears's performance – received generally a remarkable press reception:

The *New York World-Telegram*, 23 December:

A new work by Benjamin Britten, young English composer, was introduced by Daniel Saidenberg and his Little Symphony at Town Hall last night. The world is the richer for it. Titled Les Illuminations, the composition is for voice and string orchestra, in effect, a setting of poems by the French impressionist Arthur Rimbaud. It is a masterpiece.

The relationship between voice and orchestra is intimate, yet with the intimacy that does not preclude an occasional independence. There are strange cadences and meters in the voice line, sometimes, which are a music in themselves. And the orchestral pattern glows with rich colors and strong rhythms, which make perfect contrast for other moments when the mood is vaporous, sensitive, poetically fine and tender.

Peter Pears, tenor, was the soloist in the work and a creditable accomplishment he turned in, considering that the writing for the voice asks just about everything of a singer, particularly slithery glissandos. At the conclusion the audience cheered, shouted 'Bravi!' and generally carried on. Mr Britten took several bows from a box.

The *New York Sun*, 23 December:

Mr Saidenberg had the honor of sponsoring a new score of authentic interest and musical distinction – the new work by the Americanized Angle Mr Britten.

The accomplishment of Mr Britten was all the more remarkable since the texts of the nine poems by Arthur Rimbaud meant absolutely nothing to this listener. Impressionistic they certainly are and may be expressionistic, too; mysticism pursues mysticism and the whole is pretty confusing. But the important fact is that they mean something to Mr Britten, and that something was enough to compel from him an expression of imposing fantasy and musicianly resource. Considering the amount of so-called absolute music which one tolerates even though a program doubtless existed in the composer's mind, one may accept this as an interesting reversal of that – program music which makes its effect because of its eloquence in an absolute sense.

It is rather difficult to define Mr Britten's idiom in this work, beyond a characterisation of it as Debussy and Stravinsky plus a little honest Britten. It is this last element, with its shrewd treatment of the tenor voice, and its constant elaboration of the string texture around it, which gives the work its arresting force.

Peter Pears did a remarkably skillful job of the difficult vocal part, especially if one considers the limited dynamic range of his voice, and Mr Saidenberg made the score's virtues as plain as he had those of Corelli's 'Christmas Concerto' earlier in the program.

The *New York Times*, 23 December:

Then there were first New York concert performances of David Van Vactor's Bagatelles for string orchestra and Benjamin Britten's 'Les Illuminations' for tenor and string orchestra, based on poems by Rimbaud, with Peter Pears, tenor, as soloist. The Van Vactor work is in a neo-classical vein, with simple, engaging themes, some of them tending to triteness. But it is lightly and gracefully worked out. The Britten score is original and expressive of the poetic world in which Rimbaud wrote. Mr Pears sang effectively in this work.

The music critic of *P.M.* was particularly impressed by Pears's interpretation:

Peter Pears did a magnificent job with the difficult solo part. It is eloquent music – wild, and yet subdued like the memory of a beautiful but terrible nightmare. The wails, tunes and sighs of the music, better than the words can alone, re-create the deep and moving experience of the poet who died insane. Among the many modern works produced hereabouts, it stands out with the brilliance of its title.

Saidenberg and his orchestra were to give a further performance of *Les Illuminations* in New York, on 21 February 1944, when Rose Dirman was the soloist.

3 The *New York Herald-Tribune* of which Virgil Thomson (1896–1989), American composer and critic, was music critic from 1940 to 1954. He studied with Boulanger in Paris in the 1920s. His review of *Paul Bunyan* had not been encouraging. He was even more scathing about this performance of *Les Illuminations*, about which he wrote in the *New York Herald-Tribune* on 23 December:

Mr Britten's 'Illuminations' throw more light on the composer than on the enigmatic figure of Arthur Rimbaud, whose verses are their verbal thread. They are ready-made modernism and ready-made music. Their French declamation and vocal line are exaggerated without being always very expressive; their instrumental accompaniment is little more than a series of bromidic and facile 'effects'. Much of the material is all too reminiscent of 'Scheherazade' and of 'Thais' even; none of it, to this listener, said anything or went anywhere. Only one of the nine numbers made any pretense at independence of line, and that one didn't keep it up more than half way through. I found the work pretentious, banal and utterly disappointing, coming from so gifted a composer. Mr Pears, who sang it [had] neither correct French diction, nor a properly trained voice.

His waspish attitude to Britten and, later, his somewhat idiosyncratic view of the English 'musical Establishment' – 'chiefly controlled by Britten and his publisher, the latter linked by marriage to the throne' (a reference to Erwin Stein's daughter Marion, and her first marriage to the Earl of Harewood, a cousin of the Queen) – are documented in *Virgil Thomson by Virgil Thomson* (London, Weidenfeld and Nicolson, 1967), pp. 343–4, 410 and 415.

361 To Serge Koussevitzky

[*Cablegram*]

AMITYVILLE, NEW YORK: 5 JANUARY 1942

THANK YOU SO MUCH AGAIN FOR WONDERFUL PERFORMANCES[1] LOOKING
FORWARD TO SEEING YOU AGAIN THURSDAY EVENING PRESS HERE
ANNOUNCED PERFORMANCE IN BROOKLYN FRIDAY   WOULD YOU PLEASE
CONFIRM AS I MUST TRY TO CANCEL CONCERT ENGAGEMENT FOR THAT
NIGHT[2]   MANY GREETINGS

BENJAMIN BRITTEN

[*Reply from Koussevitzky pencilled at foot:*]
Press announcement a mistake   Performance for NY & Brooklyn
postponed to February   Warm greetings

SK

1 Koussevitzky and the Boston Symphony Orchestra had given
performances of *Sinfonia da Requiem* in Symphony Hall, Boston, on
2 and 3 January, which Britten had attended (see PFL, plate 158).

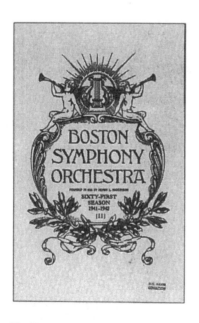

The Boston Symphony Orchestra,
sixty-first season, 1941–2;
programme cover

The first Boston performance of
Sinfonia da Requiem, 2 January 1942

Although the orchestra was scheduled to perform the *Sinfonia* at the Brooklyn Academy of Music on 9 January, the programme was changed. See, however, Letter 369.

2 We have not been able to establish whether the concert engagement to which Britten refers took place.

362 To Elizabeth Sprague Coolidge

c/o Dr. Mayer,
Long Island Home,
Amityville, N.Y.
January 6th 1942.

My dear Mrs. Coolidge,

Here is the programme that you asked for – I took the liberty of signing it! It was so disappointing that you were unable to come, because really Koussevitzky gives the most wonderful performance of my piece, & I really think the orchestra is the best I have ever heard. However he is playing it again at the end of the month in Boston,[1] and I do hope that you will be able to hear it then.

It looks as if I will be leaving the country in about a week's time, as there seem to be plenty of boats going now. It is sickening that I haven't been able to see more of you, and I was so sorry that you were feeling so poorly last week. However as soon as this horrible war is over, I hope to come back at once to this country – I have made so many good friends, and have really had so successful a time here – and then I hope to get to know you really well, and continue a friendship that has begun, I feel, so promisingly! I will give messages from you to Mrs. Bridge, who will be so keen to hear how you are first-hand. I took the great liberty of using your name as a reference the other day, on the exit permit which I have to have before leaving the country. I don't think for a moment that they will bother you, but I do hope all the same that you do not mind.

With warmest wishes for better health, and all possible good luck until I see you again.

Yours affectionately,
BENJY

1 A performance that did not materialize.

363   To Albert Goldberg

123, Louden Avenue,
Amityville, N.Y.
January 20th 1942

My dear Albert,

Please forgive the long silence, but life has just been one damn thing after another – if you ever had tried to leave this country in our year of grace 1942 you'd know what I mean – what with exit permits, priorities, sailing permits etc. etc. etc. To say nothing of the life's work that must continue – which has included dashes to Boston (to hear Koussevitsky do a wonderful show of the Sinfonia) & Philadelphia (to hear Wittgenstein wreck my diversions), and numerous masterpieces of course to be produced. All in all I've been busy, about as busy as <u>you</u> usually are!

Peter & I still don't know when we're sailing, but it may be any day now. The next time you hear from me I'll be the other side of the ocean. Please give my regards to all the orchestra, and thank them for the good time they gave me. It sounds a platitude, but really that little visit was one of my happiest memories of this country.[1]   I hope this mess will be over sooner than we expect & that I can be back & then I can come west & have some more adventures with you all!

Enclosed is a photo I once promised you: and also the score of Berkeley's which I have been meaning to show you.[2]   I do wish you could see your way to doing it. It is quite a slight piece, but very charming & ought to sound well on the strings. Parts can be obtained from Galaxy Music Corporation (17 W46, NYC). Let me know what you decide, because I'd like to tell him when I get back – he's had a tough time in the air-raids in London.

Well, Albert, my dear – excuse scribble, but am as usual hurried – it's been grand knowing you. We'll meet again sometime –

Greetings to Harold, & all the best to you,

Yours,
BENJAMIN

1 Britten refers to the concert in which he took part on 24 November, after which Goldberg wrote to him on the 26th, enclosing

a complete set of press notices. Gassmann's piece [see note 1 to Letter 353] burns me up. He has just started on this job and is turning out exactly the way I expected. He is a pupil of Hindemith and passes as a composer, although the only two things of his I have heard would hardly entitle him to that classification.

Remi Gassman, American composer and critic, was Professor of Theory at Orchestra Hall, Chicago.

2 Berkeley's *Serenade*, Op. 12, for strings, composed in 1939.

364 To Benjamin Britten
From W.H. Auden
[DMBA, *pp. 160–63; typed*]

> as from 1504 Brooklyn Avenue
> Ann Arbor (I move in Tuesday)
> Saturday [31 January 1942]

Dearest Ben,

Very guilty about not having written. Perhaps I can't make myself believe that you are really leaving us. I need scarcely say, my dear, how much I shall miss you and Peter, or how much I love you both.

There is a lot I want to talk to you about, but I must try and say a little of it by letter. I have been thinking a great deal about you and your work during the past year. As you know I think you [are] the white hope of music; for this very reason I am more critical of you than of anybody else, and I think I know something about the dangers that beset you as a man and as an artist because they are my own.

Goodness and Beauty are the results of a perfect balance between Order and Chaos, Bohemianism and Bourgeois Convention.

Bohemian chaos alone ends in a mad jumble of beautiful scraps; Bourgeois convention alone ends in large unfeeling corpses.

Every artist except the supreme masters has a bias one way or the other. The best pair of opposites I can think of in music are Wagner and Strauss. (Technical skill always comes from the bourgeois side of one's nature.)

For middle-class Englishmen like you and me, the danger is of course the second. Your attraction to thin-as-a-board-juveniles, i.e. to the sexless and innocent, is a symptom of this. And I am certain too that it is your denial and evasion of the ~~attractions~~ demands of disorder that is responsible for your attacks of ill-health, ie sickness is your substitute for the Bohemian.

Wherever you go you are and probably always will be surrounded by people who adore you, nurse you, and praise everything you do, e.g. Elisabeth, Peter (Please show this to P to whom all this is also addressed). Up to a certain point this is fine for you, but beware. You see, Bengy dear, you are always tempted to make things too easy for yourself in this way, i.e. to build yourself a warm nest of love (of course when you get it, you find it a little stifling) by playing the lovable talented little boy.

If you are really to develop to your full stature, you will have, I think, to suffer, and make others suffer, in ways which are totally strange to you at present, and against every conscious value that you have; i.e. you will have to be able to say what you never yet had had the right to say – God, I'm a shit.

This is all expressed very muddle-headedly, but try and not misunderstand it, and believe that it is only my love and admiration for you that makes me say it.

Here are one and a half more movements. The second half of the fourth movement will be about the Taxing of the People.[1]

All my love to you both, and God bless you

WYSTAN

1 *For the Time Being* (Auden's 'Christmas Oratorio'): see note 2 to Letter 397.

365 To Benjamin Britten
From W.H. Auden

1504 Brooklyn Avenue
Ann Arbor.
Michigan
Tuesday[1] [February 1942]

Dearest Ben,

Thanks so much for your letter received this morning: I write at once to correct a misunderstanding. Of course I didnt mean to suggest that your relationship with Peter was on the school boy level. Its danger is quite the reverse, of you both letting the marriage be too caring. (The escape for the paederast is that a marriage is impossible). You understand each other so well, that you will always both be tempted to identify yourselves with each other.

I know how tiresome it must be waiting around. I, of course, hope that the migration will be finally cancelled.

Will send you some more Oratorio soon.

Much love
WYSTAN

1 Probably the 10th or 17th (Auden had moved into Brooklyn Avenue on 3 February). In the interim, clearly, Britten had replied to Letter 364. His reply has been lost.

366 To Peggy Brosa

We're <u>definitely</u> sending the photos to-morrow. Barbara's address is: 11, Tryon House, Mallord St., Chelsea, S.W. 3.

c/o William Mayer M.D.
The Long Island Home, Amityville, N.Y.
Feb. 15th 1942

Dearest Peggy,

Thank you so very much for your sweet letter. As you see, we are still around and waiting 'the call'. Getting fed up with the waiting I called the Cunard line the other day & they said there wasn't a boat 'in sight' – what that means, I don't exactly know, but I am afraid it looks as if we're in for a long wait, and now there's this new crisis.[1] (I'm afraid I'm selfish enough to think how it will directly effect [sic] <u>us</u> – but I suppose it's human). It isn't that I'm so keen on leaving – but the waiting is getting abit trying. But I <u>have</u> at last started working again – not very good, but at least pushing a pen around![2] That's why I've been so bad & not answered your letter before. How sweet of Toni to think of Lord Moyne[3] – but I honestly think that it would be dreadfully difficult for him to do anything for us.

There seem to be only two possible courses – (1) that we get some official music jobs, connected either with the services or organising music (2) or just become C.O.s.[4] I think the first will be easier for me because of my commissions – Benny Goodman, the new one for a Harp Concerto,[5] & now the Koussevitzky opera one has come thro' (<u>secret</u> please!).[6] If you think Lord Moyne could help at all, <u>and</u> you & Toni know him well enough to write, & say casually that Peter & I are good musicians etc. etc. (!!), then if the position came up,[7] he'd know who we were.

I do hope your cold is better, and hasn't gone down to your chest. What a rotten time you've been having – it was infuriating that your time here was so messed up. But it was grand to get a glimpse of you, though the time was so terribly short. We have seen abit of the Titleys since then, were over to dinner last night – rather marred by Bill over-drinking abit – & Mildred looked so terribly unhappy.

The pyjamas are <u>wonderful</u>. We both wear them all the time, (only at night actually, haven't got round to wearing them in the day-time yet!,) they are so warm & comfy! The weather's been awfully raw the last few days and really they keep out all the draughts most beautifully! They'll be ideal for the boat & England, & no central-heating. Thank you so very much. Wouldn't you like us to send Toni a pair?

I had lots of mail from England the other day – from Ethel Bridge, who was well & had received our Xmas parcel & was very pleased with it. Marge has taken out a new lease of life – she <u>is</u> a phenomenon! Beth & Kit, very unhappy over everything – hating the war, & the boredom. Poor dears, I am afraid Churchill's[8] flowery phrases can't have done much to relieve their worries this afternoon – what an impossible old gas-bag he is, just like a Baptist minister! I wish he, and all that crowd would go. If they <u>are</u> going to have a war, I wish they'd do it properly – actually, well, you know what I feel – & we all feel . . .

Apologies for the long rambly letter – but it is late at night, & I've been working quite hard to-day. When does Toni go to Seattle? Give him my love, & all good wishes.

Had a battle (financial) with B & H the other day, & <u>won</u> – by going downtown to Max Winkler, & appealing to him as man-to-man . . . !!!   I asked for a statement of monies owing to me, & they sent me one showing that <u>I owed them</u> more than $1,000!!

The dirty swine ——

Much love, take care of yourself.

BEN

Love from all here.

Peter is copying out enormous bits of Beethoven, Wagner, etc. etc. because Max Winkler wants the new violin book. Is it alright to send them along soon for Toni to bow & finger at his leisure? It is good to have a chore like this to do, at this time, so that's why we're doing it now.

1 See Letter 369 from Pears to the Brosas. The 'crisis' was the possibility of being drafted for military service in the USA.

2 One of the works that was taking shape at this time was the *Hymn to St Cecilia*, Op. 27. Britten's reference to 'working again' should also be read in the context of his remark to David Rothman, which we attempt to elucidate in note 1 to Letter 351. There was indeed a significantly mute period from the completion of the *Scottish Ballad* and *An American Overture* in October 1941 until March/April 1942 when, on the journey home, he completed the *Hymn* and *A Ceremony of Carols*, Op. 28. It is that 'block' to which Beata refers in TP, where, misleadingly, her remark seems to be linked with the difficulties Britten had with the composition of the *Sinfonia da Requiem*.

3 The first Baron Moyne (1880–1944), statesman and Colonial Secretary from 1941 to 1942. He was assassinated in Cairo in November 1944.

4 Conscientious Objectors to military service.

5 Britten had been approached by Edna Phillips, the American harpist. A signed contract (dated 28 February 1942) between Britten and Phillips required the proposed concerto to be composed by 1 August, and scored by 31 October. The composer was to receive $1000 as a fee, Miss Phillips retaining a five-year period of exclusivity. The concerto was not composed, and perhaps never started: no sketches survive. See, however, Letter 374.

6 The commission from Koussevitzky to compose *Peter Grimes*. The Koussevitzky Music Foundation was established after the death of Mme Koussevitzky (on 11 January), and all works commissioned by it were required to be dedicated to her memory, as was *Peter Grimes*, when completed in 1945. According to a long article in *Time*, 16 February 1948, published to coincide with the first performance of the opera at the Met., 'Koussevitzky gave [Britten] $200 a month for five months to write an opera. Says Koussevitzky: "If he had asked more we would have paid it".' Britten must have discussed the proposal with Koussevitzky when he was in Boston in January for the performances of the *Sinfonia da Requiem*, and perhaps again in New York in March. In this letter he clearly refers to written confirmation of the commission.

It was also at about this time that Britten approached Christopher Isherwood to collaborate with him and Pears on the project, inviting Isherwood to write the libretto – a characteristic example of his turning to friends from the past who had the appropriate experience to participate in a new scheme. Isherwood rejected the offer in a letter written on 18 February 1942 from Haverford, Pennsylvania: see PGPB, p. 35, where the letter is reproduced in full. In 1981 Isherwood added a further comment about his decision to refuse Britten's offer:

How fortunate that I *didn't* attempt to write the opera! I was absolutely convinced that it wouldn't work. And, when I saw it on stage, I was astonished – I mean, of course, as a dramatic piece – I never doubted that Ben, as a composer, could rise to *any* occasion!

(PGPB, p. 36)

Undoubtedly, it was a similar attachment to former collaborators that led the composer, on his return to England, to approach Montagu Slater.

7 Lord Moyne had been much involved in the creation of CEMA, the Council for the Encouragement of Music and the Arts, the wartime forerunner of the Arts Council. Perhaps the 'position' to which Britten refers was connected with the new organization.

8 British Prime Minister and wartime leader from 1940 to 1945. Singapore had been attacked by Japanese forces on 8 February.

367 To Kit Welford
[EWB, *pp. 174–6*]

c/o Dr. Mayer,
Long Island Home,
Amityville, N.Y.
March 1st 1942

My dear Kit,

Your letter arrived a few days ago, very much delayed like all the mail these days. Thank you very much for it. I am sorry I have been so bad about writing lately, but I'm afraid I can never get up much enthusiasm about letter-writing, finding that a pen for me moves more easily in crotchets than in letters; and also, these days, when things happen so quickly, & the general outlook changes so fast, that it is hopeless to write about one's life at all, knowing perfectly well that the letter will be hopelessly out of date on arrival. Anyhow, as you would imagine, my life has been, like everyone else's over here, changed somewhat by the declaration of war,[1] and still to this moment I am not quite sure what will happen to me. I have certain things I want to do & which I may or may not be able to do – when I know I'll let you & Beth know, of course. Until this happens, one tries to go on working – luckily, I believe in my work, and so don't fall into the obvious dangers of half-heartedness, which so many artists feel like these days – but working is difficult, because there are so many distractions, endless red-tape, business matters etc. which have nothing to do & seriously interfere with the extraordinarily complicated matter of writing music. Actually, I have had a pretty good success this season, far and away better than any other – Koussevitsky has taken me up big, and I have had good successes with a string quartet, Les Illuminations (which Peter has sung a few times) and a show with the Philadelphia under

Ormandy.[2]   Which is all gratifying. But what really worries me
now is that I have reached a definite turning point in my work,
& what I most want is to be able to think & think & work & work,
completely undistracted for a good period of time. If it were in
normal times this would be completely possible – but, my problem
is only that of probably about 40,000,000 young ambitious young
men. I cannot tell you how much I agree with and admire your
letter. I am so pleased that you have thought things out so
carefully. From a very different angle I have come to an identical
point-of-view (re discipline & obedience) – but in art, as you
know, the bias is to the other direction, that of anarchy and
romantic 'freedom'. A carefully chosen discipline is the only
possible course.[3]   I am terribly sorry that you are having such a
difficult time. It is only small comfort to think that so many others
are in similar positions, and that it can't last for ever.

America has been strange since the actually [sic] entry into the
war. At first there was terrific excitement, 'unity' (how often have
we heard that word!), and flag waving. Now most of the first two
have disappeared – after all the Pacific is a mighty long way away,
and bad news (vide, China, Spain, Poland, London, Coventry ad
infinitum) grows boring after atime, unless you happen to have
a brother or an aunt near the danger spot. Politics are filthy here,
as you know, and so after the first shock, people are squabbling
in the highest places as before. The flag-waving remains, because
so many people like doing it, and adore wearing uniforms (without
exception hideous) – but it makes me sick, especially as I loathe the
Star-Spangled-Banner, and its awkward harmonies. There has been
a certain effort to ban German & Italian music, which hasn't luckily
succeeded, & apart from some ludicrous restrictions on enemy
aliens (99% refugees of course – everyone knows that most of the
fifth columnists are settled citizens of, maybe, German extraction)
people have kept their heads. Of course everyone is numbered,
docketed, finger printed, photographed, registered – but one gets
used to that. The Radio, you mentioned 'news', is fantastic here of
course. On the medium wave-length, there must be 100 different
stations everyone can get – & from every one is blared forth the
most startling news items, preceeded, interrupted & concluded
by the most blatant and, usually, intimate advertisements.

Newspapers, except maybe the Times, are completely unreliable.
The magnates have just discovered, I gather, that good news sells
best, so judging by head-lines, the Jap fleet has been sunk twice-
over, Singapore was invincible until a day or so before it fell,[4] ditto,

the Phillipines,[5] Rangoon,[6] & I suppose Java[7] et al. There is here as much anti-British feeling as there is Anti-Yank with you. The British are stupid here – so superior, and the Gneisenau & Scharnhorst episode,[8] Libyan news,[9] & Singapore coming all together have made so many little arm-chair strategists & 'know-alls' go about saying that the British have never won a war & now are depending upon Russia & America to do the job. Churchill goes over big – especially the flowery phrases . . . . well . . . . Cripps[10] has a good press, too. But India stinks. So might their own treatment of the negros, but that doesn't occur to them. The thing that really is bringing the war home is the rationing of tyres, & sugar (consequently Coca-Cola).

I am putting a note to Beth in this – please tell her all the news – I haven't got time to write her a long letter I'm afraid. I was delighted to hear about the Yacht designing;[11] I haven't been able to get a copy of the magazine yet, but I'm hoping too. It must have been a thrill. Have you anymore coming along?

Please excuse writing – never my strongest point!

Yours ever,

BEN.

1 America had entered the war on 8 December 1941.

2 Eugene Ormandy (1899–1985), American conductor of Hungarian origin. He became sole director of the Philadelphia Orchestra in 1938, an appointment he held for over forty years.

3 This sentence and Britten's preceding comments probably reflect the letter that he had received from Auden in January (see Letter 364 and Donald Mitchell, 'Introduction in the Shape of a Memoir', in DVDM, pp. 21–3.)

4 On 15 February Singapore had surrendered to the Japanese.

5 A Japanese invasion force had made a landing at Lingayen on 21 December and reached Manila on 2 January 1942.

6 Rangoon had fallen to the Japanese on 10 March.

7 Japanese forces had landed on Java on 28 February.

8 Sister battleships of the German Navy which invariably operated together. During 1941 both ships were harboured at Brest where they were subjected to continual aerial attacks. To escape, they broke out from Brest in February 1942, bound for Germany in a daring operation via the English Channel. They were struck by mines, but reached port.

9 On 21 January Rommel had launched a new offensive in the Western Desert.

10 Sir Stafford Cripps (1889–1952), statesman and lawyer. Leader of the
    House of Commons and Lord Privy Seal in 1942 and Minister of
    Aircraft Production from 1942 to 1945.

11 Kit Welford had taken up yacht-designing and won a competition.
    An article by him was published in *Yachting Monthly* in the summer
    issue of 1941.

368 To Beata Mayer

c/o William Mayer, M.D.
The Long Island Home
Amityville N.Y.
March 3rd 1942

My dear Beatty,

So sorry to have come into the office yesterday in such a dismal
state – it was very selfish of me, only you shouldn't give the
impression of being so sympathetic. I've got to remember that even
if things do seem just about at their bloodiest for me, that it is
exactly the same for about 140 millions of other people. Sorry!

I hope Max[1] has heard about his exam.

I expect to be in sometime later this week and we'll drown our
sorrows in the Russian Tea Room.[2]

Much love to you, in haste,

BEN

1 Max Wachstein (1905–1965), who was to be Beata's first husband,
   was a doctor.

2 On West 57th Street, famous as a rendezvous for New Yorkers and
   close to Carnegie Hall.

369 To Antonio and Peggy Brosa
From Peter Pears and Benjamin Britten

Amityville Long Island, N.Y.
Tuesday [10 March 1942]

My dear Peggy and Toni

You see the familiar heading – We are Still here – but really only
for a few days more now – The incompetence and stupidity of
official America is finally overcome. Our draft board has graciously
permitted us to be off, and off we go early next week. In the
meantime we have been busying ourselves with the next volume
of the Violin book, which Winkler says he would like to have as

soon as you have finished it. If Tony thinks he can't manage to
correct the proofs (when they arrive) probably he could get B &
H to have them done for him, or perhaps some student at Madison
could do them. It hardly seems worth sending them back to
England.

Life goes on here in much the same way – Tempers are apt to
get a little quicker in these days, and William finds the Home a
little trying. Bill Titley is probably going into the Navy quite soon
& Mildred will be more or less in charge. (This may be hush-hush!)

It was so lovely to see you both here and in New York. It made
such a difference to all these boring days waiting. I should like to
think we should be seeing you again before we go, – but this time
it looks fairly certain. The only good thing is that they've just
waited long enough so that Ben will be able to hear the Sinfonia,
when Koussy does it here in Brooklyn on Friday & in Carnegie
on Saturday.[1] Wittgenstein is also playing his piece on Friday at
3.30–4.30 on CBS. Do listen if you can, tho' I expect it will be bad.

Elizabeth is much better from her grippe, though this waiting
doesn't help her either. William is well again too. Michael turned
up for the weekend, improved by the shaving of his upper lip and
in good form. We see Beata a lot, who finds that grand old all-
English firm of Boosey & Hawkes harder to bear each week. We
had lunch with her the other day when who should come
bouncing in but La Reine d'Escondido, (Ethel, not the other one)
from whom we received the Cut Direct! We saw Gene & Janet[2] –
he very white and puffy, she amusing.

One of [the] things about going back is that we shall be arriving
at such a heavenly time –   April is such a marvellous month.
Think of seeing real spring again –   Oh! Peggy and Toni, when
shall we all see it together again.   Pray God, it will be soon.

I must stop as Ben wants to write a P.S.

> Much love to you both, my dears.
> Yours always
> PETER

Dearest P. & T.

As Peter has told you it is soon now – & in some ways I'm glad,
as this wait hasn't been fun. But now – how I wish I weren't
going —— there are so many people I love here and life in
England isn't going to be fun. But pray God it won't be for long,
and that we'll all be together again soon. Do write sometimes and

let us know how civilisation is going! C/o Barbara, or Ralph
Hawkes will always reach us.

I do hope you don't mind doing the Violin book, Toni – but in
a way it may be a good investment – when we're old and gray it
may be nice to have $10 a year to buy candies with –!

I'll give your love to everyone. It'll be lovely but a bit difficult to
see Ethel again.

I do hope that those old —–'s (guess who?)[3] will get you some
date to play the old concerto again Toni; but perhaps when we
meet I'll have a nice new one for you! So glad Seattle was such a
success. Hope old T.B.[4] wasn't too impossible.

All my love, take care of yourselves
& pray for us occasionally!
Au revoir.
BENJY

1 On the 13th and 14th, which reinstated the cancelled performances
   in January. Heinsheimer recalled that Richard Burgin, Koussevitzky's
   assistant conductor, gave an additional performance of the *Sinfonia*
   in New Haven ('Born in Exile', *Opera News*, 42/7, 10 December 1977).

2 Eugene Goossens and his second (American) wife, Janet (née Lewis),
   whom he had married in 1930.

3 Probably a reference to the management of Boosey & Hawkes' Artists' Bureau.

4 Sir Thomas Beecham, who was conductor of the Seattle Symphony
   Orchestra, 1941–3.

370 To William and Elizabeth Mayer

Johnson Line, Sweden.
Boston
Wednesday [25 March 1942]

My dearest William & Elizabeth,

Just in case we are allowed to send letters from here —– this is
just to surprise you! I don't think one can say much because I am
sure that all one has observed on board must be extremely secret
and not to be given away till we reach England. Well – nine days
from New York to Boston![1]   Not an exciting story, in fact <u>very,
very</u> boring. We are now lying here for repairs, but God knows how
long for. We're hoping against hope to be allowed on shore, but
doesn't seem likely.

Can't say much about life on board, but, although it might be
more uncomfortable & food could be alot worse, the change from
Amityville is just too great. We are really only now fully realising
what a civilised life we have been living with your dear selves.
Well – goodbye for the present to that; let's hope it won't be for
long. In the meantime, look after yourselves; be good & careful
(as Barbara always says!), and we'll all be together again quite soon.

No more – I hope they'll let some of this thro'. Love from us
both.

Wednesday – your day in New York, William[2] – how horrible it
is not being with you.

P.T.O.

BEN

P.S.   I was unfortunately not allowed to bring any of my last-minuit
music (M.S.) – censors took it. But I told them to send it to
Heinsheimer when it was cleared with a note asking him to send
it to me in London when it was cleared. Could you please,
Elizabeth, remind him to do this as soon as possible, since there's
a lot of important stuff among it.[3]

[*PP's hand*:] Much much love to you both!

PETER

1 Britten and Pears boarded the MS *Axel Johnson* at New York on 16
March. The event, as we have seen in note 3 to Letter 297, was
recorded in Mrs Mayer's diary: 'I bring B. and P. to the boat at
3 p.m.' In the margin she wrote: 'The Ides of March'. After waiting
several days in New York and stopping at other places on its journey
up the coast, the boat reached Boston on 25 March; but the actual
crossing was made from the port of Halifax, Nova Scotia. The total
journey took, it seems, nearly five weeks, but only twelve days of
these were spent on the Atlantic. Mrs Mayer's diary for 17 April, the
day they arrived in England, reads: 'Cable from Ben and Peter.'
Throughout the voyage Britten was busy composing the *Hymn to St
Cecilia* and *A Ceremony of Carols*, Op. 28 – the former is inscribed 'At
sea, M.S. Axel Johnson, 2 April 1942', and the latter, 'At sea, M.S.
Axel Johnson, Spring 1942'.

The New York customs authorities relieved Britten of the manuscripts he was carrying, presumably on the grounds of security,
perhaps suspicious that they represented some form of coded message or information. On arrival, his manuscripts were yet again temporarily confiscated, this time by the English authorities. See note 3
below and PFL, plate 159.

2 The Long Island Home maintained a New York office, where prospective patients were interviewed. Letter 386 suggests that Dr Mayer
was in weekly attendance on a Wednesday.

3 Elizabeth Mayer retrieved the composer's music and wrote to him
on 8 April:

I have been in the city on Monday last [6 April], and thanks to my authorizing
papers I got everything that belongs to you, at least I think it is everything.
Everybody was very nice and polite, and regretted, the only nuisance is
really that you may have needed the Music, and there was also quite a
bunch of blank MM [trade name] paper which you may have needed. The
important thing is that it is here with me, and I thought it best to wait until
you tell me where to send it. I even think I might send it by a personal
messenger. Should I not have photostatic copies before trusting it to the
winds and waters? There are the Michelangelo Sonnets, the little Sketchbook,
the School-Anthem ['God, who created me' (H.C. Beeching)], four sheets of
the Ode [Hymn to St Cecilia] and six double-sided pages of the Clarinet
Concerto, and one sheet: Moderato ma commodo (Hymn?) [Voluntary in
D minor, for organ solo].

All the above manuscripts were returned to Britten with the exception
of the pages from Hymn to St Cecilia and the organ voluntary. In 1980
these became part of the Elizabeth Mayer Collection at the Archive,
along with a number of other highly important manuscripts, including the composition sketches of the Violin Concerto, Les Illuminations, Diversions and the First String Quartet.

To Beata Mayer
From Peter Pears and Benjamin Britten
[Picture postcard:Band Stand in Public Gardens,
Halifax, Nova Scotia, Canada]

[Halifax]
[31 March 1942]

Beatty dear,

So far so good though God how slow & boring! This town is the
bottom of the pit – Much love to you. We have finished the Vanilla
Gipfeln![1] They were fine –

PETER

Much love,
BEN.

1 Vanilla Kipferln, a Viennese speciality: hazelnut cookies, halfmoon in
shape, and much relished by Pears and Britten. These were probably
made as a farewell gift by Beata's Viennese mother-in-law to be, Mrs
Wachstein.

The Return to England:
The Writing of *Grimes*
1942–1945

'Who can turn skies back
and begin again?'
Peter Grimes Act 1 Scene 2

Chronology: 1942–1945

Year	Events	Compositions
1942	*17 April*: Britten and Pears arrive home. They register as conscientious objectors and are later exempted from military service. Britten required to write radio incidental music and give concerts for CEMA. He lives at Snape *22 July*: UK première of *Sinfonia da Requiem* at Proms *September*: Moves to 104a Cheyne Walk, SW10, with Pears *23 September*: First performance of the *Michelangelo Sonnets*, at Wigmore Hall, London *22 November*: First performance of *Hymn to St Cecilia* (BBC broadcast) *5 December*: First performance of *A Ceremony of Carols*, in Norwich	*April*: *Hymn to St Cecilia*, Op. 27 (Auden) *A Ceremony of Carols*, Op. 28 *July–September*: BBC: *Appointment* (Norman Corwin); *An American in England* (with CBS, New York; Corwin); *Lumberjacks of America* (Ranald MacDougall); *The Man Born to be King* (Dorothy L. Sayers); *Britain to America* (with NBC, New York; MacNeice)
1943	*February*: Moves to 45a St John's Wood High Street, NW8, Britten's and Pears's London home until 1946 *March–April*: Britten in hospital with measles *15 October*: First performance of the *Serenade*, with Pears and Dennis Brain as soloists, at Wigmore Hall	*February*: BBC: *The Four Freedoms, No. 1: Pericles* (MacNeice) *March–April*: *Serenade*, Op. 31 *May*: Prelude and Fugue, Op. 29, for strings *July*: *Rejoice in the Lamb*, Op. 30 *October–November*: BBC: *The Rescue* (Edward Sackville-West) *December*: *The Ballad of Little Musgrave and Lady Barnard*
1944	*January*: Begins work on the composition of *Peter Grimes*	*November*: *Festival Te Deum*, Op. 32 BBC: *A Poet's Christmas*: 'A Shepherd's Carol' and 'Chorale after an Old French Carol' (Auden)

Year	Events	Compositions
1945	*8–13 March*: Gives recitals in Paris with Pears *7 May*: Germany surrenders *8 May*: VE Day marks end of European war *7 June*: First performance of *Peter Grimes* at Sadler's Wells, London *July*: Concert tour with Yehudi Menuhin of German concentration camps, including Belsen *6 and 9 August*: Atomic bombs dropped on Hiroshima and Nagasaki *14 August*: Japanese surrender. VJ Day marks end of Pacific war *21 November*: First performance of String Quartet No. 2, at Wigmore Hall *22 November*: First performance of *Donne Sonnets*, at Wigmore Hall	*10 February*: *Peter Grimes*, Op. 33 *19 August*: *The Holy Sonnets of John Donne*, Op. 35 *October*: Theatre: *This Way to the Tomb* (Ronald Duncan) String Quartet No. 2, Op. 36 *December*: Film: *Instruments of the Orchestra* (*The Young Person's Guide to the Orchestra*, Op. 34)

372 To Elizabeth Mayer
From Peter Pears

108A Castelnau
Barnes S.W. 13.
London[1]
April 19th 1942.

Dearest Elizabeth –

It was so wonderful to have your two dear letters – Ben & I collected them when we went up to Boosey & Hawkes the day after we arrived[2] (I was unlucky. My letter hasn't arrived yet –   I hope it will & that it isn't lost –   I'm sure it isn't because of the change of address, as I've had several other letters forwarded from there). Your writing, every word you write, even the paper & the type, all bring us back so closely together that it's as if we never left you. Indeed we haven't. These last three years are part of us all –   They <u>are</u> our very selves. They have meant more to me than any other years of my life.   I only <u>began</u> to live three years ago – and my life will only go on again when Ben and I come back to you, Elizabeth. This cannot be called life here. It is just an intermission.

We had a prolonged and rather boring journey. We sat in New York for several days & again in other places on the way up the coast – & the actual Atlantic crossing only took twelve days – but they were spent in the most desolate company – callow, foul mouthed, witless recruits. How we missed you and William – we went over every Amityville routine from William's turning the heat down to your pouring your Rum into your tea, trying to get spirited back to you – alas! the boat went on. The whole thing took nearly 5 weeks. Ben worked very well on the boat. They took away his St. Cecilia & Clarinet Concerto ms. away from him at the N.Y. customs, so he wrote it [the *Hymn*] all out again and finished it (very lovely!) and also wrote 7 Christmas carols for women's voices & Harp![3] Very sweet and chockfull of charm! We had rather a miserable cabin, very near the huge provisions Ice box, and the smell & heat were intolerable, & it was difficult for him as people seemed to whistle up & down the corridor all day! But he was very patient. I, of course, couldn't sing at all – & then when we got to England, they took away his MS. again – though they say they will forward them all.

Coming back here has been the most odd and mixed experience. The countryside looking dazzlingly green – uniforms everywhere

– destruction so cleared up that it looks like peacetime planning –
the starchy food that fills but does not nourish – no fruit or cream
at all – little butter – three eggs a month – and so on – but one's
friends are very glad to see one & couldn't be more welcoming.
My father and mother are both looking a lot older & have moved
house to a rather pleasant flat with a lovely little garden full of
daffodils & hyacinths. The English gardens are lovely, and the trees
are very fresh and green. The sun seems to take hours to set here.
Ben and I sat on the platform when we went down to see Beth,[4]
and it was warm and lovely, and the sun barely moved. Ralph
was exceedingly pleased to see Ben, so was Arthur Bliss whom he
went to see at the BBC.   I called Basil[5] at Birmingham; he was
delighted and surprised to hear me, but I can't see him just yet –
it's too expensive to go down there & he is very busy. The Quartet
is in print & looks very nice.   Your pictures arrived at Barbara's –
very welcome.   It is lovely to have them, they are so good of you
and will carry us over till we see you again. What a good idea of
yours it was to have Lotte[6] down to Amityville, so that we could
have you in your proper setting – !   Our plans are of course
vague.   We have to register as pacifists which will take a little
time. I hope very much that I shall be able to work with the
Quakers[7] – I think I shall join them. If only I were a better person!
    Last night there was the enclosed cutting in the paper. I'm
dreadfully afraid it means Roger[8] has gone. It is bitterly sad. It
was such a vile job & such hideous company. Alas! alas! he was a
sweet dear person.
    Dearest Elizabeth, all my love to you. I think of you always.
Your letters make me cry but they make me brave too. Write again.
Embrace William & Beata for me.

always your
PETER.

1   Pears's parents' address, which they shared with a friend, Margot
    Baker. Britten and Pears stayed there on their return from the USA,
    and Pears was to use his parents' address as a post restante until he
    and Britten moved to 104A Cheyne Walk in September. Mrs Pears
    was to write to Elizabeth Mayer on 14 September:

    [. . .] the boys as I call them have not yet got their own flat and are moving
    about very often people lending them their flats, they long to be settled but
    the flat must be near the B.B.C. as so much of their work is there.

2   They had disembarked at Liverpool on 17 April.

3   *A Ceremony of Carols*: see note 5 to Letter 374.

4 At Northwood. See also EWB, p. 177, for Beth's account of her brother's return.

5 Basil Douglas (b. 1914), English music administrator and agent. He was educated at Oxford and after coming down aspired to be a singer, which took him to study in Germany, to Munich and the Mayer family. After his return to London he shared the Charlotte Street flat with Pears and Trevor Harvey and thus got to know Britten. From 1936 to 1950 he was on the music staff of the BBC, and then at Britten's and Pears's request, became General Manager of the English Opera Group until 1959. He later founded the artists' agency which bears his name.

6 Lotte Jacobi (1896–1990), the distinguished photographer. See PFL, plates 149–53, and obituaries in the *Independent*, 11 May, *The Times*, 12 May, and the *Guardian*, 6 May 1990. See also Kelly Wise (ed.), *Lotte Jacobi* (Danbury, New Hampshire, Addison House, 1978), in which will be found a magnificent joint portrait of Britten and Pears at Amityville in 1939 and of Auden in New York in 1946 (plates 64 and 65).

7 On returning from the USA and taking up residence in London, Britten and Pears were in close touch with Friends House, the centre of the Friends War Relief Service. It was natural for the two pacifists to make this connection, the more so as Pears had distinguished Quaker forebears – he was a descendant of Elizabeth Fry. In May, Britten was to inform his Tribunal that he might find 'a spiritual home' with the Quakers (see note 1 to Letter 375). The Friends House connection was to lead to Britten and Pears generating a series of four concerts given in aid of the Friends War Relief Service and to their getting to know Olive Zorian, the violinist (see note 4 to Letter 458), who was herself a Quaker and a member of the Friends House Meeting. The Quaker connection was to extend beyond wartime, and Pears and Britten continued to give concerts at Friends House in the fifties and sixties, including a memorial concert for Zorian on 26 November 1966.

Two letters from Pears's mother, Jessie, addressed to Mrs Mayer, show how close members of the family perceived Britten's and Pears's wartime musical activities and the progress of their careers:

[*18 November 1943*]

I don't know how often you hear from Peter & Ben, they are both very busy men and doing wonderfully well at their work. Ben is composing some very good works that are broadcast, for Peter to sing to, as well as other music, they work together so well, and Peter as well as belonging to the Sadlers Wells Opera Coy, does a lot of singing & teaches, and works for the Friends.

[*Undated*]

Our very dear Peter is going ahead in his profession, and I am glad to say he is able at the same time to help the war cause by singing at concerts, in fact getting concerts up for the Quakers they are doing such wonderful work, Peter by one concert made £30 and another at Glasgow £70 a packed house. Benjamin is very busy also he is down in the country so I seldom see him, he is such a dear.

8 Roger Burney (1919–1942), a friend of Britten and Pears, but especially of Pears. He was born of a military family, was educated at Wellington and Cambridge, where he held a Kitchener Scholarship at Peterhouse. While at university he became a convinced pacifist but changed his views after the sinking by the Germans of the *Athenia*, a British passenger liner. He then enlisted in the Royal Navy, serving as a Sub-Lieutenant in the Royal Naval Volunteer Reserve. While on active service he had visited New York in 1941, when Elizabeth Mayer's Diary records various meetings with Burney, Britten and Pears in October and November. Burney was a member of the crew of the French submarine *Surcouf*, lost with all hands in February 1942. Britten was to include him among the four dedicatees of *War Requiem* (Source: James Rusbridger).

Letter envelope addressed to Roger Burney: 'Return to Sender Ship Overdue'

373 **To Ursula Nettleship**
From Peter Pears

~~67 Hallam St. W. 1.~~
108A, Castelnau,
Barnes, S.W. 13.
Riverside 5751
[April 1942]

My dear Ursula,

Ben and I are back at last! and would awfully like to see you. Are
you ever in London nowadays? I know you're working terribly
hard with CEMA[1] – it sounds wonderful work. But do let
me know if there's a chance to see you. There's such a lot to talk
about –

Much love to you
PETER

1 A contemporary publicity document outlined the role of CEMA:

> The central policy of the Council is to maintain the highest possible standard
> in our national arts of music, drama and painting at a time these things are
> threatened and when, too, they may mean more in the life of the country
> than they have ever meant before. An essential part of the plan is to carry
> the arts to those places which, for one reason or another, are cut off from
> their enjoyment. Thus it is hoped to give encouragement and refreshment
> to populations suffering from the strain and anxiety of war, while, at the
> same time, substantial help will be given to the professional artists engaged.

Eric Walter White (1905–1985), the pioneering Britten biographer,
was secretary of the organization from 1942. He continued to work
for the Arts Council (which replaced CEMA in 1946) until 1971. He
contributed much to the early development of serious Britten studies.
See also Rory Coonan, 'Beacon of culture in a wartime blackout',
Independent, 23 August 1990, in which the author outlines the role of
CEMA in wartime and its evolution in 1946 into the Arts Council of
Great Britain.

374 **To Elizabeth Mayer**

P.S. Thank you for doing so much about the MS. B & H cabled
Heinsheimer to send them all over air-mail at once so I do hope
that they've done it. Any more bothers?

11, Tryon House,
Mallord St., S.W. 3.[1]
4 May 1942

My dearest Elizabeth,

What lovely letters my dear. Thank you so very much for them,
and for doing all you have done. I am sorry not to have written
before, but life has been absolutely hectic, and what is more I've
expected everyday that there would be a big piece of news, such
as what I am going to do for the next year or so . . . to tell you,
and that it would be better to wait a day or so before writing. But
it never happens, & so we together will go thro' the tribunal.[2]
It won't be pleasant, but what is these days? Except, of course,
being with the family here, and some very dear friends. People
haven't changed – merely accentuated their qualities – the nice
ones, much nicer, & the unpleasant ones, a little worse. The first
impression of the country is a sort of drab shabiness. All the
excitement of the 'blitz' (except for isolated spots) has died down,
& people seem very, very tired. Musical life doesn't really exist,
except for this extraordinary demand for organised sound, which
makes people crowd into the Albert Hall, to hear bad orchestras,
conducted by mediocre conductors, under the worst acoustic
conditions possible, play a few popular classics (mainly Beethoven,
& then only 3, 5, or 7). Scarcely a musical life. But maybe more
exists outside London; one thing this war has done is to tend to
decentralise things. So far people have all been nice to me, and
there has been no suggestion of vindictiveness. In one or two
places, <u>over</u>-kindness, which makes one suspicious. We (P. & I)
have played all the new stuff to Ralph – the Michelangelo made a
great impression – & on the strength of it Peter has had this Tales
of Hoffmann offer (to sing Hoffmann) which will be splendid
experience for him.[3] He's singing <u>so</u> well, & everyone is surprised
& delighted – especially Basil, who seems to have grown up
enormously. Enid & Montagu Slater are delightful & we have
seen a lot of them – M. has taken to Grimes like a duck to water
& the opera is <u>leaping</u> ahead. It is very exciting – I must write &
tell Koussey about it. He has splendid ideas. It is getting more and
more an opera about the community, whose life is 'illuminated'
for this moment by the tragedy of the murders. Ellen is growing
in importance, & there are fine minor characters, such as the
Parson, pub-keeper, 'quack'-apothecary, & doctor. The St. Cecilia[4]
is finished (on the boat, as well as 7 Christmas Carols[5] – one had

to alleviate the boredom!) – very quiet & reserved. I think quite
nice. Dedicated to you, my dear, if you'll have it. Not the big
thing yet, but that'll be later. My mind is busy with Harp Concerto,
and the Sonata for orchestra,[6] in the moments when the opera
doesn't dominate everything. So you see, I'm not impotent yet – if
<u>only</u> one had the chance to work. But I'll make it, never fear! I
go backwards & forwards from Beth (Northwood) to Barbara
(Chelsea) – mostly at the former. They are such dears, and seem
immeasurably improved – but perhaps I've just got the distance
that was necessary to appreciate them. Very sympathetic &
thoughtful & unselfish in every way. Hedli & Louis Macneice I've
seen alot of, & they're nice too. Louis very important, & writing
impressive works for the BBC. – rather more impressive
bombastically than aesthetically——

So glad that Wystan has the Guggenheim[7] – how does that affect
the army position? I do hope he can avoid that, & get on with
work he can really do. And Colin[8] too. No word from either of
them, but I must write myself, when I get a second.

Well, my dearest E., I miss you more than I can say – at every
turn. How I shall get on in all these tribu-lations to come without
you I don't know. But your photos, & knowing that you're thinking
about me, help alot. And to have known you & been with you
helps most of all. And dear William too – give him lots of love from
me, & Beata, of course too. Do tell her from me that returning to
Europe isn't all that one imagines – it is pretty sordid, and although
the country is <u>unbelievably</u> beautiful (& the cuckoo!!), the accent
is horrible, and there is a provincialism & lack of vitality that makes
one yearn for the other side.

Love to you all , to Chris & Michael when you see them. Isn't it
hell about Roger? Poor, poor dear – & poor us too without him.
Please write again & soon.

All my love,
BEN

1 Barbara Britten's flat in Chelsea. Britten used his sister's flat as his
   London base until late in 1942. He was writing from a new address
   in November. See Letter 399.

2 See note 1 to Letter 375. Pears's tribunal, however, took place later
   than Britten's first hearing.

3 Pears sang the role of Hoffmann (in Offenbach's opera) for the first
   time on 6 May at the Strand Theatre, London, in a production by
   George Kirsta for Albion Opera Limited, conducted alternately by

Walter Susskind and Hans F. Redlich. Pears shared the role with the English tenor, Henry Wendon (1900–1964), who had made his operatic début at the Old Vic as Radames (*Aida*) in 1925.

In a letter to Elizabeth Mayer, dated 10 May, he wrote:

My particular excitement was that I was asked at very short notice to sing the title role in "Tales of Hoffmann" now running here in an elaborate production. Oddly enough, I wasn't at all nervous at my first performance last Wednesday afternoon & apparently was a big success & am going on tour in two weeks when we have finished in London. It's a big role with a lot of singing, & though I haven't even now after 4 performances sung it as well as I should like to, it goes across alright! I do wish you could be here to see it! I have to wear a beautiful long blue Victorian coat, & make violent love & generally behave in a very Wertherian fashion! But it's very good experience.

The success of the production led to a national tour, including Scotland. (See Letters 376 and 383.)

4 Britten had certainly begun to consider (if not actually to compose) his setting of Auden's *Hymn to St Cecilia* in the summer of 1940. Auden wrote to him on 15 July from Williamsburg, Massachusetts:

I shall be delighted too to enlarge St. Cecilia; I was only afraid of making her too fat. I will wait though till you come and I can discuss with you exactly what is best.

and later that same year:

Here is another movement for the Cecilia Ode. I tried to do yet another but it didn't come off. If you really need it, though, I'll try again.

In August and September Britten and Auden had met in Massachusetts, where work on the *Hymn* continued.

Composition of the work, however, would appear not to have been resumed until June 1941, when a first performance was contemplated by the Elizabethan Singers (Meg Mundy, Helen Marshall, Jane Rogers, Peter Pears and Bruce Boyce), to take place in New York sometime during late 1941. But Britten was unable to complete the work, and when he departed from the United States in March 1942 he had composed only the first two stanzas. The eight pages that comprise the first stanza were confiscated by Customs officials in New York, while the remaining pages of the second stanza, the earliest version of the scherzo, 'I cannot grow', were left in Britten's possession. While crossing the Atlantic, he rewrote from memory (though not without some minor modifications) all that he had so far composed, finally completing the work on 2 April on board the MS *Axel Johnson*. The final refrain was to undergo further revision.

The first performance, a broadcast, was given later in the year by the BBC Singers conducted by Leslie Woodgate on St Cecilia's Day, 22 November, as part of the 'Music-Lover's Calendar' programme, in which Alec Robertson (see note 1 to Letter 407) discussed the patron saint of music. Britten presented the manuscript fair copy of his *Hymn* to Robertson with the inscription: 'For Alec Robertson with love after his ''birthday broadcast'' BB'. Britten, as is well known, shared his birthday with the saint.

The *Hymn* was dedicated to Elizabeth Mayer. After Britten's return to England, Auden was to write, on 8 July, 'Longing to hear the St. Cecilia. Elizabeth played me the opening bars which sounded very beautiful.' (This must have been a performance from the manuscript confiscated by the Customs and re-possessed by Mrs Mayer.) In the same letter, he continues:

Since I saw you I've bought the Mozart Requiem [. . .]. Also the album you did with Colin [*Balinese Ceremonial Music*]. How well you play, dearie [. . .]. I was delighted to hear of Peter's success. Give him my love, and tell him I hope he is getting orchids from sailors.

The postscript reads: 'I envy you the English Countryside.'

In 1943, after the work's first performance and publication, Auden was to write on 23 March: 'Have just got <u>St. Cecilia</u> and think it <u>lovely</u>. Thank you, my dear.'

5 *A Ceremony of Carols*, Op. 28, for treble voices and harp. The use of a harp as accompaniment may have been stimulated by the unfulfilled commission for a harp concerto by Edna Phillips. Peter Pears, in an interview with Louis Chapin ('Peter Pears talks about Benjamin Britten', *Keynote*, April 1978, pp. 8–15), recalled that

Ben had previously been asked to write a concerto by the harpist [Carlos] Salzedo, but had declined. Undaunted, Salzedo had sent him a technical manual, and that was his source of information.

Pears's recollection requires one modification: Britten did, indeed, study two harp manuals written by Salzedo, but they had belonged to Edna Phillips. These are now in the Archive: *Modern Study of the Harp* (New York, 1921), and *Method for the Harp* (New York, 1929).

The majority of the texts Britten set are to be found in *The English Galaxy of Shorter Poems*, chosen and edited by Gerald Bullett (London, Dent, 1939; Everyman's Library Edition No. 959), purchased by the composer in Halifax, Nova Scotia, in March 1942, on the return journey to England. It seems clear that finding the anthology sparked off the work. The volume contains five of the poems (all annotated by Britten in pencil) which appear in the finished piece:

'There is no rose' (p. 5)
'I sing of a maiden' [Britten: 'As dew in Aprille'] (p. 6)
'This Little Babe' (p. 115)
'In freezing winter night' (p. 113)
'Adam lay ibounden' ['Deo Gracias'] (p. 4)

Also marked (but not to be set) was 'I saw a faire maiden' (p. 7).

Transcribed on the flyleaf and inside back cover of the volume are four additional texts:

(i)   a version of the Seven Joys of Mary, 'The very first blessing that Mary had', in Britten's hand;

(ii)   Balulalow ('O my deare hert') in Britten's hand;

(iii)   an inaccurate transcription of 'Hodie Christus natus est!', the Antiphon for the Magnificat at Second Vespers of the Nativity, in Pears's hand;

(iv)   a Latin sentence in Britten's hand, 'Hodie apparuit in Israel: Per Mariam Virginem est natus est [Rex]', a version of the last part of the text from the fifteenth-century German carol 'Resonet in Laudibus/Joseph Lieber, Joseph mein'.

Items (i) and (iv) were not set. Item (ii) ultimately became No. 4b in the published sequence, although Britten's source for Wedderburn's text of 1567 remains obscure. Item (iii) is of greater interest. Pears probably wrote out the Antiphon from memory – omitting the line 'Salvator apparuit' – by recalling Sweelinck's motet 'Hodie Christus natus est', which includes the exclamation 'Noe', absent from the liturgy. The Sweelinck formed part of the proposed repertory of the Elizabethan Singers, and Britten himself possessed a copy of the motet dating from the early 1930s. His pencil annotations indicate that he performed from it, probably when a member (in the early thirties) of the Arnold Foster Madrigal Choir. However, it was Pears's inaccurately remembered Antiphon, 'Hodie Christus natus est', that Britten first set, but ultimately he discarded it in favour of the correct liturgical form with its own plainsong tune (see Letter 407). This he used as a Procession/Recession, thereby anticipating the framing device found some twenty years later in the Church Parables.

Thus the seven completed carols referred to by Britten in this letter and by Pears in his letter to Elizabeth Mayer (No. 372) were made up of the five printed in the English Galaxy, 'Balulalow' and the first version of the 'Hodie'.

After Britten's return home, he substituted the plainsong 'Procession' and 'Recession' for the original 'Hodie'; but the music of the discarded item was used for a new carol, 'Wolcum Yole!'. 'Spring Carol' was also added to the collection. The texts for 'Wolcum Yole!' and 'Spring Carol' were included in Come Hither: A Collection of Rhymes and Poems for the Young of all Ages, made by Walter de la Mare (London, Constable, 1928), although it is not known for certain that this book was Britten's textual source. In this form (i.e. without No. 4a, 'That yongë child', and No. 7, the Interlude for solo harp) the work was first performed on 5 December 1942 in the Library of Norwich Castle by the women's voices of the Fleet Street Choir, conducted by T.B. Lawrence, with Gwendolen Mason (harp). The following year Britten revised the cycle, adding one new carol, 'That yongë child', and the harp Interlude, and also made provision for the piano to be used in place of the harp. Throughout, the order of the movements had undergone continual change, indicated on the composition sketch by a mixture of numbers:

1.	Procession (Recession)			1
2.	'Wolcum Yole!'			2
3.	'There is no rose'		2	3
4a.	'That yongë child'	MS missing		
4b.	'Balulalow'	2b.	4	4 changed to 5
5.	'As dew in Aprille'	3	5	5 changed to 6
6.	'This little babe'	4		6 changed to 7
7.	'Interlude'			7
8.	'In freezing winter night'			7
9.	'Spring Carol'			9
10.	'Deo Gracias'	MS missing		

The final version, published in 1943, was first performed on 4 December 1943 at the Wigmore Hall, London, by the Morriston Boys' Choir, conducted by the composer, with Maria Korchinska (harp). The work was dedicated to Ursula Nettleship.

6 The Sonata's compositional history is cloudy, but it seems likely that it began life as a 'Partita' for chamber orchestra. In the composer's American sketchbook (a 12-stave Schirmer MS Book No. 9, interleaved with blank pages, bound in dark green boards) there is a page of sketches for a 'Partita – chamber orchestra' with the themes for four movements written on one or two staves:

'Catch'   – four bars of $\frac{7}{8}$ similar in outline to the round 'Old Joe has gone fishing' from Act I scene 2 of *Peter Grimes*
'Tarantella' – two single bar fragments marked 'tutti'
'Overture' – D major with French dotted figures, marked 'ww/ str./harp'
'Fugue'   – the fugue subject, in D major

The 'Catch' is a fascinating example of Britten importing into his opera an idea that one would have assumed to be theatrical from the outset. In his interview with Lord Harewood (*People Today*, BBC Radio, 1960), Britten remarks, when talking about his compositional methods, 'The actual writing on the paper is *not* the moment of inspiration. That comes much earlier in [a composer's] life – he may not even be aware of it.' A little later in the same interview he goes on to describe the famous round in the pub scene of *Grimes*, without, however, mentioning – perhaps having forgotten – its first notation (which was only the outline of the $\frac{7}{8}$ tune) in another context altogether, which thus neatly supports his own speculations:

I don't know if you remember in the end of the first act, there's a storm and in the pub the tempers are getting strained and Auntie suggests that they should sing a song. Well, if one thinks of it dramatically, songs don't – aren't – in such a situation in a pub, organised by a conductor beating time – they're taken up very much one after another. Someone thinks of a tune and the others follow on. [. . .] That, in musical, technical terms is a round, where one voice sings a tune and then goes on to another but while he goes on to the second one the next character comes on and sings the first strain. Well, there is a case where one decided that a round was the most suitable dramatic form, and so one had to write a round. [. . .] That is a matter of intellectual exercise as one writes a short phrase and then one has to write another phrase to fit that, and what makes one a good or bad composer is to make these phrases sound natural and not contrived.

Among Britten's composition sketches dating from this time there is also an 'Overture and Fugue' for piano concertante, strings and timpani, based on the fragmentary sketches in the American sketchbook. This would appear to be as far as the 'Partita' project went.

There is one final incomplete composition sketch of a movement for orchestra in C major among Britten's unidentified manuscripts from this period, possibly from the summer/autumn of 1942 (see also Letter 397). The movement is marked 'I', indicating a multi-movement work, possibly the Sonata for orchestra.

The only refererence to the Sonata among the Boosey & Hawkes correspondence is a letter from Ralph Hawkes to the composer, dated 28 June 1943: ' "Sonata for Orchestra". If possible, to be completed before November so that it may have its première at an Albert Hall concert early in the New Year.'

7 Auden applied for, and was awarded, a Guggenheim Fellowship worth about $2000 to allow him to complete his 'Christmas Oratorio', *For the Time Being* (first published by Random House, New York, 1944). He was summoned to an American military draft board in September 1942, and rejected on the grounds of his homosexuality. In 1945, however, in the uniform of a US Army major, he took part in the 'United States Strategic Bombing Survey' in Germany, whose task was to discover from the civilian population the effects of Allied bombing. (See HCWHA, pp. 324 and 333–6.)

8 Colin McPhee was awarded a grant by the Guggenheim Foundation in 1942, for 'preparation of a book on Balinese music', with a renewal the following year. *A House in Bali* was published by the John Day Company, New York, 1946. See Carol J. Oja, *Colin McPhee (1900–1964): A Composer in Two Worlds*, Ph.D. dissertation, City University of New York, 1985, pp. 329–90.

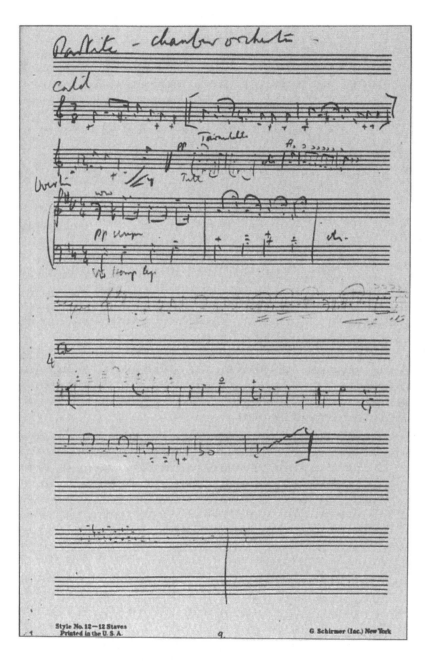

Sketch for Partita for chamber orchestra; an additional sketch for the First String Quartet appears on the same page. The bars marked 'Tarantella' found their way into the Vivace of the Second String Quartet

The first page of the composition sketch for the incomplete Sonata for Orchestra

375   **Statement to the Local Tribunal for the Registration of Conscientious Objectors.**[1]

[*Typed*]

May 4th 1942.

Since I believe that there is in every man the spirit of God, I cannot destroy, and feel it my duty to avoid helping to destroy as far as I am able, human life, however strongly I may disapprove of the individual's actions or thoughts. The whole of my life has been devoted to acts of creation (being by profession a composer) and I cannot take part in acts of destruction. Moreover, I feel that the fascist attitude to life can only be overcome by passive resistance. If Hitler were in power here or this country had any similar form of government, I should feel it my duty to obstruct this regime in every non-violent way possible, and by complete non-cooperation. I believe sincerely that I can help my fellow human beings best, by continuing the work I am most qualified to do by the nature of my gifts and training, i.e. the creation or propagation of music. I have possibilities of writing music for M.O.I.[2] films, and for B.B.C. productions,[3] and am offering my services to the Committee for the Encouragement of Music and Art. I am however prepared, but feel completely unsuited by nature & training, to undertake other constructive civilian work provided that it is not connected with any of the armed forces.

BENJAMIN BRITTEN

1   Britten's Local Tribunal took place in London on 28 May, the Tribunal comprising three members and a Chairman, Mr G.P. Hargreaves. The composer was accompanied by Stuart Morris (see note 1 to Letter 381). The Tribunal's report of the hearing was as follows:

Mr [Canon] Stuart Morris represented the applicant. Applicant says: – I cannot destroy a man's life because in every man there is the Spirit of God. I was brought up in the Church of England. I have not attended for the last five years. I do not believe in the Divinity of Christ, but I think his teaching is sound and his example should be followed. I believe in letting an invader in and then setting him a good example. Denmark has allowed the Germans in and has not yet got them out, but time is short so far. I do not object to the civil defence forces. I object to joining the forces and helping in the killing. I will join the RAMC [Royal Army Medical Corps]. I do not know what the other non-combatant services are. I think with the Quakers I might find a spiritual home. I have written music for a pacifist song [*Pacifist March* (1937)], and a pacifist film [*Peace of Britain* (1936)]. There would be no non-combatant corps if it were not for the Army.

The Tribunal's unanimous decision (received by Britten on 3 June) was that he be registered 'as a person liable under the Act to be called-up for service but employed only in non-combatant duties'. For details of Britten's successful appeal to the Appellate Tribunal, see Letter 397.

2 The Ministry of Information was formed immediately after the outbreak of war in September 1939, and seized the opportunity to use films as part of wartime propaganda. A Film Division was created, which called on the expertise of the GPO Film Unit, for which Britten had composed music during the thirties. In 1940 the GPO Film Unit was re-formed as the Crown Film Unit.

In fact, Britten never composed incidental music for any wartime MOI films, though William Walton (who was attached to the MOI Film Division from 1940) and Montagu Slater (who became Head of Scripts) may well have tried to secure film work for the composer. Both Slater and Walton were to appear as witnesses at Britten's appeal later in the year. For further details of the MOI Film Division and the Crown Film Unit, see Elizabeth Sussex, *The Rise and Fall of British Documentary: The Story of the Film Movement founded by John Grierson* (Berkeley, University of California Press, 1975), pp. 112–60.

3 Britten's skill as a composer of radio incidental music was well known before the war and it is not surprising to find the BBC keen to obtain his services for similar work in wartime, though up to March 1941 it had been BBC policy not to employ conscientious objectors.

Pears wrote to Elizabeth Mayer on 10 May: 'He has been warmly welcomed back – & has already been asked to do music for the radio show with Louis MacNeice.' This was music for three programmes (all written by MacNeice) which formed part of two related series, a joint collaboration between the BBC and CBS, New York: *Britain to America* Series I, No. 9: 'Britain through American Eyes', broadcast on 20 September; *Britain to America* Series II, No. 4: 'Where do I come in?', broadcast on 7 November; and *Britain to America* Series II, No. 13: 'Where do we go from here?', broadcast on 3 January 1943. The music in each programme was performed by the London Symphony Orchestra, conducted by Muir Mathieson.

Laurence Gilliam, the producer, invited Britten to compose incidental music for other BBC productions broadcast to the USA, including the six-part series, *An American in England*, written by Norman Corwin and produced by Edward R. Murrow, which was intended to inform an American audience about wartime conditions in Britain (June–August 1942).

A note to Murrow from Gilliam with regard to the Corwin programmes was written on 9 July. In it he set out Britten's credentials as he saw them:

. . . . Britten, as you know, has just come back from the United States and is registered as a conscientious objector. His status has not been decided yet but will be I gather quite soon. I have spoken to him and I gather his line is anti-killing but anti-Fascist in all other respects. He himself is most anxious for his music to be used in this type of work . . .

On 22 July, however, Britten seems to have concluded that his involvement in the Corwin series was under threat, on grounds that excited him to protest to Dallas Bower, the Director of the BBC Features Department:

Benjamin Britten telephoned me just after lunch to say that, at the rehearsal of his 'Sinfonia da Requiem' this morning which is being performed at the Promenade Concert this evening, D.M. [Arthur Bliss] somewhat violently implied that he considered Britten's employment for the Corwin programmes to be unfortunate. Britten takes this in no way as a criticism of his abilities as a musician but entirely as a matter of his political views.

If you will recollect, I raised this matter before any question arose regarding Britten's employment, I discussed it with you, and I discussed it with Edward Murrow. Naturally Corwin was also informed. The view of Columbia [CBS] was that for practical reasons they would prefer Britten to other composers, and that his political views were absolutely no concern of theirs. They wanted a first-class composer and musical director.

It appears that D.M. considers that Walton, Bax, and Vaughan Williams might be represented on these programmes.

This was a contretemps of some significance because it may well have fuelled a later row in 1943, involving some of the same issues and some of the same people. See Britten's letter to Bliss (No. 437) and note 1 to Letter 99.

On the day before Gilliam wrote to Ed Murrow he had supplied Britten with a statement to present to the Appellate Tribunal:

This is to bring to the notice of the Tribunal considering the case of Mr Benjamin Britten that Mr Britten has been commissioned by us to write music for a series of important broadcast programmes designed to explain this country to listeners in America, and we hope to be able to use Mr Britten's services for musical composition in connection with a large number of similar programmes in the immediate future. Apart from Mr Britten's musical qualifications for this work, he is particularly valuable to us in having recently returned from America, having worked with broadcasting organizations in the United States, so that he is in a better position than other composers to do this work with the utmost efficiency. May I hope that these considerations of national interest may weigh with you when this case is considered?

Mrs Bridge also provided Britten with a testimonial, the last paragraph of which includes a striking parallel with the first act of Britten's later pacifist opera, *Owen Wingrave*, (1970):

I remember going for walk with him through Kensington Gardens & Hyde Park & showing him the gay uniforms of the soldiers at Hyde Park (or Knightsbridge) Barracks & he would turn away & say 'I hate all of it & what it stands for'. Never could one interest him in soldiers even to play with, & this passionate hatred has remained with him all through these years that I have known him. His whole outlook on life has been a living, genuine, & conscientious protest against war & all that it means. Knowing the very high opinion of his gifts & character which my husband held & which I deeply share, I consider that these gifts would be of greater value to the country if employed in an unmilitary way.

One listener in the United States brought a sceptical ear to bear on *An American in England*. Auden wrote to Britten on 11 September, 'Have heard some of these Monday night broadcasts. I do feel sorry for you. God, what trash.'

376 To Elizabeth Mayer

> As from: 11, Tryon House,
> Mallord St., S.W. 3.
> May 17th 1942.

My dearest Elizabeth,

Your last lovely [letter] arrived two days ago when I was down in Snape with Beth & Kit – very appropriately, because it was the perfect place to receive such a letter! I am so sorry, my dear, that you have not been well. But these last few weeks must have been very trying – so much more for you than for us, because we have been seeing new things, & remaking so many old acquaintances, & been so occupied – not always cheerfully, of course – that the time has flown, & there hasn't been much time to think. Of course, I am horribly homesick for my American home – there's no use pretending I'm not: And above all, for you, my dearest Elizabeth. I got out a map the other evening & spent ages showing Beth & Kit where you all lived, where we went, & what we did when we got there – most nostalgic, and I felt more than ever, that the greater part of my life must be spent with you all on your side of the Atlantic. Of course this place has its wonderful sides – Snape – Snape is just heaven. I couldn't believe that a place could be so lovely. The garden was looking so neat & intentional, & the house is so comfortable and so lovely to look at – & the view . . . over the village to the river & marshes beyond. It is the perfect holiday-residence, there's no doubt about that. Although it is so difficult to get to – so few trains running, & then so full – & one must hire a car to get out the six miles from Saxmundham – I am going to go there alot in the next few weeks before the cloud bursts and I am caught in the red tape and other horrid affairs that are looming ahead of both of us. Next week Montagu & Enid Slater are coming down with me, & we shall get atmosphere for & discuss 'Peter Grimes' – which is going so excitingly now. Yes – in a few weeks now, Peter & I will be in it up to our necks. One's friends, & even the general public, are very kind & understanding – but the official mind, that unfortunately has the decisions to make, is extremely unpleasant, & there has been alot of unnecessary misery & worry (& even prison) of late, which is discouraging to think about. But the knowledge that you, my dear, are thinking about us, & the fact of knowing you helps so tremendously.

Peter sang so well, acted so delightfully, and was such a ravishing personality on the stage, in Hoffmann, that everyone was delighted & more than surprised. (I wasn't). There's no doubt that when this present situation is over that he has a great time ahead on the opera stage. Even now I feel he may have more chances than we expect – whatever opinions people may have, there must be tenors & heroes – & here is such a tenor & hero! We thought so much of you and William at his first performance! I do hope things are going well with the Home now – that things are settling down. I will write notes for William & Beate to put in this – please will you give them to them? Love to Christopher & Michael too. Is Michael still in the same place? Do let us know when Chris gets his scholarship or whatever. How really <u>stupid</u> of Bonner[1] to have given up his school. Really, people do have the oddest conceptions of their duty.

I haven't seen Gustel Scherchen yet, but I hope to be able to go to Cambridge soon for a few days. Wulff has just been moved – but where to, I don't know. Beth goes up to Buxton, Derbyshire, to live near Kit this week, & I shall go on staying around with Barbara, Enid & Montagu & at Snape until I know my plans. Really, the food isn't at all bad – the rationing seems very efficient, & one can still eat at Restaurants without cards. One misses sweet things & sugar most of all, especially after the abundance in America. But there are the nightingales to make up for it – one sang most beautifully all through an air-raid last week! Love from Barbara & Beth – Sebastian is to have a brother (or sister!) in the

fairly distant future! Much, much love my dearest. Take great care
of yourself – Great Expectations!

BEN

1 The headmaster of a small, private, progressive school in Redding,
   Connecticut. Christopher Mayer was a pupil there, and visited by
   his family and Britten and Pears.

377 To Beata Mayer

As from 11 Tryon House,
Mallord St., S.W.3.
May 17th 1942.

My dear Beatty,

First of all, please congratulate Max on his grand success.[1] I am
terribly pleased, & it must be an immense relief to all three of you.
Let's hope he'll be able to get a real good job now. I was also glad
to hear that you'd chucked up working on Saturdays now – a
damned good idea! I suppose you're letting down the old firm
gradually – you won't work on Fridays next, & then Mondays –
& then you'll just deign to ring them up once a week to see how
they're doing! But it serves them right. But actually, my dear, I
do hope you haven't given it up because you're sick? Anyhow with
all the expert medical advice around you, you ought to get better
quickly. But the best advice is always stay in bed nice & late, &
keep nice & warm even if it means sitting on radiators! Talking
of that, I don't know how you'd get on over here – because the
houses are <u>freezing</u>. People never light fires till late afternoon and
there's no central heating of course – & the English Spring is alright
aesthetically, but it can be darned chilly! I just shiver & run at the
nose all the time! Food's not so bad, really pretty good considering
– but there ain't no little nice things, & no mid-night scavanging
of the ice-boxes – because there ain't no iceboxes neither. Otherwise
it's quite good being back. Nice seeing lots of people you haven't
seen for ages. The nice people are much nicer, & the nasty ones
much nastier. Peter & I shall be in for pretty good hell before
long, but at least we're given time to breathe first & to get
orientated. Probably means farm-work, but we'll see. (It <u>may</u> be
prison!! – but there are lots of things worse these days, & at least
it'll be rent free!) I like my nephew Sebastian alot. He's pretty
naughty, but full of charm, & very intelligent. This letter is being

abit haphazard, because he's dashing round the house dragging his train & shouting "All the Way from America" at the top of his voice! Ralph Hawkes is well, incredibly busy & prosperous & important. Disapproves of me madly,[2] but has found that arguing is useless, & now lables me as a hopeless eccentric and leaves me alone! But my music seems to have been pretty popular since I've been away & I've come back to quite alot of money! – but it'll all go in taxes I suppose – & anyhow eating in restaurants is most bloody expensive – &, Beatty, there's just <u>no</u> drink to be got. One has to pay about 60 cents for a cocktail which tastes like & has about the same effect of a glass of coloured water. I can't think how you'd get on. Peter was a riot in Tales of Hoffmann (he took the lead & learned it in a week) – really terribly good. I think he's in for a grand success in opera now – people were terribly impressed. Well, old thing, I must stop this now. Please forgive the scribble – & anyrate, <u>you</u> might scribble me a line sometime, & tell me all the dirt.

Love to Max & Mrs. W. and lots to yourself,

BEN

1 Max Wachstein had passed his final examinations and subsequently took up an appointment as pathologist at the hospital at Middletown, New York. This was his first job, after immigration to the USA.

2 Of Britten's pacifist views.

378 To Benjamin Britten
From Peter Pears

New Theatre, Hull.

Wednesday 1.0 p.m.

[after 16 May and before 24 May 1942]

My own darling –

Just a note to tell you that I love you – & that I haven't yet had an answer to my reply paid telegram tho' there maybe one at the Theatre (I haven't been there yet). Anyway I can't do any thing about it, 'cos we have a matinée tomorrow as luck would have it & I <u>have</u> to do one or the other show. I'm writing to the Clerk to the Tribunal to explain my absence <u>if</u> they decide to have it tomorrow. What more can I do?

The broadcast was a success I think & Basil wants me to do a

"Songs for Everybody" in August.[1] Most of the Hoffmann Company listened & enjoyed it.

The music you sent to Liverpool hasn't <u>yet</u> arrived. I don't know what's happened to it.

Apparently Geoffrey Dunn[2] got Exemption at his appeal to go on with his work, teaching & singing etc. Frank Howes appeared for him & was very eloquent. Couldn't you get Ralph Hawkes to appear & speak for you? Have you heard any more?

7.0 pm

Just heard, my honey bee, My Tribunal is postponed –   They don't say till when.

I love you, I love you, I love you – always.

P.

Iris[3] has just been turned out of her flat by the Thatchers, & suggested taking a lovely one in Manchester Square, of which we could have bottom half at £2 a week, sharing bath & Kitchen. Quite separate. What do you think? Might be useful but complications could arise. Love. Love.

1 The broadcast remains untraced. On 23 August Pears was to sing in a BBC broadcast, *Songs for Everybody*, presented by Basil Douglas, with Gwen Catley (soprano), the Midland Chorus and BBC Midland Light Orchestra, conducted by Rae Jenkins.

2 English tenor (1903–1981), translator and opera producer, who was to write the libretto for Malcolm Williamson's opera, *English Eccentrics*, first performed at the 1964 Aldeburgh Festival.

3 Iris Holland-Rogers, a friend of Pears and a good linguist. She made English translations of Britten's French Folk-song Arrangements, and for the English Opera Group, in 1958, a translation, with Pears, of Monteverdi's *Il ballo delle ingrate*.

379 To Benjamin Britten
From Peter Pears
[*Pencil*]

Glasgow

<u>Sunday evening</u>

[24 May 1942]

My darling, my beloved darling, I just don't know how I'm going to face not having you for five weeks – In fact, I know I'm not going to try, because I shall steal away for a weekend at all costs, before I die of desparation – If this is anything like what I am to expect, I may as well give up now – & I'm sure this is not bad really – a dreary journey, a frightful city, a bleak room, a landlady like the Ugly Duchess, no hot water, fire which wont burn, nothing but sausages till Tuesday, & then coping with emergency rations – the list is endless & above all no you. I don't think you really know how much I need you and want you always.

<u>Wednesday</u> [27 May]

I'm sorry this letter's hasn't gone on before, but you know as a matter of fact there's no news and all I want to say to you isn't news but as old as the hills!

It was heavenly to speak to you last night and the night before. The difficulty of getting anyone by telephone at any time is acute here. Incompetent & unbelievably slow. I got on to Basil last night after endless efforts & talked to him about my singing for him. I think I may try Carmen, Manon, & Lalo in English. It should be allright.

Thank you ever so much for your telegram today about my tribunal. It's a relief – the complication would have been too intense – I <u>do</u> hope you've found a solicitor. I shall be with you all the time my darling tomorrow at 10 on – I pray it won't be too unpleasant.[1]

By the time you get this it will be all finished. How I hope you will be happy. If you would like me to come down for Sunday & Monday, I might easily manage it. (leave Glasgow 9.0 pm Sat, arrive Euston 7.0 am Sunday etc)   I should love to come, or would you rather that I put it off till the following weekend?

Any how my honey bee I love you, love you, love you & I expect your call tomorrow evening at 9.30.

[*illegible*] your sweet heart
always your loving
P

1 Britten's Tribunal was to take place the next day, on 28 May.

380   To Peter Pears
[*Pencil*]

11 Tryon House,
Mallord St, S.W. 3.
June 1st [1942]

When do you arrive this week-end? – come soon, please

God – you blighter.

Here am I – wasted a bob on wiring you, & then cut short a
pleasant evening with Stephen Spender[1] to be back at 9.30 in time
for your call – to find you'd rung at 9.10 (If I'd taken a taxi I should
have been in in time for that call – so that much for good
resolutions). I then cajolled the exchange into giving me a call by
10.15 (there being over an hour's delay), which the sweet things
did by 10.10 – &, if you please, 'Mr. Pears has just gone out.' No
wonder I'm cross. Why the hell can't you organise your times abit
– why the hell don't you do what you say, be in till 10.15 – why
the hell – well, & so on. And all because I wanted to speak to
you so badly. Boohoo. Boohoo.

[. . .] why can't you be in when I want you – Sorry. But I miss
you so much – & it's Thursday since I spoke to you. Friday's do
with Pierrot Lunaire & Façade was pretty awful really.[2] Horrible
audience, snobby – and stupid. The pieces very faded – &
Constant Lambert completely inaudible. Hedli did remarkably well
– & since I'm feeling peevish with you tonight – I think you might
have sent that wire to her. And did you write to the Tribunal[3] &
thank them??? Nag, nag. I know – but it's darned good for you.
Afterwards there was a horrible party at the Savoy, where I was
dragged away from a nice table with Hedli, Louis, Willie, Constant
& all, to sit with [. . .] (of all people) Sidney Beer!!![4]   I was livid.
They all got (Hedli etc) so beootifully tight & I remained
desparately sober. Boohoo – why don't you stick around instead of
dashing up to Scotland – God, if you prefer the Scotch to me, I'd
better pack up shop & go – but, perhaps, it's the Bally[Ballet]-Boys.
How are they?

Then I went down to Sophy & Arnold (senior) & Humphry for
the week-end – & I thought that was going to be disastrous –
Sophy was feeling ill & Arnold (home on leave) was military & very
tired, & I was terrified of arguments. However everyone cheered
up on Sunday – Humphry is a sweet & engaging kid (5½); & had a
long walk with Arnold, & we all motored over to Bradfield[5] where

Sophy sang with an amateur (and how) orchestra under Finzi ("I prefer this to those horrible professionals" sort of thing – ugh!) quite prettily, & there were some sweet things around (who are filling my mind now, because of course if one can't rely on . . . one must have something . . etc. you old she-deville). I'm too sleepy to go on with this diary – but I came back this morning & saw Wulff, then 'How Green was my Valley' (easier than talking to him – but a <u>lousy</u> picture)[6] then Spenders, & then waiting for you . . . but we <u>Won't</u> go into that again. Because anyhow I love you very much, & I wish to God (reverently, this time), you were here in bed with me. The enclosed sweet note came from William [Mayer], whom you MUST write to AT ONCE – SEE?!!

> All my love, you old so & so.
>
> B

1 Stephen Spender (b. 1909), English poet and critic. He was educated at Oxford, where he first came under the influence of Auden. After Oxford he lived in Germany for a time and during the Spanish Civil War was engaged in propaganda work for the Republican cause. His verse play, *Trial of a Judge*, was mounted by the Group Theatre in 1938. After the war, during which he was a member of the National Fire Service, Spender spent much time lecturing in the USA, but from 1970 was Professor of English at University College, London. He was married twice, the second time (in 1941) to Natasha Litvin, the concert pianist. He was knighted in 1983.

Spender recalls meetings with Britten at this time in his *Journals 1939–1983*, edited by John Goldsmith (London, Faber and Faber, 1985), p. 58:

The war was a time of entertaining friends – survivors, fire-watchers, non-combatants, or soldiers on leave. Benjamin Britten came to see us on his return from America, and also our older friends, Forster, Eliot, Elizabeth Bowen.

See also note 2 to Letter 165 and Addenda, pp. 1338–9.

His brother was Humphrey, the photographer and painter (b. 1910), another Gresham's old boy, whom Britten met occasionally in the thirties (see, for example, DMBA, p. 128). His brilliant photographs of England were of apiece with the realist and unglamorous documentary ideals of Mass-Observation and the GPO Film Unit. He was also the photographer of some of the original Group Theatre productions. See Humphrey Spender, *Worktown: Photographs of Bolton and Blackpool taken for Mass-Observation 1937–8* (Brighton, Gardner Centre Gallery, University of Sussex, 1977); and *'Lensman': Photographs 1932–52* (London, Chatto & Windus, 1987).

2 Schoenberg's *Pierrot lunaire*, conducted by Erwin Stein, with Hedli

Anderson as reciter, and Walton's entertainment, *Façade* (with Constant Lambert and Hedli as reciters), were performed at the Aeolian Hall, on 29 May. It was one of a series of concerts promoted by Boosey & Hawkes.

3 As Pears was touring in *The Tales of Hoffmann*, the Tribunal had agreed to postpone his hearing.

4 Sidney Beer (1899–1971), English conductor, who, in 1941, founded the National Symphony Orchestra.

5 The public school near Reading, Berkshire.

6 *How Green was my Valley* (US, 1941) based on Richard Llewellyn's novel about a Welsh mining community, directed by John Ford and featuring Walter Pidgeon and Maureen O'Hara.

381 To Stuart Morris[1]

11, Tryon House,
Mallord St., S.W. 3.
June 3rd [1942]

Dear Mr. Morris,

The enclosed have just arrived, & I send them on to you as you have all my papers.[2] I have to go away to-day until the end of the week on business, but if I may call & see you on Monday 8 June and talk the whole matter over, I should be very pleased. I see they have omitted the 'rider' to the sentence – about it being a "waste". Could I also bring Peter Pears, whose case we had postponed, to see you also? I know it would help him a great deal to talk to you.

Many thanks as always,

Yours sincerely,
BENJAMIN BRITTEN

1 Canon Stuart Morris (1890–1967), who from 1939 to 1943 was General Secretary of the Peace Pledge Union and Liaison Officer to the Central Board of Conscientious Objectors. He was again General Secretary from 1946 to 1964. See note 2 to Letter 388, and Sybil Morrison, *The Life and Work of Stuart Morris* (London, Peace Pledge Union, n.d.). Britten was a sponsor of the PPU from 1945 until his death. His *Pacifist March* of 1937 (words by Ronald Duncan) was written for and published by the PPU. See also DMBA, pp. 67–78.

2 Britten had been informed of the Tribunal's verdict and now needed to prepare his appeal, which was heard sometime in August/September. (See Letter 382.)

382 Appeal to the Appellate Tribunal

[June 1942]

That the Local Tribunal failed to appreciate the religious background
of my conscience trying to tie me down too narrowly to a belief
in the divinity of Christ. I don't seek as suggested to pick & choose
from his teaching, but I regard the whole context of his teaching &
example as the standard by which I must judge. It is for this reason
that my conscientious objection covers non-combatant as well as
combatant service in the army. The reference to the RAMC & non-
combatant service in the summary of further evidence does not
fairly represent what I tried to convey to the Tribunal. I could not
conscientiously join the RAMC or the non-combatant corps
because by so doing I should be no less actively participating in the
war than if I were a combatant against which service the Tribunal
recognised the validity of my objection. I realise however that in
total war, it is impossible to avoid all participation of an indirect
kind but I believe that I must draw the line as far away from direct
participation as is possible. It is for this reason that I appeal to be
left free to follow that line of service to the community which my
conscience approves & my training makes possible.[1]

BENJAMIN BRITTEN

Certificate of Registration in Register of Conscientious Objectors, 3 May 1943

1 The Appellate Tribunal granted him unconditional exemption. In this
context it is worth bearing in mind that if Britten had not declared
himself a pacifist and had been called up for military service, he
would almost certainly have been found medically unfit.

By a strange coincidence, the Chairman of the Appellate Tribunal
was Sir Francis Floud, the father of Britten's schoolfriend, Peter
Floud. In a note from 1965, written on the occasion of Sir Francis's
death, Britten wrote to his daughter, Mollie, 'He was so good to me
when I was at Gresham's once, & of course a wise & sympathetic
judge at my tribunal in the war [. . .].'

383 To Elizabeth Mayer

As from: 11, Tryon House,
Mallord St., S.W. 3.
June 5th, 1942.

My dearest Elizabeth,

I am afraid this can't be the long elaborate letter that it should
be – with so many things to talk to you about – as I haven't got
much time. I am actually down in the country staying for a few
days with Montagu & Enid Slater, and working with M. hard on
the libretto of Peter Grimes. It is going so well & I'm very keen on
his whole attitude to the subject – Very simple, full of respect for
Crabbe, and with real stage experience. My ideas are crystalizing
nicely, and I think that, given opportunity, we can make a really
nice thing of it. How I wish you were here to discuss it with us –
but I have a feeling that it really won't be long before we are
together again; it just must be! Life goes on here with a certain
amount of excitements. Peter is away in Scotland singing, but we
manage to telephone pretty often. With luck he'll be down for this
week-end – a bit extravagant, maybe, but there is so much to talk
about. I had my tribunal last week, and I must say it wasn't much
fun. A charming & intelligent man, head of the organisation
helping such as I, came with me and helped plead my case. On
the whole they were sympathetic, but of course one is swimming
against the stream and one isn't given any help. I have passed my
first hurdle, exemption from combatent work, but I still have to
fight what I am given to do – digging trenches & roads, etc. That'll
be in a month or so, when I am given a chance to appeal. I have
a fair chance of getting what I want to do as the Appeal court is
smaller, & more intimate. The real trouble is that the whole
question is impossible to argue, especially with legal minds. It's a

thing you either feel or don't feel, and I'm afraid my efforts at explanation were incredibly lame. However . . . Peter's has been postponed, as he was away in Scotland. It'll be when he gets back. I am glad to have had the experience of it, to warn him of certain things to say or to avoid saying.

Well, my dear, I got Beata's announcement[1] the other day, and I am so pleased. I am really sure it is the best thing for her; after all she has known Max now for a long time, and has gone into it with her eyes wide open. I think too, that in these unsettled days it is good to have ones private life as settled as possible. Will she give up B & H now?[2] I should think that that would be a good thing for her, as the work is so disturbing, and she doesn't really like the people. What news of Michael & Chris? I am looking forward to your next letter – it seems ages since the last one arrived; but then I'm greedy about letters – it seems so easy to loose touch with things over the other side, and it is a thing I am so particularly keen not to do. Not that people are being nasty over here; remarkably (and suspiciously!) nice, and nothing is too much trouble for them to do – Louis MacNeice has been particularly helpful. It is merely that, however much I love this country, I feel that, come what may, half of my life is now tied up with America.

By-the-way, my dear, I have a horrible request. I am having considerable trouble with my income-tax over here (just another little worry!). Luckily there is a good man,[3] a positive genius in buff forms!, who is helping me. But he says that I must have all my figures of earnings in America – so could you please look through my papers & see whether you can find details of both my earnings & expenses in 1940–41, & 1941–42 (I can't remember when the fiscal year begins – either January or March isn't it?). If you can't find them, I expect the accountant who did them for me (what <u>was</u> his name! – he lived on the corner of 5th Avenue, & 23rd St. – the regular B & H man)[4] will have a copy; and at any rate B & H would have a copy of the <u>earnings</u>. If you could possibly send them by air-mail, & send a carbon copy by sea, I should be more than grateful. I can't think why I didn't bring them, except that I didn't think for a moment that they'd be necessary. It's this wretched solicitor (Nicholson) who has messed up everything, and put all the inspectors in a bad humour! I am afraid the Michelangelo Sonnets haven't arrived yet – what has happened about them. The trouble is that they can't be printed until this good copy arrives – the only copy here is so illegible – and I am so keen to get them out as soon as possible.⁵ The folk-songs & the St. Cecilia (your piece) are being done now.⁶

It is a wonderfully hot day, out here. The weather has been superb ever since we arrived (except for a general weeping last week), & this week is the climax of it; but I believe it is sizzling in town. O God, if only the world could get straight, what a wonderful place it would be. There is so much I want to do, if there were only time & opportunity.

I saw Sophie (Wyss) & Arnold Gyde the other week-end. Very nice, not at all changed. I saw Wulff too, but he was rather altered, I am afraid. The ghastly time he has had, has made him rather vindictive, and hard. However, in time, he may soften, because underneath he is an awfully sweet boy. Perhaps if he could find the right girl whom he could marry – but his dictatorial manner, I should think, would put most girls off.

Beth and family have moved North to Buxton – I miss them, but I hope to go up soon. I spend most of the time with Barbara, or the Pears, or out here. I hope to go again to Snape with Montagu & Enid next week-end. Forgive this idle scrawl, my dear. The weather has gone to my head, & I can't think intelligently (strange condition for me!!). But all the same it is nice to imagine that I'm just prattling on to you.

Write soon, please. Tell me all the news. Nothing from Wystan, or Christopher [Isherwood], or Colin or Aaron yet. Just stir them up please – I am so keen to hear their news, & I hate to feel that they're forgetting me!

All my love – take care of yourself. Love to Edith – how is she? Any more children yet?! I was terribly touched by her remarks about the sea & storm – what a lovely, ingenuous person.

(I have to send this to catch the mail at once, so haven't time to write the note to William I meant to. So please give him my love & I'll write in a day or two).

BEN

1 Beata Mayer and Dr Max Wachstein had been married on 20 May.

2 Beata was to remain in the employment of the Artists' Bureau of Boosey & Hawkes Inc, New York, until November 1942.

3 Britten's accountant, Leslie Periton (1908–1983), acted for the composer for some thirty-five years, and was a highly regarded friend and counsellor. He was a financial adviser to the Aldeburgh Festival and English Opera Group, one of the four original executors of Britten's Estate, and a Trustee of the Britten–Pears Library. He quali-

fied in 1929 and joined A.T. Chenhalls in 1942, becoming a Senior Partner. See PFL, plate 417.

4 Lovit Hollander, 175 Fifth Avenue, New York.

5 The manuscript was dispatched to the London offices of Boosey & Hawkes by Heinsheimer on 22 June. See note 3 to Letter 370.

6 The first volume (British Isles) of Britten's Folk-song Arrangements was published in 1943 in versions for high and medium voice and piano. *Hymn to St Cecilia* was first published in 1942.

384 To Beata Wachstein
[*Incomplete*]

11 Tryon House, Mallord St., S.W. 3.
June 6th 1942.

My dear old Beatty,

So you're a respectable married woman at last – what must it feel like!! But I'm so very glad, & convinced that you & Max have done the best possible thing. I'm sure you'll feel much more stabilized, especially in these horrible times when any blasted thing might happen. I'm sure you'll go on being happier & happier together, knowing you both – bless you, my children! Mrs. Wachstein (senior) must be tickled pink. Did you get any of the family along to the ceremony, or was it all a deadly secret? How I should have loved to have been there to hold the baby – o, sorry, of course that's abit premature. Still, I hope, I shall be around when any other auspicious event is happening! Will you keep on with B & H, or has the glorious moment occured when you can cock a snook at the gang there? What are Max's plans? Is he getting a job out of town? Heavens, there is so much I want to know – what a bloody nuisance this bit of water is in between us; what fun it would be to meet, all of us, at the Russian Tea-Room, & have a cocktail, or preferably a few cocktails, and then stagger out onto 57th Street! How you'd get on here, I can't imagine – drinks are impossible to drink, even when you can get them, which isn't often, & then at what a price. For a good cocktail, or a nice bit of Rum one would sell one's soul. Mostly one drinks pints & pints of very watery beer, with no effect – except a very mundane one. Otherwise food's not so bad, although, one very seldom feels full for any length of time. Meat's so short, & one stuffs on starches & they don't satisfy for long. I am still hanging around, not knowing what's going to happen to me (I am afraid this letter has

had a bad hiatus) – when I got to the middle of the above sentence
I was overcome by really terrific heat and went straight to bed.
That was Saturday. It is now Thursday – life having been hectic in
the interim. Peter came down from Scotland overnight, arriving
on Sunday morning. I walked <u>five</u> miles to the station (Chelsea to
King's Cross) by 7.10 in the morning (started at 5.50) to meet him –
I'm pretty proud of that! We had two busy days, ending up with
Les Illuminations at the Wigmore Hall, sung by Sophie.[1] It was a
great success, but not half as good as the other shows we've heard![2]
Then I came down to Princes Risborough to work on the opera
with Montagu Slater, which I have been doing ever since, and have
only just got round to the letter again. Very sorry). To return to
our muttons – I still don't know what I shall be allowed to do. I
have had my first tribunal, which was pretty lousy, I admit. (Peter
got his postponed as he was on tour). After a long struggle I was
given exemption from combatent service, but made to do non-
combatent work (digging trenches etc.). I'm going to appeal against
that, but I don't know what chance there is of getting work which
I really believe in to do. It's an awful shame, because there's loads
of stuff I can do – I've had offers from Government Film companies,
the BBC, and lecture tours to the troops etc., to say nothing of
commissions etc. But I think it's highly unlikely that I'll be allowed
to do it. Probably I shall get farm work – pretty hard work, but at
least constructive. Peter I think will fare better, since he is
connected with the stage, & he is more likely to be allowed to
continue that – they're so keen on keeping up the morale.

I was amused by your description of the Ulli visit.[3] The woman
seems a poor specimen. But I'm not so sure that I shouldn't agree
with some of the things she said about my countrymen. They can
be very annoying, especially when you've known Americans.
Awfully snooty, & lacking in vitality. But there are lots of nice
things about them – & I do think they live in the most beautiful
country in the world. It is looking absolutely heavenly at the
moment. Snape is a dream. I'm going there this week-end – with
Montagu & Enid – which will be nice if the weather's good. I'm
looking forward to the time when I'll be able to show it to you
too.

Barbirolli is over here at the moment – but not exactly friendly!
I'm afraid the two old gizzards[4] have been telling him stories
about us – I wonder if they told him the truth – though . .!! Luckily
no one thinks anything of them over here, in fact everyone is
beautifully catty about them, – which I listen to & gloat over. We

have been very lucky so far; no unpleasantness about being away; in fact people think it's rather nice of us to have come back – certainly very silly! I still really don't know why I did it – except that I happened to feel that it was the right thing. But I am quite certain that when this mess is over (& Astrologers say hostilities will cease in Europe in the late fall!!) I'll come running

1 A performance given on 8 June, with the Boyd Neel String Orchestra conducted by Boyd Neel, as part of the Boosey & Hawkes Concert Series. The remainder of the programme comprised: Copland's *Quiet City* (George Eskdale, trumpet; Natalie James, cor anglais); four Chinese folk songs sung by C.Y. Hzieh; Lekeu's *Adagio*; four Greek folksongs arranged by Mátyás Seiber (Sophie Wyss, soprano); and Shostakovich's Concerto for piano, trumpet and strings, Op. 35 (Noel Mewton-Wood, piano; George Eskdale). *Les Illuminations* was the only item broadcast by the BBC.

2 Britten refers to Pears's performances of *Les Illuminations* in the USA.

3 Ulrica Mayer was living with a Mrs Greenhouse at the time.

4 Ethel and Rae Robertson.

385 To Peter Pears

11 Tryon House, Mallord St SW3.
June 12th 1942.

My darling – It was so heavenly to hear your voice, a few minutes ago. But don't those blasted minutes shoot by? One never has time to say what one wants, but anyhow over that cold instrument one never could say what one wants. It'll just have to wait until Saturday week. How grand that'll be. I do need you so desparately – I'm afraid I get such fits of depression when you're not around. I have been feeling all this beastly business so heavily on me recently, and the horrible loneliness – but I mustn't get sentimental, even if the radio is playing the Vltava![1] Dear Elizabeth, & dear William & Beate. What lovely people to know – & above all, my darling, what a lovely person you are to know – I don't know what I have done to deserve you! I talked about you to Margot the other night for hours – I don't know what she thought of it! But I don't care neither – I don't care who knows. I am just going to write off to Basil to tell him I've done the songs for you.[2] I talked the matter of the arrangements & the new translations[3] with Leslie Boosey this afternoon & he was very interested. I must get copies of them from Iris.

The opera is going well – I am delighted with Montagu's attitude to it, & he's steaming ahead. I'm afraid he <u>may</u> get called up as the M.I.5 (a sort of FBI) are putting obstacles in his way of getting the MOI job, because he's a party member – a nice paradox with the new 'alliance'!! I do hope he won't have to go.[4]

I had dinner with Barbara & Helen – & of course they both ask tenderly after you – you've made quite a hit, my dear, but that's nothing extraordinary is it!! I must write some letters now,

All my love. I'll expect a wire on Monday to Snape.

B.

<u>Don't</u> please give the score away – they're <u>scarce</u>.[5]

1 The second of the cycle of six symphonic poems, *Ma Vlast* ('My Fatherland') by Smetana.

2 The *Michelangelo Sonnets*.

3 Perhaps the transcriptions of Schubert's 'Die Forelle' and Schumann's 'Frühlingsnacht' for voice and small orchestra made by Britten around this period. Both the Schubert and Schumann songs used English rather than German texts.

4 Slater was a member of the Communist Party. The 'new alliance' refers to the pact between Soviet Russia and the Allies against Nazi Germany.

5 Probably a dyeline copy of the *Michelangelo Sonnets*.

386 To William Mayer

11, Tryon House, Mallord St., S.W. 3.
June 17th 1942.

My dearest William,

I am so sorry to have left your letter so long unanswered, but I have been horribly busy & generally occupied since it arrived. Anyhow, it cheered me up enormously to get it, to find out all you'd been doing, and to hear how you are. It's so good to know you're going on doing all the nice old things that I know so well – going up to New York on Wednesday, going for drives at the week-end (how's the gasoline lasting? and the tyres?), and listening to the radio etc. etc. Please go on doing them till I come back, which will be as soon as this beastly mess is over!

I am so glad that the new regime is working so well – it must be a relief to you, because I remember how worried you were about it. How are all the doctors? Tillim[1] as negatavistic as ever? Does Miss Biser[2] loosen up ever? What a bad thing about the fire, but damned lucky that no one was hurt.[3] I must say I'm glad I wasn't around, because I'm scared stiff of that kind of thing, & shouldn't have been any use to you at all! I don't like the alarms here one bit, but apart from bumps in the distance, nothing has happened actually near us so far. I go to Snape, the Mill, as often as possible, and it is looking absolutely wonderful. Hurry up your citizenship papers and come over soon, because I'm aching to show it to you. It is awfully comfortable, & almost the only house in England that has central heating – but I promise you never to let it get above 70°! The garden is grand & we are busy planting vegetables.

I wish you could see Peter on the operatic stage – he is really staggering! Looks very good, & acts wonderfully, & his voice is really sounding grand. We'll see him as Otello at the Metropolitan before long![4] It is very good for him to have such a success, & he's blossoming out as a result. The other day there was an important performance of Les Illuminations – but not, alas, by him. I nearly died, because the woman who sang it got a completely wrong idea of it, & everyone thought she was so good. But he'll show them when he gets a chance. He gets down to London occasionally for the week-end.

I am working hard on the opera libretto with Montagu Slater, and it is going along well – sticking close to Crabbe and our original sketch.[5] I hope to be able to send along a copy when it is done. I don't know when I shall be able to start the music, because still my plans are extremely vague. I'll let you know when anything definite happens – it is all rather worrying, but with the red pills I manage all right! Dear William, forgive this being such a short, scrappy letter – but I'm rather rushed, & anyhow there's not much news. Do write again soon, because it keeps America from becoming too remote, which is a great danger these days – one is awfully inclined to think this is the only kind of existence. Could you please send on the enclosed note to Wystan[6] – I haven't got his address?

> With lots of love to you all.
> Take care of yourself.
> BEN

---

1 *recte* Tillum, one of the psychiatrists at the Long Island Home.

2 Miss Beiser from the Long Island Home.

3 There had been a fire at the Home.

4 Pears was eventually to make his début at the Met. at the age of sixty-four, as Aschenbach in *Death in Venice*.

5 See Philip Brett, ' "Fiery Visions" (and Revisions): *Peter Grimes* in Progress', in PGPB, pp. 47–50.

6 The letter has not survived.

387   To Bobby Rothman[1]

11, Tryon House,
Mallord St., Chelsea, S.W.3.
June 24th 1942.

My dear old Bobby,

You cannot imagine how pleased I was to get your letter yesterday – so pleased, that instead of leaving it for a month to answer (as I usually do!) I am writing to you right away – I should be working, too, actually, but don't tell anyone! I was sorry to hear that you've been sick; that must have been a bore for you. But I hope you're fit again now, and can bathe and all that. I was awfully glad to hear all your news, to hear about the rationing of gas and sugar, and your 'dim-outs'; because I like to know all about you all, & how you are living these days. It seems such a very long time since I saw you that Sunday in Amityville, and I don't want to lose touch with you.

Well – lots of things have happened to me these last few months. The journey across was more boring than anything else. Of course it was a bit scaring at first, but I soon got used to that and did lots of work. The real trouble was that ours was a rather decrepid old boat (a Swedish freighter) and everything went wrong with her. To start with, after leaving the dock, we sat for four days just off the Statue of Liberty while the steering was being repaired. It was annoying not to be allowed on shore, especially as we were not allowed any books until we were outside American waters (fear of codes or something). Then we went up the coast, & lay for four more days off some bay or other, while the steering was being repaired <u>again</u> – this happened for about ten days, while we limped slowly up to Halifax where we stayed for five days! It was awfully boring, as it was such a small ship, & not many people to talk to. Luckily some of the crew were very nice, & also there was on board a French Professor & Peter & I practised our French on

him, so we didn't altogether waste our time. The Convoy system
was very interesting; when we next meet I'll tell you all about it.
We didn't have any bad experiences – except for one fearfully bad
storm when the rafts got washed loose & began crashing around
the deck, & one horrible night when our funnel caught fire & we
stood quite still for ages, attracting all the submarines for miles – so
we expected! All in all we took 30 days – a long time. But I was
quite sure that we should arrive safely, & didn't worry much.

It has been very strange getting back here, & seeing how
everything is after three years. It has been nice seeing all my
friends again, and they don't seem much changed. But the towns
have changed a great deal. There is really a great deal of damage
– the city of London is a terrible sight, and all over the place there
are houses down – all cleared up now, but looking rather like the
gaps where teeth have been pulled out. And everywhere is very
shabby. I have been in several alarms, & have heard lots of guns,
& distant 'bumps' but so far, luckily nothing very near – & I'm
pretty glad too! The sirens make the most horrible wailing noise,
like hundreds of gigantic cats, & they always make my stomach
turn upside down![2] The black-outs are quite amazing; it is
extraordinary how difficult it is to find your way about even in
places you know quite well. Also buses are inclined to stop very
early – which I always forget & have to walk miles home late at
night. The food situation isn't really so bad – abit short of meat,
& sweet things – & I look back very greedily to all the cream I used
to have in America! Luckily there is still alot of coffee, so I'm
happy – ! I go quite alot to my old Windmill in Suffolk County
(quite near Southwold!) which I think I told you about – & I am
organising the garden to plant vegetables so that we shan't starve
in the winter. But I'm not so hot as a gardener! I shall of course
be called up, but I am appealing to be allowed to do fire-fighting,
or ARP [Air Raid Precaution] or farming, or something useful like
that. – There, Bobby, if you have had the energy to plough through
all this! – that is an idea of what things are like over here. A bit
different from good old U.S.!! I laughed when you said you had
9 gallons of gas a week – people have about 4 a <u>month</u> here, and
there won't be any private cars after the end of this month.
However it is good exercise to bicycle – keeps my weight down
quite alot! How's your weight now? I expect you're putting on
some – I'm still about 128 as I used to be. Peter's losing hard –
he has been singing opera all over the country since he got back &
making lots of money! I am writing an opera, all about a fishing

village, full of storms, & sailing boats, & murders – very exciting!
The song I wrote for you is now being printed – I'll send you a
copy when it's done – mind you sing it!!! How's Joan's piano
getting on? What is she learning? Thank Emma for her note, &
for correcting your spelling – tell her I should like her to correct
mine – I know it's all wrong, – but I hope you can understand
what I mean! Give my love to all the family, & tell your father to
write me a note sometime – & to send me the photos he took of
us – especially, the one when I was holding you up like a sack of
coals! I should love some photos of you bathing & sailing, because
it'll be a long time before I see any of that kind of thing again. I'm
glad you'll be allowed to have your boat still. Are you going to
be allowed that sailing dinghy?! And write again soon old thing –
you can't tell how nice it is to hear all your news.

Be good – some hope . . . !

With much love,

BEN

Please give the enclosed note to Mrs. Sturmdorf.[3]

1 The son of David Rothman. It was to Bobby that Britten dedicated
his arrangement of the Somerset folksong, 'The trees that grow so
high'. See PFL, plate 127.
2 Britten was later to re-create the authentic wailing sound of the air-
raid sirens in the eleventh song, 'The Children', from his Soutar
cycle, *Who are these children?*, Op. 84 (1969). See also note 3 to Letter
155.
3 Mrs Regina Sturmdorf, Mrs Rothman's aunt.

388 To Ethel Astle[1]

c/o Boosey & Hawkes Ltd.,

295, Regent St., W. 1.

August 2nd 1942

My dear Miss Ethel,

I was terribly pleased to get your lovely letter, & to find that you
hadn't quite forgotten me after all these years! I was glad to hear
all your news, and to tell from your letter that you haven't changed
abit! It is grand that you are still going on teaching – grand that
the young can go on benefiting from your great experience &
knowledge. I can never say enough how much I personally
benefited from your teaching, & knowing you all those years. I

often remember things you used to tell me! I don't play the piano
very much these days, but this autumn I am going to do some 2
piano work with Clifford Curzon[2] who is a good friend of mine –
& a really <u>grand</u> pianist. Have you heard him? Funnily enough,
who should be his neighbour but Tressie![3] I was introduced to
her (!) by him the other day, & we laughed alot at such a
coincidence! I see quite abit of her. I am afraid there is not much
time now to tell you all my news. I don't quite know what will
happen to me in the future. Owing to my Christian views I am
having Tribunals & things like that but I have so much work to do
for the BBC that I hope they will be lenient to me. I see alot of
Barbara & Beth (& her growing family!) – not so much of Robert
who doesn't come much to town. I had a telephone talk to Basil,[4]
& hope to see him & Hilary soon. The latter seems to be very
promising. If ever I come in your direction, which is quite
possible, I would love to see you – & if ever you come to London
– please be <u>sure</u> & send me a card, & we can meet & talk over
the good old days, & the good days that I am sure are to come!
And please, even if we don't meet, let me know always what you
are doing.

   With much love & many thanks always,

                                        Your affectionate
                                        BENJAMIN

1 See note 2 to Letter 4.
2 Clifford Curzon (1907–1982), English pianist. He was a student at
  the Academy from 1919. In the late 1920s he worked with Schnabel
  in Berlin and then in Paris with Nadia Boulanger. On 13 August
  1980, at his London home, Curzon recalled his first meeting with
  Britten and Pears and the subsequent continuities and discontinuities
  of an important personal and professional relationship. We transcribe
  verbatim the notes of the conversation made by Donald Mitchell:

  Curzon originally came into touch with Britten and Pears on their return
  from the USA in 1942, not through music, but through their shared pacifism.
  Curzon was a committed pacifist himself and had working for him as a
  secretary at this time Stuart Morris, who was a notable pacifist and was
  indeed arrested at one stage and imprisoned for disseminating anti-Churchill
  leaflets. Clearly, Britten's connection with Morris came about through
  Curzon. Curzon added in this context that Britten returned to the UK wanting to be an active not a passive pacifist.
     Curzon made clear that his musical friendship with Britten was in the
  main, after 1942, a professional one, that is, they set themselves up as a
  duo. We might remember that this follows a pattern that had already
  emerged, albeit tentatively, in Britten's professional activities pre-war, before

he went to the States, e.g. the partnership with Adolph Hallis. So Curzon was following in this same tradition.

Curzon and Britten were close during this wartime period because of their pacifist and musical interests. He feels the friendship after the war would in any case have become less close, because Curzon emerged as a prominent solo pianist and Britten emerged as a composer, principally. But in any event they fell out over Britten's Piano Concerto, the first performance of the revised version of which Curzon was supposed to give. But evidently Britten was very late in supplying Curzon with the draft of the revised slow movement which was not ready even just ten days before the performance and was arriving page by page through the post. Curzon was unable to cope with this last-minute drama and told Britten that he would have to find someone else to play the work. This led to some unease and coolness, but the friendship was patched up eventually and towards the end of Britten's life the old association was restored – Curzon thinks on a deeper level than before.

The intense irritation on Curzon's part over the Piano Concerto affair found expression in a letter from his wife, Lucille, addressed to Erwin Stein at Boosey & Hawkes, dated 26 November 1945, which opened:

As to-day has brought neither the promised letter from Ben, nor the promised telephone call from you, Clifford is letting Sidney Beer know that he will be unable to play the Britten Concerto on February 26th, owing to the impossibility of getting into touch with Ben either by post or telephone. Under these conditions, it would obviously be impossible to arrange the necessary rehearsals, or to achieve the collaboration the work demands.

and ended:

As for the lack of professional courtesy involved (quite apart from any question of previous personal relationship) it is of a degree that I believe even the greatest of composers could hardly expect any serious artist to understand.

It is evident, however, from a letter to Britten from Ralph Hawkes, dated 28 August 1944, that Curzon had intended to perform the original version of the concerto early in 1945. See also Eric Roseberry, 'Britten's Piano Concerto: the Original Version', *Tempo*, 172, March 1990, who writes (p. 10, n. 1):

The correspondence on Curzon's side seems to indicate that a temporary break-down of relations had occurred between the two men as a result of Curzon's desire to acquire temporary some performing rights with respect to the new version.

In January 1944, Britten and Curzon recorded the *Introduction and Rondo alla Burlesca*, Op. 23, No. 1 (Decca K1117), and *Mazurka Elegiaca*, Op. 23 No. 2 (Decca K1118). Curzon also performed Britten's *Holiday Diary*, Op. 5, and – eventually – the revised version of the Piano Concerto, Op. 13 (see note 2 to Letter 140). Britten gave Curzon the manuscript fair copy of *Holiday Diary*, inscribing it: 'For Clifford who made them his. BB'. The manuscript is now in the Archive.

In Curzon's later years he was known for his distinguished interpretations of Mozart and Schubert, and was a frequent performer at the Aldeburgh Festival. In 1970 he recorded Mozart's Piano Concertos in D minor (K.466) and B flat major (K.595) with the English Chamber Orchestra conducted by Britten. These performances were not released immediately as Curzon, characteristically, was dissatisfied with them. They were released with his agreement in 1982, but not until after his death, on Decca sxl 7007.

In 1931 he married the American-born harpsichordist Lucille Wallace (1898–1977), for whom Britten composed cadenzas for Haydn's Harpsichord Concerto in D major (Hob. XVIII:II) in 1943/4.

Curzon and Britten gave the British premières of the *Introduction and Rondo alla Burlesca* and *Mazurka Elegiaca* at the Arts Theatre, Cambridge, on 25 April 1943, and on 10 July in the same year, of *Scottish Ballad*, with the London Philharmonic Orchestra conducted by Basil Cameron, as part of a Promenade Concert. Curzon was a contributor to TBB, pp. 67–70, in which he recalled an early play-through of *Peter Grimes* by Britten at the piano.

3 Tressie Gabriel (née Tyson), who had known the Britten family in Lowestoft, before she moved to Highgate in North London.

4 Basil Reeve, who had also been a pupil of Miss Astle's, and his sister, Hilary.

389 To Mary Behrend

104A. Cheyne Walk, S.W.10.[1]
August 6th [1942]

Dear Mrs. Behrend,

Do please forgive me in being so long in answering your nice letter about Sinfonia.[2] But I have been more than usually busy the last month, in addition to which I have been wandering rather vaguely from place to place until I shall know what I am allowed to do.

I was happy about the show – with all its defects it was a much better performance than I had expected, a grand reception, & on the whole kind criticisms.[3] I think it's being done again in London soon, and then I hope with a better performance that you will feel more convinced by the sections that puzzle you at the moment.

I hope you are all well. I was so sorry to miss George when he was in town. If you see him will you thank him very much for his nice letter, & tell him I hope to get round to answering it fully one of these days.

I don't yet know what will happen to me, but I have so much music for BBC. Features to write that I hope to get a certain amount of deferment whatever the final judgement on me is (what I am now waiting for –) – and deferment these days is golden!

I do hope I shall see you some time. When ever you come to town, I wish you would let Peter & me have a card – we are usually at the same address, which for the next two weeks is the above. After that – well, as usual, I don't know!

With many thanks again,

Best wishes to you all,
Yours,
BENJAMIN B

1 Britten and Pears had moved to this address, the house of Ursula Nettleship. Pears wrote to Elizabeth Mayer on 24 November:

We still haven't found a nice place to live in London, though we have tried everywhere. We have been staying these last months in the house of a friend who is in the country all the week, but we hope to find somewhere soon. It's very difficult not being able to unpack one's things.

2 The first performance in England of the *Sinfonia da Requiem* had been given on 22 July, when the London Philharmonic Orchestra was conducted by Basil Cameron in the BBC Promenade Concerts season. The *Sinfonia* had been the subject of an introductory article – 'Britten's New Symphony' – by Ralph Hill, in the *Radio Times*, 17 July, preceded by J.A. Westrup, 'The Virtuosity of Benjamin Britten', in the *Listener*, 16 July.

3 In the *Observer*, 26 July, William Glock wrote:

My first introduction to Britten's Sinfonia da Requiem was a finely printed score sent to me by Boosey and Hawkes; my second introduction was a gramophone record on which the composer himself analysed the symphony with a degree of reverence which most of us would rather reserve for Byrd or late Beethoven.

I suggested last week that Bartók and Stravinsky have adopted almost the whole of the European tradition, Bartók by gradual penetration into the past, Stravinsky as an expert horticulturist. Now the Requiem symphony derives from Liszt, from Mahler, from Fauré, perhaps also from Berg, and, if I may wear Savonarola's cowl for a moment longer, I should say that to belong so entirely to the late nineteenth century is to court the very essence of staleness.

Britten is the most professional of all our composers; the second movement of this symphony, for example, is an automatic [?authentic] achievement which not even Horowitz could surpass in his own sphere. But what interests everyone who has the cause of English music at heart is the character behind this professionalism. Up till now most of us have been saying that Britten fritters away his talent; and we inspect each work in the hope of finding an extra inch of depth. But wouldn't it be just as sensible to suppose that his musical accomplishment does, in fact, fully reflect its source; and that it is not technical ease which leads him to hell but a nineteenth-century fever and melancholy that hold him back from heaven? I can imagine anxious surveyors pouncing on the 'Lacrymosa' of the new symphony and saying 'the foundations are stronger than they have ever been'. Yet I'm not sure that this is true. In 'Les Illuminations', Rimbaud served as an incitement; here, the Requiem Mass. But there is less reference between words and music in the latter; I wasn't surprised when an excellent musician said that the first movement reminded him of 'Citizen Kane'.

Even so, I admire this movement tremendously. I don't know many others who could design such an emotional piece without letting it take *them* in hand, or control such a long crescendo without flagging. And although we can take Britten's orchestral imagination for granted by now, the invention here is on the Berlioz–Mahler level. I have already mentioned the second movement. The third ('Requiem aeternam') could be described in terms of the Paradiso, Liszt, and Fauré. In effect, it lacks pregnant material and doesn't strike home as the 'Lacrymosa' does. I hope the symphony will soon be heard again, if only for the sake of the first movement.

The analytical gramophone record to which Glock refers was a recording of a broadcast Britten gave on the *Sinfonia* on 19 July, as part of the BBC magazine programme, *This Week at the Proms*, presented by Alec Robertson. No trace of the recording exists, but part of Britten's script was reproduced in the *Listener*, 30 July, p. 138, 'How a musical work originates':

'The actual origin [of a work] is usually very difficult to define', he said. 'Personally, I always have a number of ideas floating around: ideas of either a tune or a rhythm or a particular timbre (what the Americans call "sonority"), or most usually ideas of the form of a work. The incentive which makes one develop or extend these ideas may originate from many different sources. It can come quite simply from a conductor or performer saying that he can use a certain kind of work, in which case one would hunt around in one's idea box to see what would be suitable. Or a great personal experience can set one going, or even sometimes one may feel the need of celebrating either a private or a public event. I do not say for a moment that some external reason is essential, that the ideas may not develop into a complete work of their own accord; but in my experience it is usually some such incentive as those I have mentioned that is necessary.'

See also note 14 to Introduction, p. 64.

A review by Bonavia appeared in the *Daily Telegraph*, on 23 July:

The title of the symphony must not be taken too literally. Mr Britten appears to have been more concerned with the presentation of his materials than with the material itself, which, however, serves his purpose well.

The presentation recalls Holst, for Britten, too, relies largely for his effects on new combinations of instruments. Holst, however, believed in broad, hearty tunes and contrasts of themes. Britten builds up each movement on one subject, which is introduced in different ways but hardly developed in the classical sense.

The symphony is the work of a virtuoso of the orchestra, and under Basil Cameron was played with the care for niceties of balance such a work deserves.

The Times wrote on the same day:

It is a concise work in three continuous movements entitled 'Lacrymosa', 'Dies Irae', and 'Requiem Aeternam'. The first is the most original, it persistently develops one calamitous theme, continuously varied but never giving place to a direct contrast. The second is, as one would expect, a macabre movement of the scherzo type. Presumably it was Berlioz who first associated the words of the sequence of the *Missa pro defunctis* with the idea of a dance of death. This movement is very elaborately scored until the unholy revelry subsides into a final andante. This seems actuated by a more genuinely musical feeling than what precedes it. The simple melody on the flutes against an angular bass figure creates a sense of unusual beauty, which goes far to justify the strange ways through which the composer has reached his *molto tranquillo*.

390 To Ernest Newman[1]

104A, Cheyne Walk, S.W.10.
Flax. 6825
Sept. 18th 1942

Dear Mr. Newman,

Thank you so much for your letter, which has remained so long unanswered —— I am afraid overwork and illness has wrecked my correspondence these last months. I was so sorry to hear that you had been so ill; I do hope you have recovered completely now after your rest. It would be very nice if we could meet sometime – but I am afraid the next few weeks are bad for me to come down to Tadworth – I have so much travelling for CEMA, & other occupying & troublesome work to do! But if you ever come to town, I should love it if you could call me here (for the next two weeks), & we could lunch or dine —— Even at Pagani's if you wish, but I would honestly rather not. What I mean is, that I am not choosy!

I do hope it will be possible for you to hear my new Michelangelo Sonnets at the Wigmore next Wednesday.[2] But if you cannot get there, I would be only too happy to arrange a performance for you someother time at your convenience. I am so keen for you to hear

them, as I am pleased with them myself – a very rare occurence
with me!

With best wishes,

Yours sincerely,
BENJAMIN BRITTEN

1 English critic, scholar and author (1868–1959) and a leading Wagner-
ian (publication of his four-volume biography was completed in
1947). He was chief music critic of the *Sunday Times*, 1920–58, in
which capacity he wrote about many important Britten premières, of
the operas especially.

2 See Letter 391.

391   To Ursula Nettleship

[after 23 September 1942]

Dear Ursula,

Hope everything is O.K. for you. I am just off to Berryfield
Cottage, Princes Risboro' (343)[1] till Friday.

Wednesday night was a <u>grand</u> success.[2] Peter sang wonderfully
& everyone was quite astounded. We were booked to record it
for HMV immediately after the show!!![3] I hope everything is going
well with you. Don't work too hard!

See you Friday – but I may ring up before to have a chat.

Love
BEN

1 The country cottage of Montagu and Enid Slater. Britten was no
doubt going there to work with Slater on the libretto for *Peter Grimes*.

2 The first public performance of Britten's *Seven Sonnets of Michelangelo*,
Op. 22, was given by the composer and Pears (the dedicatee) on 23
September at the Wigmore Hall. The programme also included John
Ireland's Violin Sonata No. 2 in A minor (played by Eda Kersey
(violin) with Ireland at the piano); the first English performance of
Bartók's *Contrasts* for violin, clarinet and piano (Kersey, Frederick
Thurston (clarinet), Ilona Kabos (piano)); and Bliss's Clarinet Quintet
(Thurston with the Griller String Quartet).

The *Michelangelo Sonnets* were an immediate success. The music
critic of *The Times* wrote on 25 September:

Britten ranges widely through foreign as well as English literature for his
words, and now sets seven sonnets of Michelangelo with the same certainty
of touch as he previously achieved with the French of 'Les Illuminations'.

The idiom contains nothing to perplex the listener and nothing to incommode the singer. They are, in fact, true songs, 'fine songs for singing' – or so Mr Pears, who returns with his pleasing voice grown more robust and his skill consolidated by experience, easily persuaded us. For though they are big songs they made a singularly direct appeal.

Ferruccio Bonavia, *Daily Telegraph*, 24 September:

The first Boosey and Hawkes concert of the season, given at Wigmore Hall last night, introduced two novelties: Béla Bartók's 'Contrasts' for violin, clarinet and piano, and Benjamin Britten's setting of seven sonnets by Michelangelo for tenor voice and piano.

[. . .]

Britten's sonnets made a much deeper impression, for even at this first hearing some rare and valuable aspects of the work were evident. The writing is lyrical and, at the same time, utterly unconventional. Every sonnet has an essentially musical core which is yet a true reflection of the poet's emotion.

The reception left no possible doubt as to the pleasure the audience had derived from the performance of Peter Pears and the composer, who accompanied him.

Gerald Abraham, writing in the *Observer*, 27 September, was presumably alluding in his final sentence to the influence of Ravel's *Histoires naturelles* (see also p. 931):

Bartók's corpus of work gives us a standard by which to judge everything new he writes: the trouble with Britten is that he seems to have no standards even for his own guidance. 'Nella penna e nell' inchiostro è'l alto e'l basso e'l mediocre stile,' sang Peter Pears – a little too rumbustiously – in the first sonnet, and the composer kept on reminding us of this truism, aiming at (and sometimes achieving) the lofty style, collapsing into banality, but (thank Heaven) avoiding the rolled golden mean of competent mediocrity. As in 'Les Illuminations', he has set himself a difficult problem though not quite so difficult this time, and solved it by using a crib.

Edward Sackville-West, in the *New Statesman and Nation*, 3 October:

After the interval came the first performance of Benjamin Britten's *Seven Sonnets of Michelangelo* for tenor and piano. I suggest that these are the finest chamber songs England has had to show since the seventeenth century, and the best any country has produced since the death of Wolf. It was high time the long, sinuous, rhetorical Italian line reappeared in English vocal music, which was dying of a surfeit of Brahms, on the one hand, and of folk tunes on the other. One could take a phrase from one of these sonnets and refer it to Puccini; but the point really is that that phrase is an echo of another in *Falstaff*, and that one again an echo of still another in, say, *l'Incoronazione di Poppaea*. By sheer sense of style, working in close harmony with profound emotion, Britten has revived a whole tradition in these songs. The experience was indescribably moving – the more so as the means are extremely economical; the accompaniment is often a mere outline, never more than a simply followed figure. To have attempted to set these sonnets, which equal Shakespeare's in subtlety of thought and feeling, was a courageous act; it could only succeed supremely or fail completely. The enthusiasm of a numerous audience made clear which was the case. More, much more, could profitably be written about these superbly beautiful songs; here I have only the space to add that the singer, Peter Pears, is something of a portent, too. It is long since we heard an English tenor with a voice at once so strong, so pure and so sweet.

In a letter to the composer Geoffrey Bush, dated 29 September (see LFBML, p. 253), John Ireland, Britten's former teacher at the College, was to write:

I also had to practise a bit, in order to play the piano part of my 2nd violin sonata at the Boosey & Hawkes concert on September 23rd – the novelties of this concert being new works by Bartók and Britten – the latter, settings of 7 Sonnets (in Italian) by Michelangelo, sung by Mr Pears and the Composer – very effective. Britten's detractors, while admitting the effectiveness, said – 'a pastiche of Verdi, Bellini & Donizetti'. I feel hardly competent to judge. In some ways the music seemed very Italian, also the treatment of the voice part – but some current English harmonies were not entirely avoided. If I can find it, I will enclose the programme so that you can form some opinion of the motif of these songs – but please return it [. . .]

The letter continued:

There are <u>too many</u> composers whose names begin with B. Bach, Beethoven, Brahms – Bax, Bliss, BRITTEN, Bantock, Bartók, Bush, Busch – and others I don't at this moment recall.

Ernest Newman had accepted Britten's invitation to attend. He wrote in the *Sunday Times*, 27 September:

Benjamin Britten's setting for tenor voice and piano (Peter Pears and the composer) of seven sonnets by Michelangelo are evidently of exceptional quality, but the style is so unexpectedly different from that of Mr Britten's other recent works, and the Italian words (unfortunately not printed in the programme) sped past us sometimes at so rapid a pace, that one can record only the general impression made by the first performance. I was particularly struck by the way in which the words and the sense and the emotional impulse of three or four lines of a poem at a time would be caught up and fused into a single ardent musical phrase. The sooner we can have the score for study the better.

3 Pears and Britten recorded the *Sonnets* for His Master's Voice on 20 November, at the EMI Recording Studios, Abbey Road, London. They were released on HMV B9302 and C3312 in November 1942. The recording, Britten's and Pears's first joint disc, was as successful as the first performance had been. Pears wrote to Elizabeth Mayer on 13 February 1943:

We have recorded the Michelangelo for HMV and they have sold enormously. It is remarkable (or isn't it remarkable, Elizabeth) how much everyone loves the Sonnets. We do them to very simple audiences & they all say it is what they have been waiting for. They have made a tremendously deep impression.

Evidence of the 'deep impression' and immediacy of the records'
circulation to which Pears refers is to be found in an entry in the
diary of Frances Partridge made only a few days before Pears's letter
to Mrs. Mayer was written:

9 February
When [Lawrence Gowing] asked me over to listen to records I went somewhat unwillingly, but I'm very glad I did, for they were Benjamin Britten's
<u>Michelangelo Sonnets</u>, and I felt I was hearing a work of genius for the first
time. We sat listening in Lawrence's tiny sitting-room, with the window
open wide and rain falling softly on the tufts of violets outside. We played
the records right through twice, but can one trust these certitudes?
(Frances Partridge, *A Pacifist's War* (London, Hogarth Press, 1978), p. 158)

 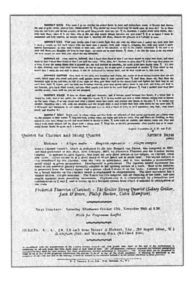

The first performance of the *Michelangelo Sonnets,* 23 September 1943. The programme
included translations of the texts by Elizabeth Mayer and Peter Pears

392 To Peter Pears

The enclosure is for obvious reasons! – I am cabling to-day.

104A. [Cheyne Walk]
Sept. 25th 1942

Darling – Here are the shirts, & I have put a hank & a sock in
too in case you need them. I miss you just dreadfully – in fact it
is difficult to take much interest in what one's doing without you
around. How are things with you? I hope you weren't too tired

to sing well last night, & the next few days won't be too bad. Relax as much as possible – stay in bed late in the mornings, & above all wrap yourself up & <u>don't</u> go around without a coat – this weather is so awful. There – that's what you get if you attach unto yourself a . . . . ! I was at the Wigstein playing the Celeste last night.[1]

Quite nicely, but it's a pukey little instrument – I nearly pushed it over trying to make a noise on it! I found counting the bars a trial tho' – Dennis Brain[2] helped me, & we got on alright, except one spot when I had (in the Durey) to do the same thing for about 12 bars & forgot to count them. However, when Reginald Goodall[3] started looking angry, I decided to stop! Everyone is crazy over you, old thing – infact I'm getting quite jealous! John Davenport was rhapsodic (maybe a little to Lennox's disappointment??) – strange people at the Wigstein last night said, <u>where</u> had you been all this time. Above all, the little stage shifter there, who'd been at it there 40 years, said you were <u>remark</u>able (he didn't know we had any particular (hm) friendship) & that you could & would make for yourself the greatest possible career, & 'I've heard Caruso & Morel,[4] too!' Quite lyrical; & to get praise from that kind of person is sumpin! – all the while Sophie was screaming away, & not a word from him about her. I was nice to her, & it was quite easy. The folk song idea is dropped (thank goodness) (probably – thro' Decca),[5] & she wants me to play Fauré for her – I said, well maybe I was signed or going to be for HMV & she seemed contented to leave it at that. I'm too fond of her to be rude, & not interested enough to be critical.[6] In other words, just weak, weak, weak. I know, you old so & so. All my love, my heart. Saw Wulff yesterday, & he was impossible – but Barbara's going to take him on now – says I shouldn't see him much, with which opinion I am in complete agreement.

> Much love, you old success you. Ring or write.
> Love to Esther,
> B

1 *Les Six*, the last (24 September) in a series of three concerts of French music given under the auspices of the French National Committee at the Wigmore Hall. Britten played the celeste in Durey's *Images à Crusoe* (Perse; 1918) for voice, string quartet, flute, clarinet and celeste, and Tailleferre's *Images* (1918) for eight instruments (piano, flute, clarinet, string quartet, and celeste).

The artists taking part were Sophie Wyss, Irene Kohler (piano), Geoffrey Gilbert and Gareth Morris (flutes), Peter Newbury (oboe), Bernard Walton (clarinet), John Alexandra (bassoon), Dennis Brain (horn), Leonard Hirsch and Gerald Emms (violins), Max Gilbert (viola), Kathleen Moorhouse (cello), Adrian Beers (double-bass), Britten (celeste) and Reginald Goodall (conductor).

2 Dennis Brain (1921–1957), son of Aubrey Brain. Brain made his début in 1938, playing much chamber music. Britten first met him during the war when he was principal horn in the RAF Orchestra. He recalled this first encounter in a tribute, 'Dennis Brain (1921–1957)' in *Tempo*, 46, Winter 1958, pp. 5–6:

> I first met Dennis in the early summer of 1942. I was writing incidental music for a series of radio commentaries on war-time England which were being broadcast weekly to America at the ungodly hour of 3am [*An American in England*]. The orchestra was that of the RAF, in which he was the first horn. I well remember being approached by him at one of the rehearsals, over, I think, some technical point in a solo passage. (Needless to say, having heard his playing in the first programme of the series I took every opportunity to write elaborate horn solos into each subsequent score!). We soon became friends [. . .]

Norman Del Mar, the conductor, was a horn player in 1942 in the RAF Orchestra, along with Brain. In 1989, he remembered this first meeting between Brain and Britten from a slightly different point of view. He recalls Brain asking Britten if he would write a horn concerto for him. Britten responded to this immediate invitation – characteristic of Brain it seems – by questioning him in detail about the technical potential of the horn and what special effects might be persuaded from it. Del Mar remembers the composer asking the horn player if he could hit a top C directly out of the blue (i.e. without approaching it), for example, and his questions to Brain about the fluctuating pitch that can be produced by stopping and unstopping with the hand, from a closed to an open position in the bell, and the harmonics that can be produced on the natural horn. It seems that Brain demonstrated these techniques on the spot to Britten, for his illumination, and, it must have been, to his satisfaction. It is these very devices that emerge in the *Serenade*, which was written with Brain in mind (the top C and fluctuating pitch both emerge in the setting of Blake's 'Elegy').

Brain's beauty of sound and virtuosity of technique led many composers to write works for him, including Britten (*Serenade*; *Canticle III*) and Hindemith. After his tragic death in a car accident Britten began to compose an 'In Memoriam' for four horns and orchestra, incorporating part of the 'Lyke Wake Dirge' from the *Serenade*, but it remained unfinished.

3 Reginald Goodall (1905–1990), English conductor. He studied piano and conducting at the College, 1925–6 and 1929–30, and again, 1932–6, while also visiting Europe to observe many of the leading conductors of the day. His association with Britten began in the

thirties with the Macnaghten Concerts, where he conducted the first performance of Britten's *Te Deum in C major* (in its orchestral version) in 1936. In 1944 he made his début at Sadler's Wells and on 7 June 1945 conducted the historic first performance of *Peter Grimes*. The following year, Goodall shared the first production of *The Rape of Lucretia* at Glyndebourne in 1946 with Ansermet, and in 1947 he conducted *Lucretia* for the English Opera Group. He joined the music staff of Covent Garden in 1946 and thenceforth conducted much of the basic repertory: he not only returned to *Peter Grimes*, but was also to conduct revivals of *Gloriana*. His stature as a Wagner conductor of the first rank began in 1968 with a series of performances at the English National Opera of *Die Meistersinger*, followed by *Parsifal* and a complete *Ring* cycle in English. He was knighted in 1985. Obituaries appeared in the *Independent*, the *Guardian* and *The Times* on 7 May 1990. A supplement to the *Independent*'s obituary was published on 21 May, from which it seems that Britten promised Goodall an exclusivity in performances of *Grimes* in England for the first two years of the opera's life. It also accounts for the circumstances which led to the gift by Goodall of the compositions sketch of the opera to the Britten–Pears Library. (Source: Isador Caplan.)

4 Enrico Caruso (1873–1921), Italian tenor. Victor Maurel (1848–1923), French baritone, who was chosen by Verdi as the first Iago (1887) and the first Falstaff (1893).

5 However Sophie Wyss and Britten later did record two of his French Folk-song Arrangements. See note 2 to Letter 425.

6 Beth writes in EWB, p. 93:

When Ben and Peter Pears returned from the States in 1942, Ben wanted Peter to sing *Les Illuminations*. This caused a rift between the Gydes and Benjamin. Arnold Gyde was furious and thought Sophie should have sung it. Sophie told me that she would rather have remained friends with Ben and did not mind too much, but her husband could not forgive the slight he felt Sophie had received.

393 To Bobby Rothman

P.S Did you get your sailing boat this Summer? I hope so – but don't tell your father or mother I said so!

As from: 11, Tryon House,
Mallord St., S.W. 3.
Sept. 29th 1942.

My dear old Bobby,

You must think I'm a pretty bad correspondent for having left your last letter so long unanswered. But, as usual, I have been terribly, horribly busy, and it is only now that I am in bed with 'flu that I can find a moment to write and thank you for all the news, & the 'photos, and to ask you many, many questions about what you're all doing, & how you all are. Your letter came very quickly – only 9 days; quite a record. But in the winter or fall it usually takes much longer. Nothing at all in your letter was censored – I think it is only if you give exact positions of bombs, or military information that things are cut out – but you mustn't mention the weather at the moment, I don't think, at least, not from this side.

Well – what kind of a summer have you had, old thing? Lots of bathing & sailing, I suppose. Gosh – how jealous that makes me feel. Do you know, even in this small country, I have only seen the sea twice, & haven't bathed once! That's a poor summer for you. I've played tennis, maybe three times, but pretty bad stuff, as it was always raining, & anyhow the balls were so lousy – tennis balls are things you can't get for love or money. I have been working like a trojan the whole time – I wrote ten programmes for the Radio in just over two months – seven of which went direct to you – (6 on C.B.C., one on NBC.).[1] Did you hear any of them? There wasn't much music, only little bits describing a man walking along the street, and the blackout (& that is black, I can tell you!) and things just to liven the show up a bit. But the shows themselves were pretty good. I have also been travelling around the country for a society called CEMA, which is run by the Government in order to give people music who otherwise don't get it (you see, inspite of you not being so crazy over it, a lot of people do like it a good deal!!!). We go to small villages, & play on pianos all out of tune, when some of the notes won't go down & those that do won't come up, and altogether have a pretty hectic time. The travelling is not so hot either – there are very few trains, and one seldom gets a seat and they usually stop at every station (much worse than the Long Island Railroad!), & in between stations too! Just occasionally we are able to go by car when there is no railway near – but the CEMA car, which has to do for seven counties, has only enough gas to do 200 miles a month – so that's not much is it? By-the-way driving in the blackout isn't much fun, especially on country roads that you don't know well, & when all sign-posts have been removed! I've got completely & utterly lost more than once, but so far, touch wood, I haven't driven into a ditch! I have been in quite a few air-raids, but with nothing very near; just abit noisy. But I'm not nearly so scared as I was at first – you get quickly used to them. The only thing that gives me the heeby-

jeebies are the sirens, which make the most horrible noise all
going up & down at different moments. But people don't take
much notice of them at the moment, unless something happens
to drop pretty close!

I am looking forward to hearing how you enjoyed your camp &
what you did there. Where was it this year? Did you take any
'photos, & anyhow when are you going to send those ones you
promised me? I liked the ones you sent very much, especially the
one of me holding you up – it doesn't look there as if you weighed
110 lbs.! I suppose you've grown alot since I saw you – I wonder
how long it'll be before I see you all again. I'll try & keep the air-
mail blue stamps going, if you write back before long that's to say – !
I wonder how different this winter will be from the usual one for
you. I suppose you'll feel the gas & rubber rationing abit – but
apart from sugar you aren't short at all, are you? Here it's quite
good really, except for the luxuries (for us!) of cream, eggs, &
butter & jams; but no one looks starving & I haven't lost any weight
so far. Well, Bobby, old sport, give the enclosed notes to your
father & Mrs. Sturmdorf, please, & when you write back, do it
yourself & don't let Emma correct it for you! After all, I am not
so hot at spelling either!

Love to all the family, & lots to yourself, & write soon & tell me
lots of news,

BEN

1 In addition to the series, *An American in England*, Britten also refers
to *Britain to America* (Series I, No. 9): 'Britain through American
eyes', written by Louis MacNeice and first broadcast by CBS on 20
September. See also PR, pp. 625–8.

394 To David Rothman

As from: 11 Tryon House,
Mallord St, S.W. 3.
Sept. 29th 1942.

My dear David,

I was delighted to get your letter – really thrilled & both Peter &
I read & re-read it lots of times. It gave such a wonderful picture
of your life, that I know so well and cannot hear too much about.
I really felt very homesick for you all – which I am afraid I very
frequently do feel! Life is so completely different over here, one's
perspectives are so absolutely changed, that those three glorious

years I spent in the States are becoming more & more dreamlike in
quality – and a very beautiful dream it was too! But in many ways
too, I am very glad to be back here – there is so much good work
one can do, and thank God I am allowed to do it, and one feels
in a more direct contact with one's own people. I am enjoying
seeing all my friends & family of course, and I must say I have
been welcomed back professionally in the most wonderful way.
(One always has one's enemies of course, and they enjoy having
a stick to beat one with). I have had so much work offered me that
it is quite embarrassing – for which I must be very grateful,
especially as it is work which is constructive in these most terrible
destructive days. Peter is continuing in his successful way – he had
an enormous success the other day in singing some new songs of
mine, and you should hear his voice now – it's quite startling! If
he knew I were writing he'd send his love to all of you; he is talking
about you & his enjoyable times in Southold; actually he is on
tour at the moment, & I have come to the country to work – &
have gone straight to bed with 'flu (which is why this writing is
so eccentric!). This is only a note, David, to apologise for not having
answered your lovely letter before (to encourage you to write again
too!); I hope to have time to write fully later on. I hope Joan gives
you as much pleasure from her piano as ever – give her my love –
& Emma too, is she married yet? – & to your dear wife, and lots
to young Dave [ie Bobby], look after yourself, & don't forget –

Your

BENJAMIN

395 To Thomas Pitfield[1]

As from: 11, Tryon House,
Mallord St., S.W.3.
Sept 29th 1942

Dear Mr. Pitfield,

Yes, I do remember meeting you at the O.U.P., but that must
have been many years ago, since I haven't had anything to do
with that respected firm for a very long time!

You interest me very much when you say that you also are a
C.O. It is extraordinary how many of one's colleagues are with
one in this, and if not actually with, are extremely sympathetic. I
meet a bit of opposition, it is true, but I should think, compared
to the last war, or to America, very little. At my first Tribunal I had

a pretty sticky time, inspite of Stuart's efforts, and only got Non-combatent. The appellate was far more sympathetic. I hope you didn't fare too badly. If you are ever in London (the above address usually gets me eventually), I should very much like to meet you again.

Many thanks for having written,

With best wishes,
Yours sincerely,
BENJAMIN BRITTEN

1 Thomas B. Pitfield (b. 1903), English composer, artist and poet, who studied at the Royal Manchester College of Music, the staff of which he joined in 1947. He became Professor of Composition, a post he continued to hold when the College was merged with the Northern School of Music in 1972. He retired in 1973. His works include a piano concerto, a Concert Piece for orchestra and a choral trilogy.

396 To Mary Behrend

As from: 11 Tryon House,
Mallord St, S.W. 3.
Sept 30th 1942

My dear Mrs. Behrend,

I am so glad that you understand about your concert – it is such a pity but things have just got abit out of hand at the moment & I have got to go carefully. But in the near future I do hope you'll let us do something for you.

I was delighted, & so will Peter be when I tell him, that you were so pleased with the Michelangelo. I was rather nervous about presenting them, as a matter of fact, since we had done them together so much, so far, to friends & in such intimate circumstances, & it seemed cruel to parade them in the cold light of the Wigmore Hall. However the reception really warmed my heart. We are doing them very soon again for the National Gallery, & for H.M.V., which will be nice.

Do let me know when you have any definite news about George. I am so anxious for him.[1]

With many greetings to you both
Yours,
BENJAMIN B

P.S.   Please forgive the sketchiness of this scrawl, but I have been laid up with a particularly virulent kind of 'flu this week.

1 The Behrends' son, in the Eighth Army, had been on embarkation
leave and was now at sea en route for Egypt.

397 To Elizabeth Mayer

As from: 11, Tryon House,
Mallord St., S.W. 3.
Sept. 30th 1942

My dearest Elizabeth,

At last there is time for a quiet chat with you! I really felt that
the moment would never come. True, in this case, it is an 'ill
wind', because it is only the fact that I have been down with 'flu
for a few days & am still in bed that I have got a moment to write
to you, my dearest, who are always in my thoughts. Do not worry
about me, because it is <u>nothing at all</u> serious; just merely abit run
down after this hurricane of work, & general condition caused by
lack of Vitamin this or that – or so my nice new doctor, a
Norwegian, tells me. She takes me very seriously & I have bottle
after bottle of the most revolting medicines to take (Usually I
forget them until Barbara jumps on my tail, or Enid, or Ursula, or
anyone else around!). Well, my dear, where does one start? Or
perhaps one doesn't bother to get any order into it – just chats and
sees what comes first into one's mind. First of course is some
first-hand (via telephone) news of you & William via Basil Wright.[1]
I could have wished for another emissary, someone who knew
you or me or Wystan better, but he is nice & brought me back some
little news of you. He loved seeing William, & gave me himself
your lovely letter. Actually he didn't get back until quite recently,
being longer in Canada than he expected. He brought with him the
Oratorio[2] which, I must say, knocked me all of a heap. It is so
wonderful to think of our dear Wystan going on writing & writing
this grand stuff, not oblivious of, but seeing through & digesting,
all the ghastly things around us, & impervious to stupid criticism.
He seems more like a giant when one is removed from him than
ever. I had a sweet letter from him this morning giving me news
of you, & saying that he is out of the Army – for what reason I
don't know, but the main thing is that he <u>is</u> out, & can go on
with his superb work. I am so terribly glad that both you and he
can be together so often – although I feel pangs of jealousy to
think of it! But this can't last for ever, & I know we'll be together
before too long again. Talking of army, you know that I got the best
possible result at my second Tribunal?[3] I am now left completely

free to go on with my work. It wasn't nearly as agonising as the
first; Stuart Morris who was my council was very good, & both
Montagu Slater & William Walton were excellent witnesses – & I
got myself one of those (for me) rare rays of light, when
everything seemed so clear & simple, in spite of the fact that I had
been up all night at a Radio show,[4] and I wasn't caught by any
of the childish inanities, which usually defeat the most intelligent
'Objectors'!! I was terribly relieved by it of course, & immediately
started feeling guilty about the whole situation – why was I able to
go on working while so many others . . . . etc. etc. However, that
was just reaction I suppose, & I've made up for it by doing this
load of work which otherwise I wouldn't touch, & also by having
the insults & embarrassments which are pretty frequent even in
1942. However, my real friends are so sweet – even young Piers
Dunkerley (you remember!), who is having such a stinking time in
convoy work, spends as much time as possible with me. We were
at Snape together a week ago! My dearest, why am I boring you
with all these stupid little details? Merely because I feel you are
with me – & in fact I'm sure it was you who suddenly pulled your
usual divine strings & gave me that clearness on my day of
Tribulation! Poor old Peter is not through yet & is still waiting. It
is awfully trying for him, but he is singing better than ever and
caused really a great sensation with the first performance of the
Michelangelo last Wednesday! I sent you a cable about it – which
I hope you got. It was very exciting, but how I wish you'd been
there. I was dreadfully nervous – after all the wonderful times we
had with it – with Mrs. Mahler, & Werfel[5] & the Wolfs,[6] do you
remember? – it was rather like parading naked in public. But the best
happened & it was most warmly received & we have at once been
engaged to repeat it in several places – at the National Gallery[7] &
also P. was signed to record it for H.M.V. (our Victor) & so, who
knows, before long we'll have a nice copy sent to you! He is
singing so beautifully now – everyone, even the old enemies,
admits it at last. I have just finished the second proofs of your
St. Cecilia[8] – I hope to be able to post you your copy very soon.
That is down for performance in December; it is such an intimate
little piece that I can't hope for any success with it, but I hope it'll
give one's friends a little something – above all, I hope my dearest,
it'll give you a little of what I always want to give you, & I really
think it will. What other news? O, the Sinfonia[9] is going very well
– performances scheduled for London again, Manchester,
Liverpool, Stockholm even – & they are going to print a new

edition of it. "Les Illuminations" goes on steadily – mostly with
Sophie, I'm afraid, although Peter has shown people now how it
really goes. Did I tell you how disappointing her show of it is? So
hopelessly inefficient, subjective & (of all things) so coy &
whimsey!!! We did it together (P. & I) for Russian relief the other
night,[10] to the great joy of Madame Maisky[11] who has become
quite a fan of mine – & I think we may do a complete programme
for her Russian fund before long. What else? – O, Clifford Curzon
(an excellent pianist, who has become a great friend of ours, & his
American wife) & I are to do the 2 piano stuff & the Ballad soon
– shades of the two gizzards! No one can tackle the quartet yet, for
it's just too darn difficult, apparently. And I'm writing . . . ? –
well, my Sonata for orchestra limps along between radio jobs, my
Christmas Carols (for children's voices & harp) are nearly done,
the opera libretto is finished (& excellent too)[12] & I'm doing separate
vocal works with Louis MacNeice,[13] whom we see a great deal of,
& with Montagu Slater, at whose house I'm now in bed and Enid
is looking after me so beautifully – & Carol (youngest of three,
do you remember the lovely photograph?) keeps me amused. She
has a new dog – a small pekenese who is being mauled about by
her. How's old Jippy, by-the-way? How does he get on without his
Master's Voice? I must make a record & send it!! I see Barbara
quite alot – in fact I dine with her at least once a week, & quite
often spend nights with her, since getting about in the black-out
is so difficult. Actually the flat, or rather small house, where Peter
& I are living till our own flat materialises (which will be when
either, or both, of us has time to think about it), is quite near her
– just on the Embankment. It belongs to Ursula Nettleship, a dear
person who runs alot of these CEMA Concerts in Villages & small
towns all over the East of England. Whenever possible Peter or I,
mostly together, do concerts for her. We go all over the place,
under the strangest conditions – playing on awful old pianos –
singing easy, but always good, programmes – & really have the
greatest successes with the simplest audiences. The worst part is
the travelling – which is no fun these days – what trains there are
are packed (seldom one gets a seat), and terribly slow, & of course
at night very very dim & dismal. One is never sure at any place
whether one will be able to be put up or not, so it is quite
adventurous! However, I feel it is absolutely worth it, because, as
we have so often agreed, it does get music really to the people,
finds out what they want & puts the emphasis on the music, & not
the personality of the artist, or their previous fame. One starts

completely from 'scratch' as it were, since more often than not, they haven't even heard of Schubert – much less, Britten or Pears!!

How I loved the picture William sent of Pemaquid[14] Point, & what heartrending memories it brought back! I do so hope you enjoyed it & came back refreshed. But your hot weather sounds very trying – altho' here one would have given alot for a little of it – I don't think I've ever felt so cold; what this winter's going to be like I just daren't imagine! And I was almost forgetting to thank you for the enormous trouble you took over my accounts – thank you so very much, my dear, it was sweet of you, & must have been a most colossal bore. But it has given me all I want to know – unless my accountant rakes up something new. I am still in a bit of a jam about taxes, but have no doubt that they'll be settled before long. It is all abit ludicrous, with mounting prices & colossal taxes – one gets abit reckless & says – let the future take care of itself which I trust it will!! By-the-way, my dear, I don't know if you still can send things – but if you can, could you possibly send any shirts or so that I left behind – especially the sports ones with big collars. I am so short of them & never dreamed that they would be so useful! What news of Michael & Christopher? I hope they're getting on as well as they always seem to. And Ulli? Beata I am going to write a note to in William's which I hope to be able to write tomorrow – & to Wystan, & Aaron & Colin and so many, so many, that I just <u>can't</u> get round to. Do you know I have been writing letters (just silly business ones) for two days & <u>still</u> am no where near clear yet. O – for the help of your typewriter! Dearest Elizabeth, Enid is just going to post and must take this, so I'll say au revoir for the moment. You know, even if I don't write, how much I think of you and love you. It's no good, my life is just not complete until I get back to you; you don't realise how desparately I need you! My dearest love to William, and to all my good friends you may see, & so much, that I can't begin to say, to you from your devoted

BENJAMIN

1 In 1942 Wright was visiting North America on behalf of John Grierson and the Ministry of Information (see Elizabeth Sussex, *The Rise and Fall of British Documentary* (Berkeley, University of California Press, 1975), pp. 135–6).

2 In October 1941, while teaching undergraduates at the State University of Ann Arbor, Auden began work on a long poem provisionally entitled 'A Christmas Oratorio' (later to be called 'For the Time

Section I

BASS SOLO

My shoes were shined, my pants were cleaned and pressed,
And I was hurrying to meet
    My own true Love:
But a great crowd grew and grew
Till I could not push my way through,
    Because
A star had fallen down the street;
When they saw who I was,
The Police tried to do their best.

Semi-chorus I
(off)
Semi-chorus 2

Joseph the Just was sober and staid,
He chiselled a living from the carpentry trade;
Mary his love, was alone a lot;
That leads to trouble, believe it or not.

B.S.

The bar was gay, the lighting well-designed,
And I was sitting down to wait
    My own true Love:
A voice I'd heard before, I think,
Cried - "This is on the House. I drink
    To him
Who does not know he is too late;"
When I asked for the time,
Everyone was very Kind.

S-C I
S-C 2

Joseph the Worker sweated away
With hammer and plane through the heat of the day.
Mary, his sweetheart, sat in the wood,
Catching a chill that changed her for good.

B.S.

Through cracks, up ladders, into waters deep,
I squeezed, I climbed, I swam, to save
    My own true Love:
Under a dead apple tree
I saw an ass; when it saw me
    It brayed;
A hermit sat in the mouth of a cave;
When I asked him the way,
He pretended to be asleep.

S-C I
S-C 2

Mary the Modest was met in the lane
By Someone or Something she couldn't explain.
Joseph the Honest looked up and God's eye
Was winking at him through a hole in the sky.

B.S.

Disjointed items stopped my life to say
How proud they were to satisfy
    My own true Love:
Hair, muscle, clothing, noses, necks,
A prince's purse, a sailor's sex
    Appeal;
And my horns grew up to the sky;
When I asked if they were real,
All giggled and ran away.

S-C I
S-C 2

Mary the Maiden, merry and mild
Walked down to the brook and came back with a child.
Joseph the Gentle is a jilted Jew.
Where's the wild father, The fun is on you.

B.S.

Where are you, Father, where?
Caught in the jealous trap
Of an empty house I hear
As I sit alone in the dark
Everything, everything,
The drip of the bath-room tap,

A page of Auden's typed libretto for the 'Christmas Oratorio', with suggested deletions marked by Britten

Being'). It was intended as a major work for Britten to set to music. Simultaneously, it was conceived as a memorial to Auden's mother and as a private coming to terms with his crisis-ridden relationship with Chester Kallman, achieved through religious faith.

While only one example has survived of Britten's letters to Auden, much of the chronology of Auden's work on the Oratorio and Britten's in the main geographically distant collaboration may be gleaned from the poet's letters to the composer. Auden had written to Britten at Amityville on 11 November 1941:

I have sketched out the First Movement of the Oratorio (1.Chorus and semi-chorus Pride. 2. Narrator. 3. Trio. 4. Narrator. 5. Chorus) and am starting on the 2nd Movement which opens with a boys' chorus.

(Berg Collection, New York Public Library)

On 27 November, Britten, accompanied by Pears and Elizabeth Mayer, travelled to Ann Arbor to stay with Auden, where the composer and poet naturally discussed their new project.

Auden continued working at the Oratorio in the New Year, sending sections to Britten as they were completed. He had written in late January (Letter 364):

Here are one and a half more movements. The second half of the fourth movement will be about the Taxing of the People.

(Berg Collection)

On 8 July, and with the composer now back in England, Auden wrote:

I shall really finish the Oratorio by the end of the month. I would of course like to have more time for revisions, but we shall see. I wrote several alterations in the parts you have, but will send two copies of the whole work as soon as it is done.

Auden did indeed complete the Oratorio and entrusted one typescript (now held in the Archive) to Basil Wright, who delivered it to the composer; a second typescript (also in the Archive) was sent to Britten via Auden's father. Both copies show evidence of having been used by the composer, but perhaps most interestingly, the second copy has a list of characters with voices assigned, inscribed in Britten's hand:

Narrator
Soloists:

	Soprano	(Mary)
	Alto	(Star)
	Tenor	(God)
	Bass	(Joseph)
	3 Magi	(Tenors)
	3 Shepherds	(Basses)
	Boys' Chorus	(S.S.A.A.)
	Semichorus	(S.A.T.B.)
	Chorus	(S.S.A.A.T.T.B.B.)

(Another, less interesting typescript is also in the Archive. It is an incomplete carbon which lacks the first two pages and has been only slightly annotated by Britten).

Auden dispatched to Britten a detailed set of instructions on 11 September:

I sent you the completed MS of the Oratorio via Basil Wright. I do hope it arrived safely. (I had lunch with Basil and Grierson – you can imagine how awful it was). If it didn't arrive, I've also sent a copy to my father via Clipper and told him to get in touch with you [. . .]

As you know the directions as to voices etc are purely tentative on my part. In the Massacre of the Innocents section, between parts 2 and 3, there should be an orchestral interlude, I think, representing the massacre itself, leading into the lament (part 3). The shepherds song (O lift your little pinkie) should be either jazz or Folk-song (Guitar – concertina – bagpipe or what-have-you) dont you think? In the final bit of all (He is the Way etc) it strikes me that you might want some Amens. (e.g. . . . .unique adventures. Amen. . . . . for years. Amen. . . . . dance for joy. Amen). If you do, just ad lib them as you feel inclined.

Please write and tell me if you've got it, if you like it, and if you want any changes made. . . . Delighted to hear you got through your tribunal O.K.

In this same letter Auden comments on Shostakovich's Seventh ('Leningrad') Symphony: '[. . .] as a whole, I thought it pretty awful, though obviously the work of a musician, the voulu political art of a guilty individual'.

In spite of Britten's obvious ardour for the text there is little evidence that the composer made progress with the piece in the winter of 1942–3. Auden was to write again, on 23 March 1943:

(a)   Have just got St. Cecilia and think it lovely. Thank you my dear.
(b)   Re Oratorio (For the Time Being) cut
    1)   the ballad verses in St. Joseph (Joseph the Joiner was sober & staid etc).
    2)   the limericks in the Magi bit.

As I think about it, I feel convinced that the whole thing is a piece of chamber music, calling for small orchestra and a choir of a dozen, ideally, for radio performance.

Though of course you would do something totally different and better, I think the Drei Groschen Oper is an example of how words can be set so as to be heard. There are of course places where you should let yourself go.

Do drop me a line to tell me if you have had any ideas. [. . .] I miss you and Peter very much indeed. Give him my love, and take lots yourself.

Peter Pears, in a letter to Humphrey Carpenter (18 April 1980), recalled Britten's reactions to Auden's text:

The parting of the ways (from Auden) began, as it seems to me, with the so-called, by Ben, 'Christmas Oratorio', which Ben had expected as a text for music, but it turned out to be a major opus, quite unsuitable without vast cuts for an Oratorio libretto. My memory (very bad) tells me that Ben realised then that he could not take Wystan seriously as a librettist and/or

Wystan could not take him (Ben) seriously as a composer. He, Ben, was hurt and bored by this. I do remember the receipt of 'For the Time Being' and how Ben was bitterly disappointed with, for instance, the Fugue (a few syllables are enough for a Fugue) – Wystan wrote 7 stanzas of 10 lines each. [. . .] and one of [the] things Ben had learnt from Paul Bunyan was that in creating new large scale musical works it was of the utmost importance that the poet and composer should work together from the outset. When a large section of the work arrived, Ben was desperate at how far Wystan had gone ahead without him and he was much more confident of himself as a composer now, so he abandoned the whole idea. We had, too, decided to come back to England, which Wystan highly disapproved of, and so came the cooling. Ben was on a different track now, and he was no longer prepared to be dominated – bullied – by Wystan, whose musical feeling he was very well aware of. Anyway Ben was thinking about Peter Grimes and perhaps he may be said to have said goodbye to working with Wystan with his marvellous setting of the Hymn (Anthem) to St. Cecilia [. . .]

Pears's recollections are clearly of special importance. But his memory on occasion could be faulty, and as our research shows, detailed discussion of the Oratorio continued *after* Britten's departure from the USA. The impression left by examining the documentary evidence is not quite one of the composer finding his collaborator totally inflexible, nor one of disappointment in the quality of the text itself, which he described as 'grand stuff [. . .] like a giant [. . .] superb work'. It is interesting, indeed, that Britten's and Auden's friendship seems to have been little affected by the departure of Britten and Pears from the States and that the composer's esteem for the poet was still at a high point in the autumn of 1942 and even later. For example in November 1944, in two letters to Pears (Nos. 487 and 489), Britten was to write, 'Wystan has sent his book [. . .] The Oratorio is as lovely and grand as ever', and '[. . .] my God there'll be a part for you in the Oratorio! It's a superb piece.' The 'goodbye' was certainly to come, but later than Pears suggested and perhaps factors other than the abortive 'Christmas Oratorio' enterprise were also involved. Some have thought that the final rupture may have been generated by Auden's adverse reaction to *Billy Budd*, which he had seen in Paris in 1952, when he had also met Britten. (See MKBB, p. 160.) However, a year later, in 1953, Auden was invited to make what proved to be his first and last appearance at an Aldeburgh Festival, when he gave a lecture on 26 June, the subject of which was 'to be announced'. In a letter to Eric Walter White on 30 June, Britten wrote, 'Auden has come and gone, giving a most provocative (& fine!) Lecture [. . .]'. See, however, Addenda, pp. 1338–9.

It is clear from a letter dated 2 July 1943 from Auden to Britten that the composer had made at least one successful attempt to persuade Auden to revise the text. Auden replied:

Enclosed are a list of alterations to the Oratorio. I hope you will be relieved at no longer having to set <u>piles</u>.

In the event Britten did not set any of the text at this period. However, in 1944 he composed a Chorale ('after an old French Carol'), 'Our Father, whose creative will', and 'A Shepherd's Carol' ('O lift your little pinkie') for a BBC radio programme, *A Poet's Christmas*, broadcast on 24 December by the BBC Singers conducted by Leslie Woodgate, and produced by Edward Sackville-West. See also Charles H. Miller, *Auden: An American Friendship* (New York, Scribner's, 1983) p. 74, in which appears a recollection by Strowan Robertson of 'how hurt Wystan was when Benjy abandoned the project'.

The 'Shepherd's Carol' was first published by Novello in 1962. 'A Shepherd's Carol' and the 'Chorale' received their first concert performances on 14 December 1961 at Grosvenor Chapel, South Audley Street, London W1, by the Purcell Singers conducted by Imogen Holst. (The same concert also included Lennox Berkeley's contribution to *A Poet's Christmas*, his setting of Frances Cornford's 'There was neither grass, nor corn'.) A BBC copyist's score of the 'Chorale' appeared in facsimile in the *Score*, 28 January 1961, pp. 47–51, and was commercially recorded by the Elizabethan Singers conducted by Louis Halsey on Argo ZRG 54 24 (1963).

3 The Appellate Tribunal had granted him unconditional exemption. Ralph Hawkes submitted a written testimonial on Britten's behalf to the Chairman of the Tribunal. See also MKWW, p. 116.

4 One of the series, *An American in England*, broadcast live to the USA at 3 a.m. London time.

5 Alma Mahler-Werfel, née Schindler (1879–1964), and her husband, the novelist, Franz Werfel (1890–1945). A dyeline copyist's copy of the *Michelangelo Sonnets* (held at the British Library) is inscribed to Alma Mahler in Britten's hand and dated February 1942, Amityville. The Mayers' visitors' book shows the signature of Alma Mahler and Franz Werfel on 1 January. It is likely that Pears and Britten performed the *Sonnets* for the Werfels on this occasion and later sent the copy for Alma, who had returned to California with her husband. After this first meeting, she wrote to Britten from the hotel where she was staying in New York:

> St. Moritz On-the-Park
> Fifty Central Park South
> New York
> [Postmarked 19 January 1942]

My dear Mr Britten,

I was hoping to see you before you are going away and I was longing to see Mrs Mayer also. But I was ill – 8 days and could not move out of bed. Now it is better and I do hope to see you in the Mahler concert on Thursday!

<u>Friday</u> we are leaving here. [*word illegible*] <u>Ring</u> me up in the morning –
please – Perhaps we find a moment to see each other. No – please! <u>come</u>
<u>Wednesday afternoon to us!</u> Many many thanks and greetings to your charm-
ing parents [presumably the Mayers] and to you and for that wonderful
singer!

Yours
ALMA MAHLER WERFEL

Excuse my English.

Britten was to meet Mrs Mahler once again when on tour in Califor-
nia in the autumn of 1949. A collection of letters and cables from
Alma to Britten up to the 1960s is in the Archive. His last orchestral
song-cycle, the *Nocturne*, Op. 60, was dedicated to her. See also Peter
Stephen Jungk, *A Life torn by History: Franz Werfel 1890–1945* (London,
Weidenfeld and Nicolson, 1990).

6 Kurt and Helene Wolff, publishers and founders of Kurt Wolff Verlag
in Munich, where they were friends of the Mayers. In America they
founded Pantheon Books, New York.

7 The repeat performance at the National Gallery took place on 22
October. In 1943, Britten and Pears performed the *Sonnets* at the
Wigmore Hall, on 27 February, at the Arts Theatre, Cambridge, on
25 April and again in London (at Charlton House) on 2 May. The
first broadcast performance, which took place on 20 July on the BBC
Home Service, was instigated by Lennox Berkeley, who was then
employed by the BBC, and wrote to Britten on 6 June:

I've at last got them to fix a provisional date for the Michelangelo Sonnets,
in the Home Service – you will be hearing about this soon, but don't say
anything about it to anyone until you do, as technically it has nothing to do
with me.

The broadcast of the *Michelangelo Sonnets* was the subject of an introductory article by Ralph Hill, 'National Gallery Concerts', in the *Radio
Times*, 16 July.

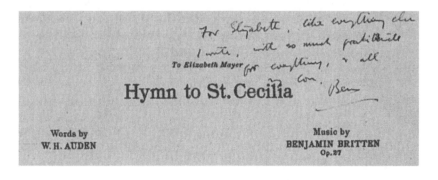

Britten's dedication of the published edition of the *Hymn to St Cecilia* to Elizabeth
Mayer

8 *Hymn to St Cecilia*, Op. 27, was first published in 1942. The first public performance was to take place on 28 November at the Wigmore Hall, when the BBC Singers were conducted by Leslie Woodgate.

'G.A.' [Gerald Abraham] wrote in the *Observer*, 6 December:

The outstanding feature of the third Boosey and Hawkes concert at the Wigmore Hall on November 28 was the first non-broadcast performance of Britten's 'Hymn to St Cecilia', an unaccompanied choral setting of a poem by Auden. The most certain of all contemporary British composers in technical approach, Britten is the least certain in assessing the value of his inspiration; he can never distinguish between the divine spark and the spark of the firework manufacturer; but in this work he has not invoked St Cecilia in vain. It is not merely that the 'Hymn' *sounds* well; Britten's music almost always does. This is music that will probably last when Mr Britten's Roman candles are long burnt out.

9 The London Philharmonic Orchestra was to give the second performance on 6 December at the Orpheum, Golders Green, London, on this occasion conducted by Constant Lambert. The pocket score of the *Sinfonia* was published by Boosey & Hawkes in 1944.

10 Britten had been one of the signatories in an exchange of greetings between British composers and their Russian colleagues on 26 August.

11 The wife of the USSR Ambassador in London.

12 Philip Brett, in PGPB, pp. 58 *et seq.*, speculates that the libretto was completed at Christmas. This letter, unknown in 1983 to Professor Brett, reveals an earlier date of completion.

13 Britten had made an incomplete setting of MacNeice's 'Cradle Song' ('Sleep, my darling, sleep') while in America, probably in 1941 or early 1942; it now forms part of the Elizabeth Mayer Collection at the Archive. The poem was published in MacNeice's collection, *Plant and Phantom* (London, Faber and Faber, 1941), p. 86. After his return to England, Britten completed a new setting of the same poem for voice and piano, no doubt because of his renewed association with MacNeice and his wife, Hedli Anderson. It remained unperformed and unpublished: the manuscript is in the Archive.

14 The Mayers had been on holiday at Pemaquid Point, Maine, during July and August.

The first page of Britten's second and complete setting of Louis MacNeice's 'Cradle Song'

398 To William Mayer

As from: 11, Tryon House,
Mallord St., S.W. 3.
Oct. 3rd 1942.

My dearest William,

I <u>am</u> sorry that there has been this long silence, but please believe
that it isn't because I'd forgotten all about you – far from it, you
are in my mind (conscious & unconscious!) the whole time –
wondering what you are doing, how the general Amityville
position is, whether the general war situation is affecting you
personally and how Jippy is too! How home-sick I feel for
Amityville! You were right when you used to say, driving along
the Merrick road[1] that there would be many things that I should
be home-sick for. Well, there are – in particular the colossal social
freedom of the States. So many things over here seem so petty now
one has known the other. The lack of enterprise worries one. And
too, the opportunities for art are so much greater in the new
World. Above all I feel homesick for the heavenly atmosphere of
Amityville – the really warm friendship and understanding that
we felt, greater than I have ever known before & shall ever know
again – until we come back to the States to you again – which,
pray God, can be sooner than seems possible at the moment. I am
glad that you are taking this room in New York.[2] I hope it'll be
the opening of a new door for you, & I am sure that in the present
trying conditions it is best for you to do it gradually like this. I
suppose you have lots of patients who are just champing for you
to arrive. How is Fine [Kahler], by the way? And Brigitte [Steiner]?
Do give them my love when, & if you are seeing them these days.
Well, I am keeping pretty busy these days – I have been welcomed
back very warmly – much more so than I would have dreamed
possible, and I think that is a very good sign, don't you – because
people could be so very nasty. Certainly a few are, but not my
friends, or the people who hand out jobs!! I am glad you heard
some of the CBS broadcasts. Unfortunately they were done under
very trying circumstances – in a terrible rush, in the midst of other
troublesome things, in other people's houses, without any peace
or quiet (how I regretted Amityville!) – & so really I am surprised
that they came out as passable as they did! But I've told the Radio
people now that I want to [do] much less of that kind of thing –
just a few nice programmes now & then. I'll let you know when

anything nice is broadcast. In the meantime I am trying to get on
with some old things that I want to get finished, getting on very
well with the opera (the first draft of the libretto is done – how I
wish you could be in on these discussions, I am sure you would
have some good ideas. Do you remember when we & Otto[3] drove
& talked it over? How is he – my love to him please), and I do lots
of concerts with Peter all over the place. I think you really would
be delighted with his voice & singing now – it has developed
enormously, ever since coming back. It is so much stronger &
richer. He does the Michelangelo & the Illuminations[4] to make you
cry now. We are making records of the former, & hope to send
you a copy soon – & also the latter if it can be arranged.

Conditions are not going to be too pleasant I am afraid this
winter. The food is not bad but it gets me down abit, & I'm always
having colds & 'flu & other things. However, I'm under a good
doctor who is doing things for it. There's not much fuel, or means
of keeping warm – but luckily my American clothes will help
counteract that. I haven't been very near any bombs yet, although
in these tours over the East of England one occasionally has
excitements, and the Mill is fairly noisy sometimes. But everything
is still standing there – & I go a great deal when I want to relax –
because, strange as it may seem, there is something impersonal
about that kind of excitement which makes it easier to cope with
than the 'busyness' & hectic rush that London is these days – I've
never known it to be so full (you can't get into a hotel or get rooms
for love or money) – unless of course the raids get too bad. Well,
my dear William, enough of this meandering. Please take it in the
spirit in which it is meant – that I love you very much & just want
to have a casual chat with you as we were always doing in the
good old days. Would you please send the enclosed note to Colin,[5]
if you know where he is. How do you really think he is. I have
had some pretty depressed notes from him.

Very, very much love, & all the luck in the world,

Your

BENJAMIN

1 The Merritt Parkway, the first highway to traverse Connecticut.

2 Dr Mayer, from late September, had interviewed prospective patients
in Manhattan, on 61st Street, between Park and Lexington, sharing
his office with Dr Herbert Howe, physician to Artur Rodzinski and
Toscanini. Dr Howe also made Toscanini's batons for him.

3 Otto Zoff: a writer and fellow immigrant of the Mayers, who had

known him in Munich. He was also active in the theatre. For an analysis of the 'Amityville drafts' of the libretto for *Peter Grimes*, see PGPB, pp. 48–50.

4 Internal memoranda (May 1943) at Boosey & Hawkes between Ralph Hawkes and Lesley Boosey indicate that there was a proposal by Walter Legge for Maggie Teyte to record *Les Illuminations* for HMV. Britten fiercely opposed this plan and the project was dropped. Pears was to record the Rimbaud songs twice: with Eugene Goossens and the New Symphony Orchestra (1954, Decca LXT 2941), and with Britten and the English Chamber Orchestra, at the Kingsway Hall, London, in December 1966 (released 1967, Decca SXL 6316).

5 Colin McPhee had written to Britten from Woodstock, New York on 21 July:

How nice to have your letter, and I'd have answered before only I've been low with malaria. [. . .]

I'm here for the summer, two miles from town, in an attractive little place, although it's lonely as hell, as I hate Woodstock people and there's no one else around.

[. . .] I'm not doing much in the way of work, and as for the Guggenheim, that was a drop in a bucket that leaks like a sieve. Next spring if I'm not in the army I'll be in the gutter [. . .]

During the early 1940s McPhee was subject to periods of acute depression. His feeling of his being ignored as a composer was worsened by his precarious financial position. See also Carol J. Oja, *Colin McPhee (1900–1964): A Composer in Two Worlds*, Ph.D. dissertation (City University of New York, 1985), pp. 281 *et seq*.

399 To Enid Slater

104A, Cheyne Walk, S.W. 10.
Nov. 23rd, 1942.

My dearest Enid,

How grand of you to get 'Where Angels'[1] for me. I have wasted hours reading it since it arrived, & love it as much as ever. God – what a cruel book, but how funny, & how damnably real. Thank you, my dear, a great deal. It was sweet of you.

This is written very late at night, after a hell of a day, & my fever which has been on me all the week hasn't left me yet. But the specialist, as I've told Montagu in detail, says that there's nothing organically wrong with me. Merely he thinks that either because of too much B & M (Sulphur Nilamide etc.),[2] or too much flu in my life, that I have no resistance to germs & I've got to undergo a hell of a cure to get that right. Depressing, but not so depressing (or romantic!) as T.B. or operations or what not! I don't quite know what the cure is yet, but he's warned me that it'll mean giving up coffee!! O law.

Love to the kids – tell Carol not to go <u>too</u> far. . . . . but I'm afraid Peter won't be bald in 14 years, & <u>just</u> as dangerous! How are you my dear? Much love, & many thanks for the Forster.

BEN

1 E.M. Forster's novel, *Where Angels Fear to Tread*, first published in 1905 by Blackwood.

2 Sulphanamide. It was manufactured by May & Baker and known as 'M & B'.

400   To Peter Pears

104A Cheyne Walk,   SW. 10.
Nov. 23rd 1942

My darling,

My hand is falling off, my eyes are falling out, my bottom is aching with so much sitting on, & I'm so sleepy that I can't think, but I must write a note to tell you one or two things, & to say that you are in my thoughts all the time, & that I make myself a bore by talking about you all the time. Sir John W. (who is about 60, & proud of it, tough & very very, o so, Scottish)[1] finds nothing organically wrong with me (luckily he didn't ask me about my morals, which might make the decision not unanimous), but finds that I have practically no resistance to germs whatsoever – he suspects as a result of the Sulpha Nylamide in 1940 – it has that effect occasionally – & must have a long cure – I don't exactly know what he wants yet, but is going to write to me details, send me stuff & says I must give up coffee!!   Boohoo. I was with him nearly 1½ hours, & was pretty well exhausted by the inquisition. However I had a nice lunch with Louis & Hedly, who were sweet, (& I have quite changed my mind <u>again</u>!), & then a mad afternoon, with Stein, printers, copyists, & harpists, & then back here by 7.0 to have a cheerful evening with the telephone & a few letters. And you my darling? Hedli tells me that last night wasn't much fun to sing.[2] Too bad. I'm sorry they didn't realise what they weren't appreciating. I hope the week won't be too strenuous & that Mabel[3] will be simple & easy. Do you know your stuff yet? Try & come back on Friday if you can, but if it's too tiring just don't bother. I can stick another week.

I am still a little disturbed by our saturday night tiff –   Worrying as to whether I am not good for you – not caring enough for your health & work. But, in all humbleness I say it, give me a chance to reform, my dear. I swear in the future I will look after you. Only I just can't bear the thought of separation. I just don't live in times like these.

Take care of yourself.

And need I say it – I love you.

B.

Wire me if you want your ration book[4] – I leave for Snape midday Wednesday.

1 Sir John Weir (1879–1968), physician to King George VI and a leading advocate of homoeopathy.

2 Pears and Hedli Anderson had given a concert in Washington (Co. Durham).

3 Mabel Ritchie.

4 Ration books had been issued in September 1939 but were not brought into use until January 1940. Food, clothes and petrol were the major items for which rationing was introduced.

401 To Benjamin Britten
From Peter Pears

In the train
[?23 November 1942]

My beloved darling –

I've just left you & we haven't started yet – I <u>have</u> to write down again just what you mean to me. You are so sweet taking all the blame for our miserable tiffs,[1] our awful nagging heart-aches – but I know as well as I know anything that it is really <u>my</u> fault. I don't love you enough, I don't try to understand you enough, I'm not Christian enough. You are <u>part of me</u>, and I get cross with you and treat you horribly and then feel as if I could die of hurt, and then I realise why I feel so hurt and aching. It's because you are part of me and when I hurt and wound you, I lacerate my very self. O my darling do forgive me. I do love you so dearly and I want you so dreadfully. I am so ambitious for you, as I am for

myself. I want us both to be <u>whole</u> persons. This division is
deadly. One see one's faults, decides what to do, & doesn't do it.
We have got to have more control over ourselves, to <u>know where
we're going</u>. I don't know how I shall bear not having you again –
and even next week no better –

And I do love you so, my darling. Even these quarrels & agonies
have their uses. They make me love you all the more.

Goodnight, my darling boy –

I kiss you.

P.

1 This letter is undated and we cannot be sure that it relates to the
'tiff' to which Britten refers in the preceding letter. However, it seems
possible that Pears's next letter (No. 402) was a response to Letter
400. The letter above seems to make sense when sited between them.
See also Letter 405.

402 To Benjamin Britten
From Peter Pears

<u>Worcester</u>

[late November 1942]

My darling –

It was lovely to have your letter this morning and to feel you
with me again. I hate being away from you so terribly. I have
such plans of our life together. Do let us start as soon as possible,
getting the right place and relaxing and working together. I do so
love you my darling and this maddening life of perpetual motion
is no good. Enjoy Snape – how I wish I were with you, and give
my love to it.

Mabel is being awfully sweet. She is a very sensitive good artist
– sometimes as a person that funny Christian Science streak
appears, a sort of solemn obstinacy – but she is very serious and
understanding.

Another factory today. Much nicer small audience but nice
people.

O my pussy cat –

O a matterofat

I love you my darling.

P.

403 To Peter Pears

You arn't free to sing the Sonnets to Glock[1] on Monday evening next, are you? Can you let me have a card about this?

104A. [Cheyne Walk, London, S.W.10.]
[early December 1942]

My darling,

So sorry that our conversation was so uncommunicative – but Ursula was in the room & I couldn't say much. We have patched up our little scrap, but I find living here very difficult. She has been in bed all day & had to be waited on abit.

Anyhow, it was heaven to hear your voice, & to know you'd written. Now I look forward to the letters. So sorry you have such a vile journey, & are working so hard. But we'll have a quiet time this Friday & Saturday – what heaven; I can scarcely wait for it, my darling. I go tomorrow to Mrs. Bridge – Friston Field, East Dean 316. It'll be heavenly to be there, all away from this ghastly rush. But I'll have my time cut out to do all this work.[2]

By-the-way the Bank has sent on my pass-book, so there's no need to worry about that. So sorry to have bothered you my darling – in fact I never seem to do <u>anything</u> but bother you do I? But I promise that when we're living alone together that I really will behave outside as I feel inside about you – & need I say how that is? Never never have I or could I love anyone as I love my darling.

Be careful,
B.

1 William Glock (b. 1908), English musical administrator, pianist, edu-cationalist and critic. After Cambridge, Glock studied with Schnabel in Berlin (1930–33). He was a distinguished pianist, but it was in other fields that he became known to the public. Glock joined the *Observer* (1934–45), of which he became chief music critic from 1939. He founded the Summer School of Music at Bryanston in 1948 – later known as Dartington Summer School – and remained Director until 1979. In 1949 he founded and edited the *Score*, a music periodical which appeared until 1961. It was in that year's January issue (No. 28) that Britten's 'Chorale (after an old French Carol)' was first published. From 1959 to 1973 he was Controller, Music, at the BBC, where he introduced a radical policy with regard to contemporary music which had a far-reaching impact on musical life throughout the country. He was knighted in 1970. See also Peter Heyworth, 'Sir William

Glock at 80: A Tribute', and David Drew, 'The Score: An Open Letter to Sir William Glock on the Occasion of his 80th Birthday', in *Tempo*, 167, December 1988, pp. 19–23.

John Amis, in *Amiscellany* (London, Faber and Faber, 1985), p. 134, recalls first seeing Glock in wartime on the platform of the Wigmore Hall in a Britten context:

Peter Pears was to sing the *Seven Sonnets of Michelangelo* but the composer was ill and therefore unable to play the piano so William came on as a substitute, wearing Air Force blue. At that time William was constantly writing about contemporary music in the columns of the *Observer*, but this was one of the few occasions I can recall when he played any of it in public.

Sir William writes in a private communication (1989):

As to the Michelangelo Sonnets, I only remember, really, the rehearsals with Peter at my flat in Hampstead, and the great pleasure I had at the performance. Later on, Peter and I gave a broadcast of the Sonnets in the BBC Indian Service, I think, somewhere underground in Oxford Street. That I do remember because I arrived in London very tired after night duty in the RAF, and made a slip in the first bar or two that has often haunted me since.

Lennox Berkeley was at the Wigmore Hall concert and wrote about it to Britten in an undated letter:

It was disappointing that you weren't able to play at the concert and the songs lost a great deal, but William did extremely well considering that he did it at such short notice, and Peter sang particularly well I thought.

He added a postscript: 'The Michelangelo sound more beautiful every time. I shall never tire of them.'

It was in fact from Berkeley that Britten, while in the USA, had received a letter (5 January 1940) drawing his attention to Glock's singular gifts:

I don't think you ever met William Glock, Observer critic, and an extremely good pianist. He's living here too. You'd like him a lot. He's very austere, and a terrifyingly severe critic – but it really means something with him – he's got a standard which is a real one, and he knows about music – I mean knows what it's about, and is able to detect at once anything 'extra-musical' – i.e. having nothing to do with music.

2 At the end of June Ralph Hawkes had written to Britten, listing the projects and commitments that had occupied the composer during the first half of the year and were to occupy him in the future. Some of them, however, were never to materialize. Hawkes's list comprised: *Rejoice in the Lamb*; *Serenade*; *Ceremony of Carols*; Sonata for orchestra; and cadenzas for concertos by Mozart (flute) and Haydn (harpsichord). As an afterthought, Hawkes adds,

Beyond these you should start no other new composition but devote yourself – upon the completion of the above works – to the Opera for Koussevitsky, the Ballet for Sadler's Wells and the Cantata [*The Rescue?*] for the BBC.

404 To Benjamin Britten
From Peter Pears

Birmingham
[before 7 December 1942]

My darling –

Just a line to say Good Morning and how are you? I should like to wake you up with a kiss but I guess I shall have to postpone that for a couple of days more.

Many thanks for your letter & the forwardings. Sweet letter from Michael. I've answered Joan Cross saying Yes with pleasure. I'm afraid next Monday night is no good for Glock. I have a Christmas Oratorio at Hitchin [7 December], though I shall be back that night late. I've been seeing various people here, all rather nice. But factory concerts are real agony – the getting up and imposing one's music through a mike past clattering plates is only just compensated for by the pleasure it seems to give some of the people. But it is bitter agony.

Much much love my only b.

Your loving
P.

Lot of love to Eth.

405 To Peter Pears

Friston Field, Nr. Eastbourne, Sussex.
East Dean 316
[early December 1942]

My darling man,

Eth is just going off to the post; I hadn't realised that it went so early, – so this can only be a scribble, to say how your letters have been life & breath to me. My darling – to think I have been so selfish as to make you unhappy, when you have so much strain, & such hard work to bear. But I too have come out of this week-end a better person. I seem to be getting things into order abit. Again it seems to be a matter of 'O man, know thyself' – & of knowing what I really want – & living that knowledge. I promise, my darling. . . . . .

It is lovely being here. You must come soon & consummate it.

Eth is an angel, & I think I make her very happy coming. We talk always about you.

I don't think the maisonette that I saw yesterday will do – too far away, too many rooms & abit gloomy. But we can go & look again on Saturday. I called you last night, but you were already out, I'm afraid. I'll try again to-morrow night. Meantime – I live for Friday, & you.

My man – my beloved man.

B.

406   To Benjamin Britten
From Peter Pears

Midland Hotel [Birmingham]
[early December 1942]

My boy – It was such heaven hearing your voice – I woke up again at once – I'd been wiling away the time re-reading Mr. Norris of which I've found a Penguin.[1]

You know, I've been thinking an awful lot about you and me. I love you with my whole being, solemnly and seriously. These last times have made me realise how serious love is, what a great responsibility and what a sharing of personalities – It's not just a pleasure & a self indulgence. Our love must be complete and a creation in itself, a gift which we must be fully conscious of & responsible for.

O my precious darling, parting from you is such agony – Just hearing your voice is joy.

Goodnight, my Ben –

Sleep well, I shall think of you all the time –
Your loving man
P.

Lots of love to Eth.

1 *Mr Norris Changes Trains*, the novel by Christopher Isherwood, first published by the Hogarth Press in 1935.

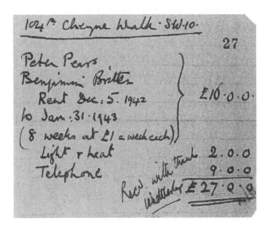

Receipt for accommodation at 104a Cheyne Walk, London SW10, signed by Ursula
Nettleship

407 To Alec Robertson[1]

[Typed]

104a, Cheyne Walk,
Chelsea, S.W.10
17th December, 1942

My dear Alec,

So sorry not to have answered your many and valuable letters
before but I have been madly busy. Anyhow the Plainchant was
perfect for the procession and recession.[2] The whole lot of carols
has been performed about half a dozen times with, I am told,
great success, although I was not there to hear. It is going to be
done at the National Gallery next Monday,[3] if you can be in town
to hear it would be nice, and I should like your comments.

I loved the article you wrote in the Gramophone,[4] it ought to sell
lots of sets. I hear they are going very well – certainly every shop
I go to has sold out. Have you heard them yet? Considering the
circumstances I think they might be a lot worse.

Peter and I go to Suffolk for Christmas and we both hope to see
you when we get back. By the way he is singing Tamino for Sadlers
Wells in January.

[Handwritten: Much love]
BENJAMIN

1 English scholar (of Gregorian chant), author and broadcaster

(1892–1982). From 1920 to 1930 he was lecturer in, and later head of, the Gramophone Company's Education Department. In 1934, he was ordained and held an appointment at Westminster Cathedral, London, until 1938 when he resumed his professional activities. (In 1969, after his retirement, Robertson returned to the priesthood.) In 1940 he joined the BBC Gramophone Department and from 1943 was appointed chief producer of music talks on the Third and Home programmes. He established a conspicuous reputation as a producer and inimitable if idiosyncratic broadcaster. Robertson wrote numerous books, one of the last of which was entitled *Requiem: Music of Mourning and Consolation* (London, Cassell, 1967), and included a study of Britten's *War Requiem*. For Robertson's eightieth birthday in 1972, Britten composed a three-part canon on the plainchant 'Alleluia' from the *Ceremony of Carols*. See also *A Symposium for Alec Robertson* (Stanbrook, Abbey Press, 1972).

2 It was Alec Robertson who supplied Britten with the plainsong melody, 'Hodie Christus natus est', which he used for the Procession and Recession of *A Ceremony of Carols*. See also note 5 to Letter 374 and GE, pp. 45–8.

3 The first London performance of Britten's *Ceremony of Carols* was given by the women's voices of the Fleet Street Choir, conducted by T.B. Lawrence, on 21 December.

4 Robertson contributed an article to the *Gramophone*, December 1942, pp. 94–5, about Britten's *Michelangelo Sonnets*. His review of Pears's and Britten's HMV recording appeared in *Gramophone*, January 1943, in which he wrote:

In recording these songs, Peter Pears was, I believe, facing the microphone (I mean, the gramophone variety) for the first time and with a most difficult task to perform. He had shown complete mastery of his material at the Wigmore Hall recital and that is, of course, discernible on the records: but his command of his voice is not quite so evident. In general it is excellent and he does many lovely things with a voice bright and ringing, if not yet quite flexible enough to get it freely away from him.

Criticisms are of small matters. There is certain breathy hollowness of tone at the ends of some phrases on low notes. This sounds untidy.

Sometimes the tone is rather too white, but the singing is nearly always alive and vital. In the matter of diction Mr Pears could learn something from John McCormack. At present he does not do justice to the Italian 'r' and once, I am sure involuntarily, he pronounces 'chi' as 'she' instead of 'kee'. These, as I have said, are but small criticisms which are only made because the singer would wish to be judged by the standard he is aiming at – the highest. He must have brought much hard work and deep thought to have achieved an interpretation of this fine quality. It hardly seems fair that Benjamin Britten should play the piano as well as he does. So many gifts united! The accompanying is, indeed, splendid. This is best shown in the last song.

408 To Steuart Wilson[1]
BBC

104A Cheyne Walk, London, S.W.10.
Jan. 6th 1943.

Dear Mr. Wilson,

I am writing at the request of Mr. Lennox Berkeley.[2] I am free to play my "Scottish Ballad" for two pianos & orchestra with the BBC orchestra on February 16th. The other pianist who plays the work with me is Clifford Curzon, who, I have ascertained, is also free on February 16th.[3] The timing of the piece is exactly 13 minutes, & the scoring is for 2 Flutes, 2 Oboes, 2 Clarinets, 2 Bassoons, Double bassoon (which can be omitted), 4 Horns, 2 Trumpets, 3 Trombones, Tuba, Timpani, 2 Percussion & Strings.

I should be much obliged to have a confirmation of the date, with times of rehearsals, & the name of the conductor.

With best wishes,
Yours sincerely,
BENJAMIN BRITTEN

1 The BBC's Overseas Music Director for a time during the war.
2 From 1942 to 1945, Berkeley was on the music staff of the BBC, planning orchestral programmes.
3 The performance, given by the BBC Symphony Orchestra (Section B) under Clarence Raybould, was broadcast in the BBC European Service. This was the result of a suggestion from Berkeley, who was employed by the European Service at the time (he was almost immediately to be moved to the Home Service Music Section). 'This would not constitute a public performance,' he had written to Britten on 31 December, 'if you want to reserve that for a more important occasion.' In fact the first public performance in England was to take place in July: see note 2 to Letter 388.

409 To Ronald Duncan

104A Cheyne Walk, S.W.10.
January 9th 1942 [1943]

I'm sorry, Ronny, I had hoped that I could have come & stayed with you for that month in Feb–March, but now my sister, who is also about to have a child,[1] has taken up residence in Snape, & I'm afraid I have to come down here (where I'm writing this letter

from) quite frequently, & daren't be away so long. But I do mean
to come & see you sometime soon – If not in Feb, certainly later
in the Spring. I should love it when I am clear of immediate work
& domestic worries. Do let me know how Rose Marie[2] fares, &
the details of the child.

If you are near the Radio, do listen in on Jan. 25th & 27th (don't
know times, so you'll have to spend 2d on the R.[Radio] Times!)[3]
How goes everything? Stuart's[4] arrest has blighted everything this
Christmas, which otherwise would have been a pleasant one for
me.

I saw Henry Boys the other day for ½ an afternoon. He was on
good form & asked alot after you.

Much love,
BENJY

1 Britten's niece and Pears's god-daughter, Sarah Charlotte (Sally) Welford, b. 13 January 1943.

2 Duncan's wife, Rose-Marie (née Hanson), was expecting their first
child, Roger, Britten's godson.

3 Britten's *Hymn to St Cecilia* and *A Ceremony of Carols* (first broadcast
of the unrevised version) were performed on 25 January by the Fleet
Street Choir, with Margaret Ritchie (soprano) and Gwendolen Mason
(harp), conducted by T.B. Lawrence. On the 27th, Basil Cameron
was to conduct the BBC Symphony Orchestra in a broadcast from
the Corn Exchange, Bedford, of *Sinfonia da Requiem*.

4 Stuart Morris had been arrested on a charge (undisclosed) under the
Official Secrets Act. His trial was held *in camera* and he was sentenced
to nine months' imprisonment. See Sybil Morrison, *The Life and Work
of Stuart Morris* (London, Peace Pledge Union, n.d.), pp. 6–7, and
Martin Ceadel, *Pacifism in Britain, 1914–1945* (Oxford, Clarendon
Press, 1980), pp. 310–12.

410 To William Glock

c/o Miss U. Nettleship,
104a, Cheyne Walk,
London, S.W.10.
January 25th 1943.

Dear William,

I ought to have written ages ago to thank you & Clement[1] for
having sent me the score of the Mozart Bb Concerto – but since

Christmas I have been nearly worked off my head, & scarcely written a single letter. Anyhow thank you so much for letting me have it – it is a work which has tremendous significance for me, & I was desparate because I couldn't pick up a score anywhere.[2]

Do let me know when you next can get to London, as I should love to see you again. The above address will reach me until the first week of February – after that I'll let Clement know the new one (Peter & I move to St. Johns Wood[3] – much more convenient).

May I say how tremendously happy your Observer articles have made me?[4] That goes for Peter too.

With love to both of you,
& many thanks again,
yours
BENJAMIN BRITTEN

1 Clement Glock, a scene-painter at Covent Garden, Glock's first wife.

2 The miniature score of K.595 (Leipzig/Vienna, Eulenburg, n.d.), bearing both Glock's signature and Britten's initials, is in the Archive. Britten was to conduct a performance of the concerto on 16 June 1965 in Blythburgh Church as part of the 18th Aldeburgh Festival, with Sviatoslav Richter and the English Chamber Orchestra.

3 45A St John's Wood High Street, London NW8, was Pears's and Britten's London home until 1946. Pears was to write to Elizabeth Mayer on 13 February:

> [. . .] we have taken this maisonette and are in the middle of moving in. The difficulty is in finding anyone to do things for one these days, carpenters, electricians etc. However we hope to be in it in a week. It will be lovely to have our own things around us again, and my piano – The flat is rather big, plenty of rooms, and we have a housekeeper, who has a baby girl, to look after us and cook for us etc.   So at last we shall be able to lead a fairly regular life in London, which has been impossible so far. It was very exciting going round choosing curtain materials – I wish you had been there. You can imagine how I enjoyed it and Ben loathed it! They are nice curtains – rather expensive – everything is, now – and I managed to find some coconut matting instead of carpet, which is impossibly expensive.

See also PFL, plate 163.

4 In the week preceding the date of this letter, Glock had compared Shostakovich and Britten in the columns of the Observer on 17 January:

> In analysing Shostakovitch's music one is tempted to take up some attitude towards the many edicts which either ban or accompany his works, and thus to make confusion more rampant than it need be. However, Nicholas Slonimsky (the author of 'Music since 1900') has recently written an article

in which Shostakovitch's career is described with sympathetic detachment. From this sensible exposition we can follow the various changes of faith culminating in the one which finds literary expression in the November number of 'Our Time' and musical expression in the 'Leningrad' Symphony, and we can also appreciate the well-defined habits of rhythm and melody and instrumentation – such as the tremolo for strings and woodwind in the finale of the fifth symphony, which Slonimsky describes as 'cutting like an acetylene torch through the fanfare of the brass'.

Such a simile would not occur to us in thinking of Britten's music. Nor would his music ever suggest such a manifesto as 'the denial of mystical moods (à la Scriabin), of all hopelessly sombre moods (à la Tschaikowsky), the restriction of the sphere of refined subjective lyricism, the urge for vigorous and pointed rhythms expressing the spirit of industrialism' which seemed a natural comment on Shostakovitch's works in the late twenties. By comparison, Britten's world is instinctive and almost accidental. His invention is poured into his melody, his long lines, his orchestral colour, the harmonies which safeguard the first two, can be rather spidery and uncomforting. Shostakovitch, if more virile, is also more obvious and hardened. He does not sacrifice harmonic appeal; his surprises are those which are easiest to bear, namely, surprises of instrumentation.

Both have been influenced by Mahler, who is the lock between the main canals of nineteenth- and twentieth-century music. But whereas Shostakovitch has learned from Mahler's modernist technique and has borrowed his grandiose gestures for the 'great canvas of symphonic art' which is the 'Leningrad' Symphony, Britten is a much more serious disciple, with the risks and refinements which that implies. So we can see the fundamental difference in practice. In the 'Leningrad' Symphony Shostakovitch appeals to an audience as immense as that which has capitulated in this country to the Warsaw Concerto. Britten addresses himself on the other hand to a semi-private gathering because we have not yet begun to demand the full use of his powers.

411   To Mary St John Hutchinson[1]

45A, St. John's Wood High St.,
N.W.8.
Feb. 25th 1943.

Dear Mrs. Hutchinson,

As you ask I am sending the details of our April 25th concert[2] to Mr. Higgins.[3] I am sorry to have delayed in doing so, but I have only just been able to see Clifford Curzon to discuss the matter with him. The programme I suggest is roughly: – Schubert – (Fantasia [in F minor] for 4 hands [D. 940], Songs, 4 Impromptus) <u>interval</u>, Me (7 Sonnets of Michelangelo, 2 piano pieces (first perf. in England), Folk song arrangements).

I think we should be billed – C.C. (pianist), P.P. (tenor), B.B. (composer–pianist).

One very important matter though – could you please find out what pianos we could have – Clifford has bad memories of Cambridge apparently! – including size? He says there is a good Grotrian Steinweg, and a Bösendorfer at the Music Schools. Could we have the use of either of them? If this is not your business, could you please pass it on to the right quarter.

I am so glad we can fix this.

Your sincerely,
BENJAMIN BRITTEN

1 Mary St John Hutchinson, née Barnes (1889–1977), wife of the barrister, St John Hutchinson (1884–1942). She was a close friend of the economist, Maynard Keynes, and a member of the Bloomsbury circle of writers and artists.

2 The concert took place at the Arts Theatre, Cambridge. The programme differed slightly from the one outlined in the letter:

   1 Schubert *Lebensstürme* (D.947)
                Andantino varié (D.823/2)
                Curzon and Britten

   2 Schubert Abschied, (D.957/7)
                'Die Forelle', (D.550)
                'Ach neige, du Schmerzensreiche', (D.564)
                   (completed by Britten, first performance)
                'Am See', (D.746)
                'Auflösung', (D.807)
                Pears and Britten

   3 Schubert Sonata in B flat, D.960
                Curzon

   4 Britten   *Seven Sonnets of Michelangelo*, Op. 22
                Pears and Britten

   5 Britten   *Introduction and Rondo alla Burlesca*, Op. 23 No. 1.
                Mazurka Elegiaca, Op. 23 No. 2
                   (first British performance)
                Curzon and Britten

   6 Britten   Folk-song arrangements:
                'Bonny Earl o' Moray'
                'Little Sir William'
                'I wonder as I wander'
                'The King is gone a-hunting'
                'Heigh-ho! Heigh-hi!'

3 Presumably a member of staff of the Arts Theatre.

FRIENDS HOUSE, EUSTON ROAD, N.W.1

LARGE MEETING HOUSE, *(opposite Euston Station)*   Buses 14, 18b, 30, 68, 73, 77

PETER PEARS Tenor

BENJAMIN BRITTEN Pianoforte

SUNDAY, 28 FEBRUARY, 1943, 2.45 p.m.
(doors open 2.15)

PROGRAMME INCLUDES : the DICHTERLIEBE of SCHUMANN ;   HANDEL'S
" Love Sounds the Alarm " and " Let me wander " ; GLUCK'S " Ah mon ami " and
" Unis de la plus tendre enfance " (from Iphigénie) ; and settings of Welsh, Scottish,
French, and American folk-songs by BENJAMIN BRITTEN.

THIRD CONCERT OF A SERIES ARRANGED BY FRIENDS HOUSE
MEETING OF THE SOCIETY OF FRIENDS FOR FRIENDS WAR RELIEF SERVICE
(registered under War Charities Act 1940)

ADMISSION BY PROGRAMME, 2/–, at doors, or in advance from usual agencies
or F.W.R.S. at Friends House, as above (send stamped envelope).   Tel: Euston 5896
LAST OF THIS SERIES OF CONCERTS :   MARCH 28th.

Recital at Friends House, London NW1, on 28 February 1943

412 Julian Herbage BBC
From Peter Pears

> 45a, St. John's Wood High St.
> N.W.8.
> Primrose 5826.
> [early March 1943]

Dear Julian Herbage –

This is just in case you haven't heard already, to let you know that Ben Britten is smitten with measles and asked me to tell you that he won't be able to play in the Messiah for you.[1] He's very sorry about it, but he's had a very bad attack of it, and the doctor's opinion is that he mustn't do any work atall until nearly the end of April –

> Yours sincerely,
> **PETER PEARS.**

The above is our new (and permanent) address and telephone number.

1 Presumably the harpsichord continuo. Later, Britten was to undertake a similar role in performances of Bach's *St John Passion* conducted by Imogen Holst at the Aldeburgh Festivals of 1954 and 1957, in which Peter Pears was the Evangelist.

413   To Erwin Stein

[*Pencil*]

[Ward 14] Grove Hospital,
Tooting Grove, S.W. 17.[1]
Monday
[Postmarked 8 March 1943]

My dear Erwin,

Thank you for your nice letter. It cheered me up alot to get it –
& I did need cheering up! I am glad things are going well, & that
people liked the old Michelangelo again. Thank you for telling me
about the Matinées Musicales. One of the nurses lent me her
radio, & I got it rather badly, but I did manage to hear it all.[2]
I thought more of it came off than at the first show – although
the orchestra still was pretty bad. But this 'tempo' question is so
hopeless! I suppose one does feel it more deeply when one's own
children (even if they're step-children) are concerned. But the Moto
Perpetuo seemed to me to fail completely, just because it was that
much too slow. Don't you think that Metronome marks might help
that abit? Anyhow we must call it Prestissimo. I thought the 1st
3 movements made some kind of an effect (The flute is an
improvement in no. 1 (instead of glock.)). The 4th still worries
me. Musically it's the most interesting I feel – but I have had a
guilty feeling at the back of my mind for ages that it was too
subtle. But we haven't heard it played yet. I felt last night that the
Bassoon needn't have been so bad – only with such stupid
conducting the poor dear never had a moment to take his time
(Zeit lassen!). It sounded awfully odd, I thought. I do hope that
you were able to listen, & am eager for your comments. I am afraid
it'll never be as popular as Soirées – but it may give that a rest
from time to time; and Freddy Ashton is keen to do them both into
a ballet (which of course they were intended for).[3] Do you think
there should be a note about this in the score i.e. ———— written at
the request of Lincoln Kirstein, to form with Soirées Musicales a
ballet to choreography by Ballanchine for the S. American tour –
summer 1941 – of his (L.K.'s) American Ballet – or words to that
effect!!

I am doing lots of reading, but also lots of planning & thinking!
I am really going to 'cry up' these measles for getting me out of
lots of these boring jobs, as I have so many things to get done. Did

I ever tell you about the Clarinet concerto? I am intrigued by the Nocturne idea for Voice & Horn.[4] No more now. Thank you again for your letter – & looking forward to seeing you when I'm out of this place.

Yours,
BEN

1 The fever hospital to which Britten had been sent for a severe attack of measles. He convalesced at Snape until the end of April.

2 The first English performance of *Matinées Musicales* (a BBC Forces Service broadcast) had been given on 22 December 1942 by the BBC Midland Light Orchestra, conducted by Rae Jenkins. The second broadcast performance was given on 7 March by the BBC Scottish Symphony Orchestra, under Guy Warrack.

3 No details of any such Ashton ballet have been traced.

4 Which was to become the *Serenade* for tenor, horn and strings, Op. 31.

414 To Enid Slater
[*Pencil*]

Grove Hospital,
Tooting Grove, SW17.
<s>February</s> Monday
[Postmarked 8 March 1943]

My dear Enid,

How sweet of you to send those books. They saved my life – I was just getting so weary of the old Horizons[1] that a good Samaritan Doctor had lent me. I haven't looked much at the de la Mare yet, but it looks a nice convalescing kind of tale – But the Constable[2] I'm lapping up. It is most beautifully done – & gives a wonderful picture of the conditions artists then worked in. My, how I admire that man! Apart from having an almost sexy love for his paintings, I admire his extraordinary oneness of purpose, & character to go on with lack of success. He was rather a sweet person too, & must have been lovely when young. Young Dunthorne[3] was a pet! Anyhow, thank you my dear – it is sweet of you to have done it.

There's nothing to report – except air raids – this place attracts planes like honey does wasps – & the guns drive one nearly crazy.

However, they don't usually go on long. But the kids cry so, which is disturbing.

I am getting slowly & surely better. Barbara & Peter had special permission to visit me yesterday, which was lovely, & thought I was looking very well! I have to stay about another 10 days, & then I'm off to Snape for abit. No jobs for 2 months – isn't that heavenly!

How's Montagu? Give him my love & say I hope the work's going well. Please give the enclosed note to Bridget.

And much love, & <u>many</u> thanks again,

BEN

1 The monthly review of literature and art edited by Cyril Connolly, founded in 1940 and published until January 1950. (See Michael Shelden, *Friends of Promise: Cyril Connolly and the World of Horizon* (London, Hamish Hamilton, 1989).) It was in *Horizon* during 1944 (June, July, August issues) that three important articles by Edward Sackville-West (see note 4 to Letter 416) were to appear, 'Music: Some Aspects of the Contemporary Problem', the second and third of which were devoted to Britten and Tippett. Sackville-West's articles are especially significant for the history of the reception – and perception – of Britten's music after his return to England in 1942. They were in the main extremely positive in tone. 'Benjamin Britten and Michael Tippett', he concluded, 'are potentially great composers who have it in their power to change, for generations to come, the podgy and obstructed expression which has for a century and a half degraded the face of English music.'

Some of his specific judgements now read oddly, particularly in the light of the comprehensive exploration and re-evaluation of Britten's pre-war music since the composer's death. He writes, for example, of the 'unpleasant Piano Concerto, with its meagre materials and its hollow emphasis on sonority', and, while finding more to admire in the Violin Concerto, estimates it to be 'an occasional piece, though serious enough in its own way: the beauty of the *Passacaglia* and final coda belongs to that of all "made" music'.

These adverse views would seem to have their roots in that widespread opinion, current in the thirties and persisting well beyond that decade, that 'early' Britten was all technique and no content. The influential pervasiveness of that assessment can be gauged when we read Sackville-West writing in terms like these (and after all, *he* had come to praise Britten, not damn him): 'The surface brilliance, the versatility, the passion for applause, that were the bane of Britten's early music, will continue to lie in wait for unguarded moments'; and elsewhere he remarks that it was with the *Sinfonia da*

Requiem that Britten had 'at last forsaken the primrose path of mere charm'.

Mere charm? One cannot but notice that nowhere in Sackville-West's essays is there a mention of that dazzling and uncomfortable *chef-d'oeuvre* of 1936, *Our Hunting Fathers* – which goes to show how by 1944 the work had dropped like a stone out of the public consciousness and out of the awareness of Britten's friends, even of one as discerning and enthusiastic as Sackville-West. It must have been his ignorance of the most remarkable of the Britten–Auden collaborations (and, of course, ignorance of *Paul Bunyan* in 1941, though he cannot be blamed for that, since no doubt the composer himself kept quiet about it) that allowed Sackville-West to dismiss Auden's influence on Britten so perfunctorily and erroneously as 'chiefly political and becomes imperceptible after *Les Illuminations*'.

A final aspect of special note is his commentary (pp. 117–18) on 'work in progress', the first act of *Peter Grimes*, 'which should, I believe, prove an English equivalent of Berg's *Wozzeck*'. It says something about the association of critic and composer at this time that Britten was willing to collaborate in a preview of his unfinished opera.

2 Presumably Andrew Shirley's 1937 edition of C.R. Leslie's *Memoirs of the Life of John Constable*.

3 John Dunthorne Jr (1798–1832), Constable's life-long friend and studio assistant in the 1820s.

415 To Ralph Hawkes

[*Pencil*]

Grove Hospital,
Tooting Grove, S.W. 17.
March 9th 1943.

My dear Ralph,

Many thanks for your letter. Congratulations on the deal![1] I don't think you'll ever regret it. What is the next step now – will you issue new scores of the Rosenkavalier & the others? or is there stock enough? I hear from America that Szell had a terrific success with Salome at the Met. – so that's a good start for you! Have you made your press announcement yet?

Yes – isn't this a major bore? – at <u>my</u> age too – Measles at Tooting! However it's a pretty good compulsory rest, & I'm rather enjoying myself doing nothing – except plan new works (you'd tremble if you knew the new schemes that are afoot!). I am being treated with terrific deference – all the doctors flock round the celebrated composer & pretend they know all my pieces! But they lend me books, which is a good thing. I shall have to stay in at least a week more, I'm afraid, as I've had what they call a 'sharp' attack, & then

I'm supposed to go away for two or three weeks. (An old man like me can't throw off these things easily!!) So it looks like goodbye to the film[2] – & I'm not all that sorry because it would have been a <u>terrific</u> work, & would have held up the Ballet[3] & the Opera[4] too long – To say nothing about the Sonata![5] I am afraid, Ralph, it's too risky to promise the Prom. people that definitely. It may be done, but I <u>won't</u> hurry this piece – it's got to be 100%. Besides I very much doubt whether the Proms is the best place to bring out a work like this. It'll be very difficult & the rehearsal there is too short. Anyhow, they'll have one 1st perf. in England,[6] so let them be content with that – & why do they never do an older piece? – the Violin Concerto, Variations, Les Illuminations or the Folk Songs[7] with Peter? What about the Sinfonia? I'm glad you liked the Matinées. They brought me in a squeaky little set, & I thought the Matinées sounded rather a 'hang-over' kind of morning! But I think the piece'll go alright. Freddy Ashton wants me to save the ballet rights of the two together (as they were originally done by Kirstein & Ballanchine in S. America) for him here – & I think he'd do it well. Has the poor dear got his ballet from Willy yet?[8]

O, Ralph could you please ask Stein to get someone to send me along the scores of the Bartok 2 piano Sonata & the Divertimento,[9] & if by <u>any chance</u> there <u>is</u> a spare vocal score of the Rosenkavalier[10] around there is nothing I should like better to do to wile away the hours than to pick the old man's brains for my opera! But don't worry if there's not – by-the-way, the Medical Superintendent here says that I needn't have my books baked on departure – he'll just say mystic words instead so <u>if</u> there were this score I shouldn't harm it, beyond a few germs!! Yes I remember the performance well – with you, & Figaro too! I was knocked flat. Wasn't it the Dresden Opera?

I'll let you know from time to time how I go along & what complications I pick up!

The best of luck to you, & many congrats. on the deal.

Yours ever,

BEN

P.S.   This is a pretty gloomy hole, & the food is rather comic, & it has a fatal attraction for Jerry planes! They all centre here – God knows why – & the noise is something unbelievable! However I'm in a single room & the nurses are very attentive – so I shouldn't complain!!

1 Boosey & Hawkes had secured rights to the Fürstner catalogue, which contained the operas of Richard Strauss, along with many other of his works.

2 A Boosey & Hawkes Memo of 31 December tells us that Britten

called here yesterday and politely declined the commission which had been offered him by Gabriel Pascal Productions to write the musical score to Shaw's <u>Caesar and Cleopatra</u>, the reason being that the script did not appeal to him but mainly that in doing it he would accomplish absolutely nothing towards the solution of his own problem as a composer. The fact which upset him mostly in the script was the burning of the Library at Alexandria. He said that the money did not interest him.

The score was eventually composed by Georges Auric, and the film featured Claude Rains and Vivien Leigh in the title roles.

3 The Sadler's Wells Ballet probably commissioned a ballet from Britten in late 1942 or early 1943, for on 13 February Pears had written to Elizabeth Mayer: 'Ben is doing a ballet for Sadler's Wells, on the Mark of Cain, very exciting.'

On the same day as Pears's letter Hawkes had written to Britten about a postponement of the project:

I have seen Bobby Helpmann and the postponement of your Sadler's Wells Ballet does not worry anyone. I shall hope to fix the matter so that Montagu Slater be paid a flat fee of Fifteen to Twenty Guineas outright to cover his work, leaving you the enjoyment of any fees which may accrue from performances.

It seems that Slater had provided a scenario and presumably Robert Helpmann (1909–1986), the Australian-born choreographer, dancer and director, was to choreograph the ballet.

Britten must have sent Slater's scenario to Sackville-West, who responded in a letter which allows us a glimpse of what Britten and his collaborator had in mind:

Thinking over the plot of your ballet, I feel moved to protest once more against this grotesque impropriety of removing the brand-mark from Judas the moment he is dead. I can imagine that you do not care for the gross heresy involved in imputing instant absolution to a suicide; but apart from this aspect, it makes nonsense of your story (which is, after all, founded on Christian ethics), since, if all an evil-liver has to do to achieve heaven is to kill himself when he has had enough, life becomes altogether too simple an affair & your characters lose all interest.

Do, I beg you, reconsider what may seem to you an absurdly small point lest [sic] what would, in fact, very greatly annoy people who might otherwise enjoy the ballet.

The project makes its final appearance in Hawkes's correspondence with the composer in a letter dated 28 June, when he lists all the work Britten has to accomplish – six items in addition to *Peter Grimes*, this ballet proposal and incidental music for the BBC. Given the work-load, it is hardly surprising that the ballet was abandoned. *Grimes* increasingly became the creative priority.

4 In the event Britten was not able to begin the composition sketch of *Peter Grimes* until January 1944. See Letter 446.

5 Sonata for orchestra: see note 6 to Letter 374.

6 Of the *Scottish Ballad*.

7 The first performance of Four British Folk-songs ('The Bonny Earl o' Moray', 'Little Sir William', 'Oliver Cromwell', 'The Salley Gardens') for voice and orchestra had been given on 13 December 1942 at the Odeon Theatre, Southgate, London, by Peter Pears with the New London Orchestra, conducted by Alex Sherman.

8 Walton's ballet in five scenes, *The Quest*, to a scenario by David Langley Moore after Spenser's *Faerie Queene*, with choreography by Frederick Ashton, and scenery and costumes by John Piper. It was first performed on 6 April 1943 at the New Theatre, London, by Sadler's Wells Ballet with Margot Fonteyn and Robert Helpmann. See also Stewart R. Craggs, *William Walton: A Thematic Catalogue of his Musical Works* (London, Oxford University Press, 1977), pp. 134–9; and Neil Tierney, *William Walton: His Life and Music* (London, Robert Hale, 1984), pp. 105–8.

9 Sonata for two pianos and percussion, composed 1937, published by Boosey & Hawkes in 1942, and *Divertimento* for string orchestra, composed 1939, published in 1940. Britten's copies of these scores are in the Archive.

10 Richard Strauss's three-act opera (1911).

416 To Peter Pears
[*Pencil*]

Grove Hospital,
Tooting Grove, S.W. 17.
March 11th 1943

My darling –

One stamp left, so whom to use it for . . . ? As if there could be any question ——!!! My dearest, I am thinking about you all to-day, rehearsing Tamino &, I hope, practising abit, & to-night you'll look so beautiful & sound so wonderful, I know.[1] How I wish I could see you – I really think I **must** come up to Blackpool for the Rigoletto.[2] Do you mind? – if I'm well enough? Then I should get a Flute as well and I want to see it so badly.

I am going to do lots of work on P. Grimes today, to see what

really is wrong with it.[3] And then I shall write a long letter to
Montagu & hope he can fix it abit. I am sure it isn't <u>fundamentally</u>
hopeless, there are too many things I like about it. For one thing
it goes <u>naturally</u> into operatic form – it doesn't embarrass me to
think of those people, singing, & singing English. And another,
I see so clearly what kind of music I want to write for it, & I <u>am</u>
interested in the people & the situations, & interested in a musical
way. It isn't often that one can get an opera scheme that comes so
near what one wants. I'm beginning to feel that Montagu may
not be the ideal librettist; but who? Wystan, well – there are the
old objections, & besides, he's not to hand. Louis – more or less
the same objections, & I don't know how I could work with him.
Eddy[4] – well, perhaps; let's see how the Rescue[5] turns out – I
doubt whether he again is a good enough poet, whether he isn't
too pretentious, again. It'll be interesting to see what Tony
Guthrie[6] has done. Yes, I think I must come to Blackpool!

I've just had a sweet letter, with no complications!, from Eddy.
He makes quite a promising suggestion about the Scot. Ballad.[7]
I think we malign him, you know: I know he's a neurotic, but
at least he can control himself!

A long letter from Robert – he's persuaded Marjorie[8] to see a
doctor – wonder of wonders! – I wonder if it'll do any good, but
it's an effort in the right direction. If she's ordered away for a rest,
it might solve matters abit.

I love the Swift, my dear – it was sweet of you to bring it for me.
The Graham Greene that Enid sent is a very good tale, with a
strong atmosphere. But awfully disturbing! I had to be comforted
by the Mahler[9] after reading it last night – what a miracle that
work is – I think I have almost more <u>affection</u> for that piece than
for any I know.

No news, my darling! I go on. Didn't sleep so well last night,
because the tooth was abit restless, & it got so awfully hot in here
– with the fire & no windows open (because of black out). But
thank god no alerts[10] – but I mustn't be a fool about them; think of
what the Germans are going through now – poor devils. How I
wish to God it would all stop. I feel every day that it goes on
longer makes things worse – takes us all further into the mire of
hate & hopelessness.

It was heaven to see you for that nice long time – Sorry if I was
very quiet – but it was nicest just to lie quietly & to watch you,
& know you were there. If it is difficult for you to come on Sunday

– don't bother; it's more important for you to rest. (But if you do come – it would be lovely!) Good luck & everything in Sevenoaks & with learning & practising.[11] I'm with you in thoughts every moment, my own darling. Take care of yourself. Don't get cold.

Immer dein

B.

1 Pears had auditioned for Joan Cross and her colleagues at Sadler's Wells on 15 December 1942, and first sang the role of Tamino in Mozart's *Die Zauberflöte* at the New Theatre, London on 19 January 1943. This performance, conducted by Lawrance Collingwood, was repeated on 11 March at the Grand Theatre, Leeds, and at Blackpool on 1 April. In January 1951 he was to appear as Tamino in a production at the Royal Opera House, Covent Garden, conducted by Erich Kleiber.

2 Pears was to sing his first Duke in Verdi's *Rigoletto* in Blackpool on 3 April, with the Sadler's Wells Opera Company conducted by Norman Feasey.

3 The day before, Britten had written to Enid Slater, 'the more I think of P. Grimes the more I like it & get excited over it. The trouble is that I don't think anyone'll be able to bear it on the stage.'

4 Edward Charles Sackville-West (1901–1965), a cousin of the writer, Vita Sackville-West (1892–1962). He was educated at Eton, where his outstanding gifts as a pianist manifested themselves. But literature was his first interest, and he wrote his first novel, *Piano Quintet*, in 1925. Sackville-West was widely read, fluent in French and German, and conspicuously well versed in European art and literature. He wrote the standard critical biography of Thomas De Quincey, *A Flame in Sunlight* (1936).

During the war he joined the Features and Drama Department of the BBC, where he probably first encountered Britten, although it may have been Berkeley who brought Sackville-West and Britten together. Michael de-la-Noy, in his biography *Eddy: The Life of Edward Sackville-West* (London, The Bodley Head, 1988), p. 205, writes that 'all that seems reasonably certain is that they knew each other well enough before the war to have collaborated on *The Rescue* within months of Britten's return from America'. We can find no evidence, however, to support this suggestion. Among Sackville-West's best work was the two-part play, *The Rescue* (see note 5 below), based on Homer's *Odyssey*, with music by Britten. This has proved to be one of the most enduring works created specifically for radio. On 30 August, before the launch of *The Rescue*, he was to produce (with Stephen Potter) for the BBC Home Service a programme entitled *The Living Spirit of France*, in which modern French poetry and music were selected by Raymond Mortimer and Lennox Berkeley. The soloists were Pears and Britten. Among the readers of the poems was Peggy Ashcroft. Sackville-West inherited the family title and became fifth Baron Sackville in 1962.

It is clear that after his return from the USA, and the consequent geographical separation from Auden, Britten found in Sackville-West a skilled and sympathetic literary adviser, collaborator and perceptive critic. He helped Britten with the choice of texts for the *Serenade*, and it was to him that the overall dedication of the work was made. He was also influential in selecting the words for *Rejoice in the Lamb*.

After the first publication of *Peter Grimes* in 1945, he contributed a substantial account of the work to the symposium published as Sadler's Wells Opera Book No. 3 (*Benjamin Britten: Peter Grimes*, edited by Eric Crozier (London, The Bodley Head, 1945), pp. 27–55). This long essay, its own merits aside, remains of some historic importance, since it must have represented thoughts and ideas about the opera with which the composer was in agreement (or at least to which he did not object).

While the professional relationship was obviously productive, the personal relationship was complex and sometimes painful. There was a period in the 1940s when Sackville-West's letters showed how deeply he was attached to, and attracted by, Britten: in some instances these begin 'My dear White Child', an image taken from Auden's 'St Cecilia' Hymn. Perhaps it was indication of a possessiveness that Britten found difficult to accept. In a letter from the year of their closest collaboration, Sackville-West rather overwhelmingly hailed him as 'a heavenly genius and potentially the greatest composer of the new era', but the friendship was to wane, although the two men were still in occasional correspondence as late as 1959. See also Michael de-la-Noy, op. cit., pp. 200–20 *passim*.

5 *The Rescue* was first broadcast in a production by John Burrell on 25 and 26 November, when the BBC Symphony Orchestra was conducted by Clarence Raybould. The extensive music comprises some eighty individual items. These include background music, interludes and songs. Recurring themes and motives are used to characterize and identify the characters. There have been six subsequent productions since 1943, the most recent in 1988. Desmond Shawe-Taylor, in a private communication, recalls that 'at one time Eddy hoped that [*The Rescue*] might have been recast in operatic form; and Ben <u>seemed</u> for a while to be interested'. See also Lewis Foreman, 'Benjamin Britten and *The Rescue*', *Tempo*, 166, September 1988, pp. 28–33, and PR, pp. 412–24 and 636–53. In the third of his 1944 *Horizon* articles Sackville-West wrote of his own response to the music of *The Rescue*:

His talent for vocal writing, combined with a striking dramatic sense, seems to indicate a born composer of operas. I have already mentioned his aptitude for finding phrases that delineate the visible world, as well as those which express character. Examples are to be found all through his work, but nowhere more remarkably than in the incidental music which he wrote for my own broadcast drama, *The Rescue*. During the composition of this score, which contains some very beautiful stuff, I was continually struck by the unerring instinct with which Britten hit upon the right musical backing for whatever it was I had written, or – alternatively – rose imaginatively to any occasion the script presented for quasi-independent music.

One of the most positive and discerning of responses to the work came from David Jones, the poet and artist (1895–1974), who was to write in a letter dated 18 May 1956, after a revival of the drama, produced by Val Gielgud and broadcast on the Third Programme on the 16th:

I listened to Ed. Sackville-West & Ben Britten's thing based on the Odyssey. You know how I loathe that music & rhetoric thing, as e.g. in various works of radio'd entertainment that need not here be named. Well, for once I thought it did come off. I suppose because of the real genius of Britten as a composer, and I thought Ed. S.W.'s words awfully good too. It was all of a piece and very moving in places. It did one good thing to me. It made me re-read the Odyssey.

See *Dai Greatcoat, A Self-portrait of David Jones in his Letters*, edited by René Hague (London, Faber and Faber, 1980), p. 168.

See also the published text of the drama, *The Rescue, A Melodrama for Broadcasting based on Homer's Odyssey*, orchestral score by Benjamin Britten, with six illustrations to the text by Henry Moore (London, Secker and Warburg, 1945), with a Preamble by Sackville-West in which he discusses his collaboration with the composer in some considerable and interesting detail (pp. 15–16) and draws attention to what he felt to be 'our one major miscalculation', in Part II, 'the transition music which should carry the listener with Odysseus and Telemachus on their journey down the mountain, signally failed to do so because, coming after a scene which had lasted thirty minutes, the imagination demanded a more spacious relaxation'.

6 Sir (William) Tyrone Guthrie (1900–1971), director and theatre designer. Guthrie was appointed in 1933 as director of plays at the Old Vic and Sadler's Wells, where he raised theatrical standards with a number of famous productions. In 1945, the year of Joan Cross's resignation from Sadler's Wells, he undertook the administration of the opera company. In 1947 he became a director of the English Opera Group (see PFL, plate 212) and produced *Peter Grimes* at Covent Garden. A year later, he was to produce for the first time Britten's realization of *The Beggar's Opera*, at Cambridge, on 24 May. (See PFL, plates 219–20.) Guthrie has written of his association with *Peter Grimes* in his autobiography, *A Life in the Theatre* (London, Hamish Hamilton, 1960), pp. 197 and 226; and 'Out of Touch', *Opera News*, 31, 28 January 1967, pp. 8–11. He was knighted in 1961.

7 This letter seems not to have survived.

8 Britten had written to his sister Beth on 10 March:

> Barbara sent me Robert's last letter – poor dear, he & Marjorie are really leading a cat & dog life now – open warfare. However much longer can it go on, I wonder? I should think that this might bring things to a head. But I can't see Marjorie giving him up – that's all. I've written him a long & sympathetic letter.

9 The Fourth Symphony, of which Britten had purchased a miniature score in Vienna on 3 November 1934 and heard a performance the following day. At the 1961 Aldeburgh Festival he was to conduct a performance of the work, with Joan Carlyle (soprano) and the London Symphony Orchestra, having a few days before made a BBC studio recording, a copy of which is in the National Sound Archive. See also Donald Mitchell and Philip Reed, Catalogue for *Perspectives on Mahler and Britten*, an exhibition at the Britten–Pears Library, Aldeburgh, as part of the 38th Aldeburgh Festival, 7–23 June 1985.

10 Air-raid warnings.

11 Pears had a concert in Sevenoaks on 13 March and moved on to Kidderminster two days later.

417 To Ralph Hawkes

Grove Hospital,
Tooting Grove, S.W.17.
March 12th, 1943.

My dear Ralph,

You shouldn't have done it – ! I only wondered if there was an old score knocking around the place, & here comes a beautiful new one, with your kind note. Thank you more than I can say. I can scarcely contain myself to write this note – you see, I've never seen a score of Rosenkavalier, & I am impatient to see how the old magician makes his effects! There's a hell of a lot I can learn from him![1]

I am afraid my opera won't be as lush or glittering as this one – after all there is a difference between Vienna & Suffolk!! – but I have great hopes of it, once we get the libretto right. I am working on it again now, with some new improvements in view. By-the-way I have a feeling that I can collaborate with Sadlers Wells opera abit in the future – it would be grand to have a permanent place to produce one's operas (& I mean to write a few in my time!) It may mean cutting down means abit (no 4 flutes or 8 horns!) – but that doesn't hurt anyone – look at the Magic Flute or Figaro, with just a tiny orchestra. It's the ideas that count. This is only a scheme at the back of my mind, but I have a hunch that it's at the back of theirs too, as Joan Cross[2] & Tony Guthrie want to see me about something. Don't say anything about it yet, tho'.

Thank you also for the Bartók, which I am intrigued to see, also. That man is a real master. Even when one feels temperamentally unsympathetic to the music, one can but admire the skill and complete integrity of it.

I am slowly getting on, thank God; but it takes a time to get over these childish diseases! I expect to get out at the beginning of the week & have been ordered straight down to Snape for a few weeks. But I will telephone you on the way through.

I hope everything is prospering with you. Is the great new deal public yet?

With best wishes & more thanks than I can say – you've given me many hours of real bliss, & instruction too!

Yours ever,

BEN

1   Something of what he learned from the 'old magician' surely surfaces . in the quartet (trio) for women's voices in Act II of Peter Grimes. To the best of our knowledge, he never professionally performed any works of Strauss, and only two works were ever included in the programmes of the Aldeburgh Festival during Britten's lifetime. Britten's unexpectedly positive response to Rosenkavalier was not sustained. He was to write to Pears in December 1971 after hearing one side of a recording of the opera: 'it's dreadful music, & really rather shocking'.

2   Joan Cross (b. 1900), English soprano. After study with Holst at St Paul's Girls' School and at Trinity College of Music, she began her professional career in 1924. She was principal soprano with Sadler's Wells Opera from 1931 to 1945, directing the company under difficult wartime circumstances during 1943 to 1945. She took the bold decision to stage Peter Grimes in June 1945, herself creating the role of Ellen Orford (see PFL, plates 183 and 187). She went on to create many other major Britten roles: the Female Chorus in The Rape of Lucretia (1946); Lady Billows in Albert Herring (1947); Elizabeth I in Gloriana (1953); and Mrs Grose in The Turn of the Screw (1954). She was a co-founder of the English Opera Group. In 1948 she founded the Opera School with Anne Wood, which later became the National Opera School. She maintained her long connection with Britten and Pears, appearing regularly as a teacher at the Britten–Pears School for Advanced Musical Studies at Snape from 1974 to 1984. Joan Cross

was of the first importance to Britten, as artist, colleague, collaborator and friend. See also her contributions to TBB ('The Bad Old Days'), pp. 175–84, and PPT, pp. 22–3, where she writes:

Strange that at least two of the music staff of that time (1943) had doubts about offering you [Pears] a contract, convinced that the voice was not operatic material! I, on the other hand, felt equally convinced that you would prove more than valuable. I'm glad I overruled my colleagues [. . .].

See also the Earl of Harewood's celebratory appreciation of her career, 'Joan Cross – a birthday celebration', in *Opera*, 41/9, September 1990, pp. 1032–9.

418 To Erwin Stein
[*Pencil*]

Grove Hospital,
Tooting Grove, S.W. 17.
March 12th 1943.

My dear Erwin,

Many thanks for your long & very interesting letter. I am glad you found time to write it because there is nothing that keeps me so cheerful as letters – especially interesting ones! Otherwise one gets awfully bored with just reading, altho' I've got some grand stuff to read – King Lear[1] (I'm ashamed to say I've never read before!), & life of Constable (a favourite painter of mine), some amusing modern novels, the Debussy criticisms[2] (disappointing I thought); my precious Mahler 4th (which I think I have more genuine affection for than for any piece in the world) & the miniature score of Magic Flute!! And that is not all, by any means. I find that I can't concentrate long enough now to do much detailed work – I just make up fantastic schemes for the future. The Clarinet concerto in which I've got interested in again was one I started sketching for Benny Goodman – but it'll be ages before I do it – don't worry! O – & one bit of good work I'm doing is on the opera libretto – I am finding lots of possibilities of improvement, especially the character of Grimes himself which I find doesn't come across nearly clearly enough. At the moment he is just a pathological case – no reasons & not many symptoms! He's got to be changed alot.[3] But even then, I am convinced that it is right for me to do this opera. I am too interested in it for me to drop it now. Even if it doesn't come out very well, it'll be experience.

Why don't you do this book you talk about? I know it would be a terrific work – but what rewarding work! With all your long experience it ought to be a most valuable contribution to the appalling inadequate musical literature.[4] The question of tempi is fascinating. I can't help feeling you know that there is only one tempo for every piece of music – at least, maybe one tempo for one person! Maybe it's something to do with heartbeats or slow or fast metabolism!! I know I suffer agonies when I feel the tempi wrong. But why, I can't say. I think association has alot to do with it – that is why gramophone records are so dangerous; one gets used to the tempo whether it's right or wrong (just as one gets used to, & expects the breaks at the end of the records!!) But, Erwin, you haven't got time to read my somewhat disturbed & incoherent remarks! One day, we'll have the long talks that we have promised each other so long; perhaps now we're settled in St. John's Wood something can happen.

I am feeling slowly better & better. It's a slow progress, & the worst trouble is depression – but I'll get over that. I expect to come out on Tuesday or Wednesday & go straight down to Snape – don't you dare tell anyone I'll be in town, will you, or that beastly telephone will start ringing!

I am glad you agree about the Sonata. I can't hurry this piece, it's got to be 100%, & it's very difficult to do. However, I hope to be able to show you something fairly soon.

How's everything going with you? No hitches I hope. Glad & surprised about the Illuminations in S. Africa! How goes the Sinfonia? Anymore misprints?[5] Please give my love to Mrs. Stein,[6] & to Marion.[7] I hope they're well. The flowers are still lovely.

With all good wishes & many thanks,
Yours ever,
BEN

Ralph has just sent me the vocal score of Rosenkavalier – don't worry I shan't be influenced by him, but what incredible skill, & stage craft!

Your metronome marks have just come – the only one I'm not sure about is no 3 – aren't you a bit fast? His seem quite crazy – but I can't be certain about this until I check up on a metronome. I've been trying to do it with my pulse – but it won't work![8]

1 In the 1960s, Britten was seriously to consider *King Lear* as the subject for an opera. His annotated copy of Shakespeare's play, acquired at this time, is in the Archive.

2 Debussy's *Monsieur Croche the Dilettante Hater* [*Monsieur Croche anti-dilettante*], (London, Williams & Norgate, 1927).

3 In reply to a comment by Murray Schafer (*British Composers in Interview* (London, Faber and Faber, 1963), pp. 116–17) – 'The Grimes of your opera is rather different from the Grimes of Crabbe's poem' – Britten said:

> A central feeling for us was that of the individual against the crowd, with ironic overtones for our own situation. As conscientious objectors we were out of it. We couldn't say we suffered physically, but naturally we experienced tremendous tension. I think it was partly this feeling which led us to make Grimes a character of vision and conflict, the tortured idealist he is, rather than the villain he was in Crabbe.

See also PGPB, pp. 180–89 and 190–96.

4 Stein was to work on this project for many years. He was never quite to complete it. A major proportion of the text, under the title of *Form and Performance*, with a foreword by Britten, was published posthumously by Faber and Faber in 1962.

5 Britten probably refers to the faulty first engraved full score of *Sinfonia da Requiem*, published in the USA by Boosey and Hawkes, Inc., in 1942, which had to be corrected and republished in London. See note 3 to Letter 389 in which is reproduced a review from the *Observer*, July 1942. This contains a specific mention of a published score which was evidently available before the first English performance of the *Sinfonia*.

6 Sophie Stein (1882–1965), wife of Erwin.

7 Marion Thorpe (née Stein; b. Vienna, 1926) came to England with her parents in 1938. She had first met Britten at the Queen's Hall in 1939, at the first performance of *Ballad of Heroes*. In 1944 the Steins moved into Britten's and Pears's St John's Wood maisonette, their flat having been destroyed by fire. From this time on she became and remained an intimate friend of both Britten and Pears. She gave up her career as a concert pianist when she married the Earl of Harewood in 1949. For their wedding, Britten composed his anthem, *Amo Ergo Sum*, Op. 46. The marriage was dissolved in 1967, and in 1973 she married the Rt Hon Jeremy Thorpe (b. 1929), Leader of the Liberal Party from 1967 to 1976. In 1963 she founded, with Fanny Waterman, the Leeds International Pianoforte Competition for which Britten wrote a 'compulsory piece', *Night Piece* (the second and last work for solo piano that Britten published during his lifetime). She was appointed a Trustee of the Britten–Pears Foundation in 1985, in which year she compiled and edited PPT.

8 See Letter 413.

419 To Peter Pears
[*Pencil*]

Old Mill, Snape, Suffolk.
March 21st 1943.

My darling –

It is such heaven to hear your voice, even if only over the telephone. But doesn't it seem ages since last Sunday! – and now we still have to wait until Friday. Still, it's not too bad; think of all the other married couples who are separated for everso much longer!!

I am so relieved you will have one free day. By-jove, you do deserve it. I have been thinking of you all the time, working like a nigger, & hoping you've not been getting too tired. Iris [Holland-Rogers] said you sang simply beautifully yesterday, what a curse it is that I haven't been able to do these concerts with you[1] – but at least I've been able to write things for you,[2] – better than nothing. It is lovely that you are enjoying Rigoletto – I bet it'll be good. I have been studying the score carefully, & have lots of ideas about it! I wonder if they agree with yours.

I was <u>very</u> impressed with Joan Cross on Monday, you know. She has the most lovely <u>warm</u> quality in her voice – really the only English Soprano who does something to ones middle like Lehmann does. Her top doesn't seem terribly free tho' – but probably thats lack of practice. One thing I noticed at the broadcast – you know when the two voices are singing high in octaves, the soprano (owing to the higher frequencies) nearly always drowns the tenor – but it was <u>not</u> so this time. You were finely audible all the time. The voice sounded <u>good</u> you know. I can see why Guty[3] was pleased.

I called Iris & she comes on Tuesday. I think she'll enjoy it here. It is very quiet – Beth is occupied with the kids all the time (Sebastian grows more ravishing every day!) & I shall still be spending alot of time lazing in bed (like now). But I don't think she'll mind, will she? Beth's trying to fix with Christine & Mrs. Burrows[4] so that she hasn't anything to do.

I hope Margaret <u>hasn't</u> got measles. Poor Mrs. Neilson will be worried if she has.[5]

Much love, my only darling. Take <u>great</u> care of yourself – & you'll have a lovely rest next weekend.

Here's Elizabeth's letter – what a pity she didn't get yours.

All my love – my P.

B.

1 Pears gave several CEMA recitals during the week following this letter: 20 March at Hayward's Heath (Schumann's *Dichterliebe* and Britten's Folk-song Arrangements, with Norman Franklin, piano); with Clifford Curzon, on 22 March; at Witham, Essex, on the 24th, and Silver End on the 25th.

2 Britten composed his *Serenade*, Op. 31, for tenor, horn and strings during March–April, selecting the texts from two sources: *Poems from the Works of Charles Cotton*, newly decorated by Claude Lovat Fraser (London, Curwen Press, 1922), for the opening 'Pastoral', and *The Oxford Book of English Verse 1250–1900*, chosen and edited by Arthur Quiller-Couch (Oxford, Clarendon Press, 1927), for all the remaining texts except the 'Elegy' (Blake). On the inside back cover of the latter volume the composer has scribbled a list of numbers under the heading 'Night', referring to nocturnal poems contained in the anthology. One of these, Tennyson's 'Summer Night' ('Now sleeps the crimson petal, now the white'), was actually set by Britten, though it remained unknown until the discovery of the composition sketch by Marion Thorpe, among her father's papers, in 1986. It was published by Boosey & Hawkes in 1989. Its most intriguing musical feature is the presence of the rocking accompanimental 'sleep' motif used by Britten in his later orchestral song-cycle, *Nocturne*, Op. 60. Thus in a hitherto unsuspected way, the *Serenade* precisely anticipates the later cycle, which is exclusively dedicated to sleep and dreams. At the time of the composition of the *Serenade* Berkeley wrote in an undated letter to Britten: 'I am rather excited about your setting "Now sleeps the crimson petal" – curiously enough it is right for you to set; I see that very clearly.' (Roger Quilter's setting of the same text had been a favourite song of Mrs Britten's: see Introduction, note 12, p. 64.) See also Donald Mitchell, ' "Forms more real than living man": Reflections on Britten's *Serenade* and *Nocturne*', in the programme for the Peter Pears Memorial Concert, given at Friends House, London, on 3 April 1987, and the same author's, ' "Now sleeps the crimson petal": Britten's other "Serenade" ', *Tempo*, June 1989, pp. 22–7.

When the vocal score of the *Serenade* first appeared Britten sanctioned the use of viola or cello to replace the horn, and special instrumental parts were made available from the publishers. It seems clear, however, that the composer never envisaged the substitute instruments taking part except as a practical means of making possible a domestic performance or rehearsal of the work, i.e. for voice and piano, with viola or cello.

Interestingly, Howard Ferguson, Britten's old College associate, had made a setting of 'The Lyke-Wake Dirge' for baritone and orchestra in 1928, as the second of his *Two Ballads*, Op. 1, first performed on 26 January 1930, with which Britten may have been familiar.

The composition sketch (damaged) for the song discarded from the final version of
Serenade, 'Now sleeps the crimson, petal, now the white' (Tennyson's 'Summer Night')

3 Julius Guttman, the singing teacher with whom Pears studied during 1943.

4 Christina Podd and Theresa Burrows were domestic helpers at Snape.

5 Britten's and Pears's housekeeper in London. Margaret was her daughter.

420 To Ralph Hawkes

The Old Mill, Snape, Suffolk.
March 22nd, 1943.

My dear Ralph,

Thank you for your letters. I em enjoying myself down here – taking life very easily, & doing a certain amount of easy work at leisure (I have completed nearly three of the horn songs since I got here!). I am looking forward to hearing yours & Stein's decision on St. Cecilia.[1] If you think it necessary, you could send a copy here & I could telephone my impressions so as not to waste time.

About the Goehr matter,[2] my feelings are these: while I see your point, I can't help feeling that it might be a good thing to have a first performance <u>outside</u> the B & H concerts. It might counteract any unfriendly comments on your boosting me, or suggestions that I can't get performances elsewhere. You will have had 1st performances of the Michelangelo, St. Cecilia, the Quartet (& if you want them later in the summer Clifford Curzon & I could do the 2–piano pieces) already this season. Please don't think me difficult. If you stick to your point I am quite willing to give way, only I should like Goehr to do them with his orchestra at your concert. Let me know what you think.

When are you off to sea? Good luck in all your ventures – !

Yours,

BEN

1 Their decision concerned the first recording of *Hymn to St Cecilia*, by the Fleet Street Choir, conducted by T.B. Lawrence, made in January 1943, of which Britten evidently disapproved. Hawkes wrote to Britten on 23 March:

I have listened to the <u>St Cecilia</u> recordings; there is no doubt that they are not perfect but the second takings are probably better than the first, although having improved some of the parts which were out of tune in the first, they have fallen down slightly on different parts in the second. I am afraid it is a case of not being able to get perfection with this Choir in this work but under present circumstances I would not advise you to try and stop the recordings being issued. I think that we are all extremely critical about this and whilst I entirely agree that we should be so, I think our criticisms need not be carried too far in this particular case. It appears that permission has been given for the recording, and, therefore, legally, I could not stop their issue [. . .]

Stein feels as I do – one can always pick holes in this sort of work and under these circumstances but as I do not feel that the Fleet Street Choir will do any better, I think that we should accept the fact that they have done their best and in any event we shall get a lot of performances of the records; in all probability we may get some human performances as a result, which are much better.

The recording was issued on Decca к 1088–9 in May. It was still available when *The Record Guide* by Edward Sackville-West and Desmond Shawe-Taylor was published by Collins in 1951, when the authors referred to a performance that 'leaves much to be desired'.

2 Britten had promised the first performance of the *Serenade* to Walter Goehr (1903–1960), British conductor of German birth and father of the composer Alexander Goehr (b. 1932). It was probably his activities as conductor of the Morley College Choir and Concerts Society that brought him into contact with Britten and Pears. Another mutual friend was Michael Tippett.

Hawkes had written to Britten on 19 March:

I have been thinking about the pieces for String Orchestra, Voice and Harp [*sic*; probably a mistyping of horn] and your promise to Walter Goehr in connection with them. I am afraid there will be difficulty if he wants to do the First Performance because our Concerts at the Wigmore were specially designed for the First Performance of works of this nature and above all things, as a 'Shop Window' for new works by you and others; in fact, I have looked upon the launching of your new works there with considerable pride. I think, under the circumstances, I must deny Walter Goehr the pleasure of doing them, since they are exactly what we should reckon to do next Season or at a later Concert this Summer. This may place you in somewhat of a difficulty with Goehr and I shall be glad if you will let me know whether you feel this to be the case. I will write to him and explain the situation but in view of the fact that he is running Concerts of not unsimilar character at the same Hall, I feel that if he did these works, it would be almost a 'slap in the face' for us. People might well say that it was strange that notwithstanding our Concerts we were unable to give the First Performance of our most prominent young composer's works.

See, however, Letter 421.

421 To Ralph Hawkes

Old Mill, Snape, Suffolk.
March 29th, 1943.

My dear Ralph,

I am sorry not to have answered your last letter before; no excuse, just sheer laziness, I'm afraid! I am much better, getting up earlier, even doing a little gardening, which will make me more prepared for the fray towards the end of next week!

Re the Goehr matter[1] – of course there are unfriendly remarks (which kind friends without fail bring to ones ears!) about your patronage of me – that couldn't help occurring, & it doesn't bother me at all. All I felt was that it is always wisest to avoid giving ones enemies more ammunition than one can help. I can give you chapter & verse if you like when we meet but I suggest we have more worth-while things to talk about on those rare occasions, & anyhow there's nothing one can do about it!

I still feel it would be nice to let Goehr do these pieces, not only because I think he's a good conductor, but because I feel that otherwise I should let him down. But I am prepared not to make any more fuss if you insist, if you see what can be done about engaging him for the concert you intend. I will write to him as nicely as I can to apologise. Incidentally there is one major point – it isn't certain that the pieces will be completely ready by the date of his concert, so maybe there is no need for the worry!

Thank you for sending on Rev. J.W.A. Hussey's letter[2] – yes, I am sure something will materialise before September. Will you write him a note saying so, or shall I? Incidentally, was the letter written direct to me or to you?

I quite agree about the St. Cecilia records; they are better than the first, & though not ideal, will probably give people some idea of the piece. I am writing to Sarton[3] about it. It is a pity, but the moral is, don't get measles!

When do you go off? Do let me know if anything occurs. I expect to get to town at the end of next week, & will call you to see if you are still around.

With best wishes,
Yours,
BEN

1 Goehr had replied to Hawkes on 26 March:

I have not been well for several weeks. And Britten (who was ill too) did not give his decision until after I had left London. That was the reason that I could not approach you – But, in any case, I thought Britten would have done that when he promised to write these songs for my concert. – However, I have substituted a repeat performance of 'Illuminations' in my programme for the 15th May. And I need not say that I shall be very pleased to perform the new songs later in one of your concerts if that can be arranged.

The first performance of the *Serenade*, Op. 31, was in fact to be conducted by Walter Goehr with Pears and Dennis Brain (horn), as part of the Boosey & Hawkes Concert at the Wigmore Hall, London, on 15 October. The programme also included the first concert performance of Berkeley's *Divertimento* for small orchestra and Stravinsky's ballet music, *Pulcinella*.

2 The Very Reverend John Walter Atherton Hussey (1909–1985), Vicar of St Matthew's Northampton, 1937–55, was also Canon of Peterborough Cathedral from 1949 to 1955, and Dean of Chichester from 1955 to 1977. For over forty years Hussey encouraged church patronage of the arts and was responsible for commissioning Henry Moore, Graham Sutherland, Marc Chagall, John Piper and Ceri Richards. He also sought the collaboration of Auden and many contemporary composers: Britten (*Rejoice in the Lamb*), Tippett, Walton, Rubbra, Berkeley and Bernstein.

Hussey had first approached Walton, who had declined the invitation. He then wrote to Britten on 22 March:

I have been wondering whether you would consider the possibility of a commission (on whatever terms you think suitable) to write some music for our Jubilee celebrations next September. I had nothing very definite in mind – perhaps a four-part anthem. Ours is only a voluntary choir of men's and boy's voices, but a great effort has been made throughout the history of this magnificent church to maintain a high level for such resources. We are also fortunate to possess a superb organ (Walker's).

A great point has always been made of the annual Dedication and Patronal Festival on S. Matthew's Day, and this year, 1943, sees the Jubilee, and we are most anxious to mark the occasion with a Festival which will be worthy. If you feel that there is any possibility of this suggestion bearing fruit, I would of course be pleased to send fully any particulars for which you might wish. I very much hope that you may be able to manage something, however small. Please do if you possibly can.

He added a postcript:

On reading through this letter I feel more than ever how impertinent it is to send it, but I hope you will forgive me and put it down to enthusiasm for a great 'bee' of mine – closer association between the arts and the Church.

Britten agreed to Hussey's request (see Letter 424) and composed *Rejoice in the Lamb* [Jubilate Agno], Op. 30, with words by Christopher Smart, a festival cantata for chorus, with treble, alto, tenor and bass solos and organ. It was first performed on 21 September. Britten was also to compose his *Prelude and Fugue on a Theme of Vittoria* for organ to celebrate the 1946 commemoration of St Matthew's Day. See also Walter Hussey, *Patron of Art: The revival of a great tradition among modern artists* (London, Weidenfeld and Nicolson, 1985); Michael Nicholas, *Muse at St Matthew's: A Short History of the Artistic Traditions of St Matthew's Church, Northampton* (Northampton, n.d. [1968]), which includes a list of the musical works Hussey commissioned; and MKWW, p. 262. Hussey's private collection of art works now hangs at the Pallant House Gallery, Chichester.

3 Harry G. Sarton (1906–1951), head of Decca's Artist and Repertoire Department, 1935–51.

422 To Benjamin Britten
From Peter Pears

> Opera House
> Blackpool.
> Tuesday [early April 1943]

My darling –

I'm just writing this before I go to bed, just to tell you how much I love and miss you – and that last weekend was pure heaven but not long enough. The journey up and all was fairly hectic although Blackpool is half empty and I found a room at a very expensive but comfortable hotel where I still am. There is a waitress looking after me who adores opera (she will have been 4 times in these two weeks) and she gives me everything I shouldn't have – lots of extras, etc.! So I'm not doing so bad. Though there is no-one to take your place curiously enough!

I'm afraid if you want to see me in Rigoletto you'll have to come here on Saturday or Southport on Wednesday, as I shan't be doing any in London. I'm doing Traviata instead so I shall have [to] learn that fairly quick too. The Rig. Costumes have arrived and are quite stupendous! The rehearsals are going very well too & I'm falling into the part easily.

Will you please buy a bottle of Complevite in Sax [Saxmundham] & take it? It's the same as Pregnavite only doesn't sound so rude! and please do take it with pleasure & not grumpily! please to please me. Promise to obey!

How are the songs?[1] I do hope I didn't damp your poor old enthusiasm too much about them – Don't be discouraged.

Don't forget, my darling, that I am only as critical as I am because I have high standards for you.

All my love, my honey –

always your

P.

Use your sweet ration before the end of the week!

1 *Serenade.*

423 To Peter Pears

Old Mill, Snape, Suffolk.

~~March 31st 1943~~

April 1st 1943

My darling,

These telephone conversations are so damnably unsatisfactory, when there is someone in the room, & one cannot say what one feels. I am sorry about it, but at anyrate it was glorious to hear your voice, & to know that you had found rooms. You old blighter, you promised me <u>faithfully</u> that you'd ring on Monday – I was so worried about you arriving there with no where to go – & I sat up till mid-night waiting! You beast! Still you are forgiven, as usual.

Things go on the same here – I work alot, (don't worry, the Nocturnes[1] will be worthy of you by the time I've finished!) correct proofs, write letters (mostly to Ralph or Decca), go long walks with Iris, & have rather beastly alerts – Monday night was nasty, & closer than Sunday – Still it might be much worse, & on the whole I am enjoying myself alot. If only you were here – you <u>must</u> start giving up jobs so you can work & do things you <u>want</u> to do. It is infuriating about no Rig. in London. Are you sure that's final? Can't you give up some little job to do it – I am sure it will be so good. But anyhow Traviata[2] will be, too, and there will obviously be a chance to show Londoners a good Duca later. But what a sweat to learn it so quickly – lucky we chose a programme for Cambridge that doesn't need much work. I'm looking for winners for you in the Schubert albums – I think I've found some, too.

It was so heavenly to have last week-end with you. I do love you so, you know, & loathe being without you. Next week is too far off still, & you have so much to do before it. Nevermind, I'm sure it'll all be grand, & relax as much as you possibly can.

Iris is well, & I think liking being here. Beth is fond of her & they get on very easily. Sally is sweeter than ever, & Sebastian, if possible, naughtier than ever. But I like him all the same, he is very attractive & strong-willed. What a handfull for uncle later!

The Goehr situation has clarified abit. His turning the cheek has conquered Ralph who now agrees to letting him conduct the Nocturnes at the BH concert later – the best arrangement since there's now no hurry, for me or for you to learn them.

The post – as usual. Much love & all luck in the world for all your shows – a good Duca, a good St. Matthew,[3] Alfred & all!

My darling man.
Dein
BEN

Love from Iris, Beth, Seb, & Sal.

1 *Serenade.*

2 Pears sang Alfredo in Verdi's *La Traviata* for the first time on 29 April at Sadler's Wells Theatre, London, conducted by Herbert Menges.

3 Reginald Jacques directed the Bach Choir and Jacques Orchestra in their annual performance of Bach's *St Matthew Passion* at the Royal Albert Hall, London, on 11 April, with Eric Greene (Evangelist), Norman Walker (Christus), Elsie Suddaby (soprano), Mary Jarred (alto), Pears (tenor) and William Parsons (bass). Pears, though singing the tenor arias at this performance, was later to become an outstanding Evangelist in both Bach Passions. He recorded the *St Matthew* twice – with Klemperer in 1962 (Columbia SAX 2447–50) and with Karl Münchinger in 1965 (Decca SET 288–91) – and the *St John* twice, both times in English – with David Willcocks in 1960 (Argo ZRG 5270–72) and with Britten in 1972 (Decca SET 531–3).

424 To Revd Walter Hussey

Old Mill, Snape, Suffolk.
April 5th 1943.

Dear Mr. Hussey,

My publishers have forwarded your letter to me here, where I am recuperating from an illness. As I also have a 'bee' about closer connection between the arts & the Church, I am sure that I shall have an idea before next September for an anthem for your jubilee. Something lively for such an occasion, don't you think? Tell me your ideas, & the size of your choir, including details of capabilities (quite confidential, of course!), & whether male or female altos, & I'll see what can be done. It'll have to be printed of course, so what is the latest date that you would like it for rehearsal?

With best wishes,
Yours sincerely,
BENJAMIN BRITTEN

425 To Elizabeth Mayer

Old Mill, Snape, Suffolk.
April 6th 1943.

My darling Elizabeth,

What a <u>lovely packet</u>! Thank you so very very much – for the sweets which are like gold these days, one never seems to get enough, & so many lovely kinds too! It is so very sweet of you to take the trouble to send them, especially as you must be so busy with all the moving & the worrying & planning of this distressing time for you all.[1] But if you could have seen our faces on the arrival of the package, & the excitement over the opening (Sebastian was delirious with joy!), it would have seemed worth while to you I know. I go back to London on Thursday & I'm taking loads to Peter who has been madly working, rushing all over the country & in need of a little extra food!

Well, my dear. I am glad in a way that you have taken the plunge – although you have been so considerate and not grumbled at all in your letters, both of us had expected it. It will be a bit difficult at first, but it seemed out of human hands to make the Amityville ménage work properly. What a pity. I am anxiously awaiting plans & addresses. I heard actually first from David Rothman who wrote such a sweet & loving letter about you both – then William's came this morning, but still saying nothing definite. Until I hear I'll go on sending to Amityville, because stupidly I've left the N. York address in London.

Well, so much has happened here since I last wrote – far too long ago. Peter & I are now very comfortably settled in 45A, St. Johns Wood High St., London, N.W.8., with a nice housekeeper, &, touching wood, things ought to be very comfortable. I haven't seen much of it because, as I believe Beth told you, I went & caught measles (!) & was packed away into a fever hospital – which was rather unpleasant in these times in an outlying part of South

London. However I've been lucky & avoided all complications & after three weeks of Snape air I am feeling quite fit to return to the fray in two days' time. I've not wasted my time as I've practically completed a new work (6 Nocturnes) for Peter [and] a lovely new young horn player Dennis Brain, & Strings, which is coming out soon. It is not important stuff, but quite pleasant, I think. St. Cecilia has been recorded, not too well, but gives an impression, the 2 piano pieces (me & Clifford Curzon!) are about to be, some new French folk-songs I've arranged² (alas, not sung by Peter, & the Quartet³ are all to be done by Decca – I must devise a way of getting them to you.

My dear – don't worry about us ever in the noisy times you read in the paper – it is only a nuisance, & not serious. I don't like it, true, but it is extraordinary what you can get used to, & it is nothing compared to what so many people are going thro' all over this poor continent.

We are so happy here in Snape, Beth & the children, Kit, when he can get away, & the same for Peter, & a dear friend (Iris Rogers) who has had such terrible operations has been recuperating here for 2 weeks, as well. I long for the time when you can see it. It must be soon. So lovely to hear the news of Beata – I must write to her soon, but I know you all realise how much there is to do, & how impossible letter writing is. But you manage so much, my darling; how you get through it all, beats me! And the New Yorkers which arrive so regularly – if in a rather strange order! We read them with avidity & pass them on to many grateful friends. Please give my love to all my good friends – I hope they're well. How is life in general with you – I hope not too complicated with rations & restrictions? Sorry this is so short & scrappy, my dearest, but I know you understand my limitations & my love.

BEN

Beth meant to write in this but what with cleaning & feeding the babies & the house she really hasn't had a moment, but she <u>will</u> write soon & thank you for Sally's beautiful parcel which was a great success & the owner is very proud of it.

1 See Letter 426.
2 All settings were to be recorded in May by Sophie Wyss and Britten, and released on Decca M568 in 1944.

3 This recording was not made. The First String Quartet was in fact first recorded in the USA, by the Galimir Quartet, and released on Esoteric ES504 in 1951.

426 To William Mayer

Old Mill, Snape, Suffolk.
April 6th 1943.

My dearest William,

Your note arrived this morning saying that you had resigned. It was not a shock, since David Rothman had given us an idea of it about a week ago. I think you have done wisely; it was too worrying for you, & anyhow these times are worrying enough for you. Once the shock of the change is over, & you are comfortably settled either in a nice little apartment in New York or a new hospital, I am sure you'll feel much better. I am terribly eager to hear what you've decided. Do write at once & tell us. How I wish we were with you to discuss all the details, & to plan, & to help you as you so often have helped us! But I can imagine so many things that you do, the New York trips & the gramophone, & Jippy (how will he like the move?) & the visits to Beate, that it is almost like being with you! But a year is a long time – let's hope it won't be another one before we are together again – either here or with you. I am longing to show you this place, inspite of the neglect in the garden (it is impossible to get people to work in it) it is looking really lovely, & it is really <u>very</u> comfortable – central heating throughout! – almost American! I have been here for about three weeks & go back to town on Thursday – feeling better for the recuperation – wasn't it crazy to get measles at my age! But luckily, altho' I felt pretty rotten with it, I missed all complications. But I am sure if you'd been here with your little boxes of magic, I should never have caught it!

Peter is with Sadlers Wells Opera company these two weeks – doing Magic Flute, Rigoletto, & rehearsing Traviata. He is singing so well, & acting with such abandon, that he is well on the way to becoming an operatic star. I wish you could see him, & we all could discuss his performances. <u>When</u> I write it, & <u>if</u> it is put on here, I hope he'll do the principal part in Peter Grimes.[1] The ideas are going well, but I haven't had time to start it yet.

How tragic about Fay.[2] I was terribly sorry to hear she was ill;

but judging by what you say, it must have been a relief. But poor Meta[3] – is she still staying on at Amityville?

How are you getting on with all the new regulations and restrictions; are they a great bore? I have got used to them here now, but luckily I don't have to cope with the food situation myself! The sweets you sent have been terribly welcome – I miss the lack of them most of anything, I think. Did I ever thank you for the Almanac – which I leave open at Nov. 22nd always so people can see the entry!! Thank you so much for sending it, & all the other, many other things you have sent, & are always sending. How can I thank you, dear William, for being so kind? Except perhaps by saying over & over again, how much I love you & think of you in all your difficulties & praying we shall all be together soon again.

BEN

1 The first indication that the role of Grimes was intended for Pears. In the draft of a cast list dating from mid-1942 the role of Grimes was envisaged for baritone. See PGPB, p. 56.

2 Dr Titley's secretary.

3 An occupational therapist at the Long Island Home.

427 To Enid Slater

Old Mill, Snape, Suffolk.
April 7th, 1943.

My dear Enid,

Thank you so very much for the 'copies'[1] which arrived this morning. You have done a really wonderful job, & I am thrilled with them. I should like to discuss with you the possibility of a ½ plate sometime soon; there's one idea I have.[2] Also, thank you very much for doing the others, & sending them off. I am awfully glad we've done this, & hope that the authorities don't keep them too long, as it comes at a bad time for the Mayers, & may cheer them up abit. In the meantime I must brace myself for your bill!

So sorry, this week-end is no good. It is Peter's only one in town for a long time & I am going up to-morrow to spend it with him. I do want to see you both soon – will you be up next week anytime? I don't know how long I'll be staying yet – all depends how I bear up. I'm much better, but it takes ages to get fit, & I get horrible attacks of depression (I've been down with it in the last four or five days – how did you guess!) But it'll be over soon, & I've done some good work here. Could you please tell Montagu that I'm writing him about P.G., & want to see him badly. Has he done anything about his ulcers? I've written to A & B [Anna and Bridget] at school – hope they get the cards.

Much love, my dear, & many thanks again
BEN

1 Prints of existing photographs.

2 Possibly Britten was considering a publicity photograph, of which multiple copies might be made.

428 To David Rothman

45A, St. Johns Wood High Street, N.W.8.
May 7th 1943
[Letter started on the 7th but apparently not
dispatched until the 22nd: see Letter 429]

My dear Dave,

It is disgracefully late to write & thank you for the lovely parcel – but I know you realise how complicated ones life is now-a-days, & since that lovely surprise arrived things have been quite out-of-hand; so letter-writing has been pushed right on one side, especially of letters to friends so far away & so dear, letters that one wants to take trouble over, & that one can enjoy writing. My dear Dave – you cannot imagine the excitement that your most wonderful parcel caused. I was down at my wind-mill in Suffolk, to where it was forwarded, staying with my sister & her two young children (one, the very young one, only 3 months old now!) Finding the Manna in the desert must have been like that! – To see such quantities of sweets, & candies, & crackers & biscuits, Sebastian, aged four, was not the only one whose eyes bulged with excitement. The mittens too are much appreciated – I gave one pair to my sister who was very pleased with it, & kept one for myself. David, I don't know how to begin to thank you adequately. I know how busy you are & how wrapped up in your own strenuous life, & those of your dear family; how you found time to think of us, much less pack up the parcel & choose the lovely contents, beats me. However, knowing David, I shouldn't be surprised! The sweets are <u>still</u> being enjoyed by Peter & me – I saved a lot to bring up to London so Peter could have some too, & he joins with me in all my thanks. Thank you also for your lovely letters which give both of us so much pleasure, & which enable us to imagine so clearly the lives which you are all living now. It must be very strange & complicated for you; much more so, perhaps, than for people over here who have never had such a high standard of living as the Americans, & who don't really miss it so much. Is the rationing complicated? Does it affect the store; I mean with tickets or vouchers etc.! Here, of course, nearly everything is controlled – & those things which aren't are very difficult to obtain, except in out-of-the-way places – and expensive too! Peter & I had the most difficult time getting this new apartment into working order, & spent pounds and pounds too. Simple things like carpets & curtains present almost insuperable difficulties these days. However, now, it is looking quite nice, & we are lucky in having a grand housekeeper who cooks, & shops, & copes with rations, & looks after us splendidly. She is worth her weight in gold (or candies!), as any form of domestic service is almost impossible to get now. Unfortunately, our entry here was somewhat marred by my catching a measle bug & being whisked away to a Fever Hospital for a few weeks! It was a pretty dismal place, ugly & sordid – but I had a better time than most of the inmates by sheer favouritism! – And friends were wonderful to me sending me books & extra food. But it is a wretched disease to get at my advanced age, & leaves you feeling very low – & liable too to catch colds & other depressing germs (infact now I am in bed with a touch of bronchitis!). But Peter & I have taken off a couple of weeks in June, & if we're lucky & get some sun, that may put things right!

It is hard to realise that it is a whole year since that Sunday when you all drove over to Amityville to say 'au revoir' to us, & what a year it has been! Personally we have both been very, very fortunate. Peter has had a success passing all bounds – he is permanently with Sadlers Wells Opera, & a very glamorous & popular heroe he makes! I have had some nice successes, and get all the work & more than I want, & in fact my chief trouble is in saying 'no' to people! Of course like everyone else, these days, one is doing about three people's work, & one has a permanent feeling of weariness. But, how lucky one is to be doing constructive work – it is so ghastly to hear these bombers roaring over at night (in both directions); so much trouble & sacrifice for nothing.

I hear that the Amityville situation is now eased abit. It was a great worry to us, feeling so far away & able to do nothing. But your letters to them [the Mayers] helped & comforted them alot – I hope you are able to go & see them occasionally – They are so devoted to you.

No more now, dear David – thank you more than I can say for the really lovely & most exciting parcel. We have enjoyed it so much. Please forgive this being in Bobby's envelope – but I know how he loves to have the stamps, & to be the addressee. Love to all of you. How is Joan progressing with the new teacher? – And Emma – & your dear Wife!

Love & thanks from both of us,

BEN

429 To Bobby Rothman

Perhaps this <u>had</u> better be the last journey of the Air Mail ticket – it's looking abit weary.

The Old Mill, Snape, Suffolk.

May 22nd 1943.

My dear old Bobby,

You must have thought that I had forgotten all about you – it's such ages since I wrote. But although I don't get around to writing letters I do think about you alot, and anyhow how could I forget you when I have a large photo of you staring at me all the time when I'm working (and I can assure you that's most of the time)!

[. . .] We've been having some noisy times, as you've probably read. Do you remember what I told you about what I thought would happen to me in raids? Well, I do admit I get pretty scared, but what gets me down most is the lack of sleep. There's days when the flak is so terrific one can't stay in bed because of being near windows, so down we have to troop under the stairs, & that's the end of sleep for abit – & does one feel bad tempered the next day! But it's not bad really, nothing to what those poor devils are going through in Europe.

I have been down here at the old Windmill for a few days. Whenever I have got a lot of writing to do I come down here because it's quieter than London, & when the telephone calls cost

½ $1 as opposed to a nickel, the telephone doesn't ring so often.
I do some work in the garden – but not nearly enough; in some
places the weeds are over a foot high; & the stinging nettles are
very vicious, & prosper madly unless one can get at them with a
fork. I think I'll have to get you to come over after the war & do
some digging for me. Perhaps you'll learn something about
horticulture in the interim – it'll be useful! Peter is well, but
suffering from singing too much & too loud & too high (he does
on an average 5 concerts a week!). He is becoming a regular star;
you should see the crowds of adoring females outside the theatre
after his shows – I get quite bad-tempered waiting for him
sometimes. We have competitions to see who can get asked for the
most autographs, & are about all-square, I think. The other night
after a concert at Blackpool (the English Coney-Island) we were
followed for about a mile after the concert by three kids, no bigger
than you!, who apparently couldn't pluck up enough courage to
speak to us. Eventually they did, & they were fans of <u>mine</u> – so
Peter was cross. But he often scores over me.

Well, Bobby – how are you? I hope you'll have as good a time
this summer as you did last – it's crazy how time flies. You must
be enormous now – I shouldn't think I'll know you when we meet.
Send me photos from time to time so I can keep up with you. I
don't change much – my hair's not white yet, but I don't feel as
young as I used to!

I ought to write to the rest of the family, but I just haven't got
the time or the strength! Give them my love & special messages
to Mrs. Sturmdorf: tell her I love her letters, & will write soon (I
hope): to Emma, hope she likes being married: to Joan, hope she's
practising hard – & just general greetings all round.

I'm going to try & devise ways of getting my records to you.
Peter & I did some for H.M.V. (the English Victor) and Decca is
recording alot of my stuff, & I'm going to do some playing soon.
But the means of getting them to you will be difficult – but I think
I can manage somehow.

Lots of love – take care of yourself, & write soon again,

BEN

P.S. You address letters quite correctly, but the posts are abit mad
sometimes. Your last letter was about a month in coming.

430 To Elizabeth Mayer

Old Mill, Snape, Suffolk.
May 22nd 1943.

My darling Elizabeth,

Your last lovely letter (the surface-mail one) arrived this morning
– sent on by Barbara, because I am here doing an especial pressure
of work & it's easier & quieter (in every way!) than London. Beth,
alas, is no longer here. It was worrying Kit too much her being
so near the coast, & certainly she has lost her nerve abit since Sally
came; so they decided to move till one knows what is going to
happen. Maybe she'll come back after the Summer. Anyhow it's
lovely here, & I can work easily. Your letter before, with the news
of the postponement of your moving arrived in interesting
circumstances – it was Peter's first Traviata with Sadlers Wells –
Barbara handed it to me just as the performance began – & at the
end of the show, I went round & we read it together in his
dressing room. It was a most <u>lovely</u> show, & a great success. How
we wished you & William could have been there – but soon, after
all this, you'll hear & see him on the stage, where he is so charming,
& looks & sounds so good. They are very pleased with him. I
don't know what to say about the postponement[1] – from this
distance it is impossible to judge. But I trust you both so implicitly
that I'm sure you've done the right thing. At anyrate you'll have
time to think now – we were both, so worried about you. What
a wonder Beate is! The photos are lovely – an excellent one of Chris
– & the most lovely one of you all. I'm going to get Enid to enlarge
it so I can add it to my picture gallery in 45a. Poor Montagu (Slater)
has been most terribly ill – almost no hope, but by some miracle
& an operation has pulled through. I dashed down to spend the
bad day with Enid, who was distracted.[2] He'll have to go slow
for abit, but with luck will soon be fit. My other friends seem well
– there are beginning to be some horrible gaps now, but so far
no one very close. Piers is away somewhere on a cruiser; I hear
from him regularly but he can't say where he is. Louis & Hedli
are round the corner still – Hedli, <u>very</u> near her time![3] Henry Boys
is in the army, but so far in England. One great new friend Peter
& I have made, an <u>excellent</u> composer, & most delightful &
intelligent man, Michael Tippett is having a bad time & may have
to go to prison (you can guess what for)[4] – but he is brave & says
he won't mind, but nevertheless we're all fighting to keep him

out. My dear – don't blame Peter for not writing – he is working
nearly to death, & for certain reasons he cannot refuse much of
it. I have insisted on <u>ten</u> days break in June; & I'm hoping he can
get through until then. His throat has been troubling him too. It
is all the trouble of too much work – Sadlers Wells love him so &
want him now for the Barber (as well as Magic Flute, Traviata, &
Rigoletto, each learned in 2 weeks!)[5] – choral societies want him,
& of course we do recitals all over the place together (nearly
always with the Sonnetts – recent places have been Oxford,
Cambridge, Greenwich, Liverpool, London (for the sixth time!)).[6]
He <u>can</u> do it, but it worries him that he can't practise enough.
When he has got time off, he can't relax; it is a full time job
looking after him, I can assure you. How I wish, by some miracle,
that we were all together again – I feel that you are the only
person who could cope with the situation! This is all to say – forgive
him not writing; it is all he can do to get thro' the most urgent
business letters. And we talk of you & think of you every day –
can't you feel the rays working?!

It is lovely to think of you playing (still in Amityville) & being
all together, sometimes lessons with Colin, & sometimes playing
with Toni. I expect the piano sounds lovely now it's tuned – how
I wish I could bang it out of tune again for you! Do you know
that I'm going to do some more playing now – I'm doing the
Scottish Ballad with Clifford Curzon again at the Albert Hall soon
– & we're going to do some records together – my pieces, &
probably the Schumann & the Mozart (pace the little Owls!).[7] I'm
also doing some more records with Peter (probably the folk-songs
& some Schubert).[8] So I'm busy, you see. I am abit worried by
my excessive local success at the moment – the reviews that the
Sonnetts, St. Cecilia, the Carols, & now the Quartet have had, &
also the fact that Les Illuminations is now a public draw! It is all a
little embarrassing, & I hope it doesn't mean there's too much
superficial charm about my pieces. I think too much success is as
bad as too little; but I expect it's only a phase which will soon pass.
Luckily Peter & Michael are rigorous critics – but how I miss you
& Wystan. There is one great critic here, Erwin Stein (late of
Universal, Vienna), who is a great help. But I think I told you about
him and his charming wife (from Mechlenburg, not Schwerin, but I
think Strelitz) – who are so good to us both – they are almost
second Mayers – but no, that's just not possible. The Mayers are
unique.

My dear – I am so tired that I can't think what I'm writing, & I

want to go to bed to get some sleep before the black-birds begin
to arrive! It isn't bad, just one gets abit weary having to get out of
bed so often! But talking of _real_ birds – the nightingales here are
heaven – I still think they are the loveliest of all songsters.

I do hope you are well & taking the greatest care of yourself –
and William, too – I hope he's well. Give him lots of love, & say
I'll answer his letters, so dear, soon.

Forgive the scribble my dearest – but I know you don't mind
how bad or stupid the things are I say – as long as I write! But
what a pale comparison writing is with talking – & _when_ will that
be possible? All my love, as ever,

BEN

P.S.   I can't understand why Wystan never got his St. Cecilia[9] –
except that posts are very unreliable these days. We can't do much
about sending many copies – unless Heinsheimer reprints over in
U.S.A.   But I'll talk to B & H about it all.

1 The postponement of the long-contemplated resignation of Dr Mayer
   from his post at Amityville.
2 Slater had a history of severe ill health: see PGPB, p. 44.
3 Of the birth of her daughter, Corinna.
4 Michael Tippett (b. 1905), English composer. Britten and Tippett
   struck up a warm friendship. Pacifism and Morley College had
   brought the two men together. Tippett composed two song-cycles
   for Pears and Britten, _Boyhood's End_ (1943) and _The Heart's Assurance_
   (1950–52); and he dedicated his Concerto for Orchestra (1962–3) to
   Britten in honour of the latter's fiftieth birthday. Britten likewise
   dedicated _Curlew River_ to Tippett 'in friendship and admiration', to
   honour his sixtieth birthday. As early as December 1942, Britten was
   enthusiastic in his response to Tippett's showing him _A Child of Our
   Time_: 'What a grand work the Oratorio is & a performance _must_ be
   arranged soon.' (See LFBML, p. 255.) Berkeley, after attending that
   first performance (on 19 March 1944, with Joan Cross and Pears
   among the soloists), wrote an undated letter to Britten which interestingly represents a view of Tippett that was probably current among
   his fellow composers:

   I was very pleased with Michael's piece – it has much real beauty, but it is
   not easy to assimilate from one hearing. I felt that it was rather too complicated and I kept wishing that he could simplify his style a little; I had a
   feeling that it might become rather hysterical at any moment – and also I
   thought his treatment of the words was too arbitrary – particularly as regards
   stresses, which was perhaps not always quite happy. However these are
   only first impressions, and things like that – particularly in the case of

something as new and individual – often turn out to be absolutely right when one knows the work better. And in any case it is marvellous to find somebody in this country besides yourself who really can write living music. After you, he's a long way ahead of any of the other younger composers.

Tippett registered as a Conscientious Objector in 1940 and was directed to undertake non-combatant military duties. His appeal was unsuccessful and he refused to comply with the Tribunal's order. In June (1943) he was sentenced to three months' imprisonment in Wormwood Scrubs; remission meant that he was released on 21 August. There was a legendary prison meeting on 11 July between Tippett, Pears and Britten, a full account of which is given by John Amis, *Amiscellany: My life, my music* (London, Faber and Faber, 1985), pp. 173–4, and which Tippett himself related in a letter to Evelyn Maude, written in Wormwood Scrubs on the 5th: 'On Sunday we [the prison orchestra] are to play in chapel, in the middle of a recital by Peter Pears & Ben Britten – all v. amusing.' It was with Britten and Pears that Tippett had breakfast on the day of his release. See also *A Man of Our Time*, exhibition catalogue (London, Schott, 1977), and LFBML, pp. 259–61.

For further details of the friendship between the two composers, see 'The Composer's View: A Selection of Letters from Michael Tippett to Benjamin Britten', edited by Philip Reed, Programme Book of the Britten–Tippett Festival, London, 1986, pp. 64–7. See also Britten's contribution to *Michael Tippett: A Symposium on his Sixtieth Birthday*, edited by Ian Kemp (London, Faber and Faber, 1965), pp. 29–30. It was in Tippett's fine 1976 obituary of Britten that he wrote:

I want to say, here and now, that Britten has been for me the most purely musical person that I have ever met and I have ever known. It always seemed to me that music sprang out of his fingers when he played the piano, as it did out of his mind when he composed.

The obituary was re-published in Tippett, *Music of the Angels: Essays and Sketchbooks of Michael Tippett*, edited by Meirion Bowen (London, Eulenburg Books, 1980), pp. 82–4, along with other recollections of Britten.

5 Pears first sang the role of Almaviva in Rossini's *Barber of Seville* on 21 July in London, conducted by Norman Feasey.

6 Pears and Britten had given recitals in Cambridge (with Curzon) on 25 April (for the complete programme, see note 2 to Letter 411); at Charlton House, Greenwich, in aid of Friends War Relief Service on 2 May (Handel, Purcell, Schumann's *Dichterliebe*, Britten's *Michelangelo Sonnets* and Folk-song Arrangements); at the Crane Theatre, Liverpool, on 3 May (same programme as at Greenwich); at the Town Hall, Oxford, on 5 May (Handel, Purcell, Schubert, *Michelangelo Sonnets* and Folk-song Arrangements). The London concert remains unidentified.

7 Probably Mozart's Sonata in D (K.448) for two pianos, and Schumann's *Andante and Variations*, Op. 46, for two pianos. However, no recordings were made of music for two pianos (or piano duet) by either composer. The 'little Owls' – Ethel and Rae Robertson, because of their short stature.

8 Britten and Pears first recorded a group of Folk-song Arrangements in January 1944: 'The Salley Gardens', 'Little Sir William' and 'Oliver Cromwell'. These were released in 1944, on Decca M 555. They recorded three Schubert songs for Decca in January 1946 – 'Am See' (D.746), 'Die Forelle' (D.550) and 'Nacht und Träume' (D.827) – which were never released. Test pressings are in the Archive. (Pears and Britten re-recorded 'Nacht und Träume' much later, in 1968, on Decca SXL 6722.) Their first Schubert recording to be issued was not made until 1950: 'Auf der Bruck' (D.853) and 'Im Frühling' (D.882), HMV DB21423 (1952).

9 A copy of the published score.

A CHILD OF OUR TIME

An Oratorio by

MICHAEL TIPPETT

The first performance of this work will be given at the
ROYAL ADELPHI THEATRE, *on Sunday*,
March 19th, at 2.30, by JOAN CROSS,
MARGARET McARTHUR, PETER PEARS,
NORMAN WALKER, LONDON REGION
CIVIL DEFENCE & MORLEY COLLEGE
CHOIRS, *and the* LONDON PHILHAR-
MONIC ORCHESTRA *conducted by* WALTER
GOEHR. *(It will be preceded by the Mauerische
Trauermusik (K477) and the Symphony in G minor
(K183) of* MOZART*)*.

AN ACCOUNT OF THE ORATORIO IS GIVEN OVERLEAF

Tickets may be obtained from the Box Office (Temple Bar 7611)

(1d.

Announcement of the first performance of Michael Tippett's oratorio, *A Child of Our Time*, on 19 March 1944

431   To Alec Robertson

45A St Johns Wood High St.,
N.W.8.
May 24th 1943

My dear Alec,

Yes, I'm sorry I wrote crossly – but I was sick about the Mahler (& W. Legge)[1] and also that you weren't going to review St. Cecilia, & say how <u>atrocious</u> you thought the performance is – as it is, some other nit-wit in the Gramophone didn't even notice it[2] (& Eric Blom calls it 'unbelievably perfect'):[3] Do you <u>really</u> think I should pass that? It all happened when I had measles, & permission to record was given behind my back; all sickening & resulted in sordid scenes. Decca are making up for it now, but I <u>can't</u> understand T.B. Laurence passing them. So that was why – imagine me prostrating myself before you in repentance – I'm so sorry for my paddy; but it's been a difficult time what with over-work, & work going badly, & Peter's throat, & goodness knows what else. Please send a postcard saying 'forgiven' (or not, as the case may be!).

I enjoyed your Tschaikovsky talk yesterday[4] – but the BBC orch sounded abit wheezy after the records!

I'm in Snape for two or three days – lovely quiet after the bangings last week. I'm back in town on Tuesday.

Love to you,
Yours
BEN

1 English musical administrator (1906–1979), who was employed by the HMV Gramophone Company (later EMI Records), 1927–64. In the 1930s he initiated a series of subscription societies for producing limited recorded editions, which included the songs of Hugo Wolf and Mahler's *Das Lied* and Ninth Symphony. (The mention of Mahler and Walter Legge in this letter probably refers to a postponed record-ing of one of Mahler's works.) During the war Legge was in charge of ENSA concerts for troops. Post-war he produced numerous impor-tant recordings, many with the Philharmonia Orchestra which he founded in 1946. He was married twice: to Nancy Evans (see note 3 to Letter 496), and later to the German soprano, Elisabeth Schwarz-kopf. See also the latter's *On and Off the Record: A Memoir of Walter Legge* (London, Faber and Faber, 1982).

2 A review by W.R. Anderson of the Fleet Street Choir's recording of

Britten's *Hymn to St Cecilia*, conducted by T.B. Lawrence, appeared in the May issue of *Gramophone*.

3 In the *Birmingham Post*.

4 Robertson had given an interval talk during a BBC Symphony Orchestra concert conducted by Clarence Raybould, the second half of which included Tchaikovsky's Fourth Symphony.

432 To Revd Walter Hussey

45A, St. John's Wood High St.,
N.W.8.
May 28th 1943.

Dear Mr. Hussey,

Please forgive my rudeness in not having answered your letter. I have been terribly busy, & anyhow those two days, Wednesday & Thursdays, were impossible for me, I am afraid. Could I let you know <u>when</u> I have got the words worked out exactly, & then perhaps we could meet, & discuss it in detail. I am afraid I have gone ahead, and used abit about the cat Jeffrey, but I don't see how it could hurt anyone – he is such a nice cat.[1]

Please excuse haste & scribble. I will get in touch with you, then, in a week or so. The piece is going well, & I am pleased with it. Christopher Smart is a great inspiration, & I hope you'll be pleased too.

Yours sincerely,
BENJAMIN BRITTEN

What is the exact date of the Festival – Edward Sackville-West who helped me with the selection of words, & Sir Kenneth Clark[2] both want to come down to it – ?

1 *Rejoice in the Lamb*: the passage at Fig. 11 for treble solo, 'For I will consider my Cat Jeoffrey'.

2 Kenneth Mackenzie Clark (Baron Clark; 1903–1983), English art-historian. He was Keeper of the Department of Fine Art at the Ashmolean Museum, Oxford, 1931–3, and Director of the National Gallery, London, 1934–45. He was knighted in 1938. When the English Opera Group was formed in 1947, Clark was among the directors of the new company. He was Chairman of the Arts Council, 1953–60. His BBC Television series, *Civilisation*, broadcast in 1969, brought him popular acclaim. He wrote two volumes of autobiography, *Another Part of the Wood* (London, John Murray, 1974), and *The Other Half*

(London, John Murray, 1977), and contributed some memories of his Suffolk childhood to TBB, pp. 39–44. A biography of Clark by Meryle Secrest was published in 1984 (London, Weidenfeld and Nicolson), p. 210 of which reminds us that he was invited to lecture at the first Aldeburgh Festival in 1948 and at many subsequent Festivals.

433 To Mary Allen[1]
BBC

45a High Street,
St. John's Wood, N.W.8.
June 29th 1943.

Dear Miss Allen,

I am so sorry to have to refuse your invitation to supply music for the production of Uncle Arthur, because it is a play I'm very fond of & I should have loved to have had a shot at thinking up the right noises for it.[2] Unfortunately the next fortnight is too impossibly busy for me to take on any other work, much as I should have liked to. Couldn't you possibly give me more notice in the future, because I am so very booked up these days?

I do hope you get someone really good for the job, & many apologies for letting you down.

Yours sincerely,
BENJAMIN BRITTEN

P.S.   The above address usually reaches me more quickly than the Snape one you wrote to ——

1 Mary Allen, BBC Drama producer, 1927–63.
2 A radio play by John Pudney, 'A moral fantasy for organ and voices', which had been first broadcast in 1937, with music by Jack Clarke. In that same year Britten had collaborated with Pudney and Auden in Hadrian's Wall.

434 To Revd Walter Hussey

[Walter Hussey's typed questionnaire is printed in roman type; Britten's replies and additional comments are printed in italic type. The cancellations are Britten's.]

[Postmarked 23 August 1943]

QUESTIONNAIRE![1]

(Five minutes only – I hope – are necessary for this paper.
Candidates should attempt all questions).

1 On page 8 of the Cantata it should be "which cloatheth the naked"?
   Yes.

2 On p. 8 it should be Jakim, not Takim? (This is according to the book and Old Testament!)
   Jakim

3 On p. 28 the first two rhimes of the Shawm should be "Lawn fawn"? "sound bound" belong to the trumpet. (Note. The Shawm is the predecessor of the oboe!)
   [Britten underlined "Lawn Fawn".]

4 I wish the punctuation and use of Capitals to be printed $\left\{ \begin{array}{c} as \\ \text{not as} \end{array} \right\}$ in the book, and ~~not as~~ in the music copies

5 ~~I return MS with alterations and additions~~ $\left\{ \begin{array}{l} \text{Please} \\ \text{delete} \\ \text{as} \\ \text{necessary} \end{array} \right.$
   I do not return copy of MS but will pass same. –
   ~~I think the whole suggested MS is fearful.~~

6 Do you wish any reference to Mr. Sackville-West in the MS, and if so what?
   Not necessary – actually I didn't use much of his suggested script.

   Note: I hope you wont delete any of the laudatory phrases in the MS. Most of the readers just wont know these things unless they are told! The Editor will accept full responsiblity for the MS and will not reveal that you have seen it!

7 $\left\{ \begin{array}{l} \text{~~I enclose~~} \\ \underline{\text{I should not think of enclosing!}} \end{array} \right.$ a note of comment and and explanation to be printed with the MS.

8 I hope to visit Northampton next on *Sunday* and intend to arrive at *late afternoon if there's a convenient train*, I should like a bed for the night(s) of *Sunday, please.*

9 What a confounded nuisance you, and the choir, are!
  Here! Here! (not at all really)

Signed: *E.B. Britten (minor)*
*(School Certificate – 5 credits)

*In addition to this startling qualification, it might interest you to know I was also a valuable member of all the elevens, Victor Ludorum, held record for several years for Throwing the Cricket Ball (until broken by a beastly little boy in a gale), apart from my highly distinguished career in the Junior Tennis World. So now you know the stature of the composer you're dealing with – !

Seriously tho' – I think your article[2] is perfectly adequate (apart from the dubious grammar of the first sentence (!)). The only suggestion is that you qualify the Hallelujah[3] abit – quiet? escstatic? reserved?. . . . . I also suggest that this section be printed in italics as it is in the nature of a refrain?

I take your word for all the corrections – I certainly meant to follow the printed text exactly (except for one deliberate change 'instruments are by their rhimes').

Thank you more than I can say for being so good to my young Wellingtonians.[4] Hope they weren't too much of a nuisance.

I'll let you know Sunday train.

In haste
BENJAMIN B.

1 Hussey had various queries about the text of *Rejoice in the Lamb* and addressed these to Britten in the shape of a questionnaire, which Britten returned with his answers duly inscribed. The text of the cantata was to be included in the service book for St Matthew's Day, 21 September 1943, the date of the first performance.

2 Hussey included a short article on *Rejoice in the Lamb* in a small booklet published at the beginning of September which gave a few facts about St Matthew's Church, Northampton, and details of the forthcoming celebration on the 21st. The article is reproduced in Walter Hussey, *Patron of Art: the revival of a great tradition among modern artists* (London, Weidenfeld and Nicolson, 1985), pp. 8–9.

3 *Rejoice in the Lamb*, Fig. 9.

4 Perhaps a school party from nearby Wellington College, where Kenneth Green (see note 10 to Letter 443) was art master.

435   To Revd Walter Hussey

45A St. John's Wood High St.,
N.W. 8.
Sept. 26th 1943.

My dear Walter,

It was all a great experience for me, & my thanks are really due to you for enabling me to have it, & for making it so worth while materially! I do hope that I have given you something which will be of more lasting value than just for this particular occasion, but it was a very beautiful & moving occasion.[1] I should like to talk to you alot about it sometime.

Please convey to Mr. Barker[2] & the extremely efficient & charming choir and soloists, how much I appreciate their great efforts in learning my piece at such short notice, & so very thoroughly. They are really very excellent, & Mr. Barker's own part was most intelligently & sensitively done. I have seldom heard such rhythmic playing from an organist.

Please forgive me not writing to them direct, but I am so tied up with work, & the horribly-boring 'incidentals'[3] to work, that I have no time at all, I'm afraid. How did the anthem go on Sunday? I am looking forward to knowing whether they got as lost in the $\frac{11}{8}$s as I did in the procession on the 21st![4] Greetings to you & many thanks again.

Yours,
BENJAMIN BRITTEN

1   Such was its importance that *The Times* published a notice of the jubilee celebrations on 22 September:

Mr Britten has a way of choosing recondite texts for setting to music. The words of the cantata 'Rejoice in the Lamb' are by Christopher Smart, an eighteenth-century poet in whom genius and madness were near together. The theme is 'Benedicite omnia opera', and some of the Lord's humblest works, the cat and the mouse, for instance, are called upon to testify to the glory of God. The naïvety of some of the 10 short sections strikes no note of incongruity in church; it very well might in a concert hall if the whole were scored for orchestra and sung by a large chorus. The cantata is correctly described therefore as a festival cantata, since it has little in common with the church anthem. The organ part requires light and extremely dexterous handling. Indeed the organ accompaniment is as unusual as the choice of words and is a matter of considerable technical interest; it is sometimes marked *presto*, or *leggiero*, and produces effects intermediate between those of the keyboard and the orchestra. As usual with Britten, the words evoke the musical imagery, but there is also a great deal of sound and straight-forward vocal writing for both choir and soloists. The spirit of the curious, vivid poem has been caught and a work not to be placed in any of the usual categories, but certainly beautiful, is the outcome of a commission by the Church for a modern work of religious art. The organist and choir of St Matthew's Church appeared to find no difficulty in its execution and performed it with simple reverence.

2 Charles Barker, the acting organist and choirmaster of St Matthew's.

3 Britten refers to his music for *The Rescue*.

4 Two bars before Fig. 7.

436 To Imogen Holst[1]

[IHB, *p. 39; incomplete*]

45a St. John's Wood High Street,
N.W.8.
Oct. 21st 1943

My dear Imogen,

I can't tell you how pleased I was to get your letter: partly because Peter & I were so glad (& relieved) to hear that you and some others had got some pleasure out of that caricature of a recital last week,[2] but primarily it was so moving to learn that my music means so much to you. I am not so self-confident ever to be blasé about appreciation, but when it comes from a musician of your standing, & from a section of musical life which I have hitherto imagined so unsympathetic to me,[3] it is inexpressibly moving & valuable to me. It is also encouraging that you too sense that 'something' in the air which heralds a renaissance. I feel terrifically conscious of it, so do Peter, & Clifford, & Michael Tippett & so many that I love & admire – it is good to add you to that list! Whether we are the voices crying in the wilderness or the thing itself, it isn't for us to know, but anyhow it is so very exciting. It is of course in all the arts, but in music, particularly, it's this acceptance of 'freedom' without any arbitrary restrictions, this simplicity, this contact with the audiences of our own time, & of people like ourselves, this seriousness & above all this professionalism. One mustn't and can't deny the many heavenly genius[es] of the last century, but it is also a greater sympathy with the earlier centuries that marks this thing perhaps the most clearly.

As you see, I have no aptitude at all for expressing myself in words – this is only an effort to continue the contact that I feel your letter has made with me, in writing, since there never seems to be a chance of talking when I am in Dartington!

Thank you more than I can say for troubling to write. Did I ever tell you that I have the strongest recollection of riding on top of a bus with your father[4] – I think, from Notting Hill Gate, to Kensington High Street? That was the only time, alas, I ever met him.

With best greetings to you, from Peter too,

BENJAMIN

1 Imogen Holst (1907–1984), English composer, conductor, teacher and writer. She was the only child of the composer Gustav Holst (1874–1934), and became a dear and much valued friend and colleague of Britten, for whom she worked as music assistant between 1952 and 1964. She studied composition, piano and conducting at the Royal College (1926–30), where she was awarded the Cobbett Prize (1928) and an Octavia Hill travelling scholarship (1930).

In 1931 she began to earn her living by exercising her considerable gifts as a practical musician, with an especial bias towards the teaching and training of amateurs. From 1932 to 1938 she was a member of the music staff at the English Folk Dance and Song Society. In January 1940 she was appointed one of six travelling musicians, paid for by the Pilgrim Trust, charged with inspiring and organizing musical activities in rural areas all over the country. The scheme was soon taken over by CEMA, under whose auspices she first met Pears and Britten. (She and Britten had not coincided at the College.) From 1943 to 1951 she was the Director of Music in the Arts Department at Dartington where she built up a remarkable and unusual training school (later to become Dartington College).

In the autumn of 1952 Britten, then engaged on *Gloriana*, asked her to come to Aldeburgh to help him in the laborious task of preparing vocal and full scores of the opera, due to be presented the following June. In fact she lived in Aldeburgh for the rest of her life, working closely with Britten both as his music assistant, and, of course, on Festival affairs, for which her practical experience and professionalism were so aptly suited. With Pears's encouragement she formed and trained a small professional choir, the Purcell Singers, with whom she gave many concerts in London, Aldeburgh and elsewhere during the 1950s and 1960s. She joined Britten and Pears as an Artistic Director of the Aldeburgh Festival in 1956, retiring from active duties in 1977.

From 1964 until her death she devoted more time to her own writing, particularly to matters concerning the music of Gustav Holst about which she naturally felt uniquely responsible. She wrote short

biographies of Bach, Britten (IHB), Byrd and Holst, undertook schol-
arly editions of Purcell, Schütz and Holst, and compiled the *Thematic
Catalogue of Gustav Holst's Music* (London, Faber Music, 1974).

There can be no doubt that Imogen Holst's friendship was very
important to Britten. He admired and respected her opinions, scholarship and skilled practicality (especially in the field of amateur
music, in which he tended to feel at a disadvantage), and was ever
grateful for her unstinting generosity of time and labour, so freely
given whenever he needed it. See also Imogen Holst, 'Working for
Benjamin Britten', *Musical Times*, 118, March 1977, pp. 202–6; Rosamund Strode, 'Imogen Holst', *R.C.M. Magazine*, 80/2, Summer Term
1984, pp. 69–72, and *Imogen Holst at Dartington*, edited by Peter Cox
and Jack Dobbs (Dartington, The Dartington Press, 1988).

2 Pears and Britten had given a recital at Dartington on 10 October, in
the Barn Theatre, the programme of which comprised songs by
Handel and Purcell (realized by Britten), a group of Folk-song
Arrangements, Tippett's Cantata *Boyhood's End* and the *Michelangelo
Sonnets*.

3 It was very likely to the musical 'establishment' based on the College,
where Imogen Holst herself had been a student, that Britten was
referring here.

4 It seems probable that the occasion of this only meeting with Gustav
Holst had taken place on 15 November 1932, at the second of the
Macnaghten–Lemare concerts held at the Ballet Club (Mercury
Theatre). Britten's diary entry concludes: 'Walk back with G. Finzi
& G. Holst.'

437 **To Arthur Bliss**[1]
BBC
[*Typed*]

45a, St. John's Wood High Street,
N.W.8.
October 27th., 1943.

Dear Mr. Bliss,

Thank you for your letter.

I have naturally heard all the reasons you have given, both to
Mr. Ralph Hawkes and to members of the Features and Dramas
Dept. as to why I should not be allowed to conduct the B.B.C.
Orchestra in the forthcoming productions of "THE RESCUE". I must
confess at once that I find them entirely unsatisfactory; I made the
arrangement to conduct, not, of course, because of any misgivings

about Mr. Raybould's work but because I have had experience in this line and working, as I have been, in the closest collaboration with the author and the producer, I had thought that under my own direction much trouble would have been saved and the best results obtained.

Realizing that if I did not proceed with the writing of the music (as I myself had intended) the Show would have to be cancelled, out of friendship for the author, Mr. Sackville-West, I have decided to complete the Score but I shall take no further part in the production.[2]

I write this to you instead of saying it personally because I wish to make a protest in writing about the breaking of an implied contract and wish to save any further embarrassment.

Yours sincerely,
BENJAMIN BRITTEN

1 Bliss was Director of Music at the BBC from 1942 to 1944.

2 Of *The Rescue.*

438 To Peter Pears

[Swansea]
[18 November 1943][1]

My darling ——

This is only a scribble just to tell you who I can remember to have been asked for next Monday – 3 Steins, 2 Slaters, 1 Martin, 1 Rogers, 1 Cross, 1 Johnson? 1 Britten (Barb.), 1 Hurst, 1 Curzon, your darling self, & me. Any more? I can't remember. (Berkeley?)[2]

It was heaven to hear your voice, & to know you're feeling better. Practise hard & get the golden box back in its proper working order again. Something goes wrong with my life when that's not functioning properly.

It's been nice here, only Erwin had one hell of a cold, which I've picked up of course. The little boys are abit of a worry, but I think will be fine in the end. They sing so well, that one gets cross with Simms that it's not perfect.[3]

I go to Dartington tomorrow, & then back to home & thou on Monday – early train. Sing nicely in Wales – I'll be thinking of you.

I find Theocritus, even in these ghastly translations,[4] very

moving. Au revoir, my Hercules – I nearly signed myself Hylas,[5]
but at nearly 30 that's alittle exaggerated!

But any how, all my love, my heart ——

B

1 Britten was in Wales with Erwin Stein for rehearsals of *A Ceremony of Carols*. He writes on Thursday 18 November and travels to Darting-ton on Friday the 19th, intending to return to London on the morning of the 22nd for the planned birthday celebration. Letter 439 shows how this intent and event were foiled by influenza, while Letter 441 brings news of the substitute birthday party.

2 Britten was running through the guest list for his abortive thirtieth birthday party on Monday 22 November. Martin = Christopher: see note 1 to Letter 439. Rogers = Iris Holland Rogers. Johnson = Eliza-beth (Liz) Johnson, a friend of Pears's.

3 Britten was preparing the Morriston Boys Choir (from Swansea) for the first performance and gramophone recording of the revised ver-sion of *A Ceremony of Carols*, which was to take place on 4 December 1943 at the Wigmore Hall, London. Ivor Simms was their choir-master. The recording was released on Decca AK 1155–7 in 1945. In Sackville-West's and Shawe-Taylor's *The Record Guide* (London, Collins, 1951), p. 147, the performance of the *Carols* was praised for having 'a congruity with the spirit of the music which is unlikely to be surpassed'.

4 *The Idylls of Theocritus with Blow and Moschus and the War Songs of Tyrtaeus*, literally translated into English prose by the Revd J. Banks with metrical versions by J.M. Chapman (London, G. Bell, 1911). Britten's copy is in the Archive.

5 In Greek mythology, a favourite of Hercules, and his companion on the expedition of the Argonauts.

439 To Revd Walter Hussey
[*Pencil*]

Yarner Farm,
Dartington,
Totnes, Devon.[1]
Nov. 23rd, 1943.

My dear Walter,

I am afraid that our luck is badly out. I arrived here last Friday for a quiet week-end, and got landed with such a virulent 'flu bug that I am afraid I shan't be able to leave this bed for several

days and there's not the faintest chance of me being able to get
to Northampton for Saturday's celebration.[2] It is very disappointing
because I was looking forward to it so much & hoping at last to
meet Henry Moore.[3] However, do give him & all of you my
greetings, & I hope the choir sing the anthem [*Rejoice in the Lamb*]
as nicely as they usually do. I shall certainly be with them in spirit.

Please give my greetings to Mrs. Cotton[4] & say how sorry I shall
be to miss her cooking – but that before long I hope to lie in that
lap of luxury again! – & indeed I do.

With apologies to you & please excuse scribble, but this is all I
can do at the moment!

Yours,

BEN

1 Britten was staying with Christopher and Cicely Martin. Christopher
(1902–1944), was the Administrator of the Arts Department at Dartington Hall, 1934–44. See also Letter 443.

2 Hussey had commissioned a sculpture for St Matthew's from Henry
Moore who had hoped to have the work ready by the middle of
November. This date had to be postponed but it seems as if Britten
had not been kept informed about the change of plan. The unveiling
of the *Madonna and Child* did not in fact take place until February
1944, when Britten was again thwarted in his attempt to attend. See
note 1 to Letter 453.

3 Henry Moore (1898–1986), English sculptor. For Moore's statement
about his *Madonna and Child*, distributed at the unveiling ceremony,
see *Henry Moore on Sculpture*, edited by Philip James (London, Macdonald, 1966), pp. 220–23.

Moore later became acquainted with Britten and Pears, and in 1967
he lent a major example of his work (*Two Piece Reclining Figure*, a
half-size model for the New York Lincoln Center piece) to stand
outside the newly opened Snape Maltings Concert Hall. Similar large
bronzes by him have been on display there in the succeeding years,
through the generosity of the sculptor himself and of the Henry
Moore Foundation.

4 Hussey's housekeeper.

440 To Peter Pears
[*Pencil*]

Yarner Farm,
Dartington,
Totnes, Devon.
Telephone, Totnes 3132
Nov 24th 1943

My darling –

This is only to say what absolute heaven it was to see you, and how sweet it was of you to come all these weary miles to cheer me up – which it did, with a vengeance.

I only hope you don't feel too weary after it, & were able to charm all their old hearts with Vasek as usual! I'm afraid it was selfish of me, but I can't be unselfish where you're concerned – I just want you so terribly that all my usual control evaporates. I am feeling loads better – still a bit wobbly, & the beastly old boil is a nuisance still, so it looks like Monday, not Saturday as I'd hoped for, but I am much more cheerful, & not such gloomy company as I was when you were here. But thank you so much for bringing all those heavenly presents with you – I love the Bali pictures[1] – quite crazy over them – & the Michelangelo too – tho' I haven't got down to the texts yet. I had some more nice letters this morning, so I've really had a pretty good birthday, inspite of germs & things. Take care of youself my heart, sing nicely at Melksham, & have some good Guties[2] & sing better & better. Hedli says the Rescue is going pretty rockily with not enough rehearsal & that no one believes I'm really ill! – sick making that. Maybe I'll listen abit & gloat tonight.[3] Cecily sends love & says I'm still a good patient which no one seems to believe!

Much love, heart – I love you so, everyday more. Be nice to me – even at 30!

Your own,
BEN

I stupidly wrote on 2 sheets instead of one, & I haven't got time to fill up this middle bit as I have got to have a rest & the post goes before I wake up & I want you to have this tomorrow to let you know I love you – which you never guessed, did you?

1 A welcome present because of the interest in Bali stimulated by McPhee.

2 Singing lessons with Julius Guttman.

3 Britten must be referring to the first performance of *The Rescue* which was broadcast successively on 25–26 November, in which case he either misdated this letter or wrote 'tonight' but meant 'tomorrow'.

441 **To Sophie Stein**
     [*Pencil*]

Yarner Farm,
Dartington,
Totnes, Devon.
Nov. 26th 1943.

My dear Sophie,

I do hope Peter found a moment when he got back from his flying visit here, & before he started off on his travels again, to ring you up & tell you of the excitement your lovely cake gave us all. We had it on the Tuesday (the first day I was eating) after supper, & Peter & Cicely Martin sat round the bed on which the cake sat & we all ate our health and yours, too, in just the light of thirty candles & the lebenslicht – it was a pretty sight! But so sickening that you couldn't share it with us. However, when I'm back & well, we'll have our party and celebrate properly. Sophie, my dear, it was sweet of you to send that cake, so big & beautiful, with all those exciting candles which one never sees nowadays, <u>and</u> all those lovely messages; thank you, thank you!

I hope you are all well; that Erwin wasn't any the worse for travelling with his nasty cold. It was sweet of him to come to Wales with me, & he was a great moral support. Don't upset yourself too much over the terrible news these days; maybe the end won't be as far off as it seems, & then people will get down to behaving properly again. But I do feel for you, my dear, in all this time – if that is any comfort to you.

Please forgive me not writing very much, & that in pencil; because I still get abit weary – this germ is such a beastly one. But I did just want you to know how your cake & the candles cheered us all up. Thank you so much again.

Lots of love to you all three – it is so lovely that we have got to know you – it shows that out of the greatest evil some good can come.

Your affectionate
BEN

442   To Ralph Hawkes

45A St. Johns Wood High St.,
N.W. 8
Dec. 5th 1943

My dear Ralph,

I do hope that your alarming 'change of face' about approaching Sidney Beer to release Dennis Brain on January 16th[1] isn't going to dish us completely! I had gathered that it was a mere formality, that a solo date would seem a good enough reason for the release, & that anyhow we all thought (Dennis included) that you would be able to manage to obtain it. You see for artistic reasons I want so badly that the Serenade should be done again and quickly – I like the work and want to get people to know it. And for business reasons, Les Illuminations simply won't draw the audience that the Serenade would – and as we are ourselves footing the bill to a considerable sum (for us) this has a particular importance! As you indicated yesterday that it wasn't Sidney Beer who would object (when I offered to approach him myself), I gather that it can't be for <u>artistic</u> reasons that there might be objections – surely no performance at the Friends House could affect a possible one at the Albert Hall? And even, were this possible, I feel rather bitter that I should have to wait even longer for the second performance of a work which I particularly like. (And anyhow, Mr. Holt[2] showed absolutely <u>no</u> interest in, was even rude to me about, the work at your Savoy party after the first performance).

So <u>please</u>, Ralph, please reconsider the matter. It means so much to me. Dennis is so keen to do it too, – if you hadn't seemed so confident about it, I should never have set my heart on it so –

I may wait to hear those boys again at the Gallery on Tuesday, especially as I have got to see a specialist on Monday afternoon (I had intended to go to Snape to work late on Monday) so maybe I shall see you sometime soon. I think we shall have some <u>excellent</u> records of the Carols with Korchinska & the choir; they were wonderful up at the studios today.[3]

Yours ever,
BEN

P.S.   If we had a taxi waiting outside the hall we <u>could</u> rush Dennis B. back to the Albert Hall in time for the second half (Eroica Symphony) which has the important horn solo – if Harold Holt would agree – ???

1 Britten refers to the impending second performance of the *Serenade*,
   given at Friends House, Euston Road, London, on 16 January 1944,
   by Pears, Dennis Brain and an *ad hoc* orchestra conducted by Walter
   Goehr. Although Brain had been engaged to play in an orchestral
   concert at the Royal Albert Hall on the same evening, he was granted
   permission to be at Friends House for the first half and had to rush
   off to the Albert Hall in the interval, to be ready for the second half
   of the orchestral programme. There was a thick fog that night. In an
   interview with Rosamund Strode in 1987, Ethel Farrell (she and her
   husband were Wardens of Friends House, 1925–56) recalled that at
   the performance of the *Serenade*,

   Ben went to one door and Peter the other, trying to find some transport,
   and just as Dennis came off the platform a man came along in a car in
   Euston Road, and Ben stopped him and asked him if he was going anywhere
   near the Albert Hall, and he said no, the nearest he was going was Marble
   Arch; so Ben said, 'That's better than nothing' – and they bundled Dennis
   in [. . .]

2 Harold Holt, the English artists' agent.

3 The Morriston Boys' Choir with Maria Korchinska repeated their
   performance of *A Ceremony of Carols* at the National Gallery, London,
   on 7 December. The recording was made between the first performance and this repeat.

443 To Elizabeth Mayer

The New Yorkers arrive regularly, and are a constant joy to us &
to many friends – thank you for that as well as for so many other
things!

I'm writing to William & Beate right away.

> Old Mill, Snape, Suffolk
> as from 45a St. Johns Wood High St NW 8.
> Dec. 8th 1943

My darling Elizabeth,

It is awfully difficult to know how to start a letter like this — ! I
feel so <u>dreadful</u> about the long silence; not really so <u>guilty</u>, because
I know you understand, & I have been dreadfully worried by
overwork, but I don't like not having been in communication with
you for so long. But even that isn't true, because we don't need
that actuality, do we? Whatever happens, or doesn't happen, you
know I'm thinking of you, & praying for you, & feeling close to
you. Now – where to start . . . . ? I really suppose it must be

since the summer since we really communicated – at anyrate since
your move. How I long to hear how that has all gone! Do you
like the new apartment? How many patients has William got, &
how does he like being free? How do you like living all the time
in New York; as little as you expected, or more? Have you been
well, or was the strain (emotional and/or physical) of leaving
Amityville too great? I do hope sometime you can feel up to writing
an answer to all these questions. Don't feel bad that you haven't
written, because that'll make you put off writing even longer! . . .
it does with me; the gap seems so large that the effort required
to bridge it seems too great! With me, it is so long since I last wrote
that it is hopeless even to try & catch up, & so we shall just sit &
chat, in pen & ink!

Well – my life has been made up of the usual ingredients – work
– friends & relations – crises! The first goes on well. Since the
Summer I have written, well, completed the Carols I started last
year – now called a Ceremony of Carols, which have had a series
of thrilling shows by a choir of little Welsh boys (from a school in
the poorest part of Swansea) and a great Russian harpist, Marie
Korchinska.[1] This has meant many journeys to Wales to rehearse,
& then they all (35!) came up to town & sang the piece many
times, & to record it, so I hope there'll be some nice records to
send you soon. People seem to love the piece, & altho' it has been
only printed about a month, the 1st edition is just on sold out, I
hear (the same with the Sonnetts (2ce) [twice] & St. Cecilia). I
have my great friends for my work, and at the moment they seem
easily to outweigh my enemies – but for how long, one can't say,
nor does it matter. Then, I've written a Prelude & Fugue for Boyd
Neel's tenth birthday, or rather his orchestra's – I made a present
of a separate part for each member in the fugue – 18 in all, so it
took some doing! This was in July.[2] Then I had a lovely
commission from a Church in Northampton, for an aniversary. The
very enterprising vicar (Mr. Hussey) commissioned a Madonna &
Child from Henry Moore (very good) & an anthem from me. I set
a section of Rejoice in the Lamb of Christopher Smart (which
Wystan introduced me to in the States) – quite simple, in about 10
sections. I'll send you a copy soon, as I like it alot at the moment.
Then, I wrote a Serenade (words from Cotton, Tennyson, Blake,
Jonson, Keats etc.) in 6, or seven pieces for Horn & Tenor &
strings. There is a wonderful young horn player called Dennis
Brain, who plays as flexibly and accurately as most clarinettists,
& is a sweet & intelligent person as well. He did the first

performance; I leave you to guess who did the singing! – and we
had a lovely show, with wonderful enthusiasm and lovely notices.[3]
Then there has been a new BBC radio version of the Return of
Odysseus, done by Edward Sackville-West, a friend of mine,
sensitive & with good taste, but (entre nous) not a great poet,
and, after all this does need a great poet to stand up to one's
memories of Homer. However the BBC put it on in lavish style,
on two evenings with full orchestra and about 1½ hours of music –
which has taken some writing! That brings us to the present, when
I am quickly scribbling a short choral work for a prison camp in
Germany where some friends of mine are, & where there is a choir
& enthusiasm for my tunes![4] And THEN I start the OPERA – for
production next Summer![5] Isn't that exciting? I shall be here most
of next 3 or 4 months doing it. To complete the work picture – add
many recitals with our Peter, quite abit of conducting (Les
Illuminations, St. Cecilia, Carols etc.), 2 piano shows with Clifford
Curzon. Peter has had trouble with his voice, poor dear – over-work.
But he's got a grand doctor who helps him (Sillizer, a Czech), and
he's over that now. But he has had the success of the season with
Vazék in the Bartered Bride – which is a most moving bit of acting;
funny, but oh, so sympathetic![6] The voice is developing well too,
& losing none of the old quality either. He sang at the old Princess
de Polignac's funeral the other day – we had both just got to
know her & were very fond of her.[7] You know about her – & her
connection with Fauré, Debussy, Ravel, etc.?? – I see alot & will
see much more of Beth, Sebastian & Sally. Kit is now, by a miracle,
out of the RAF & in a hospital in Nottingham, & the family is
going on living here at the Mill. You know we have sent no less
than three lots of photos of us all to you this year, & apparently
none has arrived – ? 2 by sea, 1 by air; but we will go on trying. It
is a pity, because the kids look so wonderful at the moment,
especially Sebastian in your lovely blue jersey and the stockings –
which he is very proud of! He is a very gay kid, with a passion
for words. He goes to school in Snape, which he enjoys alot, &
wrote his first letter to Barbara the other day. Sally is becoming a
real person, with a charming character. How I long for you to see
them – it can't be long now, can it? The friends we see most of
now are: Enid & Montagu Slater (his libretto is excellent for Grimes
now), who are both well & busy. Louis & Hedli MacNeice, & new
daughter Corinna, who is a big bouncing infant, & fond of her
godfather! Clifford & Lucille Curzon, who are perpetual comforts
to us both physically & spiritually – they have a lovely house up
in Highgate with lovely food, & both of them are first-rate artists.

Peter & I spent a few heavenly days with them in their cottage up
in the Lakes in September.[8] Christopher & Cecily Martin – he is
doing a government survey of the arts, & we all help him on
occasions – he is unearthing some important things. They are
both charming & intelligent people, & live most of the time in
Dartington Hall, Devon (where he is art-director) – which you
know about? Peter and I will be spending Christmas there as P.
has to be in Wales[9] on Boxing day, & Snape is too far away. Who
else – ? – well, many, many, because I am so lucky in my friends;
I have the nicest friends in the world, I know – but oh, would
that you were in the midst of them, my dear; how complete you
would make the circle, & how they would all adore you!

Kenneth Green is distressed that there is no way of coping with
the Miriam problem[10] – her letters to him are so unsatisfactory, &
he can't make her see reason. But he has written to you about all
this. We see him alot now, since Mrs. Behrend – a good friend &
splendid patron of the arts has commissioned him to do a painting
of Peter & me together![11] We must somehow get a picture of that
to you!

When I spoke of crises I didn't mean anything drastic; only the
inevitable ones that arise when one has any kind of public life,
and more especially any kind of principles! But somehow we always
have weathered them, because we always have some good friends
who stand by us. One particularly nasty one has had such
repercussions that have I believe resulted in a very high-
positioned potentate's resignation – no bad thing if true. We have
both been well physically, and extremely lucky in the raids, which
are often noisy, but nothing so far near us. I must say I don't enjoy
them, but Peter doesn't turn a hair – ! Our house in St. John's Wood
hasn't been awfully satisfactory because the housekeeper has been
ill for about 2 months & it has been difficult to cope with the
ordinary things of life; but here again we have been lucky – friends
have helped us, & Barbara of course has been a tower of strength.
She is a sweet thing, & I long for you to know her. She isn't awfully
well in herself – dreads the sirens, & lives thro' tortures of dread
every night, which she has perfect reason to too, poor dear! But
we see alot of her, and she does wonderful work which she enjoys
& which occupies her.

And now, my dearest, good night. How I wish I could talk with
you instead of pushing this inadequate pen! I can't begin to thank
you for all the things you've done & sent for us – the things, little
things so valuable in the household, & for one's work & one's play
that are so difficult, if not impossible to get now. You are so

thoughtful, & so generous, and so full of unselfish love. Please give my love to everyone, & tell them that I <u>will</u> one day get round to writing, & explain why – please! Love from everyone here, & from Peter who joins with me in all this, & who is so good and hardworking, and so long-suffering with me! God bless you, & keep you – Mozart & Michelangelo watch over you —— your devoted

BEN

P.S.   Christmas cards may arrive from all the Slater children, Ann, Bridget & Carole who are always talking about you!

1 Maria Korchinska (1895–1979), the Russian-born harpist. Korchinska had occasionally worked with Britten during the 1930s at the GPO Film Unit, notably on *Night Mail* (1936), and later gave many first performances of contemporary works.

2 Britten misremembers the month. In fact, the first performance took place on 23 June, at the Wigmore Hall.

3 *The Times*, 16 October:

Britten's new work, composed for this concert, and sung by Mr Peter Pears, is a song-sequence for tenor, horn, and string orchestra. The idea and lay-out are original, so too is the actual stuff of the music. Yet, as in most of Britten's work, the originality is not strained nor far-fetched, but arises out of a fundamentally simple conception (a melody for horn, wonderfully played by Mr Dennis Brain, in this Serenade), and it uses much of the ordinary stock-in trade of composition (in the figures of the accompaniments of the songs in this cycle, for instance). He has taken half a dozen English poems – Tennyson's 'The splendour falls' and the Lyke Wake Dirge among them – and looked at them with fresh eyes.

Robin Hull in the *Sunday Times*, 17 October:

The Boosey & Hawkes concert at the Wigmore Hall on Friday evening was notable for two first performances: Lennox Berkeley's Divertimento for small orchestra and Benjamin Britten's Serenade for tenor voice, horn, and string orchestra.

Lennox Berkeley's talent certainly lies in the direction of the miniature, and his Divertimento proved a thoroughly competent and attractively scored little work, which sets out to entertain and succeeds more or less. Benjamin Britten's Serenade is a romantic and sensitive setting of lyric poems by Tennyson, Blake, Ben Jonson, Keats, and others. The skilfully conceived music has wit, colour and delicate poetic feeling. It is indeed a striking work.

Peter Pears sang with beautiful tone and phrasing but his musical concep-tion as a whole seemed a little too precious and over-refined. The horn playing of Dennis Brain was a remarkable exhibition of control and intelligent artistry.

William Glock in the *Observer*, 24 October:

Five years ago I used to listen rather sadly to my predecessor, Fox-Strang-ways, while he told me of his good fortune as a young man in being able to hear Brahms's maturest works as they came out. Now I feel differently for in Benjamin Britten we have at last a composer who offers us visions as great as those. His new Serenade, op. 31, a set of six songs for tenor, horn, and strings, surpasses everything else of his in strength and feeling.

Let me take the first of these songs: a setting of Cotton's 'The Day's grown Old' and try to hint at its quality in technical terms. The atmosphere is there from the beginning, for the vocal part is drawn like a shadow over the orchestral accompaniment: against the sleepy measure in the strings, the words are phrased in common time and in an unbroken rhythm with the most imaginative effect.

Every detail is cared for: entirely different meanings are expressed, through the smallest variations in the original material, and conversely these variations impress the shape of the song as a whole on one's mind. Again, the setting of Tennyson's 'The Splendour Falls' is made memorable not only by the dazzling illumination of the string writing and by the fervour of the vocal line, but by a classical simplicity of contrast between one verse and another – it may only be an interval widening from a fourth to a fifth in the course of three verses, or the basses playing pizzicato, then not at all; then with stirring independence. Or take the first four lines of the Keats sonnet 'O Soft Embalmer': the waving voice part and the bounding lines of the accompaniment, climbing slowly in the violins and descending slowly in the basses, leave a tracery that can be carried in one's head.

I would like to be able to analyse each song at length: failing that, I can only mention Blake's 'O Rose, thou art sick' with its horn solo expressing the very essence of the words, and the lovely recitative for voice that follows the fifteenth-century Dirge with its tune repeated nine times, whilst the tossing wiry accompaniment in the orchestra gathers strength and then relinquishes it; and Ben Jonson's Hymn to Diana in which Dennis Brain played the fleet and misty horn solo as perfectly as one could imagine. Peter Pears struggled manfully with the high tessitura in the voice part. Few indeed, will be able to sing or play this Serenade; and though one may bless the friendship of Pears and Britten for the Michelangelo Sonnets and this later work I'm anxious to hear some solo songs whose style and technique are less demanding. Meanwhile HMV or Columbia or Decca should record this Serenade as soon as possible and the BBC should see that the country is made aware of its new masterpiece.

Among the audience at the première was the American composer, Marc Blitzstein, with whom Britten had had a brief acquaintance in New York. His response was not favourable. Eric Gordon, in his biography of the composer (*Mark the Music: The Life and Work of Marc Blitzstein*, New York, St Martin's Press, 1989), writes (p. 243):

I hear he was frightened off by my warning (to him at a party) that the next time we met I was going to ask him how he squared his conscientious objection to the war with doing propaganda work for the BBC, etc. That may be malicious, but then, I am, and with pleasure in certain cases.

4 *The Ballad of Little Musgrave and Lady Barnard*, completed on 13 December at Snape, for male voices and piano. It was first performed in February 1944 in a Prisoner of War Camp at Eichstätt, Germany,

and dedicated to 'Richard Wood and the musicians of Oflag VIIB – Germany – 1943'. Richard Wood was the brother of Anne Wood. In *Tempo*, 7 June 1944, an account of an 'ambitious music festival given [. . .] at Eichstätt Oflag VIIB' was published, part of which ran as follows:

The festival consisted of six events, ranging from choral and symphonic items to folk-dancing and a jazz-band. The programme of the symphony concert, in which an orchestra of twenty-nine players was conducted by Lieut. Richard Wood, consisted of Rossini's 'Barber of Seville' Overture, Mozart's D major flute Concerto (soloist, Maurice Waterhouse), Elgar's Three Bavarian Dances and Schubert's fifth Symphony. A choral and orchestral programme included excerpts from 'The Magic Flute', Bach's 'Cantata for the New Year', and madrigals and part-songs. On this occasion a male-voice choir of twenty-eight singers (choirmaster, Fred Henson) gave the first performance of Britten's 'Ballad of Little Musgrave and Lady Barnard', specially written for and dedicated to Richard Wood and the musicians of Oflag VIIB.[. . .] The festival appears to have been directed with pro-fessional competence, the eight-page printed programme listing the names of those responsible for stage directions, scenery, stage properties, lighting, wardrobe, box-office and publicity.

An account of this 'festival behind barbed wire' also appeared in *The Times*, on 2 March 1945, which included the following commen-tary on Britten's *Ballad* by the conductor, Lieutenant Wood:

Its reception apparently was mixed, for the conductor writes: 'The choir (35 to 40 voices) started by cordially disliking the work but finally they all thoroughly enjoyed it. It grew on us all the time and the audience took to it immediately or were at least brought up short by it. [. . .] It was perfor-med four times.'

See also Richard Wood, 'Music in P.O.W. Camps in Germany, 1940–45', *Making Music*, May/October 1947.

5 A reference to a possible first performance in the USA (see Letter 445). The first proposed production date in England was to be April 1944. The opera was not to be staged finally until 7 June 1945.

6 Pears first sang the role of Vašek on 10 November, in London, in a production directed by Eric Crozier and conducted by Lawrance Collingwood. He sang the part again in a new production at the Royal Opera House, Covent Garden, in 1955, directed by Christopher West and conducted by Rafael Kubelik.

7 Princess Edmond de Polignac (1865–1943), was born Winnaretta Eugénie Singer, daughter of the sewing-machine inventor, who left her an immense fortune. She married twice, on the second occasion to Prince Edmond de Polignac. She was a generous supporter of the arts and musicians, of Stravinsky in particular. Ravel dedicated his *Pavane pour une infante défunte* to her. It seems that Britten and Pears first met her in 1942 at a lunch party at the Café Royal, London,

given by Alvilde Chaplin, a friend of Lennox Berkeley's. See Michael de Cossart, *The Food of Love: Princess Edmond de Polignac (1865–1943) and her Salon*, (London, Hamish Hamilton, 1978).

8 Britten and Pears were to visit the Curzons' cottage in the Lake District (Cumbria) on one further occasion in wartime, when Britten played through what he had so far completed of *Peter Grimes*: see Clifford Curzon, 'Twenty Years Ago' in TBB, pp. 68–70.

9 In Merthyr Tydfil.

10 Miriam, temporarily resident in the USA with their son Gordon, was the wife of Kenneth Green (1905–1986), Suffolk-born artist and stage designer. Green and Britten first met in 1942 when the composer returned from the USA: the meeting was brought about by a chance encounter of Britten and Gordon Green (the artist's son) at Amityville. Green designed the Sadler's Wells production of *Così fan tutte* in 1944, in which Pears sang, and was responsible for the costumes and sets for *Peter Grimes* the following year. See also PGPB, pp. 41–3 and 88–9, and PFL, plates 180 and 183–7.

11 See PFL, plate 231. This is the double portrait now in the National Portrait Gallery, London. A further portrait of Britten by Green, also painted in 1943, is in the Archive: see PFL, plate 235.

444   To Mary Behrend
[*Postcard*]

The Old Mill, Snape
[Postmarked 9 December 1943]

Lovely to get your letter – I feel so happy when you like what I do, and set great store by it. I think the little boys were enchanting – the occasional roughness was easily overweighed by their freshness & naivety – something very special.[1] I do hope you will like Kenneth's picture; Peter & I rush down again for 24 hours next week. At the moment I am at Snape trying to get my spirits up after 'flu! – & also starting the opera.

Much love to you both,
BEN.

1 The performance on 7 December given by the Morriston Boys' Choir.

WIGMORE HALL
BOOSEY & HAWKES CONCERTS
under the direction of the Boosey & Hawkes Concert Committee

THIRD SEASON

2nd CONCERT, FRIDAY, 15th OCTOBER, 1943, at 6 p.m.

Notes by EDWIN EVANS
(Author's Copyright)

Dennis Brain (Horn) - Peter Pears (Tenor) - Winifred Radford (Soprano)
Frederick Woodhouse (Bass)
Orchestral Ensemble Conducted by Walter Goehr (Leader Maria Lidka)

Divertimento for Small Orchestra   LENNOX BERKELEY
(First Concert performance)   (1903)

Prelude - Nocturne - Scherzo - Finale

Lennox Berkeley was born at Boar's Hill, near Oxford. He studied in Paris with Nadia Boulanger from 1926 to 1933. During that time a Concerto for small orchestra was performed by the London Contemporary Music Centre. Since then his works have included an oratorio, *Jonah*, broadcast in 1936 and performed the following year at the Leeds Festival; an Overture performed in 1936 at the Barcelona Festival of the International Society for Contemporary Music; a ballet, *The Judgment of Paris*, produced at the Sadler's Wells in 1938; the Psalm, *Domini est terra*, performed at the London Festival of the I.S.C.M. in June 1938 and repeated in September at the Worcester Festival; a *Serenade for Strings*, performed by the L.C.M.C. in 1940; *Introduction and Allegro for two pianos and orchestra* performed during that year's Promenade Concerts; and the *Symphony* performed there this year. He has also composed chamber music. The *Divertimento*, composed in 1942, was commissioned by the B.B.C. and broadcast for the first time on October 1st, 1943. The title is to be taken in the literal or classical sense. It is light and easy to listen to, which brings it into line with the Strings Serenade of 1940 rather than with the composer's more austere works. The Prelude develops two themes, both of which are heard in the episode connecting the second of them with the *reprise* of the first. The slow movement, which strikes the only sombre note in the work, is a Nocturne, free in form. The Scherzo is somewhat extended but of classical type, with a Trio. At the end of the movement the Trio begins again, as if about to be repeated, but is cut short by the final chord. Preceded by a short introduction the last movement is in Rondo form.

Serenade for Tenor-Voice, Horn and String Orchestra, op. 31.   BENJAMIN BRITTEN
First performance   (1913)

Prologue - Pastoral (Cotton) - Nocturne (Tennyson) - Elegy (Blake) -
Dirge (Anon.) - Hymn (Jonson) - Sonnet (Keats) - Epilogue

This work has only recently been finished. It was specially written for to-night's performers.

INTERVAL

Price : 3d.

The first performance of the *Serenade* on 15 October 1943: the programme

445 To Henry Wood

45a, St. John's Wood High St., N.W. 8.
Dec. 14th, 1943

My dear Sir Henry,

I am sorry that your letter has lain so long unanswered, but I have been suffering from a dismal combination of 'flu and overwork, and letter-writing has got a bit overlooked, I am afraid!

I am honoured that you ask me for a first performance for your 50th season of the Promenade Concerts and I do hope something can be arranged. The trouble is that I have no orchestral work unperformed at the moment, and that I am just embarking on an enormous commitment – the writing of a full-length opera, scheduled for performance this next summer in the U.S.A.[1] – so it doesn't look as if I can possibly get a new work written by the beginning of the season. Would you, however, like the first performance of an orchestral excerpt, or some kind of set piece with voices out of it?[2] I am very much afraid that this is the only thing I can offer.*

I am so glad you are putting down the Scottish Ballad again.[3]

With best wishes,
Yours sincerely,
BENJAMIN BRITTEN

*The title of the opera is 'Peter Grimes' – but that is all the information I can give you at the moment.

1 At this stage, clearly, Britten was still thinking that the première of *Grimes* (a commission from Koussevitzky) would take place in the USA. This was to change in the light of his discussion with Sadler's Wells, a change made with Koussevitzky's consent, who was to inform Hans Heinsheimer in New York, 'I am happy to hear that Benjamin Britten is about to complete the opera I commissioned to him. I shall certainly have no objections if the opera will have a performance at Sadler's Wells Theatre in London next season.' (Ralph Hawkes to Britten, 28 April 1944.) The opera's American first performance was given on 6 August 1946 at Koussevitzky's Berkshire Music Festival at Tanglewood, conducted by Leonard Bernstein and produced by Eric Crozier.

2 See, however, Letter 455. The 'Four Sea Interludes' and 'Passacaglia' from *Peter Grimes*, Opp. 33a and 33b, were published as independent orchestral items after the launch of the opera in 1945.

3 *Scottish Ballad* was given as part of a Prom concert by Britten and
Clifford Curzon, with the London Philharmonic Orchestra conducted
by Basil Cameron, on 17 June 1944.

446 To Peter Pears

Snape
Jan. 10th 1944

My own darling P.,

You can't imagine how my thoughts have been with you thro'
all your travels & concerts this week – I don't believe you have
really been out of my mind for ten seconds all together. I can't wait
to hear how Samson went,[1] & whether you were pleased with
yourself, & if they liked you – not that there could be much doubt
of that! I hope the travelling wasn't too impossible, & that you
managed to get food, & comfortable seats & all. Where do you stay
this week? I trust you have remembered to get yourself a hotel.

I ought really to have got this off so that you would have it on
arrival, but I have been so busy all the days, & so lazy all the
evenings, I am afraid, and anyhow I have been waiting to get yours
(which I hope'll arrive in the morning) to see if there is anything
particular to answer. Well, at last I have broken the spell and got
down to work on P.G.. I have been at it for two days solidly and
got the greater part of the Prologue done. It is <u>very</u> difficult to keep
that amount of recitative moving, without going round & round
in circles, I find – but I think I've managed it. It is also difficult to
keep it going fast & yet paint moods & characters abit. I can't wait
to show it to you. Actually in this scene there isn't much for you
to do (I haven't got to the love duet yet);[2] it is mostly for Swallow,
who is turning out quite an amusing, pompous old thing! I don't
know whether I shall ever be a good opera composer, but it's
wonderful fun to try once in a way!

Otherwise I do nothing at all, except a little reading, and one or
two letters (after my great burst of correspondence on Friday).
The kids seem well, & are terribly sweet – don't forget Sally's 1st
birthday on 13th, by the way. Sebastian's a real honey and gets
more charming every day – in ten year's time he'll be a real menace,
I'm afraid! Beth is well, rather worried & over-worked because
Christina's ill & away, & Joyce may get called up;[3] but nothing
definite yet, luckily & it may not happen.

And you – you old so-and-so – I miss you most dreadfully. I

suppose we'll have to get used to this separation, but it's hellish hard. I wouldn't have dreamed that I could miss someone so much. I suppose you're so busy that you seldom give me a thought – but just now & then, think of me thinking of you! Take care of yourself – look both ways in crossing roads, wrap up well, & don't get your feet wet – because you belong to me! Ring up from time to time because it gives me strength to go on.

Love to Joan, & tell her, that in spite of her

P.G.'s going to be a knock-out!

All my love,

my darling,

B.

1 Handel's oratorio; we have not been able to locate the performance.

2 Fig. 9: 'the truth . . . the pity . . . and the truth . . .', the duet for Grimes and Ellen Orford.

3 Joyce Burrows, Mrs Burrows's daughter.

447 To Bobby Rothman

The Old Mill, Snape, Suffolk.

Jan. 12th 1944

My dear old Bobby,

Of course you don't really deserve a letter from me – do you realise that your last letter to me is dated Jan 9th 1943! I admit I haven't been much better, but I am one up on you. So please rectify the matter, at once, sir. I want to know how you are, what you're doing, how you are enjoying yourself and all that kind of thing, and if you have a new photo send it along, because I am almost forgetting what you look like. It'll soon be two years, do you know, since we undertook that perilous journey? but I must say it doesn't seem like it to me.

I haven't been doing much that would amuse you, since I wrote last. Travelling around the place giving concerts, sitting still and writing loads of music, recording & broadcasting & all that kind of thing – very boring. I also had 'flu, but there is nothing extraordinary in that – have you had it in the present epidemic? – I see that something like 13% of Americans had it, & it was quite as bad here. Those who didn't go to bed went around looking as if they ought to be there, & generally feeling sore with life. I conveniently arranged to have my dose staying in a very comfortable house of a friend, with plenty of food (not that I felt like it, tho') and general creature-comforts.

I have also spent alot of time at the Mill here, where I come whenever I can, as it is very pleasant, especially as I have a sister living here with her two kids, so the place is kept running nicely for me.

The kids are nice, tho' young, one's just one & the other nearly five. The boy (5) is very noisy, & cheerful, with a passion for drain-pipes, boilers and is everlasting digging in the garden, making sewer systems & other sordid things. But he's nice & we are very tolerant of each other. The garden is still waiting for you to come & do some digging in – I can't be bothered with such hard-work, & I only remove the more gigantic weeds when they become a nuisance! Actually it's quite impossible to get a regular man to come in & do any work, & so the whole thing's gone to pieces, I am afraid.

We have been having a nice quiet time from the air the last few weeks – I hope it goes on that way, as I don't like it any more than I told you I would! But luckily we've not had it as badly as they did before – only nuisance raids, which keep you up at night abit. Actually what keeps one awake here most is bombers going in the other direction, & knowing how I feel when they come here, I can't feel pleased for people on the other side, when they go out.

How are you getting on with your rationing – is it getting more & more complete? If you are a skilfull manager you can make do with the food, but lots of people find it very difficult. We still can have enough gas to run our car here on shopping expeditions & meeting trains – but tyres are a problem.

Did you have a good Christmas? – I was in Devonshire for mine, Peter came too, & we stayed with friends & had a grand time.

Well, take care of yourself, old thing – & write a note soon saying how you are & what you're doing.

Love to you & all the family,
BEN

448 To Revd Walter Hussey

[*Postcard*]

Old Mill.
[Postmarked 26 January 1944]

All set – in diary as well – for 19th – I shall be coming in the
morning from Stafford – can I have a run thro' with the choir
about mid-day, do you think?[1] Philip Skinner[2] is now at 43B,
Cornwall Gardens, sw7, and would love an invitation. The opera
forges ahead – so no time for more – greetings to you all.

BEN

1 Britten and Pears were to give a recital in Stafford on 18 February,
   the day before Britten had been invited to conduct the choir of St
   Matthew's, Northampton, in a performance of *Rejoice in the Lamb*, at
   the unveiling ceremony of Henry Moore's sculpture, *Madonna and
   Child*, on the 19th. See, however, note 1 to Letter 453.
2 Unidentified.

449 To Piers Dunkerley

Old Mill, Snape, Suffolk.
Feb. 8th 1944

My dear old Piers,

   I am awfully sick to miss you this week in London: had it been
at any other time I should have come up especially to see you,
but I absolutely cannot at the moment. I have got this darned opera
to get done, & I have so few days free from concerts that I just
have to stick at it when I can – see? But I am very disappointed.
So do let me know when ever you can get to town again, or even
when you can get here for a few days, & I'll raise heaven & hell to
fit in with you. Have a good time, & for goodness sake take care
of yourself, & let me know where you're going to be when ever
you know.[1]
   Beth & all the kids send their love – they're all well & bouncing.
Sally is a honey & would win your susceptable heart, I know.
Sebastian is very naughty, but nice too.
   The opera is shooting ahead, so that's all right – Peter is singing
his head off & travelling all over the place (he did 60 hours train-

sitting in 8 days, not long ago). Excuse scribble, but I'm too weary
to write better.

Love, & so sick to miss you,

BEN

1 In June, Dunkerley was to be taken prisoner in France.

450 To Ralph Hawkes

The Old Mill, Snape, Suffolk.
Feb. 10th 1944

My dear Ralph,

When I was up last week I hoped to be able to see you for a
moment, but couldn't make it; and as it doesn't look as if I shall
be up again for some time (the old opera keeps me hard at work!),
I thought I'd write you a note about my ideas for your proposed
leaflet on B.B.! I must say, when Dr. Roth[1] showed me a sketch for
it, I was abit horrified. If you remember it was about 16 pages of
flattering press notices, & read rather like an advertisement for a
patent medicine. After all, any one who has had a little publicity
could produce such a document about himself with a little careful
editing! I didn't really see any point in it. There seem to me to be
two ways of doing the job – (i) a kind of catalogue, with as many
descriptive details of each piece as can be got in (such as
instrumentation, details of works, duration – and even a press
notice or two to show how it was received, if you think fit) – and
also, if you think it necessary, a few biographical details of the
criminal's life! (ii) a short critical study of the more important
pieces to date, more like a booklet with a page or so to each work,
and with a dispassionate (tho' probably, on the whole,
favourable!) summing-up. To which of these do you incline? I think
probably the first is a more practical scheme – and that I have'nt
yet got enough gray hairs for the second.[2] About people to write
the notes – for (i) probably it is best to regard it as merely a clerk's
job, & not get anyone pretentious to do it, except perhaps for the
general note at the beginning which might be a little more
objective & critical (but preferably not written by a critic) – for (ii),
well that is a more difficult matter – probably Sackville-West or Glock,
tho' I doubt whether either have time: what do you think?

The opera is going well, but I am making enormous changes all the while in the libretto – so perhaps it's a good thing that we didn't send it to Koussie.

We've got some good records now of the 2–piano pieces & the Folk-songs.

How are you? Don't over-work.

Please give my regards to Mrs. Hawkes.

Yours,

BENJAMIN B

1 Dr Ernst Roth (1896–1971), English music publisher of Czech birth. Roth was born in Prague and studied law, music and philosophy at the university there. In 1922 he began a career in music publishing, first with Universal Edition in Vienna (head of publications from 1928) and later at Boosey & Hawkes in London, following the annexation of Austria by Germany in 1938. He was the dedicatee of Strauss's *Vier letzte Lieder* (1948). In 1963 he was to become Chairman of Boosey & Hawkes. See Ernst Roth, *The Business of Music: Reflections of a Music Publisher* (London, Cassell, 1969); Willi Schuh, 'Ernst Roth 1896–1971', *Tempo*, 98, 1972, pp. 4–8, and letters to Roth from Strauss, Stravinsky and Kodály in the same issue (pp. 9–20); and George Newman, 'Ernst Roth: A Personal Recollection', *Tempo*, 165, June 1988, pp. 37–40. He contributed an enthusiastic account of the première of *Peter Grimes* to *Picture Post*, 30 June 1945. Correspondence between Roth and Britten is owned by the Paul Sacher Stiftung, Basel.

2 Britten's first scheme was adopted for this 'leaflet' and all subsequent catalogues of his works.

451 To Peter Pears

[*Pencil*]

Snape

[before 11 February 1944]

My darling –

This is only a scribble to say a few things that one can't say over the bloody telephone. I love you, I love you, I love you. I am hopelessly homesick without you, & I only live every day because it brings the day, when we shall be together, nearer. Take care of yourself – <u>don't</u> sing too soon, & rest as much as you can. I shall listen to you on Friday – I do hope it goes well, & Sunday too.[1]

After a slow start P.G. is now swimming ahead again – I've nearly finished the scene! Montagu & I have made some good

improvements I think, & I'm writing some lovely things for you to
sing – I write every note with your heavenly voice in my head.
Darling – I love you more than you can imagine. I'm just incomplete
because half of me is in Manchester!

All my everything,

B.

1 On 11 February Pears took part in a broadcast concert from the BBC,
  Manchester, with the BBC Northern Orchestra conducted by Richard
  Austin (ENSA [Entertainments National Service Association] Music
  Adviser, Northern Region). He was soloist in Mozart's concert aria,
  'Misero! o sogno! . . . Aura che intorno' (K. 431). He gave a further
  broadcast from Manchester on the 13th, in which he sang Janáček's
  Diary of a young man who vanished (English translation by Iris Holland
  Rogers), with Emelie Hooke (soprano) and Walter Susskind (piano).

452   To Sophie Stein

The Old Mill, Snape, Suffolk.
Feb. 24th, 1944.

My dear Sophie,

This is only a note to say how I am thinking of you & praying
for you through all these beastly nights. It is really horrible for
you. You know that you can always come here, don't you, if you
want a rest. Not that it is always quiet here, unfortunately, but I
think much less worrying than London. Besides, you know that
my sister Beth is relying on you coming to help her with the
children in March, when her nurse goes off on a holiday. You will
come, won't you? Any time in March will do. I hope there won't
be any bother about you getting permission from the authorities.[1]
Would it be a help if we applied from this end?

In the meantime, take care of yourself and all the family too –

With love,

BEN

1 The Steins, Austrian émigrés, were exempted by the Secretary of
  State from special restrictions applying to aliens during the war.
  However, they needed to apply to the local chief superintendent of
  police for permission to make visits to restricted areas, i.e. the Suffolk
  coast.

453   To Revd Walter Hussey

Old Mill, Snape, Suffolk.
Feb. 28th, 1944.

My dear Walter,

I am so sorry that you had such a difficult day, & I feel guilty
that I added to the difficulties. But I couldn't make it – my arm
was playing me up to such a degree that I <u>had</u> to cope with it. It
is still a bore, but getting better luckily. You seem to have had a
good gathering of celebrities. I should very much liked to have
meet Henry Moore, & I am longing to see his Madonna.[1]
Whenever this pressure eases I will come down to see it & you all
again. I am amused at W. Walton turning up, & to hear that he
liked R. in the L., because he doesn't make it a secret that he
doesn't like my later pieces! But I expect the lovely singing of the
choir won him over.

Please excuse scribble, but I am wildly busy!

Yours ever,
BEN

By the way – <u>what</u> was the name of the young Canadian airman I
met at yours[2] not long ago? – there are two letters from him
champing for answers, and I <u>can't</u> read his signature!

1   Walter Hussey wrote of the occasion of the unveiling of Moore's
Madonna and Child in his memoir, *Patron of Art*, (London, Weidenfeld
and Nicolson, 1985), pp. 39–40:

Saturday, 19 February, was an exceptionally cold day, and there had been
enemy bombing in London during the night before. [. . .] Unfortunately a
bomb had fallen on the line and the party from London were terribly delayed.
[. . .] By half-past two, the time at which the ceremony was due to start,
they still had not arrived. Benjamin Britten, who was due to conduct *Rejoice
in the Lamb*, could not get there. [. . .] But William Walton had come over
from Ashby St Ledgers. His relations with Britten were somewhat strained
at that time, and when I jokingly, and perhaps naughtily, suggested that *he*
should conduct the Cantata, he replied that that would really 'put the cap
on it'! I liked to think, perhaps without cause, that his being there that day
helped to make relations easier.

As this letter shows, however, it was Britten's arm that kept him
away, not enemy action.

2   Good Suffolk usage, i.e. 'your place'.

454 To Benjamin Britten
From Peter Pears
[*Incomplete*]

[On the train]
[1 March 1944]

& after waiting till 12.30 am at the Central Hotel, was very kindly
allowed to share a room with another man. And so here I am on
my way back to Liverpool, having spent £5 & 36 hours on an
entirely useless journey, & having had two breakfasts & a railway
station lunch between Tuesday & Thursday nights (I expect!). What
Ibbs[1] will say I don't know. I shall just have to invent a late train
into Liverpool. Oh bunch! & it was all really because I was too tired
on Tuesday night to check up on the train.   If only I thought I
should learn from this sort of mistake! But I know only too well
that I don't profit by my mistakes – I'm such a hardened old
sinner. I don't suppose I shall ever be asked to Greenock again.
They took good care to tell me that they specialised in asking new
artists. Heddle Nash & Isobel Baillie had both made their Scottish
première there, & had been back 3 or 4 times!! Oh dear, oh dear!
& it was 23 guineas too!
   Are you warm at the Mill? I do hope so & that there's plenty of
coke. There's deep snow up here – I longed to get off & see
Lucille [Curzon] as I passed through Cumberland! Oh for a holiday!
I expect it's Freudian my missing trains. I just can't cope with the
work – & I couldn't have wanted to do anything <u>less</u> than <u>sing</u> at
<u>Greenock</u>! Ben my darling, Peter Grimes was quite madly
exciting![2] Really tremendously thrilling. The only thing you must
remember is to consider that the average singer hasn't much gift
for intensity off his own bat, so make sure that the tempi etc make
a tense delivery inevitable. Actually I feel very much that you
have already done this, only you know what most singers are; the
bit I was thinking of was Swallow in the Prologue. Can it sound
pompous at that pace? Aggressive yes – & perhaps that's enough.
The more I hear of it, the more I feel that the queerness is
unimportant & doesn't really exist in the music (or at any rate
obtrude) so it mustn't do so in the words. P.G. is an introspective,
an artist, a neurotic, his real problem is expression, self-expression.
Nicht wahr? What a part! Wow!

All my love my B. yr devoted

P.

1 Ibbs and Tillett, the London concert agency 1906–1990.
2 Britten had evidently played through to Pears what he had so far composed of the opera.

455 To Julian Herbage
BBC

45a St. John's Wood High Street,
26th March, 1944.

My dear Julian,

Please forgive the lateness of this, but your letter followed me around on my travels, & since it eventually reached me I've had no time for letter-writing.

I am afraid I have bad news for you about the opera excerpts. Although it is progressing as well as can be expected (in between dashing all over the country!), in the section I have already sketched there is nothing suitable, complete enough, for a concert performance. Of course, as I work ahead something may easily crop up – but I expect you want to know definitely now. I feel very sorry about it, as I did really want to produce something new for Sir Henry Wood this year; but I did explain to him, when he wrote that I just _had_ to get the opera done, & that it wasn't by any means certain that there would be suitable extracts from it, although I hoped there would be.

With best wishes,
Yours sincerely,
BENJAMIN BRITTEN

456 To Ronald Duncan

Old Mill, Snape, Suffolk.
April 7th 1944.

My dear Ronnie,

What a one you are! Here I am up to my eyes in opera & spiritual crises & you expect me to drop everything & write you two songs.[1] Still, maybe I'll have a shot (but _no_ promises), if you'd be so gracious as to let me know what kind of background, accompaniment, there'll be – full orch.? barrel-organ?? What kind of voice, high, low? – it makes a difference, you know. But, seriously, I wish you'd give me more notice – because I've been turning everything down for the last six months, BBC, Films (including Shaw's Caesar & Cleopatra, which I admit gave me pleasure to do!).

There may be a chance of Peter Pears & me paying you a visit in July – would that be possible or convenient? I'd love to see you again.

Love,

BENJY

1 Duncan's request must have been connected with his masque and anti-masque, *This Way to the Tomb*, for which Britten composed the incidental music (including three songs) in 1945. The two songs asked for here would have been 'The red fox, the sun' and 'Morning'. The play was first produced by the Pilgrim Players directed by E. Martin Browne at the Mercury Theatre, London, on 11 October 1945. Duncan's inscription on the flyleaf of the published text of the play (London, Faber and Faber, 1946) reads: 'For Ben, who made this play stand up. With much love. Ronnie'. Robert Speaight, who played Father Anthony, wrote a brief account of the first production in *A Tribute to Ronald Duncan by his friends* (Hartland, The Harton Press, 1974), pp. 54–5. An *a cappella* chorus, 'Deus in adjutorium meum', which formed part of the masque, was posthumously published by Boosey & Hawkes in 1983. All three songs, under the title of *Evening, Morning, Night*, for voice and harp or piano, were published by Boosey & Hawkes in 1988.

457 To Peter Pears

Old Mill

[before 9 April 1944]

My darling,

This is just to wish you a very, very happy Easter, & to tell you how I wish I were with you.[1] Have a nice rest, if you can, go to Michael, and relax as much as possible. I wish you were here; when I think of the old days when you could just hop into the car & arrive at anytime day or night, I want to cry. But perhaps they'll come again, one day, & one will be able to put all one's mind on one's work – I think that's one reason why Grimes is being such a brute at the moment. Still, I am over the worst now, and I can at least see ahead.

Working at the Schöne Müllerin with you is going to be heaven. I think we ought to do a wonderful show of it.[2] But I think I shall have to transport this awful old piano to the Wigmore – I am making such nice noises on it!

I'm waiting for your call tomorrow night – I do hope Wales wasn't too awful, but I would give alot to have been there to hear your voice – lucky Welsh!

Ursula was here yesterday – & Barbara has got here now safely for Easter & is enjoying herself. Isn't it tragic about Michael Halliday being missing.[3]   I feel very odd about it now – poor silly old dear that he was.

All my love my dearest darling,

B.

Had a note from Cecily – nothing definite about TB. yet.[4]

1 On Good Friday, 7 April, Pears was in Brecon singing Mendelssohn's oratorio, *Elijah*. The Michael to whom Britten refers might have been Michael Weekes, a friend of Pears's from the 1930s.

2 Britten and Pears gave their first performance of Schubert's song-cycle on 30 April at the Wigmore Hall, London, sharing the concert with Clifford Curzon, who played Schubert's Piano Sonata in D major (D. 850). *The Times* music critic (almost certainly Frank Howes) wrote on 2 May:

> The Schubert recital at Wigmore Hall on Sunday consisted of the Piano Sonata in D, opus 53, played by Mr Clifford Curzon; and *Die schöne Müllerin* song cycle, sung by Mr Peter Pears, with Mr Benjamin Britten accompanying; performances of an excellence which a large audience was quick to appreciate.
>   [. . .]
> Mr Pears, singing in German, had the double advantage of possessing the right kind of voice (a lyric tenor: too often we hear these songs, transposed or overweighted by deeper voices), and also of an accompanist who could make a positive contribution to the style and poetry of the music. In matters of taste, as of phrasing and tempo, this excellent partnership earned fresh regard for these almost too famous songs. There might have been more 'bite' and variety; the singer tended too much to a melodious sameness of tone-colour. But apart from a slight pinching of production on sustained notes the singing was admirably free of strain or affectation, and achieved much of the genuine Schubertian eloquence, in which the intimate lieder style must so often be reconciled with the claims of 'pure' singing and bel canto.

   Pears and Britten were to record *Die schöne Müllerin* in 1959 for Decca (released on sxl 2200 in 1960).

3 See note 1 to Diary for 10 November 1932.

4 Christopher Martin suffered from tuberculosis and was to die unexpectedly on 6 August, in hospital, after an operation.

WIGMORE HALL

Wigmore Street W·I

Sunday, April 30th

at 3 p.m.

CLIFFORD

CURZON

PETER

PEARS

BENJAMIN

BRITTEN

Schubert Recital

Piano Sonata in D major, Op. 53
Song Cycle : "Die Schöne Müllerin"

TICKETS (inc. tax) 8/6, 6/-, 3/-
may be obtained at Box Office, Wigmore Hall,
usual Ticket Offices and
IBBS & TILLETT
I 2 4 Wigmore Street, W.I (Wel. 8 4 I 8)

The Favil Press Ltd. (T.U.)

Announcement of Curzon–Pears–Britten recital, Wigmore Hall, 30 April 1944

458   To Ursula Nettleship

Old Mill, Snape, Suffolk.
April 21st, 1944.

My dear Ursula,

In great haste, but Beth believe it or not – she says she's busier than I am: moot point, which is more nuisance, opera than 2 kids? Wants me to write and say that everything is now fixed <u>this</u> end for June 10th, Snape Village Hall, & would you go ahead & book the people, & send tickets & bills etc. Everyone is panting to work for it.[1] Head (M.)[2] is a good idea – who for others – o, of course I'd forgotten the diseuse, she's a good idea (even tho' her name may be immemorable to me). Perhaps Winnie Roberts[3] – or do you think more glamour – O. Zorian?[4]

So glad you liked the piano pieces [*Holiday Diary*] – I have an awfully soft spot for them still – they just recreate that unpleasant young thing BB. in 1934 – but who enjoyed being BB all the same . . . !!

Did you hear the Serenade.[5]

P.G. leaps ahead.

When are you here?

I am afraid it looks as if Schöne Müllerin is out of luck – Peter is hopelessly booked up that week, & on the only free day (Sat. 29th) must rest. But there'll be other chances.

Love from all here,

BEN

[*illegible postscript*]

1 See Letter 464.

2 Michael Head (1900–1976), English composer, singer and pianist, who frequently gave recitals, accompanying himself at the piano.

3 Winifred Roberts, Australian-born violinist and wife of the organist and conductor, Geraint Jones. She was a pupil of Brosa's and in late 1939 or early 1940 had attended a play-through of Britten's Violin Concerto by Brosa with Henry Boys at the piano (see also Letter 481). On 5 October Britten was to perform his Violin Concerto with her under the auspices of the London Philharmonic Arts Club ('the Composer at the piano'). It was Brosa who introduced the concerto to Roberts, with whom on occasion Britten would play the Mozart duos for violin and viola. There were also times when Pears felt his voice failing him and he was unable to complete a programme, whereupon she would step in at short notice and play a Mozart sonata, with Britten as her accompanist.

4 Olive Zorian (1916–1965), English violinist. In 1942 she formed the Zorian String Quartet (in which Norina Semino was cellist), which gave notable premières and early performances of works by young British composers, Britten (String Quartet No. 2, 1945) and Tippett (String Quartet No. 3, 1945–6) among them. Between 1952 and 1957 she led the English Opera Group Orchestra. She was married to John Amis (b. 1922), the broadcaster. See also Amis, *Amiscellany: My life, my music* (London, Faber and Faber, 1985), pp. 181–2.

5 Broadcast on 20 April, with Pears, Brain and the Boyd Neel Orchestra, conducted by Boyd Neel.

49a The Old Mill, Snape (photo, Adolphus Tear)

49b The Old Mill: Britten's piano

50 London, 1942, Britten and Wulff Scherchen (now in the services); a snap taken
by a street photographer in the vicinity of Trafalgar Square. On this occasion Britten
bought and inscribed a copy of *Les Illuminations*: 'For Wulff of course – Benjamin B.
September 1942 i.e. 3 years too late'

51a   Capt. Piers Dunkerley,   51b   Erwin Stein and his wife, Sophie
Royal Marines

52a This photograph may have been taken on the occasion of a 'Salute the Red Army' event at the Royal Albert Hall on 23 February 1944, or when Shostakovich's 'Leningrad' Symphony was first performed in Britain on 22 and 29 June 1942. The presentation is being made by Sir Arnold Bax; the other composers present were (left to right) Granville Bantock, Britten and Ireland (see Letter 397)

52b Members of the Sadler's Wells company, c.1944/5; left to right: Pears, Lawrance Collingwood, Reginald Goodall, Joan Cross, Ivor Newton

53a Sadler's Wells, *c.*1943, *La Traviata:*
Pears as Alfredo (photo, Jon Vickers)

53b Sadler's Wells, *c.*1943, *The Bartered Bride:*
Pears as Vašek (photo, Alexander Bender)

53c *The Bartered Bride:* Pears with Rose Hill as Marenka

54 Britten and Pears in the garden at Sandhill, Aldeburgh, May 1948

55a The Snape marshes; this photograph by Enid Slater may have been sent to Britten in America in 1939 (see Letter 192)

55b Snape Bridge, winter 1943; left to right: Britten's niece, Sally, in pram; Beth; Pears with Britten's nephew, Sebastian; Britten

56a Family group in 1941; left to right: Barbara, Kit Welford, Helen Hurst; Sebastian on Beth's lap

56b Britten and Beth, with Sebastian, 1943

57a Snape, c.1944: Britten with Sebastian (photo, Enid Slater)

57b On the beach, c.1946/47: Britten with Sally (photo, Enid Slater)

58   Montagu Slater, the librettist of *Peter Grimes* (photo, Enid Slater)

59a Pears and Britten at the Old Mill, Snape, *c*.1944 (photo, Enid Slater)

59b and 59c Kenneth Green, costume designs for *Peter Grimes*: left, Ellen Orford; right, Grimes

60a   *Peter Grimes*, the original Sadler's Wells production, 7 June 1945, Act I; the designer was Kenneth Green (photo, Angus McBean: © Harvard Theatre Collection)

60b   Britten and Eric Crozier, the producer of *Peter Grimes*, 1945

61a *Peter Grimes*, 1945: Act II, scene 1 (photo, Angus McBean:
© Harvard Theatre Collection)

61b *Peter Grimes*, 1945: Act I, scene 2 (photo, Angus McBean:
© Harvard Theatre Collection)

62a Eric Crozier
in the T.V. studio, 1938

62b Pears at the Old Mill, Snape, *c.*1944
(photo, Enid Slater)

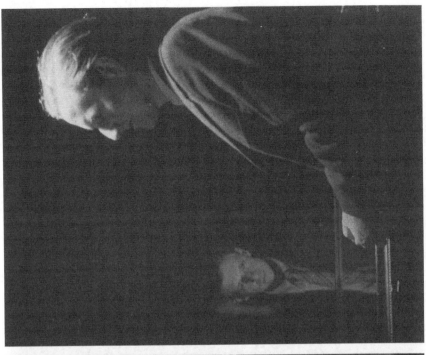

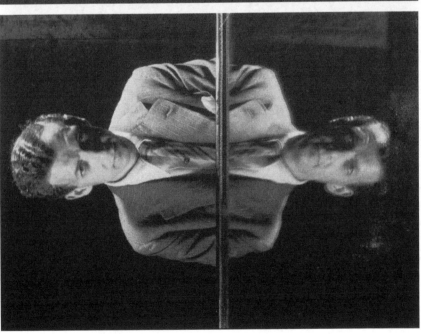

63a Britten, August 1945 (photo, Cecil Beaton: © Sotheby's)

63b Pears and Britten, August 1945 (photo, Cecil Beaton: © Sotheby's)

64   Britten, 1945 (photo, Angus McBean: © Harvard Theatre Collection)

459   To Mary Behrend

Old Mill, Snape, Suffolk.
May 9th 1944

My dear Mary,

That was a heavenly week-end! Thank you so very much for it;
it was just what both of us were needing so desparately – quiet,
peaceful, beautifully comfortable (how you manage that food &
drink in this wartime I can't imagine), & with the stimulation of
really intelligent & wise conversation. Thank you both so much. I
don't know whether Peter will find a moment to write (you know
how rushed he is this week) but if he doesn't, all this goes for him
too!

Please tell Bow that I was so impressed by his constructive
criticism of 'Peter Grimes' that I have already mentioned these
points to Montagu Slater, who is seriously considering them, & will
I think adopt them. It was sweet of you both to take so much
trouble over it. I have been hard at it since I got down here last
night – & please forgive me if I don't write more now, because it
is absorbing me at the moment. But I did want you to know at
once how very much both of us enjoyed ourselves with you.

With much love to you both,
Yours ever
BEN

460   To Peter Pears

Snape
May 9th [1944]

My honey,

I don't know when I'm going to have the joy of hearing your
voice on the telephone again – tonight you're being eaten by lions
(lucky things);[1] tomorrow, you're fire-watching (lucky fire)[2] – so I
thought I'd write a scribble to say I love you & miss you terribly,
& long for Monday. It was heaven – the week-end, quietly alone
with you; the B's are such sweet hosts, and it couldn't have been
[more] lovely could it? I've written them a note – & said you
probably won't have time to write.

It's nice here (as nice as it can be ohne dich) Sebastian is sweet,
so is Sally, & Beth seems in good form. The opera is going ahead

at last, & the garden looks nice. Only the aeroplanes are bloody, bloody, all the time.[3] Ursula is around – but mostly with the local hostlery.

I gather you didn't have time to see Erwin – but no matter. Little Sir W.???[4] Take care of yourself, my darling – nurse that heavenly voice of yours – We must do a superb Serenade.[5] See you Saturday at 12.30 for lunch. The Rothmans have sent a lovely parcel of cookies & candies – I'll bring some up for you!

All my love, my dearest,

BEN.

Of course the real reason for writing is that you must be running out of a certain commodity for railway trains ——

1 Probably a reference to the pursuit of Tamino by wild beasts in Act II of the *Magic Flute*.

2 Householders took turns to fire-watch during air-raids. But in the light of note 1 above, it is more probable that this is a reference to the famous scene in *Bohème* when Rodolfo (another Pears role) feeds the flames of the attic stove with his manuscripts.

3 Many airfields were located in East Anglia during the war because of the region's proximity to the Continent.

4 Clearly a reference to Britten's Folk-song Arrangement 'Little Sir William', but the context is obscure.

5 On 25 May, Pears, Dennis Brain and the Boyd Neel String Orchestra conducted by Britten recorded the *Serenade* for tenor, horn and strings for Decca (released on AK 1151–3 in 1945). They returned to the studio for an additional recording session on 8 October.

461 To Erwin Stein

Old Mill, Snape, Suffolk.
May 10th, 1944.

My dear Erwin,

Re one of our most eminent, & certainly our most efficient conductor[1] —— it is the old, old story of trying to change the <u>degree</u> of friendship. At the present moment, in his eyes at any rate, there have been two different conditions in our relationship – (i) an intimate one ('let me be father to you'), mostly on one side, need I say (ii) complete enmity. How (i) progressed to (ii) is of no importance, save that it is a sordid little matter, & which, as I told

you, cannot be explained or remedied. The problem is to find
condition (iii) obviously lying between (i) and (ii). Can that be done?
I think so, if the party concerned is big enough, controlled enough,
& if both sides want it badly enough. Certainly I suppose we both
want it – but I have my doubts as to whether the party has the
first qualities. It isn't made like that – it is far too vain & pompous,
too craving after that particular kind of emotional set-up, &
frankly, Erwin, I am too occupied, & getting too old to be bothered
with any more of that, especially when (as I think) the party isn't
really first-rate. But, if you think there is a way of achieving
condition number (iii) I am of course prepared to discuss it with
you! only you must remember that I don't think the matter really
of importance – that a few extra performances (admittedly good
ones) are worth all that bother & pother!

I am up on Saturday as I told you – and until then hard at Grimes.

Love to you, Sophie & Marion

Yours ever,

BEN

1 We cannot be certain about whom Britten was writing. Might it have
been Sargent, who was then principal conductor of the Liverpool
Philharmonic Orchestra, or – and perhaps more likely – Barbirolli,
who had returned to England in 1943 and taken on the Hallé Orchestra at Manchester? The association with Barbirolli dated back to the
American years. Sargent at this time, however, was showing a lively
interest in Britten's new works, for example twice performing the
Serenade with Pears and Brain and programming *Les Illuminations*
(with Pears) and the *Sinfonia da Requiem*.

462 **To Benjamin Britten**
From Peter Pears
[*Pencil*]

[In the train]
[11 May 1944]

My own beloved heart's darling, this is only just a line to tell you
that I think of you all the time, even when I'm being eaten by
lions or thrown to the Lady of Shalott,[1] or, as now, just waiting at
some station on the way to Stoke on Trent. You are with me all
the time and I plan absurdly, and day-<u>dream</u> stupidly with you all
the time. (We have just passed a station apparently called Earl's

Cement! V. odd!) Perhaps I'm even more conscious of you when
I'm away from you than when you're with me. Am I rather horrid
to you actually sometimes? Because I couldn't be nicer to you when
you aren't here! <u>Does</u> that help at all? My honey. I think also a
lot about reality & time & space & such trifles, as a result of your
not being here & yet being here. I do love you quite terribly –
   I <u>had</u> to sing Bohème last night to the Queen & the Princesses
(their first opera – most unsuitable I should have thought!) & we
were informed that we gave pleasure![2] My father & mother were
madly excited about it. It was Vic. Sladen[3] as Mimi – not bad at
all & no bad mistakes but Collingwood really stinks. Phew! it's
dirty music! However it's all probably a good training for Peter
Grimes, which is after all what I was born for, nicht-wahr? I shall
be glad when this week's over, & Monday night comes round!
Mrs. Nielson is looking after me frightfully well & has very sweetly
been taking food to my mother. She's allright really when she
has time to be.

FRIDAY noon.

Last night went very well. They like me, I think, & of course [wanted]
your, as encore, "Wonder – wander";[4] as indeed, they [did at]
Llanelly. I have to keep you with me as much as possible! And I
have now got through ⅔rds of my 5th rate music for the week!
Wow! Shalott is as odiferous as her vegetable names also! &
what a pome! Tennyson being very un-queer & boring.
Maurice J. is quite an efficient accompanist, & Kathleen Ferrier a
nice singer.[5] By the way, I've got to do Barber on Monday!!

Much much love

from

P

1 This was a cantata (1942) by Maurice Jacobson (1896–1976), a setting
  of 'The Lady of Shalott' for tenor, chorus and orchestra. The performance is described in Winifred Ferrier, *The Life of Kathleen Ferrier*
  (London, Hamish Hamilton, 1956), p. 56. Ferrier also participated as
  pianist with Jacobson, with the Newcastle String Orchestra conducted by the composer. In the first half of the concert, given by the
  Etruscan Choral Society at the Victoria Hall, Hanley, she and Pears
  had sung songs and duets. Jacobson was not only a composer but
  also a celebrated accompanist.

2 Given at the New Theatre, London, on 19 May, in the presence of
  Queen Elizabeth, the consort of George VI, and her two daughters.

3 Victoria Sladen (b. 1910), English operatic soprano.

4 'I wonder as I wander'; see note 1 to Letter 497.

5 The English contralto (1912–1953), who was the first Lucretia in 1946.
  Britten probably first heard her in *Messiah*, at Westminster Abbey in
  1943. See also his recollections of Ferrier, 'Three Premières', in
  Kathleen Ferrier: A Memoir, edited by Neville Cardus (London, Hamish
  Hamilton, 1954), pp. 54–61, in which he recalls the three works –
  Lucretia, Spring Symphony, and *Canticle II: Abraham and Isaac* – in which
  Ferrier took part; Maurice Leonard, *Kathleen: The Life of Kathleen Ferrier
  1912–1953* (London, Hutchinson, 1988), pp. 83–92, 142–3, 201–3, and
  253–4; and Charles Risby, *Kathleen Ferrier* (London, Robert Hale,
  1955). Britten contributed to a BBC Radio documentary about Ferrier,
  A Voice is a person, in (?)1967.

463 To Elizabeth Mayer

Old Mill, Snape, Suffolk.
May 13th 1944.

My darling Elizabeth,

Please, please forgive the long silence – I know you will, but I
am so grieved that it is so much longer than I intended it to be.
The trouble is that I only have time for letter-writing when I'm
down here (which, alas is scarcely 50% of my time now), & of
late I've been working so hard that when the evening comes my
eyes just give out, & I can't make myself use them any more! It
isn't that they are bad, but I've been working at great pressure. So
you see, letters so overdue to you get put off & off, and now I
can scarcely remember when I last wrote. Anyhow I know it was
not since your lovely parcel to me – with the socks, the candies
& the lovely lemon cristals. You really are the most generous and
thoughtful creature – how you always put your finger exactly on
what we need, beats me! And the heavenly parcel that arrived for
Beth & the kids to day – you should have seen their faces, Beth
about the stockings & maple sugar, Sebastian about the different
candies & the soap (particularly the smell!), & Sally crazy about
the crinkly paper (being that age!). You really are so terribly good
– and to complete the picture I was wearing your lovely sweater
& socks too! So we were very Elizabeth-conscious! but that I am
always, my dearest, it doesn't need socks to make me that. Your

last letter was an utter delight; Peter handed it to me just before a
performance of the Bartered Bride – (I'd been spending a few days
at Wellington with Kenneth Green – talking over Così fan tutte[1]
(for which he's doing the sets – Sadler's Wells) & of course,
Grimes). Clifford Curzon was with me for the show – & we both
adored Peter's creation of Vazék, a most brilliant & tender piece
of acting & then after, when we were back together at St. John's
Wood, we devoured your letter, every word, every comma,
together. You seemed so close to us, with your exquisite pictures
of your life in your little place – how we yearn to see it – but
above all, how we long for you to come here, & see Snape. It is
looking so lovely now – garden growing, children growing, & the
view as heavenly, as Constable, as ever. The nightingales sing night
and day, but fail, alas, to drown the interminable groan over-
head, which casts an evil slur over everything. What hell it is. I
scarcely know how to face the immediate future, but one must
work & work, otherwise there is only madness. I was delighted
with your news about Christopher. I know how terribly close he
is to you, & how the other job appalled you[2] – but if one wants a
thing terribly badly, one always gets it – and that is why I know
we'll all be together before long, & you can hear Peter sing, hear
the new pieces, & we can talk, and talk –

Life goes on from event to event. Peter, Clifford & I have a
Schubert recital, at the Wigmore Hall – the first of a projected
series of one-composer concerts that we 3 (& with Lucille Wallace
(Mrs. Curzon) harpsichord as well later) intend. He did the big
D major Sonata, & we the Schöne Müllerin!! How we should have
loved you to be there, & your criticisms! I think on the whole it
was good – Peter had had an abominable 2–weeks – including
2 Rigolettos, 2 Bohèmes (new part, very glamorous!), 3 Bartered
Brides, 2 Serenades (my new piece), Das Lied von der Erde, Dream
of Gerontius[3] (for 1st time) & then the Schöne Müllerin. And his
voice stood it, & sounded as good at the end as at the beginning
– could you imagine that four or five years ago? At the end of it
I took him away for a few days, & we had some heavenly peace &
quiet together, spiritually (as always when together) as well as
physically. He is now travelling around, singing, singing, & I am
here for a few days on Grimes (getting better & better, I think) &
then I go to Leicester to play the Scottish Ballad with Clifford.[4] That
reminds me – of course this is free to be played, it was never
restricted. It is now in final proofs, as well as the Introduction &
Rondo, & as soon as ever it is out I'll have copies sent to your

new 2–piano team;[5] it would be lovely if they could play it. Don't worry my dearest if things don't go well for me in the States; I don't, because I know how fickle the musical public is, & how superficial their judgements (although I was a bit grieved by Colin's attack on the Michelangelo Sonnets)[6] —— things go excitingly here – big audiences, 90% young people too, & Sweden Switzerland, Portugal all do my stuff, as well as the Middle-East, S. Africa, & even a German prison-camp – I sent a new piece out to some friends there! So there's no need to worry – all that matters is that I write better & better stuff. It is exciting that dear Wystan goes from strength to strength. I knew he would. I shall have to be an older & better composer before I get round to the Oratorio, but I am going to, one day. I am going to write to him one day, & Chris. too – perhaps I'll have time next week, when I shall spend a few days in Devon with Christopher Martin, again, poor dear, down with T.B. – So he needs much cheering.

It was lovely to see the snap of Beate – she looks as lovely as ever. I am so terribly glad that she's so happy with Max. I hope he won't have to go.[7] Please give them my (& Peter's) love. The Rothmans write regularly & send most lovely things – Dave is an angel – I dread Bobby having to go too – his last letter was so sweet, & the photos of his yacht & himself unbelievable. I feel it a wonderful contact that you are able to see them. Soon there'll be new records to send, Carols, String Quartet,[8] 2–piano pieces (with C.C.), Folk songs, & above all the Serenade. I'm arranging for a copy of the Smart [*Rejoice in the Lamb*] to be sent for you to play over to yourself!

My love to William, as ever – I hope work goes better & better – to Michael, Wystan & all my dear, dear friends. All this comes from our Vibrant Young Friend[9] too – we are one.

All the love in the world – take care of yourself –

Your
BEN

1 The Sadler's Wells production of Mozart's *Così fan tutte* (with Pears as Ferrando and Joan Cross as Fiordiligi) was first performed on 29 August, produced by Sasha Machov and conducted by Lawrance Collingwood.

2 Christopher Mayer had been assigned to the Army Medical Corps, to be trained as a medical helper. He was called up from Yale, served in the Pacific, but returned there post-war to complete his degree.

The job that appalled Mrs Mayer may have been duties undertaken at the training camp which preceded his assignment as a medic.

3 Pears had sung in *Rigoletto* in London on 21 April and 2 May, conducted by Herbert Menges; in Puccini's *La Bohème* in London on 27 and 28 April, conducted by Collingwood, in a production for Sadler's Wells by Tyrone Guthrie; in the *Bartered Bride* in London on 25, 29 April and 3 May; in the *Serenade* on 20 April, a BBC broadcast, and at the Wigmore Hall with Brain and the Boyd Neel Orchestra, conducted by Boyd Neel, on 26 April; in *Das Lied* at the Stoll Theatre, London, on 23 April; and in *Gerontius* at Bristol on 22 April.

4 A performance given by the (amateur) Leicester Symphony Orchestra, conducted by Basil Cameron, at the De Montfort Hall, Leicester, on 14 May.

5 Celius Dougherty, American pianist and composer, and Vincent Ruzicka, a prominent two-piano duo known to the Mayers.

6 In an article entitled 'Scores and Records' (*Modern Music*, 21/1, November–December 1943, pp. 48–9) McPhee had written:

The *Seven Sonnets of Michelangelo*, for tenor and piano, say nothing at all to me. They are baroque and pompous show-pieces, pastiches that hold little interest. The Pucciniesque vocal line is brilliantly written, the Italian text admirably set. But there is little if anything personal in this music, and I am always amazed at the apparently great urge in Britten, a man of real musical gifts, to turn out one more genre-piece. Where the satisfaction lies I cannot understand.

7 Beata's husband volunteered for service in the US Army as a medical officer, but he was directed to continue in his post as pathologist at the Middletown Hospital.

8 See note 3 to Letter 425.

9 Elizabeth Mayer had written to Britten on 20 April:

My God, what a stunning photo of dear Peter is going to come out in Vogue in the next issue! He is much slimmer, but really wonderful, the 'vibrant young Tenor' as the caption says, and then your dear person looking at me (at last) from the background of the picture [. . .] the whole is under 'London Spotlight'.

464   To Peter Pears

I asked Erwin for the Grieg myself, so don't worry (ha, ha,). I've
done my C.O. thing have you?[1]

Old Mill,
Snape.
June 12th 1944

Honiest, bunchiest,

It was lovely to hear your voice over that unspeakable machine
last night & Saturday. Sorry I was so involved on Sat. & so
depressed on Sun. – but the latter is a thing which usually happens
when I'm away from you; so we'd better not be apart too long or
I may shrivell altogether up in my depression. My bloody opera
stinks, & that's all there is to it. But I dare say that I shall be able
to de-odourise it before too long – or I'm hoping so. The week-end
was abit hectic – helping organise the concert, the artists, & the
village after. It's much easier to play than organise, I find –
especially difficult is showing people into their seats – I couldn't find
the numbers, & o – the confusion when people sat down in the
wrong ones! However, it went well – Korchinska played well,
Winnie Roberts so-so, but Michael Head's abit dim – but then most
singers (save one – who . . . who?) are to me. Ursula's still
around, which is un peu disturbing I find. All that coupled with
news[2] doesn't exactly help P.G. but I hope to be clearer in the old
head from now onwards.

Kalmus[3] wants us on Sept. 28th to do Boyhood's End, Berg &
Mahler at Wigstein for BH.[4]   Is that too soon do you think, &
did we definitely promise Johnny Amis for his club?[5]   I'd like to
do it then, because it comes in my 'off' week; but we can discuss
all this when we meet.

Abelard is a knock-out; I read it in about 2 days (really read it,
too!) and it kept me awake nearly all one night. It's agonising,
but one reaches the end feeling better for it. What torments those
two suffered – poor angels – do take care of yourself my dearest
– lock your door at night – unless of course you do really want to
sing the top F in I Puritani![6] I'm now reading Emma[7] to sooth
myself.

The kids are well, if a bit over excited – Sebastian got wild with
joy at so many visitors to flirt with & enchant, & we are rather
feeling the consequences! But he's a honey, & so is your god-child[8]

too, you know. She walks now, & says hallo (in a cockney accent
– most startling!)

Excuse scribble, my darling – but I want you to get this. Don't
feel too bad about the Sadlers W. Op. Co. See Joan, talk her round
– you've got lots of influence over her, and you must use it. Ralph
Hawkes wont be any better, you know.[9]

I love you, I love you, I love you. Take care of yourself – &
practise the Grieg.[10]

All my love,

BEN

1 Perhaps an obligation to make an official return of the activities they
had agreed to undertake as conscientious objectors.

2 The Allied invasion of France – 'D-Day' – had taken place on 6 June.

3 Dr Alfred A. Kalmus (1889–1972), Austrian-born music publisher.
He joined Universal Edition, Vienna, in 1909. Political events forced
him to emigrate to England where he set up the London office of
Universal Edition in 1936. In 1939 he – and his office – became part
of the Boosey & Hawkes organization. In 1949, Universal Edition
had its independence restored, with Kalmus again as its head.

4 The concert, at the Wigmore Hall, London, was the first of a series
of four promoted by Boosey & Hawkes. The programme was as
follows: Berg: five of the *Seven Early Songs*: 'Nacht', 'Die Nachtigall',
'Im Zimmer', 'Liebestod', 'Sommertag'; Bartók: *Improvisations on Hungarian Folksongs*, Op. 20 (Peter Stadlen, piano); Britten: *Phantasy*,
Op. 2 (Leon Goossens, with the Carter String Trio); Tippett: *Boyhood's
End*; Mahler: five songs: 'Rheinlegendchen', 'Ich ging mit Lust', 'Der
Tamboursg'sell', 'Blicke mir nicht in die Lieder', 'Um schlimme Kinder
artig zu machen'; and Roussel: *Serenade*, for flute, harp and string
trio (John Francis, flute; Maria Korchinska, harp; Carter String Trio).

5 The London Philharmonic Arts Club, started in wartime by John
Amis, and an offshoot of the London Philharmonic Orchestra. It met
twice a week. The Tuesday programmes alternated record recitals
('the best classical and contemporary music') with studio recitals
of the Committee for the Promotion of New Music. The Thursday
programmes introduced 'Recitals, Talks, Lectures, Brains Trusts and
other features'. Peter Pears and Norina Semino, the cellist (who on
occasion took part in CEMA recitals with Pears and Britten), were
among the artists who appeared at the Club, along with Louis Mac-
Neice, Alec Robertson, Boyd Neel, Alan Bush, Howard Ferguson,
Michael Tippett, Walter Bergmann, the Zorian Quartet, and many
other well-known musicians. See Jerrold Northrop Moore, *Philharmonic Jubilee, 1932–1982: A Celebration of the London Philharmonic*

Orchestra's Fiftieth Anniversary (London, Hutchinson, 1982), in which an example of the Club's publicity material is reproduced.

6 *Peter Abelard*, the novel by Helen Waddell, medieval scholar and translator (1889–1965), published in 1933. Abelard (1079–1142) was the most brilliant scholar, teacher at the University of Paris, theologian and rational thinker of his day, but his popular fame rests on a tragic love story. While he was tutoring Héloïse, the niece of Fulbert, a canon of Nôtre-Dame, the couple fell in love, had a child and secretly married. Fulbert took a cruel revenge and had Abelard castrated by hired ruffians (hence Britten's reference to the 'top F'). The lovers were separated – Héloïse banished to a nunnery and Abelard disgraced – but they nevertheless managed to communicate through a famous correspondence. Abelard suffered much persecution for his alleged heresy, was imprisoned and sought refuge in one monastery after another, ending his days in Cluny. Héloïse became a revered and celebrated abbess, famous for her learning. She died in 1163 and was buried in Abelard's tomb.

Britten thought seriously about using Abelard as a possible operatic subject and talked about it to his librettist Ronald Duncan after the composition of *Lucretia*. Later, in 1948, Eric Crozier attempted a text for a concert piece for Pears and Nancy Evans. Neither proposal was finished and both were eventually abandoned. (See RDBB, pp. 99–102.)

7 The novel by Jane Austen.

8 Sally Welford.

9 Britten refers to discussions about the proposed production of *Peter Grimes* by Sadler's Wells. See also Letter 468. Eric Crozier has documented in detail the troubled pre-history of the first production of *Grimes*, i.e. the many difficulties, problems and controversies that attended the opera's birth. In the main, these can be identified as the consequences of the hostility of the company – the chorus and principals – to the enterprise, and to Cross and Pears personally. Joan Cross remembers (1989) that it was the chorus in particular which was resistant to the project. Yet further dissension, ironically, was generated by the opera's success in 1945, which led to the withdrawal of the work from the Sadler's Wells company's repertory, at the composer's request, and to the resignation of Joan Cross, Pears and Crozier. See Crozier, ' "Peter Grimes": An Unpublished Article of 1946', *Opera*, 16/6, June 1965, pp. 412–16. Differences of opinion and a threatened resignation attended the first broadcast of the opera which finally took place on 17 July 1945. See report in the *Daily Mail*, 16 July.

10 Songs by Grieg, 'To the Motherland', 'A Bird's Cry' and 'The Hunter',
were in the current repertory of Pears and Britten. It is to these songs
that Britten refers in his afterthought at the head of this letter.

465   To Benjamin Britten
From Peter Pears

Hippodrome Theatre
Coventry.
[15/16/17 June 1944]

My bee –

It was lovely having your letter this morning and I am sitting
down right away to send one back to you with my love, my love
and my love.

I had a fearful time on Monday when I arrived here trying to
find digs and it wasn't until 8.30 that evening that I got
somewhere, and pretty averagely boring it is. Tiny bed-room, &
general living-dining room with a dog that persists, and flowers
that make me sneeze! So I spend most of my day out and about!
But what a life touring must be for the poor unfortunate chorus
& orchestra. Everything must depend on their digs. If they are
alright, then life is tolerable, if not, then life is unspeakable! I shall
certainly stay in Hotels whenever I can. There's at least room to
move about in! But there's no studio to practice in or anything!

I don't believe your opera stinks. I just don't believe it; anyway
if it does, by all means be-Jeyes it,[1] and have it as sweet as its
writer for me when I see it. I shall definitely try to catch the 5.26
from here which is due at Euston at 7.50 on Saturday, so I may quite
possibly hear you, & shall eat with you, & sleep with you!

I'm sorry you had such a hectic week end – I should like to have
been there to have been shewn to my seat by you! Give Ursula
my love & tell her to go away! I won't have you being badgered
by people. In my digs of course, I wake up to loud wireless at 8.0
& then news at 9.0, and I come home to news at 9.0 – though I
must say no one really seems to be interested in the war as such.
I think they would all like it ended at once. It must be too appalling
across there just now & every town destroyed.

I will write to Johnny Amis about September 28th – I'm inclined
to say 'yes' to Kalmus, for Michael's[2] sake apart from other things,
as I couldn't really do another date till December & by then we
shall probably be in the middle of our Band concerts,[3] won't we?

& we can always polish off a date for Johnny some other time say
in December – I mean, for Johnny, we can do what we like &
know, whereas we shall have to work at Berg & Mahler, nicht
wahr?

Much love to you. I simply cannot make up my mind about the
Gallery[4] – We won't have too much time to work it, enough for
a certain amount of newish –

Will this do:

Il mio tesoro (Don Giovanni) Concert Aria: Misero! o sogno o son desto (K. ?)	Mozart	Yes please! such a good one to begin with & you play it so well!

Am See
Ach! neige
Dass sie hier gewesen   Schubert
Vom Mitleiden Maria
Auflösung

To the Motherland
Bright Night
W[ind] & Wave
By the Stream   Grieg
A bird's cry
The Hunter

Goldenhair
When you are old & grey
Dweller or Adoration
Go not happy day
or   Frank Bridge
Adoration
? So perverse

1 Jeyes Fluid, a well-known brand of disinfectant.
2 Michael Tippett.
3 Presumably engagements on behalf of CEMA.
4 A programme devised for the National Gallery concert series.

466   To Miss Cook
BBC

45a St. John's Wood High Street,
June 14th 1944.

Dear Miss Cook,

Thank you for your letter. As far as I can remember, 'Down the Danube etc.' came from a show called Hadrian's Wall, which I did with W.H. Auden from North Regional (Newcastle) in either 1937 or 8.[1] I am afraid that I haven't a copy, & I don't know if one can be traced anywhere in the BBC archives; but I seem to remember a fruitless search for this music in 1939.

With apologies,
Yours sincerely,
BENJAMIN BRITTEN

1 The year was 1937. Miss Cook was writing on behalf of Elizabeth Poston, English composer and pianist (1905–1987), who was a member of the BBC music staff 1940–45, and became Director of the European Service.

467   To Peter Pears

Old Mill, Snape.
June 29th 1944

Honey, my darling,

I am nearly crazy with worry about you – praying that you can get some sleep & arn't too worried. It is the bloodiest business and I can't wait to get you out of it all. What a curse about the windows. I do hope the damage isn't too great, & can be easily put right.[1]

Things are nice here, but I've been having rather a difficult time. Work won't go well, & the news about Piers,[2] & worry about you & Barbara & all, is adding up to quite a depression. But it will all be dispelled on Saturday, & won't we enjoy ourselves!

I hope you called Sarton about the records, & that Erwin has sent the Carol ones on to St. Johns Wood as I asked him. It'll be nice to take them to Ludlow.[3]

No more now, my darling. I love you more & more every day, & long to see you. Hope the voice is as golden as ever!

All my love, & life,
BEN

1 Damage caused by one of the flying-bombs released by the Germans during the last stages of the war. The first flying-bomb (V-1) had dropped on London on 13 June. The first rocket (V-2) was to land in Britain on 8 September. The south of the country was hardest hit.

2 See Letter 470.

3 Pears's old school, Lancing, had been evacuated to two host institutions, Ellesmere College, Shropshire, and Denstone College, near Uttoxeter, Staffordshire (both Woodard Corporation schools, like Lancing) during June–July 1940. For the rest of the war Lancing was dispersed among four locations near Ludlow, Shropshire. See Letter 470.

58 To Peter Pears

Old Mill
July 12th [1944]

My darling,

Not a sound, or a tinkle, from you so I thought I would scribble a hallo to you before I dash down to the post – having been writing over-due letters since lunch. How are you – my beautiful? I hope the journey was OK. & that you found rooms all right. Let me know <u>soon</u> where you are, because I loathe not knowing.[1] I had a hectic day in London – those things around <u>all</u> day, with bumps & sirens galore – had lots to arrange, saw Ralph & fixed about P.G. at the Wells (I've written to Joan)[2] – had to arrange about letters with Post Office (Kay[3] is gone away); they're all being sent to Barbara (since we're going away from here soon, there didn't seem any other central address), & she's being posted with your address (<u>when</u> I know it!).

I've had a letter (crossing mine) from Ronnie O.kaying 22nd.[4] Beth says she'll take Mrs. Neilson if the Wells don't open in London – as I shouldn't think they will.[5] But do let me know soon – & ring up, or write – because I <u>do</u> love you & want to hear from you, because I <u>miss</u> you – see – honey?

All my love.

B.

1 Pears was in Sunderland from 12 to 22 July, on tour with Sadler's Wells, singing in Rossini's *Barber of Seville* (12th), Verdi's *Rigoletto* (18th), and Puccini's *Bohème* (22nd).

2 The choice of theatre for the launching of *Peter Grimes* had been the cause of some concern. See Letter 487.

3 Unidentified.

4 Britten and Pears were to take a short holiday in Devon from 23 to
  29 July, staying with Ronald Duncan.

5 See, however, Letter 470 where Britten refers to the opera company's
  return to London. At about this time Pears wrote to Britten from
  Sunderland, 'I'm afraid it looks as if London season is on – only
  thing is Joan has written to Chris that if we give up, can we evacuate
  to Dartington & rehearse there. Nice idea!', while in Letter 473 he
  indicates that the season was to open with the *Bartered Bride* (on 7
  August, at the Prince's Theatre). Presumably Beth and Mrs Neilson
  would not have attended the performance as London was under
  siege from the air.

469 To Peter Pears

Old Mill
July 16th 1944

Honey darling,

I hope all is well with you. It was lovely to hear your voice
yesterday – altho' we had so much beastly business to talk over.
Don't worry about mail – it is turning up regularly at Barbara's
already, & she only hasn't sent yours on because it was only
printed matter, & any how she hadn't your exact address until
yesterday. So don't be cross no more!

Well, your scene with the apprentice is going on well.[1] It is
difficult to do, & I get terribly upset by what I'm creating, but it
is nearly done, & I think will be good & effective. There's alot of
stuff for you to get your teeth in to!

I can't write much to-day – It is the first warm day we've had,
& Beth & the kids are going to take tea out & have a bathe at
Iken;[2] & if I can get enough of P.G. written I'm going with them.

Sorry that Sunderland is such a stinking hole. Never mind – not
much longer, & we'll be together in Devon! Let me know as soon
as you know your August plans, as I have to make various
arrangements.

Be good, my honey – I miss you & long for you terribly.

All my love.

B.

1 *Peter Grimes*, Act II scene 2, at the end of which the apprentice falls
  to his death.

2 On the river Alde, near Snape.

470 To Elizabeth Mayer

The Old Mill, Snape, Suffolk.
July 19th, 1944.

My darling Elizabeth,

It is such ages since I wrote that I have no idea when it was,
what I have to thank you for, or to acknowledge. Anyhow you
are used to me now, & my bad ways! But thank you for everything
– even the things that I have forgotten at the moment, but I
enjoyed enormously at the time! & the New Yorkers which arrive
very haphazardly, but in great numbers (never too great!), &
Beth's Vogue,[1] with the smashing photo which arrived yesterday!
Peter's wire[2] was a great joy, & one felt a great & tangible
connection with you. I am sorry if you have worried about us, but
I hope our message reassured you.

It is indeed a strange time – like living in an H.G. Wells fantasy,[3]
with everything unbelievable until you meet it face to face, & then
terrifying! Luckily we only caught the newest horrors for a week
or two at the beginning, but that was nasty enough. We had a
lot of concerts together around London (& Southern England!), &
they had to be done under harrassing conditions. Now, apart
from crossing London from time to time, we are away – Peter with
the opera in Sunderland & the North, me here at Snape, then for
a tiny holiday together in Devon, & then alas the opera must go
back to London. But I hope to persuade Peter to live outside –
where at least he can sleep soundly! He is well – singing very well,
tho' much too often, busy rehearsing Così fan tutte the next
production with Joan Cross, & sets by Kenneth Green (a real family
production!) – he will be lovely in that, you can imagine. When,
o when will you be able to see him on the stage, & come to some
of our recitals – perhaps this lunacy will be over before long, &
then we can slowly recover together! There is so much to talk about,
to play & to hear that I am certain we shall get new life together.
At the moment one only gets rest with friends (how right Wystan
is about this) & in one's work. The opera is going well – I've just
finished Act II, & it is the next production after Così at the Wells.
Isn't that thrilling! It is becoming a bigger affair than I expected
and so topical is to be unbearable in spots! I am yearning to see it
on the stage – with Peter, Joan Cross, & Kenneth's sets, & perhaps
me conducting!

Beth & the kids are well – she is overworking with all her chores

& her teaching; Sebastian more mischievous, & Sally more
adorable than ever. It is peaceful here, in one way, not as you
might guess in another. Barbara is in London, & very low, poor
darling. This is almost the last straw I'm afraid, but I help all I can,
& she gets away for weekends usually. So far all my friends are
well, thank God, except Piers who is missing, tho' may be a
prisoner. It makes one sick with anxiety.

I spent a lovely week at Peter's old evacuated school in
Shropshire, not long ago – when he was nearby with the opera.
Esther Neville-Smith his old friend there was sweetness &
intelligence itself – one of the people definitely for you to meet
when you come over. The children were nice, & we sang & played
to them, & I talked music, music (especially one young one who
is a wonder). These days, artists (of every kind) & children are the
only sane people.

Thank you for the crazy but well-meaning Accent[4] article! Really
criticism is at a low ebb – but was it ever higher? Things go well
with me here – in Sweden, Portugal, Switzerland, & other pleasant
places. But I don't worry that America is so hard to conquer,
except that it means you hear so few performances. (I must say
Colin's outburst in Modern Music made me sad, but I think of
him with as much affection as ever). I hope to send you the
Serenade records & Carol records before long – they won't be
issued for some time tho' I'm afraid, the new horror is holding up
things somewhat, & there are sides we must re-do.

My love (& usual apologies!) to all my dear friends, who aren't
any less dear because I don't write or hear from them! How is
dear William – I hope that the practice flourishes. I pray that you
have good news of Christopher & Michael.

Always love to Beate – & so much my dearest to you too.

BEN

1 Elizabeth Mayer was sending the *New Yorker* to Britten and Pears
   and *Vogue* to Beth.
2 Probably greetings from Elizabeth Mayer for Pears's birthday on 22nd
   June.
3 H.G. Wells (1866–1946), English novelist and writer of science fiction,
   e.g. *The War of the Worlds* and *Things to Come*.
4 We have been unable to trace this article.

471   **To David Rothman**

Peter is making some lovely new records – mostly of my music – I
am going to try & get copies to you soon.

Old Mill, Snape, Suffolk.
July 20th, 1944.

My dear Dave,

It is ages since that lovely parcel of candies & cookies – all things
quite impossible to get over here now – arrived from you, & I feel
really ashamed that I haven't written before to you. But I know
you will understand, since conditions are rather hectic here now,
& continuing with one's normal work is no easy matter! Please
forgive me, anyhow, & accept my very great gratitude for a really
lovely present, that gave so many of us such great pleasure for a
great length of time! Thank you, my dear.

And your letter too – that was a great joy: I have read and re-
read it many times – it gives me such a clear picture of your life,
in spite of war and the long lapse of time (doesn't it seem ages
since Peter & I left you all!) so little changed. Bobby must be a
great joy & help to you – he writes so sweetly & modestly about
all his doings. And Joan too – I am so glad you are so pleased
with her progress. I knew she would leap ahead when she found
the right person to take her in hand. I should like to hear her in
the Chopin Ballades! And Emma & her husband – and your wife.
It is lovely to have news of them; & I long to see them all again
– what fun it would be if it were over here! I feel you would love
this place – in peacetime when it is quiet over-head & around, &
we have got the garden into working order. At present my sister
& her children are still here, & it is a boon to me to have them,
& to know that when I am away (which is often) that the house is
being looked after and used. The kids are grand companions –
but then I have always loved children!

Peter is up north luckily at the moment – he is touring with the
opera, & occasionally he comes down south to do a recital or so
with me,[1] so we see each other fairly frequently. Then we are going
to have a short holiday – <u>one week</u>, all he can take off this year!
– together in Devonshire next week. After that the opera returns
to London, which I pray will be quieter than it is now. We had a
lively time there at the beginning of these new horrors – we were
around a great deal with concerts to give, and didn't enjoy it
much! It is pretty tiring, as you can well imagine, & how people

who have to stay in it all the time can bear it, is beyond me. There
is so little relief from anxiety too, with this new onslaught in France.
So many of one's friends are there, & it seems so close to one's
daily life. Pray God that it'll soon be over & humanity will return
to reason & kindness again – but even when the war is over I am
afraid that latter quality will be a very rare thing. I feel terribly for
you Dave with Bob growing up, but perhaps things will be changed
before he reaches the call-up age, & even if he has to go will go to
something quieter, or only nominal duties. By-the-way, a friend
of mine, who was struck by the photo he sent of himself and crew
in "Kestrel", would love to borrow the negative & copy it. Could
you please send it? – and any new ones of you all that you have.
I cherish photos of the good days in America. Please tell Bobby
that I loved his last letters & am answering them as soon as I can
manage, but life is difficult for letter-writing.

Love to you all, & again a thousand thanks for your lovely present.
With every good wish, from both Peter & me –
BEN

1 On the date this letter was written, Britten and Pears gave a recital
at Melksham, Wiltshire.

472 To Revd Walter Hussey

Grey House, Burghclere, Newbury[1]
as from Snape
[Postmarked ?July 1944]

Dear Walter,

Please excuse silence – caused by over-work & flying-bombs!.
The plans for Sept 21st are going ahead from our end. Are they
from yours? Our plan now is to have a 'cello, as we want to do
some religious music with continuo.[2] So I have asked Norina
Semino, who has agreed – & we will probably also play the Chopin
Sonata[3] (which is good). We will work out a possible programme
(with Rejoice in the Lamb in the middle) & let you know later.
I hope you are all well – please excuse haste.

Yours ever
BEN

1 Britten was staying with the Behrends.

2 See Letter 477.

3 In G minor, Op. 65.

473   **To Elizabeth Mayer**
      From Peter Pears

45a High St.
St. John's Wood
London N.W.8.
August 6th [1944]

Dearest Elizabeth –

At last here I am, sitting down with pen and paper to write to
you, who have written so many lovely letters to me, and I not
one to you for <u>so</u> long. You are such a wonderful correspondent,
Elizabeth,! you write often and sweetly – and never an impatient
demand for an answer! You have spoiled me! and I have just
collected from my mother's flat the birthday parcel which arrived
while they were away on holiday – I had the pleasure of sharing
all the goodies with her. Thank you so much, my dear! Heavenly
candies and wonderful socks!

When did I last write to you? Oh dear! over a year ago, I'm afraid
– so there should be lots of news for you – but actually Ben tells
me, he has let you have all the news. It has been the most terrifically
busy time, both for him and for me. Sometimes I don't know how I
have managed all the endless travelling & then singing at the end
of it. It's been wonderful experience, if only it doesn't go on too
long and wear me out. One can't really get a proper holiday. The
five days I had last month have to last me till after Christmas, but
I am very strong physically – & in myself I am benefiting from it,
I hope. Besides, people seem to love Ben's & my work so much
that it's always refreshing work – one receives, while one is giving.
We have done the Sonnets everywhere, and always people take to
them as if they had been waiting for just that very experience. And
now of course since last October, there has been the Serenade,
which is subtle and beautiful and haunting, with a wonderful
setting of the Blake poem "O rose thou are sick". We have just
made records of it with Boyd Neel's Orchestra for Decca, but we
shall do them again better soon, & when they are out, you must
have them. Now Ben talks of George Herbert & John Donne (the
Sacred Sonnets perhaps)[1] and also the St. Francis Mass from the
Missal. Do you know it? I don't – We can't get a copy of the Missal

alas. Peter Grimes is now two-thirds done. The 2nd Act is
finished, & Ben is starting the Third with confidence. We are
planning to do it with the Sadler's Wells Opera next April. The first
Act is quite terrifyingly intense, from first note to last. Quite
shattering. The 2nd is warmer & more relaxed, though it has the
death of the boy at the end —   It will be terribly difficult to do,
for me especially, as the part is so dramatic it needs a Chaliapin –
& my voice is still lyrical and not dramatic. However, it was a
year before I could tackle the Sonnets, do you remember, and now
they say I sing them best of anything. So perhaps I shall reach
Grimes by April – !

It has been wonderful having Michael Tippett as a fellow-artist
& composer whom we can both wholly admire and love, and then
Clifford Curzon & Lucille Wallace are dear friends and musicians.
We have the feeling here that in these dark times the seed is
slowly growing. English music is really appearing again as music
and itself, free of odd nostalgias & preoccupations with non-
musical ideas! I do so long for you to know all of them & share our
vitality and confidence and, in spite of everything, gaiety. You
would love it & understand. Michael's music is more complex than
Ben, but it is slowly being recognised, & the Cantata from W.H.
Hudson of his that we do, has made many friends – as well as
enemies. Kenneth Green is another – a real painter – his portrait
of Ben (my first picture as collector) is lovely – always different,
every day – like Ben! Kenneth has done some ravishing sets and
costumes for "Così fan Tutte", which we are busy rehearsing now
& will produce in 3 weeks. What wonderful music! I am now
singing (or have been until recently) Tamino, Duke in Rigoletto,
Alfred in Traviata, Almaviva in "Barbiere", Vashek the stutterer
in "Bartered Bride", Rudolfo in "Bohème", & now Ferrando in
"Così" —— Enough for 18 months!

We are very excited about Wystan's new book[2]. I wonder how
much he has altered the Oratorio – & when will it appear here?
Give him much love if you see him.

It was wonderful to hear of Chris being in the Medical Corps –
I do hope that he keeps clear of the worst. It is a relief that Michael
is still at home. We had a little contact with America when we saw
Marc Daniels, Meg Mundy's husband, here some time ago, &
now young John Mundy is here.[3] I shall see him tomorrow night.
We open in London again with "the Bartered Bride" & he is
coming & we shall dine with him after. Ben had also a note from
Lincoln who is here, but we haven't seen him yet. Bruce Boyce[4]

is here too, & came to the Wigmore Hall in April, when Ben & Clifford & I gave our Schubert concert, we doing the Müllerin for the first time!

I would very dearly love to visit you and William in your new home – new to you [us], if no longer to you. It sounds very lovely and characteristic. I am so very glad that things go well. We always have both your pictures on our mantelpiece so you are always with us. How I long to go on from where we stopped, Elizabeth dear. Perhaps we shall find that we have both been going on together all this while. D'you remember your little poem about the trees and their roots? My roots are stronger than they were, I fancy – so are Ben's too. He is a lovely mature person, no less vital but stronger and broader, & we have been very lucky in being often together, & above all in being able to go on with our work.

What have you been reading? Berdyaeff's "Slavery & Freedom"[5] is very good. I discovered George Eliot recently, & found her wonderfully good mostly, & so modern. Also [T.S.] Eliot's friend, for whom he wrote the Waste Land,[6] is a very remarkable poet, whom I only started on the other day – and Hölderlin! 'In the middle of life' is a perfect little poem.[7]

Dear Elizabeth, I must stop and go to rehearse. Much love to you, my dear, & to William, bless him. Don't worry about us. We will meet soon – & I will try to write again sooner –

Your loving friend

PETER

1 Settings of Donne were to be composed in 1945 (see note 2 to Letter 507) and Britten was to set words by George Herbert in his *Antiphon*, Op. 56b, for choir and organ, in 1956. His first published setting of the Mass – not the 'St Francis Mass' – was the *Missa Brevis*, Op. 63, composed in 1959.

2 *For the Time Being* (New York, Random House, 1944), published on 6 September. The first English edition (London, Faber and Faber) was published on 2 March 1945.

3 Meg and John Mundy, the children of John and Clytie Mundy. Meg was first soprano in the quintet of Elizabethan Singers, and the dedicatee of Britten's Folk-song Arrangement, 'O can ye sew cushions?' The Mundys were descended from the Elizabethan madrigal composer, John Mundy.

4 Canadian baritone (b. 1910), later a member of the English Opera Group. He sang Macheath in the 1950 Aldeburgh Festival production of *The Beggar's Opera*. Boyce, along with Pears, was a member of the

Elizabethan Singers, and had taken part as a guest artist in a concert of the Southold Town Choral Society on Long Island on 13 May 1941, conducted by Pears. See Letter 312.

5 Nicolas (Nikolai Alexandrovich) Berdyayev (1874–1948), Russian philosopher, whose *Slavery and Freedom* was widely discussed when it was first published in England in 1943.

6 Ezra Pound.

7 Britten was to set this text – 'Hälfte des Lebens' – in his *Sechs Hölderlin-Fragmente*, Op. 61, 1958.

474 To Marie Rambert[1]

The Old Mill, Snape, Suffolk.
Aug 23rd 1944

Dear Mde Rambert,

Thank you so much for your letter. I was glad to hear that the Telegraph account[2] was a mistake – but, of course, sorry that your Walter[3] had had such a terrible experience. But how incredibly stupid these journalists are – lucky one isn't as stupid at one's own job as they are! I do hope by now that a correction has been printed (I don't see the Telegraph), because I am tired of receiving abusing letters saying 'what a terrible thing to write – about D day!' You will insist on this? please!

I am longing to see the little ballet, tho, and I hope the poor boy will have strength and inclination to finish it before long. Is the season going well? I know how terribly trying these conditions are, & I think it very brave of you to carry on as you are.

With best wishes,
In haste,
Yours sincerely,
BENJAMIN BRITTEN

1 English dancer, teacher and ballet director, of Polish birth (1888–1982). Rambert was married to Ashley Dukes (1885–1959), English dramatist, theatre manager and critic, and opened her ballet school, first known as the Marie Rambert Dancers, in London in 1920. This became the Ballet Club in 1930 (performing at Dukes's Mercury Theatre), and the Ballet Rambert from 1935. She was one of the pioneers of modern British ballet and an indefatigable promoter of new choreographers. She was created DBE in 1962.

2 In the *Daily Telegraph*, 14 August, under the heading 'Theatre Notes', the paper's Theatre Correspondent had referred to the Rambert Ballet opening the next day at the Lyric, Hammersmith, adding that 'during the season an invasion day ballet, with music by Benjamin Britten, is promised'. Clearly it was this grotesque suggestion – perhaps malicious – which had caused Britten embarrassment. If a correction did appear in the paper, we have been unable to locate it.

3 Walter Gore (1910–1979), British dancer and choreographer. Gore danced in the first season of the Rambert Dancers, and was with the Ballet Rambert intermittently until 1949. He choreographed Britten's *Simple Symphony*, the first performance of which was to be given by the Ballet Rambert at the Theatre Royal, Bristol, on 19 November. This is the 'little ballet' to which Britten refers in his last paragraph.

475 To Mary Behrend
[*Postcard*]

The Old Mill, Snape, Suffolk.
August 26th 1944

My dear Mary,

I cannot attempt to thank you & Bow for your great kindness to both of us last week. You really were goodness itself. I only hope that you arn't too tired after all the extra hard work which our stay entailed. Anyhow, now that the two burdens will have departed, perhaps you will have a little time to rest! It was especially sweet of you to allow me to stay with Peter; as you know I was terribly worried about him, & it made all the difference that I could be with him in what was rather a trying attack.

I got through my day in London all right. The train up was not too crowded & on time, & I did most of the things I wanted to at the house. The opera went down well with the 'powers' at Sadlers Wells, & most arrangements are now complete for the production. I caught my train here easily, but the journey down was a nightmare – 1½ hours late. I felt that, lovely as it would have been, I had better not come back to Burghclere – I had burdened you enough as it was! Please thank Julie[1] for all her cooking, & her kindness in providing for Peter this week. And many, many thanks to both you & Bow for your sympathy, patience & infinite kindness.

With love,
BEN.

1 Julia ('Juley'), the Behrends' daughter (1915–1969).

476   To Mary Behrend
[*Postcard*]

Old Mill, Snape
[Postmarked 28 August 1944]

Thank you so much for sending on my sweet ration – I'm afraid I was very stupid, & also left a copy of Trollope's Doctor Thorne around too – could someone (perhaps Elwyn)[1] bring that up to town some day? – no hurry tho'. Peter got here for 24 hours last week, & seems much better except for abit of Bronchitis. But a pity he couldn't take off the time the Doctor said.

The opera goes on well, & I'm working very fast – it looks like a race between the war & it . . . to be over first, but I pray the former will win!

Much love to you all,
BEN

1 Elwyn Brook-Jones, the actor, who had married Julia Behrend in 1940.

477   To Revd Walter Hussey

Old Mill, Snape.
August 28th 1944.

My dear Walter,

Sorry for the long – silence. I'm just very busy, that's all!   Glad you like the idea of Semino coming – it won't cost you anything, because like Peter & me she's doing it for love!

Suggestion for programme:[1]

Arias:

Sound an alarm	Handel
Deeper & Deeper still –	
Waft her Angels	Handel
In Native Worth	Haydn
'Cello & Piano: Sonata	Chopin
Tenor, 'Cello & Piano:	
2 Solo Anthems	Maurice Greene (arr. BB)

Rejoice in the Lamb   ——   BB

Folk song arrangements   BB
'Cello Solos
Ten. 'Cello & Piano:
   My heart ever faithful   Bach
   Thanks be to God   Handel

                        ?   ?   ?

If you are in a hurry, and approve of that have the programmes
printed right away, & we can make announcements of details
ourselves (Solos & Folk-songs).
   Alas I cannot see how we can be there in the morning of the
21st. I am up to my eyes – so is Peter – & so is N.S. [Norina
Semino]. But give my love to Bishop Lang!² Could you find
somewhere for Norina to stay please – & can we stay with you?
   Please excuse scribble – but 24 hours per diem simply isn't
enough!

                                                      Yours ever,

                                                            BEN

1 The programme finally contained the following works:

Handel Arias:	'Sound an alarm' (*Judas Maccabaeus*) 'Deeper and Deeper Still' and 'Waft her Angels' (*Jephtha*)
Haydn	'In Native Worth' (*The Creation*)
Bach	Sonata for Cello and Piano [probably one of three sonatas for viola da gamba and harpsichord (BWV 1027–9)]
Maurice Greene	Two solo Anthems for Tenor: accompaniment arranged for cello and piano by Britten: 'Blessed are they that dwell in Thy House' 'O praise the Lord'
Britten	*Rejoice in the Lamb*
Schubert Songs:	'Thou are Sweet Peace' ('Du bist die Ruh' D. 776) 'Release' ('Auflösung' D. 807) 'The Almighty' ('Die Allmacht' D. 852) Cello Solos
Bach Arias:	'My heart ever faithful' ('Mein gläubiges Herze'), from Cantata 68, 'Also hat Gott die Welt geliebt'

'Thanks be to God' [commonly
attributed to Handel but, in fact, a pastiche by Siegfried Ochs (1858–1929)]

2 William Cosmo Gordon Lang, Baron Lang of Lambeth (1864–1945),
Archbishop of Canterbury, 1928–42.

478 To Ronald Duncan

Old Mill, Snape, Suffolk.
Sept. 13th 1944.

My dear Ronnie,

Thank you for the lovely Carol[1] – it is a beaut. But surely it's a
version of the one I set in the Ceremony of Carols (q.v.)? I hope
I can set it one of these days, when I get the other setting well into
the background – At the moment it's rather a pet of mine.

Please thank Rose Marie for her note & the cutting – which I was
tickled to see – when I'm low (as now) even such crazy accounts
as that give one abit of a kick – such is human nature (or mine).

Since reading Pound's A.B.C.[2] I've gone all Chaucerian. I have
a vague scheme of setting some of the shorter bits as he wrote
them (if one can find out how to pronouce them – can one?), unless
it would be too precious. But they're wonderful pieces. How goes
the Anti-Masque[3] – & (hopefully) plans for the Tales?[4]

By-the-way, can't anything be done about helping Pound[5] – he's
obviously a great man, & we haven't so many that we can go
around spilling their blood?

Love to you all. Grand about Roger's walking – how about his
sister's talking?

Hope you're Barley's all stooked??!!

Love
BENJI

1 Duncan had sent a carol (adapted from an early fifteenth-century
text), 'This song's to a girl', a version of 'As dewe in Aprille', which
Britten had already set in A Ceremony of Carols. Duncan replied: 'Have
looked at the Carol you set – obviously it's the same thing as one
I've "translated". No wonder we were both attracted to it! And
strangely too, months ago I toyed about with "Adam lay i
bounden"[. . .].'

2 Pound's ABC of Reading (London, Routledge & Kegan Paul, 1934),
re-issued by Faber and Faber in 1951, pp. 98–114.

3 The second part of Duncan's *This Way to the Tomb*, a Masque and Antimasque. See note 1 to Letter 511.

4 Britten and Duncan were planning an opera based on Chaucer's *Canterbury Tales*. Duncan was to write in his memoir, RDBB, p. 43:

> While Ben and I were working on *This Way to the Tomb* and *Peter Grimes* we were already busily hatching up another opera. He had said he wanted to write a comedy or two or three one-act comedies which might somehow be linked together. Eventually we settled on *The Canterbury Tales* and decided to select three, using the pilgrims as a link through an overture, two interludes and an epilogue. We drafted out a synopsis and later I started to write a libretto basing the first part on the *Nun's Tale*.

Neither the synopsis nor libretto draft has survived. See also RDBB, pp. 45, 56, 84, and 99–101, and Letters 490, 492 and 496.

5 For a full account of Pound's wartime broadcasts in Italy which led to his arrest on a charge of treason and eventual confinement in an American asylum – 'the statutory place of detention for all Federal prisoners regarded as insane' – see Humphrey Carpenter, *A Serious Character: The Life of Ezra Pound* (London, Faber and Faber, 1988), pp. 566–848.

479 To Mary Behrend

Old Mill, Snape, Suffolk
Sept. 18th 1944

My dear Mary,

Too stupid of me. My edition (& it's one of a rather precious set) is Bell & son, a sort of grey 'art-leather' – the York Edition. I saw it last on the round table in the hall – by the window. There is no hurry as long as I know it's there – Elwyn can bring it up sometime.

Please excuse scribble, but I'm off to-morrow for a day or two & hasten to send your copy back to you.[1]

It has been a great relief to know that Peter has been so comfortable at Spanish Place,[2] & it is sweet of Juley & Elwyn to put up with him. His throat still seems bad, tho', & I hope he can bully the C? into letting him have some time off soon.

The Opera is going well – & it is grand to know that a person with such fine instinctive taste as yourself believes in it, and me. It is worth all the pompous criticisms in the world! That you also believe in Michael, helps too – because I know him to be so frightfully good.

Much love to you all, and many, many thanks for everything,

Yours,

BEN

1 Trollope's novel. See Letter 476.

2 2 Spanish Place Mansions, London W1, was owned by John Behrend but became the home of Julia and Elwyn on their marriage.

480   To Peter Pears

[?October 1944]

Honey darling,

So sorry to miss you on the 'phone this morning. I rang at about 10.30 thinking that you were going to be there all the morning to rehearse with Norman.[1] But Mrs. N.[2] said you'd gone, so I didn't have the comfort of hearing your voice as I'd hoped – But I hope you'll be phoning one evening before too long. I'm writing this as I shan't be able to phone you, not knowing where you are.

I've phoned Ralph & written Joan saying that she will get her contract at once (she wrote me).[3] Also about orchestra – I hope there's not going to be any hitch in that direction. The scoring's going quite fast – done about ⅔ prologue in a day & a half.[4] Enid [&] Carol here to-night. Montagu tomorrow morning. Hope it'll be quiet for them – we had an exciting evening, but I must say it's more bearable when you can see things happening – quite a fine firework display! I've started the Evening Hymn[5] – what a piece that is! I've also fallen flat for Fairy Queen.[6] It's a marvel. But tell me, where can one find out the plot & dialogue? What's it all about – whence the Chinaman?[7] Sadlers Wells must do it before long. I'll fix rehearsals with the Zorians – preferably on Wed. aft. with me & Thursday morning at Northampton.[8] Couldn't you possibly get there the evening or night before – or if you're coming on a sleeper – get off at Peterboro' & avoid the double journey? Please phone about this.

Lots of love, my beloved one. Do rest & take it easy. Refuse all dates!

Your

B.

1 Norman Franklin, the accompanist.

2 Mrs Neilson, the housekeeper.

3 Presumably the contract between Boosey & Hawkes and Sadler's Wells for the first production of *Grimes*.

4 The scoring of *Peter Grimes* was completed on 10 February 1945.

5 'Now that the sun hath veiled his light', from Purcell's *Harmonia Sacra*, realized by Britten. It was published in 1947 as one of *Three Divine Hymns*, along with 'Lord what is man?' and 'We sing to him'.

6 Purcell's score for the five-act, anonymous adaptation of Shakespeare's *A Midsummer Night's Dream*, first performed in 1692. It was with a production of the work, conducted by Constant Lambert, that Covent Garden re-opened in 1946. With Imogen Holst, Britten was to make a concert edition (devised by Pears) of *The Fairy Queen* for performance at the 1967 Aldeburgh Festival, published by Faber Music in 1970. When in the school orchestra, at Gresham's in 1930, Britten recorded in his diary on 21 May, 'We are doing Selecs [Selections] Purcell's Fairy Queen music for the play, Merchant of Venice.'

7 'Dance for the Chinese Man and Woman: Chaconne', from Act V.

8 A CEMA concert given by Britten, Pears and the Zorian String Quartet, one of a series that took place in cathedrals and churches. It was broadcast from St Matthew's, Northampton, on 19 October, and comprised Orlando Gibbons: Three-part Fantasia No. 8 for strings; Dowland: Tenor Solos including 'Thou mighty God' (from *A Pilgrim's Solace*); Purcell: 'Evening Hymn' (realized Britten); Mozart: String Quartet in B flat (K. 458); Buxtehude: Two cantatas for tenor, two violins, cello and continuo: 'For God so loved the world' ('Also hat Gott die Welt geliebt') and Easter Cantata, 'O fröhliche Stunden'.

481 To Winifred Roberts

[*Typed*]

Old Mill, Snape,
Suffolk
Oct. 10th 1944

My dear Winnie,

Thank you for your sweet note. But it was quite the wrong way round – it was I who should have thanked you for all your hard work, & for giving a very moving show of my piece.[1] I think it went remarkably well, even if everything you may have set your heart on may not have come off exactly as you wished. But a first performance is always more exacting than the subsequent ones, & I'm sure the next ones will please even hyper-critical you!

People were most impressed with you, you know, & I hope an orchestral performance or performances will materialise as a result. I'll see what I can do from my end. In the meantime enjoy your concerts & practising & pave the way for a really big future I'm sure you've got ahead.

With love,
BEN

PS. I liked Arthur Oldham[2] alot – & I hope we shall be able to work together quite abit.

1 On 5 October Winifred Roberts (with the composer at the piano) had performed Britten's Violin Concerto at the Fyvie Hall, Upper Regent Street, London, under the auspices of the London Philharmonic Arts Club.

2 English composer (b. 1926), pianist and chorus-master. Oldham studied at the College with Herbert Howells and privately with Britten, one of his very few pupils, to whom he had been introduced by Winifred Roberts). He made the vocal scores of a number of Britten's works, including *Saint Nicolas* and the *Spring Symphony*. He was music director of the Ballet Rambert from 1946 to 1947 and adapted Arne's *Love in a Village* for performance at the 1952 Aldeburgh Festival. He was chorus-master of the Scottish Opera, 1966–74, and of the London Symphony Orchestra Chorus, 1969–74. As this letter suggests, he was to work as Britten's amanuensis. In 1945 he was to rehearse and direct the incidental music for *This Way to the Tomb*.

482 To Henry Willcock[1]

Old Mill, Snape, Suffolk.
Oct. 11th, 1944

My dear Henry,

Where <u>did</u> you get that extraordinary postcard? Unless you were Mass-observing pre-war seaside resorts. I rang up Ham. 2975 when I was in London for odd days last week but without success. Now I'm down here up to my eyes in overdue work, but I shall be around a bit at the end of month, & if we can fix anything I should love to see you again & congratulate you personally if you are by now a father – as I hope you are.

My life is hopelessly complex & involved in every possible direction – but I have got used to not being able to cope with it, & don't worry any more. But I do worry about my writing which deteriorates daily – sorry.

Yours ever,
BENJAMIN B

1 A school friend (1913–1976). He was a member of Britten's house, Farfield, 1923–32. The postcard (now in the Archive), of Britten and his sister, Beth, walking along the Lowestoft promenade, was found by Willcock in a street photographer's window. Willcock's daughter in a private communication explains that her father 'was at the helm (or at least shortly to be at the helm) of the social research organization Mass-Observation'. She recalls her grandmother apparently throwing away 'a stack of Britten's letters in a house move decades ago – much to my father's chagrin'. In 1972, Britten wrote to her, 'Please send my love to your father. I often think about him and how nice he was to me.'

483 To Peter Pears

[after 19 October 1944]

Honey my darling,

It was an oasis in a desert of loneliness to see you last week – yes I know one meets lots of people, & the house here couldn't be much fuller, but I only come alive when you're around, and things mean much more when we're together. However I've got so much to do (& so have you too, I know, you wicked old thing careering around like this) that I hope the next fortnight will fly like the wind, & we'll be together in Shropshire anyhow for a night, & then the week in Bristol won't be so far off.[1]

I had a valuable day in London – saw lots of people, worked with Montagu, Eric, Clifford (after his broadcast & dinner with him & Eddy, I went up to Highgate), Basil Wright about the film,[2] & altogether got lots of things "off". Now I'm here, working at pressure with Arthur Oldham (he is very quick, & a great help) before Erwin comes tomorrow to chase me.

Take care of yourself, my honey darling, rest & don't work too hard. Everyone (even Ursula) seems to have liked the broadcast, so forget that bloody man.[3] All my love, for ever & ever. Ring or write or something – please, soon.

Love, love. xxxx

BEN

1 Britten and Pears were in Shropshire on 2 November and in Bristol at the end of November (see note 6 to Letter 487).

2 *Instruments of the Orchestra* (1946): see note 7 to Letter 514.

3 Clearly a reference to adverse criticism of Pears's broadcast from Northampton on 19 October.

484   To Benjamin Britten
From Peter Pears

Newcastle
[October 1944]

My honey –

These two letters for you, & a lot of love from me.

Bless you! Staying at Durham Heavenly place. Superb place –
spent this morning on my knees in the Cathedral almost in tears.
Somehow I find beauty nowadays almost too much. It's like Rejoice
in the Lamb. That is still your best yet you know.

Much much love
P.
PTO.

Met Cyril Smith & Phyllis Sellick here.[1] Badly wanted copies of
Scottish Ballad to play in Portugal in December – Can't get any
satisfaction from Boosey & Hawkes – Couldn't you get 2 proof
copies to them?

Nice people!

Love
P.P.

1 Cyril Smith (1909–1974) and Phyllis Sellick (b. 1911), the English
  pianists who married in 1937, and who from 1941 gave frequent
  performances of music for two pianos. Smith suffered a thrombosis
  in 1956 which made him unable to use his left arm; however, a year
  later he and his wife began to appear together playing music for
  three hands, a genre they made very much their own. He published
  an autobiography, *Duet for Three Hands*, in 1958.

485   To Ursula Nettleship
[*Post Office postcard*]

Old Mill, Snape.
[Postmarked 31 October 1944]

Thank you for your card – so glad you approved of the concert – I
thought it a good one too, & the Buxtehudes straight from heaven.
The Purcell Hymn will eventually be published along with the other
ones I've mauled about – but I don't know yet exactly when. I

hope you're well – all more or less well but poor Snape is rubbing itself having been war-wounded for the first time 2 nights ago.[1]

Love,

BEN

1 A flying-bomb had fallen on a farm in Priory Lane. See EWB, p. 182. The composer James Butt, who during this period also acted as a musical assistant to Britten in return for composition lessons, later recalled that

another 'doodle-bug' missed the tower of the Mill by four feet at approximately 1 am in the morning, and villagers told me that if it had been only four feet lower Benjamin Britten, Beth Welford, Beth's children Sally and Sebastian and I would all have been blown to smithereens.

('Lord Britten: Some Recollections', *East Anglian Daily Times*, 5 December 1978)

Among Mr Butt's other memories is the occasion of his first visit to Snape:

I remember helping to score 'The Ballad of Lady Barnard and Little Musgrave' which Ben had written for a POW camp in Germany, transposing songs for Sir Peter Pears for a Radio Eireann broadcast, checking the proofs of *Les Illuminations*, and in return was given some tuition in the craft of composition [. . .] concentrating on variation form.

He also recalled an occasion when Britten played some Beethoven:

I told him that I'd been learning the notes of the five Beethoven piano concertos. 'Ah, yes,' he said, 'You know, I think this has always been rather a lovely sound,' and sat down to play the last 22 bars of the first movement of the 'Emperor', most gracefully and without effort.

486 To Peter Pears

Old Mill, Snape.
[after 28 October and before 2 November 1944]

My heart –

before I go further – please sit down at once and write me a card to Yarner Farm, Dartington, Nr. Totnes,[1] saying when & where we are performing at Shrewsbury on Thursday – & also one to Esther too. Please, my dear, otherwise I'll have palpitations not knowing where or what to do.

Now – how are you? Not too dreadfully tired, I pray, & able to get abit of rest occasionally. How was Hiawatha?[2] How did 'he'd

seen he said a . . . .' whatever it was, go? (a good sentence that).
I suppose you didn't get to Lucille. Maybe you'll go later.

Things are so-so here – Snape is rather licking its wounds after
it's 'incident', which has complicated people's lives abit. We've
had the house full of Sievekings'[3] little relations – their house being
uninhabitable. Poor Arthur Oldham's nice old lady (who'd fed
him up with eggs & butter etc.) has all her windows in, and her
ceilings down, & so he can't go <u>there</u> any more. Poor Beth, who
has been worked terribly hard, helping people to clear up too, &
has had Erwin here as well, is putting him up here. But I think
it's probably a good thing I am away next week to give her some
rest, & a chance for Jemima-James[4] to develop nicely. The kids of
course are having a whale of a time, but my work has suffered abit
– especially as Lennox's stuff had to go off in the middle of it all.
I've sent off an armchair to 45a as well, which we can spare from
here.

Aunt Effie died on Wednesday – poor old thing, it was abit of a
miserable end for her, but Barbara's been sweet, and comforting.
It's a moral for one – a life entirely selfish ending up with only an
unwilling family to care.

I had a tough evening yesterday – Arthur came by the 8.9 – no
taxis could meet, & so I took out the Morris & the battery (again)
conked, & I had to cycle in – wait for 40 mins on the station & walk
out with him, arriving 10 pm! I slept like a log all night as a result.

Sophie's at it again – another long letter – including a nice lot of
copies of press cuttings, showing how good she & I are together –
the woman's a moron. How can a person be so daft? I must say
my tolerance is wearing abit thin. My darling – only till Thursday
now – it's getting near, isn't it.

All my love. I'm writing a nice back-ground for you to sing
against.[5] Be careful.

Your B.

1 Britten was staying with Cicely Martin, whose husband had died in
August. On 2 November Pears and Britten gave a recital at Shrewsbury Technical College: Dowland: 'Awake sweet love', 'In darkness
let me dwell', 'Now, o now, we needs must part'; Purcell: 'Not all
my torments', 'There's not a swain', 'I'll sail upon the dog-star'
(realized Britten); Schubert: 'On the bridge' ('Auf der Bruck' D.853), 'To
Music' ('An die Musik' D.547), 'In Springtime' ('Im Frühling' D.882),
'The Trout' ('Die Forelle' D.550), 'The Almighty' ('Die Allmacht'
D.852) Britten: *Seven Sonnets of Michelangelo*, Op. 22; Folk-song

Arrangements: 'The Salley Gardens', 'The Bonny Earl o' Moray', 'Little Sir William', 'The King is gone a-hunting', and 'Heigh-ho! Heigh-hi!'.

2 Pears had taken part in a performance of Coleridge-Taylor's *Hiawatha* in Liverpool on 28 October, with Joan Hammond, Tom Williams and the Welsh Choral Union conducted by Malcolm Sargent.

3 Lancelot de Giberne Sieveking (Lance Sieveking, 1896–1972), producer for BBC Radio and Television, who lived at the White House, Priory Lane, Snape.

4 Beth was expecting her third child, Elizabeth Ellen Rosemary ('Roguey') who was born on 21 April 1945. For Beth's memories of this period see EWB, pp. 182–3.

5 Britten was scoring *Peter Grimes*.

487 To Peter Pears

Old Mill
Nov. 8th 1944

My honey darling,

I hope you got the parcel. I sent it off on Monday – or rather I got the Neilson to do it, after having coped with Val Drewry.[1] I got back here on Tuesday, & on your advice, there's no one here this week, & I'm getting ahead with the Te Deum[2] & Motet.[3] The former is going well, nothing very important, but slightly honey.

I hope things aren't going too badly with you – that you are able to cope with everything in your old inimitable way. I think of you every moment, & hate not to know what's happening exactly to you. Is there a chance of you being able to get to London next week? It looks as if I shall be there from Wed. to Sat. (15–18) – since Charles Munch[4] of Paris Orch. is over here and doing the Variations all over the place, & the only place I can catch it is at Wembley on Friday.[5] But don't tire yourself, honeyest, because we'll be together in Bristol for quite abit.[6]

I had a nice week-end at Lancing;[7] had a long go at Jasper[8] re Charles, & Charles re Jasper. The boy is really a nice thing, & has an astounding really genuine musical mind. But whether he'll be a composer, the Lord knows.

I went to see Emmie Bass about the Dartington Festival,[9] & she is writing to Joan re dates & things. As far as I can see, & she agreed, you & Joan are the only snags – all the rest can do it. So if you <u>can</u> work it – for Christopher's sake[10] – or even one week of it – do please try. I'm writing to her direct about it.

I had a long 'go' with Eric on the opera – as far as I can see, you were quite wrong in your hunch – it was only Joan's nerves – because things are advancing rapidly from Eric's end – <u>if</u> only they can find a theatre. Eric is standing out against Princes[11] for it – v. rightly too.

Excuse scribble, my darling – but I only wanted to send my love, & wish you luck with the 'Child'.[12] Give Michael my love, & say how much I wish I was there for it. Sing nicely, as ever – & write or ring if you can possibly. I don't see why everyone else should hear your voice, & me never –

Wystan has sent his book; the Tempest is <u>very difficult</u>, but got lovely bits. The Oratorio is as lovely and grand as ever.[13]

All my love how I wish I were with you

B.

1 A friend of Berkeley's and the dedicatee of his Six Preludes, Op. 23, for piano, composed in 1944.

2 The *Festival Te Deum*, Op. 32, for chorus and organ, composed 8–9 November for the Centenary Festival of St Mark's, Swindon. It was first performed there on 24 April 1945.

3 Britten refers to one of his two settings of Auden made at this time, probably the 'Chorale (after an old French carol)'. See also note 2 to Letter 489.

4 Charles Münch (1891–1968), French conductor and violinist. From 1938 to 1946, he was conductor of the Société des Concerts du Conservatoire de Paris and conductor of the Boston Symphony Orchestra in succession to Koussevitzky, 1949–62.

5 On 17 November.

6 Pears was to be in Bristol, from 28 November, singing in *Così*, to 1 December, when he and Britten gave a recital. Britten apparently joined him on 29 November, possibly in time to attend the première of the ballet based on the *Simple Symphony*.

7 At the school's wartime location in Shropshire.

8 Jasper Rooper (1898–1981), English composer and Director of Music at Lancing (1926–49), who had been a pupil of Vaughan Williams. His pupil was Charles Dakin. Rooper formed Lancing's 'Concert Club' in 1945, which opened with a recital by Pears and Britten. See Basil Handford, *Lancing College: History and Memoirs* (Chichester, Phillimore, 1986).

9 A letter from Peter Cox to Leonard Elmhirst, written on 12 October, explains the idea of the Festival:

We are just trying to arrange a really exciting music festival under Ben's direction. It is to be a teaching festival and to cover Imo's work for the year. We are hoping to have the Grillers, Clifford Curzon, Joan Cross, Peter Pears and Ben – and if we can possibly manage it about 100 students, who will have to sleep in barns & goodness knows where. The plans are very much in the melting pot, but they are certainly promising.

10 The proposed Festival did not take place in 1945, but there was arranged in its place a weekend of music, 14–15 July, which also served as a memorial to Christopher Martin. The Saturday concert included Tippett's *Boyhood's End* (with Pears and Britten), and on Sunday excerpts from *Grimes* were performed by Cross, Pears and Britten.

A leaflet describing the event is of some interest because of its reference to the 'Berkshire Festivals' (associated with Koussevitzky and his Boston orchestra) with which Britten would have been familiar while living in the States:

Just before he died, Christopher Martin, the Administrator of the Arts Department, planned with Benjamin Britten to run an Annual Music Festival at Dartington on the lines of the Berkshire Festivals in the United States. A group of eminent soloists under the direction of Benjamin Britten, and, later, a String Orchestra, was to come to Dartington for three weeks or a month during the summer, not only to give public performances but to teach; the students were to be young professionals drawn from all over the country.

Owing to prevailing circumstances it has been necessary to postpone our first Festival until 1946, but the principal artists who were coming this year, suggested that we should arrange in its place a Week-End of Music to be held in memory of Christopher Martin.

11 Prince's Theatre, Shaftesbury Avenue, London. See also Eric Crozier, ' "Peter Grimes": an Unpublished Article of 1946', *Opera*, 16/6, June 1965, p. 414, who had written to Joan Cross on 21 October:

Tony [Guthrie] told me this morning that the Govs. had decided it was most unlikely S.W. could be opened next Spring, and were in favour of extending the Princes' lease until July, which would, of course, mean our doing 'Grimes' there. This really does depress me, the more I think of it. [. . .] My feeling is that, much as I hate the let-down of postponements, it has to be decided whether it is better to stage 'Grimes' inadequately and under conditions of great strain and difficulty, (the production itself will be strain enough on all departments, God knows), or whether to postpone until the autumn by which time S.W. might be ready? Or alternatively, try for the King's Theatre, Hammersmith, and stage 'Grimes' there?

I am not trying to make difficulties about this, or to look for them – but I do feel strongly that circumstances are gradually manoeuvring us into a position that in six months' time will seem impractical and foolhardy. Maybe I am just jittering – but I shall be very glad to know what your opinion is.

12 Tippett's oratorio, *A Child of Our Time*. The performance took place in Liverpool on 11 November, with Joan Cross and Pears among the soloists, and the Liverpool Philharmonic Orchestra conducted by Malcolm Sargent.

13 *For the Time Being*. This volume also included 'The Sea and the Mirror': 'A Commentary on Shakespeare's The Tempest'.

488 To Benjamin Britten
From Peter Pears

Theatre Royal
Glasgow.
[8/9 November 1944]

My own B –

It was completely heavenly seeing you & working with you. Work with you is totally different in kind from any other sort. It becomes related to life immediately, which is more than any of the other stuff I do, does (including "Così"). And being with you was being alive instead of half dead. Thank you so much, honey. Now have I got to wait until Bristol? I wonder if I can slip back for the 15th. Don't rely on it, but among other things, we ought to do some work at the Debussy for Dec. 10th[1]. I have written to Felix[2] retracting the Lutenists. I don't really think they fit in, & besides we must concentrate on Debussy & Folk Songs.

Much much love
Take care of yourself.

P.

The enclosed may please you.[3]

1 A 'Concert de musique française' at the Wigmore Hall, London, in which Pears and Britten performed Debussy's *Trois poèmes de Stéphane Mallarmé* and *Trois ballades de François Villon*, and four of Britten's French Folk-song Arrangements. The programme also included Debussy's and Ravel's String Quartets played by the Zorian Quartet.

2 Felix Aprahamian?

3 The enclosure has not survived.

489 To Peter Pears

[Old Mill, Snape]
[11 November 1944]

Honey darling – it was heaven hearing you last night after all this long time – much too long. I ache for you.

I am just this moment off to town – to make this ruddy speech which is giving me the creeps![1] However – no one really expects me to be able to speak so I suppose it doesn't really matter! I wonder what you'll think of the Te Deum, the Eddy bits – I've done 2 as they were so tiny. The last will, I believe, make you smile.[2]

So glad about everything. Sing better & better – & my God there'll be a part for you in the Oratorio! It's a superb piece.

The enclosed letter came this morning[3] – can you find time to scribble a note to her.

All my love – my darling

B.

1 See Letter 491.

2 'O lift your little pinkie', the second of the two Auden settings mentioned in note 3 to Letter 487. Edward Sackville-West ('Eddy') was the producer of the BBC feature for which these items were composed (see note 2 to Letter 397).

3 This has not survived.

490 To Ronald Duncan

[Postcard]

Old Mill, Snape.
[14 November 1944]

So sorry about the long silence – but life's damned hectic at the moment. I'm glad you've done the Anti Masque; I'm longing to see it. Also most excited about the Chaucer – which Tales have you thought of?? I hope it's still all right for Peter & me to come to you the last two weeks of Jan. We've set our hearts on it, and would cry if it weren't O.K. How's your sister?[1] Give everyone my love. (I'm in London Dec. 8th – 15th. Any good??)

Love

BENJI

1 Duncan's sister was in the Royal Cancer Hospital, Fulham Road, London, SW3, convalescing after a major operation.

491 To Peter Pears

Old Mill, Snape, Suffolk.
Nov 20th 1944

Honey darling,

Such ages since I heard from you or of you. Where are you; hows everything going; and above all, <u>are</u> you going to be able to get to London next Friday, as I am planning to be there too, & longing, longing for it?

Lots has happened since we spoke – I've been in London, had a mad rushed time, did 200 things in 3 days, got back here mid-day Saturday, with Eddy – had a nice week-end, & now I'm back at the score again.[1] As I told you I got the Te Deum and 2 Motets done, & they're now in the hands of printers & copyists etc.

My speech went quite well[2] – I spoke about 10 minutes, without notes, about necessary of travel for young artists – not as well as I'd hoped, but better than I feared. What I found was that I could think when I was standing on my hind-legs which I'd always doubted. It was a pretty putrid show otherwise – the bright spot being of all people Stephen Spender, who was surprisingly nice & sympathetic.

I stayed those 3 days with Barbara – killing 2 birds – giving the Steins room,[3] and letting them get their furniture in place (it looks very nice now), & also being with poor old Barbara who's not at all well – running a permanent temperature, & D & V.[4] Nerves alone I think.

Then there was a dinner given by the French Ambassador for Charles Munch which I had to go to – very posh, (he sent <u>his car</u> for me as I had to be late!! – I'd forgotten what it felt like to glide through the London streets in a thing that size!) Rather dull people there, but Mlle Nicole Herriot[5] was nice, & he's a real charmer – <u>and</u> a damn good conductor, as I found the next night at Wembley. The L.P.O.[6] isn't so hot an orch., but he made them play wonderfully, & had a very good idea of the piece. I believe the piece was wonderful when played by the BBC under him[7] – did you hear it? It seems to have made quite a sensation around the place – & I must say I thought bits of it had worn well. I've been asked to conduct the L.P.O in the Sinfonia on Jan 6th[8] – on the strength of this, I think. Russell[9] was all over me.

I also saw Clifford, Peter Cox[10] & had a long meeting with Eric. I gather things are moving towards Covent Garden abit[11] – but the betting's on P.G. at Sadler Wells, I think now. The reproduced vocal score is _lovely_! Most beautifully written & reproduced.[12]

Kit was here too for the week-end – & most surprisingly Eddy clicked well with him & Beth – & we had a pleasant weekend altogether. He has got nice things about him – & with me is very simple & intelligent. We _walked_ over to Iken Rectory – burgled the house, & inspected it thoroughly – & it has such _immense_ possibilities that I've found out the agent & written to him. It is the most divine spot, & the house isn't half bad.[13] So there – my honey – see what love can do.

Please excuse hurry, but I've got to get on with score. Michael's sick that you can't do Dec. 24th with Liverpool Phil. when he conducts the Child. I s'pose you can't get out of the Messiah?

I can scarcely wait till Friday.[14] I'm seeing about hotel for Bristol – possibly Wed. Thursday – & trains.[15]

All my love.
love you, darling.
BEN

1 Of _Peter Grimes_.

2 We have been unable to identify the occasion.

3 See note 7 to Letter 418.

4 Diarrhoea and vomiting.

5 Probably the daughter of Edouard Herriot, the French politician, who was interned in Germany for part of the war.

6 London Philharmonic Orchestra.

7 Münch had conducted a performance of the _Frank Bridge Variations_, with the BBC Symphony Orchestra, on 15 November. A copy of the first American edition of _Sinfonia da Requiem_, presented to Münch by the composer with the inscription 'A mon cher ami et le grand maître,/Charles Münch – with happiest memories./aufwiedersehen!/ Benjamin Britten', is in the Archive. It has apparently been used by Britten as a conducting score at some time; the date of its presentation to Münch is unknown.

8 At this sponsored 'Saturday Book' Concert at the Royal Albert Hall, London, Britten and Poulenc were to be soloists in the latter's Concerto in D minor for two pianos and orchestra, with the London Philharmonic Orchestra conducted by Basil Cameron. Britten con-

ducted his *Sinfonia da Requiem*, while the remainder of the programme, Mendelssohn's *Ruy Blas* Overture and Tchaikovsky's Fifth Symphony, was conducted by Cameron.

9 Thomas Russell (1902–1984), first a member (viola) of the London Philharmonic Orchestra, then its Secretary, when the orchestra became independent and a co-operative (1939), and finally Managing Director in 1945. He founded and edited the bi-monthly journal, *Philharmonic Post*. He was dismissed in 1952, to headlines in the *Daily Telegraph* of 1 December 1952, Orchestra's Communist Chief Goes / 4 Resign after L.P.O. dismissal / "Witch Hunt Victim" Claim'. Russell's remarkable personality and career are documented in Jerrold Northrop Moore, *Philharmonic Jubilee 1932–1982* (London, Hutchinson, 1982). See also Russell, *Philharmonic Decade* (London, Hutchinson, 1944), with an introduction by J.B. Priestley, Merion and Susie Harries, *A Pilgrim Soul: The Life and Work of Elisabeth Lutyens* (London, Michael Joseph, 1989), and Kennedy's *Boult*, pp. 323–6.

10 Peter Cox had been Christopher Martin's assistant at Dartington. He took over as Administrator of the Arts Department after Martin's death.

11 Nothing came of this option. The Royal Opera House, Covent Garden, in any event, was not to reopen until January 1947. Britten's publishers, Boosey & Hawkes, had an interest in the theatre, which was undoubtedly the reason for the floating of the idea at this time. In an interview with John Higgins in *The Times*, 1 June 1985, 'Giving Birth to Peter Grimes', Joan Cross remembered that:

> It was Guthrie who was to stage the first Covent Garden *Grimes* two years later in 1947, a production which also made its way to Brussels and the Paris Opéra. The Royal Opera House, very much a rival to Sadler's Wells in the reopening stakes, had also wanted *Grimes*, but Britten chose the smaller theatre for the première because he thought the work would have greater impact in an intimate house.

12 Materials prepared for the rehearsal and first performance of the opera. The engraved vocal score was to be published in 1945.

13 The first indication that Britten might move from the Old Mill at Snape, but he was unable to bring the negotiations for the purchase of the Rectory to a successful conclusion. In 1947 he was to move to 4 Crabbe Street, Aldeburgh.

14 24 November, when Britten and Pears were next to meet each other in London.

15 See note 6 to Letter 487.

492 **To Ronald Duncan**
[*Post Office lettercard*]

Old Mill, Snape.
Nov. 23rd 1944

My dear Ronnie – apologies as usual, & many many thanks for
letting me have the Tomb complete. I've not read it thoroughly yet,
but the Anti looks up to the Masque which is remarkable. But won't
Father Divine of U.S.A. (with his millions of militant negroes) be
after you?[1] Martin Browne[2] is a curse – I <u>must</u> leave on Dec. 15th
– & can't very well be back until after Xmas – so it'll just have to
wait until then. But it doesn't make all that difference as I shall still
be hacking away at the opera until at least then. It's exciting about
the Chaucer – I haven't yet finished re-reading the Millers Tale –
but I think it has the makings of being fine, for, I think, the 3rd
one, don't you? I think we want a Tragedy, Love one, & Comedy.
I'm slowly ploughing thro' them – but get no time for reading
these days.

Love to you all – & longing to see you again –

BEN.

1 Father Major J. Divine (b. ?, d. 1965) was one of the most eccentric
   and controversial religious leaders that America has produced. He
   was a black man, born George Baker, who became the leader of a
   communal group in Brooklyn which became known as the Universal
   Peace Mission Movement. His followers believed that he fulfilled
   both the Second Coming of Christ and the Messianic expectation of
   Judaism. The heyday of the movement was in the 1930s when Father
   Divine staged elaborate feasts for his followers in the black ghetto
   during the Depression.
2 Elliott Martin Browne (1900–1980), who was to produce Duncan's
   This Way to the Tomb on 11 October 1945. Browne was closely associated with the revival of religious poetic drama. He had produced
   Eliot's *Murder in the Cathedral* in 1935 and was to produce all Eliot's
   subsequent plays.

493 **To Mary Behrend**
[*Post Office lettercard*]

Snape
[23 November 1944]

So sorry – I'm afraid 2–4th is no good – I'm in Liverpool then.[1] But
I'm hoping that I can fit some time in the following fortnight. Can

I let you know when things get sorted out abit? Poor Henry must
be getting fed up with me,[2] but life's too dreary at the moment,
& difficult to cope with! I'm off on my travels tomorrow again –
but the opera's progressing nevertheless.

Much love to you & Bow
BEN

1 Britten was attending a performance of *Les Illuminations*, sung by
 Pears, with the Liverpool Philharmonic Orchestra conducted by
 Malcolm Sargent.

2 Britten was sitting for the portrait by Henry Lamb (see PFL, plate
 234), which was finished in 1945. He was to write again to Mrs
 Behrend on 7 January,

> I am terribly sorry that I haven't been able to get down to you for him to
> finish the masterpiece – but, as I know you realise, things are dreadfully
> difficult at the moment. When the opera score gets completed I'll have
> time to think & I hope to manage it then.

> See also Keith Clements, *Henry Lamb: The artist and his friends*
> (Bristol, Redcliffe Press, 1985), which mistakenly attributes the por-
> trait to 1947. Clements's biography includes information about the
> Behrends and their patronage of Lamb.

494 To Revd Walter Hussey

[*Post Office lettercard*]

45a, St. John's Wood High St.,
N.W.8.
Dec. 8th, 1944

Dear Walter,

Thank you for your sweet note – I was glad to get your birthday
wishes. I still feel that it's best to do with out the CEMA aid for
the Sutherland[1] – Peter & I'll come back & help you raise money
from time to time! I have mentioned the matter to Lennox Berkeley
who would some time like a letter from you, if you feel you'd like
something from him.[2]

I have just done a Te Deum for Swindon, which I think may
interest you! By-the-way, do you say <u>Sabaoth</u>?   – I
hope you do!

I am going to read the letters of E. Underhill[3] – she was obviously
a great woman, but surely C. Williams[4] is wrong – the early
Christian Church <u>was</u> pacifist, until Constantine(?) made it the
official religion, & it became political??? Please excuse this scribble

– but I'm wildly busy, still I'm going to get time to bring Boyd Neel (for Decca) to you to hear the choir sing R. in the L.[5]

With love,

BEN.

1 Graham Sutherland (1903–1980) had been commissioned by Hussey to provide a painting for St Matthew's, Northampton. His *Crucifixion*, about which Hussey writes in *Patron of Art* (London, Weidenfeld and Nicolson, 1985), p.50 – 'Britten and Pears came and gave a recital in the church entirely free and asked that all the proceeds should be put in the box [. . .] "for the commissioning of works of art for the church" ' – was unveiled on 16 November 1946.

2 Berkeley's *Festival Anthem*, a setting of George Herbert's 'The Flower', was first performed at St Matthew's on 21 September 1945. See Hussey, op. cit., pp. 94–6.

3 Evelyn Underhill (Mrs Stuart Moore: 1875–1941), English religious writer.

4 Charles Williams (1886–1945), who edited *The Letters of Evelyn Underhill*, published in 1943. He was a novelist, poet, dramatist, literary critic and theologian.

5 *Rejoice in the Lamb*: Boyd Neel acted in an advisory capacity to the Decca Record Company. However, Decca did not record the cantata at this time.

495 To Mary Behrend

45a St. Johns Wood High St, N.W.8.

Feb. 10th 1945

My dear Mary,

I ought to have written ages ago – but it's this wretched opera which has taken every one of my not-compulsory-active-moments! I am terribly touched that you'd like a quartet of me, & honoured too.[1] As you know, I value your criticism & appreciation very highly, and you couldn't give me a higher testimonial than this. I have had a quartet at the back of my mind for sometime, & your sweet offer will do alot towards bringing it to life. Just <u>when</u> that can be it's difficult at the moment to say. I have actually just this moment written 'End' to the opera score.[2] I have a small film to write for the Board of Education,[3] and some incidental music to Ronald Duncan's masque. I want badly to complete a sonata for orchestra (already started), & there is a big Xmas show to be

written & arranged for the Wells, fairly soon.[4] Then I have the
opera arrangements (coaching & rehearsals), my concerts with
Peter including a Paris visit. This all sounds formidable I know, but
by the autumn, especially with this sweet incentive from you I ought
to be ready to start it. I shall hate to discuss a fee with you, & I
wonder how we can arrive at such a thing. But it'll have to be by
word of mouth, because it'll be necessary to find exactly <u>what</u> you
will want in the way of rights & things. But let's wait until we meet,
which I am sorry won't be next week. Of course it <u>was</u> very short
notice, but my Oxford concert was cancelled & I had two free
days! Actually now, I think I'd better go to Manchester & rehearse
with Peter & see about the opera. Thank you for your invitation
which I should have loved to have accepted, but I couldn't just sit
still at this moment, blissful as it would have been. When we
come back from France (end of March) I hope we can arrange
something.

Thank you again for your lovely idea –
& with much love to you both,
BEN.

1 The result of this commission was to be Britten's String Quartet
   No. 2 in C, dedicated to Mary Behrend. See also Letter 513.
2 The date of this letter, 10 February, in fact appears at the end of the
   manuscript full score of *Peter Grimes*.
3 *Instruments of the Orchestra*.
4 See note 3 to Letter 500.

496 To Ronald Duncan

as from: 45a, St. John's Wood High St., N.W.8.
Feb. 24th 1945.

My dear Ronnie,

This written in enormous haste & in Joan Cross's dressing room
in the Opera House![1] (I am in the middle of opera and all its
consequences now.) The trouble is that Peter & I have now got to
leave for Paris on 5th[2] & so it looks as if we shall miss you – blast
it. Anyhow the Serenade at the Albert Hall was to be postponed
as the Horn player is not yet back from the States. So if you
cannot be in London later (I shall be there for a bit at the end of
the month) I shall have to see Martin Browne alone – shan't I?

I'm terribly sorry about it, but it is unavoidable – the passages across are so few & far between & we've got to fit in with them as much as possible. But I hope it won't be so long before we meet. I've talked to Eric Crozier[3] about the Chaucer – & he wants to discuss several points with you – & good ones, too. He's very intelligent & clear-sighted. That too'll have to wait. We are having a terrific time with Grimes – & Peter & I are pretty well re-writing his part. Montagu agreed to the new mad-scene, & I kept your part in it fairly quiet, altho' I murmured that you helped us abit![4] Actually your work in that omens well for our future work together, I think.

I hope all your troubles with the cold spell & its consequences are over now – what a time you had with all the furniture swimming around! Sounds like the Sorcerer's apprentice. Please give my love to Rose Marie & the children – hope Roger's behaving himself, & that the Pin-up Girl's as pictorial as ever.

Peter sends his love, & would write only the poor child's worked off his feet & through his vocal cords – 6 concerts in a row before the Paris trip.

Terribly sorry, Ronnie about 6th – but we must coincide before long.

Are you well – & no more nervous troubles – seriously?

Much love,
BEN

I <u>must</u> find an envelope big enough for <u>St. Anthony</u>.[5]

1 Between 12 February and 1 March Pears was singing with Sadler's Wells Opera at the Manchester Opera House in *Così* (12, 16 and 24 February), *Barber of Seville* (23 February), *Rigoletto* (26 February) and *Bartered Bride* (27 February and 1 March).

2 While in Paris (France had been liberated by the Allies in August 1944), Britten and Pears gave three concerts under the auspices of the British Council. On 8 March they broadcast from the Théâtre des Champs-Elysées (for Radiodiffusion France) a programme that comprised Haydn's Symphony No. 92 (Orchestre National, conducted by Manuel Rosenthal) and Britten's *Les Illuminations, Soirées Musicales* and *Matinées Musicales* (conducted by the composer). On the 10th and 11th Britten and Charles Münch conducted the orchestra of the Société des Concerts du Conservatoire de Paris at the same theatre, when the programme included Weber's *Oberon* overture, Schubert's 'Unfinished', Mendelssohn's *Midsummer Night's Dream* Scherzo, Britten's *Serenade* (Pears and Lucien Thevet) and *Sinfonia da Requiem* (presumably conducted by the composer), and Bliss's *Le*

Phénix, 'Hommage à la France'. This was Bliss's march for orchestra, *The Phoenix*, composed in 1944. Finally, Britten and Pears gave a British Council recital at the Salle de l'ancienne conservatoire on 13 March, performing 'Have you seen but a whyte lilie grow?'; Dowland's 'Come again, sweet love doth now invite' and 'Come, heavy sleep'; four Purcell/Britten realizations: 'I'll sail upon the Dog-star', 'Turn, turn thine eyes', 'There's not a swain', 'On the brow of Richmond Hill'; and 'The Queen's Epicedium'; and Britten's *Michelangelo Sonnets* and French Folk-song Arrangements ('La belle est au jardin d'amour', 'Eho! Eho!', 'Le Roi s'en va t'en chasse', and 'Quand j'étais chez mon père').

3 Eric Crozier (b. 1914), English producer and librettist. Crozier had been play producer in the first years of BBC Television (1936–9) and in 1944 was producing operas for Sadler's Wells, notably Smetana's *Bartered Bride* with Pears as Vašek. His work with the company culminated in the première of *Peter Grimes* in 1945.

He went on to produce *The Rape of Lucretia* at Glyndebourne the following year, and subsequently collaborated with Britten as librettist of *Albert Herring* (1947), *Saint Nicolas* (1948), *Let's Make an Opera* (1949) and (with E.M. Forster) *Billy Budd* (1951).

Crozier was a co-founder of the English Opera Group in 1947 and of the Aldeburgh Festival in 1948. He also wrote the commentary for the published score of *The Young Person's Guide to the Orchestra*, Op. 34.

In 1949 he married the English mezzo-soprano, Nancy Evans (b. 1915), who shared the role of Lucretia with Kathleen Ferrier in the first performance of the opera. She created the role of Nancy in *Albert Herring*, and in 1947 Britten wrote *A Charm of Lullabies*, Op. 41, for her. Crozier contributed a memoir of his collaborations, 'Staging First Productions: I', to *The Operas of Benjamin Britten*, edited by David Herbert (London, Hamish Hamilton, 1979), pp. 24–33. See also 'An Albert Herring Anthology', compiled by Eric Crozier, Donald Mitchell, Philip Reed and Rosamund Strode, in the Glyndebourne Festival Programme Book 1985, pp. 113–23. For at least a decade, from the early forties until the early fifties, Crozier was an active, productive and influential figure among Britten's creative partners.

His misgivings about the Chaucer project related to the bawdiness of the text, which he felt worked against the possibility of 'The Miller's Tale' in the theatre – 'and I told Ben and Duncan it could not be done'.

It was Eric Crozier who chose Leonard Thompson to be the first boy apprentice in *Grimes*. Leonard's local priest, Paul Gedge (shades of *Herring*!), was a friend of Crozier's who had an interest in organizing children's theatre. It was from this group that Crozier sought 'the first John'. Leonard Thompson, in a letter to Pears (30 July 1979), recalls

meeting Eric in the vicarage garden, knowing nothing at all about music and little more about acting, and somehow or other being chosen to play John. [. . .] It was, of course, a most important day in my life, but there was certainly no sense of occasion on my part. I can remember thinking how courteous Eric was [. . .] And so to Wolverhampton [where the Sadler's Wells Company was on tour] where I first met you and Ben. [. . .] the first opera I ever heard was the *Bartered Bride,* in which you sang Vašek. It was one of Ben's many kindnesses to walk with me around the town, telling me the story of the opera we were to hear. You above all will know of Ben's deep knowledge of (it certainly seemed to me) *all* forms of music and it gave me a foundation for a love of opera which has persisted to this day. [. . .] Every evening, usually after tea, Ben and I would walk around and I learned about the lives of the composers concerned and the highlights to watch for. It certainly was a unique series of lessons from a unique man.

4 Duncan had assisted Britten in revising the so-called 'Mad Scene' in Act III scene 2 of *Grimes.* The revisions were made at West Mill, Duncan's home in North Devon. The 'cold spell' to which Britten refers (and which included a heavy fall of snow) had kept him at work indoors with Duncan. See PBPG, pp. 81–6, and RDBB, pp. 37–9.

5 Britten refers to the Masque from *This Way to the Tomb,* of which St Antony is protagonist.

497   To Sylvia Spencer
[*Postcard*]

45A St. Johns Wood High St.,
N.W.8.
[?1945]

Sorry for long silence, but work & 'flu have completely occupied me these last few months. Sorry, also, that I can't or couldn't let you have a copy of 'I wonder as I wander' – copyright reasons outside my control! But I hope they'll get straightened someday, as I want to hear you blow it —— [1]

Best wishes,
BENJAMIN BRITTEN

1 Britten made an arrangement of 'I wonder as I wander' by John Jacob Niles (1892–1980), in the mistaken belief it was a folksong and in the public domain. The discovery that the song had been composed and was still in copyright (it had been published in the USA by G. Schirmer in 1944) meant that he was unable to publish his version.

In recitals, Pears sang Niles's tune unaccompanied, and Britten interpolated interludes of his own invention. The earliest known performance was given by Pears and Norman Franklin on 20 March 1943 as part of a CEMA concert at Hayward's Heath. The various manuscripts used by Britten and Pears are in the Archive.

498 To the Rt Hon R.A. Butler[1]
Council for the Encouragement of Music and the Arts

> 45A St. John's Wood High St.,
> N.W.8.
> March 20th 1945.

Dear Mr. Butler,

Thank you for your kind invitation to join the CEMA Music Panel, which I have much pleasure in accepting. I will do my best to attend the quarterly meetings, inspite of the extensive touring that I have to do – because the scheme is one in which I am very interested.[2]

> Yours sincerely,
> BENJAMIN BRITTEN

1 Richard Austen Butler (1902–1982), created Baron Butler of Saffron Walden in 1965. He was Minister of Education (1941–5) in Churchill's wartime government. The Butler Education Act of 1944 laid the foundations of post-war reforms in the maintained sector of English education: its overt aim was to provide a full secondary education for all and give equivalent status to all types of secondary schools.

2 Britten was a member of the Music Panel until December 1947.

499 To Maurice Gendron[1]

> 45A, St. Johns Wood High St.,
> N.W.8.
> May 2nd 1945

Mon cher Maurice,

I am so sorry not to have written before – but what with the opera rehearsals, with the concerts with Peter, the travelling, & my own writing, life has been very busy. And also I have been waiting till I had some plans to suggest to you, something about your coming over here. Would the month of September be possible?

I have spoken about you to many people, & I think something
fine can be arranged for you. There are many possibilities – some
concerts with the London Philharmonic Orchestra (possibly the
Schumann, Haydn or Dvorak), the Prokofiev with the B.B.C.,[2] the
Fauré Recital with Peter & me,[3] & possibly some other recitals
with me, including the Stravinsky, Debussy, & my Suite when I
have done it for you.[4] When there is something definite fixed,
you will be sent an invitation, formal & official, & I hope you can
arrange with M. Erlanger[5] to come here. We look forward with
eagerness to your coming, & to renewing our friendship, so
strongly begun in Paris.

    This is only a short letter which I hope our new mutual friend
Monique Haas[6] will be able to give you. She has had a good
success here, & Peter & I were delighted to meet her.

    Eh bien, mon cher, à bientôt,

With much love from us both.

Your friend,

BENJAMIN BRITTEN

P.T.O.

P.S.   Please remember Peter & me to all our new friends in Paris,
Roland, Marie Laure, Marie Blanche,[7] and many others. We are
always talking about you & the lovely time we had in Paris.

1 Maurice Gendron (1920–1990), French cellist and conductor whom
   Britten met in Paris during March. He was invited to appear at the
   Aldeburgh Festival of 1960, when he played Chopin's G minor Sonata
   (with Michèle Boegner, piano), Bach's Sonata in G minor (BWV 1029,
   with George Malcolm, harpsichord), and the D major Suite (BWV
   1012, for unaccompanied cello); and again in 1963, when he replaced
   an indisposed Rostropovich in piano trios by Mozart, Bridge, Schubert and Beethoven (with Yehudi Menuhin and Britten), and gave a
   recital with Britten which included the composer's Cello Sonata, Op.
   65. See also obituaries of Gendron by Noël Goodwin (*Independent*)
   and Yehudi Menuhin (*Guardian*), and in *The Times*, 22 August 1990.

2 In fact, Gendron was to give the first performance in Western Europe
   of Prokofiev's Cello Concerto, Op. 58, with the London Philharmonic
   Orchestra conducted by Walter Susskind, on 9 December, at the Stoll
   Theatre, Kingsway, London.

3 On 10 December, at a National Gallery Concert in London, Pears,
   Gendron and Britten gave a Schubert – Fauré programme comprising
   Schubert: Sonata in A minor, 'Arpeggione' (D.821); songs: 'Am Grabe
   Anselmos' (D.504), 'Du bist die Ruh' (D.776), 'Auflösung' (D.807),

'Am See' (D.746), 'Nacht und Träume' (D.827) and 'Der Musensohn' (D.764); and Fauré: Cello Sonata No. 2 in G minor, Op. 117.

4 On 2 December Gendron and Britten gave a recital at the Wigmore Hall, including the Debussy Cello Sonata (1915) and one of the Fauré sonatas. The Stravinsky was probably the *Suite Italienne* (1932), arranged from *Pulcinella*. The suite Britten mentions was never composed, nor any other piece, despite Gendron's many requests over a long period. On 18 December 1960 Britten was to write to the cellist:

I wanted to write to you personally before you heard a tiny bit of 'cello news from rumours – when Rostropovich was over here recently I heard him play, & was enormously taken by him, both as an artist and as a man. He knew a great deal of my music intimately, and expressed a great wish to come & play at the Festival here. We of course agreed – for many reasons, not least that it is a wonderful thing for a fine Soviet artist to come to such a festival. I therefore am writing him a short 'cello work (a kind of Sonatina on which I am now working) [this was to become the Sonata in C, Op. 65, for cello and piano]. This in no way influences my strong friendship and enormous musical admiration that I feel for you. But realising that most likely you will feel slighted by this, I wanted to write to you myself and explain. The Festival audiences won't in any way forget your wonderful performances here (above all the superb unaccompanied Bach), & if you ever forgive me (!) will very much want you to come back & play for us.

Gendron replied generously in a letter (written in English) dated 9 January 1961:

I do understand your admiration for Rostropovich who is the only cellist I do admire without reserve. I am pleased to know that you will write for cello and am looking forward to play your work if I may, that is to say, if there is no exclusivity for the moment.

Of course, deep in my heart I would have loved you to have written it for me but may be one day I shall have a concerto!

No dearest Ben, nothing can change my friendship, my deep affection and the great admiration I have for you.

5 M. Philippe Erlanger, Minister for Foreign Affairs in France at the time.

6 Monique Haas (b. 1909), French pianist.

7 Roland Baurdarca, a name that appears on a list of names and addresses in Britten's hand under the heading 'Paris visit'; Marie-Laure, Vicomtesse de Noailles, society hostess and friend of many musicians; Marie-Blanche de Polignac, who was daughter of the couturier Lanvin and a professional singer who sang in Nadia Boulanger's choir. Both women were prominent members of Parisian society.

Marion Thorpe recollects that Britten and Pears, on their return to London, commented on the contrast between the 'smart' set they had met, who lived in style and could afford the black-market prices of the time, and others for whom life was still very hard in post-Liberation Paris. (See also Michael de Cossart, *The Food of Love: Princess Edmond de Polignac (1865–1943) and her Salon* (London, Hamish Hamilton, 1978). A London-based French friend, Tony Mayer, helped in the arrangements for the trip; during the war years, he was *chargé de mission* at the French Embassy and responsible for organizing, with the help of Felix Aprahamian, the series of *concerts de musique française* given at the Wigmore Hall. See also Letter 392.

500 To Revd Walter Hussey

[*Picture postcard:*
Bridgnorth from the Castle Hill]

Crown Hotel, Bridgnorth. [Shropshire]
[Postmarked 13 May 1945]

Thank you for your letter. I'm sorry you haven't heard yet from Poulenc,[1] but I think he's coming back soon. Actually Auden turned up the other day on his way [home] but again he'll be back soon & we'll tackle him then.[2] The Swindon Te Deum wasn't a great success; the choir was completely incompetent, & a great disappointment! So glad you liked Eric's Christmas piece.[3] We're all here, – a nice spot, going in daily to Wolverhampton for rehearsals – where the opera is.[4] Mind you keep June 7th![5]

Love from us both,

BEN

1 Presumably a commission had been offered by Hussey to Francis Poulenc (1899–1963), French composer and pianist. Britten and Poulenc had first met as soloists in Poulenc's two-piano concerto at a 'Saturday Book' LPO Concert conducted by Basil Cameron on 6 January at the Albert Hall. They remained firm friends and Poulenc's two-act opera, *Les Mamelles de Tirésias* (1944), was given its first English performance by the English Opera Group at the 1958 Aldeburgh Festival, with Pears as the Husband, Britten and Viola Tunnard at the piano and Charles Mackerras conducting. In 1963, Poulenc was to contribute to TBB, 'Hommage à Benjamin Britten', p. 13. At the 1954 Aldeburgh Festival, Britten included four songs by Poulenc in a recital, and at the 1964 Festival, in a concert dedicated to Poulenc's memory, Britten and Pears performed the song-cycle, *Tel jour, telle nuit* (Paul Eluard), a work they had first performed together in 1943. In the 1964 Programme Book the two men wrote in a joint note:

To the average Englishman, Francis Poulenc's music may have appeared that of the typical French composer: witty, daring, sentimental, naughty. In fact Francis was very easily depressed, shockable, unsure, and liable to panic. No one who saw it will ever forget his agony in a boat on Thorpeness Meare, and it was really his horror of the sea which finally stopped him from coming back to Aldeburgh in 1958 to play in *Tirésias*. [. . .] He put a high value on Sincerity: he was himself too innocent to be insincere. The two sides of his art (as represented by the *Stabat Mater* and *Les Mamelles*) were supposed to be very clearly and consciously juxtaposed; on the contrary it was one of his most adorable qualities that he was incapable of being anything but himself – a delightful friend and lovable musician.

2 Auden wrote to Britten on 30 January 1946 from New York:

Have had a letter from the Rev. Hussey of Northampton asking me to do something for his festival and saying that you would be prepared to provide the notes. My present idea is to do a special Litany for St. Matthew's Day which I suppose would be intoned, preceded by a chorale and followed by an anthem. If your musical ideas demand it, you can revise the order of the two stanzas, and if it is too long, just pick the stanza you prefer.

Britten never set the Anthem (which he was to receive from Auden in February) and the poet's 'Litany and Anthem for St Matthew's Day' was first read on 21 September 1946 at Northampton in a festival of sacred music and poetry that included Britten's *Rejoice in the Lamb* and *Festival Te Deum*. See also Hussey, *Patron of Art* (London, Weidenfeld and Nicolson, 1985), pp. 83–7.

3 Eric Crozier writes (in a private communication):

This is almost certainly a reference to the play *Christmas in the Market Place*, which I translated from the French of Henri Ghéon. It was published first in 1944 and several times reprinted. I staged the play for the Pilgrim Players of Canterbury, with E. Martin Browne (a friend of T.S. Eliot, and producer of all his plays) in the leading part. It was also staged in a church in Margaret Street by Rupert Doone, with décor and costumes by Robert Medley. Walter Hussey probably read it with a view to performance at Northampton.

In 1944 there had been some discussion of a 'Christmas production' by Sadler's Wells in which Crozier was hoping to involve Britten. He wrote to Joan Cross on 21 October:

Ben Britten turned up unexpectedly in London yesterday, and wanted to see me about 'Grimes', so we had a long time together clearing various points up. I tackled him about the Christmas production, and found him most sympathetically inclined to the idea and willing to choose, arrange or compose music. He couldn't have been more helpful, and I think the next step is for the Administration to make him a definite offer for doing the work, so that he can count on that, and make allowances of time, for any other things he plans to do next year. He thinks T.S. Eliot should be asked to do the text, or would have liked to work with Auden on it, if the latter weren't six thousand miles away. I don't agree with the idea of Auden: Eliot would be a major scoop, though possibly a bit dry and cerebral, and might accept if it were sure Ben was to be the music collaborator. En tout cas,

WIGMORE HALL

BOOSEY & HAWKES
FOURTH **CONCERTS** SEASON

THURSDAY, MAY 31st, 1945, at 7 p.m.

Concert-Introduction to

PETER GRIMES
*An Opera in three acts and a prologue
derived from the poem of George Crabbe
by Montagu Slater*

Music by

Benjamin Britten

given by the producer and the principal
characters of the forthcoming production of

The Sadler's Wells Opera

on the 7th of June

•

Price 6d.

I

General Introduction by TYRONE GUTHRIE

II

An Outline of the Opera by ERIC CROZIER

The Musical Illustrations given by :

Peter Grimes, a fisherman ...	PETER PEARS
Ellen Orford, a widowed school-mistress	JOAN CROSS
Auntie, landlady of "The Boar"	EDITH COATES
Nieces, chief attractions of "The Boar"	BLANCHE TURNER / MINNIA BOWER
Balstrode, a retired sea-captain...	RODERICK JONES
Swallow, lawyer and magistrate...	OWEN BRANNIGAN
Mrs. Sedley, a rentier widow ...	VALETTA JACOPI
Ned Keene, apothecary	EDMUND DONLEVY
Bob Boles, a Methodist fisherman	MORGAN JONES
Mr. Horace Adams, the Rector...	TOM CULBERT

The scene of the opera is *The Borough*,
a small East Coast fishing-town, in 1830

Producer · · · · · ERIC CROZIER
•
At the piano · · BENJAMIN BRITTEN

The concert introduction to *Peter Grimes*, Wigmore Hall, 31 May 1945

"Peter Grimes," *Benjamin Britten's* first opera, was commissioned early in 1942 by *Serge Koussevitsky*, in memory of his wife, *Madame Natalie Koussevitsky*, who had recently died. The first performances were to be given under *Koussevitsky* at the Berkshire (New England) Festival of the Boston Symphony Orchestra. This proved unpractical in wartime, and the first production was arranged for England with the Sadler's Wells Opera.

Preliminary work on the libretto began in 1942. The composition of the music took from January, 1944, until February, 1945, when rehearsals immediately began for the re-opening of Sadler's Wells Theatre in June.

George Crabbe (1755-1832), from whose poem "The Borough" *Montagu Slater* derived the situation and characters of the opera, was born at Aldeburgh in Suffolk. *Benjamin Britten* was born in a house on the sea-front at Lowestoft, twenty-five miles north of Aldeburgh, and has lived nearly all his life in the district.

Crabbe was a realist. At a time when poetic fashion shunned "low" subjects, he set out to describe the daily life of The Borough—Aldeburgh—in all its meanness and familiarity. In basing their opera on his poem, the composer and librettist have broken away from the romantic scenes and heroic situations of operatic fashion, setting their action and their people in a homelier native background.

E.C

Ready for the first performance June 7th

PETER GRIMES. Libretto

with a cover design by Kenneth Green

Price 2/6

Published by BOOSEY & HAWKES Ltd.,
295 REGENT STREET, W.1

•

No. 3 of Sadler's Wells Opera Books:

Benjamin Britten's
PETER GRIMES

*Essays by Benjamin Britten, E. M. Forster,
Montagu Slater and Edward Sackville-West
Illustrated with stage and costume designs by
Kenneth Green*

Price 2/6

Published by
JOHN LANE, THE BODLEY HEAD Ltd.

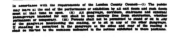

The programme for the first performance of *Peter Grimes*, Sadler's Wells, 7 June 1945

Ben's willingness and liking for the idea itself seems to indicate a first step on the right foot – [. . .]

The concept outlined by Crozier seems to reflect the shape of the radio features for the BBC on which Britten had worked in 1937 and 1938, i.e. *The Company of Heaven* and *The World of the Spirit*, which presented a similar mix of text and music built round a biblical theme (angels) or religious festival (Whitsun). The 1944 proposal – of which Crozier now has no recollection – did not materialize. One notes Britten's thoughts of Eliot or Auden as possible textual collaborators.

4 The Sadler's Wells company was at the Grand Theatre, Wolverhampton, 8–18 May, performing *Rigoletto* (8th and 12th), *Così* (14th and 18th), and *The Bartered Bride* (15th).

5 The date of the forthcoming first performance of *Peter Grimes*.

501 To Mary Behrend

[*Postcard*]

[after 7 June 1945]

Dear Mary,

I shall try madly to catch 6 p.m. on 3rd – I have a recording that afternoon, but with luck I should make it! Don't worry about 4th – I'm good with Women's Institutes! I don't know about Peter – it depends on Sadlers W. dates. Grimes is on 20th, 25th, 29th June. 17th(?) 21st July. We are all excited about the way it's going. Please excuse rush – but I know you understand!

Love to you & Bow,
BEN

502 To Mrs Wright[1]

45A St. John's Wood High St.
N.W. 8
June 18th 1945.

Dear Mrs. Wright,

Thank you for your kind letter of appreciation about Peter Grimes. I am awfully glad you liked it. We are all of course very excited that it is going so well, & that people are turning up so numerously to see it. It looks as if the old spell on British opera may be broken at last![2] I am glad that Basil will be able to see it on Wednesday. I hope to catch sight of him after it.

I hope you are well, and not too busy – a dreadful disease these days!

> With many thanks again for your letter,
> Yours ever,
> BENJY

1 The mother of Basil Wright, the film director.

2 It is clear that it was beginning to dawn on Britten that the performance of *Peter Grimes* on 7 June had been more than an important
première, that in fact it might prove to be an event with altogether
larger reverberations – as indeed was to be the case.

We reproduce the reception of the work by music critics of the
major dailies, the weeklies and Sunday newspapers, beginning with
Frank Howes's assessment in *The Times*, 8 June:

> It is a long time indeed since a new full-length opera by an English composer
> has thrown down its challenge for acceptance into the small number of
> works that will hold the stage and add something new to musical experience.
> It is a happy augury for the Sadler's Wells opera that Britten's *Peter Grimes*
> should make the return to its old home after five years of itinerant exile. It
> is a good omen for English opera that this first-fruit of peace should declare
> decisively that opera on the grand scale and in the grand manner can still
> be written. Expectations ran high and were not disappointed.
>
> The first test of a new opera is whether its dramatic appeal comes straight
> off the stage to the listener. *Peter Grimes*, making one or two feints at an
> episodic method, proceeds by sharp turns of the dramatic screw to situations
> of great power which, intensified by orchestral music of diabolical cunning,
> explode in climaxes that leave no room for doubt about this essential quality.
>
> The next test for an opera is whether it demands fine singing and supplies
> opportunities for it. In *Peter Grimes* the chief character is Public Opinion and
> the protagonist who plays it is the chorus. Everything, from the intonation
> of the General Confession to crowd scenes unparalleled outside the Russian
> operas and embracing public house catches, unison work-songs, brawls, and
> voices off, is provided in profusion by the composer. The name-part requires
> the interpretation of schizophrenia which makes Purcell's 'Mad Bess' look
> simple. Lyrical moments are rarer, but they are there for tenor and soprano,
> as is traditional and right.
>
> The third test is not essential for success, since successful operas have
> been written without it – originality in the substance of the music. Britten
> has a way of hitting on a device, an apparently simple but deceptively
> ingenious bit of figuration, for example, which seems right almost to obvious-
> ness once it is revealed. The opera is filled to the brim with this effortless
> originality and spills over with interest. The composer is very bold in what
> he does and his audacity succeeds everywhere but in the last scene of all.
> Here there is much unaccompanied solo singing, the orchestra fades away
> into silence and then at the critical moment for the first time in more than
> two hours of music the spoken voice intrudes. Possibly if the silent action

was retained and the voices restored to *mezza voce* this scene would be less precarious.

The first performance went well. In Mr Reginald Goodall the company has discovered an operatic conductor with a talent for dramatic music, and his piloting of chorus and orchestra through a complex score was the chief factor in the opera's successful performance. Mr Peter Pears, as Peter Grimes, commanded all the vocal resources required for a great and exacting part, though he was not completely convincing as a sadist. Miss Joan Cross provided the element of tenderness and repose in a context of tension, and Mr Roderick Jones judged to a nicety the prominence required by the man who turned the scale from tolerance of evil to action against it.

On 15 June the music critic of *The Times* returned to the topic under the sub-title 'Second Thoughts':

The plot, which is derived from Crabbe's poem 'The Borough', deals with the life of a Suffolk fishing town of 1830 and the main drama goes on inside the frame of the corporate life of the place, which is therefore depicted by a number of vignettes of persons and episodes of their doings. These minor characters include the landlady of The Boar Inn, her complaisant 'nieces', a retired sea-captain who ultimately precipitates the culminating act in the drama of Peter Grimes, a seedily respectable widow, and a Methodist fisherman, besides the functional persons of the Borough, magistrate, rector, doctor, schoolmistress, and even the local carrier. These characters come over clearly as individuals and add up, with the aid of a chorus, into a community. The chorus is very important alike in its dramatic function as the public opinion which clashes with the personality of Peter Grimes, and in the quantity and variety of the music it has to sing. By every argument of tradition and probability an English opera is likely to do well on a choral foundation, but in point of fact this opera is more like some Slavonic models in its dramatic use of the chorus than any of the more familiar types of opera. Thus the curtain of the penultimate scene is a choral hue-and-cry for Peter Grimes, boldly conceived on simple lines to strike with such concentrated impact as to make it the climax of the opera. Elsewhere the chorus gets a church service, which the composer uses in antiphony with the soprano heroine's arioso, a catch which alternates with and ultimately overwhelms the confused counterpoint of a tavern brawl, and a sunny work-song of fisherfolk mending their nets, which sets before the audience the permanent life of the Borough, within which the personal tragedy of Grimes is enacted.

There are thus two parallel dramas running concurrently, and some criticism will no doubt be directed at this structural peculiarity; there is on the one hand the even life of the borough and on the other the tempestuous tragedy of Grimes, who is at loggerheads with it. The opera begins with what is formally a prologue to both dramas, an inquest on Grimes's apprentice, in which we meet the chief characters of both. The first scene of the first act develops the conflict between them. The next scene is set in the inn, and we appear to be in for still another *genre* picture of small town life, but between the two scenes another character has made its appearance – the sea. In this entr'acte Britten has written salt-water music of unequalled intensity – the sting and the crash and the scream of great waters have never before been caught and translated into music with such fidelity, not even in *The Flying Dutchman*, for this is not onomatopoeic imitation but a universal-ized image of the sea itself in tempest. This storm music punctuates the human music of the inn every time the door opens. And then just as one begins to wonder when the other drama will begin to move Grimes bursts in, like the Flying Dutchman himself, and in an aria sets out the better side of his nature, which has hitherto only been seen under the cloud of his unpopularity.

Grimes is then a dual personality, and the role will set a problem of interpretation which may defeat singers of less intelligence than Peter Pears. The composer, however, has taken out an insurance against any defects of characterization in the libretto, in his own music, and in his interpreter by writing from this time on music of such dramatic intensity that one is prepared to accept Grimes as an instrument of a malign fate. The last scene, in which Grimes is sent to a death by his own act, is the most problematical. A second hearing did not wholly remove, though it certainly modified, the impression that the use of the speaking voice, after the fortissimo of the chorus and the incisiveness of the orchestral scene-painting have been exhausted, is a dangerous intrusion of an alien element. Some re-timing of the stage action may be necessary if the deliberate but hazardous passage from climax to anti-climax, from tragic night to common day, is to make the bold effect which the composer has conceived so truly to life.

Ferruccio Bonavia wrote in the *Daily Telegraph*, 8 June:

Sadler's Wells Theatre, which has been closed since September 1940, was reopened last night for the first performance of Benjamin Britten's 'Peter Grimes' – the first opera written by this brilliant and prolific young composer.

Success in the concert room does not inevitably lead to success in the opera house but, let it be said at once that 'Peter Grimes' equals and, in some respects, surpasses Mr Britten's previous essays in the choral and symphonic field.

This opera has force, vitality, beauty. The first scene ends with two solil-oquys of poetry which have a haunting loveliness. All through, the atmos-phere is that of the theatre and not the concert room.

The composer has been captivated by George Crabbe's 'The Borough', an early 19th-century poem describing the 'wild amphibious' race then inhabit-ing Aldeburgh in Suffolk, where the poet 'with the sour name and the sweet countenance' was born and bred.

Determined to avoid anything smacking of conventional opera, the com-poser and his librettist, Montagu Slater, have given us an opera which has neither love-duet nor hero. Peter is played by the tenor, the protagonist in most operas. But he does not and is not meant to engage very deeply our sympathies.

He is first introduced as standing trial for the murder at sea of his appren-tice: he is then seen treating brutally the boy who has taken the place of the first apprentice. We see him finally, a raving lunatic, putting out to sea to seek death in drowning.

The dramatic interest is not in the clash of passion, but in the realistic picture of grim life and of the character which in the early nineteenth-century rioted in the East Anglian borough. One woman stands out from the crowd, the gentle schoolmistress whom Peter loves. But as love does not affect his actions its value as a dramatic theme is not important.

In the music that accompanies the action, Mr Britten has shown that he possesses the rare and most valuable gift of characterisation.

The opera was produced with unusual care. Excellent performances were given by Joan Cross (Ellen) and Peter Pears (Grimes), well supported by the rest of the company and by the orchestra conducted by Reginald Goodall.

Scott Goddard, in the *News Chronicle*, 8 June:

Benjamin Britten's 'Peter Grimes' is no child's play. The tale is fierce, its development tragic, and the music fascinating as much when it fails, as it sometimes seems to do, as when it so notably succeeds.

With that there is the emotional force it has in itself, and that other emotion it lends and receives from the action. It is an astonishing work to meet for the first time.

The performance was good, and will improve. Peter Pears as Grimes, the maddened fisherman, gave a profoundly sympathetic rendering of the part for which he will be remembered. Singing and acting were of one piece, and intensely moving. So too, the Ellen of Joan Cross, the one woman who stood by Grimes.

The chorus of villagers who, with their mean social instinct, hound Grimes into lunacy, are as important in the plot as the principals. This choral writing is one of Britten's most remarkable achievements and the singing was splendid.

All the orchestral writing is effective, and as soon as the conductor, Reginald Goodall, can get a better balance the value of this will tell.

Will this new opera succeed? The public is fickle, and on its unstable temperament all depends no matter how good the work or how fine the performance.

Sadler's Wells has taken a chance, and deserves to pull it off. 'Peter Grimes' is a work that must not be ignored by those who admire originality and take the art of opera seriously.

Eric Blom, in the *Birmingham Post*, 8 June:

Those who know their Crabbe will recognise the title as that of one of the short character sketches in narrative verse in 'The Borough', and they can hardly fail to say that this is about the last literary subject in the world which can be imagined in the form of an opera. It is gloomy, harrowing and depressing in the extreme, whereas the fundamental fact about opera is, historically and in the matter of its general practice, that it is festive – and to this even such grim specimens as 'Elektra', 'Wozzeck' and 'A Lady Macbeth of Mtsensk' are not altogether exceptions. Opera is also, including these three, concerned with many characters, even where it bears the name of one. Again, in the opera things must happen, and happen swiftly and variedly. It is obvious that the original 'Peter Grimes' lives up to none of these conditions: turned into an opera, it would seem to be fore-doomed to failure.

Was Britten's first opera a failure at Sadler's Wells to-night? The answer is that it was a decided success, both as an event and as a work of art. Not an unqualified success in everybody's eyes or ears perhaps. It can be criticised as

being too harsh, as departing too far from the original with all those characters which are the librettist's invention, not Crabbe's at all, and so on. But
for my part I have no doubt whatever that Britten's opera is a modern work
of the first importance, a work of genius, an opera so impressive and original
that only the most absurd prejudice will keep it out of the great foreign
opera houses.

It is not depressing or, if it is, then one must call 'King Lear' depressing,
which is not to say that Britten is another Shakespeare, but merely that great
tragic art does not dampen the human spirit, but elates it.

I refrain from mentioning the cast, for I propose to do so when the Sadler's
Wells company brings 'Peter Grimes' to Birmingham – and this is just a
roundabout way of asking that they should.

But it must be said that Eric Crozier's extremely vivid production and
Kenneth Greene's most evocative settings do much to create an atmosphere
of haunted moods that would be creepy if it were less poetical. It is the
music, however, which is the well spring of this atmosphere. It is full of
eerie sounds, of tense terrifying silences, of monotonous sea waves, and in
one scene a recurrent fog horn has a horrid fascination. At the same time,
it is music that always has an admirable shape and life of its own. 'Peter
Grimes' is not only a great opera, it is also a great composition.

In the *Sunday Times*, for three weeks from 10 June, Ernest Newman
devoted three long articles exclusively to the opera, but only in one
of them (the second) did he touch rather briefly on the music:

Mr Britten, having a drama on his hands that must be allowed to have its
full say in the matter of music v. drama – or, if we prefer it, music plus
drama – is confronted with much the same problem as Wagner was, and he
solves it in basically the same way, though with modern modifications in
detail. The quite static moments in so realistic a drama are necessarily few.
Consequently the episodes of set lyrical outpouring are rare – a few passages
for Grimes or Ellen Orford: the final scene of Peter's madness, the fine
reflective trio for the four female characters in the second act, etc. (This, by
the way, is not a gaffe on my part, though there are four singers, the music
is in three real parts, the Two Nieces singing in unison.) The greater part of
the stage action is carried on in a sort of song-speech that keeps us faithfully
as possible to the accents and rise and fall and easy flow of ordinary speech,
while the orchestra 'points' what is being said in a curiously effective way.

Apart from the more lyrical episodes I have just mentioned, the main
burden of intense emotional expression is laid on the orchestra in a number
of interludes which sum up the emotional significance of what has gone
before or prepare us for what is to come. They are of great power and
masterly musicianship; particularly impressive are the prelude (and postlude)
to the opera that defines the grey atmosphere of the hard-bitten little fishing
town, the brooding night-piece that introduces Act III, and the superb passacaglia between the first and second scenes of Act II. The whole texture,
musical and dramatic, of the opera is admirably unified, in spite of the many
genres it employs, ranging from almost naked speech to music at its fullest
power; but to listen to it in the right way the spectator must approach it
from its own standpoint, not that of any previous operatic species.

In the *Observer*, on 10 and 24 June, William Glock, like Howes in *The Times*, offered first and second thoughts about *Grimes*:

The opera begins very cleverly with a prologue in which Grimes and The Borough are shown at once in tragic opposition, and this prologue, a court inquiry, also serves to introduce us within the first few minutes to all the principal characters. Grimes is romanticized in various ways, by giving him a string accompaniment while the others have only woodwind and brass; by spreading his words out to twice the length of the magistrate's when he repeats the oath, and by introducing an almost Beethovenian pathos when Grimes asks the accuser to be brought into the hall so that 'the case won't go on in people's minds'. Here, in fact, is the technique by which everything is as sharply focused as possible; could Verdi have been there he would have sat back in admiration if not always in comfort. For this first act, whether curiously or not, has often rather a waspish sound; and the sensuous contrast with Acts 2 and 3 is very marked.

It is in keeping with Britten's creative 'innocence' that he should grasp at every kind of resource, and give us in 'Peter Grimes', every level from the most elementary operatic manoeuvre to the purest poetry. Thus we find naïve comments by the chorus, or the melodramatic tone and eerie instrumentation of such a phrase as 'murder most foul it is'; we also find disturbingly beautiful things such as Grimes's vision of the world as it might be, 'wrapp'd round with kindness like September haze' (end of Act 2), and thrilling choruses such as the Round in the first act and the hymn of hate in the third, culminating in those tremendous shouts of 'Grimes, Grimes'.

But I think the most masterly writing of all is in the church scene at the beginning of Act 2. Here, against the background of a church service – hymn, prayers, the Benedicite and the Creed – there is a first scene between Ellen and Grimes's new boy apprentice, and then between Ellen and Grimes. The service has two functions, to contrast the ordinary life of The Borough with the special drama going on outside, and also to intensify the drama itself. I can only describe the main points very crudely, the lines of the hymn crowding closer together at the first climax, the priest switching violently from B natural to E flat at 'O Lord open thou our lips', as Ellen discovers that Grimes has wounded the boy; the Benedicite being sung in a feverishly swift flow of quavers as Peter and Ellen begin to quarrel; and then the Creed being left in mid-air so that all the speed and excitement can finally be concentrated on the stage. Such simple effects belong to genius; and despite a few derivative phrases I think that this whole scene would stand its ground anywhere.

The performance was splendid. Peter Pears spared no effort of physique or imagination in his portrayal of Grimes, while Joan Cross, as Ellen Orford, sang with ardour, dignity, and a beautiful quality of tone. Reginald Goodall's conducting I liked very much; he seemed to combine an experienced control of stage and orchestra with a musicianly enthusiasm which sometimes rose to the level of evangelical zeal. But then, as the chorus also showed, it is a most thrilling work. Don't miss it.

And 24 June:

During the last fortnight, I have heard and read several comments on 'Peter

Grimes', the new opera in the Sadler's Wells repertory, which describe it as a fierce and challenging work. What spoiled babies we have become. I should have thought that the most noticeable thing about Britten was his gift for making statements of undoubted originality in terms which everyone could understand. There are no technical advances in 'Peter Grimes'. It is, in fact, an entertainment of the highest class in which broad inspirations are worked out with an entirely traditional sagacity.

Besides his attachment to Aldeburgh and the sea, there were surely two excellent reasons which drove Britten to write his opera; on the one hand the constructive and dramatic possibilities of the Borough in opposition to Grimes; on the other hand, Grimes himself, in a version dictated partly by operatic needs, but still more by Britten's. insight into that emotional range his music could most perfectly express. In the choruses he could show his élan and his mastery of every resource of development and climax. In planning the various scenes of Borough life in the Boar, in church, in the dance hall – he could call upon a never-ending flow of 'ideas'. And into his study of Grimes he could pour the kind of music that he could imagine at an intense level throughout.

[. . .]

I would like to add a last comment on Britten's treatment of the words. Nowhere in 'Peter Grimes' is there anything stiff or self-conscious; and it would be futile to examine his music for evidence of some consistent and over-riding experiment in technique. Where characterisation is wanted, we find Swallow's neat and rapid interrogation in the Prologue, Auntie's comically vigorous accents in the Boar, and Grimes's cadenza-like passage, sung in the final scene to his own name – a great arc of notes to a single syllable. So perhaps one should look at those details which are not influenced by any direct dramatic intention. I think there are two noticeable things. First, Britten achieves flexibility quite often by balancing the emphasis of the bar-lines (or of certain beats within the bar) against the natural emphasis of the words. Secondly, he very rarely changes the time-signature, but employs every subtlety in order to place the words freely and easily without dullness or heaviness or those endless triplets which are so disheartening in their effect.

In the weeklies, Philip Hope-Wallace wrote in *Time and Tide*, 14 June, a commentary of unusual penetration which seems in some respects remarkably to anticipate Philips Brett's pioneering essay in PGPB, 'Britten and Grimes', pp. 180–89:

It is Britten's grasp of the craft of opera which so excites here. His great originality as a musician is not, never has been, in doubt. A parodist of the wittiest, he has the clearest possible sense of his *own* style. Every bar of this long and rich score is stamped with individual character. The handling of the orchestral mass, the complex choral 'draughtmanship' never fumble; the extended melodic idiom, indeed the whole cast of the melody with its sparse evocative accompaniments, is the very stuff of expressive vocal writing; and with it goes a feeling for texture and for climax which are the hall mark of a musician of the first quality.

But – and here one must begin to qualify – an effective opera could be made with only a tenth of the originality and imagination here evident, and *Peter Grimes, qua* opera, exhibits in the matter of operatic craft a defect which if not cardinal is none the less likely to work strongly against the general acceptance of the work into the main stream of music drama and against its chances of holding the stage. Powerfully though it evokes the atmosphere of a harsh way of life in an East Anglian fishing village, it just fails to make explicitly enough either in music or drama its essential and difficult 'hidden' theme of its hero's divided nature. (I write after one performance in which the role was diffidently sung and in which the words were often fatally inaudible, but the defect was clear enough and no object is served by glossing it over.)

Montagu Slater's libretto would seem to have extracted from Crabbe's curious poem not merely the crowded surface picture (inevitably over-crowded, for the real hero of the *poem* is the *Borough*); but also some of the essence of a tragic conflict in a man's soul. Yet in the collaboration not enough light falls on this central theme which is finally the sole claim on dramatic interest.

Fisherman Grimes, you remember, is a moral outlaw in this Suffolk village. His only ally is the schoolmistress, Ellen (a wonderfully realised secondary figure in the opera). Between her and his desire to court her, stands his poverty, his half visionary madness and his reputation of ill-using his apprentices. It is the accidental death in his service of a boy from the workhouse which provokes the village to the man-hunt which ends with Grimes drowning himself. These tragic external events make the 'story' of the opera as we have it, but the inner nature of the man and his motives – a wonderful subject for music – have very largely to be accepted on trust. In short, this hero remains curiously negative and the conflict of his divided heart is not disclosed.

Or put it that those passages, those strokes by which the revelation is made, are not sufficiently prominent or arresting to clue up the whole composition into a dramatically cogent whole. This arises from some failure, too complex to analyse here, in solving the problem of operatic tempo: the 'rate' at which the action unfolds itself in music and at which attention is alternately seized and relaxed: the way, in short, in which the audience's sympathy or interest are sought. It may be that at subsequent performances the problem will be seen to have been solved in some fashion too novel to 'bite' at a first hearing. But the impression persisted that Grimes had not been allotted his proper dominant position in the scheme – at any rate with anything commensurate to the entirely successful originality and strength wherewith the other secondary interests (the life of the place and the reactions of Grimes's fellows) are placed before us. The music which presents Grimes himself – in the witness-box, in his fierce approaches to Ellen, in that half-drunken outburst which silences the brawling pub, above all in that curious scene of muttering self-communing, shut away in his hut with the speechless workhouse waif – is music of an uncannily chilled and angu-ished sort; disturbing, but stopping just short of the required revelatory power. We never really meet the man. His death breaks no heart. His suicide is a mere item of police court news. Is this deliberate? I think not.

Desmond Shawe-Taylor contributed two articles to the *New States-man and Nation* on 9 and 16 June:

I know that operas are not ethical treatises, and that I shall be accused of taking too literal a view of a poetic creation. Maybe. But is there not some-thing shocking in the attempt to win our sympathies for a character *simply because* he is an outlaw and an enemy of society – and no more questions asked? What I am quite prepared (especially after the Wigmore Hall concert) to believe is that the richness and dramatic power of Britten's music will enable us to ignore (for the time being) an adolescent conception of man and society which is in sober truth indefensible. In the theatre we may well be lulled into acquiescense; but at home, shall we not begin to wonder?

And 16 June:

The moment the curtain rises (there is no overture) the spectator is seized by a powerful impression of competence. Everything happens rapidly, clearly and inevitably. The business before the Borough Court is transacted with despatch – as though music were quite the simplest and most natural of mediums in which a Coroner's Inquest could be conducted. Different though the mood is, one thinks of the opening of Verdi's *Falstaff*, there is the same effect of speed and precision. A bustling, pompous little tune gives us the self-important magistrate; a shrill figure in the wood-wind the bickering, gesticulating crowd. And Grimes? His romantic, larger-than-life personality is immediately established in purely musical terms by the remote modulations and soft string chords which underpin his slow answers and repetition of the Oath. Thus, in the first ten minutes, before any set pieces bring up the question of 'inspiration', we are convinced that the composer is a born opera-writer. In the light of all that follows, this impression of naturalness, ease and sheer competence may seem a slight virtue to insist on, but it is not. It is the pre-condition which makes all the later flights of imagination possible; it is that quality, the lack of which has strewn the history of English opera with so many distinguished corpses.

Competence assured, poetry steals in with an unaccompanied duet between Grimes and the schoolmistress Ellen Orford. The curtain drops, and the flat, salty, windy coast is magically evoked in an orchestral interlude; bare, grace-noted minims on the higher strings, clean arpeggios on the harp, soft chords on the brass. It looks so simple, that innate pictorialism of Britten's which we have already admired in the *Serenade*, and now it serves so well the broader need of opera; when the curtain rises we see only what we have already heard. These preludes and interludes, of which there are six in all, form a major item in the musical design; they are about equally divided between the pictorial and the psychological. Here almost alone, the composer unleashes the full power of the orchestra, elsewhere subduing it most carefully to allow the voices to dominate and the words to be heard; also, they are the only respect in which he departs from the generally late Verdian lay-out of the score. I am not referring to the musical idiom, but to the division of the score into set-pieces, arias, ensembles and choruses, linked by recitatives which slip insensibly into *arioso*. He shows great mastery too of a kind of operatic writing known as the *scena* of which a notable example, containing perhaps the most expressive and touching music in the whole opera, occurs in the first scene of the second act. Here Ellen and the new apprentice sit down in the Sunday morning sunshine, while the hymns and responses of matins float out through the open church door; she talks to the boy (who won't answer) and falls into a reverie. Musically, the idea of a soprano occupied with her own troubles against a liturgical background is as old as Gounod's *Faust*; but with what freshness and skill Britten has treated it. There is the device, borrowed from broadcasting, of 'fading up' and 'fading down' the two component parts of the scene, and there is a subtle musical interrelation between them; as when a theme is picked up from the church service and adapted, in a most affecting manner, to form the substance of Ellen's lament. Such things are 'tricks'; but, like a poet's skill in versification, they are the necessary foundation for the noblest ideas.

At first hearing the first two acts may seem a trifle episodic. Later, the realisation that the chorus is as much the protagonist as Grimes himself partly removes this impression; we begin to see the big choral scenes, not as so much 'atmosphere' or 'colour' but, like those of *Boris Godunov* or *Turandot* (both of which they often recall), as one of the mainsprings of the action. The last act, however, immediately makes an impression of intense and concentrated dramatic power. There is a steady rise in the temperature of the first scene, from the rough, burlesque gaiety of the Moot Hall dances, a moment of almost Schubertian charm, when the Rector goes off to water his roses, Ellen's lovely 'embroidery' aria, up to the electrifying climax of that tremendous series of cries which herald the man-hunt: 'Peter Grimes! Peter Grimes!' This call resounds, distant and mysterious now in the sea-mist, through the final scene, which is also punctuated by the boom of the fog-horn. This is the background of another *scena*, for the distraught Grimes, in which snatches of remembered melody, almost in the manner of the *cadenza* in Elgar's *Violin Concerto*, flicker by out of the past. As we reach the last hours before dawn, all colour and sound drain out of the world: the chorus is silent, the orchestra is silent, at last Grimes himself is silent. In the intense stillness, and with profoundly dramatic effect, occur the only lines of spoken dialogue in the work. They are spoken by the honest sea captain Balstrode: 'Sail out of sight of the land, and sink your boat.' Wordlessly, Grimes obeys. After a long pause life returns: dawn breaks, the mist disperses, the music on the high strings which began Act I comes back again, the townsfolk begin to go about their daily business; we reach 'the cold beginning of another day'. It is a wonderful conception, which needs perhaps another two or three minutes of music for full realisation.

Beverley Baxter, in the *Evening Standard*, 9 June, under the title 'One Man Against the Mob':

With the courage of youth Britten casts aside all conventions. There is no love duet, no coquetting Musetta or melodious Mimi, no Prize or Flower song. 'My theme is of the mob and the sea,' he seems to say, 'and the orchestra tells their story.' Never for a moment does the orchestra cease to comment and to dramatise.

In the first act the music is so harsh and relentless that the ear cries for mercy, but Britten's retort is: 'Did the people show mercy to Peter Grimes?' In the whole of the long first act there is hardly a touch of beauty in the score, and none at all of tenderness.

The harmonies are modern and discordant, as if the composer himself were some kind of robot with a hatred of mankind. 'There is no bodily pleasure in it,' said a well-known operatic tenor to me as he went out for a breath of air.

In the next two acts the cruelty remains, but beauty begins to emerge, fitfully, reluctantly, and one's senses become stirred to unusual excitement.

It was an inspired performance by singers and orchestra alike, so excellent in the acting that one can only assume that the rehearsals must have gone on for weeks. There was one exquisite moment when four *soprani* sang, and if we remembered the Trio from Rosenkavalier it did not mean that Britten was imitating it.

The best of the whole work is towards the finish, where Peter, hunted like a rat, sings of what might have been. In the distance there is the fog-horn, and the manner in which the composer brings the singer's voice into unison with the horn is intensely dramatic. And I am still haunted by the deep chords of the orchestra as if the sea were waiting for its human sacrifice, knowing that it could afford to wait.

To Reginald Goodall, the conductor, to Peter Pears as Peter Grimes, to Joan Cross as the kindly school teacher, to Eric Crozier as the producer, to the orchestra, to the other soloists and to the only grand opera chorus which ever really acted I offer my congratulations and my thanks. As for Benjamin Britten, young as he is, this opera will outlive him.

Four tail-pieces:
Time, 7 June:

Critical judgements apart, it was a big night at 'The Wells'. *Peter Grimes* was England's first new opera in almost ten years. The score called for some 200 singers and musicians. Gallery oldtimers had set up their camp stools in ticket queues 24 hours in advance. Ecstatic music-lovers kept throwing bouquets at the cast and composer until the historic old stage was carpeted with flowers. The peerage showed up in more furs, white ties and tiaras than Londoners had seen since the war began.

Joan Cross, in *The Times*, 1 June 1985, recollected the impact of the première:

At first we didn't know. There was silence at the end and then shouting broke out. The stage crew were stunned: they thought it was a demonstration. Well, it was but fortunately it was of the right kind. My main memory was of being given a great bowl of waterlilies by Peter and Ben which I took straight off to the Savoy. Why waterlilies? Well, they were original, weren't they? Everything Peter and Ben did was original.

One other thing I'm sure of and that is the high quality of the orchestra playing. They were probably a very moderate band individually, but that night they pulled out all the stops for Reggie Goodall and I count him the supreme *Grimes* conductor.

Goodall's memory of the first performance was different at least in one important respect. He had not found the orchestral playing adequate to the virtuoso demands of Britten's score, perhaps because many of the country's best orchestral players had been and were still in the armed forces.

An interesting account of the first performance of *Grimes* was contributed by Scott Goddard, in his chapter on Britten, to *British Music of Our Time* (Harmondsworth, Pelican, 1946), pp. 217–18:

There had been much publicity over this production, valuable for the event itself, though it did no good to the work. Generous enthusiasm was immediately countered by spiteful antagonism, each answering each before the opera had even been seen. It became impossible to mention the work without discussion degenerating into argument. Nothing could be discovered of its artistic quality, so heavy was the cloud of sociological, political, even ethical bickering surrounding *Peter Grimes*. It may at least be granted that no English opera has ever had such a press. When at length *Peter Grimes* was heard, it was found to be finer as a work of art, less tendentious as a vehicle for ideas, less portentous as a manifesto than friends or enemies had implied.

'Critic' in the *New Statesman* (Summer 1945):

I can vouch for the truth of the following incidents on a single-track bus journey last Saturday. They seem almost to amount to proof that we are becoming a nation of high-brows. A friend boarded a 38 bus at Green Park, asked the conductor whether he went past Sadler's Wells. 'Yes, I should say I do,' he replied. 'I wish I could go inside instead. That will be threepence for Peter Grimes.' All the way to Roseberry Avenue, a young man sitting next to my friend whistled the Tarantella from Walton's *Façade*; it is not an easy tune to whistle and the whistler did *not* get off at Sadler's Wells. But my friend did, and as he left the bus he heard the conductor shouting at the top of a loud voice: 'Sadler's Wells! Any more for Peter Grimes, the sadistic fisherman!'

The last was a favourite story of Peter Pears's. See also PBPG, pp. 153–62.

In 1950, E.J. Dent, who had been very closely associated with the development at Sadler's Wells of English opera and opera in English, wrote a letter to the composer Bernard Stevens (12 June) in which he summed up his views to date – some of them surely eccentric – of Britten's operas, and of *Grimes* in particular:

I have been reading fifty or sixty opera librettos and almost as many operas, and what always infuriates me is the obvious aiming at some already hackneyed popular effect of commercial opera. *Peter Grimes* held me (and I saw three different productions, two in London and one in Budapest, which was the best of all by far) by its sincerity and integrity as a whole, though I was annoyed by certain tricks of effect at times.

I come to the conclusion that it is a mistake to try to write highly 'poetical' and 'literary' librettos. The poet ought to concentrate entirely on drama and absolute truth to human nature, however unreal or fantastic the story may be; and always to use the very simplest words which everybody can understand at first hearing. Secondly, always to make the characters talk in their own character, and to avoid carefully all temptation to put the author's own private philosophy of life into their mouths. This if properly carried out does not at all prevent the poet's own personality coming through the whole drama, as the great dramatists of the past have shown us. Prospero for instance talks of a good deal of 'philosophy' but it is all within the character of Prospero himself.

One bad fault of *Peter Grimes*, I thought, was that the minor characters like Auntie and Boles so often talk *at* each other, and *to* the audience, and do not really engage in conversation, talking *to* each other. But perhaps Slater would reply that people of their education and manners do very often express their feelings regardless of the people they are talking with, and do just talk into the blue. But I can't think it makes good drama on the stage.

Much of the same applied to the chorus at times, especially in the scene following the Inquest (and during the Inquest – though I must say the Inquest scene is masterly as a whole and about the best 'exposition' of an opera I have ever known) where they have a long sustained tune. It is a poor tune, and you don't really hear any words; it is really survival (to some extent modernized) of the old-fashioned 'opening chorus' of soldiers, gypsies or 'gentlemen of Japan'. The other bad patch, I always felt, was the much admired ensemble of the women after the men go off to lynch Peter at the hut. I find it musically boring and vocally ill-contrived, also utterly static; and it is inappropriate that Ellen should join in block harmony with Auntie and the nieces. The Budapest producer at least had the sense to make her stand very much apart from them.

Boles was always a great character thrown away. When I went to the preliminary lecture at the Wigmore Hall [on 31 May 1945], before the first SW [Sadler's Wells] production, and extracts were sung, I got the impression that Boles (very well sung by Morgan Jones) was going to play a great part in the opera; but he didn't, and at CG [Covent Garden] it was worse still, because the part was sung by . . .

Why has Britten dropped Slater as a librettist? If they had gone on working together we might have had another opera on the level of Grimes and better, if they both learned (and in collaboration) something from experience. But with Ronald Duncan poor B.B. fell out of the frying-pan into the fire, and every mistake of inexperience made by him with Slater was intensified instead of being corrected. I enjoyed *Herring* as an amusing triviality but don't think I want to see it again; *Lucretia* is just dreadful. I saw *Grimes* about a dozen times and was always deeply gripped and moved by it.

See *Bernard Stevens and his Music*, compiled and edited by Bertha Stevens (London, Kahn & Averill, 1989), pp. 150–53. See also note 3 to Letter 181.

The programme for the first performance of *Peter Grimes*, Sadler's Wells, 7 June 1945

The action of the opera takes place in THE BOROUGH, a small East Coast Fishing-town, early in the nineteenth century

ACT I —Prologue	.....	.....	.....	.....	.....	A Court Room in the Moot Hall
Scene 1	.....	.....	.....	.....	.....	The High Street. A few days later
Scene 2	.....	.....	.....	.....	.....	Inside "The Boar." The same evening
ACT II—Scene 1	.....	.....	.....	.....	.....	The High Street. Some weeks later
Scene 2	.....	.....	.....	.....	.....	Peter Grimes' hut
ACT III—Scene 1	.....	.....	.....	.....	.....	The High Street. Three days later
Scene 2	.....	.....	.....	.....	.....	The same. Early the following morning

(NOTE.—The Management would be grateful if applause were reserved until after the final scene of each act, as the musical action is continuous.

Produced by ERIC CROZIER
Scenery and Costumes by KENNETH GREEN

Scenery made in Sadler's Wells Workshops and painted by Henry Bird. Costumes made in the Sadler's Wells Workrooms under the direction of Maria Garde ; and by H. Sparrow
Properties by Harry Adams (Old Vic Workshops)   Joan Cross's Wig by Gustave
Wigs by " Bert "

THE STORY OF THE OPERA

In the life of his Suffolk fishing-town Peter Grimes fits uneasily. He lives alone, visionary, ambitious, impetuous, poaching and fishing without caution or care for consequences, and with only one friend in the town—the widowed schoolmistress, Ellen Orford. He is determined to make enough money to ask her to marry him, though too proud to ask her till he has lived down his unpopularity and remedied his poverty.

He fishes with the aid of an apprentice, bought, according to the custom of the time, from the work-house. In the Prologue he is chief witness in an inquest on his first apprentice and the verdict is accidental death. In Act I he is boycotted but obtains a second apprentice, whom Ellen goes to fetch for him and promises to care for. In Act II she discovers he has been using the boy cruelly. Frightened, Peter takes the boy down the scar of a recent landslide under which he moors his boat, and the boy falls down the cliff. When it is discovered that the boy is dead a hue-and-cry from the Borough sets out to find Peter, who commits suicide by scuttling his boat just out of sight of the town. This is in the small hours of the morning. The Borough wakes up and goes on with its life as usual.

Musical Director	.....	.....	.....	.....	.....	.....	LAWRANCE COLLINGWOOD
General Manager	.....	.....	.....	.....	.....	.....	BRUCE WORSLEY
Stage Director	.....	.....	.....	.....	.....	.....	ERIC BASS
Stage Manager	.....	.....	.....	.....	.....	.....	JOHN GREENWOOD
Chorus Master	.....	.....	.....	.....	.....	.....	ALAN MELVILLE
Secretary	.....	.....	.....	.....	.....	.....	SHEILA FERGUSSON
General Manager	.....	(for Old Vic and Sadler's Wells)	.....	GEORGE CHAMBERLAIN

SMOKING IS NOT PERMITTED

In accordance with the requirements of the Lord Chamberlain—
1.—The public may leave at the end of the performance by all exit doors and such doors must at that time be open.
2.—All gangways, passages and staircases must be kept entirely free from chairs or any other obstruction.
3.—Persons shall not in any circumstances be permitted to stand or sit in any of the gangways intersecting the seating, or to sit in any of the other gangways. If standing be permitted in the gangways at the sides and rear of the seating, it shall be strictly limited to the number indicated in the notices exhibited in those positions.
4.—The safety curtain must be lowered and raised in the presence of each audience.

503 **To Imogen Holst**

[IHB, *pp. 42–3; incomplete*]

> 45a, St. John's Wood High St.,
> N.W. 8.
> June 26th 1945

My dear Imogen,

Thank you for your kind letter about Peter Grimes. I am so glad that the opera came up to your expectations, & it is sweet & generous of you to write so warmly about it. I must confess that I am very pleased with the way that it seems to 'come over the foot-lights', and also with the way the audience takes it, & what is perhaps more, returns night after night to take it again! I think the occasion is actually a greater one than either Sadler's Wells or me, I feel. Perhaps it is an omen for English Opera in the future. Anyhow I hope that many composers will take the plunge, & I hope also that they'll find as I did the water not quite so icy as expected!

I am looking forward to the 14th–15th. So sorry that the programmes were so long in coming along; but Clifford's little temperament threw our plans out, & we were simply too exhausted to start thinking of new ones. I suggest that the Sunday Evening informal one should be three operatic groups from Joan C, Peter, & me (Mozart, Verdi, me – Solos & Duets) with Clifford doing pieces in between. When do you want details of that?

Many thanks again for your lovely letter, & with best wishes,

> Yours ever,
> BEN

504 **To Peter Pears**

> 45A, [St. John's Wood High St., N.W.8.]
> [?22 July 1945]

My darling,

This's only a scribbled note because I'm very sleepy, haven't practiced the old Kreutzer[1] at all, & want to go to bed soon.

I hope the journey wasn't too bad, & also that you aren't too lonely. It was bloody that you had to go off – we all felt miserable at leaving you, but none so incurable as I! But Joan will be arriving to-morrow, & that won't be so bad. See alot of her – she loves you dearly & needs you.

I slept till 10.30 (after drugs!) this morning, & spent most of the morning in bed. This afternoon at the British Council working out the records & casting.[2] Eric is going to be engaged by them as producer to manage everything, so things are under control. He's seeing Peter Cox to-morrow too. We plan opening May or June, with the New Op. Co.[3]

Well, honey darling, I go off to-morrow 3.0. Pray for me. I only hope Yehudi[4] remains nice. How I wish it were you! However – it isn't for long, & it can't be as bad as I imagine!

Take great care of yourself, my darling. You know how I love you, & believe in you.

Bless you
All my love
B.

1 Beethoven's Sonata in A minor, Op. 47, for violin and piano, which Britten was preparing for his visit to German concentration camps in the aftermath of Germany's defeat, as accompanist of Yehudi Menuhin. Nine concerts in five days were given under the auspices of the United Nations Relief and Rehabilitation Association. The visit was arranged by the Jewish Committee for European Relief and Britten was probably away between the 23rd and 30th July. See also Letter 505.

2 A complete recording by Decca of *Peter Grimes* under the auspices of the British Council had been proposed. This never happened, one consequence of the arguments and dissension within Sadler's Wells that ironically attended the success of the opera. (See also Eric Crozier, ' "Peter Grimes", an Unpublished Article of 1946', *Opera*, 16/6, June 1965, p. 415.) In July 1948, however, after the first production of the opera at Covent Garden, Pears, Cross and the Chorus and Orchestra of the Royal Opera House, Covent Garden, conducted by Reginald Goodall, recorded several excerpts from the opera for HMV. These recordings took place on the 14th and 16th, under the composer's supervision, and comprised 'Glitter of waves' (Act II scene 1), the 'Embroidery' aria (Act III scene 1), and the sixth orchestral interlude and Grimes's 'Mad' scene (Act III scene 2). It is not known why these excerpts were not issued at the time. Susana Walton, in her biography of her husband *William Walton: Behind the Façade* (Oxford, Oxford University Press, 1988), p. 125, recalls:

At that time the British Council had a recording panel, for which William was a consultant. When asked whether *Peter Grimes* should be recorded, William replied that, as funds available were so scarce, something less commercially viable should be selected. Britten was much offended. The opera was not recorded for another ten years.

The excerpts were finally released in 1972, as part of a set – 'Stars of the Old Vic and Sadler's Wells' (EMI RLS 707) – celebrating the Sadler's Wells Opera's golden days. In 1959 Britten's own complete recording, with Pears as Grimes, was issued on Decca SXL 2150–52.

There is an interesting history attached to this 1959 recording. Jeremy Cullum, who was Britten's secretary at the time, remembered in conversation with Rosamund Strode (1990), that Britten was 'in considerable pain when conducting the preparatory rehearsals for the recording of *Grimes.*' It appears that – 'while shaving' – he had 'managed to put his shoulder out'. Evidently, the story continues, Goodall came to the rescue, and although Britten conducted the actual takes he (Goodall) did all the preliminary rehearsing and sorting out (and presumably the trial takes), which of course accounted for more than half the physical effort involved. No doubt Britten was contractually bound to conduct the finished product (recorded at Walthamstow Assembly Hall) if he possibly could, and the mere fact of his having such a perfect deputy would doubtless have allowed him to relax a bit and un-stiffen.

On 20 December 1958 Britten wrote to Goodall:

I shall never forget your kindness & generosity in coming to help me out on the last days' recording of Peter Grimes. It was typical of you – also typical was the way you conducted the piece, without any preparation at all.

I am most grateful to you – & send my thanks along with best Xmas wishes to you & your wife –

This fascinating narrative means that the 1959 recording of *Grimes* might be thought to combine the composer's interpretation with that of the man who conducted the work's première in 1945, an interpretation itself much admired by the composer. After all, it seems, Goodall in one important sense left behind him a complete recorded version of his celebrated performance of *Grimes.*

3 The new operatic venture organized under the banner of Glyndebourne, which was to promote the first production of Britten's next opera, *The Rape of Lucretia*, with a libretto by Ronald Duncan. It was to be first performed on 12 July 1946 and marked the reopening of Glyndebourne after the war. The alternating casts included Pears, Joan Cross, Kathleen Ferrier and Nancy Evans, and the conductors were Ernest Ansermet and Reginald Goodall (see PFL, plates 188–204). Eric Crozier was the producer.

However, in the summer of 1945, Dartington, not Glyndebourne, was proposed as the venue for the launching of the 'New Op. Co.' and *Lucretia*. According to Dartington Hall records, this was originally to have taken place in April 1946, but in March 1946 Peter Cox was to write in his Arts Administration report:

Our plans for the summer have been curtailed by the cancellation of Benjamin Britten's English Opera Company's visit to Dartington. This is a great disappointment. The costs and other practical difficulties of running this venture were such that when Mr John Christie offered the Company a home in Glyndebourne and a financial guarantee, Britten accepted it, though with some regret.

The association with Glyndebourne was short-lived, but from these performances of *Lucretia* the idea of the English Opera Group was born. It was as a visiting company that the EOG was first to perform *Albert Herring* at Glyndebourne in 1947 (see PFL, plates 212–18). See also *The English Opera Group 1946–56*, edited by Colin Graham, with a cover design by John Piper (London, 1956).

4 Britten was about to leave for Germany with Yehudi Menuhin (b. 1916), American-born violinist and conductor, now of British nationality. During the Second World War he gave numerous concerts for American and Allied troops all over the world. Menuhin had a long friendship with Britten and Pears and was a frequent performer at the Aldeburgh Festival. When Menuhin founded the Gstaad Festival in 1956, and, later, in 1968, when he became Artistic Director of the Bath Festival, Pears and Britten were among the first performers invited to take part. See PFL, plates 280–83. In his autobiography, *Unfinished Journey* (London, Macdonald, 1977), pp. 178–9, Menuhin recalled the German tour, during which the composer was persistently referred to as 'Mr Button, Mr Menuhin's secretary':

I asked the British authorities if I might visit the camps in their sector, the British gave me permission to go, Gerald Moore agreed to come with me. Then, about a week before our departure, at a party given in London by the music publishers Boosey & Hawkes, I met Benjamin Britten. Returned to England after spending the war years largely in the United States, he too was casting about for some commitment to the human condition whose terrible depths had been so newly revealed, and was immediately enthusiastic about my initiative. He urged me to take him, and Gerald Moore very gracefully gave way.
[. . .]
Before leaving London, Ben and I made an attempt at rehearsing a repertoire, only, after five minutes, to abandon it: there was so much more than we could ever do, our understanding of each other's approach seemed so intuitively sure; we put our trust in luck and musical compatibility and set off for Germany. We took with us more or less the whole standard violin literature – concerti, sonatas, little pieces – and played it, without rehearsal, two or three times a day for ten days in the saddest ruins of the Third Reich. At Belsen we played twice in one afternoon. I shall not forget that afternoon as long as I live. The inmates of the camp had been liberated some weeks earlier, the prison huts burned down, and the ex-prisoners transferred to the adjoining SS barracks, which had, among other comforts, a theatre. Men and women alike, our audience was dressed in army blankets fashioned by clever tailors among them into skirts and suits. No doubt a few weeks since

their rescue they had put a little flesh on their bones, but to our unaccus-
tomed eyes they seemed desperately haggard, and many were still in hospital. Among these was a little gypsy boy whose sweetness and pathos so
struck me that had my domestic life not been a shambles, I would have
adopted him there and then. In the thirty years since that afternoon several
members of the Belsen audiences have come backstage to make themselves
known, restored to the living in Israel, Australia or elsewhere; but the gypsy
boy I never saw again.

See also note 5 to Letter 505.

505 To Peter Pears

Old Mill, Snape, Suffolk.
August 1st, 1945.

My own darling,

It was heaven to hear your voice after this mad week. I was
terribly disappointed that you didn't call last night, & had given
up hope until your wire at 8.0 this morning, & you at 8.45! I do so
hope this lousy tour[1] isn't being too hellish for you – don't take
any notice of those ludicrous fools[2] – they couldn't matter less. Just
sing as well as you can, & spend the time with Joan & Laurence[3]
& Reggie – & think about next week when you'll be here! It seems
ages since you left on that hideous train – & what a gloomy crowd
of us meandered across Regents Park home! I can't tell you all
about the trip now as we are going off to Aldeburgh in a moment
& I want to post this before I go (I've been lazy this morning and
corrected proofs in bed[4] – & only just got up!) Yehudi was nice,
& under the circumstances the music was as good as it could be –
with all that travelling all over the country & two, & sometimes
three concerts a day. We travelled in a small car over bad roads, &
got hopelessly lost often. But we saw heavenly little German
villages, with sweetest people in them (I swear that the Teutons
are the most beautiful (& cleanest) race on earth), & we saw
completely destroyed towns (like Münster) which haven't been
cleared up & yet have over 20,000 people (looking just as clean
as ever) living, God knows where, in them. And then on the other
side there were the millions of D.P.s [displaced persons] in, some
of them, appalling states, who could scarcely sit still & listen, &
yet were thrilled to be played to.[5] We stayed the night in Belsen,
& saw over the hospital – & I needn't describe that to you. On the
whole, the Military Government seems to be doing a good job, &
not as brutal or callous as one might fear – but o – what insoluble

problems. It was good to be able to do even this minute bit – &
I'm determined to do it again, & to organise other things too.
Unnra[6] (under whom we were), British Council,[7] & Emmie[8] are
all going to help.

Honey darling – I want to see you so badly. And to tell you all.
But it isn't too bad, to wait till next week, when some of these
people have to wait for ever for their beloveds. I don't know why
we should be so lucky, in all this misery.

Plans are going ahead for the Opera Company – Dartington is
fixed, Tennants[9] are extremely interested, & Ronnie has a man
with money. Rosemary is in Hospital already (thanks to old
Barbara).[10] Ronnie is coming here this week-end, & I expect most
week-ends too.

Take all the care in the world of yourself darling. I hope to have
something to show you when you get here.

And all, all my love

B

1 Sadler's Wells was on tour in Belfast from 23 July to 9 August. Pears
   sang in the *Bartered Bride* (24, 28 and 30 July), *Bohème* (27 July), and
   Così (2, 3, 7 and 9 August).

2 The friction within the Sadler's Wells company, manifest after the
   production of *Peter Grimes*.

3 Lawrance Collingwood (1887–1982), English conductor and composer, who studied in Russia with Glazunov. He joined the staff of
   the Old Vic Theatre in 1919 and later acted as rehearsal pianist and
   chorus-master. He became principal conductor of the Sadler's Wells
   company in 1931, retiring in 1946. He conducted the British premières
   of Rimsky-Korsakov's *Snow Maiden* and *Tsar Saltan*, and Mussorgsky's *Boris Godunov*.

4 The vocal score of *Grimes*. See also Letter 509.

5 The reaction of one member of that audience luckily survives in a .
   letter written by the young Anita Lasker (b. 1925), later Mrs Peter
   Wallfisch, now cellist in the English Chamber Orchestra, who in 1945
   was an inmate of Belsen when Menuhin and Britten gave their concert on 27 July. She wrote to an aunt three days later:

   On Friday Menuhin was really here in Belsen Camp. At first there was a
   rumour that it was only for Poles, and we were absolutely furious, but then
   it transpired that this was not meant too literally, and we managed to get
   tickets without too much trouble.

   It was a beautiful evening. Both soloist and accompanist were of a simplicity regarding their attire which almost bordered on the slovenly, which
   fitted the local atmosphere perfectly. No need to mention that Menuhin

played violinistically to perfection. After all he is Yehudi Menuhin, but I must say (and I beg you not to take this as impertinence on my part) I was a little disappointed. Soulful (like I imagine Casals's playing), it was not. It had really the feeling that he was saving himself. It may well be that the prevailing atmosphere did not exactly inspire him. It was impossible to achieve silence in the hall, and I felt really ashamed of the audience. A miracle that he did not just break up in the middle.

While Anita knew who Menuhin was, she of course had no knowledge whatsoever of his accompanist, which makes her reaction all the more remarkable:

Concerning the accompanist, I can only say that I just can not imagine anything more beautiful (wonderful). Somehow one never noticed that there was any accompanying going on at all, and yet I had to stare at this man like one transfixed as he sat seemingly suspended between chair and keyboard, playing so beautifully.

Yes, who would have believed that Belsen Camp would ever hear Menuhin. By the way, they played Prelude and Fugue Bach/Kreisler, the Kreutzer Sonata, Mendelssohn Concerto, something by Debussy and several other unknown things.

We are grateful to Mrs Wallfisch for allowing us to use this letter and for her translation.

In an interview with Menuhin, conducted for TP but not used in the film, the violinist recalled that at Belsen the inmates

just sat there as though in a dream and gradually they warmed and behaved as they generally thought an audience did behave. But at the beginning there was no question of an ordinary audience; they did not applaud when the artists arrived on the stage.

In this same interview, a further recollection from an eye-witness was introduced, a member of Queen Alexandra's Military Nursing Service, working in the camp, who remembered how inspiring it was to see

these two compassionate men clad simply in shirt and shorts creating glorious melody and moving amongst the people, people who were difficult to rouse with the deadly mental lethargy which was the result of the horrors and privations they had suffered [. . .]

6 UNRRA: United Nations Relief and Rehabilitation Agency.

7 The government-funded organization, founded in 1935, 'to promote abroad a wider appreciation of British culture and civilization'.

8 Emmie Tillett, head of Ibbs & Tillett, the musical agents who acted for Britten and Pears at this time.

9 H.M. Tennant, the theatrical agents and impresarios.

10 Rose-Marie, Duncan's wife, had developed tuberculosis. See RDBB, pp. 73–5 and 82–3, and PFL, plate 200. Presumably Barbara Britten, as a social worker, had been able to pull strings on Mrs Duncan's behalf and helped secure her hospitalization.

506 To Benjamin Britten
From Peter Pears

Royal Hotel
Bangor [Co. Down, Northern Ireland]
Saturday [4 August 1945]

My own honey bee –

I got your darling letter yesterday afternoon. It was so heavenly
to have it and I read it over and over again. The days are going
very quickly really and I shall soon be with you. How I wish it was
tomorrow. My whole being longs to be with you, my darling – to
feel you and hear you and look at you. I want to hear all about
Germany. Your letter makes one hope, in spite of all the horror.

We went down to Dublin on Tuesday morning (you were already
back, thank God, – I had your wire on Monday) until Wednesday
evening, and I must say it was like a breath of heaven – no war –
no bombs – smart brightly painted house, young people in tweeds
and summer frocks instead of uniforms, and any amount of good
food. We all built ourselves up like mad, & even Ulster food
which is better than English, seems very dull. The Free State are
being very good about Europe too, they were sending over 300
milch cows & many tons of sugar to Belgium while we were there
(though they are short of sugar in Eire too). It's very Catholic of
course, and there are beggars & extreme poverty, but they are
comparatively free. The worst are the English landed gentry with
hard voices like my sister! (Honey! love you!) We are coming to
Belfast on March 2nd you & I, & Dublin is open-armed to us.[1]
They have done the Serenade & Les Illuminations (though there's
only a tiny Group of lively music lovers) & I suggested that we
should go down & do Les Ill. & you conduct it?! However let's wait
& see. (Bee! love you!)

We see very little of the rest of the Company. Anna Pollak[2] came
to Dublin with us, she's very sweet & her Dorabella is a lot better
– she could be very useful to us in small ways. She would do
anything & is mad keen & adores us. I told her a little & she
would come at the drop of a hat. There are one or two other good
singers in the Chorus, intelligent sweet & mad keen; I think we
could get pretty well anyone we wanted. All very exciting. Roderick
Jones[3] spoke to me last night again saying how sick he was at not
being able to record Grimes, genuinely sick, I think, but Legge
wouldn't let him go,[4] & these people are like Edmund – they

darent cut off from a sure job yet. (Bunch! bee!) I could go on
writing and writing and don't really know or care what I'm writing
about (Honey!) because you're back and I'm going to see you in a
week (my boy!) it's a week a whole bloody week seven days 168
hours 10080 minutes. God knows how many seconds (my beloved)
& then my own darling I shall be with you close to you my lovely
boy & you will have all of me your lover

Your self

P.

1 Pears and Britten were to give two recitals on behalf of the British
  Music Society of Northern Ireland, at Queen's University, Belfast,
  on the afternoon and evening of 2 March 1946. The programmes
  included the *Michelangelo Sonnets*, the *Holy Sonnets of John Donne*
  and Folk-song Arrangements. We have been unable to trace the
  performance in Dublin.

2 English mezzo-soprano of Austrian parentage (b. 1915), and a pupil
  of Joan Cross, who had engaged her for Sadler's Wells. She made
  her début as Dorabella, and remained with the company until 1961.
  She also sang with the English Opera Group, creating the role of
  Bianca in *Lucretia* in 1946.

3 The Welsh baritone, who was Balstrode in the original production
  of *Peter Grimes*.

4 Pears refers to Walter Legge, who was responsible for planning the
  ENSA tour by the Sadler's Wells company, which had resulted in
  the postponement of the recording. But in fact, despite Britten's
  hopes (see Letters 508 and 509), the project was never reinstated. A
  report of the 'postponement' appeared in *Tempo*, 12 September 1945,
  p. 15. The recording, by Decca, had been planned to start on the
  3rd. See also MKWW, p. 132.

507 To Peter Pears

Old Mill
Bank [Holiday] Sunday
[6 August 1945]

My darling –

Thank you for your sweet note – it was heavenly to get it & to
have it. It has made these three dreary weeks more bearable. But
we are now in the last week – thank God. I can't wait till you're
here. It's looking so beautiful and the weather's so perfect. I hope
all this horrible vaccination will be over[1] when you arrive – not that

it's bad now, but I can't bathe, & I want so badly to bathe with
you –

Your voice has just come over the telephone. I feel sick that
you're alone this week-end, but it won't be too long – Ronnie,
Kit, Barbara & Helen are all here. It's quite smooth. I am very fond
& impressed by Ronnie – & we are discussing the opera hard. I think
we can make Lucretia into a lovely piece – with you & Joan as such
commentators! My other work is slowly going ahead – but I'm
abit weary, & can't get down to much yet. But it's heaven to deal
with Donne[2] instead of Montagu!

Excuse the shortness of this, but we're just off for a picnic, &
the others are shouting. I've found a wonderful Bach fugue
(independant) for key-board. (A minor, very fast).[3]

All my love, darling.

B.

1 See Letter 509.

2 *The Holy Sonnets of John Donne*, Op. 35, completed on 19 August,
   after Britten's return from Germany and undoubtedly coloured by
   the dark experience of the tour. The cycle was first performed by
   Pears and the composer on 22 November at the Wigmore Hall,
   London. Britten had been reading Donne's poetry at least two years
   earlier. Pears had written to Elizabeth Mayer on 13 February 1943:
   'What have you been reading lately? Ben and I have been re-reading
   Donne lately – those wonderful holy sonnets, and especially the
   Hymn to God the Father.' But even while still living in the United
   States, Britten had made an incomplete sketch for voice and piano
   of Donne's 'Stay, O Sweet, and do not rise', which probably dates
   from 1941.

3 There are two independent keyboard fugues in A minor by J.S. Bach:
   BWV 958 and 959.

508 To Jean Hamilton[1]
[*Pencil*]

Old Mill, Snape.
10th Aug. [1945]

My dear Jean,

This is only a horrible note to answer your more immediate
queries – as I'm in bed, & everso sorry for myself. (infantile things
like vaccinations can be horrible when you're a hoary old man).

(1)   I tried to call the garage about your gloves while dashing thro' London without getting an answer. But perhaps you can try. Name Walter Scott – Telephone Maida Vale 0191 (??).

2)   Arthur Oldham certainly got the money & shirt & was very grateful. Perhaps he had difficulty in paying it in. I'll write him.

3)   It looks as if August is no good for us for come to you – I'm stuck here all that time working like a Trojan. But the Grimes recording may now take place late September – could we please come then?

4)   Germany was a terrific & horrific experience; emminently worth while. I'm trying to get similar parties to repeat the dose, because it is necessary. I'm getting Unrra, Brit. Council etc. on to it. Too much to write about in my present feeble state (anyhow this letter must be hell to read) – but I'll tell all about [it] when we meet. By the way I met the Taylors![2] They're real charmers, & sent lots of love to you. Yehudi was nice, & what's more a sport, which was the quality most needed on the trip.

So glad John has transferred his blue-eyedom to Morrison.[3] Hope he finds him manageable.

Lots of love to you all.

BEN

1 Concert pianist (b. 1904), the wife of John Maud (1906–1982), who, knighted in 1946, was created Baron Redcliffe-Maud of the City and County of Bristol in 1967. At this time John Maud was Permanent Secretary at the Ministry of Education (1945–52), which had commissioned the film *Instruments of the Orchestra* (see note 7 to Letter 514). Britten dedicated *The Young Person's Guide to the Orchestra* (the concert version of the film music) 'to the children of John and Jean Maud: Humphrey, Pamela, Caroline and Virginia, for their edification and entertainment'. He was in close touch with the family from the 1940s and occasionally visited them at Oxford where Maud was Master of University College (1963–82).

2 Probably Charles Taylor, leader of the Covent Garden orchestra, and his family.

3 Herbert Stanley Morrison (Baron Morrison of Lambeth; 1888–1965), Labour politician. Morrison was one of the leading architects of the Labour landslide election victory of 1945. He was Home Secretary in Churchill's wartime administration and Attlee's deputy in the post-war Labour governments.

509   To Montagu Slater

Old Mill, Snape.
Aug. 28th, 1945.

My dear Montagu,

I am so very sorry that I have left you so in the dark. The reason
is that since I got down here after my madly hectic German trip
I have been more or less laid-up. The doctor insisted on vaccination
after I was back, & now after a month my leg is still very bad, &
I spend alot of time in bed & can't really get around or down to
anything. I suppose it's just overwork; but a bore all the same as
it's putting me back so. Any how the proofs of Grimes have been
sweated thro' – I didn't bother you with them since they are word
for word the same as the Sadler's Wells performance which I
thought we'd agreed upon as being intelligible & singable.[1] If you
insist on seeing the proofs, of course ring Roth – but do remember
the urgency. Basle is already fixed[2] & wants copies, & Prague,
Paris, & Broadway (believe it or not!) are waiting, 'interested'.[3] I
never bother poets with my proofs of their stuff – at least, Wystan
never read his. But sorry if I've slipped up. I've left ''his temper's
up'', since that still seemed the most simple & singable (to that
phrase). Also, on thinking it over I felt that it could easily refer to
the middle of Peter's song, & altho' he is at this moment sitting
quietly, it could seem to them ominous, & after all he <u>does</u> scream
''get out'' a moment after.

It looks at the moment as if the powers of Evil have won & that
the recording of Grimes is off – at least temporally. Personally I
haven't got time to intrigue to this degree – & after all there the
piece <u>is</u>, & a matter of months doesn't really matter. But it's
depressing.

Germany was exhausting to a degree (9 concerts in 4 days &
miles of bumpy travel in small car each day) & most harrowing
(condition of the D.P.'s, & the Germans, & first sights of really
bombed towns). But I think it was worth doing, & Yehudi was
nice.

Love to all the family. I hope you're well.
Yours ever,
BEN

1 This letter is eloquent of the difficulties attending the writing of the
   libretto for *Grimes*. Slater was protective of the integrity of his text,
   sometimes justifiably so (see PBPG, pp. 37–9 and 62–4), sometimes

not. All the evidence suggests, however, that he was a preternaturally slow, cautious worker who did not find it easy to respond speedily or perhaps to understand the needs and priorities of a composer. Slater subsequently published the text of *Grimes* as a poem in its own right, with none of the changes imposed (as he saw it) by the exigencies of the opera house. See Montagu Slater, *Peter Grimes and Other Poems* (London, The Bodley Head, 1946). A comparison of Grimes's mad scene (Act III scene 2) as it appears in Slater's poem with the parallel passage from the libretto demonstrates the differences:

PETER:
Quietly. Here you are. You're home.
This breakwater with splinters torn
By winds, is where your father took
You by the hand to this same boat
Leaving your home for the same sea
Where he died and you're going to die.

Quietly. Here you are. You're home.
You're not to blame that he went down.
It was his weakness that let go.
He was too weak. Were you to know?
He was too weak, and so the sea
Engulfed him, and you're going to die.

VOICES:
Peter Grimes. Peter Grimes.

PETER:
You shouters there – I've made it right.
It was my conscience, my fate
Got rid of him. If you who call
Don't understand, old Swallow will.

PETER:
' Steady. There you are. Nearly home.
What is home? Calm as deep water.
Where's my home? Deep in calm water.
Water will drink my sorrows dry.
And the tide will turn.

VOICES:
Grimes!

PETER:
Steady. There you are. Nearly home.
The first one died, just died . . .
The other slipped, and died . . .
And the third will . . .
'Accidental circumstances' . . .
Water will drink his sorrows –
   my sorrows – dry
And the tide will turn.

VOICES:
Peter Grimes, Peter Grimes!

PETER:
Peter Grimes! Here you are! Here I am!
Hurry, hurry!
Now is gossip put on trial.
Bring the branding iron and knife
For what's done now is done for life . . .
Come on! Land me!
'Turn the skies back and begin again.'

It will be noted that the text from the libretto, a scene on which Britten worked with Ronald Duncan, allows for the brilliant cadenza-like recapitulation of leading musical ideas that reach back to the very opening bars of the opera. This is a dimension entirely absent from Slater's version, and which must have been devised to meet the composer's needs at this crucial formal juncture in the opera.

2 The first Swiss production of *Grimes* was to be given at Basel, on 6 May 1946, with Z. Wozniak in the title role, conducted by Alexander Krannhals.

3 The earliest performance of *Grimes* in Czechoslovakia was a Prague radio broadcast in 1947. Its first stage performance took place at Brno, on 28 June, with A. Jurecka in the title role, conducted by R. Brock. Covent Garden Opera Company took Guthrie's production to Paris

in 1948, where it was first heard on 9 June, with Richard Lewis as Grimes, conducted by Karl Rankl. The opera was not heard on Broadway. Its American première was at Tanglewood in 1946, while its first performance at the Metropolitan, New York, was given on 12 February 1948.

510 To Lucille Wallace

Old Mill, Snape, Suffolk.
Sept 8th 1945

My dear Lucille,

Your letter is now nearly a month old, & I am so sorry that it has lain all this time unanswered. As a matter of fact I haven't been frightfully well (a first vaccination at my age is no joke!), & on top of that I've been pretty busy, as Clifford will verify, & on top of everything I'm just a damn bad letter-writer. Please forgive me.

I was terribly touched by your most generous offer. It is incredibly sweet and kind of you to have thought of helping me in my ambitious schemes in the housing direction;[1] and had things turned out differently it would have been a most acceptable offer. As it happened I had already decided not to bid for the Rectory; coming on top of everything, opera and crises & all, I couldn't face it – and just as well too, as the delapidated old house, valued by some architects at about £1500, went for £6200 at the auction! But believe me, my dear, it wasn't a Harpsichord idea which was frightening me away – but just plain lack of hours & minutes.

I had hoped that you & Clifford could have come, as you said, to our little party; but when that fell through I realised it was hopeless. But thank you a thousand times, & apologies for the misunderstanding which must have seemed grotesquely rude to you.

I hope your apalling alarums & excursions over the White House[2] are calming down a bit now. What a time you've had! We're starting the same game with our old house at Lowestoft, so I do rather know what it all means.[3]

I very much want to see you both when you, & I, are back in the middle of the month. Clifford's rest-fast- cure sounds a bit drastic, but I hope it'll do him the heap of good he so obviously needs before embarking on next season.

Much love to you both, and many thanks again.
BENJIE

1 Lucille Curzon had written to Britten on 12 August:

It didn't dawn on me till fairly late in the proceedings, that you must have supposed my wanting to see you 'on business' meant <u>my</u> business. Actually it was about <u>your</u> business, i.e. your prospective house purchase.

Some Anglo-American transactions unexpectedly fell through and I at once thought of you, because for those few days before the final re-shuffle, I should have had a suitable sum available. All of this I had meant to discuss with you when you came out on the Sunday, as you had suggested. But when Sunday didn't materialize, and when I saw that the mere mention of 'business' on my part seemed to make any other meeting so difficult, I realized you had probably suspected a commission for a Hps. Concerto or something equally awkward, just at the moment when your interest in 'this quaint old instrument' has, perhaps, led you farther afield!

2 The Curzons' London home at Millfield Lane, Highgate.

3 Negotiations to sell 21 Kirkley Cliff Road, Lowestoft, which had remained in the family's possession since Mr Britten's death in 1934.

511 To Arthur Oldham

Old Mill
[September/October 1945]

Dear Arthur,

In haste.

Here is your fragment.[1] I suggest that she sings it as many times as necessary – quite slowly or remotely – but each time <u>softer</u>. If it doesn't do – call me

Good luck
BEN

1 Presumably a late addition, made during the rehearsals of Ronald
  Duncan's *This Way to the Tomb*, first performed by the Pilgrim Players
  at the Mercury Theatre, London, on 11 October. Oldham was musical
  director of the production, which ran for eighteen months. The 'fragment' forms the interpolation for an off-stage soprano: see Duncan,
  Collected Plays (London, Hart-Davis, 1971), p. 27. A review (unsigned)
  appeared in the *New Statesman and Nation*, 3 November 1945:

> Ronald Duncan's poetic Masque, with its subtle rhyming and effective satire,
> is used to convey a Chestertonian attack on materialism. It is divided into
> two parts; the first presents the temptations of St Antony, who until the last
> moment was unable to find the peace of God because, in rejecting the sins
> of the flesh, he could not cast out the sin of Pride. The second half, the
> 'Anti-masque', presents the shrine of St Antony in the twentieth century;
> on the day when the peasants expect the Saint to rise from the dead. But
> the tomb is actually haunted by a television unit which tours the world
> exposing religious pretensions, under the illusion that the living spirit of a
> saint can be photographed. The modern young things who want to expose
> the superstition of the peasants obtain no scientific results, and trample on
> St Antony when he appears. But they discover in themselves the fear of
> their own emptiness. The beautiful words of the Masque were perfectly
> enunciated by Robert Speaight, whose performance of St Antony is through-
> out beyond praise. Among the rest of an excellent cast one may mention
> particularly Frank Napier, who achieves exactly the right degree of smugness
> as a fourteenth-century disciple wishing to become famous by writing St
> Antony's biography, and the right degree of hypocrisy as a twentieth-century
> priest who does not believe in Christianity. The play falters only at the end,
> where Ronald Duncan leaves the audience unsure whether his conclusion
> supports the whole Catholic view or is only meant as an attack on the
> scientific age which thinks that the only realities are those you can record
> with a machine. Benjamin Britten's songs are finely sung by Eric Shilling.
> This is a performance of real intellectual and aesthetic value.

  One of the pianists in the performance was John (Homer) Lindsay,
  a co-student of Oldham's at the College. His recollections of his
  friendship with Britten, initiated by his participation in *This Way to
  the Tomb*, form the subject of a long interview with Donald Mitchell,
  London, 10 July 1990; Archive.

512 To Hubert Hales[1]

Old Mill, Snape Suffolk
Oct. 8th 1945

Dear Mr. Hales,

Thank you for your letter. I was glad to get news of Gresham's
& to hear that the school is now returned to Holt.

I am afraid that my interest in the School is not dictated by

inclination, but by the amount of free time at my disposal – strictly
limited! In many ways I am very grateful to the school. On the
whole I was happy there.[2] Owing, I am afraid, to mutual suspicion
between Mr. Greatorex and myself I didn't get much
encouragement or help musically, although Miss Chapman was
always very patient with my scratchings on the viola!

But in many ways I remember the school with great affection;
Basil Fletcher – now at Bristol University, when I occasionally see
him – was especially good to me.

I should like to hear news of the school from time to time – but
preferably not via Old Boy's meetings which I abhor – especially
if there are particularly promising boys in some direction when I
could help and encourage. Perhaps you could write occasionally?

Thank you for your kind congratulations. In many ways I have
been very lucky.

With best wishes,

Yours sincerely,
BENJAMIN BRITTEN

Please give my best wishes to Miss Chapman & Mr. Taylor.

1 Hales was an assistant master at Gresham's from 1924 to 1928, and
returned to succeed Greatorex as Director of Music from 1936.

2 T.A. [Blanco] White, who for a time shared a study with Britten at
Gresham's recollected in 1989:

I can only guess what anyone else thought of him. Our housemaster and
prefects will have disapproved of him, as I know they did of me; but he was
recognised as having exceptional talent and that meant allowing him to go
his own way; Holt was for its time exceptionally tolerant of anyone showing
any sort of above-average ability. I imagine that any other boys who came
to think about him at all just thought him a bit of an oddity; by no means
the only one.

513   To Mary Behrend

45A St. Johns Wood High St
N.W. 8.
[3 December 1945]

My dear Mary,

Your sweet letters have given Peter & me much happiness. Thank
you so much, & for your most generous cheque, which has helped
us to be able to send the fine cheque of over £350 to the India
Relief. You will be getting the MS of the Quartet[1] very soon – when

the engravers are finished with it. I am so glad you got pleasure from it because to my mind it is the greatest advance that I have yet made, & altho' it is far from perfect, it has given me encouragement to continue on new lines. People don't understand it as they do the Donne, but that is because those wonderful words help so.

Thank you for providing such a generous incentive to write it! Love to you & Bow – in great haste.

BEN.

1 Britten's String Quartet No. 2. The manuscript was presented by Mrs Behrend to St Michael's College, Tenbury. In 1987 the College placed it on loan to the Britten–Pears Library.

514 To Ralph Hawkes[1]

Old Mill, Snape, Suffolk.
Dec. 19th, 1945.

My dear Ralph,

I have been meaning to write to you for ages, but, as I know you realise, time for writing letters occurs so very rarely! It is really only when I manage to steal a few days down here, that I get enough leisure to think quietly. I was glad to get Clare's letter & to hear personal news of you both. You seem to be having a whale of a time – how I envy you all that comfort & luxury! This winter is being a fairly hard one, & down here especially one misses adequate fuelling – this house was designed for central heating, & is fairly cheerless without it. But still, it's nothing to Europe, of which Peter & I had a tiny foretaste not long ago, at the beginning of the cold weather. We had a fine time, in Paris, & a real wow with our recital, going to Bordeaux as well, & if we hadn't had to get back, should have gone to Lyons & Toulouse[2] as well. Actually getting back was no easy matter as we were stuck on the boat at Dieppe for two days, because of a great Channel gale, & consequently missed all our connections to Germany, to have been next on the list.

Since then everything's been rattling along. The New opera company is slowly materialising and I hope to give you definite news of this, place & dates, within a week or so. We're all very excited about it, & some fine people are joining us. I haven't started the Rape of Lucretia yet, but Ronnie Duncan is half-way thro' the libretto which I think terrific. I expect Erwin told you

about the Purcell concerts.[3] They really went well and we are
developing ambitious plans about a long series of Purcell
realisations by me! It is most wonderful music and gets
extraordinary receptions everywhere. Peter & I have done it all
over this country, & we're going to do some of the big pieces in
Amsterdam & Brussels next month.[4] The new quartet & the Donne
went well too – it's a pity you won't be there for the repeat concert
on Jan. 4th.[5] I'm just clearing up my 'chores' before getting down to
the opera – some incidental music for a play of Louis MacNeice for
BBC,[6] & the Purcell variations for the Orchestra film.[7] I'm hoping
that the latter may be useful for the ordinary orchestra repertoire,
but I'm not sure yet. Be patient, please, Ralph! I'll turn out some
orchestral pieces before long for you – but don't be too depressed
if things aren't too good about me in the U.S.A. Let matters take
their course there. I'm afraid that I am conceited enough to feel
that eventually they'll come round, as this country & the continent
have – but at the moment my music is neither ordinary enough or
shocking enough to hit them. I'm sorry, but only because of the
good orchestras on your side – not because of the audiences, the
critics, or the impressarios for whom I can't care much! But I
realise how infuriating it must be for you, and am very grateful for
what you're doing. Incidentally I'm relieved that the Dowling
Grimes[8] is off – he seems to have extraordinary theories on how to
treat serious works! I should like to have heard Mrs. Mundy's
party, and your expostulation of Grimes. I bet you did it well –
after all you heard it quite a few times here! It goes back to the
Wells on Feb. 7th,[9] but I don't have much hopes of a better show
there (they're in the most dreadful mess up there now) – it's
Zurich that I'm looking forward to – ![10]
    There's one small business matter which I ought to have
discussed with you before you left, & which is a bit overdue now,
& that is about my new Contract with you. I wonder if you would
mind if I went back to the original method of only receiving what
I earn, & when I earn it. You see, Ralph, I am scared of receiving
the large sum you mention (£600 per annum) & then (by evil
chance) having to pay some back at the end of three years. If I
needed a large sum now I should have to accept the advance
method, but I don't & I'm old-fashioned enough not to feel easy
about receiving more than I actually earn. You may say that I
probably shall earn at least £600 p.a., but one can never tell what
can happen. So please, if you don't mind let's wash it out. I
expect, however, that you will want some kind of 'Exclusivity'

contract with me? – not, I can assure you, that I'm likely to go off
to Augeners. If this is the case, perhaps you'd like a much smaller
guarantee, & not an advance of the size you mention. Perhaps
you'd let me know what you feel about this. I haven't mentioned
it to Leslie yet.[11]

Please thank Clare very much for her letter. I was very glad to
get all the gossip & messages. I hope she's enjoying the West
Coast as much as the East. I expect you'll find Hollywood jubilant
over the resounding flop of Caesar & Cleopatra! Something tells
me I was wise to steer clear of that little picture. Anyhow that
world is not for me. We have all enjoyed the food-parcels no end[12]
– thank you both everso much for the very kind thoughts. We daily
eat your healths now! We all send the season's greetings to you
both, and best wishes for the New Year. How long are you going
to be away? Don't be away too long, nor become too infatuated
with the New World. The Old World's got quite abit of life in her
yet – besides she needs you to keep an eye on her!

With many thanks, & best wishes to you both,
Yours ever,
BEN

P.S.   Please give my love to the Mayers, Mundys and all my good
friends. I'm so glad that you remembered them for the de Luxe
Grimes edition![13] It is a splendid affair, & Joan, Peter and all are
thrilled by it.

1   At this time Hawkes was head of the New York office of Boosey &
    Hawkes.

2   Pears and Britten had given a recital at the Salle du Conservatoire,
    Paris, on 20 October: 'Have you seen but a whyte lilie grow?' (Anon,
    c.1600); Dowland: 'Sorrow, stay'; Purcell (realized Britten): 'There's
    not a swain', 'Turn thine eyes' and 'On the brow of Richmond Hill';
    Schubert: 'Am See' (D.746), 'Auf der Bruck' (D.853), 'Du bist die
    Ruh' (D.776), 'Die Allmacht' (D.852); Britten: Seven Sonnets of Michel-
    angelo and four of the French Folk-song Arrangements. The pro-
    gramme was repeated on 23 October at the Ciné-Mondial, Bordeaux.

3   Two concerts were held to mark the 250th anniversary of the death
    of Henry Purcell (1659–1695). On 21 November (the anniversary of
    his death), at the Wigmore Hall, London, the programme contained
    Purcell's Four-part Fantasia for strings, No. 4 in F, and Five-part
    Fantasia, No. 13 (Fantasia upon one note), performed by the Zorian
    String Quartet with Robert Donington (viola); the Quartet also gave
    the first performance of Britten's Second String Quartet in C, Op. 36

(written in homage to Henry Purcell). Pears and Britten performed Britten's realization of Purcell's Divine Hymn, 'Lord, what is Man?', and were joined by Margaret Ritchie and Richard Wood in further Purcell items: 'Saul and the Witch at Endor', 'Fairest Isle', 'Lost is my quiet', 'Man is for the woman made', 'There's not a swain', 'What can we poor females do?', 'Pious Celinda', 'I spy Celia' and 'If music be the food of love' (3rd version). Britten's realization of Purcell's 'The Blessed Virgin's Expostulation' was sung by Margaret Ritchie, accompanied by Britten. Finally, Purcell's Trio Sonata in F (the 'Golden' Sonata) for two violins, cello and continuo was performed by Olive Zorian and Marjorie Lavers (violins), Norina Semino (cello), and Britten at the piano, again in his realization of the thoroughbass.

On 22 November, once more at the Wigmore Hall, Pears and Britten gave the first performance of *The Holy Sonnets of John Donne*. The remainder of the programme comprised: Purcell's Verse Anthem, 'My beloved spake'; 'My song shall be alway of the loving kindness of the Lord'; *The Queen's Epicedium*; Anthem: 'Why do the Heathen?' and *Ode for St Cecilia's Day* (1692).

The Times, on 24 November, published a notice of both concerts:

[Britten's] tribute to Purcell properly contained a measure of imitation; in his new string quartet he included a Chacony, and in his sonnet cycle, which Mr Peter Pears sang, he handles verbal rhythms, word painting, and the sense of line with the inspiration derived from the older master. This second string quartet is a more convincing work than the first, though it contains patches of fog in places where he is trying to do what is easier on an orchestra – namely, create a diffused sonority instead of a tissue of themes. But the themes of the three movements are clear enough and strong enough to make the work, which was played by the Zorian Quartet, pungent without being aggressive, original without strain. In Donne's 'Holy Sonnets' he had burning words to fire him. Four of the nine stood out at a first hearing; the first; 'O my black soul', with its headlong plunge into passionate sound; the sixth, a love song that sweetened the astringency of the seventeenth century with a breath of Schubert; the familiar 'At the round earth's imagined corners', with the directness of its own trumpet call, and the final funeral march, a superb conception to match the words 'Death, be not proud'. Some of the quicker ones, notably No. 2, raise again the question whether what might be called his scherzo treatment of words is as effective in fact as it is ingenious in conception. But the cycle triumphs by its sustained intensity.

There was an additional Purcell concert on 23 November (at the National Gallery, London), when Pears and Britten were joined by the Aeolian String Quartet. The programme included 3 three-part Fantasias, 2 four-part Fantasias and a Chacony, and realizations of 'Lord, what is man?', 'Evening Hymn', 'If music be the food of love' (first version), 'I'll sail upon the dog-star' and 'Sweeter than roses'.

4 Britten and Pears were to give an 'Engelsche Liederenavond' on 11 January 1946 in the Kleine Zaal of the Concertgebouw, Amsterdam:

'Have you seen but a whyte lilie grow?' (Anon, *c.* 1600); John Bartlett: 'When from my love'; Dowland: 'Sorrow, stay'; Purcell (realized Britten): 'There's not a swain', 'Sweeter than roses', and Three Divine Hymns; Britten: *Seven Sonnets of Michelangelo* and Folk-song Arrangements. We have not been able to trace the date of the Brussels concert.

5 Britten and Pears were to take part in a concert at the Wigmore Hall on 4 January 1946. The programme comprised: Purcell, realized Britten: 'Lord, what is Man' and 'A Divine Hymn' (Pears and Britten); Britten: String Quartet No. 2 (Zorian String Quartet) and *The Holy Sonnets of John Donne* (Pears and Britten); and Purcell, realized Britten: Trio Sonata in F, the 'Golden' Sonata, Olive Zorian and Marjorie Lavers (violins), Norina Semino (cello), Britten (piano).

6 *The Dark Tower*, first broadcast on 21 January 1946, produced by Louis MacNeice, with Britten's score conducted by Walter Goehr. Britten collaborated closely with MacNeice on this project, and the latter dedicated the published text to him (London, Faber and Faber, 1947). See also Barbara Coulton, *Louis MacNeice in the BBC* (London, Faber and Faber, 1980), pp. 77–83; PR, pp. 656–65; and PFL, plates 210–11.

Philip Hope-Wallace wrote about the broadcast in the *Listener* on 24 January:

And what of 'The Dark Tower'? An uncouth modern edifice, Baedeker might say. But no play by MacNeice can be passed by with indifference, and that alone is a score in radio where masterpiece and bagatelle only too often seem 'much of a muchness'. The long verse-allegory dealt with The Quest, a subject which, one remembered, had led other notable talents astray – something about Parsifal's Progress seems to bring out the bore in the liveliest spirits. We were conscious of a real poet's sensibility, of a wide power of matching new-minted phrase and stale jargon to make a language which should touch heart and mind and ear freshly. Yet the parable was very difficult to visualise; indeed, I think it was the poet's deliberate intention that it should be so. But the mind's eye, seeing nothing, was restless, and imagination refused to warm to the long-drawn dedicated venture. And yet, comparatively, how distinguished and original the idea and the idiom, with its acute musical commentary by Britten, melodrama in the true sense. But the successful mating of music and the speaking voice, of which this was an example, remains one of radio's first artistic problems. The trouble is that sooner or later – as composers of light opera have discovered – the music makes the tone of speech sound inadequate.

James Butt ('Lord Britten: Some Recollections', *East Anglian Daily Times*, 5 December 1978) recollects arriving at Erwin Stein's home 'and finding that there was an emergency to cope with [. . .] because Ben had written music for a radio play which had to be copied'.

7 *Instruments of the Orchestra* (Crown Film Unit for the Ministry of Education), produced by Alexander Shaw, directed by Muir Mathie-

son, with a script by Montagu Slater. The film featured the London Symphony Orchestra conducted by Malcolm Sargent and was first to be screened at the Empire Theatre, Leicester Square, London, on 29 November 1946. The score was completed on New Year's Eve 1945. In its concert version as *The Young Person's Guide to the Orchestra*, Op. 34, with a commentary by Eric Crozier, it was first performed on 15 October 1946 in Liverpool by the Liverpool Philharmonic Orchestra conducted by Sargent. A review of the film by Scott Goddard was published in *Penguin Music Magazine*, Vol. 3, edited by Ralph Hill (West Drayton, Penguin, 1947), pp. 64–5. Goddard describes the film as 'altogether a brilliant piece of showmanship', and once again the composer's 'cleverness' is emphasized: 'Benjamin Britten's score has nothing to learn from a bag full of monkeys or film magnates.' See also Hans Keller, 'A Film Analysis of the Orchestra', *Sight and Sound*, 16/61, 1947, pp. 30–31, where Keller writes of Britten's music:

Needless to say, it is among the best music that has ever been written for the cinema, and one may add that it is not only a young person's guide to the orchestra, but also, in an implied if unintended fashion, something of a young composer's guide to orchestration.

It was Basil Wright – working in 1945 as producer-in-charge at the Crown Film Unit – who commissioned Britten to compose the music for the film. In a letter to Eric Walter White (1 April 1948) he recalled:

Ben was very busy & it was a long time before he got down to it. But one minute after midnight, New Year's Day, 1946, he phoned me with New Year's wishes & the job finished. He played it through to me the next morning.

Shortly after this Wright left the Crown Film Unit and the project was taken over by Mathieson and Shaw.

According to a recollection of Norman Del Mar's, the performance we hear on the soundtrack of the film was conducted by Muir Mathieson, *not* by Sargent, whose principal interest was to undertake the role of instructor and narrator. This probably explains why the interpolations of spoken text make the detached impression that they do: that is precisely what they were. Footage of Sargent conducting the *Young Person's Guide* may have been used, but it was not his performance that was finally synchronized with the film.

Rosamund Strode tells us that the composer was much irritated by the BBC's practice of referring to the work as *Variations and Fugue on a Theme of Henry Purcell*, Op. 34 – its sub-title – instead of using its correct title, *The Young Person's Guide to the Orchestra*. It seems that this tradition was the result of a directive from Sargent, who may have thought the proper title altogether too frivolous in the context of concert performances. The BBC was eventually persuaded to amend its announcements.

8 Was it that Denis Dowling, the baritone, had been invited to direct the 1946 Sadler's Wells revival of *Peter Grimes*?

9 The opera returned to Sadler's Wells in 1946 for performances (with Pears in the title role) on 7, 12, 14 and 26 February; 13 and 15 March; 23 and 25 April, and 1 and 4 May.

10 *Grimes* was performed in Zürich on 1 and 5 June 1946, with Pears in the title role and Joan Cross as Ellen, conducted by R. Denzler. The soprano Lisa Della Casa sang the role of the Second Niece.

11 Leslie Periton.

12 Food rationing was still in force.

13 Boosey & Hawkes had published a specially bound edition of the vocal score signed by the composer. Pears received copy No. 2, now in the Archive, which also possesses the copy given to Reginald Goodall.

The composition sketch of *Peter Grimes*: 'Now the Great Bear and Pleiades'

BIBLIOGRAPHY

Compiled by Philip Reed

A., 'Theatre, Art, Culture' [review of first performance of *Bridge Variations*], *Salzburger Volksblatt*, 28 August 1937

A., A.H., 'Theatre, Art, Culture' [review of first performance of *Bridge Variations*], *Salzburger Chronik*, 28 August 1937

Abraham, Gerald, 'Britten, Rubbra, and Prokofiev' [review of first concert performance of *Hymn to St Cecilia*], *Observer*, 6 December 1942

Abraham, Gerald, 'This Week's Concerts' [review of first performance of *Michelangelo Sonnets*], *Observer*, 27 September 1942

Aiken, W.A., *The Voice: An Introduction to Practical Phonology*, London, Longmans, Green & Co., 1951

Aldeburgh Festival Programme Books, 1948–90

Alston, John, Interview with Donald Mitchell, Aldeburgh, 20 June 1988; The Britten–Pears Library

American Film Institute Catalogue of Motion Pictures, 1921–30, New York, Epping Bouker, 1971

Amis, John, *Amiscellany: My life, my music*, London, Faber and Faber, 1985

Ancient English Christmas Carols MCCCC-MDCC, collected and arranged by Edith Rickert, London, Chatto & Windus, 1928

Anderson, Hedli, Interview with John Evans, October 1980, Paris; The Britten–Pears Library

Anderson, W.R., 'Fleet Street Choir (T.B. Lawrence); *Hymn to St Cecilia*, Op. 27' [review of gramophone recording], *Gramophone*, May 1943

'Answers to Correspondents', *Musical Times*, October 1928, p. 920

Antheil, George, *Bad Boy of Music*, New York, Doubleday, 1945

Apel, Willi, *Harvard Dictionary of Music*, London, Routledge & Kegan Paul, 1951

Apuleius, Lucius, *The Golden Asse*, Adlington's translation (with T. Petronius Arbiter: *The Satyricon*; and Longus: *Daphnis and Chloe*), London, Simpkin Marshall, 1933

Armor, John, and Wright, Peter, *Manzanar*, with commentary by

John Hersey and photographs by Ansel Adams, London, Secker & Warburg, 1989

[Astle, Ethel], 'Mr. Benjamin Britten's First Music Teacher', *Eastern Daily Express*, 26 April 1952

Atkins, Harold, and Cotes, Peter, *The Barbirollis: a Musical Marriage*, London, Robson Books, 1983

Auden, W.H., *Another Time*, New York, Random House, 1940

——, *Collected Poems*, London, Faber and Faber, 1976

——, *Collected Shorter Poems*, London, Faber and Faber, 1966

——, *The Complete Works of W.H. Auden: Plays (with Christopher Isherwood) and other Dramatic Writings, 1928–1938* [EMWHA], edited by Edward Mendelson, London, Faber and Faber, 1989

——, *The Dance of Death*, London, Faber and Faber, 1933

——, 'The Dark Valley', in *Best Broadcasts of 1939–40*, selected and edited by Max Wylie, New York, Whittlesey House, 1940, pp. 33–43

——, *The Double Man*, New York, Random House, 1941; also published as *New Year Letter*, London, Faber and Faber, 1941

——, *For the Time Being*, New York, Random House, 1944

——, 'Honour', in *The Old School: Essays by Diverse Hands*, edited by Graham Greene, Oxford, Oxford University Press, 1984, pp. 5–6

——, 'Letter to Elizabeth Mayer', *Atlantic*, 167, January–February 1941

——, *Look, Stranger!*, London, Faber and Faber, 1936

——, 'Ode to the George Washington Hotel', introduced by Edward Mendelson, *New York Times Book Review*, 8 March 1981, p. 11

——, 'Opera on an American Legend: Problem of Putting the Story of Paul Bunyan on the Stage', *New York Times*, 4 May 1941; reprinted in Auden, *Paul Bunyan: The Libretto of the Operetta by Benjamin Britten*, with an essay by Donald Mitchell, London, Faber Music, 1988, pp. 1–4

——, *Paul Bunyan: The Libretto of the Operetta by Benjamin Britten*, with an essay by Donald Mitchell [DMPB], London, Faber and Faber, 1988

——, 'Three Songs for St Cecilia's Day', *Harper's Bazaar*, 75/14, December 1941, p. 63

Auden, W.H., and Garrett, John (editors), *The Poet's Tongue*, London, G. Bell & Sons Ltd, 1935

Auden, W.H., and Christopher Isherwood, *The Ascent of F6*, London, Faber and Faber, 1936; 2nd edition, 1937

——, *The Dog beneath the Skin*, London, Faber and Faber, 1935

——, *Journey to a War*, London, Faber and Faber 1939

——, *On the Frontier*, London, Faber and Faber, 1938

Auden, W.H., and Louis MacNeice, *Letters from Iceland*, London, Faber and Faber, 1937

Auden, W.H., and Pearson, Norman Holmes (editors), *Poets of the English Language*, New York, The Viking Press, 1950

Ault, Norman (editor), *Elizabethan Lyrics*, London, Longman, 1925

——, (editor), *Seventeenth Century Lyrics*, London, Longman, 1928

Austin, W.W. 'Aaron Copland', in *The New Grove Dictionary of American Music*, Vol. 1, edited by H. Wiley Hitchcock and Stanley Sadie, London and New York, Macmillan, 1986, p. 499

Bacharach, A.L. (editor), *British Music of Our Time*, Harmondsworth, Pelican, 1946

Badder, David, and Baker, Bob (editors), 'John Grierson', *Film Dope*, 21, October 1980, pp. 17–33

Bagar, Robert, 'Paul Bunyan: Britten Work has Première at Columbia', *New York World-Telegram*, 5 May 1941

Baker, George, Letter to the Editor, *Sunday Times*, 15 June 1941

Baker's Biographical Dictionary of Musicians, completely revised by Nicolas Slonimsky, 5th edition, New York, Schirmer, 1958

[Balanchine, George], *Choreography by George Balanchine: A Catalogue of Works*, New York, Viking, 1984

Balanchine, George, and Mason, Francis, *Balanchine's Festival of Ballet*, London, W.H. Allen, 1978

The Ballet Caravan, with an introduction by Lincoln Kirstein, New York, Frances Hawkins Concert Management, n.d. [?1938]

Banfield, Stephen, ' "Too Much of Albion?": Mrs Coolidge and her British Connections', *American Music*, Spring 1986, pp. 59–88

Barbirolli, Evelyn Rothwell, 'Ivor Walsworth 1909–78', *R.A.M. Magazine*, Spring 1979, p. 12

Barry, Edward, 'Pianist Britten Well Liked in Own Concerto' [review of first US performance of Piano Concerto], *Chicago Tribune*, 16 January 1940

Barry, Edward, [review of Chicago première of *Les Illuminations* and *Sinfonia da Requiem*], *Chicago Tribune*, 25 November 1941

Bartley, William Warren, *Wittgenstein*, London, Quartet Books, 1974

Baxter, Beverley, 'One Man against the Mob' [review of first performance of *Peter Grimes*], *Evening Standard*, 9 June 1945

Beecham, Thomas, *A Mingled Chime*, London, Hutchinson, 1944

Benney, Mark, *Low Company: Describing the evolution of the burglar*, London, Peter Davies, 1936

Berdyayev, Nicholas, *Slavery and Freedom*, translated by R.M. French, London, Bles, 1943

Berkeley, Lennox, 'The Light Music', in *Benjamin Britten: A Commentary on His Works from a Group of Specialists*, edited by Donald Mitchell and Hans Keller, London, Rockcliff, 1952, pp. 287–94

——, Prefatory Note to *Mont Juic*, London, Boosey & Hawkes, 1979

——, 'Views from Mont Juic', *Tempo*, 106, September 1973, pp. 6–7

[Berkeley, Lennox], 'Sir Lennox Berkeley: Composer of Restrained and Courteous Virtues' [obituary], *The Times*, 27 December 1989

Berthoud, Roger, *The Life of Henry Moore*, London, Faber and Faber, 1987

Biancolli, Louis, 'Britten Work Played in Carnegie Hall' [review of first performance of Violin Concerto], *New York World-Telegram*, 29 March 1940

Bird, Bailey, Interview with Donald Mitchell, April 1977; Toronto, The Britten–Pears Library

Blackwood, Andrew, 'The Arts Cinema', *Cambridge Review*, 6 May 1983, pp. 104–6

Blake, Lord, and Nicholls, C.S. (editors), *The Dictionary of National Biography, 1971–80* [DNB], Oxford, Oxford University Press, 1986

Bliss, Arthur, *As I Remember*, London, Faber and Faber, 1970; revised edition, London, Thames, 1990

Blom, Eric (editor), *Grove's Dictionary of Music and Musicians*, 5th edition, London, Macmillan, 1954

——, [review of Britten concert, Birmingham, 21 April 1939], *Birmingham Post*, 22 April 1939

——, [review of first performance of *Peter Grimes*], *Birmingham Post*, 8 June 1945

The Bloxhamist, 455, April 1945

Blum, John M., *et al.*, *The National Experience*, 6th edition, San Diego, Harcourt Brace Jovanovich, 1985

Blyth, Alan, *Remembering Britten*, London, Hutchinson, 1981

Bohm, Jerome D., 'Philharmonic Plays Britten Work for Violin' [review of first performance of Violin Concerto], *New York Herald-Tribune*, 29 March 1940

——, [review of first performance of *Introduction and Rondo alla Burlesca*], *New York Herald-Tribune*, 6 January 1941

——, [review of New York première of *Bridge Variations*], *New York Herald-Tribune*, 13 July 1939

Boito, Diane, 'Manuscript Music in the James Marshall and Marie-Louise Osborn Collection', *Notes*, 27/2, December 1970

Bonavia, Ferruccio, 'British Choral Music: Young Men's Work' [review of first performance of *A Boy was Born*], *Daily Telegraph*, 24 February 1934

——, 'Britten's Sonnet Settings: Notable New Work' [review of first performance of *Michelangelo Sonnets*], *Daily Telegraph*, 24 September 1942

——, 'Moderns in London: Contemporary Music Centre Selects New Works with Caution' [review of first performance of *Les Illuminations*] *New York Times*, 31 January 1940

——, 'Playboy of Music: Benjamin Britten's Piano Concerto' [review of first performance], *Daily Telegraph*, 19 August 1938

——, [review of first performance of *Peter Grimes*], *Daily Telegraph*, 8 June 1945

——, [review of first English performance of *Bridge Variations*], *Daily Telegraph*, 6 October 1937

——, 'A Virtuoso of the Orchestra: New Britten Work' [review of first English performance of *Sinfonia da Requiem*), *Daily Telegraph*, 23 July 1942, p. 3

'Boosey and Hawkes Concerts: Second Season Begun' [review of first performance of *Michelangelo Sonnets*], *The Times*, 25 September 1942

Boulez, Pierre, *Orientations*, London, Faber and Faber, 1986

Bowen, Meirion (editor), *Music of the Angels: Essays and Sketchbooks of Michael Tippett*, London, Eulenburg Books, 1980

Bowles, Paul, *Without Stopping: An Autobiography*, New York, G.P. Putnam's Sons, 1972

Boyd, Malcolm, 'Benjamin Britten and Grace Williams: Chronicle of a Friendship', *Welsh Music*, 6/6, Winter 1980–81, pp. 7–38

——, *Grace Williams*, University of Wales, Welsh Arts Council, 1980

Boys, Henry, 'Benjamin Britten: *Variations on a Theme of Frank Bridge*', sleeve notes for Decca x226–8, 1938

——, Interview with Donald Mitchell, 20 November 1986, Shaw, Wiltshire; The Britten–Pears Library

——, 'Musico-dramatic Analysis', in *The Rape of Lucretia*, edited by Eric Crozier, London, The Bodley Head, 1948, pp. 75–101

——, sleeve notes for recording of Mahler's Ninth Symphony, HMV DB 3613–22, 1938

——, 'The Younger English Composers, V.: Benjamin Britten', *Monthly Musical Record*, 68, October 1938, pp. 234–7

Bradshaw, M., 'Music of Benjamin Britten' [Letter to the Editor], *Listener*, 13 August 1942, p. 214

Brahms, Caryl, and Simon, S.J., *A Bullet in the Ballet*, London, Michael Joseph, 1937

Brand, Julianne, Hailey, Christopher, and Harris, Donald (editors), *The Berg–Schoenberg Correspondence*, London, Macmillan, 1987

Brecht, Bertolt, *Die Massnahme*, Frankfurt-am-Main, Suhrkamp Verlag, 1972

Brett, Philip (compiler), *Benjamin Britten: Peter Grimes* [PGPB], Cambridge, Cambridge University Press, 1983

——, ' "Fiery Visions" (and Revisions): *Peter Grimes* in Progress', in Philip Brett (compiler), *Benjamin Britten: Peter Grimes*, Cambridge, Cambridge University Press, 1983, pp. 47–87

Brian, Havergal, 'On the Other Hand' [review of first performance of *Ballad of Heroes*], *Musical Opinion*, September 1939, p. 1018

Briggs, H.B., and Frere, W.H., *A Manual of Plainsong for Divine Service Containing the Canticles Noted, the Psalter Noted to Gregorian Tones, Together with the Litany and Responses*, London, Novello, 1902

Briggs, Susan, *Keep Smiling Through*, London, Weidenfeld and Nicolson, 1975

——, *Those Radio Times*, London, Weidenfeld and Nicolson, 1981

Britten, Benjamin, ' "As You Like It": Walton's Music', *World Film News*, 1/7, October 1936

——, 'Britten Looking Back' [BBST], *Sunday Telegraph*, 17 November 1963, p. 9

——, 'Chorale after an Old French Carol', *The Score*, 28 January 1961, pp. 47–51

——, *A Complete Catalogue of his Works*, London, Boosey & Hawkes, 1963

——, *A Complete Catalogue of his Published Works*, London, Boosey & Hawkes and Faber Music, 1973; with supplement, 1978

——, *The Composer and the Listener*, BBC Radio, 1946; published as 'How to become a Composer', *Listener*, 7 November 1946

——, 'How a musical work originates' *Listener*, 30 July 1942, p. 138

——, 'Dennis Brain (1921–1957)', *Tempo*, 46, Winter 1958, pp. 5–6

——, 'Les Illuminations' [programme note], The Britten–Pears Library

——, Interview with Henry Comer, CBC, 11 April 1968; The Britten–Pears Library

——, 'An Interview' [with Charles Osborne], *London Magazine*, 3/7, October 1963, pp. 91–6

——, 'A Holiday Diary' [programme note], 1944; British Library, Clifford Curzon Papers

——, Letter to the Editor [re *Sinfonia da Requiem*], *Radio Times*, 18 January 1946

——, 'The Marriage of Figaro' [review], *Opera*, 3/5, May 1952, pp. 308–9

——, 'My Dear Michael', in *Michael Tippett: A Symposium on his Sixtieth Birthday*, edited by Ian Kemp, London, Faber and Faber, 1965, pp. 29–30

——, 'On Behalf of Gustav Mahler', *Tempo*, 2/2, American Series, February 1942, p. 5; reprinted in *Tempo*, 120, March 1977, pp. 14–15

——, *On Receiving the First Aspen Award* [BBAA], London, Faber and Faber, 1964

——, *People Today* [Interview with the Earl of Harewood], BBC Radio, May/June 1960; The Britten–Pears Library

——, Piano Concerto [programme note], Henry Wood Promenade Concert Programme, 18 August 1938; reproduced in PFL, plate 111

——, Prefatory Note [to the String Quartet in D (1931)], London, Faber Music, 1975

——, sleeve note for recording of the *Simple Symphony*, Decca LW 5163, 1956

——, 'Three Premières', in *Kathleen Ferrier: A Memoir*, edited by Neville Cardus, London, Hamish Hamilton, 1954, pp. 54–61

——, 'Variations on a Theme of Frank Bridge, Op. 10' [programme note], 16th ISCM Festival Programme Book, London, 1938

——, 'A Visiting Composer Sees America', New York Times, 24 March 1940; reprinted as 'An English Composer Sees America', Tempo, 1/2, American Series, April 1940, pp. 1–3

Britten, Benjamin, and Berkeley, Lennox, Mont Juic [programme note], The Britten–Pears Library

Britten, Benjamin, and Pears, Peter, 'Francis Poulenc, 1899–1963', Aldeburgh Festival Programme Book, 1964, p. 23

Britten, Beth, My Brother Benjamin [EWB], Bourne End, The Kensal Press, 1986

Britten, Robert, Notes of Conversation with Donald Mitchell, 16 November 1977; The Britten–Pears Library

Brome, Vincent, J.B. Priestley, London, Hamish Hamilton, 1988

'Brosa Finds American Stay Rewarding Despite Brief Joust with Ellis Island', Musical Courier, 15 May 1940

Brosa, Peggy, Interview with Donald Mitchell, 9 September 1977, London; The Britten–Pears Library

Broue, Pierre, and Temime, Emil, The Revolution and the Civil War in Spain, translated by Tony White, London, Faber and Faber, 1972

Brown, Ivor, 'Johnson over Jordan' [review of first performance], Observer, 26 February 1939

——, [review of On the Frontier], Observer, 19 February 1939

——, 'Westminster Theatre: Timon of Athens' [review of first performance], Observer, 24 November 1935

Brown, Jason, 'Benjamin Britten: The Lowestoft Man who thinks in sound', Lowestoft Journal, 31 January 1948

Buckle, Richard, in collaboration with John Taras, George Balanchine: Ballet Master, London, Hamish Hamilton, 1988

Bullett, Gerald (editor), The English Galaxy of Shorter Poems, London, Dent, 1939 (Everyman's Library Edition No. 959)

Burbank, Richard, Twentieth Century Music, London, Thames and Hudson, 1984

Burke, Sir Bernard (editor), Burke's Geneological and Heraldic History of the Peerage, Baronetage and Knightage, Privy Council and Order of Precedence, London, Shaw, 1938

Burra, Peter (editor), Farrago, Oxford, Simon Nowell Smith, 1930–31

——, (under pseudonum of 'James Salkeld'), 'For a Song', Farrago, 4, December 1930, p. 34

——, 'Music Festival at Barcelona', The Times, 21 April 1936

——, 'The Novels of E.M. Forster', in The Nineteenth Century and After, 116 [1934], pp. 581–94

Bush, Alan, In My Eighth Decade and Other Essays, London, Kahn & Averill, 1980

Butt, James, 'Lord Britten: Some Recollections', *East Anglian Daily Times*, 5 December 1978

Butt, L.A., [review of first performance of *Stay Down Miner*], *Left Review*, 2/9, June 1936

Calder, Angus, and Sheridan, Dorothy (editors), *Speak for Yourself: a Mass-Observation Anthology, 1937–49*, London, Jonathan Cape, 1984

Calvocoressi, M. D., 'From My Note-Book' [review of first performance of *A Boy was Born*], *Musical Opinion*, April 1934

Campbell, Margaret, *The Great Cellists*, London, Gollancz, 1988

Capell, Richard, 'Benjamin Britten Novelty' [review of first performance of *Our Hunting Fathers*], *Daily Telegraph*, 26 September 1936

——, 'Musicians of the Left: A Spanish Elegy by Benjamin Britten' [review of first performance of *Ballad of Heroes*], *Daily Telegraph*, 6 April 1939

——, [review of first performance of *Temporal Variations* and *Two Ballads*], *Daily Telegraph*, 16 December 1936

Caplan, Isador, 'Sir Reginald Goodall' [supplementary obituary], *Independent*, 21 May 1990

Cardus, Neville, 'Cardus on Solomon', *Guardian*, 24 February 1988

——, (editor), *Kathleen Ferrier: A Memoir*, London, Hamish Hamilton, 1954

Carner, Mosco, *Alban Berg: The Man and The Work*, London, Duckworth, 1975

'Carols and Organ – Young Lowestoft Composer's Works Performed' [review of first performance of *A Hymn to the Virgin* and 'I saw three ships'], *Lowestoft Journal*, 10 January 1931, p. 7

Carpenter, Humphrey, *A Serious Character: The Life of Ezra Pound*, London, Faber and Faber, 1988

——, *W.H. Auden: A Biography* [HCWHA], London, Allen & Unwin, 1981

Carr, Virginia Spencer, *The Lonely Hunter: A Biography of Carson McCullers*, New York, Anchor Books, 1976

Cassidy, Claudia, 'On the Aisle: Britten Introduces Concerto with Goldberg' [review of American première of Piano Concerto], *Journal of Commerce*, 16 January 1940

Catto, Max, *They Walk Alone: A play in three acts*, London, Martin Secker, 1939

Ceadel, Martin, *Pacifism in Britain 1914–1945*, Oxford, Clarendon Press, 1980

Chamber's Biographical Dictionary, 2 volumes, Edinburgh, Chambers, 1974

Chambers, Colin, *The Story of the Unity Theatre*, London, Lawrence and Wishart, 1989

Channing, Richard, 'An Audenary House', *Harpers & Queen*, March 1988, pp. 208–10

Chapin, Louis, 'Peter Pears Talks about Benjamin Britten', *Keynote*, April 1978, pp. 8–15

Chapman, Ernest (compiler), *John Ireland – A Catalogue of Published Works and Recordings*, London, John Ireland Charitable Trust, 1968

Charpentereau, Simon, *Le Livre d'or de la chanson enfantine*, Paris, Les Editions Ouvrières, 1976

Chilvers, Ian, and Osborne, Harold (editors), *The Oxford Dictionary of Art*, Oxford, Oxford University Press, 1988

Christie, Agatha, 'Philomel Cottage', in *The Listerdale Mystery*, Glasgow, Collins, 1934

A Christmas Anthology, The Augustan Book of Poetry, London, Ernest Benn, n.d.

Clark, Jon, Heinemann, Margot, Margolies, David, and Snee, Carol (editors), *Culture and Crisis in the Thirties*, London, Lawrence and Wishart, 1979

Clark, Kenneth, *Another Part of the Wood*, London, John Murray, 1974

——, *The Other Half*, London, John Murray, 1977

——, 'The Other Side of the Alde', in *Tribute to Benjamin Britten on His Fiftieth Birthday*, edited by Anthony Gishford, London, Faber and Faber, 1963, pp. 39–44

Clements, Keith, *Henry Lamb: The Artist and His Friends*, Bristol, Redcliffe Press, 1985

Cochran, Charles B., *Cock-a-doodle-do*, London, Dent, 1941

Cohen, Harriet, *A Bundle of Time*, London, Faber and Faber, 1969

——, *Music's Handmaid*, London, Faber and Faber, 1936

Coldstream, William, Conversation with Donald Mitchell, 18 November 1978, London, The Britten–Pears Library

Cole, Hugo, 'Music with a French Accent', *Guardian*, 27 December 1989

Colles, H.C., 'Norwich Music Festival' [review of first performance of *Our Hunting Fathers*], *The Times*, 26 September 1936

——, [review of RCM Jubilee Concert], *R.C.M. Magazine*, 29/3, 1933, pp. 68–9

Colles, H.C., and Cruft, John, *The Royal College of Music: A Centenary Record 1883–1983*, London, Prince Consort Foundation, 1982

'Composer at 17 – Lowestoft Youth's Choral Songs' [review of first performance of *A Hymn to the Virgin*, and 'I saw three ships'], *East Anglian Daily Times*, 7 January 1931

Compton, Susan, *Henry Moore*, London, Weidenfeld and Nicolson/Royal Academy of Arts, London, 1988

'Concerts – Miss Betty Humby' [review of first performance of *Holiday Tales [Diary]*], *The Times*, 4 December 1934

Congdon, Don (editor), *The Thirties: A Time to Remember*, New York, Simon and Schuster, 1962

Connolly, Cyril, 'Editorial', *Horizon*, February 1940

'Contemporary Music Centre – Four Works by English Composers' [review of first performance of *Les Illuminations*], *The Times*, 31 January 1940

Cooke, Mervyn, 'Britten and the Gamelan: Balinese Influences in *Death in Venice*', in *Benjamin Britten: Death in Venice*, compiled and edited by Donald Mitchell, Cambridge, Cambridge University Press, 1987, pp. 115–28

——, *Oriental Influences in the Music of Benjamin Britten*, Ph.D. dissertation, University of Cambridge, 1988

Coonan, Rory, 'Beacon of culture in a wartime blackout', *Independent*, 23 August 1990

Cooper, Joseph, *Facing the Music: An Autobiography*, London, Weidenfeld and Nicolson, 1979

Copland, Aaron, 'A Visit to Snape', in *Tribute to Benjamin Britten on His Fiftieth Birthday*, edited by Anthony Gishford, London, Faber and Faber, 1963, pp. 71–3

Copland, Aaron, and Perlis, Vivian, *Copland: 1900 through 1942*, London, Faber and Faber, 1984

Corwin, Norman, 'London by Clipper' [from *An American in England*], in *Radio Drama in Action: Twenty-five Plays of a Changing World*, edited by Erik Barnouw, New York, Rinehart, 1945, pp. 203–19

——, *Untitled and Other Radio Dramas* [includes 'London by Clipper' and 'An Anglo-American Angle' from *An American in England*], New York, Henry Holt, 1945

Cotton, Charles, *Poems from the Works of Charles Cotton*, newly decorated by Claude Lovat Fraser, London, Curlew Press, 1922

Coulton, Barbara, *Louis MacNeice in the BBC*, London, Faber and Faber, 1980

Cox, David, *The Henry Wood Proms*, London, BBC, 1980

Cox, Peter, and Dobbs, Jack (editors), *Imogen Holst at Dartington*, Dartington, The Dartington Press, 1988

Crabbe, George, *The Poetical Works of the Rev. George Crabbe*, edited, with a life, by his son, London, John Murray, 1851

Craggs, Stewart R., *Arthur Bliss: A Bio-Bibliography*, New York, Greenwood Press, 1988

——, *William Walton: A Thematic Catalogue of His Musical Works*, with a critical appreciation by Michael Kennedy, London, Oxford University Press, 1977

Croall, Jonathan, *Don't You Know There's a War on?: The People's Voice, 1939–45*, London, Hutchinson, 1988

Cross, Joan, 'The Bad Old Days', in *Tribute to Benjamin Britten on His*

Fiftieth Birthday, edited by Anthony Gishford, London, Faber and Faber, 1963

Crozier, Eric (editor), *Benjamin Britten: Peter Grimes*, Sadler's Wells Opera Book No. 3, London, The Bodley Head, 1945

——, ' "Peter Grimes": an Unpublished Article of 1946', *Opera*, 16/6, June 1965, pp. 412–16

——, (editor), *The Rape of Lucretia*, London, The Bodley Head, 1948

——, 'Staging First Productions: I', in *The Operas of Benjamin Britten*, edited by David Herbert, London, Hamish Hamilton, 1979, pp. 24–33

Crozier, Eric, Mitchell, Donald, Reed, Philip, and Strode, Rosamund, (compilers), 'An *Albert Herring* Anthology', in the Glyndebourne Festival Programme Book 1985, pp. 113–23

Cummings, David, *The New Everyman Dictionary of Music*, originally compiled by Eric Blom, 6th edition, London, Dent, 1988

Cunningham, Valentine, *British Writers of the Thirties*, Oxford, Oxford University Press, 1988

——, (editor) *Spanish Front: Writers on the Civil War*, Oxford, Oxford University Press, 1986

Curzon, Clifford, Notes of Interview with Donald Mitchell, London, 13 August 1980; The Britten–Pears Library

——, 'Twenty Years Ago', in *Tribute to Benjamin Britten on His Fiftieth Birthday*, edited by Anthony Gishford, London, Faber and Faber, 1963, pp. 67–70

Darke, Harold, *A History of the St Michael's Singers (1916–1939)*, London, privately published, 1949

Darlington, W.A., 'A Left Theatre Production: "Stay Down Miner" ' [review of first performance], *Daily Telegraph*, 11 May 1936

Darnton, Christian, 'Finale: The Best Concert' [review of first performance of *Sinfonietta*], *Music Lover*, 4 February 1933

——, 'More Modern Music at the Ballet Club' [review of *Phantasy* Quintet and first performance of Three Two-part Songs], *Music Lover*, 17 December 1932, p. 10

Davies, William Henry, *A Poet's Calendar*, London, Cape, 1927

Davis, H.W.C. (editor), *The Dictionary of National Biography, 1912–1921* [DNB], London, Oxford University Press, 1927

Dawkes, Hubert, and Tooze, John, 'In conversation with Antonio Brosa', *R.C.M. Magazine*, 63/3, 1967, pp. 88–92, and 65/1, 1969, pp. 8–12

Dean, Basil, *Mind's Eye: An Autobiography 1927–1972*, London, Hutchinson, 1973

Debussy, Claude, *Monsieur Croche the Dilettante Hater*, London, Williams & Northgate, 1927

De Cossart, Michael, *The Food of Love: Princess Edmond de Polignac (1865–1943) and Her Salon*, London, Hamish Hamilton, 1978

De la Mare, Walter, *Come Hither: A Collection of Rhymes and Poems for the Young of all ages*, revised edition, London, Constable, 1928

——, *The Augustan Book of Modern Poetry*, London, Ernest Benn, 1925–6

De-la-Noy, Michael, *Eddy: The Life of Edward Sackville-West*, London, The Bodley Head, 1988

De Laroque, Lucinda (editor), *Debrett's Handbook 1986*, London, Debrett's Peerage, 1986

Denison, Michael, 'Sir Noël Pierce Coward (1899–1973)', in *The Dictionary of National Biography*, edited by Lord Blake and C.S. Nicholls, Oxford, Oxford University Press, 1986, pp. 186–9

Devries, Herman, 'Music in Review' [review of American première of Piano Concerto], *Herald-American*, 16 January 1940

De W., K., [concert review of a Pears–Britten recital], *North Fork Life* (Mattituck, Long Island), 19 December 1941

Dickinson, Peter, *The Eightieth Year of Lennox Berkeley*, London, Chester Music, 1983

——, *The Music of Lennox Berkeley*, London, Thames, 1988

Dickinson, Peter, and Nichols, Roger, 'Sir Lennox Berkeley' [obituaries], *Independent*, 27 December 1989

Dobbs, Brian, *Drury Lane*, London, Cassell, 1972

Dolin, Anton, *Autobiography*, London, Oldbourne, 1960

Douglas, Basil, Interview with Donald Mitchell, London, 16 November 1987; The Britten–Pears Library

Downes, Olin, 'Britten Concerto in Première Here' [review of first performance of Violin Concerto], *New York Times*, 29 March 1940

——, 'Official Opening for "Paul Bunyan" – Work Is Called Meritorious – Many of the Singers from Amateur Ranks' [review of first performance of *Paul Bunyan*], *New York Times*, 6 May 1941

Drabble, Margaret (editor), *The Oxford Companion to English Literature*, Oxford, Oxford University Press, 1985

Drew, David (editor), *Decca Book of Ballet*, London, Muller, 1958

——, *Kurt Weill: A Handbook*, London, Faber and Faber, 1987

——, 'The Score: An Open Letter to Sir William Glock on the Occasion of His 80th Birthday', *Tempo*, 167, December 1988, pp. 21–3

Duberman, Martin Bauml, *Paul Robeson*, London, The Bodley Head, 1989

Duncan, Ronald, *All Men Are Islands*, London, Hart-Davis, 1964

——, *Collected Plays*, London, Hart-Davis, 1971

——, *How to Make Enemies*, London, Hart-Davis, 1968

——, *This Way to the Tomb*, London, Faber and Faber, 1946

——, *Working with Britten: A Personal Memoir* [RDBB], Welcombe, The Rebel Press, 1981

Dukes, Ashley, *The Scene is Changed*, London, Macmillan, 1942

Dutt, (Rajini) Palme, *Fascism*, London, Martin Lawrence, 1934

Eccles, James Ronald, *My Life as a Public School Master*, privately published, n.d.

Edminston, Susan, and Cirino, Linda D., *Literary New York: A History and Guide*, Boston, Houghton Mifflin, 1976

Eggenberger, David, *A Dictionary of Battles*, London, Allen & Unwin, 1967

Ehrlich, Cyril, *Harmonious Alliance: A History of the Performing Right Society*, Oxford, Oxford University Press, 1989

Elborn, Geoffrey (editor), *To John Piper on his Eightieth Birthday*, London, Stourton Press, 1983

Elliott, Graham, *Benjamin Britten: The Things Spiritual* [GE], Ph.D. dissertation, University of Wales, 1985

Elliott, Florence, and Summerskill, Michael, *A Dictionary of Politics*, 5th edition, Harmondsworth, Penguin, 1966

Elsom, John, and Tomalin, Nicholas, *The History of the National Theatre*, London, Jonathan Cape, 1978

The Encyclopaedia Britannica: A Dictionary of Arts, Sciences, Literature and General Information, 11th edition, Cambridge, Cambridge University Press, 1910

' "Enemy aliens" remember war', *The Times*, 15 May 1990

Evans, Edwin, 'First of Three Recitals' [review of first performance of *Three Divertimenti*], *Daily Mail*, 25 February 1936

——, 'New Violin Concerto' [review of first English performance of *Violin Concerto*], *Liverpool Daily Post*, 7 April 1941

——, [review of first performance of *Our Hunting Fathers*], *Musical Times*, October 1936

Evans, John, sleeve notes for *The Heart of the Matter*, etc., EMI EL 27 0653 1, 1987

Evans, John, Reed, Philip, and Wilson, Paul (compilers), *A Britten Source Book*, Aldeburgh, Britten Estate, 1987

Ewen, David, *American Composers: A Biographical Dictionary*, New York, G.P. Putnam's Sons, 1982

——, *The Book of Modern Music*, New York, Knopf, 1943

——, *The Story of America's Musical Theater*, Philadelphia, Chiltern, 1961

F., H., [review of first English performance of *Bridge Variations*], *Sunday Times*, 10 October 1937

Farnan, Dorothy J., *Auden in Love*, London, Faber and Faber, 1985

Farrell, Edith, Interview with Rosamund Strode, 13 November 1987, Prestbury, Gloucestershire; The Britten–Pears Library

Ferguson, Howard, 'People, Events and Influences', in *The Music of*

Howard Ferguson, edited by Alan Ridout, London, Thames, 1989, pp. 7–15

'Festival of Music for the People – Benjamin Britten's New Work' [review of first performance of *Ballad of Heroes*], *The Times*, 6 April 1939

Ferrier, Winifred, *The Life of Kathleen Ferrier*, London, Hamish Hamilton, 1956

Finney, Brian, *Christopher Isherwood: A Critical Biography*, London, Faber and Faber, 1979

Fleischhauer, Carl, and Braman, Beverly W. (editors), *Documenting America, 1935–1943*, Berkeley, University of California Press, 1988

Flindell, E. Fred, 'Paul Wittgenstein (1887–1961): Patron and Pianist', *Music Review*, 32, 1971, pp. 107–27

Foreman, Lewis, *Bax: A Composer and His Times*, London, Scolar Press, 1983

——, 'Benjamin Britten and *The Rescue*', *Tempo*, 166, September 1988, pp. 28–33

——, *From Parry to Britten: British Music in Letters* [LFBML], London, Batsford, 1987

Foreman, Lewis, Hughes, Eric, and Walker, Malcolm, 'Frank Bridge (1879–1941): A Discography', *Recorded Sound*, April–June 1977, pp. 669–73

Forster, E.M., 'George Crabbe: The Poet and the Man', *Listener*, 29 May 1941

——, *A Passage to India*, Everyman's Library Edition, London, Dent, 1942

——, *Where Angels Fear to Tread*, Edinburgh and London, Blackwood, 1905

Forsyth, Cecil, *Orchestration*, London, Macmillan/Stainer and Bell, 1914

Forsyth, J.A., 'Few "People" at Their Concert' [review of first performance of *Ballad of Heroes*], *Star*, 6 April 1939

Fox Strangways, A.H., 'Christmas' [review of first concert performance of *A Boy was Born*], *Observer*, 23 December 1934; reprinted in *Music Observed*, edited by Steuart Wilson, London, Methuen, 1936

——, [review of first performance of Lennox Berkeley's *Jonah*], *Observer*, 10 October 1937

——, [review of first performance of *Our Hunting Fathers*], *Observer*, 27 September 1936

France, Anatole, *L'Orme du mail*, Paris, 1897

——, *The Merry Tales of Jacques Tournebroche*, translated by Alfred Allinson, London, 1923

Frank, Alan, 'The I.S.C.M. London Festival: June 17–24', *Musical Times*, July 1938

——, 'New Concerto', *Radio Times*, 12 August 1938, p. 16

——, [review of *Bridge Variations*], *Musical Times*, July 1938, p. 537

'Freakish Music at Florence – Mr. Britten's "Fantasia" an Oasis of Melody' [review of ISCM performance of *Phantasy* Quartet], *Morning Post*, 10 April 1933

Freud, Ernst, Freud, Lucie, and Grubrich-Smitis, Ilse (editors), *Sigmund Freud: His Life in Pictures and Words*, Harmondsworth, Penguin, 1985

Fryer, Jonathan, *Isherwood*, New York, Doubleday, 1978

G., C.D., 'New English Music' [review of first performance of *Sinfonietta*], *Daily Telegraph*, 1 February 1933

G., G., 'Britten Piece Diagnosed' [review of New York première of *Bridge Variations*], *New York Times*, 13 July 1939

Gänzel, Kurt, *The British Musical Theatre*, 2 volumes, London, Macmillan, 1986

Garland, Henry and Mary, *The Oxford Companion to German Literature*, Oxford, Clarendon Press, 1976

Gassmann, Remi, [review of Chicago première of *Sinfonia da Requiem*], *Chicago Daily Times*, 25 November 1941, p. 35

[Gendron, Maurice], obituary, *The Times*, 22 August 1990

Gillies, Malcolm, *Bartók in Britain: A Guided Tour*, Oxford, Clarendon Press, 1989

Gillman, Peter and Leni, *'Collar the Lot!'*, London, Quartet Books, 1980

Gishford, Anthony (editor), *Tribute to Benjamin Britten on His Fiftieth Birthday* [TBB], London, Faber and Faber, 1963

Glock, William, 'Music' [review of UK première of *Sinfonia da Requiem*], *Observer*, 26 July 1942, p. 2

——, 'Music', *Observer*, 17 January 1943, p. 2

——, 'Music' [review of first performance of *Serenade*], *Observer*, 24 October 1943, p. 2

——, 'Music' [review of first performance of *Peter Grimes*], *Observer*, 10 June 1945

——, 'Music' [review of *Peter Grimes*], *Observer*, 24 June 1945

Glover, C. Gordon, 'Introducing – ', *Radio Times*, 19 November 1943, p. 5

Goddard, Scott, 'Benjamin Britten', in *British Music of Our Time*, edited by A.L. Bacharach, Harmondsworth, Pelican, 1946

——, 'Contemporary Music – Choral and Piano Works at Broadcasting House' [review of first performance of *A Boy was Born*], *Morning Post*, 24 February 1934

——, 'Music of the Film' [review of *Instruments of the Orchestra*], *Penguin Music Magazine*, Vol. 3, West Drayton, Penguin, 1947, pp. 64–5

——, 'New Work is Fierce and Original' [review of first performance of *Peter Grimes*], *News Chronicle*, 8 June 1945

Goldberg, Albert, Interview with Donald Mitchell, Pasadena, California, 23 May 1989; The Britten–Pears Library

——, vignette of Britten, Goldberg/Britten papers; The Britten–Pears Library

Goldie, Grace Wyndham, 'Broadcast Drama – Three Cheers!' [review of first broadcast of *Hadrian's Wall*], *Listener*, 8 December 1937, p. 1254

[Goodall, Sir Reginald], obituary, *Guardian*, 7 May 1990

——, obituary, *The Times*, 7 May 1990

Goodwin, Noël, 'Maurice Gendron', *Independent*, 22 August 1990

——, and Christiansen, Rupert, 'Sir Reginald Goodall' [obituary], *Independent*, 7 May 1990

[Goossens, Leon], obituary, *The Times*, 15 February 1988

Gordon, Eric, *Mark the Music: The Life and Work of Marc Blitzstein*, New York, St Martin's Press, 1989

Gordon, Keith V., *North America sees our King and Queen* London, Hutchinson, n.d. [1939]

Graham, Colin (editor), *The English Opera Group 1946–56*, London, English Opera Group, 1956

Graves, Robert, *Goodbye to All That*, London, Jonathan Cape, 1929

——, *Poems 1926–1930*, London, Heinemann, 1931

Gray, Cecil, *A Survey of Contemporary Music*, London, Oxford University Press, 1924

Greco, Stephen, 'A Knight at the Opera: An Interview with Sir Peter Pears', *The Advocate* (San Francisco), 271, 12 July 1979, pp. 37–9

Green, Stanley, *Broadway Musicals Show by Show*, London, Faber and Faber, 1987

——, *Encyclopaedia of the Musical*, London, Cassell, 1976

Greene, David Mason, *Greene's Biographical Encyclopaedia of Composers*, London, Collins, 1986

Greene, Graham (editor), *The Old School: Essays in Diverse Hands*, Oxford, Oxford University Press, 1984

Gregory, Ross, *America 1941: A Nation at the Crossroads*, New York, The Free Press, 1989

Greither, Aloys, and Zweite, Armin, *Josef Scharl 1896–1954*, Munich, Prestel-Verlag, 1982

The Gresham, Holt, 1928–30

Gresham's School Register, Gresham's School, Holt

Grierson, Mary, *Donald Francis Tovey: A Biography based on letters*, London, Oxford University Press, 1952

Griffiths, Paul, *The Thames and Hudson Encyclopaedia of 20th-Century Music*, London, Thames and Hudson, 1986

Grigson, Geoffrey, *Recollections, Mainly of Artists and Writers*, London, Chatto & Windus/The Hogarth Press, 1984

Guthrie, Tyrone, *A Life in the Theatre*, London, Hamish Hamilton, 1960

——, 'Out of Touch', *Opera News*, 31, 28 January 1967, pp. 8–11

Gyseghem, André van, 'British Theatre in the Thirties: An Autobiographical Record', in *Culture and Crisis in the Thirties*, edited by Jon Clark, Margot Heinemann, David Margolies and Carol Snee, London, Lawrence and Wishart, 1979, pp. 216–18

Haddon Squire, W.H., [review of first performance of Piano Concerto], *Christian Science Monitor*, August 1938

Hague, Rene (editor), *Dai Greatcoat: A Self-portrait of David Jones in his Letters*, London, Faber and Faber, 1980

Handford, Basil, *Lancing College: History and Memoirs*, Chichester, Phillimore, 1986

Harbison, John, [review of Aaron Copland and Vivian Perliss, *Copland: 1900 through 1942*, London, Faber and Faber, 1984], *Musical Quarterly*, 71/1, 1985, pp. 95–8

Hardy, Forsyth (editor), *Grierson on Documentary*, London, Faber and Faber, 1979

——, *John Grierson: A Documentary Biography*, London, Faber and Faber, 1979

Harewood, Earl of, 'In Memoriam: Erwin Stein 1885–1958', in *Tribute to Benjamin Britten on His Fiftieth Birthday*, edited by Anthony Gishford, London, Faber and Faber, 1963, pp. 160–64

——, 'Joan Cross – a birthday celebration', *Opera*, 41/9, 7 September 1990, pp. 1032–9

——, 'The Man', in *Benjamin Britten: A Commentary on His Works from a Group of Specialists*, edited by Donald Mitchell and Hans Keller, London, Rockliff, 1952, pp. 1–8

——, '*The Rape of Lucretia*: Ronald Duncan as Librettist', in *A Tribute to Ronald Duncan by His Friends*, edited by Harold Lockyear, Hartland, The Harton Press, 1974, pp. 60–69

——, *The Tongs and the Bones: The Memoirs of Lord Harewood*, London, Weidenfeld and Nicolson, 1981

Hargreaves, Gordon, 'Robert Medley: From the Life', Aldeburgh Festival 1985 exhibition catalogue

Harries, Merion and Susie, *A Pilgrim Soul: The Life and Work of Elisabeth Lutyens*, London, Michael Joseph, 1989

Hart, James D., *The Oxford Companion to American Literature*, 5th edition, New York, Oxford University Press, 1983

Hartnoll, Phyllis (editor), *The Oxford Companion to the Theatre*, 3rd edition, Oxford, Oxford University Press, 1966

——, (editor), *The Oxford Companion to the Theatre*, 4th edition, Oxford, Oxford University Press, 1983

Harvey, Audrey, Letter to the Editor, [?] *Sunday Telegraph Magazine*, date unidentified

Harvey, Paul (compiler and editor), *The Oxford Companion to English Literature*, 4th edition, revised by Dorothy Eagle, Oxford, Clarendon Press, 1967

Harvey, Trevor, Interview with Donald Mitchell, 15 December 1980; The Britten–Pears Library

——, 'A Personal Reminiscence: Paul Wittgenstein', *Gramophone*, June 1961

Haskell, Arnold L., *Ballet: A Complete Guide to Appreciation, History, Aesthetics, Ballets, Dancers*, Harmondsworth, Penguin, 1938

Haskell, Arnold L., Powell, Dilys, Myers, Rollo, and Ironside, Robin, *Since 1939: Ballet, Films, Music, Painting*, London, Readers' Union, 1948

Headington, Christopher, *Britten*, London, Eyre Methuen, 1981

——, *Peter Pears: A Biography*, London, Faber and Faber [forthcomming]

Heinsheimer, Hans W., *Best Regards to Aida*, New York, Knopf, 1968

——, 'Born in Exile', *Opera News*, 42/7, 10 December 1977, pp. 16–17

——, *Fanfare for 2 Pigeons*, New York, Garrett Publications, 1949

——, Interview with Donald Mitchell, April 1977, New York; The Britten–Pears Library

——, *Menagerie in F sharp*, New York, Doubleday, 1947

Heller, Erich, *In the Age of Prose*, Cambridge, Cambridge University Press, 1984

Herbert, David (editor), *The Operas of Benjamin Britten*, London, Hamish Hamilton, 1979

Heyworth, Peter, 'Sir William Glock at 80: A Tribute', *Tempo*, 167, December 1988, pp. 19–20

Higgins, John, 'Giving Birth to Peter Grimes', *The Times*, 1 June 1985

Hill, Ralph, 'Britten's New Symphony', *Radio Times*, 17 July 1942

——, 'National Gallery Concerts' [introduction to *Michelangelo Sonnets*], *Radio Times*, 16 July 1943

Hindmarsh, Paul, *Frank Bridge: A Thematic Catalogue* [PHFB], London, Faber Music, 1983

Hitchcock, H. Wiley, and Sadie, Stanley (editors), *The New Grove Dictionary of American Music*, 4 volumes, London and New York, Macmillan, 1986

Hobday, Charles, *Edgell Rickword: A Poet at War*, London, Carcanet, 1989

Hobson, Harold, 'Group Theatre: Westminster – "Out of the Picture" by Louis MacNeice' [review of first performance], *Observer*, 12 December 1937

——, 'Mercury: "The Ascent of F6" by W.H. Auden and Christopher Isherwood' [review of first performance], *Observer*, 28 February 1937

——, 'Mercury: Puppet Show 1938' [review of first performance of *Spain*], *Observer*, 26 June 1938, p. 13

——, 'Westminster: The Agamemnon of Aeschylus' [review of first performance] *Observer*, 8 November 1936, p. 17

Holland, A.K., [review of Liverpool concert in aid of Spanish Civil War Relief], *Liverpool Daily Post*, 8 March 1939

Hollander, Paul, *Political Pilgrims: Travels of Western Intellectuals to the Soviet Union, China and Cuba*, New York, Oxford University Press, 1981

Holroyd, Michael, *Augustus John: a Biography*, Harmondsworth, Penguin, 1976

Holst, Imogen, *Britten* (The Great Composers), London, Faber and Faber, 1966; 2nd edition, 1970

——, *Britten* (The Great Composers) [IHB], 3rd edition, London, Faber and Faber, 1980

——, Interview with Donald Mitchell, 22 June 1977, Aldeburgh; The Britten–Pears Library

——, *Thematic Catalogue of Gustav Holst's Music*, London, Faber and Faber, 1974

——, 'Working for Benjamin Britten', *Musical Times*, 118, March 1977, pp. 202–6

Honegger, Marc, *Dictionnaire de la musique: Science de la musique*, Paris, Bordas, 1976

[Hooton, Florence], obituary, *The Times*, 24 May 1988

Hope-Wallace, Philip, 'Broadcast Drama: All Sorts and Sizes' [review of first broadcast of *The Dark Tower*], *Listener*, 24 January 1946, p. 124

——, 'Peter Grimes' [review of first performance], *Time and Tide*, 14 June 1945, p. 496

Houseman, John, 'The Men from Mars', in *The Thirties: A time to remember*, edited and with commentary by Don Congdon, New York, Simon and Schuster, 1962, pp. 583–97

Howes, Frank, 'Benjamin Britten', in *Grove's Dictionary of Music and Musicians*, 5th edition, edited by Eric Blom, London, Macmillan, 1954, Vol. 1, pp. 949–56

——, 'Macnaghten–Lemare Concert' [review of *Phantasy* Quintet and first performance of Three Two-part Songs], *Musical Times*, January 1933

——, ' "Peter Grimes": Second Thoughts', *The Times*, 15 June 1945

——, [review of first English performance of Violin Concerto], *The Times*, 7 April 1941

——, [review of Pears–Britten recording of 'The foggy, foggy dew',

HMV DA 1873], *Journal of the English Folk Dance and Song Society*, 5/3, December 1948

——, 'Sadler's Wells Opera: "Peter Grimes" ', *The Times*, 8 June 1945

Hughes, Herbert, [review of first performance of Frank Bridge's Piano Trio (1929)], *Daily Telegraph*, 5 November 1929, p. 8

Hull, Robin, 'Two New British Compositions' [review of first performance of *Serenade*], *Sunday Times*, 17 October 1943

[Humby, Betty], obituary, *R.A.M. Club Magazine*, 171, October 1958, pp. 66–7

Hussey, Walter, *Patron of Art: The Revival of a Great Tradition among Modern Artists*, London, Weidenfeld and Nicolson, 1985

Hynes, Samuel, *The Auden Generation: Literature and Politics in England in the 1930s*, London, Faber and Faber, 1979

The Idylls of Theocritus with Blow and Moschus and the War Songs of Tyrtaeus, literally translated into English prose by the Revd J. Banks with metrical versions by J.M. Chapman, London, G. Bell, 1911

Illinois Symphony Orchestra: Prospectuses for the 4th, 5th and 6th Seasons, December 1939 – June 1942

Ireland, John, Interview with Arthur Jacobs, BBC Radio, 11 August 1959

Irving, Ernest, *Cue for Music*, London, Dennis Dobson, 1959

Isherwood, Christopher, *Christopher and His Kind*, New York, Farrar, Strauss and Giroux Inc., 1976; London, Eyre Methuen, 1977

——, *Kathleen and Frank*, London, Methuen, 1971

——, *Lions and Shadows*, London, Hogarth Press, 1938

——, *Mr Norris changes Trains*, London, Hogarth Press, 1935

——, *People One Ought to Know*, illustrated by Sylvain Mangeot, London, Macmillan, 1982

Jackson, Holbrook (editor), *The Complete Nonsense of Edward Lear*, London, Faber and Faber, 1947

[Jacobi, Lotte], obituary, *The Times*, 12 May 1990

Jacobs, Arthur, *A New Dictionary of Music*, 2nd edition, Harmondsworth, Penguin, 1967

——, *The New Penguin Dictionary of Music*, London, Allen Lane, 1978

Jenkins, Roy, [review of Leo Amery Diaries], *Observer*, 7 August 1988

Jennings, Humphrey, and Madge, Charles (editors), *May the Twelfth: Mass-Observation Day – Surveys 1937 by over Two Hundred Observers*, with a new afterword by David Pocock, London, Faber and Faber, 1987

Jezic, Diane Peacock, *Women Composers: The Lost Tradition Found*, New York, The Feminist Press (City University of N.Y.), 1988

Jones, Barry, and Dickson, M.V., *The Macmillan Dictionary of Biography*, London, Macmillan, 1981

Jones, Isabel Morse, 'Coolidge Quartet Gives Works of Three Composers' [review of first performance of String Quartet No. 1], *Los Angeles Times*, 22 September 1941

Jungk, Peter Stephan, *A Life torn by History: Franz Werfel 1890–1945*, London, Weidenfeld and Nicolson, 1990

K., M.S., 'Two British Musicians Delight Audiences Here', unidentified Grand Rapids newspaper, November 1941

Kallmann, Helmut, Potvin, Gilles, and Winters, Kenneth (editors), *Encyclopaedia of Music in Canada*, Toronto, University of Toronto Press, 1981

Kästner, Erich, *Emil und die Detektive: ein Roman für Kinder*, illustrated by Walter Trier, Berlin/Grünewald, Williams Verlag, 1931

Kelleher, D.L. (compiler), *Christmas Carols, The Augustan Books of Poetry*, 2nd series, no. 18, London, Ernest Benn, n.d.

Keller, Hans, 'A Film Analysis of the Orchestra', *Sight and Sound*, 16/61, 1947, pp. 30–31

——, 'Film Music: Britten', *Music Survey*, 2/4, Spring 1950, pp. 250–51

Kelley, A. Lindsay (editor), *Kelly's Directory of Suffolk*, 19th edition, London, Kelly's Directories, 1929

Kelly, Richard J., *We Dream of Honour: John Berryman's Letters to His Mother*, New York, Norton, 1988

Kemp, Ian (editor), *Michael Tippett: A Symposium on his Sixtieth Birthday*, London, Faber and Faber, 1965

Kempton, Murray, 'The Fate of Paul Robeson', *New York Review of Books*, 27 April 1989, pp. 3–7

Kennedy, Michael, *Adrian Boult*, London, Hamish Hamilton, 1987

——, *Barbirolli*, London, Hart-Davis, 1971

——, *Britten*, London, Dent, 1981

——, *Catalogue of the Works of Ralph Vaughan Williams*, revised edition, London, Oxford University Press, 1982

——, *The Oxford Dictionary of Music*, Oxford, Oxford University Press, 1985

——, *Portrait of Walton* [MKWW], Oxford, Oxford University Press, 1989

Kenyon, Nicholas, *The BBC Symphony Orchestra: The first fifty years 1930–1980*, London, British Broadcasting Corporation, 1981

King, William G. 'Music and Musicians: About Benjamin Britten and a Symphonic Première', *New York Sun*, late March 1941

——, 'Music and Musicians: Constant Composer: About the Gifted and Very Busy Benjamin Britten', *New York Sun*, 27 April 1940

Kirstein, Lincoln, *Thirty Years: The New York City Ballet*, New York, Alfred A. Knopf, 1979

Koch, Howard L., 'Benjamin Britten: A Reminiscence', *New York State School Music News*, February 1977, p. 15

Komponisten des 20 Jahrhunderts in der Paul Sacher Stiftung, Basel, Paul Sacher Stiftung, 1986

The Koussevitzky Music Foundation: Catalog of Works, New York, Boosey & Hawkes [1958]

L., R., [review of first performance of *Sinfonia da Requiem*], *New York Herald-Tribune*, 31 March 1941

L., S., 'Music Comment' [review of Chicago premières of *Les Illuminations* and *Sinfonia da Requiem*], *Chicago Daily News*, 26 November 1941

L., W, [review of first performance of *Simple Symphony*], *Eastern Daily Press*, 7 March 1934

Lafitte, François, *The Internment of Aliens*, 1940; new edition, London, Libris, 1940

Lago, Mary, and Furbank, P.N. (editors), *Selected Letters of E.M. Forster, Volume II, 1921–70*, London, Collins, 1985

Lambert, Constant, 'Music: Britten's New Concerto' [review of first performance of Piano Concerto], *Listener*, 25 August 1938, p. 412

Landon, Ronald (editor), *Who's Who in Music*, London, Shaw, 1935

Laughton, Bruce, *The Euston Road School: A Study in Objective Painting*, Aldershot, Scolar Press, 1986

'Leading European Composers Writing Symphonic Work for 26th Centenary', *Japan Times*, 25 February 1940

Leaming, Barbara, *Orson Welles*, London, Weidenfeld and Nicolson, 1985

Lee, Russell, 'Japanese Relocation', in *Documenting America, 1935–1943*, edited by Carl Fleischhauer and Beverly W. Braman, Berkeley, Universtiy of California Press, 1988, p. 240–51

Lee, Sir Sidney (editor), *The Dictionary of National Biography, 1901–11* [DNB], London, Oxford University Press, 1920

'Left Theatre: "Stay Down Miner" by Montagu Slater' [review of first performance], *The Times*, 12 May 1936

Left Review, October 1934–May 1938

Lehmann, John, and Fuller, Roy (editors), *The Penguin New Writing*, Harmondsworth, Penguin, 1985

Leichtentritt, Hugo, *Serge Koussevitzky, the Boston Symphony Orchestra and the New American Music*, Cambridge, Massachusetts, Harvard University Press, 1947

Leonard, Maurice, *Kathleen: The Life of Kathleen Ferrier, 1912–1953*, London, Hutchinson, 1988

Lindsay, John, Interview with Donald Mitchell, 10 July 1990, London; The Britten–Pears Library

Lockyear, Harold (editor), *A Tribute to Ronald Duncan by His Friends*, Hartland, The Harton Press, 1974

'London Concerts' [review of first performance of *Ballad of Heroes*], *Musical Times*, May 1939, p. 382

'London Concerts – BBC Contemporary Concert' [review of first performance of *On this Island*], *Musical Times*, December 1937, p. 1067

'London Concerts – String Orchestras' [review of first UK performance of *Bridge Variations*], *Musical Times*, November 1937, p. 990

Longmate, Norman, *How We Lived Then: A History of Everyday Life during the Second World War*, London, Arrow Books, 1973

Low, Rachael, *Documentary and Educational Films of the 1930s*, London, Allen & Unwin, 1979

Lutyens, Elisabeth, *A Goldfish Bowl*, London, Cassell, 1972

Lutyens Work List, London, Olivan Press, 1972

Lynes, Russell, *The Lively Audience: A Social History of the Visual and Performing Arts in America, 1890–1950*, New York, Harper & Row, 1985

McC., J., 'Final Tribute Paid to Dance Teacher' [Elsie Hockey: obituary], *East Anglian Daily Times*, 28 February 1984

McCarthy, Albert, *The Dance Band Era: The Dancing Decades from Ragtime to Swing, 1910–1950*, London, Spring Books, 1974

MacDonald, Calum, 'Rebecca Clarke's Chamber Music – I', *Tempo*, 160, March 1987, pp. 15–26

MacDonald, Malcolm (editor), *Havergal Brian on Music: Selections from his Journalism, Volume 1, British Music*, London, Toccata Press, 1986

McGuiness, Brian, *Wittgenstein: A Life, Young Ludwig 1889–1921*, Harmondsworth, Penguin, 1990

McLeish, Kenneth (compiler), *Penguin Companion to the Arts in the Twentieth Century*, Harmondsworth, Penguin, 1986

Macnaghten, Anne, 'The First Fifty Years', with an afterword by Ian Horsbrugh, Programme Book for the New Macnaghten Concerts – *50 Years of New Music, 1931–81*, pp. 4–5

——, 'The Story of the Macnaghten Concerts', *Musical Times*, September 1959

'Macnaghten–Lemare Concert – New Works at Ballet Club' [review of *Alla quartetto Serioso: 'Go play, boy, play'*], *The Times*, 14 December 1933

'Macnaghten–Lemare Concerts' [review of *Phantasy* Quintet and first performance of Three Two-part Songs), *The Times*, 16 December 1932

'Macnaghten–Lemare Concerts' [review of first performance of *Sinfonietta*], *The Times*, 3 February 1933

McNaught, William, 'Broadcast Music: Mainly about Britten' [review of first English performance of *Sinfonia da Requiem*], *Listener*, 30 July 1942, pp. 156–7

——, 'The Promenade Concerts' [review of first performance of Piano Concerto], *Musical Times*, September 1938, p. 703

MacNeice, Louis (translator), *The Agamemnon of Aeschylus*, London, Faber and Faber, 1936

——, *The Collected Poems of Louis MacNeice*, edited by E.R. Dodds, London, Faber and Faber, 1966

——, *The Dark Tower and Other Radio Scripts*, London, Faber and Faber, 1947

——, *Out of the Picture*, London, Faber and Faber, 1937

——, *Plant and Phantom*, London, Faber and Faber, 1941

——, *The Strings are false: An unfinished biography*, London, Faber and Faber, 1965

McPhee, Colin, *Balinese Ceremonial Music*, New York, Schirmer, 1940

——, *A House in Bali*, New York, The John Day Company, 1946

——, 'Scores and Records' [review of *Michelangelo Sonnets*], *Modern Music*, 21/11, November–December 1943, pp. 48–9

Maine, Basil, *Elgar: His Life and Works*, 2 volumes, London, Bell, 1933

——, *New Paths in Music*, London, Nelson, 1940

——, [review of first performance of *Our Hunting Fathers*], *Eastern Daily Press*, 26 September 1936

Manchester, P.W., *Vic–Wells: A Ballet Progress*, London, Gollancz, 1943

Mann, Klaus, *The Turning Point: Thirty-five Years in this Century*, with a new introduction by Shelley L. Frisch, London, Oswald Wolff, 1984

Mark, Christopher, 'Britten's *Quatre Chansons Françaises*', *Soundings*, 10, Summer 1983, pp. 23–35

Marris, Paul (editor), *Paul Roth* (BFI Dossier No. 16), London, British Film Institute, 1982

Martin, Lyndon, [review of first performance of *Diversions*], *Philadelphia Inquirer*, 17 January 1942

Masefield, John, *Minnie Maylow's Story, and Other Tales*, London, Heinemann, 1931

Matthews, David, 'Act II Scene 1: An Examination of the Music', in *Benjamin Britten: Peter Grimes*, compiled by Philip Brett, Cambridge, Cambridge University Press, 1983, pp. 121–47

Maugham, W. Somerset, *Ashenden*, London, Heinemann, 1928

Maurois, André, *Disraeli: A Picture of the Victorian Age*, translated by Hamish Miles, London, John Lane, 1927

Mayer, Revd Michael, Interview with Donald Mitchell and Philip Reed, 22 June 1988; Aldeburgh, The Britten–Pears Library

The Medical Directory, 1932–75

Medley, Robert, *Drawn from a Life: A Memoir*, London, Faber and Faber, 1983

——, 'The Group Theatre 1932–39: Rupert Doone and Wystan Auden', *London Magazine*, January 1981, pp. 47–60

Mendelson, Edward, *Early Auden*, New York, Viking/London, Faber, 1981

——, (editor) *The English Auden: Poems, Essays and Dramatic Writings 1927–1939*, London, Faber and Faber, 1977

Menuhin, Yehudi, 'A great cellist of the French school' [obituary: Maurice Gendron], 22 August 1990, p. 39

——, *Unfinished Journey*, London, Macdonald, 1977

Mercer, Derrik, *Chronicle of the 20th Century*, London, Longman, 1988

'Mercury Theatre: "The Ascent of F6" by W.H. Auden and Christopher Isherwood' [review of first performance], *The Times*, 27 February 1937

Mg., P., 'Neue Musik in Basel' [review of Continental première of *Les Illuminations*], *Weltwoche*, 327, 16 February 1940

Miller, Charles H., *Auden: An American friendship*, New York, Charles Scribner's Sons, 1983

Mills, Charles 'Over the Air' [review of Britten's incidental music for CBS (Columbia Workshop) production of Hardy's *The Dynasts*], *Modern Music*, 18/2, January–February 1941, pp. 131–3

Mitchell, Donald (compiler and editor), *Benjamin Britten: Death in Venice* [DVDM], Cambridge, Cambridge University Press, 1987

——, *Benjamin Britten: The Early Years*, BBC Radio 3, 1980

——, *Britten and Auden in the Thirties: The Year 1936* [DMBA], London, Faber and Faber, 1981

——, 'Britten on "Oedipus Rex" and "Lady Macbeth" ', *Tempo*, 120, March 1977, pp. 10–12

——, 'A Celebration' [introductory note to concert in honour of Mayer family], Aldeburgh Festival Programme Book 1988, pp. 85–7

——, ' "Forms More Real than Living Man": Reflections on Britten's *Serenade* and *Nocturne*', Programme Book for the Peter Pears Memorial Concert, Friends House, London, 3 April 1987; revised as ' "Now Sleeps the Crimson Petal": Britten's Other "Serenade" ', *Tempo*, 169, June 1989, pp. 22–7

——, *Gustav Mahler: Songs and Symphonies of Life and Death*, London, Faber and Faber, 1985

——, Interviews with the original cast of *Paul Bunyan*, April 1977, New York; The Britten–Pears Library

——, 'An Introduction in the Shape of a Memoir', in *Benjamin Britten: Death in Venice*, compiled and edited by Donald Mitchell, Cambridge, Cambridge University Press, 1987, pp. 1–25

——, 'Jinx', in *Decca Book of Ballet*, edited by David Drew, London, Muller, 1958, pp. 414–16

——, 'Montagu Slater (1902–1956): Who was he?' in *Benjamin Britten:*

Peter Grimes, compiled by Philip Brett, Cambridge, Cambridge University Press, 1983, pp. 22–46

——, 'The Origins, Evolution and Metamorphoses of *Paul Bunyan*, Auden's and Britten's "American Opera" ' [DMPB], in W.H. Auden, *Paul Bunyan: The Libretto of the Operetta by Benjamin Britten*, London, Faber and Faber, 1988, pp. 83–148

——, sleeve note for recording of the *American Overture*, etc., EMI EL 2702631, 1986

——, sleeve note for recording of the *Quatre Chansons Françaises*, etc., EMI ASD 4177, 1982

——, 'What do we know about Britten now?', in *The Britten Companion*, edited by Christopher Palmer, London, Faber and Faber, 1984, pp. 21–45

Mitchell, Donald, and Evans, John, *Benjamin Britten: Early Chamber Music* [sleeve note], Unicorn-Kanchana DKP 9020, 1983

——, *Pictures from a Life: Benjamin Britten 1913–1976* [PFL], London, Faber and Faber, 1978

Mitchell, Donald, and Hans Keller (editors), *Benjamin Britten: A Commentary on His Works from a Group of Specialists* [DMHK], London, Rockliff, 1952

Mitchell, Donald, and Reed, Philip, 'Hedli Anderson' [obituary], *Independent*, 10 February 1990; revised version reprinted in Aldeburgh Festival Programme Book, 1990, pp. 18–19

——, 'Perspectives on Mahler and Britten', exhibition catalogue, The Britten–Pears Library, Aldeburgh, 38th Aldeburgh Festival, 7–23 June 1985

Miura, Atsushi, 'British Conductor Finds Missing Work by Britten', *Asahi Evening News*, 5 June 1987, p. 3

'Modern Music' [review of Suite, Op. 6], *Musical Opinion*, July 1938, p. 857

'Modern Music: End of Florence Festival' [review of ISCM performance of *Phantasy* Quartet], *The Times*, 9 April 1934

'Modern Music – John Ireland and Bela Bartók' [review of Suite, Op. 6], *The Times*, 22 June 1938

Moore, Jerrold Northrop, *Philharmonic Jubilee 1932–1982: A Celebration of the London Philharmonic Orchestra's Fiftieth Anniversary*, London, Hutchinson, 1982

Morris, John, *Traveller from Tokyo*, London, The Book Club, 1945

Morrison, Sybil, *The Life and Work of Stuart Morris*, London, Peace Pledge Union, n.d.

Motion, Andrew [Books section], *Sunday Times*, 26 March 1989

——, *The Lamberts: George, Constant and Kit*, London, Chatto & Windus, 1986

'Music in Chicago' [review of *Mont Juic* and *Les Illuminations*], *Music News*, 1940

'Music in the Making: Benjamin Britten', *Tempo*, 1, January 1939

'Music in the Making – News of Composers Associated with Boosey & Hawkes: Benjamin Britten' [organ themes for improvisation, 1945], *Tempo*, 12, September 1945, p. 15

'Music in Prison Camp: Festival behind Barbed Wire' [review of first performance of *The Ballad of Little Musgrave and Lady Barnard*], *The Times*, 2 March 1945

'Music Masterpieces Arrive For Emperor', *Japan Times*, 21 July 1940

'The Music Society' [review of first concert performance of *Phantasy Quartet*], *The Times*, 25 November 1933, p. 10

Musical Record, New York, 2/1, June 1941

Neel, Boyd, 'The String Orchestra', in *Benjamin Britten: A Commentary on His Works from a Group of Specialists*, edited by Donald Mitchell and Hans Keller, London, Rockcliff, 1952, pp. 237–44

Newman, Ernest, 'Britten's Concerto' [review of first English performance of Violin Concerto], *Sunday Times*, 4 May 1941

——, ' "Peter Grimes" – I', *Sunday Times*, 10 June 1945

——, ' "Peter Grimes" – II', *Sunday Times*, 17 June 1945

——, ' "Peter Grimes" – III', *Sunday Times*, 24 June 1945

——, [review of first performance of *Michelangelo Sonnets*], *Sunday Times*, 27 September 1942

——, 'Thoroughbreds', *Sunday Times*, 8 June 1941

Newman, George, 'Ernst Roth: A Personal Recollection', *Tempo*, 165, June 1988, pp. 37–40

'New Chamber Music: Boosey and Hawkes Concert' [review of first English performance of String Quartet No. 1], *The Times*, 29 April 1943

A New Pictorial and Descriptive Guide to Lowestoft, London, Ward, Lock and Co., 1900–1901

'New Priestley Play with Ballet and Music', *Observer*, 29 January 1939, p. 9

'New Theatre: "Johnson over Jordan" by J.B. Priestley [review of first performance], *The Times*, 23 February 1939

'New Works for Small Orchestra – Wigmore Hall Concert' [review of first performance of *Serenade*], *The Times*, 16 October 1943, p. 6

'News of the Day: Germany' [review of first performance of *The Ballad of Little Musgrave and Lady Barnard*], *Tempo*, 7, June 1944, p. 24

Nicholas, Michael, *Muse at St Matthew's: A short history of the artistic traditions of St Matthew's Church*, Northampton, privately published, n.d. [1968]

Nicholson, Patricia, Interview with Rosamund Strode, 1985, Lowestoft; The Britten–Pears Library

Nolan, Sir Sidney, Interview with Donald Mitchell, 11 June 1990, Aldeburgh; The Britten–Pears Library

Northcott, Bayan, 'At the service of music', *Independent*, 15 May 1990

'Norfolk and Norwich Triennial Music Festival', *Eastern Daily Press*, 22 September 1936

'A Notable Concert' [review of first performance of *Les Illuminations*], *Daily Telegraph*, 31 January 1940

O'Connor, Gary, *Ralph Richardson: An Actor's Life*, London, Hodder and Stoughton, 1982

Oja, Carol J., *Colin McPhee (1900–1964): A Composer in Two Worlds*, Ph.D. dissertation, City University of New York, 1985; published, Washington, DC, Smithsonian Institute Press, 1990

——, 'Marc Blitzstein's *The Cradle Will Rock* and Mass-song Style of the 1930s', *Musical Quarterly*, 73/4, 1989, pp. 445–75

Oliver, Daphne, 'Frank Bridge: A Memory', Aldeburgh Festival Programme Book 1979, pp. 8–10

'Opening Night' [review of first performance of *Peter Grimes*], *Time*, 7 June 1945

'Opera's New Face', *Time*, 51/7, 16 February 1948, pp. 62–8

'Orchestra's Communist Chief Goes', *Daily Telegraph*, December 1952

Orrichio, Michael, 'Martian Hoards to Repeat 1938 Invasion', *Austin-American-Statesman*, 30 October 1988

Osborne, Charles, *W.H. Auden: The Life of a Poet*, London, Eyre, Methuen, 1980

Osborne, Harold (editor), *The Oxford Companion to Twentieth-Century Art*, Oxford, Oxford University Press, 1988

Oxenham, John, *The Long Road*, London, Methuen, 1907

Page One: Major Events 1920–1988 as presented in the New York Times, New York, Times Books, 1988

Palmer, Alan, *The Penguin Dictionary of Twentieth Century History*, Harmondsworth, Penguin, 1979

Palmer, Christopher (editor), *The Britten Companion* [BC], London, Faber and Faber, 1984

——, 'Embalmer of the Midnight: the Orchestral Song-cycles', in *The Britten Companion*, edited by Christopher Palmer, London, Faber and Faber, 1984, pp. 308–28

Parker, John (compiler and editor), *Who's Who in the Theatre: a Biographical Record of the Contemporary Stage*, 11th edition, London, Pitman, 1952

Parmenter, Ross, [review of first performance of *Introduction and Rondo alla Burlesca*], *New York Times*, 6 January 1941

——, 'Morini Plays Beethoven Work' [review of first performance of *Sinfonia da Requiem*], *New York Times*, 31 March 1941

Partridge, Frances, *A Pacifist's War*, London, Hogarth Press, 1978

'Patron's Fund Concert' [review of first performance of *Three Divertimenti*], *The Times*, 28 February 1936.

Pauli, Hansjörg, and Wünsche, Dagmar, *Hermann Scherchen 1891–1966: Ein Lesebuch*, Berlin, Akademie der Kunste/Edition Hentrich, 1986

Payne, Anthony, Foreman, Lewis, and Bishop, John, *The Music of Frank Bridge*, London, Thames, 1976

Pears, Peter, 'Britten: *Sonatina Romantica*' [programme note], Aldeburgh Festival Programme Book 1983

——, 'Clytie Hine Mundy' [obituary], *The Times*, 12 August 1983

——, 'The New York *Death in Venice*', Aldeburgh Festival Programme Book 1975, pp. 9–14

——, 'San Fortunato: From a Diary', in *A Tribute to Ronald Duncan by His Friends*, edited by Harold Lockyear, Hartland, The Harton Press, 1974, pp. 96–101

Penrose, Barrie, and Freeman, Simon, *The Secret Life of Anthony Blunt*, London, Grafton Books, 1986

Performing Right Gazette, October 1934, January 1936 and January 1937

Perkins, Francis D., [review of first performance of *Mazurka Elegiaca*], *New York Herald-Tribune*, 10 December 1941

Pine, L.G., *Who's Who in Music*, London, Shaw, 1949

Piper, John, 80th Birthday Retrospective Exhibition Catalogue, London, Tate Gallery, 1983

Poulenc, Francis, 'Hommage à Benjamin Britten', in *Tribute to Benjamin Britten on His Fiftieth Birthday*, edited by Anthony Gishford, London, Faber and Faber, 1963, p. 13

Poulton, Alan (compiler and editor), *Alan Rawsthorne: Biographical Essays*, Kidderminster, Bravura Publications, 1984

——, (compiler and editor), *Alan Rawsthorne: A Catalogue of his Music*, with an introductory essay by Gerald Schurmann, Kidderminster, Bravura Publications, 1984

——, (compiler), *The Recorded Works of Sir William Walton: A Discography Celebrating Fifty Years of Recorded History, 1929–79*, Kidderminster, Bravura Publications, 1980

Potgeister, John, 'Adolph Hallis', *SAUK – SABC Bulletin*, 12 August 1968, pp. 10–11

Priestley, J.B., Interview with Harold Conway, *Daily Mail*, 4 March 1939

——, *Johnson over Jordan (the Play) and all about it (an essay)*, London, Heinemann, 1939

——, *Margin Released: A writer's reminiscences and reflections*, London, Mercury Books, 1966

'Priestley Play to Go On', *Daily Mail*, 11 March 1939

'Promenade Concert: Benjamin Britten's Piano Concerto' [review of first performance], *The Times*, 19 August 1938

'Promenade Concert: Bliss and Britten' [review of first performance of 'Marine' and 'Being Beauteous]', *The Times*, 18 August 1939

'Promenade Concerts: New Work by English Composer' [review of first English performance of *Sinfonia da Requiem*], *The Times*, 23 July 1942

The Public School Hymn Book with Tunes, edited by a Committee of the Headmasters' Conference, London, Novello, n.d.

Pudney, John, 'Britten – A Formative Recollection', Programme Book for *A Tribute to Benjamin Britten*, New Philharmonia Orchestra, 22 February 1977

——, *Home and Away – An Autobiographical Gambit*, London, Michael Joseph, 1960

'Purcell Celebration: Mr Britten's Tribute' [review of first performance of String Quartet No. 2 and *The Holy Sonnets of John Donne*], *The Times*, 24 November 1945

' "Q" Theatre: "They Walk Alone" by Max Catto' [review of first performance], *Observer*, 27 November 1938

Queen, Ellery, *The Finishing Stroke*, Harmondsworth, Penguin Books, 1967

Quiller-Couch, Arthur (editor), *The Oxford Book of English Verse 1250–1900*, Oxford, Clarendon Press, 1927

Randel, Don Michael (editor), *The New Harvard Dictionary of Music*, Cambridge, Massachusetts, Harvard University Press, 1986

Read, Herbert (editor), *The Thames and Hudson Encyclopaedia of the Arts*, London, Thames and Hudson, 1966

Reade, Charles, *The Cloister and the Hearth*, London, Trubner, 1861

'Recitals of the Week – Adolph Hallis Chamber Concert' [review of first performance of *Temporal Variations* and *Two Ballads*], *The Times*, 18 December 1936

'Recitals of the Week – Boyd Neel Orchestra' [review of first UK performance of *Bridge Variations*], *The Times*, 8 October 1937, p. 12

Reed, Philip, 'A Cantata for Broadcasting: Introducing Britten's *The Company of Heaven*', *Musical Times*, June 1989, pp. 324–31

——, 'The Composer's View: A Selection of Letters from Michael Tippett to Benjamin Britten', Programme Book of the Britten–Tippett Festival, London, 1986, pp. 64–7

——, 'Copland and Britten: A Composing Friendship', Aldeburgh Festival Programme Book, 1990, pp. 28–9

——, *The Incidental Music of Benjamin Britten: A Study and Catalogue of His Music for Film, Theatre and Radio* [PR], Ph.D. dissertation, University of East Anglia, 1987

——, 'A Rejected Love Song from *Paul Bunyan*', *Musical Times*, June 1988, pp. 283–8

Reeve, Basil, Interview with Donald Mitchell, 3 October 1986, London; The Britten–Pears Library

Reid, Alan, *A Concise Encyclopedia of the Second World War*, London, Osprey, 1974

Reid, Charles, *Malcolm Sargent: A Biography*, London, Hamish Hamilton, 1968

[Reiniger, Lotte], obituary, *The Times*, 22 June 1981, p. 14

Renard, Jules, *Poile de Carotte*, Paris, 1894

[Review of first performance of Bagatelle for violin, viola and piano], *The Gresham*, XII, October 1928 – July 1930, p. 170

[Review of *Les Illuminations*, conducted Saidenberg], *New York Times*, 23 December 1941

[Review of *Les Illuminations*, conducted Saidenberg], *New York Sun*, 23 December 1941

[Review of *Les Illuminations*, conducted Saidenberg], *New York World-Telegram*, 23 December 1941

[Review of *Les Illuminations*, conducted Saidenberg], *P.M.*, [?]January 1942

[Review of first concert performance of *Phantasy* Quartet], *Monthly Musical Record*, December 1933

[Review of first performance of *Rejoice in the Lamb*], *The Times*, 22 September 1943

[Review of first performance of *Scottish Ballad*], *Cincinnati Enquirer*, 29 November 1941

[Review of first English performance of *Bridge Variations*], *Observer*, 10 October 1937

[Review of first performance of *This Way to the Tomb*], *New Statesman and Nation*, 30/767, 3 November 1945

Richards, Bernard, Interview with Rosamund Strode, 27 May 1987, Aldeburgh; The Britten–Pears Library

Ridout, Alan (editor), *The Music of Howard Ferguson*, London, Thames, 1989

Rigby, Charles, *Kathleen Ferrier: A Biography*, London, Robert Hale, 1955

Rimbaud, Arthur, *Prose Poems from Les Illuminations*, put into English by Helen Rootham, with an introductory essay by Edith Sitwell, London, Faber and Faber, 1932

Risby, Charles, *Kathleen Ferrier*, London, Robert Hale, 1955

Roberts, Richard Ellis, 'Immortal Joy and Supernatural Power', *Radio Times*, 24 September 1937, p. 17

Roberts, Winifred, Interview with Rosamund Strode, 30 March 1985, Barnet; The Britten–Pears Library

[Robertson, Alec], *Dear Alec . . . A Tribute for His Eightieth Birthday from Friends Known and Unknown*, Worcester, Stanbrook Abbey Press, 1972

Robertson, Alec, *Requiem: Music of Mourning and Consolation*, London, Cassell, 1967

——, 'Songs: Peter Pears (tenor) and Benjamin Britten (piano): *Seven Sonnets of Michelangelo*', Gramophone, December 1942, pp. 94–5

——, [review of the HMV recording of *Michelangelo Sonnets*], *Gramophone*, January 1943

Roseberry, Eric, 'Britten's Piano Concerto: The Original Version', *Tempo*, 172, March 1990, pp. 10–18

Rosenthal, Harold, and Warrack, John, *The Concise Oxford Dictionary of Opera*, London, Oxford University Press, 1964

Rosenthal, M., and Yudin P. (editors), *A Dictionary of Philosophy*, Moscow, Progress Publishers, 1967

Roth, Ernst, *The Business of Music: Reflections of a Music Publisher*, London, Cassell, 1969

——, 'The Vision of Ralph Hawkes', *Tempo*, 78, supplement, autumn 1966, pp. 6–8

Rotha, Paul, *Documentary Diary: An informal history of the British Documentary, 1928–39*, London, Secker & Warburg, 1973

——, *Documentary Film*, 3rd edition, London, Faber and Faber, 1952

Rothenstein, John, *Modern English Painters*, III, 'Hennell to Hockney', London, Macdonald, 1984

Rubbra, Edmund, 'Britten's "A Boy was Born" ', *Radio Times*, 16 February 1934, p. 450

Rushmore, Robert P., 'Auden in Amityville', *Long Island Forum*, July 1985, pp. 131–5

Russell, Bertrand, *The Autobiography of Bertrand Russell*, Vol. II, London, Allen & Unwin, 1968

Russell, Thomas, *Philharmonic Decade*, with an introduction by J.B. Priestley, London, Hutchinson, 1944

Sackville-West, Edward, 'The Musical and Dramatic Structure', in *Benjamin Britten: Peter Grimes*, Sadler's Wells Opera Book No. 3, edited by Eric Crozier, London, The Bodley Head, 1945, pp. 27–55

——, 'Music: Some Aspects of the Contemporary Problem', *Horizon*, June/July/August 1944

——, *The Rescue: A Melodrama for broadcasting based on Homer's Odyssey*, with six illustrations to the text by Henry Moore, London, Secker & Warburg, 1945

——, [review of first performance of *Michelangelo Sonnets*], *New Statesman and Nation*, 3 October 1942

Sackville-West, Edward, and Shawe-Taylor, Desmond, *The Record Guide*, London, Collins, 1951

Sadie, Stanley (editor), *The New Grove Dictionary of Music and Musicians*, 20 volumes, London, Macmillan, 1980

Salkeld, James [Peter Burra], 'For a Song', *Farrago*, 4, December 1930, p. 34

Salter, Elizabeth, *Helpmann: The authorized biography of Sir Robert Helpmann, CBE*, Brighton, Angus and Robertson, 1978

Salzedo, Carlos, *Method for the Harp*, New York, 1929

——, *Modern Study of the Harp*, New York, 1921

Saltman, Jack (editor), *The Cambridge Handbook of American Literature*, Cambridge, Cambridge University Press, 1986

Sandburg, Carl (editor), *The American Songbag*, New York, Harcourt, Brace & Company, 1927

Sauerlander, Beata, Interview with Christopher Headington, June 1988, Aldeburgh; The Britten–Pears Library

Sawyer-Lançanno, Christopher, *An Invisible Spectator: A Biography of Paul Bowles*, London, Bloomsbury, 1989

Scarfe, Norman, *Suffolk* (Shell Guide), London, Faber and Faber, 1960

Schafer, Murray, *British Composers in Interview*, London, Faber and Faber, 1963

Schafer, R. Murray (editor), *Ezra Pound and Music: The Complete Criticism*, London, Faber and Faber, 1978

Schlesinger, Arthur M., revised by John M. Blum, 'The New Deal', in *A History of the United States since 1865, Part Two*, 6th edition, New York, Harcourt Brace Jovanovich, 1985

Schloss, Edwin H., [review of first performance of *Diversions*], *Philadelphia Record*, 17 January 1942

'School Band Din Called Vital by British Pianist – Pay More Attention to Boy Virtuosos, Urges Composer Britten', *Chicago Daily News*, 15 January 1940, p. 12

Schrecker, Ellen W., *No Ivory Tower: McCarthyism and the Universities*, New York, Oxford University Press, 1986

Schuh, Willi, 'Ernst Roth 1896–1971', *Tempo*, 98, 1972, pp. 4–8

Scott-Sutherland, Colin, *John Ireland*, Rickmansworth, Triad Press, 1980

Searle, Muriel V., *John Ireland: The Man and his Music*, Tunbridge Wells, Midas Books, 1979

Secrest, Meryle, *Kenneth Clark*, London, Weidenfeld and Nicolson, 1984

Seebohm, Caroline [Mrs Walter Lippincott], 'Conscripts to an Age: British Expatriates 1939–1945', unpublished; The Britten–Pears Library

Seymour-Smith, Martin, *Robert Graves: His Life and Work*, London, Hutchinson, 1982

Shakespeare, William, *The Art of Singing*, 3 volumes, New York, Ditson, 1898–9

Shaw, George Bernard, *The Apple Cart*, London, Constable, 1930

Shawe-Taylor, Desmond, 'Peter Grimes – I', *New Statesman and Nation*, 9 June 1945, p. 371

——, 'Peter Grimes – II', *New Statesman and Nation*, 16 June 1945, p. 387

Shead, Richard, *Constant Lambert*, London, Simon Publications, 1973

Shelden, Michael, *Friends of Promise: Cyril Connolly and the World of Horizon*, London, Hamish Hamilton, 1989

Sidnell, Michael, *Dances of Death: The Group Theatre of London in the Thirties*, London, Faber and Faber, 1984

Silber, Evelyn, *The Sculpture of Epstein*, Oxford, Phaidon, 1986

Simon, Henry, 'Paul Bunyan Gets a Fitting for Opera' [review of first performance], *P.M.*, May 1941

Skowronski, Joanne, *Aaron Copland: A Bio-bibliography*, Westport, Connecticut, Greenwood Press, 1985

Slater, Montagu, *Easter 1916*, London, Lawrence and Wishart, 1936

——, *New Way Wins: The Play from Stay Down Miner*, London, Lawrence and Wishart, 1937

——, *Once a Jolly Swagman*, London, John Lane, 1944

——, *Peter Grimes and Other Poems*, London, John Lane, The Bodley Head, 1946

Slonimsky, Nicolas, *Baker's Biographical Dictionary of Musicians*, 7th edition, Oxford, Oxford University Press, 1984

——, *Music since 1900*, 4th edition, New York, Charles Scribner's Sons, 1971

——, *Perfect Pitch: A Life Story*, Oxford, Oxford University Press, 1988

Smith, Cecil, 'Britten Will Make American Bow Tomorrow', *Chicago Tribune*, 14 January 1940

——, *Musical Comedy in America*, New York, Theatre Arts Books, 1950

[Solomon], obituary, *The Times*, 24 February 1988

Sonneck, O.G., *Beethoven: Impressions by his Contemporaries*, New York, Schirmer, 1926

The Sounding Board: Albert Goldberg, interviewed by Salome Ramis Arkatov and Dale E. Treleven, Oral History Program, University of California, Los Angeles, 1988

Spaeth, Sigmund, *Great Symphonies: How to Recognise and Remember them*, New York, Garden City Publishing, 1936

Speaight, Robert, 'This Way to the Tomb', in *A Tribute to Ronald Duncan by his friends*, edited by Harold Lockyear, Hartland, The Harton Press, 1974, pp. 54–5

Spender, Humphrey, '*Lensman': Photographs 1932–52*, London, Chatto & Windus, 1987

——, *Worktown: Photographs of Bolton and Blackpool Taken for Mass-Observation 1937–8*, Brighton, Gardner Centre Gallery, University of Sussex, 1977

Spender, Stephen, *Collected Poems*, London, Faber and Faber, 1985

——, 'Greatorex', *The Grasshopper*, 1955, p. 13

——, *Journals 1939–1983*, edited by John Goldsmith, London, Faber and Faber, 1985

——, *Poems*, 2nd edition, London, Faber and Faber, 1934

——, *The Thirties and after: Poetry, Politics, People (1933–75)*, London, Macmillan, 1978

——, *Trial of a Judge*, London, Faber and Faber, 1938

Spiegl, Fritz, 'Leon Goossens: Legendary Oboist', *Guardian*, 15 February 1988, p. 35

Spoto, Donald, *Lenya: A Life*, London, Viking, 1989

Stainer, John, and Barrett, W.A. (editors), *A Dictionary of Musical Terms*, 4th edition, London, Novello, 1889

Stansky, Peter, and Abrahams, William, *Journey to the Frontier: Julian Bell and John Cornford: Their Lives and the 1930s*, London, Constable, 1966

Stein, Erwin, 'Britten', in *The Book of Modern Music*, edited by David Ewen, 2nd edition, New York, Knopf, 1950

——, *Form and Performance*, with a foreword by Benjamin Britten, London, Faber and Faber, 1962

Stephen, Sir Leslie, and Lee, Sir Sidney (editors), *The Dictionary of National Biography* [DNB], 22 volumes, London, Oxford University Press, 1917

Stevens, Bertha (compiler and editor), *Bernard Stevens and his Music: A Symposium*, London, Kahn & Averill, 1989

Stevens, Halsey, *The Life and Music of Belá Bartók*, revised edition, London, Oxford University Press, 1964

Stevenson, Ronald (editor), *Alan Bush: An 80th Birthday Symposium*, Kidderminster, Bravura Publications, 1981

Steyn, Mark, 'A Shot of Southern Discomfort', *Independent*, 2 December 1989

Stinson, Eugene, [review of first American performance of Piano Concerto], *Chicago Daily News*, 16 January 1940

Stock, Noel, *The Life of Ezra Pound*, Harmondsworth, Penguin, 1974

Strachey, Lytton, *Elizabeth and Essex*, London, Chatto & Windus, 1928

Strode, Rosamund, 'Imogen Holst', *R.C.M. Magazine*, 80/2, Summer term 1984, pp. 69–72

——, (compiler), *Music of Forty Festivals: A List of Works Performed at Aldeburgh Festivals from 1948 to 1987*, Aldeburgh, Aldeburgh Foundation/The Britten–Pears Library, 1987

——, 'Obituary: Sir Peter Pears CBE (1910–1986)', *R.C.M. Magazine*, 82/2, Summer term 1986, pp. 39–43

Stuckenschmidt, H.H., *Margot – Bildnis einer Sängerin*, München, Piper Verlag, 1981

Summerscale, John (editor), *The Penguin Encyclopedia*, Harmonds-
worth, Penguin, 1965
Sussex, Elizabeth, Introduction to the Post Office Video Catalogue
of the GPO Film Unit, n.d.
——, *The Rise and Fall of British Documentary: the Story of the Film
Movement Founded by John Grierson*, Berkeley, University of Califor-
nia Press, 1975
[Swingler, Randall], obituary, *The Times*, 20 June 1967
Symons, Julian, *The Thirties: A Dream Revolved*, London, Faber and
Faber, 1975

Taubman, Howard, [review of first performance of *Mazurka Elegiaca*],
New York Times, 10 December 1941
Teagre, John, *The City University: A History*, London, City University,
1980
Temianka, Henri, *Facing the Music: An irreverent close-up of the real
Concert World*, New York, David McKay, 1973
A Tenor Man's Story [PPTMS], Central Television/Barrie Gavin, 1985
'Theatre Notes', *Daily Telegraph*, 14 August 1944
Thomas, Edward, 'Sir Lennox Berkeley' [supplementary obituary],
Independent, 30 December 1989
Thomas, Hugh, *John Strachey*, London, Eyre Methuen, 1973
——, *The Spanish Civil War*, 3rd edition, Harmondsworth, Penguin,
1977
Thomson, Virgil, 'Musico-Theatrical Flop' [review of first perform-
ance of *Paul Bunyan*], *New York Herald Tribune*, 6 May 1941, p. 14
——, [review of *Les Illuminations*, December 1941], *New York Herald-
Tribune*, 23 December 1941
——, *Virgil Thomson*, London, Weidenfeld and Nicolson, 1967
——, *A Virgil Thomson Reader*, with an introduction by John Rockwell,
Boston, Houghton Mifflin, 1981
Thorpe, Marion (editor), *Peter Pears: A Tribute on His 75th Birthday*
[PPT], London, Faber Music/The Britten Estate, 1985
Tierney, Neil, *William Walton: His Life and Music*, London, Robert
Hale, 1984
A time there was . . . : A Profile of Benjamin Britten [TP], London Week-
end Television/Tony Palmer, 1980
Tippett, Michael, 'Benjamin Britten: Obituary', *Listener*, 16 December
1976; reprinted in *Music of the Angels: Essays and Sketchbooks of
Michael Tippett*, edited by Meirion Bowen, London, Eulenburg
Books, 1980, p. 82–4
[Tippett, Michael], *A Man of Our Time*, exhibition catalogue, London,
Schott, 1977
Tischer, Barbara L., *An American Music: The Search for an American
musical identity*, New York, Oxford University Press, 1986

Townsman, edited by Ronald Duncan, 1938–44 (later renamed *The Scythe*)

Travers, Ben, *Vale of Laughter: An Autobiography*, London, Geoffrey Bles, 1957

Tribute to Alan Bush on his Fiftieth Birthday, London, Workers' Music Association, 1950

Vachell, Horace Annesley, *The Hill*, London, John Murray, 1905

Vaughan Williams, Ralph, 'Obituary – Sydney Waddington', *R.C.M Magazine*, 49/3, 1953, pp. 79–80

Vaughan Williams, Ralph, [review of first volume of Britten's Folksong Arrangements], *Journal of the English Folk Dance and Song Society*, 4/4, December 1943

Vaughan Williams, Ursula, *R.V.W.*, Oxford, Oxford University Press, 1964

'Veress Sends Music Fêting 26th Centenary', *Japan Times*, 11 May 1940

W., W.L., 'Lotte in Weimar' [Lotte Jacobi: obituary], *Guardian*, 15 May 1990

Waddell, Helen, *Peter Abelard*, London, Constable, 1933

Walker, Malcolm, *Benjamin Britten: Discography of commercial recordings as a performer*, unpublished

Walton, Susana, *William Walton: Behind the Façade*, Oxford, Oxford University Press, 1988

Watson, Don, *British Socialist Theatre 1930–1979*, Ph.D. dissertation, University of Hull, 1985

Watt, Harry, *Don't Look at the Camera*, New York, St Martin's Press, 1974

Weaver, J.R.H. (editor), *The Dictionary of National Biography 1922–30* [DNB], London, Oxford University Press, 1937

Weber, J.F., *Benjamin Britten* (Discography Series No. XVI), New York, 1975

'Week-end Concerts – Contemporary Music' [review of first performance of *On this Island*], *The Times*, 22 November 1937

[Weir, Sir John], obituary, *British Medical Journal*, 1 and 8 May 1971, pp. 282–3

Weisberger, Bernard A. (editor), *The WPA Guide to America: The Best of 1930s America as Seen by the Federal Writers' Project*, New York, Pantheon Books, 1985

Welford, Beth, Interview with Charles Ford, *c.* 1976/7, Aldeburgh; The Britten–Pears Library

——, Interview with Anthony Friese-Greene, 1977; The Britten–Pears Library

Wellesz, Egon, 'E. J. Dent and the International Society for Contemporary Music', *Music Review*, 7, 1946, pp. 205–8

Westrup, J.A., 'New English Music' [review of first performance of *Three Divertimenti*], *Daily Telegraph*, 26 February 1936

——, [review of first concert performance of 'Marine' and 'Being Beauteous'], *Daily Telegraph*, 18 August 1939

——, 'The Virtuosity of Benjamin Britten', *Listener*, 16 July 1942, p. 93

Whitman, Alden, 'A North Fork Remembrance', *New York Times*, 28 January 1973

White, Eric Walter, *Benjamin Britten: His Life and Operas*, London, Faber and Faber, 1970

——, *Benjamin Britten: His Life and Operas* [EWW], 2nd edition, edited by John Evans, London, Faber and Faber, 1983

——, *Benjamin Britten: A Sketch of His Life and Works*, London, Boosey & Hawkes, 1948; new edition, revised and enlarged, 1954

—— (compiler), 'Bibliography of Benjamin Britten's Incidental Music', in *Benjamin Britten: A Commentary on his Works from a Group of Specialists*, edited by Donald Mitchell and Hans Keller, London, Rockliff, 1952, pp. 311–13

Who Was Who 1897–1915, 6th edition, London, A. & C. Black, 1988

Who Was Who 1916–1928, 4th edition, London, A. & C. Black, 1967

Who Was Who 1929–1940, 2nd edition, London, A. & C. Black, 1967

Who Was Who 1941–1950, 5th edition, London, A. & C. Black, 1980

Who Was Who 1951–1960, 4th edition, London, A. & C. Black, 1984

Who Was Who 1961–1970, 2nd edition, London, A. & C. Black, 1979

Who Was Who 1971–1980, London, A. & C. Black, 1981

Who Was Who: A Cumulated Index 1897–1980, London, A. & C. Black, 1981

Who's Who 1975, London, A. & C. Black, 1975

Who's Who 1980, London, A. & C. Black, 1980

Who's Who 1987, London, A. & C. Black, 1987

Wickham Legg, L.G. (editor), *The Dictionary of National Biography, 1931–40* [DNB], London, Oxford University Press, 1949

Wickham Legg, L.G., and Williams, E.T. (editors), *The Dictionary of National Biography, 1941–50* [DNB], London, Oxford University Press, 1981.

'Wigmore Hall: A Schubert Recital' [review of Pears – Britten performance of *Die schöne Müllerin*], *The Times*, 2 May 1944

Williams, Charles (editor), *The Letters of Evelyn Underhill*, London, Longmans, 1943

Williams, E.T., and Nicholls, C.S. (editors), *The Dictionary of National Biography, 1961–1970* [DNB], London, Oxford University Press, 1981

Williams, E.T., and Palmer, Helen M. (editors), *The Dictionary of National Biography, 1951–1960* [DNB], London, Oxford University Press, 1971

Williams, Edward, 'Mary Peppin' [obituary], *Independent*, 28 August 1989, p. 13

Williams, Neville, *Chronology of the Modern World 1763–1965*, Harmondsworth, Penguin, 1975

Williams, Val, 'Lotte Jacobi' [obituary], *Independent*, 11 May 1990

Williamson, Malcolm, 'Sir Lennox Berkeley (1903–1989)', *Musical Times*, April 1990, pp. 197–9

Willson, Dorothy Wynne, *Early Closing*, London, Constable, 1931

Wilson, Steuart, 'The English Singers', *Recorded Sound*, 20, 1965, pp. 375–81

Wise, Kelly (ed.), *Lotte Jacobi*, Danbury, New Hampshire, Addison House, 1978

The WPA Guide to Illinois: The Federal Writers' Project Guide to 1930s Illinois, with a new introduction by Neil Harris and Michael Conzen, New York, Pantheon Books, 1983

The WPA Guide to New York City: The Federal Writers' Project Guide to 1930s New York, with a new introduction by William H. Whyte, New York, Pantheon Books, 1982

Wright, Basil, 'Britten and Documentary', *Musical Times*, 104, November 1963, pp. 779–80

——, *The Long View*, London, Secker & Warburg, 1974

Wright, Paul, *A Brittle Glory*, London, Weidenfeld and Nicolson, 1986

——, Notes of Conversation with Donald Mitchell, n.d., London; The Britten–Pears Library

Wood, Christopher, *The Dictionary of Victorian Painters*, London, Antique Collectors Club, 1971

Wood, Henry, *My Life of Music*, London Gollancz, 1938

Wood, Richard, 'Music in P.O.W. Camps in Germany, 1940–1945', *Making Music*, May and October 1947

Worsley, T.C., *Fellow Travellers*, new edition, London, Gay Modern Classics, 1984

——, *Flannelled Fool: A Slice of Life in the Thirties*, London, Alan Ross, 1967

Wyss, Sophie, Interview with John Skiba, *Composer*, Winter 1976–7, pp. 33–5

Yeatman, Robert Julian, and Sellars, Walter Carruthers, *1066 and All That*, London, Methuen, 1930

'Young Lowestoft Composer – Mr. Basil Maine's Tribute to Boy of 19 – Praise for English Composers' [report of 'Personalities amongst English Composers', a lecture given by Basil Maine, Norwich], *Eastern Daily Press*, 20 February 1934

ADDENDA

ADD. 1 To Harry Farjeon[1]

West Cottage Road, West End Lane, N.W.6.
Jan. 6th 1935 [*recte* 1936]

Dear Mr. Farjeon,

Thank you for writing to me about my 'Boy was Born'. I am glad you liked the work; I think it was a good show that evening.[2]

I cannot promise that I shall go on 'like that' – as you say – always. One grows up, I find. And even now after four years or so I find that there is alot in the work one wouldn't do nowadays.

However – I hope you won't be disappointed!

Yours,

BENJAMIN BRITTEN

1 English composer (1878–1948). Farjeon was a pupil of Landon Ronald and later studied with Frederick Corder at the Academy, where he was eventually to teach harmony and composition. Among his works were three operettas. He wrote many piano pieces for young players, and his sister, Eleanor, was the well-known children's writer. In *Friday Afternoons,*Britten had set a poem by Eleanor Farjeon, 'Jazz-Man' (No.10): the song was written on 15 November 1933.

She later attended the first performance of *Grimes* and wrote to the composer to thank him for it. Later still, in 1965, at the age of eighty-four, she wrote again with some recollections of a meeting at Sadler's Wells during an interval in the second performance of the opera: '[. . .] on getting back my breath after the first act [I] had stumbled downstairs and booked for all the other performances. I seem to remember [your] stammering "Is it all right?" when I reintroduced myself. I stammeringly suggested that it was.' The letter ends: 'Thank you for filling my old years with joys and wonders.' She died in 1965.

2 17 December 1935. See end of note 2 to Letter 72.

ADD. 2 To Stephen Spender[1]

43 Nevern Square, S.W.5.

May 26th 1938

Dear Stephen,

Thanks alot for the letter & for sending the poem.[2] I think it is grand, & have some ideas for setting it. I think it might go very well for Hedli – sung half-dramatically with back-cloth or something – together with Wystan's old dictator poem.[3] Perhaps the Unity [Theatre] might be interested in them as interludes in a show or revue? This is all very much in the air & I haven't thought at all about details.[4] I am <u>fearfully</u> busy at the moment – I have a concerto down for the Proms. & the thing's not nearly done yet. There's your Danton play[5] – Wystan's & Christopher's[6] – & a Ballet for Sadler's Wells[7] – & possibly one for de Basil (with Sitwell (O) !!)[8] – to be thought about.

However the Mill (apart from domestic ructions at the beginning) is peaceful. You must see it.

I heard from Wystan this morning – they seem to be having an exciting time.[9]

Yours

BENJAMIN

1 See note 1 to Letter 380.

2 Spender had written to Britten on 11 May:

Dear Benjamin,

I enclose a poem I have written which might be suitable for a song. Let me know if you would care to write music for it. I shall be home in a week.

I heard from Wystan & Christopher today. They seem to have had a very interesting time. They'll be in America by the end of this month.

Yours

STEPHEN

The enclosure has not survived and Spender does not now recall the poem he sent Britten.

3 Professor Edward Mendelson confirms our hunch that this must have been Auden's poem, 'It's farewell to the drawing room's civilised cry'. Britten in fact was to use this text later in his *Ballad of Heroes*. See note 2 to Letter 92, and note 4 to Letter 167.

4 This project seems not to have materialized.

5 *Danton's Death*, a translation by Spender and Goronwy Rees of Büchner's play. The outbreak of war prevented this Group Theatre production from taking place.

6 *On the Frontier.* See note 3 to Letter 155.

7 See note 2 to Letter 120.

8 This otherwise unidentified and unrealized project must have given rise to Pears's reference to Osbert Sitwell in Letter 134. Col. Wassily de Basil (1888–1951) founded the Ballet Russe de Monte Carlo in 1932 and was later sole director of the original Ballet Russe from 1939–48.

9 Auden and Isherwood were in China. They would make their return by way of New York.

ADD. 3 **To Benjamin Britten**
From Rutland Boughton[1]

3 July 1945

Dear Benjamin Britten,

Hearing the interludes from Peter Grimes at your Cheltenham rehearsal,[2] I was compelled to run to town for the complete work, and I rejoice in it even though my old ears cannot always accept your dissonances, though my 3 days at Cheltenham give me hope that they (my ears) are still capable of education. I am ordering the vocal score of P.G. from B. & H., in the hope of a more real understanding of the work. The relation of voices to orchestra I thought was completely satisfactory, & the scene with the fog-horn very fine.

Don't you think the lighting might be increased with advantage in some of the other scenes? It is only on a very dark night that one cannot see much better than your producer seemed to think.

With my very real congratulations
I am
Sincerely yrs
RUTLAND BOUGHTON

P.S. Is there likely to be a London performance soon after Sep. 1? On that day I am lecturing on opera at the Regent St. Polytechnic, & would like to refer to P.G. if those references could be followed up by a performance.

1 See note 7 to Diary for 10 September 1931.

2 The first concert performance of the *Four Sea Interludes*, conducted by Benjamin Britten with the London Philharmonic Orchestra, was given at the first Cheltenham Festival on 13 June 1945.

ADD. 4 To Rutland Boughton

Old Mill Snape Suffolk
Aug. 29th 1945

Dear Rutland Boughton,

Your kind & moving letter has lain very long unanswered. I am very sorry, but actually since it arrived I have been either abroad, or down here sick with the result of my <u>first</u> vaccination!

So I'm afraid my correspondence has got hopelessly behindhand. Please forgive my apparent rudeness.

I was very pleased that you got pleasure from Peter Grimes. I was very nervous about my first operatic venture, I admit, but I am rather encouraged by the kindness so many people have expressed about it. – I take it as a real compliment that such an experienced opera composer as yourself approve of it. I am afraid that there won't be any performances in London in the near future: there has been a big bust-up in the company, & the Governors of the Wells have sided with the "opposition" to Grimes, & so it doesn't seem likely that it will be revived there. But happily there seems to be possibilities of other homes for it.

I note your criticism of the final lighting. Actually the lighting generally was erratic, since the electricians had laws unto themselves – such was the state of chaos in the company! – so what you saw was probably not the intention of the producer. There should have been a spot on Peter althrough the scene.

Thank you again so very much for your letter. I was really most happy to get it.

Yours sincerely
BENJAMIN BRITTEN

II SUPPLEMENTARY ANNOTATIONS

Letter 87, note 1

The Russian Britten scholar, Lyudmila Kovnatskaya, in a highly interesting unpublished paper on Britten's *Russian Funeral*, has identified the Russian source of the melody of the work's middle section. (L. Kovnatskaya, '*Russian Funeral* through Russian ears: aural impressions and some questions', Leningrad, 1990.) For the origin of the principal tune, see DMBA, pp. 72–3.

Letter 165, note 2

Wulff's memory of Pears's performance of the Spender setting is confirmed in the most remarkable and vivid detail by an entry in William Coldstream's Notebooks, dated 17 January 1939:

In the evening Nancy, Wystan, I and a boy Wystan had met at Bryanston went to a party given by Benjamin Britten in Hallam Street. The other guests were Christopher, Stephen and Inez, Christopher's new boy friend, a German boy friend of Benjamin's and Hedli Anderson. A singer who lives with Benjamin was part host.

The evening was slightly sticky – probably because Benjamin does not like Stephen and Inez very much because he most likely knows that they don't like his music. Also the presence of two anti-boy women, Nancy and Inez, complicated the atmosphere because Benjamin likes to be with Wystan & Christopher, all boys together without disturbing foreign elements such as slightly hostile ladies or gentlemen hostile to the gay music. Stephen thinks Benjamin's music rather superficial. But then he thinks my painting very dull and uninspired. He is a natural 'highbrow'. He really likes the obscure & very serious and as Benjamin's whole work has been influenced by Wystan's teaching of carefree lucidity and the non avoidance of banality Stephen does not like the result.

Inez sat looking very self consciously composed – Nancy said that Stephen took great pains to sit near her at regular intervals & occasionally touch her as a guarantee of stable affection when in the camp of the enemy. Stephen sat next to Nancy and said 'May I hold your hand Nancy?' and giggled. Hedli Anderson came in very theatrical & self assured. 'Queen of the boys tonight'. She is really very nice & very sane. But she is like actors & actresses are, no animal existence & curiously sexless underneath an outspoken & pretendedly candid manner.

She sat on the piano and sang Wystan's songs & Benjamin played with great gusto. He likes to play all the time without stopping. He likes doing what he does well all the time. Hedli sang 'Jam Tart', 'Johnnie' and a new song called 'Tell me the truth about Love' by Wystan. Then she sang a very nice song called 'Up in a Balloon'. I think she had found the words in the British Museum. And she also sang 'Riding in the Park'. Then Stephen asked if Benjamin would play the song which he had made from Stephen's poem. I can't remember which poem it was but it was a very Stephenish one full of slightly embarrassing & very strong feelings, very personal, very big & over life size in emotion but very original and striking. It had lines like 'I rushed upstairs etc etc' – all rather like a huge nightmare. People wondered if they might laugh while it was being sung by Benjamin's singer friend. I giggled a little bit but no one laughed. Christopher looked very bright & dry like a sardonic Robin.

Nancy = Coldstream's first wife. She was later to marry Michael, one of Spender's brothers.
Inez = Spender's first wife.

'Christopher's new boy friend' = Jackie Hewit.

'Riding in the Park' = a solo version, presumably, of the famous duet from Lehár's operetta, *The Merry Widow*.

See Caroline Cuthbert, 'From William Coldstream's Notebooks', in Lawrence Gowing and David Sylvester, *The Paintings of William Coldstream 1908–1987*, London, Tate Gallery, 1990, pp. 31–6, and note 2 to Letter 126.

Letter 256, note 4

The *Tatuta Maru*, 'Japan's finest passenger liner', was to play an important role in the political crisis of 1941, when America and Japan were on the brink of war. See Edward Behr, *Hirohito: Beyond the Myth* (Harmondsworth, Penguin, 1990), pp. 291–2.

Letter 297, note 2

Prince Fuminaro Konoye was three times Prime Minister of Japan. 'Indolent, opinionated, passionate and unpredictable', he was to commit suicide in December 1945, a tragic victim of Japan's defeat. He had resigned as Prime Minister in October 1941, believing that Japan and the USA could reach agreement and avoid conflict. His musician brother, Viscount Hidemaro Konoye (1898–1973), had spent the war years in Germany. It was he who had founded the New Symphony Orchestra of Tokyo, which he conducted and which would have performed under his direction Britten's *Sinfonia* had it proved acceptable to his brother's committee. Konoye with his orchestra had made the first commercial recording, for Parlophone, of Mahler's Fourth Symphony in May 1930. See Behr, op. cit., p. 184 *et seq.*, and pp. 397–407

Letter 397, note 2

In interviews with Donald Mitchell (27 October 1990 Aldeburgh; Archive) Stephen [SS] and Natasha [NS] Spender recalled their individual memories of Britten and Pears. Perhaps not surprisingly, those recollections often centred on Auden and the members of Auden's 'circle' in the thirties:

ss: [. . .] Isherwood made a very revealing remark as a matter of fact, which I've been puzzling about ever since. I said something about Ben and he said, 'Well, Ben is like water in our hands. Ben is a very weak character and Wystan and I can do anything we like with him'. [. . .] Auden tended to think of people in the other arts as somehow kind of extensions [. . .] of his world. For instance, he had great ideas about how Bill Coldstream should paint [. . .] He extended his imagination into other people's worlds [. . .] The unwritten masterpiece of the century – the early part of this century – is the collaboration between Auden and Benjamin Britten. That ought to have been written and I think they both knew it ought to have been written.

Inevitably, both SS and NS had something to say about the rupture of the Auden/Britten friendship and the evident wound it caused the poet. The end of the relationship, SS remarked, 'was one of the deepest griefs in Auden's life', which, according to NS, manifested itself in tears: 'You mean tears, really – ?' — 'Absolutely. Tears.'

NS went on to add that after the war she would often invite Britten and Pears to the Spender household when Auden was a guest, but 'invariably there was a telegram that Ben wasn't well and couldn't come'. Furthermore, the break with Auden meant that any development or continuation of a friendship with the Spenders – occasional encounters apart – was prohibited, as NS made clear: 'We were simply regarded as – in a way we were – Wystan's closest friends in England, and therefore Ben felt reserved about us because [. . .] he knew that Wystan stayed with us'. (Isherwood felt much the same. When Donald Mitchell interviewed him in California in 1978, he remarked that the end of Britten's friendship with Auden had, in his view, led to an unmotivated and unwanted termination of *his* old friendship with Britten.)

As for the occasion that prompted the final break, both SS and NS recollect a letter from Auden having a role to play:

ss: I think that Auden said he wrote to Ben after one of his operas a very praising letter but that Auden, considering himself a great expert on opera and music and everything – and music being his real love apart from poetry – had made a few criticisms, and the letter arrived in the envelope, torn up. It was returned to him torn up in the envelope, so Auden told us.

NS adds the detail that Auden questioned in his letter the wisdom of setting 'a certain poetic metre to a certain rhythm [. . .] and the letter came back to him torn in a thousand pieces. Just an envelope, and out came the pieces of the letter. And after that Wystan gave up trying'.

Perhaps for the first time we have an account of the *event* that left the Auden/Britten friendship in pieces, like the letter. But which opera was it that gave rise to Auden's ill-fated missive? We know that Auden had been present at the Paris performance of *Billy Budd* in 1952 and had had reservations about it, as Walton's testimony suggests. Moreover, while Donald Mitchell has forgotten the source, he clearly recalls being told that Britten had been irritated by Auden's criticisms of the production, which had struck him as schoolmasterly and pedantic, e.g. discussion of the precise distance at which Billy should have been standing in relation to Claggart in the trial scene. But this was 1952; and it seems scarcely possible that an invitation would have been extended to Auden to lecture at Aldeburgh in 1953 if there had been a serious row about *Budd* the year before. Nor does it seem likely that Auden would have returned to expressing his doubts about *Budd* in a letter, so long after the event, though it could well have been the case that his adverse observations were all too vividly recalled on receipt of the letter which proved, from Britten's point of view, to be the last straw. (However, in 1961 Auden generously contributed a significant MS to the Christie's auction held to raise funds for the Aldeburgh Festival.)

The chronology of all this leads to the conclusion that it must have been *Gloriana*, first performed in 1953 some twelve days before the Festival began, in which Auden was to participate. We know that he attended a performance of the opera (see HCWHA, p. 375) and that his response was mixed, though it appears that he was full of admiration for the music. Moreover, if it were an issue about poetic metre and musical rhythm that Auden raised with Britten, then it is *Gloriana* (and not *Budd*) that offers material for debate. Could it have been Essex's Lute Song, for example, that Auden found wanting in some aspect?

The destruction of the evidence – the letter – means that we can never know what it was precisely that triggered off the explosion. It was an eruption that had been prepared by the Paris encounter over *Budd*, and exacerbated too, no doubt, by Auden's (and Kallman's) collaboration with Stravinsky in *The Rake's Progress* (1951), an enterprise – and an opera – of which Britten took a peculiarly jaundiced view. Up to mid-1953 the old friendship was still just about intact but now not strong enough to survive pontification about *Gloriana*, a work in any case that had not the happiest of public or critical receptions. The rest – despite Auden's brief appearance in the BBC TV film, *Britten at Fifty*, and his aborted effort to contribute to TBB (see DMBA, p. 109, note 24) – was a bruised silence. How odd, though, that at the very end Britten's tears came to match Auden's.

Index to Volumes One and Two

compiled by Jill Burrows

KEY TO ABBREVIATIONS

AF	Aldeburgh Festival/Foundation
arr.	arranger/arranged by
BB	Benjamin Britten
C	concert or recital performance
c	conductor/conducted by
ed.	editor(s)/edited by
EOG	English Opera Group
orch.	orchestrated
ill.	illustration
PP	Peter Pears
p	played by/solo performer(s)
R	radio broadcast
r	reader/reciter
real.	realization/realized by
S	staged performance/production
s	sung by/singer(s)
trans.	translator/translated by
transcr.	transcription/transcribed by

INDEX OF BRITTEN'S WORKS

ARRANGEMENTS, CADENZAS, EDITIONS AND REALIZATIONS

INDEX OF OTHER COMPOSERS

Underlined references indicate the main entry.

Addinsell, Richard: *Warsaw Concerto*, popularity of, 1114

Andrews, H.K.: Oboe Concerto, C (*p* Spencer; Macnaghten–Lemare), 300

Anonymous: 'Have you seen but a whyte lilie grow', C (*s* PP; *p* BB), 1244, 1287, 1289

Arlen, Harold: 'Stormy Weather', BB improvisation, 452–3

Arne, Thomas: Gavotte and Allegro, C (amateur; *p* Hoult Taylor), 118; *Love in a Village*, S (AF), 1226

Bach, Johann Christian: sinfonia (unspecified), C (*c* Mengelberg), 352

Bach, Johann Sebastian: air and gigue, C (amateur; *p* Walter Greatorex), 118; aria, C (amateur; *p* Joyce Chapman), 118; Brandenburg concertos, 899; Brandenburg Concerto No.6, C (*c* Wood), 284; Cantata No. 174, C (Sinfonia; *c* Boult), 385; *Cantata for the New Year*, C (Oflag VIIB), 1177; cello sonata (unspecified), C (*p* Semino, BB), 1221; Cello Sonata in G minor (BWV1029), C (AF; *p* Gendron, Malcolm), 1247; Cello Suite in D (BWV1012), C (AF; *p* Gendron); Chaconne from Partita in D minor (BWV1004), C (*p* Brosa), 169; *Christmas Oratorio*, C (*p* PP), 1107; Chromatic Fantasia and Fugue in D minor (BWV903); BB studies, 241; Concerto in C minor for two keyboards and strings (BWV1060), C (*p* Bartlett, Robertson; *c* Wood), 208; Concerto in C for two keyboards and strings (BWV1061), C (*p* Bartlett, Robertson; *c* Wood), 208; Concerto in D minor for two violins (BWV1043), C (domestic), 149; play-through, 147; Concerto in D minor for keyboard and strings (BWV1052), C (*p* Gieseking; *c* Boult), 216; (*p* Samuel), 99; (*p* Samuel; *c* Boult), 283; *Jesu meine Freude* motet (BWV227), R (*c* Boult), 247; 'Komm, süsser Tod' ('Come Sweet Repose') (BWV478), C (*s* PP; *p* BB), 1003; 'Mein gläubiges Herzes' ('My heart ever faithful'), C (*s* PP; *p* BB), 1221; 'Non sa che sia dolore' (BWV209), C (RCM), 259; Orchestral Suite in B minor

(BWV1067), C (*c* Wood), 208; Partita in E minor (BWV830), (*p* Harold Samuel), 218; Peasant Cantata: Mer ahn en neue Oberkeet (BWV212), C (Lowestoft Musical Society), 112; prelude and fugue (arr. Kreisler), C (*p* Menuhin, BB), 1274; Prelude and Fugue in B minor (BWV544), C (*p* Thalben-Ball), 208; Prelude and Fugue in E flat (BWV552) (arr. Schoenberg), R (*c* Schoenberg), 153; *St Matthew Passion*, C (*c* Boult), 169, 170; (*c* Jacques), 1142; at funeral of Robert Victor Britten (extract), 336; performers, 171; and PP, 1142; R, 244; records (*s* PP (Evangelist); *c* Klemperer), 1142; (*s* PP (Evangelist); *c* Münchinger), 1142; *St John Passion*, BB as harpsichord continuo, 1116; records (*s* PP (Evangelist); *c* Willcocks), 1142; (*s* PP (Evangelist); *c* BB), 1142; Sarabande, Andante and Bourrée (arr.), C (*c* Wood), 208; 'Suite No.6' (arr. Wood); C (*c* Wood), 208–9; Toccata and Fugue in D minor (BWV565), C (Lowestoft Musical Society), 150; (orch. Klenovsky), R (*c* Wood), 278; Violin Concerto in E, C (*p* Clebanoff; *c* Solomon), 913; Violin Sonata in A (BWV1050), C (*p* Alston, Samuel), 99

Badings, Henk: *Prelude to a Tragedy*, C (*c* Barlow), 932

Balakirev, Mily: songs (unspecified), R (*s* Wyss), 458, 459

Bantock, Granville: *Hebridean Symphony*, C (*c* Sargent), 166; *The Pilgrim's Progress*, and National Chorus, 169; *Sappho* overture, C (*c* Boult), 282

Bartlett, John: 'When from my love', C (*s* PP; *p* BB), 1289

Bartók, Béla: *Allegro barbaro*, R (*p* Long), 261; Burlesque No.1, R (*p* Long), 261; *Contrasts* for violin, clarinet and piano, C (*p* Kersey, Thurston, Kabos), 1076, 1077; *Divertimento*, BB requests score, 1121, 1123, 1129; and Paul Sacher, 651; *Improvisations on Hungarian Folksongs* Op.20, C (*p* Stadlen), 1204; *Mikrokosmos*, C (*p* Bartók), 561; *The Miraculous Mandarin* suite, R (*c* Wood), 240,

GENERAL INDEX

Underlined references indicate the main entry.
References in **bold type** indicate the recipient of a letter.

Donald Mitchell is our leading Britten scholar and Chairman of the Britten Estate. A close friend of the composer and his publisher for thirteen years, it was to him that Britten entrusted the task of documenting his life and work.

Since Britten's death, Mitchell has generated a vast body of critical commentary, through articles, books, radio features, television documentaries and lectures, among them the 1979 T.S. Eliot Memorial Lectures on Britten and Auden in the Thirties. He has encouraged a whole generation of younger Britten scholars.

Donald Mitchell is equally renowned as a Mahler scholar and has published three volumes in a projected four-volume study of Mahler's life and music; the second volume was dedicated to Benjamin Britten. He is currently engaged on the preparation of the third volume in this series.

Philip Reed was Staff Musicologist at the Britten–Pears Library and is rapidly achieving a reputation as one of the most gifted of the younger generation of Britten scholars. In 1997 he was appointed Head of Publications at English National Opera.

Rosamund Strode, for many years Britten's musical assistant, is Archivist and Keeper of Manuscripts at the Britten–Pears Library, Aldeburgh.

Kathleen Mitchell read history at Birkbeck College, and later became a leading figure in London education. From 1974 to 1979, she was Headmistress of Pimlico School, with its Special Music Course, in which Britten took a close interest.

Judy Young was personal assistant to Jeremy Thorpe when he was Leader of the Liberal Party before taking up her appointment with the Britten–Pears Foundation.